MASTERS OF FANTASY

MASTERS OF FANTASY

EDITED BY TERRY CARR & MARTIN HARRY GREENBERG

GALAHAD BOOKS

NEW YORK

Published in 1992 by

Galahad Books
A division of LDAP, Inc.
386 Park Avenue South
Suite 1913
New York, NY 10016

Galahad Books is a registered trademark of LDAP, Inc.
Published by arrangement with Martin Harry Greenberg and the
Estate of Terry Carr.
Library of Congress Catalog Card Number: 92-70618
ISBN: 0-88365-786-4

Printed in the United States of America.

ACKNOWLEDGMENTS

"The Rats in the Walls" by H. P. Lovecraft. From *Weird Tales*, March, 1924. Copyright © 1924 by *Weird Tales*, copyright renewed. Reprinted by permission of the Scott Meredith Literary Agency, Inc., 845 Third Ave., New York, NY 10022.

"The Woman of the Wood" by A. Merritt. From *Weird Tales*, August, 1926. Copyright © 1926 by Abraham Merritt. Copyright renewed, 1954, by Abraham Merritt. Reprinted by permission of Brandt & Brandt Literary Agents, Inc.

"Trouble With Water" by H. L. Gold. From *Unknown*, March, 1939. Copyright © 1939 by Street & Smith, renewed 1967 by Condé Nast. Copyright © 1980 by H. L. Gold. Reprinted by permission of the author.

"Thirteen O'Clock" by C. M. Kornbluth. From *Stirring Science Stories*, February, 1941. Copyright © 1941 by C. M. Kornbluth, copyright renewed. Reprinted by permission of Robert P. Mills, Ltd.

"The Coming of the White Worm" by Clark Ashton Smith. From *Stirring Science Stories*, April, 1941. Copyright © 1941, by Clark Ashton Smith, copyright renewed. Reprinted by permission of the Scott Meredith Literary Agency, Inc., 845 Third Ave., New York, NY 10022.

"Yesterday Was Monday" by Theodore Sturgeon. From *Unknown*, June, 1941. Copyright © 1941 by Street & Smith Publications, Inc., copyright renewed by Theodore Sturgeon. Reprinted by permission of Kirby McCauley, Ltd.

"They Bite" by Anthony Boucher. From *Unknown Worlds*, August, 1943. Copyright © 1945, 1972 by Anthony Boucher. Reprinted by permission of Curtis Brown, Ltd.

"Call Him Demon" by Henry Kuttner. From *Thrilling Wonder Stories*, Fall, 1946. Copyright © 1945 by Henry Kuttner, copyright renewed 1972. Reprinted by permission of the Harold Matson Company, Inc.

"Daemon" by C. L. Moore. From *Famous Fantastic Mysteries*, October, 1946. Copyright © 1946 by C. L. Moore, copyright renewed 1974. Reprinted by permission of the Harold Matson Company, Inc.

"The Black Ferris" by Ray Bradbury. From *Weird Tales*, May, 1948. Copyright © 1948 by Ray Bradbury, copyright renewed 1975. Reprinted by permission of the Harold Matson Company, Inc.

"Displaced Person" by Eric Frank Russell. From *Weird Tales,* September, 1948. Copyright ©
1948, 1965 by Eric Frank Russell. Reprinted by permission of the Scott Meredith Literary
Agency, Inc., 845 Third Ave., New York, NY 10022.

"Our Fair City" by Robert A. Heinlein. From *Weird Tales,* January, 1949. Copyright © 1949 by
Weird Tales, 1976 by Robert A. Heinlein. Reprinted by permission of the author and his
agents, Blassingame, McCauley & Wood.

"Come and Go Mad" by Fredric Brown. From *Weird Tales,* July, 1949. Copyright © 1949 by
Weird Tales. Copyright renewed by Fredric Brown. Reprinted by permission of the Scott
Meredith Literary Agency, Inc., 845 Third Ave., New York, NY 10022.

"There Shall Be No Darkness" by James Blish. From *Thrilling Wonder Stories,* April, 1950.
Copyright © 1950 by Standard Magazines, Inc. Copyright renewed. Reprinted by permission
of Richard Curtis Associates.

"The Loom of Darkness" by Jack Vance. From *Worlds Beyond,* December, 1950. Copyright ©
1950 by Hillman Periodicals, Inc., copyright © 1977 by Jack Vance. Reprinted by permission
of Kirby McCauley, Ltd.

"The Rag Thing" by Donald A. Wollheim. From *The Magazine of Fantasy and Science Fiction,*
October, 1951. Copyright © 1951 by Fantasy House, Inc.; 1969 by Donald A. Wollheim.
Reprinted by permission of the author.

"Sail On! Sail On!" by Philip José Farmer. From *Startling Stories,* December, 1952. Copyright
© 1952 by Philip José Farmer. Reprinted by permission of the author and his agents, the Scott
Meredith Literary Agency, Inc., 845 Third Ave., New York, NY 10022.

"One Ordinary Day, with Peanuts" by Shirley Jackson. From *The Magazine of Fantasy and
Science Fiction,* January, 1955. Copyright © 1955 by Shirley Jackson. Reprinted by permission
of Brandt & Brandt Literary Agents, Inc.

"That Hell-Bound Train" by Robert Bloch. From *The Magazine of Fantasy and Science Fiction,*
September, 1958. Copyright © 1958 by Mercury Press, Inc. Reprinted by permission of Kirby
McCauley, Ltd.

"Nine Yards of Other Cloth" by Manly Wade Wellman. From *The Magazine of Fantasy and
Science Fiction,* November, 1958. Copyright © 1958 by Mercury Press, Inc. Reprinted by
permission of Kirby McCauley, Ltd.

"The Montavarde Camera" by Avram Davidson. From *The Magazine of Fantasy and Science
Fiction,* May, 1959. Copyright © 1959 by Mercury Press, Inc. Reprinted by permission of
Kirby McCauley, Ltd.

"Man Overboard" by John Collier. From *The Magazine of Fantasy and Science Fiction,* March,
1960. Copyright © 1960 by Mercury Press, Inc. Reprinted by permission of the Harold
Matson Company, Inc.

"My Dear Emily" by Joanna Russ. From *The Magazine of Fantasy and Science Fiction,* July,
1962. Copyright © 1962 by Mercury Press, Inc., copyright © 1965 by Joanna Russ. Reprinted
by permission of Curtis Brown, Ltd.

"Descending" by Thomas M. Disch. From *Fantastic,* July, 1964. Copyright © 1964 by Thomas
M. Disch. Reprinted by permission of the author.

"Four Ghosts in Hamlet" by Fritz Leiber. From *The Magazine of Fantasy and Science Fiction,*
January, 1965. Copyright © 1965 by Mercury Press, Inc. Reprinted by permission of Robert P.
Mills, Ltd.

"Divine Madness" by Roger Zelazny. From the *Magazine of Horror,* Summer 1966. Copyright
© 1966 by Health Knowledge, Inc. Reprinted by permission of Roger Zelazny.

Acknowledgments

"Narrow Valley" by R. A. Lafferty. From *The Magazine of Fantasy and Science Fiction,* September, 1966. Copyright © 1966 by Mercury Press, Inc., copyright © 1970 by R. A. Lafferty; reprinted by permission of the author and his agent, Virginia Kidd.

"Timothy" by Keith Roberts. From *sf impulse,* September 1966. Copyright © 1966 by *sf impulse.* Reprinted by permission of the author and E. J. Carnell Literary Agency.

"Through a Glass—Darkly" by Zenna Henderson. From *The Magazine of Fantasy and Science Fiction,* October, 1970. Copyright © 1970 by Mercury Press, Inc. Reprinted by permission of Curtis Brown, Ltd.

"Jeffty Is Five" by Harlan Ellison appeared in *The Magazine of Fantasy and Science Fiction* (July, 1977) and in the author's collection, *Shatterday.* Copyright © 1977, 1980 by Harlan Ellison. Reprinted by arrangement with and permission of the author and the author's agent, Robert P. Mills, Ltd., New York. All rights reserved.

"Within the Walls of Tyre" by Michael Bishop. From *Weirdbook 13,* 1978. Copyright © 1978 by Michael Bishop. Reprinted by permission of the author and his agent, Virginia Kidd.

CONTENTS

Contents

INTRODUCTION

This anthology was created to fill an astonishing gap in fantasy book publishing. While there have been numerous anthologies of fantasy stories, many of them excellent, until now no one has made the effort to gather together in one volume a selection of the finest stories that have been published since the first all-fantasy magazine was born. *Masters of Fantasy* attempts just that task; it might be called the "definitive" anthology of magazine fantasy. Every story in this book originally appeared in a fantasy magazine, and the overall mixture of styles and subjects shows the rich variety of imagination that these magazines have presented.

There are no stories here from books, "slick" magazines, literary reviews, or any source other than the central genre publications. In this way we emphasize the development of a cohesive and self-aware literary movement that has brought great changes to the traditional fantasy modes. The stories are arranged in chronological order of their publications, making the pattern of development obvious.

"Fantasy" connotes different things to different people: one of us might think immediately of ghost stories, another of fairy tales, a third of the Arabian Nights or the tales of King Arthur. These were the basic types of fantasy through the nineteenth and early twentieth centuries. When magazines specifically devoted to fantasy began to appear, they started from this foundation and built an astonishing variety of new types of fantasy. The old forms were updated, new styles and techniques came into use, and even some fundamental assumptions of fantasy writers were reexamined.

Once regular magazine markets for such stories became available many new writers began to produce fantasy and they brought new approaches to the genre. Perhaps the most noticeable was the faster pace

Wright himself made the attempt in 1930 with *Oriental Stories*; when its sales proved disappointing the title was changed to *The Magic Carpet Magazine*, but this too was unsuccessful and it died after fourteen issues. In 1939, Better Publications, Inc., publishers of dozens of successful pulp magazines, entered the weird fantasy field with *Strange Stories*, which did well for a while but was discontinued after twelve issues in favor of more lucrative magazines in other genres.

These and a few other unsuccessful efforts at serious weird fiction magazines proved that the readership for them was too small to support more than *Weird Tales* itself (and *Weird Tales* was only marginally profitable). A number of publishers in the thirties tried to achieve greater sales by producing lurid magazines that combined fantasy with sex and sadism; such titles as *Horror Stories*, *Sinister Stories*, *Terror Tales* and *Uncanny Tales* published stories like "Mistress of Satan's Hounds" and "Brides for the Half-Men." Though they made money for a while, they died as the Depression waned; this was probably not a coincidence.

But at the same time, two new fantasy magazines were launched that featured types of fantasy stories radically different from those in *Weird Tales*. In March 1939, John W. Campbell added a fantasy companion to his science fiction magazine *Astounding Science-Fiction* — titled *Unknown*, it featured a more "modern" style of fantasy in which terror gave way to rigorously logical consideration of fantasy themes. Its stories were crisply written, often full of adventure, frequently humorous; Theodore Sturgeon, L. Sprague de camp, Henry Kuttner, L. Ron Hubbard and many others wrote excellent fantasies for this magazine. It lasted for four and a half years, until World War II paper restrictions forced its demise.

Almost concurrently with *Unknown*'s first issue, a new magazine called *Fantastic Adventures* appeared — edited by Raymond A. Palmer — as a companion magazine to *Amazing Stories*, it presented a mixture of styles similar to those in *Unknown* but written for a younger audience. Stories of high adventure were of course featured, but the shorter stories were often comic; they had titles like "The Strange Voyage of Hector Squinch" and "The Horse That Talked." *Fantastic Adventures* became very successful and lasted till 1953, when it combined with a newer, digest-size magazine, *Fantastic*.

The 1940s also saw the rise and great popularity of several fantasy magazines devoted primarily to reprints. *Famous Fantastic Mysteries* and *Fantastic Novels*, edited by Mary Gnaedinger, were companion magazines that featured novels reprinted from non-genre pulps and from hardcover books; these tended to be lost-race adventures by, or in the manner of, A. Merritt. The *Avon Fantasy Reader* concentrated on stories in the stories they wrote. Traditionally fantasy had usually been slow and moody, but in order to please the readers of popular fantasy magazines — all of them "pulp" magazines at first — writers learned to be more spare with their adjectives, and to get their stories moving quickly.

The first all-fantasy magazine was *Weird Tales*, founded in 1923 by publisher J. C. Henneberger, who was an admirer of Edgar Allan Poe's horror stories and wanted to promote further writing of that type. The magazine's first editor, Edwin Baird, was less than enthusiastic about the genre and the issues he produced were mostly low in quality. He published the early stories of H.P. Lovecraft, but only because Henneberger insisted; Baird's own attempts to popularize the magazine included publication of articles and stories by Harry Houdini. (These were revised or ghost-written by Lovecraft.) But sales remained poor and after a year and a half Henneberger replaced Baird with a new editor, Farnsworth wright.

Wright quickly proved to be a superb editor, establishing a reputation in the fantasy genre as towering as that of John W. Campbell was to become in science fiction. In the nearly sixteen years he edited the magazine, Wright discovered and published the work of such writers as Clark Ashton Smith, Robert E. Howard, C. L. Moore and many more — literally all the major authors of magazine fantasy in the twenties and thirties. (He also published the first story of a teenager who later became famous as Tennessee Williams.) But Wright had long suffered from Parkinson's disease and by 1940 his health was failing. When the magazine was sold to a new publisher, the editorship was turned over to Dorothy McIlwraith. Wright died later that year, mourned and lauded by his friends and associates in fantasy.

McIlwraith was a competent editor but she had to work with a severely curtailed budget (it had never been large), and *Weird Tales* favorites such as Lovecraft, Howard, and Smith had either died or stopped writing for the magazine. She published early stories by Fritz Leiber and Theodore Sturgeon, and discovered Ray Bradbury, publishing most of his excellent early fantasies. The magazine survived the forties but died in 1954, along with most of the other pulp magazines in all genres; the pulp era had come to an end.

(The magazine was briefly revived — for four issues — in the early seventies under the editorship of Sam Moskowitz. At this writing, another revival is underway with Lin Carter as editor; it is to appear as a paperback "magazine.")

Several attempts were made during the 1930s to publish other fantasy magazines that would sell to *Weird Tales*'s readership. Farnsworth from the early *Weird Tales* and those by authors who had written fantasy-horror before or outside of the pulp magazines, such as Stephen Vincent Benét, Lord Dunsany, Ambrose Bierce and William Hope Hodgson. Donald A. Wollheim, a fantasy aficionado, proved himself to be a fine editor with this series.

The 1950s began with the inauguration of several new fantasy magazines, all of them in the digest-sized format. Howard Browne edited *Fantastic*, which we've already mentioned; its early issues presented excellent stories by top writers such as Bradbury, Sturgeon, and Leiber, but its editorial budget was too high to be justified by its sales, so it merged with *Fantastic Adventures* and, offering lower rates to authors, has varied widely in quality since. There were several excellent but short-lived ventures by other publishers and editors: Damon Knight's *Worlds Beyond* lasted for only three issues; Lester del Rey's *Fantasy Fiction Magazine* presented four issues; and H. L. Gold's *Beyond* survived ten issues. The fifties, a time characterized by humdrum complacency in this country, felt no strong need for fantasy.

But the most successful new magazine of the period —and arguably the finest fantasy magazine ever published — was *Fantasy and Science*, launched late in 1949 under the editorship of Anthony Boucher and J. Francis McComas. Its early issues featured nearly as many reprints as original stories, the reprints being drawn from books and non-genre magazines; but the emphasis soon changed to new stories, at least half of which were science fiction. This enabled the magazine to survive and thrive to the present, attracting not only fantasy fans but also the science fiction readership. (SF readers apparently welcome fantasy occasionally but not as a steady diet.)

Fantasy and Science Fiction, under the editorships of Boucher and McComas, later of Robert P. Mills, Avram Davidson, Edward Ferman, and currently, Kristine Kathryn Rosch, became the "quality" magazine of fantasy; it has published most of the important fantasy stories of the last thirty years. Authors such as Richard Matheson, Zenna Henderson, R. Bretnor, Avram Davidson, Richard Cowper and far too many others to name established their reputations in its pages.

In England, Walter Gillings began editing *Science-Fantasy* in 1950; after two issues, he yielded the editorial chair to E. J. Carnell, who continued the magazine for thirteen years. Kyril Bonfiglioli replaced him and soon changed the title to *impulse*, later to *sf impulse*; Harry Harrison edited the final five issues, the last of which appeared in 1967. This magazine brought to prominence such British writers as J. G. Ballard and Keith Roberts, and the U.S. author Thomas Burnett Swain.

The fantasy readership was slow to organize, at least in comparison with science fiction fandom, but in recent years fantasy conventions have become common, and literary prizes have been established, such as the World Fantasy Award and Britain's August Derleth Fantasy Award. (Actually, the sf Hugo Award has always been open to works of fantasy, and several such stories have won.)

There has been a strong resurgence in fantasy book publishing recently, with mass-market houses like Del Rey Books, Dell, and other adopting special logos for their fantasy novels and collections. This renascence was spurred by the great commercial and artistic success of J.R.R. Tolkien's *The Lord of the Rings*, which set off a boom of so-called "high fantasy" (frequently imitative). A revival of Robert E. Howard's stories about Conan and other warrior-heroes quickly led to many new novels of "sword and sorcery"; and weird/horror fiction has again become popular, originally as a result of the republication of H. P. Lovecraft's works and currently because of the great success of writers such as Stephen King.

It is a curious fact that though fantasy has again become very popular as far as book sales are concerned, this trend has not yet been reflected in magazine publishing. The market today for short stories of fantasy is mostly confined (with the notable exception of *Fantasy and Science Fiction*) to book anthologies and semi-professional magazines.

This situation is as sad as it is peculiar — but there is the hope that readers and writers of fantasy short stories will be inspired by the rich legacy presented in the pages that follow. For as the more than a quarter of a million words of fantasy fiction in this volume indicate, fantasy magazines have produced a significant amount of quality writing over the years in a wide variety of styles, from the humorous to the tragic, from visions of charming apparitions to horrible creatures that go bump in the night.

TERRY CARR (1937-1987)
MARTIN HARRY GREENBERG
Oakland and Green Bay

The Rats in the Walls

H. P. Lovecraft

On July 16, 1923, I moved into Exham Priory after the last workman had finished his labors. The restoration had been a stupendous task, for little had remained of the deserted pile but a shell-like ruin; yet because it had been the seat of my ancestors, I let no expense deter me. The place had not been inhabited since the reign of James the First, when a tragedy of intensely hideous, though largely unexplained, nature had struck down the master, five of his children, and several servants; and driven forth under a cloud of suspicion and terror the third son, my lineal progenitor and the only survivor of the abhorred line.

With this sole heir denounced as a murderer, the estate had reverted to the crown, nor had the accused man made any attempt to exculpate himself or regain his property. Shaken by some horror greater than that of conscience or the law, and expressing only a frantic wish to exclude the ancient edifice from his sight and memory, Walter de la Poer, eleventh Baron Exham, fled to Virginia and there founded the family which by the

1

next century had become known as Delapore.

Exham Priory had remained untenanted, though later allotted to the estates of the Norrys family and much studied because of its peculiarly composite architecture; an architecture involving Gothic towers resting on a Saxon or Romanesque substructure, whose foundation in turn was of a still earlier order or blend of orders—Roman, and even Druidic or native Cymric, if legends speak truly. This foundation was a very singular thing, being merged on one side with the solid limestone of the precipice from whose brink the priory overlooked a desolate valley three miles west of the village of Anchester.

Architects and antiquarians loved to examine this strange relic of forgotten centuries, but the country folk hated it. They had hated it hundreds of years before, when my ancestors lived there, and they hated it now, with the moss and mould of abandonment on it. I had not been a day in Anchester before I knew I came of an accursed house. And this week workmen have blown up Exham Priory, and are busy obliterating the traces of its foundations. The bare statistics of my ancestry I had always known, together with the fact that my first American forbear had come to the colonies under a strange cloud. Of details, however, I had been kept wholly ignorant through the policy of reticence always maintained by the Delapores. Unlike our planter neighbors, we seldom boasted of crusading ancestors or other mediaeval and Renaissance heroes; nor was any kind of tradition handed down except what may have been recorded in the sealed envelope left before the Civil War by every squire to his eldest son for posthumous opening. The glories we cherished were those achieved since the migration; the glories of a proud and honorable, if somewhat reserved and unsocial Virginia line.

During the war our fortunes were extinguished and our whole existence changed by the burning of Carfax, our home on the banks of the James. My grandfather, advanced in years, had perished in that incendiary outrage, and with him the envelope that had bound us all to the past. I can recall that fire today as I saw it then at the age of seven, with the Federal soldiers shouting, the women screaming, and the negroes howling and praying. My father was in the army, defending Richmond, and after many formalities my mother and I were passed through the lines to join him.

When the war ended we all moved north, whence my mother had come; and I grew to manhood, middle age, and ultimate wealth as a stolid Yankee. Neither my father nor I ever knew what our hereditary envelope had contained, and as I merged into the grayness of Massachusetts business life I lost all interest in the mysteries which evidently lurked far back in my family tree. Had I suspected their nature, how gladly I would have left Exham Priory to its moss, bats, and cobwebs!

My father died in 1904, but without any message to leave to me, or to my only child, Alfred, a motherless boy of ten. It was this boy who reversed the order of family information, for although I could give him only jesting conjectures about the past, he wrote me of some very interesting ancestral legends when the late war took him to England in 1917 as an aviation officer. Apparently the Delapores had a colorful and perhaps sinister history, for a friend of my son's, Capt. Edward Norrys of the Royal Flying Corps, dwelt near the family seat at Anchester and related some peasant superstitions which few novelists could equal for wildness and incredibility. Norrys himself, of course, did not take them so seriously; but they amused my son and made good material for his letters to me. It was this legendry which definitely turned my attention to my transatlantic heritage, and made me resolve to purchase and restore the family seat which Norrys showed to Alfred in its picturesque desertion, and offered to get for him at a surprisingly reasonable figure, since his own uncle was the present owner.

I bought Exham Priory in 1918, but was almost immediately distracted from my plans of restoration by the return of my son as a maimed invalid. During the two years that he lived I thought of nothing but his care, having even placed my business under the direction of partners.

In 1921, as I found myself bereaved and aimless, a retired manufacturer no longer young, I resolved to divert my remaining years with my new possession. Visiting Anchester in December, I was entertained by Capt. Norrys, a plump, amiable young man who had thought much of my son, and secured his assistance in gathering plans and anecdotes to guide in the coming restoration. Exham Priory itself I saw without emotion, a jumble of tottering mediaeval ruins covered with lichens and honeycombed with rooks' nests, perched perilously upon a precipice, and denuded of floors or other interior features save the stone walls of the separate towers.

As I gradually recovered the image of the edifice as it had been when my ancestors left it over three centuries before, I began to hire workmen for the reconstruction. In every case I was forced to go outside the immediate locality, for the Anchester villagers had an almost unbelievable fear and hatred of the place. This sentiment was so great that it was sometimes communicated to the outside laborers, causing numerous desertions; whilst its scope appeared to include both the priory and its ancient family.

My son had told me that he was somewhat avoided during his visits because he was a de la Poer, and I now found myself subtly ostracised for a like reason until I convinced the peasants how little I knew of my heritage. Even then they sullenly disliked me, so that I had to collect most of the village traditions through the mediation of Norrys. What the people could not forgive, perhaps, was that I had come to restore a symbol so abhorrent to them; for, rationally or not, they viewed Exham Priory as nothing less than a haunt of fiends and werewolves.

Piecing together the tales which Norrys collected for me, and supplementing them with the accounts of several savants who had studied the ruins, I deduced that Exham Priory stood on the site of a prehistoric temple; a Druidical or ante-Druidical thing which must have been contemporary with Stonehenge. That indescribable rites had been celebrated there, few doubted, and there were unpleasant tales of the transference of these rites into the Cybele-worship which the Romans had introduced.

Inscriptions still visible in the subcellar bore such unmistakable letters as "DIV ... OPS ... MAGNA. MAT ..." sign of the Magna Mater whose dark worship was once vainly forbidden to Roman citizens. Anchester had been the camp of the third Augustan legion, as many remains attest, and it was said that the temple of Cybele was splendid and thronged with worshippers who performed nameless ceremonies at the bidding of a Phrygian priest. Tales added that the fall of the old religion did not end the orgies at the temple, but that the priests lived on in the new faith without real change. Likewise was it said that the rites did not vanish with the Roman power, and that certain among the Saxons added to what remained of the temple, and gave it the essential outline it subsequently preserved, making it the center of a cult feared through half the heptarchy. About 1000 A.D. the place is mentioned in a chronicle as being a substantial stone priory housing a strange and powerful monastic order and surrounded by extensive gardens which needed no walls to exclude a frightened populace. It was never destroyed by the Danes, though after the Norman Conquest it must have declined tremendously; since there was no impediment when Henry the Third granted the site to my ancestor, Gilbert de la Poer, First Baron Exham, in 1261.

Of my family before this date there is no evil report, but something strange must have happened then. In one chronicle there is a reference to a de la Poer as "cursed of God" in 1307, whilst village legendry had nothing but evil and frantic fear to tell of the castle that went up on the foundations of the old temple and priory. The fireside tales were of the most grisly description, all the ghastlier because of their frightened reticence and cloudy evasiveness. They represented my ancestors as a race of hereditary daemons beside whom Gilles de Retz and the Marquis de Sade would seem the veriest tyros, and hinted whisperingly at their responsibility for the occasional disappearances of villagers through several generations.

The worst characters, apparently, were the barons and their direct heirs; at least, most was whispered about these. If of healthier inclinations, it was said, an heir would early and mysteriously die to make way for another more typical scion. There seemed to be an inner cult in the family, presided over by the head of the house, and sometimes closed except to a few members. Temperament rather than ancestry was evidently the basis of this cult, for it was entered by several who married into the family. Lady Margaret Trevor from Cornwall, wife of Godfrey, the second son of the fifth baron, became a favorite bane of children all over the countryside, and the daemon heroine of a particularly horrible old ballad not yet extinct near the Welsh border. Preserved in balladry, too, though not illustrating the same point, is the hideous tale of Lady Mary de la Poer, who shortly after her marriage to the Earl of Shrewsfield was killed by him and his mother, both of the slayers being absolved and blessed by the priest to whom they confessed what they dared not repeat to the world.

These myths and ballads, typical as they were of crude superstition, repelled me greatly. Their persistence, and their application to so long a line of my ancestors, were especially annoying; whilst the imputations of monstrous habits proved unpleasantly reminiscent of the one known scandal of my immediate forbears—the case of my cousin, young Randolph Delapore of Carfax, who went among the negroes and became a voodoo priest after he returned from the Mexican War.

I was much less disturbed by the vaguer tales of wails and howlings in the barren, windswept valley beneath the limestone cliff; of the graveyard stenches after the spring rains; of the floundering, squealing white thing on which Sir John Clave's horse had trod one night in a lonely field; and of the servant who had gone mad at what he saw in the priory in the full light of day. These things were hackneyed spectral lore, and I was at that time a pronounced skeptic. The accounts of vanished peasants were less to be dismissed, though not especially significant in view of mediaeval custom. Prying curiosity meant death, and more than one severed head had been publicly shown on the bastions—now effaced—around Exham Priory.

A few of the tales were exceedingly picturesque, and made me wish I had learnt more of the comparative mythology in my youth. There was, for instance, the belief that a legion of batwinged devils kept witches' sabbath each night at the priory—a legion whose sustenance might explain the disproportionate abundance of coarse vegetables harvested in the vast gardens. And, most vivid of all, there was the dramatic epic of the rats— the scampering army of obscene vermin which had burst forth from the castle three months after the tragedy that doomed it to desertion—the lean, filthy, ravenous army which had swept all before it and devoured fowl, cats, dogs, hogs, sheep, and even two hapless human beings before its fury was spent. Around that unforgettable rodent army a whole separate cycle of myths revolves, for it scattered among the village homes and brought curses and horrors in its train.

Such was the lore that assailed me as I pushed to completion, with an elderly obstinacy, the work of restoring my ancestral home. It must not be imagined for a moment that these tales formed my principal psychological environment. On the other hand, I was constantly praised and encouraged by Capt. Norrys and the antiquarians who surrounded and aided me. When the task was done, over two years after its commencement, I viewed the great rooms, wainscotted walls, vaulted ceilings, mullioned windows, and broad staircases with a pride which fully compensated for the prodigious expense of the restoration.

Every attribute of the Middle Ages was cunningly reproduced, and the new parts blended perfectly with the original walls and foundations. The seat of my fathers was complete, and I looked forward to redeeming at last the local fame of the line which ended in me. I would reside here permanently, and prove that a de la Poer (for I had adopted again the original spelling of the name) need not be a fiend. My comfort was perhaps augmented by the fact that, although Exham Priory was mediaevally fitted, its interior was in truth wholly new and free from old vermin and old ghosts alike.

As I have said, I moved in on July 16, 1923. My household consisted of seven servants and nine cats, of which latter species I am particularly fond. My eldest cat, "Nigger-Man," was seven years old and had come with me from my home in Bolton, Massachusetts; the others I had accumulated whilst living with Capt. Norrys' family during the restoration of the priory.

For five days our routine proceeded with the utmost placidity, my time being spent mostly in the codification of old family data. I had now obtained some very circumstantial accounts of the final tragedy and flight of Walter de la Poer, which I conceived to be the probable contents of the hereditary paper lost in the fire at Carfax. It appeared that my ancestor was accused with much reason of having killed all the other members of his household, except four servant confederates, in their sleep, about two weeks after a shocking discovery which changed his whole demeanor, but which, except by implication, he disclosed to no one save perhaps the servants who assisted him and afterward fled beyond reach.

This deliberate slaughter, which included a father, three brothers, and two sisters, was largely condoned by the villagers, and so slackly treated by the law that its perpetrator escaped honored, unharmed, and undisguised to Virginia; the general whispered sentiment being that he had purged the land of immemorial curse. What discovery had prompted an act so terrible, I could scarcely even conjecture. Walter de la Poer must have known for years the sinister tales about his family, so that this material could have given him no fresh impulse. Had he, then, witnessed some appalling ancient rite, or stumbled upon some frightful and revealing symbol in the priory or its vicinity? He was reputed to have been a shy, gentle youth in England. In Virginia he seemed not so much hard or bitter as harassed and apprehensive. He was spoken of in the diary of another gentleman adventurer, Francis Harley of Bellview, as a man of unexampled justice, honor, and delicacy.

On July 22 occurred the first incident which, though lightly dismissed at the time, takes on a preternatural significance in relation to later events. It was so simple as to be almost negligible, and could not possibly have been noticed under the circumstances; for it must be recalled that since I was in a building practically fresh and new except for the walls, and surrounded by a well-balanced staff of servitors, apprehension would have been absurd despite the locality.

What I afterward remembered is merely this—that my old black cat, whose moods I know so well, was undoubtedly alert and anxious to an extent wholly out of keeping with his natural character. He roved from room to room, restless and disturbed, and sniffed constantly about the walls which formed part of the Gothic structure. I realize how trite this sounds—like the inevitable dog in the ghost story, which always growls before his master sees the sheeted figure—yet I cannot consistently suppress it.

The following day a servant complained of restlessness among all the cats in the house. He came to me in my study, a lofty west room on the second story, with groined arches, black oak panelling, and a triple Gothic window overlooking the limestone cliff and desolate valley; and even as he spoke I saw the jetty form of Nigger-Man creeping along the west wall and scratching at the new panels which overlaid the ancient stone.

I told the man that there must be some singular odor or emanation from the old stonework, imperceptible to human senses, but affecting the delicate organs of cats even through the new woodwork. This I truly believed, and when the fellow suggested the presence of mice or rats, I mentioned that there had been no rats there for three hundred years, and that even the field mice of the surrounding country could hardly be found in these high walls, where they had never been known to stray. That afternoon I called on Capt. Norrys, and he assured me that it would be quite incredible for field mice to infest the priory in such a sudden and unprecedented fashion.

That night, dispensing as usual with a valet, I retired in the west tower chamber which I had chosen as my own, reached from the study by a stone staircase and short gallery—the former partly ancient, the latter entirely restored. This room was circular, very high, and without wainscotting, being hung with arras which I had myself chosen in London. Seeing that Nigger-Man was with me, I shut the heavy Gothic door and retired by the light of the electric bulbs which so cleverly counterfeited candles, finally switching off the light and sinking on the carved and canopied four-poster, with the venerable cat in his accustomed place across my feet. I did not draw the curtains, but gazed out at the narrow north window which I faced. There was a suspicion of aurora in the sky, and the delicate traceries of the window were pleasantly silhouetted.

At some time I must have fallen quietly asleep, for I recall a distinct sense of leaving strange dreams, when the cat started violently from his placid position. I saw him in the faint auroral glow, head strained forward, forefeet on my ankles, and hind feet stretched behind. He was looking intensely at a point on the wall somewhat west of the window, a point which to my eye had nothing to mark it. but toward which all my attention was now directed.

And as I watched, I knew that Nigger-Man was not vainly excited. Whether the arras actually moved I cannot say. I think it did, very slightly. But what I can swear to is that behind it I heard a low, distinct scurrying as of rats or mice. In a moment the cat had jumped bodily on the screening tapestry, bringing the affected section to the floor with his weight, and exposing a damp, ancient wall of stone; patched here and there by the restorers, and devoid of any trace of rodent prowlers.

Nigger-Man raced up and down the floor by this part of the wall, clawing the fallen arras and seemingly trying at times to insert a paw between the wall and the oaken floor. He found nothing, and after a time returned wearily to his place across my feet. I had not moved, but I did not sleep again that night.

In the morning I questioned all the servants, and found that none of them had noticed anything unusual, save that the cook remembered the actions of a cat which had rested on her windowsill. This cat had howled at some unknown hour of the night, awaking the cook in time for her to see him dart purposefully out of the open door down the stairs. I drowsed away the noontime, and in the afternoon called again on Capt. Norrys, who became exceedingly interested in what I told him. The odd incidents—so slight yet so curious—appealed to his sense of the picturesque, and elicited from him a number of reminiscences of local ghostly lore. We were genuinely perplexed at the presence of rats, and Norrys lent me some traps and Paris green, which I had the servants place in strategic localities when I returned.

I retired early, being very sleepy, but was harassed by dreams of the most horrible sort, I seemed to be looking down from an immense height upon a twilit grotto, knee-deep with filth, where a white-bearded daemon swineherd drove about with his staff a flock of fungous, flabby beasts whose appearance filled me with unutterable loathing. Then, as the swineherd paused and nodded over his task, a mighty swarm of rats rained down on the stinking abyss and fell to devouring beasts and man alike.

From this terrific vision I was abruptly awaked by the motions of Nigger-Man, who had been sleeping as usual across my feet. This time I did not have to question the source of his snarls and hisses, and of the fear which made him sink his claws into my ankle, unconscious of their effect; for on every side of the chamber the walls were alive with nauseous sound—the verminous slithering of ravenous, gigantic rats. There was now no aurora to show the state of the arras—the fallen section of which had been replaced—but I was not too frightened to switch on the light.

As the bulbs leapt into radiance I saw a hideous shaking all over the tapestry, causing the somewhat peculiar designs to execute a singular dance of death. This motion disappeared almost at once, and the sound with it. Springing out of bed, I poked at the arras with the long handle of a warming-pan that rested near, and lifted one section to see what lay beneath. There was nothing but the patched stone wall, and even the cat had lost his tense realization of abnormal presences. When I examined the circular trap that had been placed in the room, I found all of the openings sprung, though no trace remained of what had been caught and had escaped.

Further sleep was out of the question, so, lighting a candle, I opened the door and went out in the gallery toward the stairs to my study, Nigger-Man following at my heels. Before we had reached the stone steps, however, the cat darted ahead of me and vanished down the ancient flight. As I descended the stairs myself, I became suddenly aware of sounds in the great room below; sounds of a nature which could not be mistaken.

The oak-panelled walls were alive with rats, scampering and milling, whilst Nigger-Man was racing about with the fury of a baffled hunter. Reaching the bottom, I switched on the light, which did not this time cause the noise to subside. The rats continued their riot, stampeding with such force and distinctness that I could finally assign to their motions a definite direction. These creatures, in numbers apparently inexhaustible, were engaged in one stupendous migration from inconceivable heights to some depth conceivably or inconceivably below.

I now heard steps in the corridor, and in another moment two servants pushed open the massive door. They were searching the house for some unknown source of disturbance which had thrown all the cats into a snarling panic and caused them to plunge precipitately down several flights of stairs and squat, yowling, before the closed door to the sub-cellar. I asked them if they had heard the rats, but they replied in the negative. And when I turned to call their attention to the sounds in the panels, I realized that the noise had ceased.

With the two men, I went down to the door of the sub-cellar, but found the cats already dispersed. Later I resolved to explore the crypt below, but for the present I merely made a round of the traps. All were sprung, yet all were tenantless. Satisfying myself that no one had heard the rats save the felines and me, I sat in my study till morning, thinking profoundly and recalling every scrap of legend I had unearthed concerning the building I inhabited.

I slept some in the forenoon, leaning back in the one comfortable library chair which my mediaeval plan of furnishing could not banish. Later I telephoned to Capt. Norrys, who came over and helped me explore the sub-cellar.

Absolutely nothing untoward was found, although we could not repress a thrill at the knowledge that this vault was built by Roman hands. Every low arch and massive pillar was Roman—not the debased Romanesque of the bungling Saxons, but the severe and harmonious classicism of the age of the Caesars; indeed, the walls abounded with inscriptions familiar to the antiquarians who had repeatedly explored the place—things like "P. GETAE. PROP...TEMP...DONA..." and "L. PRAEC...VS...PONTIFI...ATYS...."

The reference to Atys made me shiver, for I had read Catullus and knew something of the hideous rites of the Eastern god, whose worship was so mixed with that of Cybele. Norrys and I, by the light of lanterns, tried to interpret the odd and nearly effaced designs on certain irregularly rectangular blocks of stone generally held to be altars, but could make nothing of them. We remembered that one pattern, a sort of rayed sun, was held by students to imply a non-Roman origin, suggesting that these altars had merely been adopted by the Roman priests from some older and perhaps aboriginal temple on the same site. On one of these blocks were some brown stains which made me wonder. The largest, in the center of the room, had certain features on the upper surface which indicated its connection with fire—probably burnt offerings.

Such were the sights in that crypt before whose door the cats howled, and where Norrys and I now determined to pass the night. Couches were brought down by the servants, who were told not to mind any nocturnal actions of the cats, and Nigger-Man was admitted as much for help as for companionship. We decided to keep the great oak door—a modern replica with slits for ventilation—tightly closed; and, with this attended to, we retired with lanterns still burning to await whatever might occur.

The vault was very deep in the foundations of the priory, and undoubtedly far down on the face of the beetling limestone cliff overlooking the waste valley. That it had been the goal of the scuffling and unexplainable rats I could not doubt, though why, I could not tell. As we lay there expectantly, I found my vigil occasionally mixed with half-formed dreams from which the uneasy motions of the cat across my feet would rouse me.

These dreams were not wholesome, but horribly like the one I had had the night before. I saw again the twilit grotto, and the swineherd with his unmentionable fungous beasts wallowing in filth, and as I looked at these things they seemed nearer and more distinct—so distinct that I could almost observe their features. Then I did observe the flabby features of one of them—and awaked with such a scream that Nigger-Man started up, whilst Capt. Norrys, who had not slept, laughed considerably. Norrys might have laughed more—or perhaps less—had he known what it was that made me scream. But I did not remember myself till later. Ultimate horror often paralyses memory in a merciful way.

Norrys waked me when the phenomena began. Out of the same frightful dream I was called by his gentle shaking and his urging to listen to the cats. Indeed, there was much to listen to, for beyond the closed door at the head of the stone steps was a veritable nightmare of feline yelling and clawing, whilst Nigger-Man, unmindful of his kindred outside, was running excitedly around the bare stone walls, in which I heard the same babel of scurrying rats that had troubled me the night before.

An acute terror now rose within me, for here were anomalies which nothing normal could well explain. These rats, if not the creatures of a madness which I shared with the cats alone, must be burrowing and sliding in Roman walls I had thought to be of solid limestone blocks... unless perhaps the action of water through more than seventeen centuries had eaten winding tunnels which rodent bodies had worn clear and ample.... But even so, the spectral horror was no less; for if these were living vermin why did not Norrys hear their disgusting commotion? Why did he urge me to watch Nigger-Man and listen to the cats outside, and why did he guess wildly and vaguely at what could have aroused them?

By the time I had managed to tell him, as rationally as I could, what I thought I was hearing, my ears gave me the last fading impression of the scurrying; which had retreated *still downward*, far underneath this deepest of sub-cellars till it seemed as if the whole cliff below were riddled with questing rats. Norrys was not as skeptical as I had anticipated, but instead seemed profoundly moved. He motioned to me to notice that the cats at the door had ceased their clamor, as if giving up the rats for lost; whilst Nigger-Man had a burst of renewed restlessness, and was clawing frantically around the bottom of the large stone altar in the center of the room, which was nearer Norrys' couch than mine.

My fear of the unknown was at this point very great. Something astounding had occurred, and I saw that Capt. Norrys, a younger, stouter, and presumably more naturally materialistic man, was affected fully as much as myself—perhaps because of his lifelong and intimate familiarity with local legend. We could for the moment do nothing but watch the old black cat as he pawed with decreasing fervor at the base of the altar, occasionally looking up and mewing to me in that persuasive manner which he used when he wished me to perform some favor for him.

Norrys now took a lantern close to the altar and examined the place where Nigger-Man was pawing; silently kneeling and scraping away the lichens of the centuries which joined the massive pre-Roman block to the tesselated floor. He did not find anything, and was about to abandon his efforts when I noticed a trivial circumstance which made me shudder, even though it implied nothing more than I had already imagined.

I told him of it, and we both looked at its almost imperceptible manifestation with the fixedness of fascinated discovery and acknowledgment. It was only this—that the flame of the lantern set down near the altar was slightly but certainly flickering from a draught of air which it had not before received, and which came indubitably from the crevice between floor and altar where Norrys was scraping away the lichens.

We spent the rest of the night in the brilliantly lighted study, nervously discussing what we should do next. The discovery that some vault deeper than the deepest known masonry of the Romans underlay this accursed pile; some vault unsuspected by the curious antiquarians of three centuries; would have been sufficient to excite us without any background of the sinister. As it was, the fascination became two-fold; and we paused in doubt whether to abandon our search and quit the priory forever in superstitious caution, or to gratify our sense of adventure and brave whatever horrors might await us in the unknown depths.

By morning we had compromised, and decided to go to London to gather a group of archaeologists and scientific men fit to cope with the mystery. It should be mentioned that before leaving the sub-cellar we had vainly tried to move the central altar which we now recognized as the gate to a new pit of nameless fear. What secret would open the gate, wiser men than we would have to find.

During many days in London Capt. Norrys and I presented our facts, conjectures, and legendary anecdotes to five eminent authorities, all men who could be trusted to respect any family disclosures which future explorations might develop. We found most of them little disposed to scoff, but, instead, intensely interested and sincerely sympathetic. It is hardly necessary to name them all, but I may say that they included Sir William Brinton, whose excavations in the Troad excited most of the world in their day. As we all took the train for Anchester I felt myself poised on the brink of frightful revelations, a sensation symbolized by the air of mourning among the many Americans at the unexpected death of the

President on the other side of the world.

On the evening of August 7 we reached Exham Priory, where the servants assured me that nothing unusual had occurred. The cats, even old Nigger-Man, had been perfectly placid; and not a trap in the house had been sprung. We were to begin exploring on the following day, awaiting which I assigned well-appointed rooms to all my guests.

I myself retired in my own tower chamber, with Nigger-Man across my feet. Sleep came quickly, but hideous dreams assailed me. There was a vision of a Roman feast like that of Trimalchio, with a horror in a covered platter. Then came that damnable, recurrent thing about the swineherd and his filthy drove in the twilit grotto. Yet when I awoke it was full daylight, with normal sounds in the house below. The rats, living or spectral, had not troubled me; and Nigger-Man was still quietly asleep. On going down, I found that the same tranquillity had prevailed elsewhere; a condition which one of the assembled savants—a fellow named Thornton, devoted to the psychic—rather absurdly laid to the fact that I had now been shown the thing which certain forces had wished to show me.

All was now ready, and at 11 A.M. our entire group of seven men, bearing powerful electric searchlights and implements of excavation, went down to the sub-cellar and bolted the door behind us. Nigger-Man was with us, for the investigators found no occasion to despise his excitability, and were indeed anxious that he be present in case of obscure rodent manifestations. We noted the Roman inscriptions and unknown altar designs only briefly, for three of the savants had already seen them, and all knew their characteristics. Prime attention was paid to the momentous central altar, and within an hour Sir William Brinton had caused it to tilt backward, balanced by some unknown species of counterweight.

There now lay revealed such a horror as would have overwhelmed us had we not been prepared. Through a nearly square opening in the tiled floor, sprawling on a flight of stone steps so prodigiously worn that it was little more than an inclined plane at the center, was a ghastly array of human or semi-human bones. Those which retained their collocation as skeletons showed attitudes of panic, fear, and over all were the marks of rodent gnawing. The skulls denoted nothing short of utter idiocy, cretinism, or primitive semiapedom.

Above the hellishly littered steps arched a descending passage seemingly chiseled from the solid rock, and conducting a current of air. This current was not a sudden and noxious rush as from a closed vault, but a cool breeze with something of freshness in it. We did not pause long, but shiveringly began to clear a passage down the steps. It was then that Sir William, examining the hewn walls, made the odd observation that the passage, according to the direction of the strokes, must have been chiseled *from beneath*.

I must be very deliberate now, and choose my words.

After ploughing down a few steps amidst the gnawed bones we saw that there was light ahead; not any mystic phosphorescence, but a filtered daylight which could not come except from unknown fissures in the cliff that overlooked the waste valley. That such fissures had escaped notice from outside was hardly remarkable, for not only is the valley wholly uninhabited, but the cliff is so high and beetling that only an aeronaut could study its face in detail. A few steps more, and our breaths were literally snatched from us by what we saw; so literally that Thornton, the psychic investigator, actually fainted in the arms of the dazed man who stood behind him. Norrys, his plump face utterly white and flabby, simply cried out inarticulately; whilst I think that what I did was to gasp or hiss, and cover my eyes.

The man behind me—the only one of the party older than I—croaked the hackneyed "My God!" in the most cracked voice I ever heard. Of seven cultivated men, only Sir William Brinton retained his composure, a thing the more to his credit because he led the party and must have seen the sight first.

It was a twilit grotto of enormous height, stretching away farther than any eye could see; a subterraneous world of limitless mystery and horrible suggestion. There were buildings and other architectural remains—in one terrified glance I saw a weird pattern of tumuli, a savage circle of monoliths, a low-domed Roman ruin, a sprawling Saxon pile, and an early English edifice of wood—but all these were dwarfed by the ghoulish spectacle presented by the general surface of the ground. For yards about the steps extended an insane tangle of human bones, or bones at least as human as those on the steps. Like a foamy sea they stretched, some fallen apart, but others wholly or partly articulated as skeletons; these latter invariably in postures of daemoniac frenzy, either fighting off some menace or clutching other forms with cannibal intent.

When Dr. Trask, the anthropologist, stopped to classify the skulls, he found a degraded mixture which utterly baffled him. They were mostly lower than the Piltdown man in the scale of evolution, but in every case definitely human. Many were of higher grade, and a very few were the skulls of supremely and sensitively developed types. All the bones were gnawed, mostly by rats, but somewhat by others of the half-human drove. Mixed with them were many tiny bones of rats—fallen members of the lethal army which closed the ancient epic.

I wonder that any man among us lived and kept his sanity through that hideous day of discovery. Not Hoffman or Huysmans could conceive a scene more wildly incredible, more frenetically repellent, or more Gothically grotesque than the twilit grotto through which we seven staggered; each stumbling on revelation after revelation, and trying to keep for the nonce from thinking of the events which must have taken place there three hundred, or a thousand, or two thousand, or ten thousand years ago. It was the antechamber of hell, and poor Thornton fainted again when Trask told him that some of the skeleton things must have descended as quadrupeds through the last twenty or more generations.

Horror piled on horror as we began to interpret the architectural remains. The quadruped things—with their occasional recruits from the biped class—had been kept in stone pens, out of which they must have broken in their last delirium of hunger or rat-fear. There had been great herds of them, evidently fattened on the coarse vegetables whose remains could be found as a sort of poisonous ensilage at the bottom of huge stone bins older than Rome. I knew now why my ancestors had had such excessive gardens—would to heaven I could forget! The purpose of the herds I did not have to ask.

Sir William, standing with his searchlight in the Roman ruin, translated aloud the most shocking ritual I have ever known; and told of the diet of the antediluvian cult which the priests of Cybele found and mingled with their own. Norrys, used as he was to the trenches, could not walk straight when he came out of the English building. It was a butcher shop and kitchen—he had expected that—but it was too much to see familiar English implements in such a place, and to read familiar English *graffiti* there, some as recent as 1610. I could not go in that building—that building whose demon activities were stopped only by the dagger of my ancestor Walter de la Poer.

What I did venture to enter was the low Saxon building whose oaken door had fallen, and there I found a terrible row of ten stone cells with rusty bars. Three had tenants, all skeletons of high grade, and on the bony forefinger of one I found a seal ring with my own coat-of-arms. Sir William found a vault with far older cells below the Roman chapel, but these cells were empty. Below them was a low crypt with cases of formally arranged bones, some of them bearing terrible parallel inscriptions carved in Latin, Greek, and the tongue of Phrygia.

Meanwhile, Dr. Trask had opened one of the prehistoric tumuli, and brought to light skulls which were slightly more human than a gorilla's, and which bore indescribably ideographic carvings. Through all this horror my cat stalked unperturbed. Once I saw him monstrously perched atop a mountain of bones, and wondered at the secrets that might lie behind his yellow eyes.

Having grasped to some slight degree the frightful revelations of this twilit area—an area so hideously foreshadowed by my recurrent dream— we turned to that apparently boundless depth of midnight cavern where no ray of light from the cliff could penetrate. We shall never know what sightless Stygian worlds yawn beyond the little distance we went, for it was decided that such secrets are not good for mankind. But there was plenty to engross us close at hand, for we had not gone far before the searchlights showed that accursed infinity of pits in which the rats had feasted, and whose sudden lack of replenishment had driven the ravenous rodent army first to turn on the living herds of starving things, and then to burst forth from the priory in that historic orgy of devastation which the peasants will never forget.

God! those carrion black pits of sawed, picked bones and opened skulls! Those nightmare chasms choked with the pithecanthropoid, Celtic, Roman, and English bones of countless unhallowed centuries! Some of them were full, and none can say how deep they had once been. Others were still bottomless to our searchlights, and peopled by unnamable fancies. What, I thought, of the hapless rats that stumbled into such traps amidst the blackness of their quests in this grisly Tartarus?

Once my foot slipped near a horribly yawning brink, and I had a moment of ecstatic fear. I must have been musing a long time, for I could not see any of the party but the plump Capt. Norrys. Then there came a sound from that inky, boundless, farther distance that I thought I knew; and I saw my old black cat dart past me like a winged Egyptian god, straight into the illimitable gulf of the unknown. But I was not far behind, for there was no doubt after another second. It was the eldritch scurrying of those fiend-born rats, always questing for new horrors, and determined to lead me on even unto those grinning caverns of earth's center where Nyarlathotep, the mad faceless god, howls blindly in the darkness to the piping of two amorphous idiot flute-players.

My searchlight expired, but still I ran. I heard voices, and yowls, and echoes, but above all there gently rose that impious, insidious scurrying; gently rising, rising, as a stiff bloated corpse gently rises above an oily river that flows under endless onyx bridges to a black, putrid sea.

Something bumped into me—something soft and plump. It must have been the rats; the viscous, gelatinous, ravenous army that feast on the dead and the living. . . . Why shouldn't rats eat a de la Poer as a de la Poer eats forbidden things? . . . The war ate my boy, damn them all . . . and the Yanks ate Carfax with flames and burned the Grandsire Delapore and the secret. . . . No, no, I tell you, I am *not* that demon swineherd in the twilit grotto! It was *not* Edward Norrys' fat face on that flabby fungous thing! Who says I am a de la Poer? He lived, but my boy died! . . . Shall a Norrys hold the lands of a de la Poer? . . . It's voodoo, I tell you . . . that spotted snake. . . . Curse you, Thornton, I'll teach you to faint at what my family do! . . . 'Sblood, thou stinkard, I'll learn ye how to gust . . . wolde ye swynke me thilke wys? ... *Magna Mater! Magna Mater!* ... *Atys* ... *Dia ad aghaidh's ad aodaun* ... *agus bas dunach ort! Dhonas 's dholas ort, agus leatsa!* ... *Ungl* ... *ungl* ... *rrlh* ... *chchch.* ....

That is what they say I said when they found me in the blackness after three hours; found me crouching in the blackness over the plump, half-eaten body of Capt. Norrys, with my own cat leaping and tearing at my throat. Now they have blown up Exham Priory, taken my Nigger-Man away from me, and shut me into this barred room at Hanwell with fearful whispers about my heredity and experience. Thornton is in the next room, but they prevent me from talking to him. They are trying, too, to suppress most of the facts concerning the priory. When I speak of poor Norrys they accuse me of a hideous thing, but they must know that I did not do it. They must know it was the rats; the slithering scurrying rats whose scampering will never let me sleep; the demon rats that race behind the padding in this room and beckon me down to greater horrors than I have ever known; the rats they can never hear; the rats, the rats in the walls.

The Woman of the Wood

A. Merritt

McKay sat on the balcony of the little inn that squatted like a brown gnome among the pines on the eastern shore of the lake.

It was a small and lonely lake high up in the Vosges; and yet, lonely is not just the word with which to tag its spirit; rather was it aloof, withdrawn. The mountains came down on every side, making a great tree-lined bowl that seemed, when McKay first saw it, to be filled with the still wine of peace.

McKay had worn the wings in the world war with honor, flying first with the French and later with his own country's forces. And as a bird loves the trees, so did McKay love them. To him they were not merely trunks and roots, branches and leaves; to him they were personalities. He was acutely aware of differences in character even among the same species—that pine was benevolent and jolly; that one austere and monkish; there stood a

19

swaggering bravo, and there dwelt a sage wrapped in green meditation; that birch was a wanton—the birch near her was virginal, still a-dream.

The war had sapped him, nerve and brain and soul. Through all the years that had passed since then the wound had kept open. But now, as he slid his car down the vast green bowl, he felt its spirit reach out to him; reach out to him and caress and quiet him, promising him healing. He seemed to drift like a falling leaf through the clustered woods; to be cradled by gentle hands of the trees.

He had stopped at the little gnome of an inn, and there he had lingered, day after day, week after week.

The trees had nursed him; soft whisperings of leaves, slow chant of the needled pines, had first deadened, then driven from him the re-echoing clamor of the war and its sorrow. The open wound of his spirit had closed under their green healing; had closed and become scar; and even the scar had been covered and buried, as the scars on Earth's breast are covered and buried, as the falling leaves of Autumn. The trees had laid green, healing hands on his eyes, banishing the pictures of war. He had sucked strength from the green breasts of the hills.

Yet as strength flowed back to him and mind and spirit healed, McKay had grown steadily aware that the place was troubled; that its tranquillity was not perfect; that there was ferment of fear within it.

It was as though the trees had waited until he himself had become whole before they made their own unrest known to him. Now they were trying to tell him something; there was a shrillness as of apprehension, of anger, in the whispering of the leaves, the needled chanting of the pines.

And it was this that had kept McKay at the inn—a definite consciousness of appeal, consciousness of something wrong—something wrong that he was being asked to right. He strained his ears to catch words in the rustling branches, words that trembled on the brink of his human understanding.

Never did they cross that brink.

Gradually he had orientated himself, had focused himself, so he believed, to the point of the valley's unease.

On all the shores of the lake there were but two dwellings. One was the inn, and around the inn the trees clustered protectively, confiding; friendly. It was as though they had not only accepted it, but had made it part of themselves.

Not so was it of the other habitation. Once it had been the hunting lodge of long-dead lords; now it was half ruined, forlorn. It stood across the lake almost exactly opposite the inn and back upon the slope a half mile from the shore. Once there had been fat fields around it and a fair orchard.

The forest had marched down upon them. Here and there in the fields, scattered pines and poplars stood like soldiers guarding some outpost; scouting parties of saplings lurked among the gaunt and broken fruit trees. But the forest had not had its way unchecked; ragged stumps showed where those who dwelt in the old lodge had cut down the invaders, blackened patches of the woodland showed where they had fired the woods.

Here was the conflict he had sensed. Here the green folk of the forest were both menaced and menacing; at war. The lodge was a fortress beleaguered by the woods, a fortress whose garrison sallied forth with axe and torch to take their toll of the besiegers.

Yet McKay sensed the inexorable pressing-in of the forest; he saw it as a green army ever filling the gaps in its enclosing ranks, shooting its seeds into the cleared places, sending its roots out to sap them; and armed always with a crushing patience, a patience drawn from the stone breasts of the eternal hills.

He had the impression of constant regard of watchfulness, as though night and day the forest kept its myriads of eyes upon the lodge; inexorably, not to be swerved from its purpose. He had spoken of this impression to the inn-keeper and his wife, and they had looked at him oddly.

"Old Polleau does not love the trees, no," the old man had said. "No, nor do his two sons. They do not love the trees—and very certainly the trees do not love them."

Between the lodge and the shore, marching down to the verge of the lake was a singularly beautiful little coppice of silver birches and firs. The coppice stretched for perhaps a quarter of a mile, was not more than a hundred feet or two in depth, and it was not alone the beauty of its trees but their curious grouping that aroused McKay's interest so vividly. At each end of the coppice were a dozen or more of the glistening needled firs, not clustered but spread out as though in open marching order; at widely spaced intervals along its other two sides paced single firs. The birches, slender and delicate, grew within the guard of these sturdier trees, yet not so thickly as to crowd each other.

To McKay the silver birches were for all the world like some gay caravan of lovely demoiselles under the protection of debonair knights. With that odd other sense of his he saw the birches as delectable damsels, merry and laughing—the pines as lovers, troubadours in their green-needled mail. And when the winds blew and the crests of the trees bent under them, it was as though dainty demoiselles picked up fluttering, leafy skirts, bent leafy hoods and danced while the knights of the firs drew closer round them, locked arms with theirs and danced with them to the roaring horns of the winds. At such times he almost heard sweet laughter from the birches, shoutings from the firs.

Of all the trees in that place McKay loved best this little wood; he rowed across and rested in its shade, had dreamed there and, dreaming, had heard again elfin echoes of the sweet laughter; eyes closed, had heard mysterious whisperings and the sound of dancing feet light as falling leaves; had taken dream draught of that gaiety which was the soul of the little wood.

And two days ago he had seen Polleau and his two sons. McKay had been dreaming in the coppice all that afternoon. As dusk began to fall he had reluctantly arisen and begun the row back to the inn. When he had been a few hundred feet from shore three men had come out from the trees and had stood watching him—three grim, powerful men taller than the average French peasant.

He had called a friendly greeting to them, but they had not answered it; stood there, scowling. Then as he bent again to his oars, one of the sons had raised a hatchet and had driven it savagely into the trunk of a slim birch beside him. He thought he heard a thin wailing cry from the stricken tree, a sigh from all the little wood.

McKay had felt as though the keen edge had bitten into his own flesh.

"Stop that!" he had cried, "Stop it, damn you!"

For answer the son had struck again—and never had McKay seen hate etched so deep as on his face as he struck. Cursing, a killing rage in heart, he swung the boat around, raced back to shore. He had heard the hatchet strike again and again and, close now to shore, had heard a crackling and over it once more the thin, high wailing. He had turned to look.

The birch was tottering, was falling. But as it had fallen he had seen a curious thing. Close beside it grew one of the firs, and, as the smaller tree crashed over, it dropped upon the fir like a fainting maid in the arms of a lover. And as it lay and trembled there, one of the great branches of the fir slipped from under it, whipped out and smote the hatchet wielder a crushing blow upon the head, sending him to earth.

It had been, of course, only the chance blow of a bough, bent by pressure of the fallen tree and then released as that tree slipped down. But there had been such suggestion of conscious action in the branch's recoil, so much of bitter anger in it, so much, in truth, had it been like the vengeful blow of a man that McKay had felt an eerie prickling of his scalp, his heart had missed its beat.

For a moment Polleau and the standing son had stared at the sturdy fir with the silvery birch lying on its green breast and folded in, shielded by, its needled boughs as though—again the swift impression came to McKay— as though it were a wounded maid stretched on breast, in arms, of knightly lover. For a long moment father and son had stared.

Then, still wordless but with that same bitter hatred on both their faces, they had stopped and picked up the other and with his arms around the neck of each had borne him limply away.

McKay, sitting on the balcony of the inn that morning, went over and over that scene; realized more and more clearly the human aspect of fallen birch and clasping fir, and the conscious deliberateness of the fir's blow. And during the two days that had elapsed since then, he had felt the unease of the trees increase, their whispering appeal became more urgent.

What were they trying to tell him? What did they want him to do?

Troubled, he stared across the lake, trying to pierce the mists that hung over it and hid the opposite shore. And suddenly it seemed that he heard the coppice calling him, felt it pull the point of his attention toward it irresistibly, as the lodestone swings and holds the compass needle.

The coppice called him, bade him come to it.

Instantly McKay obeyed the command; he arose and walked down to the boat landing; he stepped into his skiff and began to row across the lake. As his oars touched the water his trouble fell from him. In its place flowed peace and a curious exaltation.

The mist was thick upon the lake. There was no breath of wind, yet the mist billowed and drifted, shook and curtained under the touch of unfelt airy hands.

They were alive—the mists; they formed themselves into fantastic palaces past whose opalescent facades he flew; they built themselves into hills and valleys and circled plains whose floors were rippling silk. Tiny rainbows gleamed out among them, and upon the water prismatic patches shone and spread like spilled wine of opals. He had the illusion of vast distances—the hills of mist were real mountains, the valleys between them were not illusory. He was a colossus cleaving through some elfin world. A trout broke, and it was like leviathan leaping from the fathomless deep. Around the arc of its body rainbows interlaced and then dissolved into rain of softly gleaming gems—diamonds in dance with sapphires, flame-hearted rubies and pearls with shimmering souls of rose. The fish vanished, diving cleanly without sound; the jewelled bows vanished with it; a tiny irised whirlpool swirled for an instant where trout and flashing arcs had been.

Nowhere was there sound. He let his oars drop and leaned forward, drifting. In the silence, before him and around him, he felt opening the gateways of an unknown world.

And suddenly he heard the sound of voices, many voices; faint at first and murmurous; louder they became, swiftly; women's voices sweet and lilting and mingled with them the deeper tones of men. Voices that lifted and fell in a wild, gay chanting through whose *joyesse* ran undertones both of sorrow and of rage—as though faery weavers threaded through silk spun of sunbeams, sombre strands dipped in the black of graves and crimson strands stained in the red of wrathful sunsets.

He drifted on, scarce daring to breathe lest even that faint sound break the elfin song. Closer it rang and clearer; and now he became aware that the speed of his boat was increasing, that it was no longer drifting; that it was as though the little waves on each side were pushing him ahead with soft and noiseless palms. His boat grounded and as it rustled along over the smooth pebbles of the beach the song ceased.

McKay half arose and peered before him. The mists were thicker here but he could see the outlines of the coppice. It was like looking at it through many curtains of fine gauze; its trees seemed shifting, ethereal, unreal. And moving among the trees were figures that threaded the boles and flitted in rhythmic measures like the shadows of leafy boughs swaying to some cadenced wind.

He stepped ashore and made his way slowly toward them. The mists dropped behind him, shutting off all sight of shore.

The rhythmic flittings ceased; there was now no movement as there was no sound among the trees—yet he felt the little woods abrim with watching life. McKay tried to speak; there was a spell of silence on his mouth.

"You called me. I have come to listen to you—to help you if I can."

The words formed within his mind, but utter them he could not. Over and over he tried, desperately; the words seemed to die before his lips could give them life.

A pillar of mist whirled forward and halted, eddying half an arm length away. And suddenly out of it peered a woman's face, eyes level with his own. A woman's face—yes; but McKay, staring into those strange eyes probing his, knew that face though it seemed it was that of no woman of human breed. They were without pupils, the irises deer-like and of the soft green of deep forest dells; within them sparkled tiny star points of light like motes in a moonbeam. The eyes were wide and set far apart beneath a broad, low brow over which was piled braid upon braid of hair of palest gold, braids that seemed spun of shining ashes of gold. Her nose was small and straight, her mouth scarlet and exquisite. The face was oval, tapering to a delicately pointed chin.

Beautiful was that face, but its beauty was an alien one; elfin. For long moments the strange eyes thrust their gaze deep into his. Then out of the mist two slender white arms stole, the hands long, fingers tapering. The tapering fingers touched his ears.

"He shall hear," whispered the red lips.

Immediately from all about him a cry arose; in it was the whispering and rustling of the leaves beneath the breath of the winds, the shrilling of the harp strings of the boughs, the laughter of hidden brooks, the shoutings of waters flinging themselves down to deep and rocky pools—the voices of the woods made articulate.

"He shall hear!" they cried.

The long white fingers rested on his lips, and their touch was cool as bark of birch on cheek after some long upward climb through forest; cool and subtly sweet.

"He shall speak," whispered the scarlet lips.

"He shall speak!" answered the wood voices again, as though in litany.

"He shall see," whispered the woman and the cool fingers touched his eyes.

"He shall see!" echoed the wood voices.

The mists that had hidden the coppice from McKay wavered, thinned and were gone. In their place was a limpid, translucent, palely green ether, faintly luminous—as though he stood within some clear wan emerald. His feet pressed a golden moss spangled with tiny starry bluets. Fully revealed before him was the woman of the strange eyes and the face of elfin beauty. He dwelt for a moment upon the slender shoulders, the firm small tip-tilted breasts, the willow litheness of her body. From neck to knees a smock covered her, sheer and silken and delicate as though spun of cobwebs; through it her body gleamed as though fire of the young Spring moon ran in her veins.

Beyond her, upon the golden moss were other women like her, many of them; they stared at him with the same wide-set green eyes in which danced the clouds of sparkling moonbeam motes; like her they were crowned with glistening, pallidly golden hair; like hers too were their oval faces with the pointed chins and perilous elfin beauty. Only where she stared at him gravely, measuring him, weighing him—there were those of these her sisters whose eyes were mocking; and those whose eyes called to him with a weirdly tingling allure, their mouths athirst; those whose eyes looked upon him with curiosity alone and those whose great eyes pleaded with him, prayed to him.

Within that pellucid, greenly luminous air McKay was abruptly aware that the trees of the coppice still had a place. Only now they were spectral indeed; they were like white shadows cast athwart a glaucous screen; trunk and bough, twig and leaf they arose around him and they were as though etched in air by phantom craftsmen—thin, unsubstantial; they were ghost trees rooted in another space.

Suddenly he was aware that there were men among the women; men whose eyes were set wide apart as were theirs, as strange and pupilless as were theirs but with irises of brown and blue; men with pointed chins and oval faces, broad shouldered and clad in kirtles of darkest green; swarthy-skinned men, muscular and strong, with that same little grace of the women—and like them of a beauty alien and elfin.

McKay heard a little wailing cry. He turned. Close beside him lay a girl clasped in the arms of one of the swarthy, green-clad men. She lay upon his breast. His eyes were filled with a black flame of wrath, and hers were misted, anguished. For an instant McKay had a glimpse of the birch old Polleau's son had sent crashing down into the boughs of the fir. He saw birch and fir as immaterial outlines around the man and girl. For an instant girl and man and birch and fir seemed one and the same. The scarlet-lipped woman touched his shoulder, and the confusion cleared.

"She withers," sighed the woman, and in her voice McKay heard a faint rustling as of mournful leaves. "Now is it not pitiful that she withers—our sister who was so young, so slender, and so lovely?"

McKay looked again at the girl. The white skin seemed shrunken; the moon radiance that gleamed through the bodies of the others in hers was dim and pallid; her slim arms hung listlessly; her body drooped. The mouth too was wan and parched, the long and misted green eyes dull. The palely golden hair lustreless, and dry. He looked on slow death—a withering death.

"May the arm that struck her down wither!" the green-clad man who held her shouted, and in his voice McKay heard a savage strumming as of winter winds through bleak boughs: "May his heart wither and the sun blast him! May the rain and the waters deny him and the winds scourge him!"

"I thirst," whispered the girl.

There was a stirring among the watching women. One came forward holding a chalice that was like thin leaves turned to green crystal. She paused beside the trunk of one of the spectral trees, reached up and drew down to her a branch. A slim girl with half-frightened, half-resentful eyes glided to her side and threw her arms around the ghostly bole. The woman with the chalice bent the branch and cut it deep with what seemed an arrow-shaped flake of jade. From the wound a faintly opalescent liquid slowly filled the cup. When it was filled the woman beside McKay stepped forward and pressed her own, long hands around the bleeding branch. She stepped away and McKay saw that the stream had ceased to flow. She touched the trembling girl and unclasped her arms.

"It is healed," said the woman gently. "And it was your turn little sister. The wound is healed. Soon you will have forgotten."

The woman with the chalice knelt and set it to the wan, dry lips of her who was—withering. She drank of it, thirstily, to the last drop. The misty eyes cleared, they sparkled; the lips that had been so parched and pale grew red, the white body gleamed as though the waning light had been fed with new.

"Sing, sisters," she cried, and shrilly. "Dance for me, sisters!"

Again burst out that chant McKay had heard as he had floated through the mists upon the lake. Now, as then, despite his opened ears, he could distinguish no words, but clearly he understood its mingled themes—the joy of Spring's awakening, rebirth, with the green life streaming singing up through every bough, swelling the buds, burgeoning with tender leaves the branches; the dance of the trees in the scented winds of Spring; the drums of the jubilant rain on leafy hoods; passion of Summer sun pouring its golden flood down upon the trees; the moon passing with stately step and slow and green hands stretching up to her and drawing from her breast milk of silver fire; riot of wild, gay winds with their mad pipings and strummings;—soft interlacing of boughs, the kiss of amorous leaves—all these and more, much more that McKay could not understand since it dealt with hidden, secret things for which man has no images, were in that chanting.

And all these and more were in the measures, the rhythms of the dancing of those strange, green-eyed women and brown-skinned men; something incredibly ancient yet young as the speeding moment, something of a world before and beyond man.

McKay listened, McKay watched, lost in wonder; his own world more than half forgotten; his mind meshed in web of green sorcery.

The woman beside him touched his arm. She pointed to the girl.

"Yet she withers," she said. "And not all our life, if we poured it through her lips, could save her."

He looked; he saw that the red was draining slowly from the girl's lips, the luminous life tides waning; the eyes that had been so bright were misting and growing dull once more, suddenly a great pity and a great rage shook him. He knelt beside her, took her hands in his.

"Take them away! Take away your hands! They burn me!" she moaned.

"He tries to help you," whispered the green-clad man, gently. But he reached over and drew McKay's hands away.

"Not so can you help her," said the woman.

"What can I do?" McKay arose, looked helplessly from one to the other. "What can I do to help?"

The chanting died, the dance stopped. A silence fell and he felt upon him the eyes of all. They were tense—waiting. The woman took his hands. Their touch was cool and sent a strange sweetness sweeping through his veins.

"There are three men yonder," she said. "They hate us. Soon we shall be as she is there—withering. They have sworn it, and as they have sworn so will they do. Unless—"

She paused; and McKay felt the stirrings of a curious unease. The moonbeam dancing motes in her eyes had changed to tiny sparklings of red. In a way, deep down, they terrified him—those red sparklings.

"Three men?"—in his clouded mind was the memory of Polleau and his two strong sons. "Three men," he repeated, stupidly—"But what are three men to you who are so many? What could three men do against those stalwart gallants of yours?"

"No," she shook her head. "No—there is nothing our—men—can do; nothing that we can do. Once, night and day, we were gay. Now we fear— night and day. They mean to destroy us. Our kin have warned us. And our kin cannot help us. Those three are masters of blade and flame. Against blade and flame we are helpless."

"Blade and flame!" echoed the listeners. "Against blade and flame we are helpless."

"Surely will they destroy us," murmured the woman. "We shall wither all of us. Like her there, or burn—unless—"

Suddenly she threw white arms around McKay's neck. She pressed her lithe body close to him. Her scarlet mouth sought and found his lips and clung to them. Through all McKay's body ran swift, sweet flames, green fire of desire. His own arms went round her, crushed her to him.

"You shall not die!" he cried. "No—by God, you shall not!"

She drew back her head, looked deep into his eyes.

"They have sworn to destroy us," she said, "and soon. With blade and flame they will destroy us—these three—unless—"

"Unless?" he asked, fiercely.

"Unless you—slay them first!" she answered.

A cold shock ran through McKay, chilling the green sweet fires of his desire. He dropped his arm from around the woman; thrust her from him. For an instant she trembled before him.

"Slay!" he heard her whisper—and she was gone. The spectral trees wavered; their outlines thickened out of immateriality into substance. The green translucence darkened. He had a swift vertiginous moment as though he swung between two worlds. He closed his eyes. The vertigo passed and he opened them, looked around him.

McKay stood on the lakeward skirts of the little coppice. There were no shadows flitting, no sign of the white women and the swarthy, green-clad men. His feet were on green moss; gone was the soft golden carpet with its blue starlets. Birches and firs clustered solidly before him. At his left was a sturdy fir in whose needled arms a broken birch tree lay withering. It was the birch that Polleau's men had so wantonly slashed down. For an instant he saw within the fir and birch the immaterial outlines of the green-clad man and the slim girl who withered. For that instant birch and fir and girl and man seemed one and the same. He stepped back, and his hands touched the smooth, cool bark of another birch that rose close at his right.

Upon his hands the touch of that bark was like—was like?—yes, curiously was it like the touch of the long slim hands of the woman of the scarlet lips. But it gave him none of that alien rapture, that pulse of green life her touch had brought. Yet, now as then, the touch steadied him. The outlines of girl and man were gone. He looked upon nothing but a sturdy fir with a withering birch fallen into its branches.

McKay stood there, staring, wondering, like a man who has but half awakened from dream. And suddenly a little wind stirred the leaves of the rounded birch beside him. The leaves murmured, sighed. The wind grew stronger and the leaves whispered.

"Slay!" he heard them whisper—and again: "Slay! Help us! Slay!"

And the whisper was the voice of the woman of the scarlet lips!

Rage, swift and unreasoning, sprang up in McKay. He began to run up through the coppice, up to where he knew was the old lodge in which dwelt Polleau and his sons. And as he ran the wind blew stronger, and louder and louder grew the whisperings of the trees.

"Slay!" they whispered. "Slay them! Save us! Slay!"

"I will slay! I will save you!" McKay, panting, hammer pulse beating in his ears, rushing through the woods heard himself answering that ever louder, ever more insistent command. And in his mind was but one desire—to clutch the throats of Polleau and his sons, to crack their necks; to stand by them then and watch them wither; wither like that slim girl in the arms of the green-clad man.

So crying, he came to the edge of the coppice and burst from it out into a flood of sunshine. For a hundred feet he ran, and then he was aware that the whispering command was stilled; that he heard no more that maddening rustling of wrathful leaves. A spell seemed to have been loosed from him; it was as though he had broken through some web of sorcery. McKay stopped, dropped upon the ground, buried his face in the grasses.

He lay there, marshalling his thoughts into some order of sanity. What had he been about to do? To rush berserk upon those three who lived in the old lodge and—kill them! And for what? Because that elfin, scarlet-lipped woman whose kisses he still could feel upon his mouth had bade him! Because the whispering trees of the little wood had maddened him with that same command!

And for this he had been about to kill three men!

What were that woman and her sisters and the green-clad swarthy gallants of theirs? Illusions of some waking dream—phantoms born of the hypnosis of the swirling mists through which he had rowed and floated across the lake? Such things were not uncommon. McKay knew of those who by watching the shifting clouds could create and dwell for a time with wide open eyes within some similar land of fantasy; knew others who needed but to stare at smoothly falling water to set themselves within a world of waking dream; there were those who could summon dreams by gazing into a ball of crystal, others found their phantoms in saucers of shining ebon ink.

Might not the moving mists have laid those same hypnotic fingers upon his own mind—and his love for the trees the sense of appeal that he had felt so long and his memory of the wanton slaughter of the slim birch have all combined to paint upon his drugged consciousness the phantasms he had beheld?

Then in the flood of sunshine the spell had melted, his consciousness leaped awake?

McKay arose to his feet, shakily enough. He looked back at the coppice. There was no wind now, the leaves were silent, motionless. Again he saw it as the caravan of demoiselles with their marching knights and troubadours. But no longer was it gay. The words of the scarlet-lipped woman came back to him—that gaiety had fled and fear had taken its place. Dream phantom or—dryad, whatever she was, half of that at least was truth.

He turned, a plan forming in his mind. Reason with himself as he might, something deep within him stubbornly asserted the reality of his experience. At any rate, he told himself, the little wood was far too beautiful to be despoiled. He would put aside the experience as dream— but he would save the little wood for the essence of beauty that it held in its green cup.

The old lodge was about a quarter of a mile away. A path led up to it through the ragged fields. McKay walked up the path, climbed rickety steps and paused, listening. He heard voices and knocked. The door was flung open and old Polleau stood there, peering at him through half shut, suspicious eyes. One of the sons stood close behind him. They stared at McKay with grim, hostile faces.

He thought he heard a faint, far off despairing whisper from the distant wood. And it was as though the pair in the doorway heard it too, for their gaze shifted from him to the coppice, and he saw hatred flicker swiftly across their grim faces; their gaze swept back to him.

"What do you want?" demanded Polleau, curtly.

"I am a neighbor of yours, stopping at the inn—" began McKay, courteously.

"I know who you are," Polleau interrupted brusquely, "but what is it that you want?"

"I find the air of this place good for me," McKay stifled a rising anger. "I am thinking of staying for a year or more until my health is fully recovered. I would like to buy some of your land and build me a lodge upon it."

"Yes, M'sieu?" there was acid politeness now in the powerful old man's voice. "But is it permitted to ask why you do not remain at the inn? Its fare is excellent and you are well liked there."

"I have desire to be alone," replied McKay. "I do not like people too close to me. I would have my own land, and sleep under my own roof."

"But why come to me?" asked Polleau. "There are many places upon the far side of the lake that you could secure. It is happy there, and this side is not happy, M'sieu. But tell me, what part of my land is it that you desire?"

"That little wood yonder," answered McKay, and pointed to the coppice.

"Ah! I thought so!" whispered Polleau, and between him and his sons passed a look of bitter understanding. He looked at McKay, sombrely.

"That wood is not for sale, M'sieu," he said at last.

"I can afford to pay well for what I want," said McKay. "Name your price."

"It is not for sale," repeated Polleau, stolidly, "at any price."

"Oh, come," laughed McKay, although his heart sank at the finality in that answer. "You have many acres and what is it but a few trees? I can afford to gratify my fancies. I will give you all the worth of your other land for it."

"You have asked what that place that you so desire is, and you have answered that it is but a few trees," said Polleau, slowly, and the tall son behind him laughed, abruptly, maliciously. "But it is more than that, M'sieu— Oh, much more than that. And you know it, else why would you pay such price? Yes, you know it—since you know also that we are ready to destroy it, and you would save it. And who told you all that, M'sieu?" he snarled.

There was such malignance in the face thrust suddenly close to McKay's, teeth bared by uplifted lip, that involuntarily he recoiled.

"But a few trees!" snarled old Polleau. "Then who told him what we mean to do—eh, Pierre?"

Again the son laughed. And at that laughter McKay felt within him resurgence of his own blind hatred as he had fled through the whispering wood. He mastered himself, turned away, there was nothing he could do—now. Polleau halted him.

"M'sieu," he said, "Wait. Enter. There is something I would tell you; something too I would show you. Something, perhaps, that I would ask you."

He stood aside, bowing with a rough courtesy. McKay walked through the doorway. Polleau with his son followed him. He entered a large, dim room whose ceiling was spanned with smoke-blackened beams. From these beams hung onion strings and herbs and smoke-cured meats. On one side was a wide fireplace. Huddled beside it sat Polleau's other son. He glanced up as they entered and McKay saw that a bandage covered one side of his head, hiding his left eye. McKay recognized him as the one who had cut down the slim birch. The blow of the fir, he reflected with a certain satisfaction, had been no futile one.

Old Polleau strode over to that son.

"Look, M'sieu," he said and lifted the bandage.

McKay with a faint tremor of horror, saw a gaping blackened socket, red rimmed and eyeless.

"Good God, Polleau!" he cried. "But this man needs medical attention. I know something of wounds. Let me go across the lake and bring back my kit. I will attend him."

Old Polleau shook his head, although his grim face for the first time softened. He drew the bandages back in place.

"It heals," he said. "We have some skill in such things. You saw what did it. You watched from your boat as the cursed tree struck him. The eye was crushed and lay upon his cheek. I cut it away. Now he heals. We do not need your aid, M'sieu."

"Yet he ought not have cut the birch," muttered McKay, more to himself than to be heard.

"Why not?" asked old Polleau, fiercely, "Since it hated him."

McKay stared at him. What did this old peasant know? The words strengthened that deep stubborn conviction that what he had seen and heard in the coppice had been actuality—no dream. And still more did Polleau's next words strengthen that conviction.

"M'sieu," he said, "you come here as ambassador—of a sort. The wood has spoken to you. Well, as ambassador I shall speak to you. Four centuries my people have lived in this place. A century we have owned this land. M'sieu, in all those years there has been no moment that the trees have not hated us—nor we the trees.

"For all those hundred years there have been hatred and battle between us and the forest. My father, M'sieu, was crushed by a tree; my elder brother crippled by another. My father's father, woodsman that he was, was lost in the forest—he came back to us with mind gone, raving of wood women who had bewitched and mocked him, luring him into swamp and fen and tangled thicket, tormenting him. In every generation the trees have taken their toll of us—women as well as men—maiming or killing us."

"Accidents," interrupted McKay. "This is childish, Polleau. You cannot blame the trees."

"In your heart you do not believe so," said Polleau. "Listen, the feud is an ancient one. Centuries ago it began when we were serfs, slaves of the nobles. To cook, to keep us warm in winter, they let us pick up the fagots, the dead branches and twigs that dropped from the trees. But if we cut down a tree to keep us warm, to keep our women and our children warm, yes, if we but tore down a branch—they hanged us, or they threw us into dungeons to rot, or whipped us till our backs were red lattices.

"They had their broad fields, the nobles—but we must raise our food in the patches where the trees disdained to grow. And if they did thrust themselves into our poor patches, then, M'sieu, we must let them have their way—or be flogged, or be thrown into the dungeons or be hanged.

"They pressed us in—the trees," the old man's voice grew sharp with fanatic hatred. "They stole our fields and they took the food from the mouths of our children; they dropped their fagots to us like dole to beggars; they tempted us to warmth when the cold struck our bones—and they bore us as fruit a-swing at the end of the foresters' ropes if we yielded to their tempting.

"Yes, M'sieu—we died of cold that they might live! Our children died of hunger that their young might find root space! They despised us—the trees! We died that they might live—and we were men!"

"Then, M'sieu came the Revolution and the freedom. Ah, M'sieu, then we took our toll! Great logs roaring in the winter cold—no more huddling over the alms of fagots. Fields where the trees had been—no more starving of our children that theirs might live. Now the trees were the slaves and we the masters.

"And the trees knew and they hated us!

"But blow for blow, a hundred of their lives for each life of ours—we have returned their hatred. With axe and torch we have fought them—

"The trees!" shrieked Polleau, suddenly, eyes blazing red rage, face writhing, foam at the corners of his mouth and gray hair clutched in rigid hands— "The cursed trees! Armies of the trees creeping—creeping—closer, ever closer—crushing us in! Stealing our fields as they did of old! Building their dungeon round us as they built of old the dungeons of stone! Creeping—creeping! Armies of trees! Legions of trees! The trees! The cursed trees!"

McKay listened, appalled. Here was crimson heart of hate. Madness! But what was at the root of it? Some deep inherited instinct, coming down from forefathers who had hated the forest as the symbol of their masters. Forefathers whose tides of hatred had overflowed to the green life on which the nobles had laid their *tabu*—as one neglected child will hate the favorite on whom love and gifts are lavished? In such warped minds the crushing fall of a tree, the maiming sweep of a branch, might well appear as deliberate, the natural growth of the forest seem the implacable advance of an enemy.

And yet—the blow of the fir as the cut birch fell *had* been deliberate!

and there *had* been those women of the wood—

"Patience," the standing son touched the old man's shoulder. "Patience! Soon we strike our blow."

Some of the frenzy died out of Polleau's face.

Though we cut down a hundred," he whispered, "By the hundred they return! But one of us, when they strike—he does not return. No! They have numbers and they have—time. We are now but three, and we have little time. They watch us as we go through the forest, alert to trip, to strike, to crush!

"But M'sieu," he turned bloodshot eyes to McKay. "We strike our blow, even as Pierre has said. We strike at the coppice that you so desire. We strike there because it is the very heart of the forest. There the secret life of the forest runs at full tide. We know—and you know! Something that, destroyed, will take the heart out of the forest—will make it know us for its masters."

"The women!" the standing son's eyes glittered, "I have seen the women there! The fair women with the shining skins who invite—and mock and vanish before hands can seize them."

"The fair women who peer into our windows in the night—and mock us!" muttered the eyeless son.

"They shall mock no more!" shouted Polleau, the frenzy again taking him. "Soon they shall lie, dying! All of them—all of them! They die!"

He caught McKay by the shoulders, shook him like a child.

"Go tell them that!" he shouted. "Say to them that this very day we destroy them. Say to them it is *we* who will laugh when winter comes and we watch their round white bodies blaze in this hearth of ours and warm us! Go—tell them that!"

He spun McKay around, pushed him to the door, opened it and flung him staggering down the steps. He heard the tall son laugh, the door close. Blind with rage he rushed up the steps and hurled himself against the door. Again the tall son laughed. McKay beat at the door with clenched fists, cursing. The three within paid no heed. Despair began to dull his rage. Could the trees help him—counsel him? He turned and walked slowly down the field path to the little wood.

Slowly and ever more slowly he went as he neared it. He had failed. He was a messenger bearing a warrant of death. The birches were motionless; their leaves hung listlessly. It was as though they knew he had failed. He paused at the edge of the coppice. He looked at his watch, noted with faint surprise that already it was high noon. Short shrift enough had the little wood. The work of destruction would not be long delayed.

McKay squared his shoulders and passed in between the trees. It was strangely silent in the coppice. And it was mournful. He had a sense of life brooding around him, withdrawn into itself; sorrowing. He passed through the silent, mournful wood until he reached the spot where the rounded, gleaming barked tree stood close to the fir that held the withering birch. Still there was no sound, no movement. He laid his hands upon the cool bark of the rounded tree.

"Let me see again!" he whispered. "Let me hear! Speak to me!"

There was no answer. Again and again he called. The coppice was silent. He wandered through it, whispering, calling. The slim birches stood, passive with limbs and leaves adroop like listless arms and hands of captive maids awaiting with dull woe the will of conquerors. The firs seemed to crouch like hopeless men with heads in hands. His heart ached to the woe that filled the little wood, this hopeless submission of the trees.

When, he wondered, would Polleau strike. He looked at his watch again; an hour had gone by. How long would Polleau wait? He dropped to the moss, back against a smooth bole.

And suddenly it seemed to McKay that he was a madman—as mad as Polleau and his sons. Calmly, he went over the old peasant's indictment of the forest; recalled the face and eyes filled with the fanatic hate. Madness! After all, the trees were—only trees. Polleau and his sons—so he reasoned—had transferred to them the bitter hatred their forefathers had felt for those old lords who had enslaved them; had laid upon them too all the bitterness of their own struggle to exist in this high forest land. When they struck at the trees, it was the ghosts of these forefathers striking at the nobles who had oppressed them; it was themselves striking against their own destiny. The trees were but symbols. It was the warped minds of Polleau and his sons that clothed them in false semblance of conscious life in blind striving to wreak vengeance against the ancient masters and the destiny that had made their lives hard and unceasing battle against Nature. The nobles were long dead; destiny can be brought to grips by no man. But the trees were here and alive. Clothed in mirage, through them the driving lust for vengeance could be sated.

And he, McKay, was it not his own deep love and sympathy for the trees that similarly had clothed them in that false semblance of conscious life? Had he not built his own mirage? The trees did not really mourn, could not suffer, could not—know. It was his own sorrow that he had transferred to them; only his own sorrow that he felt echoing back to him from them.

The trees were—only trees.

Instantly, upon the heels of that thought, as though it were an answer, he was aware that the trunk against which he leaned was trembling; that the whole coppice was trembling; that all the little leaves were shaking, tremulously.

McKay, bewildered, leaped to his feet. Reason told him that it was the wind—yet there was no wind!

And as he stood there, a sighing arose as though a mournful breeze were blowing through the trees—and again there was no wind!

Louder grew the sighing and within it now faint wailings.

"They come! They come! Farewell sisters! Sisters—farewell!"

Clearly he heard the mournful whispers.

McKay began to run through the trees to the trail that led out to the fields of the old lodge. And as he ran the wood darkened as though clear shadows gathered in it, as though vast unseen wings hovered over it. The trembling of the coppice increased; bough touched bough, clung to each other; and louder became the sorrowful crying:

"Farewell sister! Sister!—farewell!"

McKay burst out into the open. Halfway between him and the lodge were Polleau and his sons. They saw him; they pointed and lifted mockingly to him bright axes. He crouched, waiting for them to come, all fine-spun theories gone and rising within him that same rage that hours before had sent him out to slay.

So crouching, he heard from the forested hills a roaring clamor. From every quarter it came, wrathful, menacing; like the voices of legions of great trees bellowing through the horns of tempest. The clamor maddened McKay; fanned the flame of rage to white heat.

If the three men heard it, they gave no sign. They came on steadily, jeering at him, waving their keen blades. He ran to meet them.

"Go back!" he shouted. "Go back, Polleau! I warn you!"

"He warns us!" jeered Polleau. "He—Pierre, Jean—he warns us!"

The old peasant's arm shot out and his hand caught McKay's shoulder with a grip that pinched to the bone. The arm flexed and hurled him against the unmaimed son. The son caught him, twisted him about and whirled him headlong a dozen yards, crashing him through the brush at the skirt of the wood.

McKay sprang to his feet howling like a wolf. The clamor of the forest had grown stronger.

"Kill!" it roared. "Kill!"

The unmaimed son had raised his axe. He brought it down upon the trunk of a birch, half splitting it with one blow. McKay heard a wail go up from the little wood. Before the axe could be withdrawn he had crashed a fist in the axe wielder's face. The head of Polleau's son rocked back; he yelped, and before McKay could strike again had wrapped strong arms around him, crushing breath from him. McKay relaxed, went limp, and the son loosened his grip. Instantly McKay slipped out of it and struck again, springing aside to avoid the rib-breaking clasp. Polleau's son was quicker than he, the long arms caught him. But as the arms tightened, there was the sound of sharp splintering and the birch into which the axe had bitten toppled. It struck the ground directly behind the wrestling men. Its branches seemed to reach out and clutch at the feet of Polleau's son.

He tripped and fell backward, McKay upon him. The shock of the fall broke his grip and again McKay writhed free. Again he was upon his feet, and again Polleau's strong son, quick as he, faced him. Twice McKay's blows found their mark beneath his heart before once more the long arms trapped him. But their grip was weaker; McKay felt that now his strength was equal.

Round and round they rocked, McKay straining to break away. They fell, and over they rolled and over, arms and legs locked, each striving to free a hand to grip the other's throat. Around them ran Polleau and the one-eyed son, shouting encouragement to Pierre, yet neither daring to strike at McKay lest the blow miss and be taken by the other.

And all that time McKay heard the little wood shouting. Gone from it now was all mournfulness, all passive resignation. The wood was alive and raging. He saw the trees shake and bend as though torn by a tempest. Dimly he realized that the others must hear none of this, see none of it; as dimly, wondered why this should be.

"Kill!" shouted the coppice—and over its tumult he heard the roar of the great forest:

"Kill! Kill!"

He became aware of two shadowy shapes, shadowy shapes of swarthy green-clad men, that pressed close to him as he rolled and fought.

"Kill!" they whispered. "Let his blood flow! Kill! Let his blood flow!"

He tore a wrist free from the son's clutch. Instantly he felt within his hand the hilt of a knife.

"Kill!" whispered the shadowy men.

"Kill!" shrieked the coppice.

"Kill!" roared the forest.

McKay's free arm swept up and plunged the knife into the throat of Polleau's son! He heard a choking sob; heard Polleau shriek; felt the hot blood spurt in face and over hand; smelt its salt and faintly acrid odor. The encircling arms dropped from him; he reeled to his feet.

As though the blood had been a bridge, the shadowy men leaped from immateriality into substances. One threw himself upon the man McKay had stabbed; the other hurled upon Polleau. The maimed son turned and fled, howling with terror. A white woman sprang out from the shadow, threw herself at his feet, clutched them and brought him down. Another woman and another dropped upon him. The note of his shrieking changed from fear to agony; then died abruptly into silence.

And now McKay could see none of the three, neither old Polleau or his sons, for the green-clad men and the white women covered them!

McKay stood stupidly, staring at his red hands. The roar of the forest had changed to a deep triumphal chanting. The coppice was mad with joy. The trees had become thin phantoms etched in emerald translucent air as they had been when first the green sorcery had enmeshed him. And all around him wove and danced the slim, gleaming women of the wood.

They ringed him, their song bird-sweet and shrill; jubilant. Beyond them he saw gliding toward him the woman of the misty pillars whose kisses had poured the sweet green fire into his veins. Her arms were outstretched to him, her strange wide eyes were rapt on his, her white body gleamed with the moon radiance, her red lips were parted and smiling—a scarlet chalice filled with the promise of undreamed ecstasies. The dancing circle, chanting, broke to let her through.

Abruptly, a horror filled McKay. Not of this fair woman, not of her jubilant sisters—but of himself.

He had killed! And the wound the war had left in his soul, the wound he thought had healed, had opened.

He rushed through the broken circle, thrust the shining woman aside with his blood-stained hands and ran, weeping, toward the lake shore. The singing ceased. He heard little cries, tender, appealing; little cries of pity; soft voices calling on him to stop, to return. Behind him was the sound of little racing feet, light as the fall of leaves upon the moss.

McKay ran on. The coppice lightened, the beach was before him. He heard the fair woman call him, felt the touch of her hand upon his shoulder. He did not heed her. He ran across the narrow strip of beach, thrust his boat out into the water and wading through the shallows threw himself into it.

He lay there for a moment, sobbing; then drew himself up, caught at the oars. He looked back at the shore now a score of feet away. At the edge of the coppice stood the woman, staring at him with pitying, wise eyes. Behind her clustered the white faces of her sisters, the swarthy faces of the green-clad men.

"Come back!" the woman whispered, and held out to him slender arms.

McKay hesitated, his horror lessening in that clear, wise, pitying gaze. He half swung the boat around. His gaze dropped upon his blood-stained hands and again the hysteria gripped him. One thought only was in his mind—to get far away from where Polleau's son lay with his throat ripped open, to put the lake between that body and him.

Head bent low, McKay bowed to the oars, skimming swiftly outward. When he looked up a curtain of mist had fallen between him and the shore. It hid the coppice and from beyond it there came to him no sound. He glanced behind him, back toward the inn. The mists swung there, too, concealing it.

McKay gave silent thanks for these vaporous curtains that hid him from both the dead and the alive. He slipped limply under the thwarts. After a while he leaned over the side of the boat and, shuddering, washed the blood from his hands. He scrubbed the oar blades where his hands had left red patches. He ripped the lining out of his coat and drenching it in the lake he cleansed his face. He took off the stained coat, wrapped it with the lining round the anchor stone in the skiff and sunk it in the lake. There were other stains upon his shirt; but these he would have to let be.

For a time he rowed aimlessly, finding in the exertion a lessening of his soul sickness. His numbed mind began to function, analyzing his plight, planning how to meet the future—how to save him.

What ought he do? Confess that he had killed Polleau's son? What reason could he give? Only that he had killed because the man had been about to cut down some trees—trees that were his father's to do with as he willed!

And if he told of the wood woman, the wood women, the shadowy shapes of their green gallants who had helped him—who would believe?

They would think him mad—mad as he half believed himself to be.

No, none would believe him. None! Nor would confession bring back life to him he had slain. No; he would not confess.

But stay—another thought came! Might he not be—accused? What actually happened to old Polleau and his other son? He had taken it for granted that they were dead; that they had died under those bodies white and swarthy. But had they? While the green sorcery had meshed him he had held no doubt of this—else why the jubilance of the little wood, the triumphant chanting of the forest?

Were they dead—Polleau and the one-eyed son? Clearly it came to him that they had not heard as he had, had not seen as he had. To them McKay and his enemy had been but two men battling in a woodland glade; nothing more than that—until the last! Until the last? Had they seen more than that even then?

No, all that he could depend upon as real was that he had ripped out the throat of one of old Polleau's sons. That was the one unassailable verity. He had washed the blood of that man from his hands and his face.

All else might have been mirage—but one thing was true. He had murdered Polleau's son!

Remorse? He had thought that he had felt it. He knew now that he did not; that he had no shadow of remorse for what he had done. It had been panic that had shaken him, panic realization of the strangenesses, reaction from the battle lust, echoes of the war. He had been justified in that— execution. What right had those men to destroy the little wood; to wipe wantonly its beauty away?

None! He was glad tht he had killed!

At that moment McKay would gladly have turned his boat and raced away to drink of the crimson chalice of the wood woman's lips. But the mists were raising. He saw that he was close to the landing of the inn. There was no one about. Now was his time to remove the last of those accusing stains. After that—

Quickly he drew up, fastened the skiff, slipped unseen to his room. He locked the door, started to undress. Then sudden sleep swept over him like a wave, drew him helplessly down into ocean depths of sleep.

A knocking at the door awakened McKay, and the innkeeper's voice summoned him to dinner. Sleepily, he answered, and as the old man's footsteps died away, he roused himself. His eyes fell upon his shirt and the great stains now rusty brown. Puzzled, he stared at them for a moment, then full memory clicked back in place.

He walked to the window It was dusk. A wind was blowing and the trees were singing, all the little leaves dancing; the forest hummed a cheerful vespers. Gone was all the unease, all the inarticulate trouble and the fear. The forest was tranquil and it was happy.

He sought the coppice through the gathering twilight. Its demoiselles were dancing lightly in the wind, leafy hoods dipping, leafy skirts ablow. Beside them marched the green troubadours, carefree, waving their needled arms. Gay was the little wood, gay as when its beauty had first drawn him to it.

McKay undressed, hid the stained shirt in his travelling trunk, bathed and put on a fresh outfit, sauntered down to dinner. He ate excellently. Wonder now and then crossed his mind that he felt no regret, no sorrow even, for the man he had killed. Half he was inclined to believe it all a dream—so little of any emotion did he feel. He had even ceased to think of what discovery might mean.

His mind was quiet; he heard the forest chanting to him that there was nothing he need fear; and when he sat for a time that night upon the balcony a peace that was half an ecstasy stole in upon him from the murmuring woods and enfolded him. Cradled by it he slept dreamlessly.

McKay did not go far from the inn that next day. The little wood danced gaily and beckoned him, but he paid no heed. Something whispered to wait, to keep the lake between him and it until word came of what lay or had lain there. And the peace still was on him.

Only the old innkeeper seemed to grow uneasy as the hours went by. He went often to the landing, scanning the further shore.

"It is strange," he said at last to McKay as the sun was dipping behind the summits. "Polleau was to see me here today. He never breaks his word. If he could not come he would have sent one of his sons."

McKay nodded, carelessly.

"There is another thing I do not understand," went on the old man. "I have seen no smoke from the lodge all day. It is as though they were not there."

"Where could they be?" asked McKay, indifferently.

"I do not know," the voice was more perturbed. "It all troubles me, M'sieu. Polleau is hard, yes; but he is my neighbor. Perhaps an accident—"

"They would let you know soon enough if there was anything wrong," McKay said.

"Perhaps, but—" the old man hesitated. "If he does not come tomorrow and again I see no smoke I will go to him," he ended.

McKay felt a little shock run through him—tomorrow then he would know, definitely know, what it was that had happened in the little wood.

"I would if I were you," he said. "I'd not wait too long either. After all— well, accidents do happen."

"Will you go with me, M'sieu?" asked the old man.

"No!" whispered the warning voice within McKay. "No! Do not go!"

"Sorry," he said, aloud. "But I've some writing to do . If you should need me send back your man. I'll come."

And all that night he slept, again dreamlessly, while the crooning forest cradled him.

The morning passed without sign from the opposite shore. An hour after noon he watched the old innkeeper and his man row across the lake. And suddenly McKay's composure was shaken, his serene certainty wavered. He unstrapped his field glasses and kept them on the pair until they had beached the boat and entered the coppice. His heart was beating uncomfortably, his hands felt hot and his lips dry. He scanned the shore. How long had they been in the wood? It must have been an hour! What were they doing there? What had they found? He looked at his watch incredulously. Less then fifteen minutes had passed.

Slowly the seconds ticked by. And it was all of an hour indeed before he saw them come out upon the shore and drag their boat into the water. McKay, throat curiously dry, a deafening pulse within his ears, steadied himself; forced himself to stroll leisurely down to the landing.

"Everything all right?" he called as they were near. They did not answer; but as the skiff warped against the landing they looked up at him and on their faces were stamped horror and a great wonder.

"They are dead, M'sieu," whispered the innkeeper. "Polleau and his two sons—all dead!"

McKay's heart gave a great leap, a swift faintness took him.

"Dead!" he cried. "What killed them?"

"What but the trees, M'sieu?" answered the old man, and McKay

thought his gaze dwelt upon him strangely. "The trees killed them. See—
we went up the little path through the wood, and close to its end we found
it blocked by fallen trees. The flies buzzed around those trees, M'sieu, so
we searched there. They were under them, Polleau and his sons. A fir had
fallen upon Polleau and had crushed in his chest. Another son we found
beneath a fir and upturned birches. They had broken his back, and an eye
had been torn out—but that was no new wound, the latter."

He paused.

"It must have been a sudden wind," said his man. "Yet I never knew of a
wind like that must have been. There were no trees down except those that
lay upon them. And of those it was as though they had leaped out of the
ground! Yes, as though they had leaped out of the ground upon them. Or it
was as though giants had torn them out for clubs. They were not broken—
their roots were bare—"

"But the other son—Polleau had two?"—try as he might, McKay could
not keep the tremor out of his voice.

"Pierre," said the old man, and again McKay felt that strange quality in
his gaze. "He lay beneath a fir. His throat was torn out!"

"His throat torn out!" whispered McKay. His knife! The knife that had
been slipped into his hand by the shadowy shapes!

"His throat was torn out," repeated the innkeeper. "And in it still was the
broken branch that had done it. A broken branch, M'sieu, pointed as a
knife. It must have caught Pierre as the fir fell and ripping through his
throat—been broken off as the tree crashed."

McKay stood, mind whirling in wild conjecture. "You said—a broken
branch?" McKay asked through lips gone white.

"A broken branch, M'sieu," the innkeeper's eyes searched him. "It was
very plain—what it was that happened. Jacques," he turned to his man.
"Go up to the house."

He watched until the man shuffled out of sight.

"Yet not all plain, M'sieu," he spoke low to McKay. "For in Pierre's
hand I found—this."

He reached into a pocket and drew out a button from which hung a strip
of cloth. Cloth and button had once been part of that blood-stained coat
which McKay had sunk within the lake; torn away no doubt when death
had struck Polleau's son!

McKay strove to speak. The old man raised his hand. Button and cloth
fell from it, into the water. A wave took it and floated it away; another and
another. They watched it silently until it had vanished.

"Tell me nothing, M'sieu," the old innkeeper turned to him. "Polleau
was hard and hard men, too, were his sons. The trees hated them. The trees
killed them. And now the trees are happy. That is all. And the—souvenir—

is gone. I have forgotten I saw it. Only M'sieu would better also—go."

That night McKay packed. When dawn had broken he stood at his window, looked long at the little wood. It was awakening, stirring sleepily like drowsy delicate demoiselles. He drank in its beauty—for the last time; waved it farewell.

McKay breakfasted well. He dropped into the driver's seat; set the engine humming. The old innkeeper and his wife, solicitous as ever for his welfare, bade him Godspeed. On both their faces was full friendliness—and in the old man's eyes somewhat of puzzled awe.

His road lay through the thick forest. Soon inn and lake were far behind him.

And singing went McKay, soft whisperings of leaves following him, glad chanting of needled pines; the voice of the forest tender, friendly, caressing—the forest pouring into him as farewell gift its peace, its happiness, its strength.

Trouble with Water

H. L. Gold

Greenberg did not deserve his surroundings. He was the first fisherman of
the season, which guaranteed him a fine catch; he sat in a dry boat—one
without a single leak—far out on a lake that was ruffled only enough to
agitate his artificial fly. The sun was warm, the air was cool; he sat
comfortably on a cushion; he had brought a hearty lunch; and two bottles
of beer hung over the stern in the cold water.

Any other man would have been soaked with joy to be fishing on such a
splendid day. Normally, Greenberg himself would have been ecstatic, but
instead of relaxing and waiting for a nibble, he was plagued by worries.

This short, slightly gross, definitely bald, eminently respectable
businessman lived a gypsy life. During the summer he lived in a hotel with
kitchen privileges in Rockaway; winters he lived in a hotel with kitchen
privileges in Florida; and in both places he operated concessions. For years
now, rain had fallen on schedule every weekend, and there had been
storms and floods on Decoration Day, July 4th and Labor Day. He did not
love his life, but it was a way of making a living.

He closed his eyes and groaned. If he had only had a son instead of his
Rosie! Then things would have been mighty different—

For one thing, a son could run the hot dog and hamburger griddle,

45

Esther could draw beer, and he would make soft drinks. There would be small difference in the profits, Greenberg admitted to himself; but at least those profits could be put aside for old age, instead of toward a dowry for his miserably ugly, dumpy, pitifully eager Rosie.

"All right—so what do I care if she don't get married?" he had cried to his wife a thousand times. "I'll support her. Other men can set up boys in candy stores with soda fountains that have only two spigots. Why should I have to give a boy a regular International Casino?"

"May your tongue rot in your head, you no-good piker!" she would scream. "It ain't right for a girl to be an old maid. If we have to die in the poor-house, I'll get my poor Rosie a husband. Every penny we don't need for living goes to her dowry!"

Greenberg did not hate his daughter, nor did he blame her for his misfortunes; yet, because of her, he was fishing with a broken rod that he had to tape together.

That morning his wife opened her eyes and saw him packing his equipment. She instantly came awake. "Go ahead!" she shrilled—speaking in a conversational tone was not one of her accomplishments—"Go fishing, you loafer! Leave me here alone. I can connect the beer pipes and the gas for soda water. I can buy ice cream, frankfurters, rolls, sirup, and watch the gas and electric men at the same time. Go ahead—go fishing!"

"I ordered everything," he mumbled soothingly. "The gas and electric won't be turned on today. I only wanted to go fishing—it's my last chance. Tomorrow we open the concession. Tell the truth, Esther, can I go fishing after we open?"

"I don't care about that. Am I your wife or ain't I, that you should go ordering everything without asking me—"

He defended his actions. It was a tactical mistake. While she was still in bed, he should have picked up his equipment and left. By the time the argument got around to Rosie's dowry, she stood facing him.

"For myself I don't care," she yelled. "What kind of a monster are you that you can go fishing while your daughter eats her heart out? And on a day like this yet! You should only have to make supper and dress Rosie up. A lot you care that a nice boy is coming to supper tonight and maybe take Rosie out, you no-good father, you!"

From that point it was only one hot protest and a shrill curse to find himself clutching half a broken rod, with the other half being flung at his head.

Now he sat in his beautifully dry boat on an excellent game lake far out on Long Island, desperately aware that any average fish might collapse his taped rod.

What else could he expect? He had missed his train; he had had to wait for the boathouse proprietor; his favorite dry fly was missing; and, since morning, not a fish struck at the bait. Not a single fish!

And it was getting late. He had no more patience. He ripped the cap off a bottle of beer and drank it, in order to gain courage to change his fly for a less sporting bloodworm. It hurt him, but he wanted a fish.

The hook and the squirming worm sank. Before it came to rest, he felt a nibble. He sucked in his breath exultantly and snapped the hook deep into the fish's mouth. Sometimes, he thought philosophically, they just won't take artificial bait. He reeled in slowly.

"Oh, Lord," he prayed, "a dollar for charity—just don't let the rod bend in half where I taped it!"

It was sagging dangerously. He looked at it unhappily and raised his ante to five dollars; even at that price it looked impossible. He dipped his rod into the water, parallel with the line, to remove the strain. He was glad no one could see him do it. The line reeled in without a fight.

"Have I—God forbid!—got an eel or something not kosher?" he mumbled. "A plague on you—why don't you fight?"

He did not really care what it was—even an eel—anything at all.

He pulled in a long, pointed, brimless green hat.

For a moment he glared at it. His mouth hardened. Then, viciously, he yanked the hat off the hook, threw it on the floor and trampled on it. He rubbed his hands together in anguish.

"All day I fish," he wailed, "two dollars for train fare, a dollar for a boat, a quarter for bait, a new rod I got to buy—and a five-dollar-mortgage charity has got on me. For what? For you, you hat, you!"

Out in the water an extremely civil voice asked politely: "May I have my hat, please?"

Greenberg glowered up. He saw a little man come swimming vigorously through the water toward him: small arms crossed with enormous dignity, vast ears on a pointed face propelling him quite rapidly and efficiently. With serious determination he drove through the water, and, at the starboard rail, his amazing ears kept him stationary while he looked gravely at Greenberg.

"You are stamping on my hat," he pointed out without anger.

To Greenberg this was highly unimportant. "With the ears you're swimming," he grinned in a superior way. "Do you look funny!"

"How else could I swim?" the little man asked politely.

"With the arms and legs, like a regular human being, of course."

"But I am not a human being. I am a water gnome, a relative of the more common mining gnome. I cannot swim with my arms, because they must be crossed to give an appearance of dignity suitable to a water gnome; and my feet are used for writing and holding things. On the other hand, my ears are perfectly adapted for propulsion in water. Consequently, I employ them for that purpose. But please, my hat—there are several matters requiring my immediate attention, and I must not waste time."

Greenberg's unpleasant attitude toward the remarkably civil gnome is easily understandable. He had found someone he could feel superior to, and, by insulting him, his depressed ego could expand. The water gnome certainly looked inoffensive enough, being only two feet tall.

"What you got that's so important to do, Big Ears?" he asked nastily.

Greenberg hoped the gnome would be offended. He was not, since his ears, to him, were perfectly normal, just as you would not be insulted if a member of a race of atrophied beings were to call you "Big Muscles." You might even feel flattered.

"I really must hurry," the gnome said, almost anxiously. "But if I have to answer your questions in order to get back my hat—we are engaged in restocking the Eastern waters with fish. Last year there was quite a drain. The bureau of fisheries is cooperating with us to some extent, but, of course, we cannot depend too much on them. Until the population rises to normal, every fish has instructions not to nibble."

Greenberg allowed himself a smile, an annoyingly skeptical smile.

"My main work," the gnome went on resignedly, "is control of the rainfall over the Eastern seaboard. Our fact-finding committee, which is scientifically situated in the meteorological center of the continent, coordinates the rainfall needs of the entire continent; and when they determine the amount of rain needed in particular spots of the East, I make it rain to that extent. Now may I have my hat, please?"

Greenberg laughed coarsely. "The first lie was big enough—about telling the fish not to bite. You make it rain like I'm President of the United States!" He bent toward the gnome slyly. "How's about proof?"

"Certainly, if you insist." The gnome raised his patient, triangular face toward a particularly clear blue spot in the sky, a trifle to one side of Greenberg. "Watch that bit of the sky."

Greenberg looked up humorously. Even when a small dark cloud rapidly formed in the previously clear spot, his grin remained broad. It could have been coincidental. But then large drops of undeniable rain fell over a twenty-foot circle; and Greenberg's mocking grin shrank and grew sour.

He glared hatred at the gnome, finally convinced. "So you're the dirty crook who makes it rain on weekends!"

"Usually on weekends during the summer," the gnome admitted. "Ninety-two percent of water consumption is on weekdays. Obviously we must replace that water. The weekends, of course, are the logical time."

"But, you thief!" Greenberg cried hysterically, "you murderer! What do you care what you do to my concession with your rain? It ain't bad enough business would be rotten even without rain, you got to make floods!"

"I'm sorry," the gnome replied, untouched by Greenberg's rhetoric. "We do not create rainfall for the benefit of men. We are here to protect the fish.

"Now please give me my hat. I have wasted enough time, when I should be preparing the extremely heavy rain needed for this coming weekend."

Greenberg jumped to his feet in the unsteady boat. "Rain this week-end—when I can maybe make a profit for a change! A lot you care if you ruin business. May you and your fish die a horrible, lingering death."

And he furiously ripped the green hat to pieces and hurled them at the gnome.

"I'm really sorry you did that," the little fellow said calmly, his huge ears treading water without the slightest increase of pace to indicate his anger. "We Little Folk have no tempers to lose. Nevertheless, occasionally we find it necessary to discipline certain of your people, in order to retain our dignity. I am not malignant; but, since you hate water and those who live in it, water and those who live in it will keep away from you."

With his arms still folded in great dignity, the tiny water gnome flipped his vast ears and disappeared in a neat surface dive.

Greenberg glowered at the spreading circles of waves. He did not grasp the gnome's final restraining order; he did not even attempt to interpret it. Instead he glared angrily out of the corner of his eye at the phenomenal circle of rain that fell from a perfectly clear sky. The gnome must have remembered it at length, for a moment later the rain stopped. Like shutting off a faucet, Greenberg unwillingly thought.

"Good-by, weekend business," he growled. "If Esther finds out I got into an argument with the guy who makes it rain—"

He made an underhand cast, hoping for just one fish. The line flew out over the water; then the hook arched upward and came to rest several inches above the surface, hanging quite steadily and without support in the air.

"Well, go down in the water, damn you!" Greenberg said viciously, and he swished his rod back and forth to pull the hook down from its ridiculous levitation. It refused.

Muttering something incoherent about being hanged before he'd give in, Greenberg hurled his useless rod at the water. By this time he was not surprised when it hovered in the air above the lake. He merely glanced red-eyed at it, tossed out the remains of the gnome's hat, and snatched up the oars.

When he pulled back on them to row to land, they did not touch the water—naturally. Instead they flashed unimpeded through the air, and Greenberg tumbled into the bow.

"A-ha!" he grated. "Here's where the trouble begins." He bent over the side. As he had suspected, the keel floated a remarkable distance above the lake.

By rowing against the air, he moved with maddening slowness toward shore, like a medieval conception of a flying machine. His main concern was that no one should see him in his humiliating position.

At the hotel he tried to sneak past the kitchen to the bathroom. He knew that Esther waited to curse him for fishing the day before opening, but more especially on the very day that a nice boy was coming to see her Rosie. If he could dress in a hurry, she might have less to say—

"Oh, there you are, you good-for-nothing!"

He froze to a halt.

"Look at you!" she screamed shrilly. "Filthy—you stink from fish!"

"I didn't catch anything, darling," he protested timidly.

"You stink anyhow. Go take a bath, may you drown in it! Get dressed in two minutes or less, and entertain the boy when he gets here. Hurry!"

He locked himself in, happy to escape her voice, started the water in the tub, and stripped from the waist up. A hot bath, he hoped, would rid him of his depressed feeling.

First, no fish; now, rain on weekends! What would Esther say—if she knew, of course. And, of course, he would not tell her.

"Let myself in for a lifetime of curses!" he sneered. "Ha!"

He clamped a new blade into his razor, opened the tube of shaving cream, and stared objectively at the mirror. The dominant feature of the soft, chubby face that stared back was its ugly black stubble; but he set his stubborn chin and glowered. He really looked quite fierce and indomitable. Unfortunately, Esther never saw his face in that uncharacteristic pose, otherwise she would speak more softly.

"Herman Greenberg never gives in!" he whispered between savagely hardened lips. "Rain on weekends, no fish—anything he wants; a lot I care! Believe me, he'll come crawling to me before I go to him."

He gradually became aware that his shaving brush was not getting wet. When he looked down and saw the water dividing into streams that flowed around it, his determined face slipped and grew desperately anxious. He tried to trap the water—by catching it in his cupped hands, by creeping up on it from behind, as if it were some shy animal, and shoving his brush at it—but it broke and ran away from his touch. Then he jammed his palm against the faucet. Defeated, he heard it gurgle back down the pipe, probably as far as the main.

"What do I do now?" he groaned. "Will Esther give it to me if I don't take a shave! But how? ... I can't shave without water."

Glumly, he shut off the bath, undressed and stepped into the tub. He lay down to soak. It took a moment of horrified stupor to realize that he was completely dry and that he lay in a waterless bathtub. The water, in one surge of revulsion, had swept out onto the floor.

"Herman, stop splashing!" his wife yelled. "I just washed that floor. If I find one little puddle I'll murder you!"

Greenberg surveyed the instep-deep pool over the bathroom floor. "Yes, my love," he croaked unhappily.

With an inadequate washrag he chased the elusive water, hoping to mop it all up before it could seep through to the apartment below. His washrag remained dry, however, and he knew that the ceiling underneath was dripping. The water was still on the floor.

In despair, he sat on the edge of the bathtub. For some time he sat in silence. Then his wife banged on the door, urging him to come out. He started and dressed moodily.

When he sneaked out and shut the bathroom door tightly on the flood inside, he was extremely dirty and his face was raw where he had experimentally attempted to shave with a dry razor.

"Rosie!" he called in a hoarse whisper. "Sh! Where's mamma?"

His daughter sat on the studio couch and applied nail-polish to her stubby fingers. "You look terrible," she said in a conversational tone. "Aren't you going to shave?"

He recoiled at the sound of her voice, which, to him, roared out like a siren. "Quiet, Rosie! Sh!" And for further emphasis, he shoved his lips out against a warning finger. He heard his wife striding heavily around the kitchen. "Rosie," he cooed, "I'll give you a dollar if you'll mop up the water I spilled in the bathroom."

"I can't papa," she stated firmly. "I'm all dressed."

"Two dollars, Rosie—all right, two and a half, you blackmailer."

He flinched when he heard her gasp in the bathroom; but, when she came out with soaked shoes, he fled downstairs. He wandered aimlessly toward the village.

Now he was in for it, he thought; screams from Esther, tears from Rosie—plus a new pair of shoes for Rosie and two and a half dollars. It would be worse, though, if he could not get rid of his whiskers—

Rubbing the tender spots where his dry razor had raked his face, he mused blankly at a drugstore window. He saw nothing to help him, but he went inside anyhow and stood hopefully at the drug counter. A face peered at him through a space scratched in the wall case mirror, and the druggist came out. A nice-looking, intelligent fellow, Greenberg saw at a glance.

"What you got for shaving that I can use without water?"

"Skin irritation, eh?" the pharmacist replied. "I got something very good for that."

"No. It's just— Well, I don't like to shave with water."

The druggist seemed disappointed. "Well, I got brushless shaving cream." Then he brightened. "But I got an electric razor—much better."

"How much?" Greenberg asked cautiously.

"Only fifteen dollars, and it lasts a lifetime."

"Give me the shaving cream," Greenberg said coldly.

With the tactical science of a military expert, he walked around until some time after dark. Only then did he go back to the hotel, to wait outside. It was after seven, he was getting hungry, and the people who entered the hotel he knew as permanent summer guests. At last a stranger passed him and ran up the stairs.

Greenberg hesitated for a moment. The stranger was scarcely a boy, as Esther had definitely termed him, but Greenberg reasoned that her term was merely wish-fulfillment, and he jauntily ran up behind him.

He allowed a few minutes to pass, for the man to introduce himself and let Esther and Rosie don their company manners. Then, secure in the knowledge that there would be no scene until the guest left, he entered.

He waded through a hostile atmosphere, urbanely shook hands with Sammie Katz, who was a doctor—probably, Greenberg thought shrewdly, in search of an office—and excused himself.

In the bathroom he carefully read the directions for using brushless shaving cream. He felt less confident when he realized that he had to wash his face thoroughly with soap and water, but without benefit of either, he spread the cream on, patted it, and waited for his beard to soften. It did not, as he discovered while shaving. He wiped his face dry. The towel was sticky and black, with whiskers suspended in paste, and, for that, he knew, there would be more hell to pay. He shrugged resignedly. He would have to spend fifteen dollars for an electric razor after all; this foolishness was costing him a fortune!

That they were waiting for him before beginning supper, was, he knew, only a gesture for the sake of company. Without changing her hard, brilliant smile, Esther whispered: "Wait! I'll get you later—"

He smiled back, his tortured, slashed face creasing painfully. All that could be changed by his being enormously pleasant to Rosie's young man. If he could slip Sammie a few dollars—more expense, he groaned—to take Rosie out, Esther would forgive everything.

He was too engaged in beaming and putting Sammie at ease to think of what would happen after he ate caviar canapes. Under other circumstances Greenberg would have been repulsed by Sammie's ultra-professional waxed mustache—an offensively small, pointed thing—and his commercial attitude toward poor Rosie; but Greenberg regarded him as a potential savior.

"You open an office yet, Doctor Katz?"

"Not yet. You know how things are. Anyhow, call me Sammie."

Greenberg recognized the gambit with satisfaction, since it seemed to please Esther so much. At one stroke Sammie had ingratiated himself and begun bargaining negotiations.

Without another word, Greenberg lifted his spoon to attack the soup. It would be easy to snare this eager doctor. A *doctor!* No wonder Esther and Rosie were so puffed with joy.

In the proper company way, he pushed his spoon away from him. The soup spilled onto the tablecloth.

"Not so hard, you dope," Esther hissed.

He drew the spoon toward him. The soup leaped off it like a live thing and splashed over him—turning, just before contact, to fall on the floor. He gulped and pushed the bowl away. This time the soup poured over the side of the plate and lay in a huge puddle on the table.

"I didn't want any soup anyhow," he said in a horrible attempt at levity. Lucky for him, he thought wildly, that Sammie was there to pacify Esther with his smooth college talk—not a bad fellow, Sammie, in spite of his mustache; he'd come in handy at times.

Greenberg lapsed into a paralysis of fear. He was thirsty after having eaten the caviar, which beats herring any time as a thirst raiser. But the knowlege that he could not touch water without having it recoil and perhaps spill, made his thirst a monumental craving. He attacked the problem cunningly.

The others were talking rapidly and rather hysterically. He waited until his courage was equal to his thirst; then he leaned over the table with a glass in his hand. "Sammie, do you mind—a little water, huh?"

Sammie poured from a pitcher while Esther watched for more of his tricks. It was to be expected, but still he was shocked when the water exploded out of the glass directly at Sammie's only suit.

"If you'll excuse me," Sammie said angrily, "I don't like to eat with lunatics."

And he left, though Esther cried and begged him to stay. Rosie was too stunned to move. But when the door closed, Greenberg raised his agonized eyes to watch his wife stalk murderously toward him.

Greenberg stood on the boardwalk outside his concession and glared blearily at the peaceful, blue, highly unpleasant ocean. He wondered what would happen if he started at the edge of the water and strode out. He could probably walk right to Europe on dry land.

It was early—much too early for business—and he was tired. Neither he nor Esther had slept; and it was practically certain that the neighbors hadn't either. But above all he was incredibly thirsty.

In a spirit of experimentation, he mixed a soda. Of course its high water content made it slop onto the floor. For breakfast he had surreptitiously tried fruit juice and coffee, without success.

With his tongue dry to the point of furriness, he sat weakly on a boardwalk bench in front of his concession. It was Friday morning, which meant that the day was clear, with a promise of intense heat. Had it been Saturday, it naturally would have been raining.

"This year," he moaned, "I'll be wiped out. If I can't mix sodas, why should beer stay in a glass for me? I thought I could hire a boy for ten dollars a week to run the hot-dog griddle; I could make sodas, and Esther could draw beer. All I can do is make hot dogs, Esther can still draw beer; but twenty or maybe twenty-five a week I got to pay a sodaman. I won't even come out square—a fortune I'll lose!"

The situation really was desperate. Concessions depend on too many factors to be anything but capriciously profitable.

His throat was fiery and his soft brown eyes held a fierce glaze when the gas and electric were turned on, the beer pipes connected, the tank of carbon dioxide hitched to the pump, and the refrigerator started.

Gradually, the beach was filling with bathers. Greenberg writhed on his bench and envied them. They could swim and drink without having liquids draw away from them as if in horror. They were not thirsty—

And then he saw his first customers approach. His business experience was that morning customers buy only soft drinks. In a mad haste he put up the shutters and fled to the hotel.

"Esther" he cried. "I got to tell you I can't stand it—"

Threateningly, his wife held her broom like a baseball bat. "Go back to the concession, you crazy fool. Ain't you done enough already?"

He could not be hurt more than he had been. For once he did not cringe. "You got to help me, Esther."

"Why didn't you shave, you no-good bum? Is that any way—"

"That's what I got to tell you. Yesterday I got into an argument with a water gnome—"

"A what?" Esther looked at him suspiciously.

"A water gnome," he babbled in a rush of words. "A little man so high, with big ears that he swims with, and he makes it rain—"

"Herman" she screamed. "Stop that nonsense. You're crazy"

Greenberg pounded his forehead with his fist. "I *ain't* crazy. Look, Esther. Come with me into the kitchen."

She followed him readily enough, but her attitude made him feel more helpless and alone than ever. With her fists on her plump hips and her feet set wide, she cautiously watched him try to fill a glass of water.

"Don't you see?" he wailed. "It won't go in the glass. It spills over. It runs away from me."

She was puzzled. "What happened to you?"

Brokenly, Greenberg told of his encounter with the water gnome, leaving out no single degrading detail. "And now I can't touch water," he ended. "I can't drink it. I can't make sodas. On top of it all, I got such a thirst, it's killing me."

Esther's reaction was instantaneous. She threw her arms around him, drew his head down to her shoulder, and patted him comfortingly as if he were a child. "Herman, my poor Herman!" she breathed tenderly. "What did we ever do to deserve such a curse?"

"What shall I do, Esther?" he cried helplessly.

She held him at arms' length. "You got to go to a doctor," she said firmly. "How long can you go without drinking? Without water you'll die. Maybe sometimes I am a little hard on you, but you know I love you—"

"I know, mamma," he sighed. "But how can a doctor help me?"

"Am I a doctor that I should know? Go anyhow. What can you lose?"

He hesitated. "I need fifteen dollars for an electric razor," he said in a low, weak voice.

"So?" she replied. "If you got to, you got to. Go, darling. I'll take care of the concession."

Greenberg no longer felt deserted and alone. He walked almost confidently to a doctor's office. Manfully, he explained his symptoms. The doctor listened with professional sympathy, until Greenberg reached his description of the water gnome.

Then his eyes glittered and narrowed. "I know just the thing for you, Mr. Greenberg," he interrupted. "Sit there until I come back."

Greenberg sat quietly. He even permitted himself a surge of hope. But it seemed only a moment later that he was vaguely conscious of a siren screaming toward him; and then he was overwhelmed by the doctor and two internes who pounced on him and tried to squeeze him into a bag.

He resisted, of course. He was terrified enough to punch wildly. "What are you doing to me?" he shrieked. "Don't put that thing on me!"

"Easy now," the doctor soothed. "Everything will be all right."

It was on that humiliating scene that the policeman, required by law to accompany public ambulances, appeared.

"What's up?" he asked.

"Don't stand there, you fathead," an interne shouted. "This man's crazy. Help us get him into this strait jacket."

But the policeman approached indecisively. "Take it easy, Mr. Greenberg. They ain't gonna hurt you while I'm here. What's it all about?"

"Mike!" Greenberg cried, and clung to his protector's sleeve. "They think I'm crazy—"

"Of course he's crazy," the doctor stated. "He came in here with a fantastic yarn about a water gnome putting a curse on him."

"What kind of a curse, Mr. Greenberg?" Mike asked cautiously.

"I got into an argument with the water gnome who makes it rain and takes care of the fish," Greenberg blurted. "I tore up his hat. Now he won't let water touch me. I can't drink, or anything—"

The doctor nodded. "There you are. Absolutely insane."

"Shut up." For a long moment Mike stared curiously at Greenberg. Then: "Did any of you scientists think of testing him? Here, Mr. Greenberg." He poured water into a paper cup and held it out.

Greenberg moved to take it. The water backed up against the cup's far lip; when he took it in his hand, the water shot out into the air.

"Crazy, is he?" Mike asked with heavy irony. "I guess you don't know there's things like gnomes and elves. Come with me, Mr. Greenberg."

They went out together and walked toward the boardwalk. Greenberg told Mike the entire story and explained how, besides being so uncomfortable to him personally, it would ruin him financially.

"Well, doctors can't help you," Mike said at length. "What do they know about the Little Folk? And I can't say I blame you for sassing the gnome. You ain't Irish or you'd have spoke with more respect to him. Anyhow, you're thirsty. Can't you drink *anything?*"

"Not a thing," Greenberg said mournfully.

They entered the concession. A single glance told Greenberg that business was very quiet, but even that could not lower his feelings more than they already were. Esther clutched him as soon as she saw them.

"Well?" she asked anxiously.

Greenberg shrugged in despair. "Nothing. He thought I was crazy."

Mike stared at the bar. Memory seemed to struggle behind his reflective eyes. "Sure," he said after a long pause. "Did you try beer, Mr. Greenberg? When I was a boy my old mother told me all about elves and gnomes and the rest of the Little Folk. She knew them, all right. They don't touch alcohol, you know. Try drawing a glass of beer—"

Greenberg trudged obediently behind the bar and held a glass under the spigot. Suddenly his despondent face brightened. Beer creamed into the glass—and stayed there! Mike and Esther grinned at each other as Greenberg threw back his head and furiously drank.

"Mike!" he crowed. "I'm saved. You got to drink with me!"

"Well—" Mike protested feebly.

By late afternoon, Esther had to close the concession and take her husband and Mike to the hotel.

The following day, being Saturday, brought a flood of rain. Greenberg nursed an imposing hang-over that was constantly aggravated by his having to drink beer in order to satisfy his recurring thirst. He thought of forbidden icebags and alkaline drinks in an agony of longing.

"I can't stand it!" he groaned. "Beer for breakfast—phooey!"

"It's better than nothing," Esther said fatalistically.

"So help me, I don't know if it is. But, darling, you ain't mad at me on account of Sammie, are you?"

She smiled gently, "Poo! Talk dowry and he'll come back quick."

"That's what I thought. But what am I going to do about my curse?"

Cheerfully, Mike furled an umbrella and strode in with a little old woman, whom he introduced as his mother. Greenberg enviously saw evidence of the effectiveness of icebags and alkaline drinks, for Mike had been just as high as he the day before.

"Mike told me about you and the gnome," the old lady said. "Now I know the Little Folk well, and I don't hold you to blame for insulting him, seeing you never met a gnome before. But I suppose you want to get rid of your curse. Are you repentant?"

Greenberg shuddered. "Beer for breakfast! Can you ask?"

"Well, just you go to this lake and give the gnome proof."

"What kind of proof?" Greenberg asked eagerly.

"Bring him sugar. The Little Folk love the stuff—"

Greenberg beamed. "Did you hear that, Esther? I'll get a barrel—"

"They love sugar, but they can't eat it," the old lady broke in. "It melts in water. You got to figure out a way so it won't. Then the little gentleman'll know you're repentant for real."

"A-ha!" Greenberg cried. "I knew there was a catch!"

There was a sympathetic silence while his agitated mind attacked the problem from all angles. Then the old lady said in awe: "The minute I saw your place I knew Mike had told the truth. I never seen a sight like it in my life—rain coming down, like the flood, everywhere else; but all around this place, in a big circle, it's dry as a bone!"

While Greenberg scarcely heard her, Mike nodded and Esther seemed peculiarly interested in the phenomenon. When he admitted defeat and came out of his reflected stupor, he was alone in the concession, with only a vague memory of Esther saying she would not be back for several hours.

"What am I going to do?" he muttered. "Sugar that won't melt—" He drew a glass of beer and drank it thoughtfully. "Particular they got to be yet. Ain't it good enough if I bring simple sirup—that's sweet."

He pottered about the place, looking for something to do. He could not polish the fountain on the bar, and the few frankfurters boiling on the griddle probably would go to waste. The floor had already been swept. So he sat uneasily and worried his problem.

"Monday, no matter what," he resolved, "I'll go to the lake. It don't pay to go tomorrow. I'll only catch a cold because it'll rain."

At last Esther returned, smiling in a strange way. She was extremely gentle, tender and thoughtful; and for that he was appreciative. But that night and all day Sunday he understood the reason for her happiness.

She 'had spread word that, while it rained in every other place all over town, their concession was miraculously dry. So, besides a headache that made his body throb in rhythm to its vast pulse, Greenberg had to work like six men satisfying the crowd who mobbed the place to see the miracle and enjoy the dry warmth.

How much they took in will never be known. Greenberg made it a practice not to discuss such personal matters. But it is quite definite that not even in 1929 had he done so well over a single weekend.

Very early Monday morning he was dressing quietly, not to disturb his wife. Esther, however, raised herself on her elbow and looked at him doubtfully.

"Herman," she called softly, "do you really have to go?"

He turned, puzzled. "What do you mean—do I have to go?"

"Well—" She hesitated. Then: "Couldn't you wait until the end of the season, Herman, darling?"

He staggered back a step, his face working in horror. "What kind of an idea is that for my own wife to have?" he croaked. "Beer I have to drink instead of water. How can I stand it? Do you think I *like* beer? I can't wash myself. Already people don't like to stand near me; and how will they act at the end of the season? I go around looking like a bum because my beard is too tough for an electric razor, and I'm all the time drunk—the first Greenberg to be a drunkard. I want to be respected—"

"I know, Herman, darling," she sighed. "But I thought for the sake of our Rosie— Such a business we've never done like we did this weekend. If it rains every Saturday and Sunday, but not on our concession, we'll make a *fortune!*"

"Esther!" Herman cried, shocked. "Doesn't my health mean anything?"

"Of course, darling. Only I thought maybe you could stand it for—"

He snatched his hat, tie and jacket, and slammed the door. Outside, though, he stood indeterminedly. He could hear his wife crying, and he realized that, if he succeeded in getting the gnome to remove the curse, he would forfeit an opportunity to make a great deal of money.

He finished dressing more slowly. Esther was right, to a certain extent. If he could tolerate his waterless condition—

"No!" he gritted decisively. "Already my friends avoid me. It isn't right that a respectable man like me should always be drunk and not take a bath. So we'll make less money. Money isn't everything—"

And with great determination he went to the lake.

But that evening, before going home, Mike walked out of his way to stop in at the concession. He found Greenberg sitting on a chair, his head in his hands, and his body rocking slowly in anguish.

"What is it, Mr. Greenberg?" he asked gently.

Greenberg looked up. His eyes were dazed. "Oh, you, Mike," he said blankly. Then his gaze cleared, grew more intelligent, and he stood up and led Mike to the bar. Silently, they drank beer. "I went to the lake today," he said hollowly. "I walked all around it hollering like mad. The gnome didn't stick his head out of the water once."

"I know," Mike nodded sadly. "They're busy all the time."

Greenberg spread his hands imploringly. "So what can I do? I can't write him a letter or send him a telegram; he ain't got a door to knock on or a bell for me to ring. How do I get him to come up and talk?"

His shoulders sagged. "Here, Mike. Have a cigar. You been a real good friend, but I guess we're licked."

They stood in an awkward silence. Finally Mike blurted: "Real hot, today. A regular scorcher."

"Yeah. Esther says business was pretty good, if it keeps up."

Mike fumbled at the Cellophane wrapper. Greenberg said: "Anyhow, suppose I did talk to the gnome. What about the sugar?"

The silence dragged itself out, became tense and uncomfortable. Mike was distinctly embarrassed. His brusque nature was not adapted for comforting discouraged friends. With immense concentration he rolled the cigar between his fingers and listened for a rustle.

"Day like this's hell on cigars," he mumbled, for the sake of conversation. "Dries them like nobody's business. This one ain't, though."

"Yeah," Greenberg said abstractedly. "Cellophane keeps them—"

They looked suddenly at each other, their faces clean of expression.

"Holy smoke!" Mike yelled.

"Cellophane on sugar!" Greenberg choked out.

"Yeah," Mike whispered in awe. "I'll switch my day off with Joe, and I'll go to the lake with you tomorrow. I'll call for you early."

Greenberg pressed his hand, too strangled by emotion for speech. When Esther came to relieve him, he left her at the concession with only the inexperienced griddle boy to assist her, while he searched the village for cubes of sugar wrapped in Cellophane.

The sun had scarcely risen when Mike reached the hotel, but Greenberg had long been dressed and stood on the porch waiting impatiently. Mike

was genuinely anxious for his friend. Greenberg staggered along toward
the station, his eyes almost crossed with the pain of a terrific hangover.

They stopped at a cafeteria for breakfast. Mike ordered orange juice,
bacon and eggs, and coffee half-and-half. When he heard the order,
Greenberg had to gag down a lump in his throat.

"What'll you have?" the counterman asked.

Greenberg flushed. "Beer," he said hoarsely.

"You kidding me?" Greenberg shook his head, unable to speak. "Want
anything with it? Cereal, pie, toast—"

"Just beer." And he forced himself to swallow it. "So help me," he
hissed at Mike, "another beer for breakfast will kill me!"

"I know how it is," Mike said around a mouthful of food.

On the train they attempted to make plans. But they were faced by a
phenomenon that neither had encountered before, and so they got
nowhere. They walked glumly to the lake, fully aware that they would have
to employ the empirical method of discarding tactics that did not work.

"How about a boat?" Mike suggested.

"It won't stay in the water with me in it. And you can't row it."

"Well, what'll we do then?"

Greenberg bit his lip and stared at the beautiful blue lake. There the
gnome lived, so near to them. "Go through the woods along the shore, and
holler like hell. I'll go the opposite way. We'll pass each other and meet at
the boathouse. If the gnome comes up, yell for me."

"O.K.," Mike said, not very confidently.

The lake was quite large and they walked slowly around it, pausing often
to get the proper stance for particularly emphatic shouts. But two hours
later, when they stood opposite each other with the full diameter of the
lake between them, Greenberg heard Mike's hoarse voice: "Hey, gnome!"

"Hey, gnome!" Greenberg yelled. "Come on up!"

An hour later they crossed paths. They were tired, discouraged, and
their throats burned; and only fishermen disturbed the lake's surface.

"The hell with this," Mike said. "It ain't doing any good. Let's go back to
the boathouse."

"What'll we do?" Greenberg rasped. "I can't give up!"

They trudged back around the lake, shouting half-heartedly. At the
boathouse, Greenberg had to admit that he was beaten. The boathouse
owner marched threateningly toward him.

"Why don't you maniacs get away from here?" he barked. "What's the
idea of hollering and scaring away the fish? The guys are sore—"

"We're not going to holler anymore," Greenberg said. "It's no use."

When they bought beer and Mike, on an impulse, hired a boat, the
owner cooled off with amazing rapidity, and went off to unpack bait.

"What did you get a boat for?" Greenberg asked. "I can't ride in it."

"You're not going to. You're gonna walk."

"Around the lake again?" Greenberg cried.

"Nope. Look, Mr. Greenberg. Maybe the gnome can't hear us through all that water. Gnomes ain't hardhearted. If he heard us and thought you were sorry, he'd take his curse off you in a jiffy."

"Maybe." Greenberg was not convinced. "So where do I come in?"

"The way I figure it, some way or other you push water away, but the water pushes you away just as hard. Anyhow, I hope so. If it does, you can walk on the lake." As he spoke, Mike had been lifting large stones and dumping them on the bottom of the boat. "Give me a hand with these."

Any activity, however useless, was better than none, Greenberg felt. He helped Mike fill the boat until just the gunwales were above water. Then Mike got in and shoved off.

"Come on," Mike said. "Try to walk on the water."

Greenberg hesitated. "Suppose I can't?"

"Nothing'll happen to you. You can't get wet; so you won't drown."

The logic of Mike's statement reassured Greenberg. He stepped out boldly. He experienced a peculiar sense of accomplishment when the water hastily retreated under his feet into pressure bowls, and an unseen, powerful force buoyed him upright across the lake's surface. Though his footing was not too secure, with care he was able to walk quite swiftly.

"Now what?" he asked, almost happily.

Mike had kept pace with him in the boat. He shipped his oars and passed Greenberg a rock. "We'll drop them all over the lake—make it damned noisy down there and upset the place. That'll get him up."

They were more hopeful now, and their comments, "Here's one that'll wake him," and "I'll hit him right on the noodle with this one," served to cheer them still further. And less than half the rocks had been dropped when Greenberg halted, a boulder in his hands. Something inside him wrapped itself tightly around his heart and his jaw dropped.

Mike followed his awed, joyful gaze. To himself, Mike had to admit that the gnome, propelling himself through the water with his ears, arms folded in tremendous dignity, was a funny sight.

"Must you drop rocks and disturb us at our work?" the gnome asked.

Greenberg gulped. "I'm sorry, Mr. Gnome," he said nervously. "I couldn't get you to come up by yelling."

The gnome looked at him. "Oh. You are the mortal who was disciplined. Why did you return?"

"To tell you that I'm sorry, and I won't insult you again."

"Have you proof of your sincerity?" the gnome asked quietly.

Greenberg fished furiously in his pocket and brought out a handful of sugar wrapped in cellophane, which he tremblingly handed to the gnome.

"Ah, very clever, indeed," the little man said, unwrapping a cube and popping it eagerly into his mouth. "Long time since I've had some."

A moment later Greenberg spluttered and floundered under the surface. Even if Mike had not caught his jacket and helped him up, he could almost have enjoyed the sensation of being able to drown.

Thirteen O'Clock

C. M. Kornbluth

Peter Packer excitedly dialed his slide-rule, peering through a lens as one of the minutely scored lines met with another. He rose from his knees, brushing dust from the neat crease of his serge trousers. No doubt of it— the house had a secret attic room. Peter didn't know anything about sliding panels or hidden buttons; in the most direct way imaginable he lifted the axe he had brought and crunched it into the wall.

On his third blow he holed through. The rush of air from the darkness was cool and sweet. Smart old boy, his grandfather, thought Peter. Direct ventilation all over the house—even in a false compartment. He chopped away heartily, the hollow strokes ringing through the empty attic and down the stairs.

He could have walked through the hole erect when he was satisfied with his labors; instead he cautiously turned a flashlight inside the space. The beam was invisible; all dust had long since settled. Peter grunted. The floor seemed to be sound. He tested it with one foot, half in, half out of the hidden chamber. It held.

The young man stepped through easily, turning the flash on walls and floor. The room was not large, but it was cluttered with a miscellany of objects—chests, furniture, knick-knacks and what-nots. Peter opened a chest, wondering about pirate gold. But there was no gold, for the thing was full to the lid with chiffons in delicate hues. A faint fragrance of musk filled the air; sachets long since packed away were not entirely gone.

Funny thing to hide away, thought Peter. But Grandfather Packer had been a funny man—having this house built to his own very sound plans, waiting always on the Braintree docks for the China and India Clippers and what rare cargo they might have brought. Chiffons! Peter poked around in the box for a moment, then closed the lid again. There were others.

He turned the beam of the light on a wall lined with shelves. Pots of old workmanship—spices and preserves, probably. And a clock. Peter stared at the clock. It was about two by two by three feet—an unusual and awkward size. The workmanship was plain, the case of crudely finished wood. And yet there was something about it—his eyes widened as he realized what it was. The dial showed thirteen hours!

Between the flat figures XII and I there was another—an equally flat XIII. What sort of freak this was the young man did not know. Vaguely he conjectured on prayer-time, egg-boiling and all the other practical applications of chronometry. But nothing he could dredge up from his well-stored mind would square with this freak. He set the flash on a shelf and hefted the clock in his arms, lifting it easily.

This, he thought, would bear looking into. Putting the light in his pocket he carried the clock down the stairs to his second-floor bedroom. It looked strangely incongruous there, set on a draftsman's table hung with rules and T squares. Determinedly Peter began to pry open the back with a chisel, when it glided smoothly open without tooling. There was better construction in the old timepiece than he had realized. The little hinges were still firm and in working order. He peered into the works and ticked his nail against one of the chimes. It sounded sweet and clear.

The young man took a pair of pliers. Lord knew where the key was, he thought, as he began to wind the clock. Slowly it got under way, ticking loudly. The thing had stopped at 12:59. That would be nearly one o'clock in any other timepiece; on this the minute hand crept slowly toward the enigmatic XIII.

Peter wound the striking mechanism carefully, and watched as a little whir sounded. The minute hand met the Roman numeral, and with a click the chimes sounded out in an eerie, jangling discord. Peter thought with sudden confusion that all was not as well with the clock as he had thought.

The chimes grew louder, filling the little bedroom with their clang.

Horrified, the young man put his hands on the clock as though he could stop off the noise. As he shook the old cabinet the peals redoubled until they battered against the eardrums of the draftsman, ringing in his skull and resounding from the walls, making instruments dance and rattle on the drawing-board. Peter drew back, his hands to his ears. He was filled with nausea, his eyes bleared and smarting. As the terrible clock thundered out its din without end he reached the door feebly, the room swaying and spinning about him, nothing real but the suddenly glowing clock-dial and the clang and thunder of its chimes.

As he opened the door it ceased, and he closed his eyes in relief as his nausea passed. He looked up again, and his eyes widened with horror. Though it was noon outside a night-wind fanned his face, and though he was on the second-story landing of his Grandfather Packer's house dark trees rose about him, stretching as far as the eye could see.

For three hours—by his wristwatch's luminous dial—Peter had wandered, aimless and horrified, waiting for dawn. The aura of strangeness that hung over the forest in which he walked was bearable; it was the gnawing suspicion that he had gone mad that shook him to his very bones. The trees were no ordinary things, of that he was sure. For he had sat under one forest giant and leaned back against its bole only to rise with a cry of terror. He had felt its pulse beat slowly and regularly under the bark. After that he did not dare to rest, but he was a young and normal male. Whether he would or not he found himself blundering into ditches and stones from sheer exhaustion. Finally, sprawled on the ground, he slept.

Peter woke stiff and sore from his nap on the bare ground, but he felt better for it. The sun was high in the heavens; he saw that it was about eleven o'clock. Remembering his terrors of the night he nearly laughed at himself. This was a forest, and there were any number of sane explanations how he got here. An attack of amnesia lasting about twelve hours would be one cause. And there were probably others less disturbing.

He thought the country might be Maine. God knew how many trains or busses he had taken since he lost his memory in his bedroom. Beginning to whistle he strode through the woods. Things were different in the daytime.

There was a sign ahead! He sprinted up to its base. The thing was curiously large—painted in red characters on a great slab of wood, posted on a dead tree some twelve feet from the ground. The sign said ELLIL. He rolled the name over in his mind and decided that he didn't recognize it. But he couldn't be far from a town or house.

Ahead of him sounded a thunderous grunt.

"Bears!" he thought in a panic. They had been his childhood bogies; he had been frightened of them ever since. But it was no bear, he saw. He almost wished it was. For the thing that was veering on him was a frightful composite of every monster of mythology, menacing him with sabrelike claws and teeth and gusts of flame from its ravening throat. It stood only about as high as the man, and its legs were long, but it seemed ideally styled for destruction, to the engineer.

Without ado he jumped for a tree and dug his toes into the grooves of the bark, shinning up it as he used to as a child. But there was nothing childlike about it now. With the creature's flaming breath scorching his heels he climbed like a monkey, stopping only at the third set of main branches, twenty-five feet from the ground. There he clung, limp and shuddering, and looked down.

The creature was hopping grotesquely about the base of the tree, its baleful eyes on him. The man's hand reached out for a firmer purchase on the branch, and part came away in his hand. He had picked a sort of coconut—heavy, hard, and with sharp corners. Peter raised his eyes. Why not? Carefully noting the path that the creature below took around the trunk he poised the fruit carefully. Wetting a finger, he adjusted the placing. On a free drop that long you had to allow for windage, he thought.

Twice more around went the creature, and then its head and the murderous fruit reached the same point at the same time. There was a crunching noise which Peter could hear from where he was and the insides of its head spilled on the forest sward.

"Clever," said a voice beside him on the branch.

He turned with a cry. The speaker was only faintly visible—the diaphanous shadow of a young girl, not more than eighteen, he thought. Calmly it went on, "You must be very mancic to be able to land a fruit so accurately. Did he give you an extra sense?" Her tone was light, but from what he could see of her dim features they were curled in an angry smile.

Nearly letting go of the branch in his bewilderment he answered as calmly as he could, "I don't know who you mean. And what is mancic?"

"Innocent," she said coldly. "Eh? I could push you off this branch without a second thought. But first you tell me where Almarish got the model for you. I might turn out a few myself. Are you a doppleganger or a golem?"

"Neither," he spat, bewildered and horrified. "I don't even know what they are!"

"Strange," said the girl. "I can't read you." Her eyes squinted prettily and suddenly became solid, luminous wedges in her transparent face. "Well," she sighed, "let's get out of this." She took the man by his elbow and dropped from the branch, hauling him after her. Ready for a sickening impact with the ground, Peter winced as his heels touched it light as a feather. He tried to disengage the girl's grip, but it was hard as steel.

"None of that," she warned him. "I have a blast-finger. Or didn't he tell you?"

"What's a blast-finger?" demanded the engineer.

"Just so you won't try anything," she commented. "Watch." Her body solidified then, and she pointed her left index finger at a middling-sized tree. Peter hardly saw what happened, being more interested in the incidental miracle of her face and figure. But his attention was distracted by a flat crash of thunder and sudden glare. And the tree was riven as if by a terrific stroke of lightning. Peter smelled ozone as he looked from the tree to the girl's finger and back again. "Okay," he said.

"No nonsense?" she asked. "Come on."

They passed between two trees, and the vista of forest shimmered and tore, revealing a sort of palace—all white stone and maple timbers. "That's my place," said the girl.

II

"Now," she said, settling herself into a cane-backed chair. Peter looked about the room. It was furnished comfortably with pieces of antique merit, in the best New England tradition. His gaze shifted to the girl, slender and palely luminous, with a half-smile playing about her chiseled features.

"Do you mind," he said slowly, "not interrupting until I'm finished with what I have to say?"

"A message from Almarish? Go on."

And at that he completely lost his temper. "Listen, you snip!" he raged. "I don't know who you are or where I am but I'd like to tell you that this mystery isn't funny or even mysterious—just downright rude. Do you get that? Now—my name is Peter Packer. I live in Braintree, Mass. I make my living as a consulting and industrial engineer. This place obviously isn't Braintree, Mass. Right? Then where is it?"

"Ellil," said the girl simply.

"I saw that on a sign," said Packer. "It still doesn't mean anything to me. Where is Ellil?"

Her face became suddenly grave. "You may be telling the truth," she said thoughtfully. "I do not know yet. Will you allow me to test you?"

"Why should I?" he snapped.

"Remember my blast-finger?"

Packer winced. "Yes," he said. "What are the tests?"

"The usual," she smiled. "Rosemary and garlic, crucifixes and the secret name of Jehovah. If you get through those you're okay."

"Then get on with it," the man said, confusedly.

"Hold these." She passed him a flowery sprig and a clove of garlic. He took them, one in each hand. "All right?" he asked.

"On those, yes. Now take the cross and read this name. You can put the vegetables down now."

He followed instructions, stammering over the harsh Hebrew word. In a cold fury the girl sprang to her feet and leveled her left index finger at him. "Clever," she blazed. "But you can't get away with it! I'll blow you so wide open—"

"Wait," he pleaded. "What did I do?" The girl, though sweet-looking, seemed to be absolutely irresponsible.

"Mispronounced the Name," she snapped. "Because you can't say it straight without crumbling into dust!"

He looked at the paper again and read aloud slowly and carefully. "Was that right?" he asked.

Crestfallen, the girl sat down. "Yes," she said. "I'm sorry. You seem to be okay. A real human. Now what do you want to know?"

"Well—who are you?"

"My name's Melicent." She smiled deprecatingly. "I'm a—sort of a sorceress."

"I can believe that," grunted the man. "Now why should you take me for a demon, or whatever you thought I was?"

"Doppleganger," she corrected him. "I was sure—well, I'd better begin at the beginning.

You see, I haven't been a sorceress very long—only two years. My mother was a witch—a real one, and pretty first-class. I've heard it said that she brewed the neatest spells in Ellil. All I know I learned from her—never studied it formally. My mother didn't die a natural sort of death, you see. Almarish got her."

"Who's Almarish?"

She wrinkled her mouth with disgust. "That thug!" she spat. "He and his gang of half-breed demons are out to get control of Ellil. My mother wouldn't stand for it—she told him right out flat over a Multiplex Apparition. And after that he was gunning for her steady—no letup at all. And believe me, there are mighty few witches who can stand up under much of that, but Mother stood him off for fifteen years. They got my father—he wasn't much good—a little while after I was born. Vampires.

"Mother got caught alone in the woods one morning without her tools—unguents, staffs and things—by a whole flock of golems and zombies." The girl shuddered. "Some of them—well, Mother finished about half before they overwhelmed her and got a stake of myrtle through her heart. That finished her—she lost all her magic, of course, and

Almarish sent an ordinary plague of ants against her. Adding insult to injury, I call it!" There were real tears of rage in her eyes.

"And what's this Almarish doing now?" asked Peter, fascinated.

Melicent shrugged. "He's after me," she said simply. "The bandur you killed was one of my watchdogs. And I thought he'd sent you. I'm sorry."

"I see," breathed the man slowly. "What powers has he?"

"The usual, I suppose. But he has no principles about using them. And he has his gang—I can't afford real retainers. Of course I whip up some simulacra whenever I hold a reception or anything of that sort. Just images to serve and take wraps. They can't fight."

Peter tightened his jaw. "You must be in a pretty bad way," he volunteered diffidently.

The girl looked him full in the eye, her lip trembling. She choked out, "I'm in such a hell of a spot!" and then the gates opened and she was weeping as if her heart would break. The man stared frozenly, wondering how he could comfort a despondent sorceress. "There, there," he said tentatively.

She wiped her eyes and looked at him. "I'm sorry," she said sniffing. "But it's seeing a fairly friendly face again after all these years—no callers but leprechauns and things. You don't know what it's like."

"I wonder," said Peter, "how you'd like to live in Braintree."

"I don't know," she said brightly. "But how could I get there?"

"There should be at least one way," reflected the man.

"But why—what was that?" shot out the girl, snatching up a wand.

"Knock on the door," said Peter. "Shall I open it?"

"Please," said Melicent nervously, holding up the slender staff. The man stood aside and swung the door wide. In walked a curious person of mottled red and white coloring. One eye was small and blue, the other large and savagely red. His teeth were quite normal—except that the four canines protruded two inches each out of his mouth. He walked with a limp; one shoe seemed curiously small. And there was a sort of bulge in the trousers that he wore beneath his formal morning-coat.

"May I introduce myself," said the individual removing his sleek black topper. "I am Balthazar Pike. You must be Miss Melicent? And this—ah—zombie?" He indicated Peter with a dirty leer.

"Mr. Packer, Mr. Pike," said the girl. Peter simply stared in horror while the creature murmured, "Enchanted."

Melicent drew herself up proudly. "And this, I suppose," she said, "is the end?"

"I fear so, Miss Melicent," said the creature regretfully. "I have my orders. Your house has been surrounded by picked forces; any attempt to use your blast-finger or any other weapon of offense will be construed as resistance. Under the laws of civilized warfare we are empowered to reduce you to ashes should such resistance be forthcoming. May I have your reply?"

The girl surveyed him haughtily, then, with a lightninglike sweep of her wand, seemed to blot out every light in the room. Peter heard her agitated voice. "We're in a neutral screen, Mr. Packer. I won't be able to keep it up for long. Listen! That was one of Almarish's stinkers—big cheese. He didn't expect any trouble from me. He'll take me captive as soon as they break the screen down. Do you want to help me?"

"Of course!" exploded the man.

"Good. Then you find the third oak from the front door on the left and walk widdershins three times. You'll find out what to do from them."

"Walk how?" asked Peter.

"Widdershins—counterclockwise. Lord, you're dumb!"

Then the lights seemed to go on again, and Peter saw that the room was filled with the half-breed creatures. With an expression of injured dignity the formally-attired Balthazar Pike asked, "Are you ready to leave now, Miss Melicent? Quite ready?"

"Thank you, General, yes," said the girl coldly. Two of the creatures took her arms and walked her from the room. Peter saw that as they stepped over the threshold they vanished, all three. The last to leave was Pike, who turned and said to the man: "I must remind you, Mister—er—ah—that you are trespassing. This property now belongs to the Almarish Realty Corporation. All offenders will be prosecuted to the fullest extent of the law. Good day Mister—er—ah—" With which he stepped over the door and vanished.

Hastily Peter followed him across the line, but found himself alone outside the house. For which he was grateful. "Third oak from the left door," he repeated. Simple enough. Feeling foolish he walked widdershins three times around and stopped dead waiting for something.

What a sweet, brave kid she had been! He hoped nothing would really happen to her—before he got there.

He felt a sort of tugging at his serge trousers and stepped back in alarm. "Well?" shrilled a small voice. Peter looked down and winced. The dirtiest, most bedraggled little creature he had ever seen was regarding him with tiny, sharp eyes. There were others, too, squatting on pebbles and toadstools.

"Miss Melicent told me to ask you what I should do," said Peter. As the little leader of the troop glared at him he added hastily, "If you please."

"Likely tale," piped the voice of the creature. "What's in it for us?"

"I dunno," said the man, bewildered. "What do you want?"

"Green cloth," the creature answered promptly. "Lots of it. And if you have any small brass buttons, them too."

Peter hastily conducted an inventory of his person. "I'm sorry," he said hesitantly. "I haven't any green. How about blue? I can spare my vest." He carefully lowered the garment to the ground among the little people.

"Looks all right," said the leader. "Jake!" One of the creatures advanced and fingered the cloth. "Hmm—" he said. "Good material." Then there was a whispered consultation with the leader, who at last shouted up to Peter: "Head East for water. You can't miss it!"

"Hey," said Peter, blinking. But they were already gone. And though he widdershin-walked for the next half hour and even tried a few incantations remembered from his childhood they did not come back, nor did his vest.

So, with his back to the sinking sun, he headed East for water.

III

"Mahoora City Limits," said the sign. Peter scratched his head and passed it. He had hit the stretch of highway a few miles back once he had got out of the forest, and it seemed to be leading straight into a city of some kind. There was a glow ahead in the sky; a glow which abruptly became a glare.

"Jeepers!" the man gasped. "Buildings—skyscrapers!" Before him reared a sort of triple Wall Street with which were combined the most spectacular features of Rockefeller Center. In the sudden way in which things happened in Ellil he turned a sort of blind corner in the road and found himself in the thick of it.

A taxi roared past him; with a muttered imprecation he jumped out of the way. The bustling people on the sidewalks ignored him completely. It was about six o'clock; they were probably going home from their offices. They were all sorts of people—women and girls, plain and pretty, men and boys, slim, fat, healthy and dissipated. And striding along in lordly indifference Peter saw a cop.

"Excuse me," said Peter, elbowing his way through the crowd to the member of Mahoora's finest. "Can you tell me where I can find water?" That was, he realized, putting it a bit crudely. But he was hopelessly confused by the traffic and swarms of pedestrians.

The cop turned on him with a glassy stare. "Water?" he rumbled. "Would yez be wantin' tap, ditch, fire—or cologne?" The man hesitated. He didn't know, he realized in a sudden panic. The elves, or whatever they had been, hadn't specified. Cagily he raised his hand to his brow and muttered, " 'Scuse me—previous engagement—made the appointment for today—just forgot—" He was edging away from the cop when he felt a hand on his arm.

"What was that about water?" asked the cop hoarsely, putting his face near Peter's. Desperately the man blurted: "The water I have to find to lick Almarish!" Who could tell? Maybe the cop would help him.

"What?" thundered M.P.D. Shield No. 2435957607. "And me a loyal supporter of the Mayor Almarish Freedom Peace and Progress Reform Administration?" He frowned. "You look subversive to me—come on!" He raised his nightstick suggestively, and Peter meekly followed him through the crowds.

"How'd they get you in here?" asked Peter's cell-mate.

Peter inspected him. He was a short, dark sort of person with a pair of disconcertingly bright eyes. "Suspicion," said Peter evasively. "How about you?"

"Practicing mancy without a license, theoretically. Actually because I tried to buck the Almarish machine. You know how it is?"

"Can't say I do," answered Peter. "I'm a stranger here."

"Yeah? Well—like this. Few years ago we had a neat little hamlet here. Mahoora was the biggest little city in these parts of Ellil, though I say it myself. A little industry—magic chalices for export, sandals of swiftness, invisibility cloaks, invincible weapons—you know?"

"Um," said Peter noncommittally.

"Well, I had a factory—modest little chemical works. We turned out love-philtres from my own prescription. It's what I call a neat dodge—eliminates the *balneum mariae* entirely from the processing, cuts down drying time—maybe you aren't familiar with the latest things in the line?"

"Sorry, no."

"Oh—well, then, in came these plugs of Almarish. Flying goon-squads that wrecked plants and shops on order, labor spies, provocateurs, everything. Soon they'd run out every racketeer in the place and hijacked them lock, stock and barrel. Then they went into politics. There was a little scandal about buying votes with fairy gold—people kicked when it turned into ashes. But they smoothed that over when they got in.

"And then—! Graft right and left, patronage, unemployment, rotten food scandals, bribery, inefficiency—everything that's on the list. And this is their fifth term. How do you like that?"

"Lord," said Peter, shocked. "But how do they stay in office?"

"Oh," grinned his friend. "The first thing they did was to run up some pretty imposing public works—tall buildings, bridges, highways and monuments. Then they let it out that they were partly made of half-stuff. You know what that is?"

"No," said Peter. "What is it?"

"Well—it's a little hard to describe. But it isn't really there and it isn't really not there. You can walk on it and pick it up and things, but—well, it's a little hard to describe. The kicker is this. Half-stuff is there only as long as you—the one who prepared a batch of it that is—keep the formula going. So if we voted those leeches out of office they'd relax their formula and the half-stuff would vanish and the rest of the buildings and bridges and highways and monuments would fall with a helluva noise and damage. How do you like that?"

"Efficiency plus," said Peter. "Where's this Almarish hang out?"

"The mayor?" asked his cell-mate sourly. "You don't think he'd be seen in the city, do you? Some disgruntled citizen might sic a flock of vampires on his honor. He was elected in absentia. I hear he lives around Mal-Tava way."

"Where's that?" asked Peter eagerly.

"You don't know? Say, you're as green as they come! That's a pretty nasty corner of Ellil—the nastiest anywhere, I guess. It's a volcanic region, and those lava-nymphs are pretty tough molls. Then there's a dragon-ranch around there. The owner got careless and showed up missing one day. The dragons broke out and ran wild; they're the killingest you could hope to see. Anything else?"

"No," said Peter, heavy-hearted. "I guess not."

"That's good. Because I think we're going to trial right now." A guard was opening the door, club poised. "His Honor, Judge Balthazar Pike will see you now," said the warden. Peter groaned.

The half-breed demon, his sartorial splendor of the preceding afternoon replaced by judiciary black silk, smiled grimly on the two prisoners. "Mr. Morden," he said indicating the erstwhile manufacturer, "and Mr.—er—ah?"

"Packer!" exploded the man. "What are you doing here?"

"Haw!" laughed the judge. "That's what I was going to ask you. But first we have this matter of Mr. Morden to dispose of. Excuse me a moment? Clerk, read the charges."

A cowed-looking little man picked an index-card from a stack and read: "Whereas Mr. Percival Morden of Mahoora has been apprehended in the act of practicing mancy and whereas this Mr. Morden does not possess an approved license for such practice it is directed that His Honor Chief Judge Balthazar Pike declare him guilty of the practice of mancy without a license. Signed, Mayor Almarish. Vote straight Peace and Progress Reform Party for a clean and efficient administration." He paused for a moment and looked timidly at the judge who was cleaning his talons. "That's it, your honor," he said.

"Oh—thank you. Now, Morden—guilty or not guilty?"

"What's the difference?" asked the manufacturer sourly. "Not guilty, I guess."

"Thank you." The judge took a coin from his pocket. "Heads or tails?" he asked.

"Tails," answered Morden. Then, aside to Peter, "It's magic, of course. You can't win." The half-breed demon spun the coin dexterously on the judicial bench; it wobbled, slowed, and fell with a tinkle. The judge glanced at it. "Sorry, old man," he said sympathetically. "You seem to be guilty. Imprisonment for life in an oak-tree. You'll find Merlin de Bleys in there with you, I rather fancy. You'll like him. Next case," he called sharply as Morden fell through a trapdoor in the floor.

Peter advanced before the bar of justice. "Can't we reason this thing out?" he asked agitatedly. "I mean, I'm a stranger here and if I've done anything I'm sorry—"

"Tut!" exclaimed the demon. He had torn the cuticle of his left index talon, and it was bleeding. He stanched the green liquid with a handkerchief and looked down at the man. "Done anything?" he asked mildly. "Oh—dear me, no! Except for a few trifles like felonious impediment of an officer in the course of his duty, indecent display, seditious publication, high treason and unlawful possession of military and naval secrets—done anything?" His two odd eyes looked reproachfully down on the man.

Peter felt something flimsy in his hand. Covertly he looked and saw a slip of blue paper on which was written in green ink: "This is Hugo, my other watchdog. Feed him once a day on green vegetables. He does not like tobacco. In haste, Melicent."

There was a stir in the back of the courtroom, and Peter turned to see one of the fire-breathing horrors which had first attacked him in the forest tearing down the aisle lashing out to right and left, incinerating a troop of officers with one blast of its terrible breath. Balthazar Pike was crawling around under his desk, bawling for more police.

Peter cried, "You can add one more—possession of a bandur without a license! Sic 'em, Hugo!" The monster flashed an affectionate look at him and went on with the good work of clearing the court. The man sprang aside as the trapdoor opened beneath his feet and whirled on a cop who was trying to swarm over him. With a quick one-two he laid him out and proceeded to the rear of the courtroom, where Hugo was standing off a section of the fire-department that was trying to extinguish his throat. Peter snatched an axe from one and mowed away heartily. Resistance melted away in a hurry, and Peter pushed the hair out of his eyes to find that they were alone in the court.

"Come on, boy," he said. Whistling cheerily he left the building, the bandur at his heels, smoking gently. Peter collared a cop—the same one who had first arrested him. "Now," he snarled. "Where do I find water?"

Stuttering with fright, and with two popping eyes on the bandur, the officer said, "The harbor's two blocks down the street if you mean—"

"Never mind what I mean!" growled Peter, luxuriating in his new-found power. He strode off pugnaciously, Hugo following.

IV

"I beg your pardon—are you looking for water?" asked a tall, dark man over Peter's shoulder. Hugo growled and let loose a tongue of flame at the stranger's foot. "Shuddup, Hugo," said Peter. Then, turning to the stranger, "As a matter of fact I was. Do you—?"

"I heard about you from them," said the stranger. "You know. The little people."

"Yes," said Peter. "What do I do now?"

"Underground Railroad," said the stranger. "Built after the best Civil War model. Neat, speedy and efficient. Transportation at half the usual cost. I hope you weren't planning to go by magic carpet?"

"No," Peter assured him hastily. "I never use them."

"That's great," said the stranger swishing his long black cloak. "Those carpet people—stifling industry, I call it. They spread a whispering campaign that our road was unsafe! Can you imagine it?"

"Unsafe," scoffed Peter. "I'll bet they wish their carpets were half as safe as your railroad!"

"Well," said the stranger thoughtfully, "perhaps not half as safe . . . No; I wouldn't say half as safe . . ." He seemed likely to go on indefinitely. Peter asked, "Where do I get the Underground?"

"A little East of here," said the stranger. He looked about apprehensively. "We'd better not be seen together," he muttered out of the corner of his mouth. "Meet you over there by the clock-tower—you can get it there."

"Okay," said Peter. "But why the secrecy?"

"We're really underground," said the stranger, walking away.

Peter rejoined him at the corner of the clock-tower; with an elaborate display of unconcern the stranger walked off, Peter following at some distance. Soon they were again in the forest that seemed to border the city of Mahoora. Once they were past the city-limits sign the stranger turned, smiling.

"I guess we're safe now," he said. "They could try a raid and drag us back across the line, but they wouldn't like to play with your bandur, I think. Here's the station."

He pressed a section of bark on a huge tree; silently it slid open like a door. Peter saw a row of steps leading down into blackness. "Sort of spooky," he said.

"Not at all! I have the place ghostproofed once a year." The stranger led the way, taking out what looked like a five-branched electric torch. "What's that?" asked Peter, fascinated by the weird blue light it shed.

"Hand of glory," said the stranger casually. Peter looked closer and shuddered, holding his stomach. Magic, he thought, was probably all right up to the point where it became grave-robbery.

They arrived at a neatly tiled station; Peter was surprised to find that the trains were tiny things. The one pulled up on the tracks was not as high as he was. "You'll have to stoke, of course," said the stranger.

"What?" demanded Peter indignantly.

"Usual arrangement. Are you coming or aren't you?"

"Of course—but it seems strange," complained Peter climbing into the engine. Hugo climbed up into the coal car and curled up emitting short smoky bursts of flame which caused the stranger to keep glancing at him in fear for his fuel.

"What's in the rest of the train?" asked Peter.

"Freight. This is the through cannonball to Mal-Tava. I have a special shipment for Almarish. Books and things, furniture, a few cases of liquor— you know?"

"Yes. Any other passengers?"

"Not this month. I haven't much trouble with them. They're usually knights and things out to kill sorcerers like Almarish. They take their horses along or send them ahead by carpet. Do you plan to kill Almarish?"

Peter choked. "Yes," he finally said. "What's it to you?"

"Nothing—I take your money and leave you where you want to go. A tradesman can't afford opinions. Let's get up some steam, eh?"

Amateurishly Peter shoveled coal into the little furnace while the stranger in the black cloak juggled with steam-valves and levers. "Don't be worried," he advised Peter. "You'll get the hang of things after a while." He glanced at a watch. "Here we go," he said, yanking the whistle-cord.

The train started off into its tunnel, sliding smoothly and almost silently along, the only noise being from the driving rods. "Why doesn't it clack against the rails?" asked Peter.

"Levitation. Didn't you notice? We're an inch off the track. Simple, really."

"Then why have a track?" asked Peter.

The stranger smiled and said, "Without—" then stopped abruptly and looked concerned and baffled. And that was all the answer Peter got.

"Wake up," shouted the stranger nudging Peter. "We're in the war zone!"

"Zasso?" asked Peter, blinking. He had been napping after hours of steady travel. "What war zone?"

"Trolls—you know."

"No, I don't!" snapped Peter. "What side are we on?"

"Depends on who stops us," said the stranger, speeding the engine. They were out of the tunnel now, Peter saw, speeding along a couple of inches above the floor of an immense dim cave. Ahead the glittering double strand of the track stretched into the distance.

"Oh—oh!" muttered the cloaked stranger. "Trouble ahead!" Peter saw a vague, stirring crowd before them. "Those trolls?" he asked.

"Yep," answered the engineer resignedly, slowing the train. "What do you want?" he asked a solid-looking little man in a ragged uniform. "To get the hell out of here," said the little man. He was about three feet tall, Peter saw. "What happened?" he asked.

"The lousy Insurgents licked us," said the troll. "Will you let us on the train before they cut us down?"

"First," said the engineer methodically, "there isn't room. Second, I have to keep friends with the party in power. Third, you know very well that you can't be killed."

"What if we are immortal?" asked the troll agitatedly. "Would you like to live forever scattered in little pieces?"

"Second," said Peter abruptly, "you get out of it as best you can." He was speaking to the engineer. "And first, you can dump all the freight you have for Almarish. He won't want it anyway when I'm through with him."

"That right?" asked the troll.

"Not by me!" exploded the engineer. "Now get your gang off the track before I plough them under!"

"Hugo," whispered Peter. With a lazy growl the bandur scorched the nape of the engineer's head.

"All right," said the engineer. "All right. Use force—all right." Then, to the leader of the trolls, "You tell your men they can unload the freight and get as comfortable as they can."

"Wait!" interjected Peter. "Inasmuch as I got you out of this scrape—I think—would you be willing to help me out in a little affair of honor with Almarish?"

"Sure!" said the troll. "Anything at all. You know, for a surface-dweller you're not half bad!" With which he began to spread the good news among his army.

Later, when they were all together in the cab, taking turns with the shovel, the troll introduced himself as General Skaldberg of the Third Loyalist Army.

Speeding ahead again at full speed the end of the cavern was in sight
when another swarm of trolls blocked the path. "Go through them!"
ordered Peter coldly.

"For pity's sake," pleaded the stranger. "Think of what this will do to my
franchise!"

"That's your worry," said the general. "You fix it up with the Insurgents.
We gave you the franchise anyway—they have no right of search."

"Maybe," muttered the engineer. He closed his eyes as they went
slapping into the band of trolls under full steam. When it was all over and
they were again tearing through the tunnel he looked up. "How many?" he
asked brokenly.

"Only three," said the general regretfully. "Why didn't you do a good job
while you were at it?"

"You should have had your men fire from the freight-cars," said the
engineer coldly.

"Too bad I didn't think of it. Could you turn back and take them in a
surprise attack?"

The engineer cursed violently, giving no direct answer. But for the next
half hour he muttered to himself distraitly, groaning "Franchise!" over and
over again.

"How much farther before we get to Mal-Tava?" asked Peter glumly.

"Very soon now," said the troll. "I was there once. Very broken terrain—
fine for guerilla work."

"Got any ideas on how to handle the business of Almarish?"

The general scratched his head. "As I remember it," he said slowly, "I
once thought it was a pushover for some of Clausewitz's ideas. It's a funny
tactical problem—practically no fortifications within the citadel—everything lumped outside in a wall of steel. Of course Almarish probably has a
lot on the ball personally. All kinds of direct magic at his fingertips. And
that's where I get off with my men. We trolls don't even pretend to know
the fine points of thaumaturgy. Mostly straight military stuff with us."

"So I have to face him alone?"

"More or less," said the general. "I have a couple of guys that majored in
Military Divination at Ellil Tech Prep. They can probably give you a
complete layout of the citadel, but they won't be responsible for illusions,
Multiplex Apparitions or anything else Almarish might decide to throw in
the way. My personal advice to you is—be skeptical."

"Yes?" asked Peter miserably.

"Exactly," said Skaldberg. "The real difficulty in handling arcane
warfare is in knowing what's there and what ain't. Have you any way of
sneaking in a confederate? Not a spy, exactly—we military men don't
approve of spying—but a sort of—ah—one-man intelligence unit."

"I have already," said Peter diffidently. "She's a sorceress, but not much good I think. Has a blast-finger, though."

"Very good," grunted Skaldberg. "Very good indeed. God, how we could have used her against the Insurgents! The hounds had us in a sort of peninsular spot—with only one weak line of supply and communication between us and the main force—and I was holding a hill against a grand piquet of flying carpets that were hurling thunderbolts at our munitions supply. But their sights were away off and they only got a few of our snipers. God, what a blast-finger would have done to those bloody carpets!"

The engineer showed signs of interest. "You're right!" he snapped. "Blow 'em out of the sky—menace to life and limb! I have a bill pending at the All Ellil Conference on Communication and Transportation—would you be interested?"

"No," grunted the general. The engineer, swishing his long black cloak, returned to his throttle muttering about injunctions and fairplay.

V

"Easy, now!" whispered the general.

"Yessir," answered a troll going through obvious mental strain while his hand, seemingly of its own volition, scrawled lines and symbols on a sheet of paper. Peter was watching, fascinated and mystified, as the specialist in military divination was doing his stuff.

"There!" said the troll, relaxing. He looked at the paper curiously and signed it: "Borgenssen, Capt."

"Well?" asked General Skaldberg excitedly. "What was it like?"

The Captain groaned. "You should see for yourself, sir!" he said despondently. "Their air-force is flying dragons and their infantry's a kind of Kraken squad. What they're doing out of water I don't know."

"Okay," said the general. He studied the drawing. "How about their mobility?"

"They haven't got any and they don't need any," complained the diviner. "They just sit there waiting for you—in a solid ring. And the air-force has a couple of auxiliary rocs that pick up the Krakens and drop them behind your forces. Pincher stuff—very bad."

"I'll be the judge of that!" thundered the general. "Get out of my office!" The captain saluted and stumbled out of the little cave which the general had chosen to designate as GHQ. His men were "barracked" on the bare rock outside. Volcanoes rumbled and spat in the distance. There came one rolling crash that set Peter's hair on end.

"Think that was for us?" he asked nervously.

"Nope—I picked this spot for lava drainage. I have a hundred men erecting a shut-off at the only exposed point. We'll be safe enough." He turned again to the map, frowning. "This is our real worry—what I call impregnable, or damn near it. If we could get them to attack us—but those rocs smash anything along that line. We'd be cut off like a rosebud. And with our short munitions we can't afford to be discovered and surrounded. Ugh! What a spot for an army man to find himself in!"

A brassy female voice asked, "Somep'n bodderin' you, shorty?" The general spun around in a fine purple rage. Peter looked in horror and astonishment on the immodest form of a woman who had entered the cave entirely unperceived—presumably from some occult means. She was a slutty creature, her hair dyed a vivid red and her satin skirt an inch or two above the knee. She was violently made up with flame-colored rouge, lipstick and even eye-shadow.

"Well," she complained stridently, puffing on a red cigarette, "wadda you joiks gawkin' at? Aincha nevva seen a lady befaw?"

"Madam," began the general, outraged.

"Can dat," she advised him easily. "I hoid youse guys chewin' da fat—I wanna help youse out." She seated herself on an outcropping of rock and adjusted her skirt—Northward.

"I concede that women," spluttered the general, "have their place in activities of the military—but that place has little or nothing to do with warfare as such! I demand that you make yourself known—where did you come from?"

"Weh did I come from?" she asked mockingly. "Weh, he wansa know. Lookit dat!" She pointed one of her bright-glazed fingernails at the rocky floor of the cave, which grew liquid in a moment, glowing cherry-red. She leered at the two and spat at the floor. It grew cold in another moment. "Don't dat mean nothin' to youse?" she asked.

The general stared at the floor. "You must be a volcano nymph."

"Good fa you, shorty!" she sneered. "I represent da goils from Local toity-tree. In brief, chums, our demands are dese: one, dat youse clear away from our union hall pronto; two, dat youse hang around in easy reach—in case we want youse fa poiposes of our own. In retoin fe dese demands, we—dats me an' de goils—will help youse guys out against Almarish. Dat lousy fink don't give his hands time off no more. Dis place might as well be a goddam desert fa all de men around. Get me?"

"These—ah—purposes of your own in clause two," said the general hesitantly. "What would they be?"

She smiled dirtily and half-closed her eyes. "Escort soivice, ya might call it. Nuttin' harmful ta yer men, cap. We'll probably get tired of dem in a munt' or two and send dem off safe. You trolls are kinda cute."

The general stared, too horrified even to resent being called "cap."

"Well?" demanded the nymph.

"Well—yes," said the general.

"Okay, shorty," she said, crushing out her cigarette against her palm. "Da goils'l be aroun' at dawn fa de attack. I'll try ta keep 'em off yer army until de battle's over. So long!" She sank into the earth, leaving behind only a smell of fleur-de-floozy perfume.

"God!" whispered General Skaldberg. "The things I do for the army!"

In irregular open formation the trolls advanced, followed closely by the jeering mob of volcano nymphs.

"How about it, General?" asked Peter. He and the old soldier were surveying the field of battle from a hill in advance of their forces; the hideous octopoid forms of the defenders of Almarish could be plainly seen, lumbering onward to meet the trolls with a peculiar sucking gait.

"Any minute now—any second," said Skaldberg. Then, "Here it comes!" The farthest advanced of the trolls had met with the first of the Krakens. The creature lashed out viciously; Peter saw that its tentacles had been fitted with studded bands and other murderous devices. The troll dodged nimbly and pulled an invincible sword on the octopoid myth. They mixed it; when the struggle went behind an outcropping of rock the troll was in the lead, unharmed, while the slow-moving Kraken was leaking thinly from a score of punctures.

"The dragons," said Peter, pointing. "Here they are." In V formation the monsters were landing on a far end of the battlefield, then coming at a scrabbling run.

"If they make it quicker than the nymphs—" breathed the general. Then he sighed relievedly. They had not. The carnage among the dragons was almost funny; at will the nymphs lifted them high in the air on jets of steam and squirted melted rock in their eyes. Squalling in terror the dragons flapped into the air and lumbered off Southward.

"That's ocean," grinned the general. "They'll never come back—trying to find new homes, I suspect."

In an incredibly short time the field was littered with the flopping chunks that had been hewed from the Krakens. Living still they were, but powerless. The general shook his hand warmly. "You're on your own now," he said. "Good luck, boy. For a civilian you're not a bad sort of egg at all." He walked away.

Glumly Peter surveyed the colossal fortress of Almarish. He walked aimlessly up to its gate, a huge thing of bronze and silver, and pulled at the silken cord hanging there. A gong sounded and the door swung open. Peter advanced hopelessly into a sort of audience chamber. "So!" thundered a mighty voice.

"So what?" asked Peter despondently. He saw on a throne high above him an imposing figure. "You Almarish?" he asked listlessly.

"I am. And who are you?"

"It doesn't matter. I'm Peter Packer of Braintree, Mass. I don't even expect you to believe me." The throne lowered slowly and jerkily, as if on hydraulic pumps. The wizard descended and approached Peter. He was a man of about forty, with a full brown beard reaching almost to his belt.

"Why," asked the sorcerer, "have you come bearing arms?"

"It's the only way I could come," said Peter. "Let me first congratulate you on an efficient, well-oiled set of political machinery. Not even back in the United States have I seen graft carried to such a high degree. Secondly, your choice of assistants is an eye-opener. Your Mr. Pike is the neatest henchman I've ever seen. Thirdly, produce the person of Miss Melicent or I'll have to use force."

"Is that so?" rumbled Almarish. "Young puppy! I'd like to see you try it. Wrestle with me—two falls out of three. I dare you!"

Peter took off his coat of blue serge. "I never passed up a dare yet," he said. "How about a mat?"

"Think I'm a sissy?" the sorcerer jeered.

Peter was stripped for action. "Okay," he said. Slowly Almarish advanced on him, grappling for a hold. Peter let him take his forearm, then shifted his weight so as to hurl the magician over his shoulder. A moment later Peter was astonished to find himself on the floor underneath the wizard.

"Haw!" grunted Almarish, rising. "You still game?" He braced himself. "Yep!" snapped Peter. He hurled himself in a flying tackle that began ten feet away from the wizard and ended in a bone-crushing grip about the knees. Peter swarmed up his trunk and cruelly twisted an arm across his chest. The magician yelped in sudden agony, and let himself fall against the floor. Peter rose, grinning. "One all," he said cheerfully.

Almarish grappled for the third fall; Peter cagily backed away. The wizard hurled himself in a bruising body-block against Peter, battering him off his feet and falling on the young man. Instinctively Peter bridged his body, arching it off the floor. Almarish, grunting fiercely, gripped his arm and turned it slowly, as though he were winding a clock. Peter snapped over, rolling on the wizard's own body as a fulcrum. He had his toe in his hand, and closed his fist with every ounce of muscle he had. The sorcerer screamed and fell over on his face. Peter jammed his knee in the wizard's inside socket and bore down terribly. He could feel the bones bend in his grip.

"Enough!" gasped the wizard. Peter let him loose.

"You made it," said Almarish. "Two out of three."

Peter studied his face curiously. Take off that beard and you had—

"You said it, Grandfather Packer," said Peter, grinning.

Almarish groaned. "It's a wise child that knows its own father—grandfather, in this case," he said. "How could you tell?"

"Everthing just clicked," said Peter simply. "You disappearing—that clock—somebody applying American methods in Ellil—and then I shaved you mentally and there you were. Simple?"

"Sure is. But how do you think I made out here, boy?"

"Shamefully. That kind of thing isn't tolerated any more. It's gangsterism—you'll have to cut it out, gramp."

"Gangsterism be damned!" snorted the wizard. "It's business. Business and common-sense."

"Business maybe—certainly not common-sense. My boys wiped out your guard and I might have wiped out you if I had magic stronger than yours."

Grandfather Packer chuckled in glee. "Magic? I'll begin at the beginning. When I got that dad-blamed clock back in '63 I dropped right into Ellil—onto the head of an assassin who was going for a real magician. Getting the set-up I pinned the killer with a half-nelson and the magician dispatched him. Then he got grateful—said he was retiring from public life and gave me a kind of token—good for any three wishes.

"So I took it, thanking him kindly, and wished for a palace and a bunch of gutty retainers. It was in my mind to run Ellil like a business, and I did it the only way I knew how—force. And from that day to this I used only one wish and I haven't a dab of magic more than that!"

"I'll be damned!" whispered Peter.

"And you know what I'm going to do with those other two wishes? I'm going to take you and me right back into the good old U. S. A.!"

"Will it only send two people?"

"So the magician said."

"Grandfather Packer," said Peter earnestly, "I am about to ask a very great sacrifice of you. It is also your duty to undo the damage which you have done."

"Oh," said Almarish glumly. "The girl? All right."

"You don't mind?" asked Peter incredulously.

"Far be it from me to stand in the way of young love," grunted the wizard sourly. "She's up there."

Peter entered timidly; the girl was alternately reading a copy of the *Braintree Informer* and staring passionately at a photograph of Peter. "Darling," said Peter.

"Dearest!" said Melicent, catching on almost immediately.

A short while later Peter was asking her: "Do you mind, dearest if I ask one favor of you—a very great sacrifice?" He produced a small, sharp pen-knife.

And all the gossip for a month in Braintree was of Peter Packer's stunning young wife, though some people wondered how it was that she had only nine fingers.

The Coming of the White Worm

Clark Ashton Smith

Evagh the warlock, dwelling beside the boreal sea, was aware of many strange and untimely portents in midsummer. Chilly burned the sun above Mhu Thulan from a heaven clear and pallid as ice. At eve the aurora was hung from zenith to earth like an arras in a high chamber of gods. Wan and rare were the poppies and small the anemones in the cliff-hidden vales behind Evagh's house; and the fruits in his walled garden were pale of rind and green at the core. He saw by day the unseasonable flight of great multitudes of fowl, going southward from the isles beyond Mhu Thulan; and by night he heard the clamor of other passing multitudes

Now Evagh was troubled by these portents, for his magic could not wholly interpret them. And the rude fisher-folk on the shore of the haven below his house were also troubled in their fashion. Day by day they had gone forth through the summer in their coracles of elk-hide and willow, casting their seines: but in the seines they drew only dead fishes, blasted as

85

if by fire or extreme cold. And because of this, as the summer drew on, it came to pass that few of them fared any longer to sea.

Then, out of the north, where ships from Cerngoth were wont to ply among the Arctic islands, a galley came drifting with idle oars and aimlessly veering helm. And the tide beached it among the fishermen's boats on the sands beneath the cliff-built house of Evagh. And, thronging about the galley, the fishers beheld its oarsmen still at the oars and its captain at the helm. But the faces and hands of all were white as leprosy; and the pupils of their open eyes had faded strangely, being indistinguishable from the whites; and a blankness of horror was within them like ice in deep pools fast frozen to the bottom.

Loath were the fishers to touch the dead men; and they murmured, saying that a doom was upon the sea, and a curse upon all seafaring things and people. But Evagh, deeming that the bodies would rot in the sun and would breed pestilence, commanded them to build a pile of driftwood about the galley. And when the pile had risen above the bulwarks, hiding from view the dead rowers, he fired it with his own hands.

High flamed the pile, and smoke ascended black as a storm-cloud, blowing in windy volumes. But when the fire sank, the bodies of the oarsmen were still sitting amid the mounded embers, and their arms were still outstretched in the posture of rowing, and their fingers were clenched; though the oars had now dropped away from them in brands and ashes. And the galley's captain stood upright still in his place: though the burnt helm had fallen beside him. Naught but the raiment of the corpses had been consumed; and they shone white as marble above the charrings of wood; and nowhere upon them was any blackness left by the fire.

Deeming this thing an ill prodigy, the fishers were all aghast, and they fled swiftly to the highmost rocks. But the sorcerer Evagh awaited the cooling of the brands.

Quickly the brands darkened; but smoke arose from them still throughout the noon and afternoon; and still they were overhot for human treading when the hour drew toward sunset. So Evagh fetched water in urns from the sea and cast it upon the ashes and charrings so that he might approach the corpses. After the smoke and hissing had died, he went forward. Nearing the bodies he was aware of a great coldness; and the coldness began to ache in his hands and ears, and smote sharply through his mantle of fur. Going still closer, he touched one of the bodies with his forefinger-tip; and the finger, though lightly pressed and quickly withdrawn, was seared as if by flame.

Evagh was much amazed: for the condition of the corpses was a thing unknown to him heretofore; and in all his science of wizardry there was naught to enlighten him.

Returning to his house ere night, he burned at each door and window the gums that are most offensive to the northern demons. Afterward he perused with sedulous care the writing of Pnom, in which are collated many powerful exorcisms against the white spirits of the pole. For these spirits, it seemed, had laid their power upon the galley's crew; and he could not but apprehend some further working of the power.

Though a fire burned in the chamber, piled with fat pine and terebinth, a deadly chill began to invade the air toward midnight. And Evagh's fingers grew numb on the sheets of parchment, so that he could scarce turn them. And the cold deepened steadily, slowing his blood as if with ice; and he felt on his face the breathing of an icy wind. Yet the heavy doors and stout-paned windows were tightly closed; and the fire blazed high in no need of replenishment.

Then, with eyes whose very lids stiffened about them, Evagh saw that the room grew brighter with a light shining through the northern windows. Pale was the light, and it entered the room in a great beam falling directly upon him where he sat. And the light seared his eyes with a chill radiance, and the cold sharpened as if somehow one with the brightness; and the wind blew swiftlier out of the light, seeming no longer air but an element rare and unbreathable as ether. Vainly, with numbing thoughts, he strove to recall the exorcisms of Pnom. And his breath forsook him on the thin wind, and he fell down in a sort of waking swoon that was nigh to death. He seemed to hear voices muttering unfamiliar spells, while the bleak light and ether ebbed and flowed like a tide about him. And in time it seemed that his eyes and his flesh were tempered to endure them, and he breathed once more, and his blood quickened again in his veins; and the swoon passed, and he rose up like one that rises from the dead.

Full upon him poured the strange light through the windows. But the stiffness of cold was gone from his limbs, and he felt no more of chillness than was natural to the late summer night. Looking forth from one of the windows, he witnessed a strange marvel: for in the harbor there towered an iceberg such as no vessel had yet sighted in its seafaring to the north. It filled the broad haven from shore to shore, and sheered up to a height immeasurable with piled escarpments and tiered precipices; and its pinnacles hung like towers in the zenith. It was vaster and steeper than the mountain Yarak, which marks the site of the boreal pole; and from it there fell upon sea and land a frosty glittering paler and brighter than the light of the full moon.

On the shore below were the charrings of the beached galley, and among them the corpses incombustible by fire. And along the sands and rocks, the fisher-folk were lying or standing upright in still, rigid postures, as if they had come forth to behold the great iceberg and had been smitten by a magic sleep. And the whole harbor-shore, and the garden of Evagh, filled with that pallid splendor, was like a place where frost has fallen thickly over all.

Feeling a great wonder, Evagh would have gone forth from his house: but, ere he had taken three steps, a numbness came upon all his members, and deep sleep overpowered his senses even where he stood.

The sun had risen when he awoke. Peering out, he beheld a new marvel: for his garden and the rocks and sea-sands below it were visible no longer. In their stead were level spaces of ice about his house, and tall ice-pinnacles. Beyond the verges of the ice he saw a sea that lay remotely and far beneath; and beyond the sea the low looming of a dim shore.

Terror came to Evagh now, for he recognized in all this the workings of a sorcery beyond the power of mortal wizards. Plain it was that his stout house of granite stood no longer on the coast of Mhu Thulan but was based now on some upper crag of that stupendous iceberg he had beheld in the night. Trembling, he prayed and knelt to the Old Ones, who dwell secretly in subterrene caverns or abide under the sea or in the supermundane spaces. And even as he prayed, he heard a loud knocking at his door.

Fearfully he arose and opened the portals. Before him were two men, strange of visage and bright-skinned, who wore for mantles such rune-enwoven stuffs as wizards wear. The runes were uncouth and alien; but when the men bespoke him he understood something of their speech, which was in a dialect of the hyperborean isles.

"We serve that Outer One whose name is Rlim Shaikorth," they said. "From spaces beyond the north he has come in his floating citadel, the ice-mountain Yikilth, from which pours an exceeding coldness and a pale splendor that blasts the flesh of men. He has spared us alone amid the inhabitants of the isle Thulask, tempering our flesh to the rigor of his abode, making respirable for us the air no mortal man may breathe, and taking us to go with him in his seafaring upon Yikilth. Thee also he has spared and acclimated by his spells to the coldness and thin ether. Hail, O Evagh, whom we know for a great wizard by this token: since only the mightiest of warlocks are thus chosen and exempted."

Sorely astonished was Evagh; but seeing that he had now to deal with men who were as himself, he questioned closely the two magicians of Thulask. They were named Dooni and Ux Loddhan, and were wise in the lore of the elder gods. They would tell him nothing of Rlim Shaikorth but avowed that their service to this being consisted of such worship as is given to a god, together with the repudiation of all bonds that had linked them heretofore to mankind. And they told Evagh that he was to go with them at once before Rlim Shaikorth, and perform the due rite of obeisance, and accept the bond of alienage.

So Evagh went with the Thulaskians and was led by them to a great pinnacle of ice that rose unmeltable into the sun, beetling above all its fellows. The pinnacle was hollow, and climbing therein by stairs of ice, they came at last to the chamber of Rlim Shaikorth, which was a circular dome with a round block at the center, forming a dais.

At sight of that entity which occupied the dais, Evagh's pulses were stilled for an instant by terror; and, following upon the terror, his gorge rose within him through excess of loathing. In all the world there was nothing that could be likened for its foulness to Rlim Shaikorth. Something he had of the semblance of a fat white worm; but his bulk was beyond that of the sea-elephant. His half-coiled tail was thick as the middle folds of his body; and his front reared upward from the dais in the form of a white round disk, and upon it were imprinted vague lineaments. Amid the visage a mouth curved uncleanly from side to side of the disk, opening and shutting incessantly on a pale and tongueless and toothless maw. Two eye sockets lay close together above the shallow nostrils, but the sockets were eyeless, and in them appeared from moment to moment globules of a blood-colored matter having the form of eyeballs; and ever the globules broke and dripped down before the dais. And from the ice-floor there ascended two masses like stalagmites, purple and dark as frozen gore, which had been made by this ceaseless dripping of the globules.

Dooni and Ux Loddhan prostrated themselves, and Evagh deemed it well to follow their example. Lying prone on the ice, he heard the red drops falling with a splash as of heavy tears; and then, in the dome above him, it seemed that a voice spoke; and the voice was like the sound of some hidden cataract in a glacier hollow with caverns.

"O Evagh," said the voice, "I have preserved thee from the doom of others, and have made thee as they that inhabit the bourn of coldness and inhale the airless void. Wisdom ineffable shall be thine, and mastery beyond the conquest of mortals, if thou will but worship me and become my thrall. With me thou shalt voyage amid the kingdoms and isles of earth, and see the white falling of death upon them in the light from Yikilth. Our coming shall bring eternal frost on their gardens, and shall set upon their people's flesh the rigor of transarctic gulfs. All this shalt thou witness, being as one of the lords of death, supernal and immortal; and in the end thou shalt return with me to that world beyond the pole, in which is mine abiding empire."

Seeing that he was without choice in the matter, Evagh professed himself willing to yield worship and service to the pale worm. Instructed by his fellow-wizards, he performed the rites that are scarce suitable for narration, and swore the vow of unspeakable alienage.

Strange was that voyaging, for it seemed that the great iceberg was guided by sorcery, prevailing ever against wind and tide. And always, as they went, the chill splendor smote afar from Yikilth. Proud galleys were overtaken, and their crews were blasted at the oars. The fair hyperborean ports, busy with maritime traffic, were stilled by the iceberg's passing. Idle were their streets and wharves, idle was the shipping in their harbors, when the pale light had come and gone. Far inland fell the rays, bringing to the fields and gardens a blight more lasting than that of winter; and forests were frozen, and the beasts that roamed them were turned as if into marble, so that men who came long afterward to that region found the elk and bear and mammoth still standing in all the postures of life. But, sitting in his house or walking abroad on the berg, Evagh was aware of no sharper cold than that which abides in summer shadows.

Now, besides Dooni and Ux Loddhan, there were five other wizards that went with Evagh on that voyage, having been chosen by Rlim Shaikorth and transported with their houses to the berg through unknown enchantment. They were outlandish men, called Polarians, from islands nearer the pole than broad Thulask. Evagh could understand little of their ways; and their sorcery was foreign and their speech unintelligible to him; nor was it known to the Thulaskians.

Daily the eight wizards found on their tables all provender necessary for human sustenance; though they knew not the agency that supplied it. All were seemingly united in the worship of the worm. But Evagh was uneasy at heart, beholding the doom that went forth eternally from Yikilth upon lovely cities and fruitful ocean-shores. Ruthfully he saw the blasting of flower-girdled Cerngoth and the stillness that descended on the thronged streets of Leqquan, and the frost that seared with sudden whiteness the garths and orchards of the sea-fronting valley of Aguil.

Ever southward sailed the great berg, bearing its lethal winter to lands where the summer sun rode high. And Evagh kept his own counsel and followed in all ways the custom of the others. At intervals that were regulated by the motions of the circumpolar stars, the warlocks climbed to that lofty chamber in which Rlim Shaikorth abode perpetually, half coiled on his dais of ice. There, in a ritual whose cadences corresponded to the falling of those eye-like tears that were wept by the worm, and with genuflections timed to the yawning and shutting of his mouth they yielded to Rlim Shaikorth the required adoration. And Evagh learned from the others that the worm slept for a period at each darkening of the moon; and only at that time did the sanguine tears suspend their falling, and the mouth forbear its alternate closing and gaping.

At the third repetition of the rites, it came to pass that only seven wizards climbed to the tower. Evagh, counting their number, perceived that the missing man was one of the five outlanders. Later, he questioned Dooni and Ux Loddhan and made signs of inquiry to the four northrons; but it seemed that the fate of the absent warlock was a thing mysterious to all. Nothing was seen or heard of him; and Evagh, pondering long and deeply, was somewhat disquieted. For, during the ceremony in the tower chamber, it had seemed to him that the worm was grosser of bulk and girth than on any former occasion.

Covertly he asked the Thulaskians what manner of nutriment was required by Rlim Shaikorth. Concerning this, there was some dispute, for Ux Loddhan maintained that the worm fed on the hearts of white arctic bears, while Dooni swore that his rightful nourishment was the liver of whales. But, to their knowledge, the worm had not eaten during their sojourn upon Yikilth.

Still the iceberg followed its course beneath the heightening sun; and again, at the star-appointed time, which was the forenoon of every third day, the sorcerers convened in the worm's presence. Their number was now but six, and the lost warlock was another of the outlanders. And the worm had greatened still more in size, thickening visibly from head to tail.

Now, in their various tongues, the six remaining wizards implored the worm to tell them the fate of their absent fellows. And the worm answered; and his speech was intelligible to all, each thinking that he had been addressed in his own language: "This matter is a mystery, but ye shall all receive enlightenment in turn. Know this: the two that have vanished are still present; and they and ye also shall share even as I have promised in the ultramundane lore and empery of Rlim Shaikorth."

When they had descended from the tower, Evagh and the two Thulaskians debated the interpretations of this answer. Evagh maintained that their missing companions were present only in the worm's belly; but the others argued that these men had undergone a more mystical translation and were now elevated beyond human sight and hearing. Forthwith they began to make ready with prayer and austerity, looking for some sublime apotheosis which would come to them in due turn. But Evagh could not trust the worm's equivocal pledges; and fear and doubt remained with him.

Seeking for some trace of the lost Polarians to assuage his doubt, he made search of the mighty berg, on whose battlements his own house and the houses of the other warlocks were perched like the tiny huts of fishers on ocean-cliffs. In this quest the others would not accompany him, fearing to incur the worm's displeasure. From verge to verge he roamed unhindered, and he climbed perilously on the upper scarps, and went down into deep crevasses and caverns where the sun failed and there was no other light than the strange luster of that unearthly ice. Embedded here in the walls, as if in the stone of nether strata, he saw dwellings such as men had never built, and vessels that might belong to other ages or worlds; but nowhere could he detect the presence of any living creature; and no spirit or shadow gave response to his evocations.

So Evagh was still fearful of the worm's treachery; and he resolved to remain awake on the night preceding the next celebration of the rites of worship. At eve of that night he assured himself that the other warlocks were all housed in their separate mansions, to the number of five; and then he set himself to watch without remission the entrance of Rlim Shaikorth's tower, which was plainly visible from his own windows.

Weirdly and coldly shone the great berg in the darkness, pouring forth a light as of frozen stars. The moon rose early on the eastern sea. But Evagh, holding vigil at his window till midnight, saw that no visible form emerged from the tower, and none entered it. At midnight there came upon him a sudden drowsiness, and he could sustain his vigil no longer but slept deeply throughout the remainder of the night.

On the following day there were but four sorcerers who gathered in the ice-dome and gave homage to Rlim Shaikorth. And Evagh saw that two more of the outlanders, men of bulk and stature dwarfish beyond their fellows, were now missing.

One by one thereafter, on nights preceding the ceremony of worship, the companions of Evagh vanished. The last Polarian was next to go; and it came to pass that only Evagh and Ux Loddhan and Dooni went to the tower; and then Evagh and Ux Loddhan went alone. And terror mounted daily in Evagh, and he would have hurled himself into the sea from Yikilth, if Ux Loddhan, divining his intention, had not warned him that no man could depart therefrom and live again in solar warmth and terrene air, having been habituated to the coldness and thin ether.

So, at that time when the moon had waned and darkened wholly, it occurred that Evagh climbed before Rlim Shaikorth with infinite trepidation and loath, laggard steps. And, entering the dome with downcast eyes, he found himself the sole worshipper.

A palsy of fear was upon him as he made obeisance; and scarcely he dared to lift his eyes and regard the worm. But soon, as he began to perform the customary genuflections, he became aware that the red tears of Rlim Shaikorth no longer fell on the purple stalagmites; nor was there any sound such as the worm was wont to make by the perpetual opening and shutting of his mouth. And venturing at last to look upward, Evagh beheld the abhorrently swollen mass of the monster, whose thickness was now such as to overhang the dais' rim; and he saw that the mouth and eye-holes were closed in slumber. Thereupon he recalled how the wizards of Thulask had told him that the worm slept for an interval at the darkening of each moon.

Now was Evagh sorely bewildered: for the rites he had learned could be fittingly performed only while the tears of Rlim Shaikorth fell down and his mouth gaped and closed and gaped again in a measured alternation. And none had instructed him as to what rites were suitable during the slumber of the worm. And being in much doubt, he said softly: "Wakest thou, O Rlim Shaikorth?"

In reply, he seemed to hear a multitude of voices that issued obscurely from out the pale, tumid mass before him. The sound of the voices was weirdly muffled, but among them he distinguished the accents of Dooni and Ux Loddhan; and there was a thick muttering of uncouth words which he knew for the speech of the five Polarians; and beneath this he caught, or seemed to catch, innumerable undertones that were not the voices of any creatures of Earth. And the voices rose and clamored, like those of prisoners in some profound oubliette.

Anon, as he listened in awe and horror, the voice of Dooni became articulate above the others; and the manifold clamor and muttering ceased, as if a multitude were hushed to hear its spokesman. And Evagh heard the tones of Dooni, saying:

"The worm sleeps, but we whom the worm has devoured are awake. Direly has he deceived us, for he came to our houses in the night, devouring us bodily one by one as we slept under his enchantment. He has eaten our souls even as our bodies, and verily we are part of Rlim Shaikorth, but exist only as in a dark and noisome dungeon; and while the worm wakes we have no separate being, but are merged wholly into the being of Rlim Shaikorth.

"Hear, then, O Evagh, the truth which we have learned from our oneness with the worm. He has saved us from the white doom and has taken us upon Yikilth for this reason, because we alone of all mankind, who are sorcerers of high attainment and mastery, may endure the lethal ice-change and become breathers of the airless void, *and thus, in the end, be made suitable for his provender.*

"Great and terrible is the worm, and the place wherefrom he comes and whereto he returns is not to be dreamt of by mortal men. And the worm is omniscient, save that he knows not the waking of them he has devoured, and their awareness during his slumber. But the worm, though ancient beyond the antiquity of worlds, is not immortal and is vulnerable in one particular. Whosoever learns the time and means of his vulnerability, and has heart for the undertaking, may slay him easily. And the time for this deed is during his term of sleep. Therefore we adjure thee now by the faith of the Old Ones to draw the sword thou wearest beneath thy mantle and plunge it into the side of Rlim Shaikorth; for such is the means of his slaying.

"Thus only shall the going forth of the pale death be ended; and only thus shall we, thy fellows, obtain release from our blind thralldom and incarceration; and with us many that the worm has betrayed and eaten in former ages and upon distant worlds. And only by the doing of this thing shalt thou escape the worm's mouth, nor abide henceforward as a ghost among other ghosts in his belly. But know, however, that he who slays Rlim Shaikorth must necessarily perish in the slaying."

Evagh, in great astonishment, made question of Dooni and was answered readily concerning all that he asked. Much did he learn of the worm's origin and essence, and the manner in which Yikilth had floated down from transpolar gulfs to voyage the seas of Earth. Ever, as he listened, his abhorrence greatened; though deeds of dark sorcery had long indurated his flesh and soul, making him callous to more than common horrors. But of that which he learned it were ill to speak now.

At length there was silence in the dome; for Evagh had no longer any will to question the ghost of Dooni; and they that were imprisoned with Dooni seemed to wait and watch in a stillness of death.

Then, being a man of much resolution and hardihood, Evagh delayed no longer but drew from its ivory sheath the short and well-tempered sword of bronze which he carried at his baldric. Approaching close to the dais, he plunged the blade into the overswollen mass of Rlim Shaikorth. The blade entered easily, slicing and tearing, as if he had stabbed a monstrous bladder, and was not stayed even by the broad pommel; and the whole right hand of Evagh was drawn after it into the wound.

He perceived no quiver or stirring of the worm; but out of the wound there gushed a sudden torrent of black liquescent matter, swiftening and deepening till the sword was caught from Evagh's grasp as if in a mill-race. Hotter far than blood and smoking with strange steamy vapors, the liquid poured over his arms and splashed his raiment as it fell. Quickly the ice was awash around his feet; but still the fluid welled as if from some inexhaustible spring of foulness; and it spread everywhere in meeting pools and runlets.

Evagh would have fled then; but the sable liquid, mounting and flowing, was about his ankles when he neared the stairhead; and it rushed adown the stairway before him like a cataract. Hotter and hotter it grew, boiling, bubbling, while the current strengthened and clutched at him and drew him like malignant hands. He feared to essay the downward stairs; nor was there any place in the dome where he could climb for refuge. He turned, striving against the tide for bare foothold, and saw dimly through reeking vapors the throned mass of Rlim Shaikorth. The gash had widened prodigiously, and a stream surged from it like waters of a broken weir; and yet, for further proof of the worm's unearthly nature, *his bulk was in no wise diminished thereby*. And still the black fluid came in an evil flood; and it rose swirling about the knees of Evagh; and the vapors seemed to take the form of a myriad phantoms, wreathing and dividing obscurely as they went past him. Then, tottering giddily on the stairhead, he was swept away and hurled to his death on the ice-steps far below.

That day, on the sea to eastward of middle Hyperborea, the crews of certain merchant galleys beheld an unheard-of thing. As they sped north, returning from far ocean isles with a wind that aided their oars, they sighted in the late forenoon a monstrous iceberg whose pinnacles and crags loomed high as mountains. The berg shone in part with a weird light; and from its loftiest pinnacle poured an ink-black torrent; and all the ice-cliffs and buttresses beneath were astream with rapids and cascades and sheeted falls of the same blackness, that fumed like boiling water as they plunged oceanward; and the sea around the berg was clouded and streaked for a wide interval as if with the dark fluid of the cuttlefish.

The mariners feared to sail closer; but, full of awe and marveling, they stayed their oars and lay watching the berg; and the wind dropped, so that their galleys drifted within view of it all that day. The berg dwindled swiftly, melting as though some unknown fire consumed it; and the air took on a strange warmth between gusts of arctic coldness, and the water about their ships grew tepid. Crag by crag the ice was runneled and eaten away; and huge portions fell off with a mighty splashing; and the highest pinnacle collapsed; but still the blackness poured out as from an unfathomable fountain. The watchers thought, at whiles, that they beheld houses running seaward amid the loosened fragments; but of this they were uncertain because of those ever-mounting vapors. By sunset-time the berg had diminished to a mass no larger than a common floe; yet still the welling blackness overstreamed it; and it sank low in the wave; and the weird light was quenched altogether. Thereafter, the night being moonless, it was lost to vision. A gale rose, blowing strongly from the south; and at dawn the sea was void of any remnant.

Concerning the matters related above, many and various legends have gone forth throughout Mhu Thulan and all the hyperboreal kingdoms and archipelagoes. The truth is not in such tales, for no man has known the truth heretofore. But I, the sorcerer Eibon, calling up through my necromancy the wave-wandering spirit of Evagh, have learned from him the true history of the worm's advent. And I have written it down in my volume with such omissions as are needful for the sparing of mortal weakness and sanity. And men will read this record, together with much more of the elder lore, in days long after the coming and melting of the great glacier.

Yesterday Was Monday

Theodore Sturgeon

Harry Wright rolled over and said something spelled "Bzzzzhha-a-aw!" He chewed a bit on a mouthful of dry air and spat it out, opened one eye to see if it really would open, opened the other and closed the first, closed the second, swung his feet onto the floor, opened them again and stretched. This was a daily occurrence, and the only thing that made it remarkable at all was that he did it on a Wednesday morning, and—

Yesterday was Monday.

Oh, he knew it was Wednesday all right. It was partly that, even though he knew yesterday was Monday, there was a gap between Monday and now; and that must have been Tuesday. When you fall asleep and lie there all night without dreaming, you know, when you wake up, that time has passed. You've done nothing that you can re-remember; you've had no particular thoughts, no way to gauge time, and yet you know that some hours have passed. So it was with Harry Wright. Tuesday had gone wherever your eight hours went last night.

But he hadn't slept through Tuesday. Oh no. He never slept, as a matter of fact, more than six hours at a stretch, and there was no particular reason for him doing so now. Monday was the day before yesterday; he had turned in and slept his usual stretch, he had awakened, and it was Wednesday.

It *felt* like Wednesday. There was a Wednesdayish feel to the air.

Harry put on his socks and stood up. He wasn't fooled. He knew what day it was. "What happened to yesterday?" he muttered. "Oh—yesterday was Monday." That sufficed until he got his pajamas off. "Monday," he mused, reaching for his underwear, "was quite a while back, seems as though." If he had been the worrying type, he would have started then and there. But he wasn't. He was an easygoing sort, the kind of man that gets himself into a rut and stays there until he is pushed out. That was why he was an automobile mechanic at twenty-three dollars a week; that's why he had been one for eight years now, and would be from now on, if he could only find Tuesday and get back to work.

Guided by his reflexes, as usual, and with no mental effort at all, which was also usual, he finished washing, dressing, and making his bed. His alarm clock, which never alarmed because he was of such regular habits, said, as usual, six twenty-two when he paused on the way out, and gave his room the once-over. And there was a certain something about the place that made even this phlegmatic character stop and think.

It wasn't finished.

The bed was there, and the picture of Joe Louis. There were the two chairs sharing their usual seven legs, the split table, the pipe-organ bedstead, the beige wallpaper with the two swans over and over and over, the tiny corner sink, the tilted bureau. But none of them were finished. Not that there were any holes in anything. What paint there had been in the first place was still there. But there was an odor of old cut lumber, a subtle, insistent air of building, about the room and everything in it. It was indefinable, inescapable, and Harry Wright stood there caught up in it, wondering. He glanced suspiciously around but saw nothing he could really be suspicious of. He shook his head, locked the door and went out into the hall.

On the steps a little fellow, just over three feet tall, was gently stroking the third step from the top with a razor-sharp chisel, shaping up a new scar in the dirty wood. He looked up as Harry approached, and stood up quickly.

"Hi," said Harry, taking in the man's leather coat, his peaked cap, his wizened, bright-eyed little face. "Whatcha doing?"

"Touch-up," piped the little man. "The actor in the third floor front has a nail in his right heel. He came in late Tuesday night and cut the wood here. I have to get it ready for Wednesday."

"This is Wednesday," Harry pointed out.

"Of course. Always has been. Always will be."

Harry let that pass, started on down the stairs. He had achieved his amazing bovinity by making a practice of ignoring things he could not understand. But one thing bothered him—

"Did you say that feller in the third floor front was an actor?"

"Yes. They're all actors, you know."

"Your're nuts, friend," said Harry bluntly. "That guy works on the docks."

"Oh yes—that's his part. That's what he acts."

"No kiddin'. An' what does he do when he isn't acting?"

"But he— Well, that's all he does do! That's all any of the actors do!"

"Gee— I thought he looked like a reg'lar guy, too," said Harry. "An actor? 'Magine!"

"Excuse me," said the little man, "but I've got to get back to work. We mustn't let anything get by us, you know. They'll be through Tuesday before long, and everything must be ready for them."

Harry thought: this guy's crazy nuts. He smiled uncertainly and went down to the landing below. When he looked back the man was cutting skillfully into the stair, making a neat little nail scratch. Harry shook his head. This was a screwy morning. He'd be glad to get back to the shop. There was a '39 sedan down there with a busted rear spring. Once he got his mind on that he could forget this nonsense. That's all that matters to a man in a rut. Work, eat, sleep, pay day. Why even try to think anything else out?

The street was a riot of activity, but then it always was. But not quite this way. There were automobiles and trucks and buses around, aplenty, but none of them were moving. And none of them were quite complete. This was Harry's own field; if there was anything he didn't know about motor vehicles, it wasn't very important. And through that medium he began to get the general idea of what was going on.

Swarms of little men who might have been twins of the one he had spoken to were crowding around the cars, the sidewalks, the stores and buildings. All were working like mad with every tool imaginable. Some were touching up the finish of the cars with fine wire brushes, laying on networks of microscopic cracks and scratches. Some, with ball peens and mallets, were denting fenders skillfully, bending bumpers in an artful crash pattern, spider-webbing safety-glass windshields. Others were aging top dressing with high-pressure, needlepoint sandblasters. Still others were pumping dust into upholstery, sandpapering the dashboard finish around light switches, throttles, chokes, to give a finger-worn appearance. Harry stood aside as a half dozen of the workers scampered down the street bearing a fender which they riveted to a 1930 coupé. It was freshly bloodstained.

Once awakened to this highly unusual activity, Harry stopped, slightly open-mouthed, to watch what else was going on. He saw the same process being industriously accomplished with the houses and stores. Dirt was being laid on plate-glass windows over a coat of clear sizing. Woodwork was being cleverly scored and the paint peeled to make it look correctly weather-beaten, and dozens of leather-clad laborers were on their hands and knees, poking dust and dirt into the cracks between the paving blocks. A line of them went down the sidewalk, busily chewing gum and spitting it out; they were followed by another crew who carefully placed the wads according to diagrams they carried, and stamped them flat.

Harry set his teeth and muscled his rocking brain into something like its normal position. "I ain't never seen a day like this or crazy people like this," he said, "but I ain't gonna let it be any of my affair. I got my job to go to." And trying vainly to ignore the hundreds of little, hard-working figures, he went grimly on down the street.

When he got to the garage he found no one there but more swarms of stereotyped little people climbing over the place, dulling the paint work, cracking the cement flooring, doing their hurried, efficient little tasks of aging. He noticed, only because he was so familiar with the garage, that they were actually *making* the marks that had been there as long as he had known the place. "Hell with it," he gritted, anxious to submerge himself into his own world of wrenches and grease guns. "I got my job; this is none o' my affair."

He looked about him, wondering if he should clean these interlopers out of the garage. Naw—not his affair. He was hired to repair cars, not to police the joint. Long as they kept away from him—and, of course, animal caution told him that he was far, far outnumbered. The absence of the boss and the other mechanics was no surprise to Harry; he always opened the place.

He climbed out of his street clothes and into coveralls, picked up a tool case and walked over to the sedan, which he had left up on the hydraulic rack yester— that is, Monday night. And that is when Harry Wright lost his temper. After all, the car was his job, and he didn't like having anyone else mess with a job he had started. So when he saw his job—his '39 sedan— resting steadily on its wheels over the rack, which was down under the floor, and when he saw that the rear spring was repaired, he began to burn. He dived under the car and ran deft fingers over the rear wheel suspensions. In spite of his anger at this unprecedented occurrence, he had to admit to himself that the job had been done well. "Might have done it myself," he muttered.

A soft clank and a gentle movement caught his attention. With a roar he reached out and grabbed the leg of one of the ubiquitous little men, wriggled out from under the car, caught his culprit by his leather collar, and dangled him at arm's length.

"What are you doing to my job?" Harry bellowed.

The little man tucked his chin into the front of his shirt to give his windpipe a chance, and said, "Why, I was just finishing up that spring job."

"Oh. So you were just finishing up on that spring job," Harry whispered, choked with rage. Then, at the top of his voice, "Who told you to touch that car?"

"Who told me? What do you— Well, it just had to be done, that's all. You'll have to let me go. I must tighten up those two bolts and lay some dust on the whole thing."

"You must *what?* You get within six feet o' that car and I'll twist your head offn your neck with a Stillson!"

"But— It has to be done!"

"You won't do it! Why, I oughta—"

"Please let me go! If I don't leave that car the way it was Tuesday night—"

"When was Tuesday night?"

"The last act, of course. Let me go, or I'll call the district supervisor!"

"Call the devil himself. I'm going to spread you on the sidewalk outside; and heaven help you if I catch you near here again!"

The little man's jaw set, his eyes narrowed, and he whipped his feet upward. They crashed into Wright's jaw; Harry dropped him and staggered back. The little man began squealing, "Supervisor! Supervisor! Emergency!"

Harry growled and started after him; but suddenly, in the air between him and the midget workman, a long white hand appeared. The empty air was swept back, showing an aperture from the garage to blank, blind nothingness. Out of it stepped a tall man in a single loose-fitting garment literally studded with pockets. The opening closed behind the man.

Harry cowered before him. Never in his life had he seen such noble, powerful features, such strength of purpose, such broad shoulders, such a deep chest. The man stood with the backs of his hands on his hips, staring at Harry as if he were something somebody forgot to sweep up.

"That's him," said the little man shrilly. "He is trying to stop me from doing the work!"

"Who are you?" asked the beautiful man, down his nose.

"I'm the m-mechanic on this j-j— Who wants to know?"

"Iridel, supervisor of the district of Futura, wants to know."

"Where in hell did you come from?"

"I did not come from hell. I came from Thursday."

Harry held his head. "What *is* all this?" he wailed. "Why is today Wednesday? Who are all these crazy little guys? What happened to Tuesday?"

Iridel made a slight motion with his finger, and the little man scurried back under the car. Harry was frenzied to hear the wrench busily tightening bolts. He half started to dive under after the little fellow, but Iridel said, "Stop!" and when Iridel said, "Stop!" Harry stopped.

"This," said Iridel calmly, "is an amazing occurrence." He regarded Harry with unemotional curiosity. "An actor on stage before the sets are finished. Extraordinary."

"What stage?" asked Harry. "What are you doing here anyhow, and what's the idea of all these little guys working around here?"

"You ask a great many questions, actor," said Iridel. "I shall answer them, and then I shall have a few to ask you. These little men are stage hands—I am surprised that you didn't realize that. They are setting the stage for Wednesday. Tuesday? That's going on now."

"Arrgh!" Harry snorted. "How can Tuesday be going on when today's Wednesday?"

"Today isn't Wednesday, actor."

"Huh?"

"Today is Tuesday."

Harry scratched his head. "Met a feller on the steps this mornin'—one of these here stage hands of yours. He said this was Wednesday."

"It *is* Wednesday. Today is Tuesday. Tuesday is today. 'Today' is simply the name for the stage set which happens to be in use. 'Yesterday' means the set that has just been used; 'Tomorrow' is the set that will be used after the actors have finished with 'today.' This is Wednesday. Yesterday was Monday; today is Tuesday. See?"

Harry said, "No."

Iridel threw up his long hands. "My, you actors are stupid. Now listen carefully. This is Act Wednesday, Scene 6:22. That means that everything you see around you here is being readied for 6:22 a.m. on Wednesday. Wednesday isn't a time; it's a place. The actors are moving along toward it now. I see you still don't get the idea. Let's see . . . ah. Look at that clock. What does it say?"

Harry Wright looked at the big electric clock on the wall over the compressor. It was corrected hourly and highly accurate, and it said 6:22. Harry looked at it amazed. "Six tw— but my gosh, man, that's what time I left the house. I walked here, an' I been here ten minutes already!"

Iridel shook his head. "You've been here no time at all, because there is no time until the actors make their entrances."

Harry sat down on a grease drum and wrinkled up his brains with the effort he was making. "You mean that this time proposition ain't something that moves along all the time? Sorta—well, like a road. A road don't go no place— You just go places along it. Is that it?"

"That's the general idea. In fact, that's a pretty good example. Suppose we say that it's a road; a highway built of paving blocks. Each block is a day; the actors move along it, and go through day after day. And our job here—mine and the little men—is to... well, pave that road. This is the clean-up gang here. They are fixing up the last little details, so that everything will be ready for the actors."

Harry sat still, his mind creaking with the effects of this information. He felt as if he had been hit with a lead pipe, and the shock of it was being drawn out infinitely. This was the craziest-sounding thing he had ever run into. For no reason at all he remembered a talk he had had once with a drunken aviation mechanic who had tried to explain to him how the air flowing over an airplane's wings makes the machine go up in the air. He hadn't understood a word of the man's discourse, which was all about eddies and chords and cambers and foils, dihedrals and the Bernouilli effect. That didn't make any difference; the things flew whether he understood how or not; he knew that because he had seen them. This guy Iridel's lecture was the same sort of thing. If there was nothing in all he said, how come all these little guys were working around here? Why wasn't the clock telling time? Where was Tuesday?

He thought he'd get that straight for good and all. "Just where is Tuesday?" he asked.

"Over there," said Iridel, and pointed. Harry recoiled and fell off the drum; for when the man extended his hand, it *disappeared!*

Harry got up off the floor and said tautly, "Do that again."

"What? Oh— Point toward Tuesday? Certainly." And he pointed. His hand appeared again when he withdrew it.

Harry said, "My gosh!" and sat down again on the drum, sweating and staring at the supervisor of the district of Futura. "You point, an' your hand—ain't," he breathed. "What direction is that?"

"It is a direction like any other direction," said Iridel. "You know yourself there are four directions—forward, sideward, upward, and"—he pointed again, and again his hand vanished— *"that* way!"

"They never tol'e me that in school," said Harry. "Course, I was just a kid then, but—"

Iridel laughed. "It is the fourth dimension—it is *duration*. The actors move through length, breadth, and height, anywhere they choose to within the set. But there is another movement—one they can't control—and that is duration."

"How soon will they come ... eh ... here?" asked Harry, waving an arm. Iridel dipped into one of his numberless pockets and pulled out a watch. "It is now eight thirty-seven Tuesday morning," he said. "They'll be here as soon as they finish the act, and the scenes in Wednesday that have already been prepared."

Harry thought again for a moment, while Iridel waited patiently, smiling a little. Then he looked up at the supervisor and asked, "Hey—this 'actor' business—what's that all about?"

"Oh—that. Well, it's a play, that's all. Just like any play—put on for the amusement of an audience."

"I was to a play once," said Harry. "Who's the audience?"

Iridel stopped smiling. "Certain— Ones who may be amused," he said. "And now I'm going to ask you some questions. How did you get here?"

"Walked."

"You *walked* from Monday night to Wednesday morning?"

"Naw— From the house to here."

"Ah— But how did you get to Wednesday, six twenty-two?"

"Well I— Damfino. I just woke up an' came to work as usual."

"This is an extraordinary occurrence," said Iridel, shaking his head in puzzlement. "You'll have to see the producer."

"Producer? Who's he?"

"You'll find out. In the meantime, come along with me. I can't leave you here; you're too close to the play. I have to make my rounds anyway."

Iridel walked toward the door. Harry was tempted to stay and find himself some more work to do, but when Iridel glanced back at him and motioned him out, Harry followed. It was suddenly impossible to do anything else.

Just as he caught up with the supervisor, a little worker ran up, whipping off his cap.

"Iridel, sir," he piped, "the weather makers put .006 of one percent too little moisture in the air on this set. There's three sevenths of an ounce too little gasoline in the storage tanks under here."

"How much is in the tanks?"

"Four thousand two hundred and seventy-three gallons, three pints, seven and twenty-one thirty-fourths ounces."

Iridel grunted. "Let it go this time. That was very sloppy work. Someone's going to get transferred to Limbo for this."

"Very good, sir," said the little man. "Long as you know we're not responsible." He put on his cap, spun around three times and rushed off.

"Lucky for the weather makers that the amount of gas in that tank doesn't come into Wednesday's script," said Iridel. "If anything interferes with the continuity of the play, there's the devil to pay. Actors haven't sense enough to cover up, either. They are liable to start whole series of miscues because of a little thing like that. The play might flop and then we'd all be out of work."

"Oh," Harry oh-ed. "Hey, Iridel—what's the idea of that patchy-looking place over there?"

Iridel followed his eyes. Harry was looking at a corner lot. It was tree-lined and overgrown with weeds and small saplings. The vegetation was true to form around the edges of the lot, and around the path that ran diagonally through it; but the spaces in between were a plane surface. Not a leaf nor a blade of grass grew there; it was naked-looking, blank, and absolutely without any color whatever.

"Oh, that," answered Iridel. "There are only two characters in Act Wednesday who will use that path. Therefore it is as grown-over as it should be. The rest of the lot doesn't enter into the play, so we don't have to do anything with it."

"But— Suppose someone wandered off the path on Wednesday," Harry offered.

"He'd be due for a surprise, I guess. But it could hardly happen. Special prompters are always detailed to spots like that, to keep the actors from going astray or missing any cues."

"Who are they—the prompters, I mean?"

"Prompters? G.A.'s—Guardian Angels. That's what the script writers call them."

"I heard o' them," said Harry.

"Yes, they have their work cut out for them," said the supervisor. "Actors are always forgetting their lines when they shouldn't, or remembering them when the script calls for a lapse. Well, it looks pretty good here. Let's have a look at Friday."

"Friday? You mean to tell me you're working on Friday already?"

"Of course! Why, we work years in advance! How on earth do you think we could get our trees grown otherwise? Here—step in!" Iridel put out his hand, seized empty air, drew it aside to show the kind of absolute nothingness he had first appeared from, and waved Harry on.

"Y-you want me to go in there?" asked Harry diffidently.

"Certainly. Hurry, now!"

Harry looked at the section of void with a rather weak-kneed look, but could not withstand the supervisor's strange compulsion. He stepped through.

And it wasn't so bad. There were no whirling lights, no sensations of falling, no falling unconscious. It was just like stepping into another room—which is what had happened. He found himself in a great round chamber, whose roundness was touched a bit with the indistinct. That is, it

had curved walls and a domed roof, but there was something else about it.
It seemed to stretch off in that direction toward which Iridel had so
astonishingly pointed. The walls were lined with an amazing array of
control machinery—switches and ground-glass screens, indicators and
dials, knurled knobs, and levers. Moving deftly before them was a crew of
men, each looking exactly like Iridel except that their garments had no
pockets. Harry stood wide-eyed, hypnotized by the enormous complexity
of the controls and the ease with which the men worked among them.
Iridel touched his shoulder. "Come with me," he said. "The producer is in
now; we'll find out what is to be done with you."

They started across the floor. Harry had not quite time to wonder how
long it would take them to cross that enormous room, for when they had
taken perhaps a dozen steps they found themselves at the opposite wall.
The ordinary laws of space and time simply did not apply in the place.

They stopped at a door of burnished bronze, so very highly polished that
they could see through it. It opened and Iridel pushed Harry through. The
door swung shut. Harry, panic-stricken lest he be separated from the only
thing in this weird world he could begin to get used to, flung himself
against the great bronze portal. It bounced him back, head over heels, into
the middle of the floor. He rolled over and got up to his hands and knees.

He was in a tiny room, one end of which was filled by a colossal
teakwood desk. The man sitting there regarded him with amusement.
"Where'd you blow in from?" he asked; and his voice was like the angry
bee sound of an approaching hurricane.

"Are you the producer?"

"Well, I'll be darned," said the man, and smiled. It seemed to fill the
whole room with light. He was a big man, Harry noticed; but in this
deceptive place, there was no way of telling how big. "I'll be most verily
darned. An actor. You're a persistent lot, aren't you? Building houses for
me that I almost never go into. Getting together and sending requests for
better parts. Listening carefully to what I have to say and then ignoring or
misinterpreting my advice. Always asking for just one more chance, and
when you get it, messing that up too. And now one of you crashes the gate.
What's your trouble, anyway?"

There was something about the producer that bothered Harry, but he
could not place what it was, unless it was the fact that the man awed him
and he didn't know why. "I woke up in Wednesday," he stammered, "and
yesterday was Tuesday. I mean Monday. I mean—" He cleared his throat
and started over. "I went to sleep Monday night and woke up Wednesday,
and I'm looking for Tuesday."

"What do you want me to do about it?"

"Well—couldn't you tell me how to get back there? I got work to do."

"Oh—I get it," said the producer. "You want a favor from me. You know, someday, some one of you fellows is going to come to me wanting to give me something, free and for nothing, and then I am going to drop quietly dead. Don't I have enough trouble running this show without taking up time and space by doing favors for the likes of you?" He drew a couple of breaths and then smiled again. "However—I have always tried to be just, even if it is a tough job sometimes. Go on out and tell Iridel to show you the way back. I think I know what happened to you; when you made your exit from the last act you played in, you somehow managed to walk out behind the wrong curtain when you reached the wings. There's going to be a prompter sent to Limbo for this. Go on now—beat it."

Harry opened his mouth to speak, thought better of it and scuttled out the door, which opened before him. He stood in the huge control chamber, breathing hard. Iridel walked up to him.

"Well?"

"He says for you to get me out of here."

"All right," said Iridel. "This way." He led the way to a curtained doorway much like the one they had used to come in. Beside it were two dials, one marked in days, and the other in hours and minutes.

"Monday night good enough for you?" asked Iridel.

"Swell," said Harry.

Iridel set the dials for 9:30 p.m. on Monday. "So long, actor. Maybe I'll see you again some time."

"So long," said Harry. He turned and stepped through the door.

He was back in the garage, and there was no curtained doorway behind him. He turned to ask Iridel if this would enable him to go to bed again and do Tuesday right from the start, but Iridel was gone.

The garage was a blaze of light. Harry glanced up at the clock— It said fifteen seconds after nine-thirty. That was funny; everyone should be home by now except Slim Jim, the night man, who hung out until four in the morning serving up gas at the pumps outside. A quick glance around sufficed. This might be Monday night, but it was a Monday night he hadn't known.

The place was filled with the little men again!

Harry sat on the fender of a convertible and groaned. "Now what have I got myself into?" he asked himself.

He could see that he was at a different place-in-time from the one in which he had met Iridel. There, they had been working to build, working with a precision and nicety that was a pleasure to watch. But here—

The little men were different, in the first place. They were tired-looking, sick, slow. There were scores of overseers about, and Harry winced with one of the little fellows when one of the men in white lashed out with a long whip. As the Wednesday crews worked, so the Monday gangs slaved. And the work they were doing was different. For here they were breaking down, breaking up, carting away. Before his eyes, Harry saw sections of paving lifted out, pulverized, toted away by the sackload by lines of trudging, browbeaten little men. He saw great beams upended to support the roof, while bricks were pried out of the walls. He heard the gang working on the roof, saw patches of roofing torn away. He saw walls and roof both melt away under that driving, driven onslaught, and before he knew what was happening he was standing alone on a section of the dead white plain he had noticed before on the corner lot.

It was too much for his overburdened mind; he ran out into the night, breaking through lines of laden slaves, through neat and growing piles of rubble, screaming for Iridel. He ran for a long time, and finally dropped down behind a stack of lumber out where the Unitarian church used to be, dropped because he could go no farther. He heard footsteps and tried to make himself smaller. They came on steadily; one of the overseers rounded the corner and stood looking at him. Harry was in deep shadow, but he knew the man in white could see in the dark.

"Come out o' there," grated the man. Harry came out.

"You the guy was yellin' for Iridel?"

Harry nodded.

"What makes you think you'll find Iridel in Limbo?" sneered his captor. "Who are you, anyway?"

Harry had learned by this time. "I'm an actor," he said in a small voice. "I got into Wednesday by mistake, and they sent me back here."

"What for?"

"Huh? Why—I guess it was a mistake, that's all."

The man stepped forward and grabbed Harry by the collar. He was about eight times as powerful as a hydraulic jack. "Don't give me no guff, pal," said the man. "Nobody gets sent to Limbo by mistake, or if he didn't do somethin' up there to make him deserve it. Come clean, now."

"I didn't do nothin'." Harry wailed. "I asked them the way back, and they showed me a door, and I went through it and came here. That's all I know. Stop it, you're choking me!"

The man dropped him suddenly. "Listen, babe, you know who I am? Hey?" Harry shook his head. "Oh—you don't. Well, I'm Gurrah!"

"Yeah?" Harry said, not being able to think of anything else at the moment.

Gurrah puffed out his chest and appeared to be waiting for something more from Harry. When nothing came, he walked up to the mechanic, breathed in his face. "Ain't scared, huh? Tough guy, huh? Never heard of Gurrah, supervisor of Limbo an' the roughest, toughest son of the devil from Incidence to Eternity, huh?"

Now Harry was a peaceable man, but if there was anything he hated, it was to have a stranger breathe his bad breath pugnaciously at him. Before he knew it had happened, Gurrah was sprawled eight feet away, and Harry was standing alone rubbing his left knuckles—quite the more surprised of the two.

Gurrah sat up, feeling his face. "Why, you . . . you hit me!" he roared. He got up and came over to Harry. "You hit me!" he said softly, his voice slightly out of focus in amazement. Harry wished he hadn't—wished he was in bed or in Futura or dead or something. Gurrah reached out with a heavy fist and—patted him on the shoulder. "Hey," he said, suddenly friendly, "you're all right. Heh! Took a poke at me, didn't you? Be damned! First time in a month o' Mondays anyone ever made a pass at me. Last was a feller named Orton. I killed 'im." Harry paled.

Gurrah leaned back against the lumber pile. "Dam'f I didn't enjoy that, feller. Yeah. This is a hell of a job they palmed off on me, but what can you do? Breakin' down—breakin' down. No sooner get through one job, workin' top speed, drivin' the boys till they bleed, than they give you the devil for not bein' halfway through another job. You'd think I'd been in the business long enough to know what it was all about, after more than eight hundred an' twenty million acts, wouldn't you? Heh. Try to tell *them* that. Ship a load of dog houses up to Wednesday, sneakin' it past backstage nice as you please. They turn right around and call me up. 'What's the matter with you, Gurrah? Them dog houses is no good. We sent you a list o' worn-out items two acts ago. One o' the items was dog houses. Snap out of it or we send someone back there who can read an' put you on a toteline.' That's what I get—act in and act out. An' does it do any good to tell 'em that my aide got the message an' dropped dead before he got it to me? No. Uh-uh. If I say anything about that, they tell me to stop workin' 'em to death. If I do that, they kick because my shipments don't come in fast enough."

He paused for breath. Harry had a hunch that if he kept Gurrah in a good mood it might benefit him. He asked, "What's your job, anyway?"

"Job?" Gurrah howled. "Call this a job? Tearin' down the sets, shippin' what's good to the act after next, junkin' the rest?" He snorted.

Harry asked, "You mean they use the same props over again?"

"That's right. They don't last, though. Six, eight acts, maybe. Then they got to build new ones and weather them and knock 'em around to make 'em look as if they was used."

There was silence for a time. Gurrah, having got his bitterness off his chest for the first time in literally ages, was feeling pacified. Harry didn't know how to feel. He finally broke the ice. "Hey, Gurrah— How'm I goin' to get back into the play?"

"What's it to me? How'd you— Oh, that's right, you walked in from the control room, huh? That it?"

Harry nodded.

"An' how," growled Gurrah, "did you get inta the control room?"

"Iridel brought me."

"Then what?"

"Well, I went to see the producer, and—"

"Th' *producer!* Holy— You mean you walked right in and—" Gurrah mopped his brow. "What'd he say?"

"Why—he said he guessed it wasn't my fault that I woke up in Wednesday. He said to tell Iridel to ship me back."

"An' Iridel threw you back to Monday." And Gurrah threw back his shaggy head and roared.

"What's funny," asked Harry, a little peeved.

"Iridel," said Gurrah. "Do you realize that I've been trying for fifty thousand acts or more to get something on that pretty ol' heel, and he drops you right in my lap. Pal, I can't thank you enough! He was supposed to send you back into the play, and instead o' that you wind up in yesterday! Why, I'll blackmail him till the end of time!" He whirled exultantly, called to a group of bedraggled little men who were staggering under a cornerstone on their way to the junkyard. "Take it easy, boys!" he called. "I got ol' Iridel by the short hair. No more busted backs! No more snotty messages! *Haw haw haw!"*

Harry, a little amazed at all this, put in a timid word, "Hey—Gurrah. What about me?"

Gurrah turned. "You? Oh. *Tel-e-phone!"* At his shout two little workers, a trifle less bedraggled than the rest, trotted up. One hopped up and perched on Gurrah's right shoulder; the other draped himself over the left, with his head forward. Gurrah grabbed the latter by the neck, brought the man's head close and shouted into his ear, "Give me Iridel!" There was a moment's wait, then the little man on his other shoulder spoke in Iridel's voice, into Gurrah's ear, "Well?"

"Hiyah, fancy pants!"

"Fancy— I beg your— Who is this?"

"It's Gurrah, you futuristic parasite. I got a couple things to tell you."

"Gurrah! How—*dare* you talk to me like that! I'll have you—"

"You'll have me in your job if I tell all I know. You're a wart on the nose of progress, Iridel."

"What is the meaning of this?"

"The meaning of this is that you had instructions sent to you by the producer an' you muffed them. Had an actor, there, didn't you? He saw the boss, didn't he? Told you he was to be sent back, didn't he? Sent him right over to me instead of to the play, didn't you? You're slippin', Iridel. Gettin' old. Well, get off the wire. I'm callin' the boss, right now."

"The boss? Oh—don't do that, old man. Look, let's talk this thing over. Ah—about that shipment of three-legged dogs I was wanting you to round up for me; I guess I can do without them. Any little favor I can do for you—"

—"you'll damn well do, after this. You better, Goldilocks." Gurrah knocked the two small heads together, breaking the connection and probably the heads, and turned grinning to Harry. "You see," he explained, "that Iridel feller is a damn good supervisor, but he's a stickler for detail. He sends people to Limbo for the silliest little mistakes. He never forgives anyone and he never forgets a slip. He's the cause of half the misery back here, with his hurry-up orders. Now things are gonna be different. The boss has wanted to give Iridel a dose of his own medicine for a long time now, but Irrie never gave him a chance."

Harry said patiently, "About me getting back now—"

"My fran'!" Gurrah bellowed. He delved into a pocket and pulled out a watch like Iridel's. "It's eleven forty on Tuesday," he said. "We'll shoot you back there now. You'll have to dope out your own reasons for disappearing. Don't spill too much, or a lot of people will suffer for it—you the most. Ready?"

Harry nodded; Gurrah swept out a hand and opened the curtain to nothingness. "You'll find yourself quite a ways from where you started," he said, "because you did a little moving around here. Go ahead."

"Thanks," said Harry.

Gurrah laughed. "Don't thank me, chum. You rate all the thanks! Hey— if, after you kick off, you don't make out so good up there, let them toss you over to me. You'll be treated good; you've my word on it. Beat it; luck!"

Holding his breath, Harry Wright stepped through the doorway.

He had to walk thirty blocks to the garage, and when he got there the boss was waiting for him.

"Where you been, Wright?"

"I—lost my way."

"Don't get wise. What do you think this is—vacation time? Get going on the spring job. Damn it, it won't be finished now till tomorra."

Harry looked him straight in the eye and said, "Listen. It'll be finished tonight. I happen to know." And, still grinning, he went back into the garage and took out his tools.

They Bite

Anthony Boucher

There was no path, only the almost vertical ascent. Crumbled rock for a few yards, with the roots of sage finding their scanty life in the dry soil. Then jagged outcroppings of crude crags, sometimes with accidental footholds, sometimes with overhanging and untrustworthy branches of greasewood, sometimes with no aid to climbing but the leverage of your muscles and the ingenuity of your balance.

The sage was as drably green as the rock was drably brown. The only color was the occasional rosy spikes of a barrel cactus.

Hugh Tallant swung himself up onto the last pinnacle. It had a deliberate, shaped look about it—a petrified fortress of Lilliputians, a Gibraltar of pygmies. Tallant perched on its battlements and unslung his field glasses.

The desert valley spread below him. The tiny cluster of buildings that was Oasis, the exiguous cluster of palms that gave name to the town and shelter of his own tent and to the shack he was building, the dead-ended highway leading straightforwardly to nothing, the oiled roads diagramming the vacant blocks of an optimistic subdivision.

Tallant saw none of these. His glasses were fixed beyond the oasis and the town of Oasis on the dry lake. The gliders were clear and vivid to him, and the uniformed men busy with them were as sharply and minutely visible as a nest of ants under glass. The training school was more than usually active. One glider in particular, strange to Tallant, seemed the focus of attention. Men would come and examine it and glance back at the older models in comparison.

Only the corner of Tallant's left eye was not preoccupied with the new glider. In that corner something moved, something little and thin and brown as the earth. Too large for a rabbit, much too small for a man. It darted across that corner of vision, and Tallant found gliders oddly hard to concentrate on.

He set down the bifocals and deliberately looked about him. His pinnacle surveyed the narrow, flat area of the crest. Nothing stirred. Nothing stood out against the sage and rock but one barrel of rosy spikes. He took up the glasses again and resumed his observations. When he was done, he methodically entered the results in the little black notebook.

His hand was still white. The desert is cold and often sunless in winter. But it was a firm hand, and as well trained as his eyes, fully capable of recording faithfully the designs and dimensions which they had registered so accurately.

Once his hand slipped, and he had to erase and redraw, leaving a smudge that displeased him. The lean, brown thing had slipped across the edge of his vision again. Going toward the east edge, he would swear, where that set of rocks jutted like the spines on the back of a stegosaur.

Only when his notes were completed did he yield to curiosity, and even then with cynical self-reproach. He was physically tired, for him an unusual state, from this daily climbing and from clearing the ground for his shack-to-be. The eye muscles play odd nervous tricks. There could be nothing behind the stegosaur's armor.

There was nothing. Nothing alive and moving. Only the torn and half-plucked carcass of a bird, which looked as though it had been gnawed by some small animal.

It was halfway down the hill—hill in Western terminology, though anywhere east of the Rockies it would have been considered a sizable mountain—that Tallant again had a glimpse of a moving figure.

But this was no trick of a nervous eye. It was not little nor thin nor brown. It was tall and broad and wore a loud red-and-black lumberjacket. It bellowed, "Tallant!" in a cheerful and lusty voice.

Tallant drew near the man and said, "Hello." He paused and added, "Your advantage, I think."

The man grinned broadly. "Don't know me? Well, I daresay ten years is a long time, and the California desert ain't exactly the Chinese rice fields. How's stuff? Still loaded down with Secrets for Sale?"

Tallant tried desperately not to react to that shot, but he stiffened a little. "Sorry. The prospector getup had me fooled. Good to see you again, Morgan."

The man's eyes narrowed. "Just having my little joke," he smiled. "Of course you wouldn't have no serious reason for mountain climbing around a glider school, now, would you? And you'd kind of need field glasses to keep an eye on the pretty birdies."

"I'm out here for my health." Tallant's voice sounded unnatural even to himself.

"Sure, sure. You were always in it for your health. And come to think of it, my own health ain't been none too good lately. I've got me a little cabin way to hell-and-gone around here, and I do me a little prospecting now and then. And somehow it just strikes me, Tallant, like maybe I hit a pretty good lode today."

"Nonsense, old man. You can see—"

"I'd sure hate to tell any of them Army men out at the field some of the stories I know about China and the kind of men I used to know out there. Wouldn't cotton to them stories a bit, the Army wouldn't. But if I was to have a drink too many and get talkative-like—"

"Tell you what," Tallant suggested brusquely. "It's getting near sunset now, and my tent's chilly for evening visits. But drop around in the morning and we'll talk over old times. Is rum still your tipple?"

"Sure is. Kind of expensive now, you understand—"

"I'll lay some in. You can find the place easily—over by the oasis. And we . . . we might be able to talk about your prospecting, too."

Tallant's thin lips were set firm as he walked away.

The bartender opened a bottle of beer and plunked it on the damp-circled counter. "That'll be twenty cents," he said, then added as an afterthought, "Want a glass? Sometimes tourists do."

Tallant looked at the others sitting at the counter—the red-eyed and unshaven old man, the flight sergeant unhappily drinking a Coke—it was after Army hours for beer—the young man with the long, dirty trench coat and the pipe and the new-looking brown beard—and saw no glasses. "I guess I won't be a tourist," he decided.

This was the first time Tallant had had a chance to visit the Desert Sport Spot. It was as well to be seen around in a community. Otherwise people begin to wonder and say, "Who is that man out by the oasis? Why don't you ever see him anyplace?"

The Sport Spot was quiet that night. The four of them at the counter, two Army boys shooting pool, and a half-dozen of the local men gathered about a round poker table, soberly and wordlessly cleaning a construction worker whose mind seemed more on his beer than on his cards.

"You just passing through?" the bartender asked sociably.

Tallant shook his head. "I'm moving in. When the Army turned me down for my lungs, I decided I better do something about it. Heard so much about your climate here I thought I might as well try it."

"Sure thing," the bartender nodded. "You take up until they started this glider school, just about every other guy you meet in the desert is here for his health. Me, I had sinus, and look at me now. It's the air."

Tallant breathed the atmosphere of smoke and beer suds, but did not smile. "I'm looking forward to miracles."

"You'll get 'em. Whereabouts you staying?"

"Over that way a bit. The agent called it 'the old Carker place.' "

Tallant felt the curious listening silence and frowned. The bartender had started to speak and then thought better of it. The young man with the beard looked at him oddly. The old man fixed him with red and watery eyes that had a faded glint of pity in them. For a moment, Tallant felt a chill that had nothing to do with the night air of the desert.

The old man drank his beer in quick gulps and frowned as though trying to formulate a sentence. At last he wiped beer from his bristly lips and said, "You wasn't aiming to stay in the adobe, was you?"

"No. It's pretty much gone to pieces. Easier to rig me up a little shack than try to make the adobe livable. Meanwhile, I've got a tent."

"That's all right, then, mebbe. But mind you don't go poking around that there adobe."

"I don't think I'm apt to. But why not? Want another beer?"

The old man shook his head reluctantly and slid from his stool to the ground. "No thanks. I don't rightly know as I—"

"Yes?"

"Nothing. Thanks all the same." He turned and shuffled to the door.

Tallant smiled. "But why should I stay clear of the adobe?" he called after him.

The old man mumbled.

"What?"

"They bite," said the old man, and went out shivering into the night.

The bartender was back at his post. "I'm glad he didn't take that beer you offered him," he said. "Along about this time in the evening I have to stop serving him. For once he had the sense to quit."

Tallant pushed his own empty bottle forward. "I hope I didn't frighten him away."

"Frighten? Well, mister, I think maybe that's just what you did do. He didn't want beer that sort of came, like you might say, from the old Carker place. Some of the old-timers here, they're funny that way."

Tallant grinned. "Is it haunted?"

"Not what you'd call haunted, no. No ghosts there that I ever heard of." He wiped the counter with a cloth and seemed to wipe the subject away with it.

The flight sergeant pushed his Coke bottle away, hunted in his pocket for nickels, and went over to the pinball machine. The young man with the beard slid onto his vacant stool. "Hope old Jake didn't worry you," he said.

Tallant laughed. "I suppose every town has its deserted homestead with a grisly tradition. But this sounds a little different. No ghosts, and they bite. Do you know anything about it?"

"A little," the young man said seriously. "A little. Just enough to—"

Tallant was curious. "Have one on me and tell me about it."

The flight sergeant swore bitterly at the machine.

Beer gurgled through the beard. "You see," the young man began, "the desert's so big you can't be alone in it. Ever notice that? It's all empty and there's nothing in sight, but there's always something moving over there where you can't quite see it. It's something very dry and thin and brown, only when you look around it isn't there. Ever see it?"

"Optical fatigue—" Tallant began.

"Sure. I know. Every man to his own legend. There isn't a tribe of Indians hasn't got some way of accounting for it. You've heard of the Watchers? And the twentieth-century white man comes along, and it's optical fatigue. Only in the nineteenth century things weren't quite the same, and there were the Carkers."

"You've got a special localized legend?"

"Call it that. You glimpse things out of the corner of your mind, same like you glimpse lean, dry things out of the corner of your eye. You encase 'em in solid circumstance and they're not so bad. That is known as the Growth of Legend. The Folk Mind in Action. You take the Carkers and the things you don't quite see and you put 'em together. And they bite."

Tallant wondered how long that beard had been absorbing beer. "And what were the Carkers?" he prompted politely.

"Ever hear of Sawney Bean? Scotland—reign of James First, or maybe the Sixth, though I think Roughead's wrong on that for once. Or let's be more modern—ever hear of the Benders? Kansas in the 1870s? No? Ever hear of Procrustes? Or Polyphemus? Or Fee fi-fo-fum?

"There are ogres, you know. They're no legend. They're fact, they are. The inn where nine guests left for every ten that arrived, the mountain cabin that sheltered travelers from the snow, sheltered them all winter till the melting spring uncovered their bones, the lonely stretches of road that so many passengers traveled halfway—you'll find 'em everywhere. All over Europe and pretty much in this country too before communications became what they are. Profitable business. And it wasn't just the profit. The Benders made money, sure; but that wasn't why they killed all their victims as carefully as a kosher butcher. Sawney Bean got so he didn't give a damn about the profit; he just needed to lay in more meat for the winter.

"And think of the chances you'd have at an oasis."

"So these Carkers of yours were, as you call them, ogres?"

"Carkers, ogres—maybe they were Benders. The Benders were never seen alive, you know, after the townspeople found those curiously butchered bones. There's a rumor they got this far west. And the time checks pretty well. There wasn't any town here in the eighties. Just a couple of Indian families, last of a dying tribe living on at the oasis. They vanished after the Carkers moved in. That's not so surprising. The white race is a sort of super-ogre, anyway. Nobody worried about them. But they used to worry about why so many travelers never got across this stretch of desert. The travelers used to stop over at the Carkers', you see, and somehow they often never got any farther. Their wagons'd be found maybe fifteen miles beyond in the desert. Sometimes they found the bones, too, parched and white. Gnawed-looking, they said sometimes."

"And nobody ever did anything about these Carkers?"

"Oh, sure. We didn't have King James Sixth—only I still think it was First—to ride up on a great white horse for a gesture, but twice Army detachments came here and wiped them all out."

"Twice? One wiping-out would do for most families." Tallant smiled.

"Uh-uh. That was no slip. They wiped out the Carkers twice because, you see, once didn't do any good. They wiped 'em out and still travelers vanished and still there were gnawed bones. So they wiped 'em out again. After that they gave up, and people detoured the oasis. It made a longer, harder trip, but after all—"

Tallant laughed. "You mean to say these Carkers were immortal?"

"I don't know about immortal. They somehow just didn't die very easy. Maybe, if they were the Benders—and I sort of like to think they were—they learned a little more about what they were doing out here on the desert. Maybe they put together what the Indians knew and what they knew, and it worked. Maybe Whatever they made their sacrifices to understood them better out here than in Kansas."

"And what's become of them—aside from seeing them out of the corner of the eye?"

"There's forty years betwen the last of the Carker history and this new settlement at the oasis. And people won't talk much about what they learned here in the first year or so. Only that they stay away from that old Carker adobe. They tell some stories— The priest says he was sitting in the confessional one hot Saturday afternoon and thought he heard a penitent come in. He waited a long time and finally lifted the gauze to see was anybody there. Something was there, and it bit. He's got three fingers on his right hand now, which looks funny as hell when he gives a benediction."

Tallant pushed their two bottles toward the bartender. "That yarn, my young friend, has earned another beer. How about it, bartender? Is he always cheerful like this, or is this just something he's improvised for my benefit?"

The bartender set out the fresh bottles with great solemnity. "Me, I wouldn't've told you all that myself, but then, he's a stranger too and maybe don't feel the same way we do here. For him it's just a story."

"It's more comfortable that way," said the young man with the beard, and he took a firm hold on his beer bottle.

"But as long as you've heard that much," said the bartender, "you might as well— It was last winter, when we had that cold spell. You heard funny stories that winter. Wolves coming into prospectors' cabins just to warm up. Well, business wasn't so good. We don't have a license for hard liquor, and the boys don't drink much beer when it's that cold. But they used to come in anyway because we've got that big oil burner.

"So one night there's a bunch of 'em in here—old Jake was here, that you was talking to, and his dog Jigger—and I think I hear somebody else come in. The door creaks a little. But I don't see nobody, and the poker game's going, and we're talking just like we're talking now, and all of a sudden I hear a kind of a noise like crack! over there in that corner behind the jukebox near the burner.

"I go over to see what goes and it gets away before I can see it very good. But it was little and thin and it didn't have no clothes on. It must've been damned cold that winter."

"And what was the cracking noise?" Tallant asked dutifully.

"That? That was a bone. It must've strangled Jigger without any noise. He was a little dog. It ate most of the flesh, and if it hadn't cracked the bone for the marrow it could've finished. You can still see the spots over there. The blood never did come out."

There had been silence all through the story. Now suddenly all hell broke loose. The flight sergeant let out a splendid yell and began pointing excitedly at the pinball machine and yelling for his payoff. The construction worker dramatically deserted the poker game, knocking his chair over in the process, and announced lugubriously that these guys here had their own rules, see?

Any atmosphere of Carker-inspired horror was dissipated. Tallant whistled as he walked over to put a nickel in the jukebox. He glanced casually at the floor. Yes, there was a stain, for what that was worth.

He smiled cheerfully and felt rather grateful to the Carkers. They were going to solve his blackmail problem very neatly.

Tallant dreamed of power that night. It was a common dream with him. He was a ruler of the new American Corporate State that would follow the war; and he said to this man, "Come!" and he came, and to that man, "Go!" and he went, and to his servants, "Do this!" and they did it.

Then the young man with the beard was standing before him, and the dirty trench coat was like the robes of an ancient prophet. And the young man said, "You see yourself riding high, don't you? Riding the crest of the wave—the Wave of the Future, you call it. But there's a deep, dark undertow that you don't see, and that's a part of the Past. And the Present and even your Future. There is evil in mankind that is blacker even than your evil, and infinitely more ancient."

And there was something in the shadows behind the young man, something little and lean and brown.

Tallant's dream did not disturb him the following morning. Nor did the thought of the approaching interview with Morgan. He fried his bacon and eggs and devoured them cheerfully. The wind had died down for a change, and the sun was warm enough so that he could strip to the waist while he cleared land for his shack. His machete glinted brilliantly as it swung through the air and struck at the roots of the brush.

When Morgan arrived his full face was red and sweating.

"It's cool over there in the shade of the adobe," Tallant suggested. "We'll be more comfortable." And in the comfortable shade of the adobe he swung the machete once and clove Morgan's full, red, sweating face in two.

It was so simple. It took less effort than uprooting a clump of sage. And it was so safe. Morgan lived in a cabin way to hell-and-gone and was often away on prospecting trips. No one would notice his absence for months, if then. No one had any reason to connect him with Tallant. And no one in Oasis would hunt for him in the Carker-haunted adobe.

The body was heavy, and the blood dripped warm on Tallant's bare skin. With relief he dumped what had been Morgan on the floor of the adobe. There were no boards, no flooring. Just the earth. Hard, but not too hard to dig a grave in. And no one was likely to come poking around in this taboo territory to notice the grave. Let a year or so go by, and the grave and the bones it contained would be attributed to the Carkers.

The corner of Tallant's eye bothered him again. Deliberately he looked about the interior of the adobe.

The little furniture was crude and heavy, with no attempt to smooth down the strokes of the ax. It was held together with wooden pegs or half-rotted thongs. There were age-old cinders in the fireplace, and the dusty shards of a cooking jar among them.

And there was a deeply hollowed stone, covered with stains that might have been rust, if stone rusted. Behind it was a tiny figure, clumsily fashioned of clay and sticks. It was something like a man and something like a lizard, and something like the things that flit across the corner of the eye.

Curious now, Tallant peered about further. He penetrated to the corner that the one unglassed window lighted but dimly. And there he let out a little choking gasp. For a moment he was rigid with horror. Then he smiled and all but laughed aloud.

This explained everything. Some curious individual had seen this, and from his accounts had burgeoned the whole legend. The Carkers had indeed learned something from the Indians, but that secret was the art of embalming.

It was a perfect mummy. Either the Indian art had shrunk bodies, or this was that of a ten-year-old boy. There was no flesh. Only skin and bone and taut, dry stretches of tendon between. The eyelids were closed; the sockets looked hollow under them. The nose was sunken and almost lost. The scant lips were tightly curled back from the long and very white teeth, which stood forth all the more brilliantly against the deep-brown skin.

It was a curious little trove, this mummy. Tallant was already calculating the chances for raising a decent sum of money from an interested anthropologist—murder can produce such delightfully profitable chance by-products—when he noticed the infinitesimal rise and fall of the chest.

The Carker was not dead. It was sleeping.

Tallant did not dare stop to think beyond the instant. This was no time to pause to consider if such things were possible in a well-ordered world. It was no time to reflect on the disposal of the body of Morgan. It was a time to snatch up your machete and get out of there.

But in the doorway he halted. There, coming across the desert, heading for the adobe, clearly seen this time, was another—a female.

He made an involuntary gesture of indecision. The blade of the machete clanged ringingly against the adobe wall. He heard the dry shuffling of a roused sleeper behind him.

He turned fully now, the machete raised. Dispose of this nearer one first, then face the female. There was no room even for terror in his thoughts, only for action.

The lean brown shape darted at him avidly. He moved lightly away and stood poised for its second charge. It shot forward again. He took one step back, machete arm raised; and fell headlong over the corpse of Morgan. Before he could rise, the thin thing was upon him. Its sharp teeth had met through the palm of his left hand.

The machete moved swiftly. The thin dry body fell headless to the floor. There was no blood.

The grip of the teeth did not relax. Pain coursed up Tallant's left arm—a sharper, more bitter pain than you would expect from the bite. Almost as though venom—

He dropped the machete, and his strong white hand plucked and twisted at the dry brown lips. The teeth stayed clenched, unrelaxing. He sat bracing his back against the wall and gripped the head between his knees. He pulled. His flesh ripped, and blood formed dusty clots on the dirt floor. But the bite was firm.

His world had become reduced now to that hand and that head. Nothing outside mattered. He must free himself. He raised his aching arm to his face, and with his own teeth he tore at that unrelenting grip. The dry flesh crumbled away in desert dust, but the teeth were locked fast. He tore his lip against their white keenness, and tasted in his mouth the sweetness of blood and something else.

He staggered to his feet again. He knew what he must do. Later he could use cautery, a tourniquet, see a doctor with a story about a Gila monster— their heads grip too, don't they?—but he knew what he must do now.

He raised the machete and struck again.

His white hand lay on the brown floor, gripped by the white teeth in the brown face. He propped himself against the adobe wall, momentarily unable to move. His open wrist hung over the deeply hollowed stone. His blood and his strength and his life poured out before the little figure of sticks and clay.

The female stood in the doorway now, the sun bright on her thin brownness. She did not move. He knew that she was waiting for the hollow stone to fill.

Call Him Demon

Henry Kuttner

A long time afterward she went back to Los Angeles and drove past Grandmother Keaton's house. It hadn't changed a great deal, really, but what had seemed an elegant mansion to her childish, 1920 eyes was now a big ramshackle frame structure, gray with scaling paint.

After twenty-five years the—insecurity—wasn't there any more, but there still persisted a dull, irrational, remembered uneasiness, an echo of the time Jane Larkin had spent in that house when she was nine, a thin, big-eyed girl with the Buster Brown bangs so fashionable then.

Looking back, she could remember too much and too little. A child's mind is curiously different from an adult's. When Jane went into the living room under the green glass chandelier on that June day in 1920, she made a dutiful round of the family, kissing them all. Grandmother Keaton and chilly Aunt Bessie and the four uncles. She did not hesitate when she came to the new uncle—who was different.

The other kids watched her with impassive eyes. They knew. They saw she knew. But they said nothing just then. Jane realized she could not mention the—the trouble—either, until they brought it up. That was part of the silent etiquette of childhood. But the whole house was full of uneasiness. The adults merely sensed a trouble, something vaguely wrong. The children, Jane saw, *knew*.

Afterward they gathered in the back yard, under the big date-palm. Jane ostentatiously fingered her new necklace and waited. She saw the looks the others exchanged—looks that said, "Do you think she really noticed?" And finally Beatrice, the oldest, suggested hide-and-seek.

"We ought to tell her, Bee," little Charles said.

Beatrice kept her eyes from Charles.

"Tell her what? You're crazy, Charles."

Charles was insistent but vague.

"You know."

"Keep your old secret," Jane said. "I know what it is, anyhow. *He's* not my uncle."

"See?" Emily crowed. "She did too see it. I told you she'd notice."

"It's kind of funny," Jane said. She knew very well that the man in the living room wasn't her uncle and never had been, and he was pretending, quite hard—hard enough to convince the grown-ups—that he had always been here. With the clear, unprejudiced eye of immaturity, Jane could see that he wasn't an ordinary grown-up. He was sort of—empty.

"He just came," Emily said. "About three weeks ago."

"Three days," Charles corrected, trying to help, but his temporal sense wasn't dependent on the calendar. He measured time by the yardstick of events, and days weren't standard sized for him. They were longer when he was sick or when it rained, and far too short when he was riding the merry-go-round at Ocean Park or playing games in the back yard.

"It was three weeks," Beatrice said.

"Where'd he come from?" Jane asked.

There were secret glances exchanged.

"I don't know," Beatrice said carefully.

"He came out of a big round hole that kept going around," Charles said. "It's like a Christmas tree through there, all fiery."

"Don't tell lies," Emily said. "Did you ever truly see that, Charles?"

"No, Only sort of."

"Don't *they* notice?" Jane meant the adults.

"No," Beatrice told her, and the children all looked toward the house and pondered the inscrutable ways of grown-ups. "They act like he's always been here. Even Granny. Aunt Bessie said he came before *I* did. Only I knew that wasn't right."

"Three weeks," Charles said, changing his mind.

"He's making them all feel sick," Emily said. "Aunt Bessie takes aspirins all the time."

Jane considered. On the face of it, the situation seemed a little silly. An uncle three weeks old? Perhaps the adults were merely pretending, as they sometimes did, with esoteric adult motives. But somehow that didn't seem quite the answer. Children are never deceived very long about such things.

Charles, now that the ice was broken and Jane no longer an outsider, burst suddenly into excited gabble.

"Tell her, Bee! The real secret—you know. Can I show her the Road of Yellow Bricks? Please, Bee? Huh?"

Then the silence again. Charles was talking too much. Jane knew the Road of Yellow Bricks, of course. It ran straight through Oz from the Deadly Desert to the Emerald City.

After a long time Emily nodded.

"We got to tell her, you know," she said. "Only she might get scared. It's so dark."

"You were scared," Bobby said. "You cried, the first time."

"I didn't. Anyhow it—it's only make believe."

"Oh, *no!*" Charles said. "I reached out and touched the crown last time."

"It isn't a crown," Emily said. "It's *him.* Ruggedo."

Jane thought of the uncle who wasn't a real uncle—who wasn't a real person. "Is *he* Ruggedo?" she asked.

The children understood.

"Oh, no," Charles said. "Ruggedo lives in the cellar. We give him meat. All red and bluggy. He *likes* it! Gobble, gobble!"

Beatrice looked at Jane. She nodded toward the club house, which was a piano-box with a genuine secret lock. Then, somehow, quite deftly, she shifted the conversation onto another subject. A game of cowboys-and-Indians started presently and Bobby, howling terribly, led the rout around the house.

The piano-box smelled pleasantly of acacia drifting through the cracks. Beatrice and Jane, huddled together in the warm dimness, heard diminishing Indian-cries in the distance. Beatrice looked curiously adult just now.

"I'm glad you came, Janie," she said. "The little kids don't understand at all. It's pretty awful."

"Who is he?"

Beatrice shivered. "I don't know. I think he lives in the cellar." She hesitated. "You have to get to him through the attic, though. I'd be awfully scared if the little kids weren't so—so—they don't seem to mind at all."

"But, Bee! Who *is* he?"

Beatrice turned her head and looked at Jane, and it was quite evident then that she could not or would not say. There was a barrier. But because it was important, she tried. She mentioned the Wrong Uncle.

"I think Ruggedo's the same as him. I know he is, really. Charles and Bobby say so—and they know. They know better than I do. They're littler.... It's hard to explain, but—well, it's sort of like the Scoodlers. Remember?"

The Scoodlers. That unpleasant race that dwelt in a cavern on the road to Oz and had the convenient ability to detach their heads and hurl them at passers-by. After a moment the parallel became evident. A Scoodler could have his head in one place and his body in another, but both parts would belong to the same Scoodler.

Of course the phantom uncle had a head and a body both. But Jane could understand vaguely the possibility of his double nature, one of him moving deceptively through the house, focus of a strange malaise, and the other nameless, formless, nesting in a cellar and waiting for red meat....

"Charles knows more than any of us about it," Beatrice said. "He was the one who found out we'd have to feed R—Ruggedo. We tried different things, but it has to be raw meat. And if we stopped—something awful would happen. We kids found that out."

It was significant that Jane didn't ask how. Children take their equivalent of telepathy for granted.

"*They* don't know," Beatrice added. "We can't tell them."

"No," Jane said, and the two girls looked at one another, caught in the terrible, helpless problem of immaturity, the knowledge that the mores of the adult world are too complicated to understand, and that children must walk warily. Adults are always right. They are an alien race.

Luckily for the other children, they had come upon the Enemy in a body. One child alone might have had violent hysterics. But Charles, who made the first discoveries, was only six, still young enough so that the process of going insane in that particular way wasn't possible for him. A six-year-old is in a congenitally psychotic state; it is normal to him.

"And they've been sick ever since he came," Beatrice said.

Jane had already seen that. A wolf may don sheepskin and slide unobserved into a flock, but the sheep are apt to become nervous, though they cannot discover the source of their discomfort.

It was a matter of mood. Even he showed the same mood—uneasiness, waiting, sensing that something was wrong and not knowing what—but with *him* it was simply a matter of camouflage. Jane could tell he didn't want to attract attention by varying from the arbitrary norm he had chosen—that of the human form.

Jane accepted it. The uncle who was—empty—the one in the cellar called Ruggedo, who had to be fed regularly on raw meat, so that Something wouldn't happen. . . .

A masquerader, from somewhere. He had power, and he had limitations. The obvious evidences of his power were accepted without question. Children are realists. It was not incredible to them, for this hungry, inhuman stranger to appear among them—for here he was.

He came from somewhere. Out of time, or space, or an inconceivable place. He never had any human feelings; the children sensed that easily. He pretended very cleverly to be human, and he could warp the adult minds to implant artificial memories of his existence. The adults thought they remembered him. An adult will recognize a mirage; a child will be deceived. But conversely, an intellectual mirage will deceive an adult, not a child.

Ruggedo's power couldn't warp their minds, for those minds were neither quite human nor quite sane, from the adult standpoint. Beatrice, who was oldest, was afraid. She had the beginnings of empathy and imagination. Little Charlie felt mostly excitement. Bobby, the smallest, had already begun to be bored. . . .

Perhaps later Beatrice remembered a little of what Ruggedo looked like, but the others never did. For they reached him by a very strange road, and perhaps they were somewhat altered themselves during the time they were with him. He accepted or rejected food; that was all. Upstairs, the body of the Scoodler pretended to be human, while the Scoodler's head lay in that little, horrible nest he had made by warping space, so he was invisible and intangible to anyone who didn't know how to find the Road of Yellow Bricks.

What was he? Without standards of comparison—and there are none, in this world—he cannot be named. The children thought of him as Ruggedo. But he was not the fat, half-comic, inevitably frustrated Gnome King. He was never that.

Call him demon.

As a name-symbol, it implies too much and not enough. But it will have to do. By the standard of maturity he was monster, alien, super-being. But because of what he did, and what he wanted—call him demon.

One afternoon, a few days later, Beatrice hunted up Jane. "How much money have you got, Janie?" she asked.

"Four dollars and thirty-five cents," Jane said, after investigation. "Dad gave me five dollars at the station. I bought some popcorn and—well—different things."

"Gee, I'm glad you came when you did." Beatrice blew out a long breath. Tacitly it was agreed that the prevalent socialism of childhood clubs would apply in this more urgent clubbing together of interests. Jane's small hoard was available not for any individual among them, but for the good of the group. "We were running out of money," Beatrice said. "Granny caught us taking meat out of the icebox and we don't dare any more. But we can get a lot with your money."

Neither of them thought of the inevitable time when that fund would be exhausted. Four dollars and thirty-five cents seemed fabulous, in that era. And they needn't buy expensive meat, so long as it was raw and bloody.

They walked together down the acacia-shaded street with its occasional leaning palms and drooping pepper trees. They bought two pounds of hamburger and improvidently squandered twenty cents on sodas.

When they got back to the house, Sunday lethargy had set in. Uncles Simon and James had gone out for cigars, and Uncles Lew and Bert were reading the papers, while Aunt Bessie crocheted. Grandmother Keaton read *Young's Magazine,* diligently seeking spicy passages. The two girls paused behind the beaded portieres, looking in.

"Come on, kids," Lew said in his deep, resonant voice. "Seen the funnies yet? Mutt and Jeff are good. And Spark Plug—"

"Mr. Gibson is good enough for me," Grandmother Keaton said. "He's a real artist. His people look like people."

The door banged open and Uncle James appeared, fat, grinning, obviously happy from several beers. Uncle Simon paced him like a personified conscience.

"At any rate, it's quiet," he said, turning a sour glance on Jane and Beatrice. "The children make such a rumpus sometimes I can't hear myself think."

"Granny," Beatrice asked, "where are the kids?"

"In the kitchen, I think, dear. They wanted some water for something."

"Thanks." The two girls went out, leaving the room filled with a growing atmosphere of sub-threshold discomfort. The sheep were sensing the wolf among them, but the sheepskin disguise was sufficient. They did not know....

The kids were in the kitchen, busily painting one section of the comics with brushes and water. When you did that, pictures emerged. One page of the newspaper had been chemically treated so that moisture would bring out the various colors, dull pastels, but singularly glamorous, in a class with the Japanese flowers that would bloom in water, and the Chinese paper-shelled almonds that held tiny prizes.

From behind her, Beatrice deftly produced the butcher's package.

"Two pounds," she said. "Janie had some money, and Merton's was open this afternoon. I thought we'd better...."

Emily kept on painting diligently. Charles jumped up.

"Are we going up now, huh?"

Jane was uneasy. "I don't know if I'd better come along. I—"

"I don't want to either," Bobby said, but that was treason. Charles said Bobby was scared.

"I'm not. It just isn't any fun. I want to play something else."

"Emily," Beatrice said softly. "You don't have to go this time."

"Yes, I do." Emily looked up at last from her painting. "I'm not scared."

"I want to see the lights," Charles said. Beatrice whirled on him.

"You tell such lies, Charles! There aren't any lights."

"There are so. Sometimes, anyhow."

"There aren't."

"There are so. You're too dumb to see them. Let's go and feed him."

It was understood that Beatrice took command now. She was the oldest. She was also, Jane sensed, more afraid than the others, even Emily.

They went upstairs, Beatrice carrying the parcel of meat. She had already cut the string. In the upper hall they grouped before a door.

"This is the way, Janie," Charles said rather proudly. "We gotta go up to the attic. There's a swing-down ladder in the bathroom ceiling. We have to climb up on the tub to reach."

"My dress," Jane said doubtfully.

"You won't get dirty. Come on."

Charles wanted to be first, but he was too short. Beatrice climbed to the rim of the tub and tugged at a ring in the ceiling. The trapdoor creaked and the stairs descended slowly, with a certain majesty, beside the tub. It wasn't dark up there. Light came vaguely through the attic windows.

"Come on, Janie," Beatrice said, with a queer breathlessness, and they all scrambled up somehow, by dint of violent acrobatics.

The attic was warm, quiet and dusty. Planks were laid across the beams. Cartons and trunks were here and there.

Beatrice was already walking along one of the beams. Jane watched her.

Beatrice didn't look back; she didn't say anything. Once her hand groped out behind her; Charles, who was nearest, took it. Then Beatrice reached a plank laid across to another rafter. She crossed it. She went on— stopped—and came back, with Charles.

"You weren't doing it right," Charles said disappointedly. "You were thinking of the wrong thing."

Beatrice's face looked oddly white in the golden, faint light.

Jane met her cousin's eyes. "Bee—"

"You have to think of something else," Beatrice said quickly. "It's all right. Come on."

Charles at her heels, she started again across the plank. Charles was saying something, in a rhythmic, mechanical monotone:

> *"One, two, buckle my shoe,*
> *Three, four, knock at the door,*
> *Five, six, pick up sticks—"*

Beatrice disappeared.

> *"Seven, eight, lay them—"*

Charles disappeared.
Bobby, his shoulders expressing rebelliousness, followed. And vanished.
Emily made a small sound.
"Oh—*Emily!*" Jane said.
But her youngest cousin only said, "I don't want to go down there, Janie!"
"You don't have to."
"Yes, I do," Emily said. "I'll tell you what. I won't be afraid if you come right after me. I always think there's something coming up behind me to grab—but if you promise to come right after, it'll be all right."
"I promise," Jane said.
Reassured, Emily walked across the bridge. Jane was watching closely this time. Yet she did not see Emily disappear. She was suddenly—gone. Jane stepped forward, and stopped as a sound came from downstairs.
"*Jane!*" Aunt Bessie's voice. "*Jane!*" It was louder and more peremptory now. "Jane, where are you? Come here to me!"
Jane stood motionless, looking across the plank bridge. It was quite empty, and there was no trace of Emily or the other children. The attic was suddenly full of invisible menace. Yet she would have gone on, because of her promise, if—
"*Jane!*"
Jane reluctantly descended and followed the summons to Aunt Bessie's bedroom. That prim-mouthed woman was pinning fabric and moving her lips impatiently.
"Where on earth have you been, Jane? I've been calling and calling."
"We were playing," Jane said. "Did you want me, Aunt Bessie?"
"I should say I did," Aunt Bessie said. "This collar I've been crocheting. It's for a dress for you. Come here and let me try it on. How you grow, child!"
And after that there was an eternity of pinning and wriggling, while Jane kept thinking of Emily, alone and afraid somewhere in the attic. She began to hate Aunt Bessie. Yet the thought of rebellion or escape never crossed her mind. The adults were absolute monarchs. As far as relative values went, trying on the collar was more important, at this moment, than

anything else in the world. At least, to the adults who administered the world.

While Emily, alone and afraid on the bridge that led to—elsewhere. . . .

The uncles were playing poker. Aunt Gertrude, the vaudeville actress, had unexpectedly arrived for a few days and was talking with Grandmother Keaton and Aunt Bessie in the living room. Aunt Gertrude was small and pretty, very charming, with a bisque delicacy and a gusto for life that filled Jane with admiration. But she was subdued now.

"This place gives me the creeps," she said, making a dart with her folded fan at Jane's nose. "Hello, funny-face. Why aren't you playing with the other kids?"

"Oh, I'm tired," Jane said, wondering about Emily. It had been nearly an hour since—

"At your age I was never tired," Aunt Gertrude said. "Now look at me. Three a day and that awful straight man I've got—Ma, did I tell you—" The voices pitched lower.

Jane watched Aunt Bessie's skinny fingers move monotonously as she darted her crochet hook through the silk.

"This place is a morgue," Aunt Gertrude said suddenly. "What's wrong with everybody? Who's dead?"

"It's the air," Aunt Bessie said. "Too hot the year round."

"You play Rochester in winter, Bessie my girl, and you'll be glad of a warm climate. It isn't that, anyway. I feel—mm-n—it's like being on stage after the curtain's gone up."

"It's your fancy," her mother said.

"Ghosts," Aunt Gertrude said, and was silent. Grandmother Keaton looked sharply at Jane.

"Come over here, child," she said.

Room was made on the soft, capacious lap that had held so many youngsters.

Jane snuggled against that reassuring warmth and tried to let her mind go blank, transferring all sense of responsibility to Grandmother Keaton. But it wouldn't work. There was something wrong in the house, and the heavy waves of it beat out from a center very near them.

The Wrong Uncle. Hunger and the avidity to be fed. The nearness of bloody meat tantalizing him as he lay hidden in his strange, unguessable nest elsewhere—otherwhere—in that strange place where the children had vanished.

He was down there, slavering for the food; he was up here, empty, avid, a vortex of hunger very near by.

He was double, a double uncle, masked but terrifyingly clear. . . .

Jane closed her eyes and dug her head deeper into Grandmother Keaton's shoulder.

Aunt Gertrude gossiped in an oddly tense voice, as if she sensed wrongness under the surface and was frightened subtly.

"I'm opening at Santa Barbara in a couple of days, Ma," she said. "I—what's wrong with this house, anyhow? I'm as jumpy as a cat today!—and I want you all to come down and catch the first show. It's a musical comedy. I've been promoted."

"I've seen the *Prince of Pilsen* before."

"Not with me in it. It's my treat. I've engaged rooms at the hotel already. The kids have to come too. Want to see your auntie act, Jane?"

Jane nodded against her grandmother's shoulder.

"Auntie," Jane said suddenly. "Did you see all the uncles?"

"Certainly I did."

"All of them? Uncle James and Uncle Bert and Uncle Simon and Uncle Lew?"

"The whole kaboodle. Why?"

"I just wondered."

So Aunt Gertrude hadn't noticed the Wrong Uncle either. She wasn't truly observant, Jane thought.

"I haven't seen the kids, though. If they don't hurry up, they won't get any of the presents I've brought. You'd never guess what I have for you, Janie."

But Jane scarcely heard even that exciting promise. For suddenly the tension in the air gave way. The Wrong Uncle who had been a vortex of hunger a moment before was a vortex of ecstasy now. Somewhere, somehow, at last Ruggedo was being fed. Somewhere, somehow, that other half of the double uncle was devouring his bloody fare....

Janie was not in Grandmother Keaton's lap any more. The room was not around her. The room was a spinning darkness that winked with tiny lights—Christmas tree lights, Charles had called them—and there was a core of terror in the center of the whirl. Here in the vanished room the Wrong Uncle was a funnel leading from that unimaginable nest where the other half of him dwelt, and through the funnel, into the room, poured the full ecstatic tide of his satiety.

Somehow in this instant Jane was very near the other children who must stand beside that spinning focus of darkness. She could almost sense their presence, almost put out her hand to touch theirs.

Now the darkness shivered and the bright, tiny lights drew together, and into her mind came a gush of impossible memories. She was too near *him*. And he was careless as he fed. He was not guarding his thoughts. They poured out, formless as an animal's, filling the dark. Thoughts of red food, and of other times and places where that same red food had been brought him by other hands.

It was incredible. The memories were not of earth, not of this time or place. He had traveled far, Ruggedo. In many guises. He remembered now, in a flow of shapeless visions, he remembered tearing through furred sides that squirmed away from his hunger, remembered the gush of hot sweet redness through the fur.

Not the fur of anything Jane had ever imagined before....

He remembered a great court paved with shining things, and something in bright chains in the center, and rings of watching eyes as he entered and neared the sacrifice.

As he tore his due from its smooth sides, the cruel chains clanked around him as he fed....

Jane tried to close her eyes and not watch. But it was not with eyes that she watched. And she was ashamed and a little sickened because she was sharing in that feast, tasting the warm red sweetness with Ruggedo in memory, feeling the spin of ecstasy through her head as it spun through his.

"Ah—the kids are coming now," Aunt Gertrude was saying from a long way off.

Jane heard her dimly, and then more clearly, and then suddenly Grandmother Keaton's lap was soft beneath her again, and she was back in the familiar room. "A herd of elephants on the stairs, eh?" Aunt Gertrude said.

They were returning. Jane could hear them too now. Really, they were making much less noise than usual. They were subdued until about halfway down the stairs, and then there was a sudden outburst of clattering and chatter that rang false to Jane's ears.

The children came in, Beatrice a little white, Emily pink and puffy around the eyes. Charles was bubbling over with repressed excitement, but Bobby, the smallest, was glum and bored. At sight of Aunt Gertrude, the uproar redoubled, though Beatrice exchanged a quick, significant glance with Jane.

Then presents and noise, and the uncles coming back in; excited discussion of the trip to Santa Barbara—a strained cheeriness that, somehow, kept dying down into heavy silence.

None of the adults ever really looked over their shoulders, but—the feeling was of bad things to come.

Only the children—not even Aunt Gertrude—were aware of the complete *emptiness* of the Wrong Uncle. The projection of a lazy, torpid, semi-mindless entity. Superficially he was as convincingly human as if he had never focused his hunger here under this roof, never let his thoughts whirl through the minds of the children, never remembered his red, dripping feasts of other times and places.

He was very sated now. They could feel the torpor pulsing out in slow, drowsy waves so that all the grown-ups were yawning and wondering why. But even now he was empty. Not real. The "nobody-there" feeling was as acute as ever to all the small, keen, perceptive minds that saw him as he was.

Later, at bedtime, only Charles wanted to talk about the matter. It seemed to Jane that Beatrice had grown up a little since the early afternoon. Bobby was reading *The Jungle Book,* or pretending to, with much pleased admiration of the pictures showing Shere Khan, the tiger. Emily had turned her face to the wall and was pretending to be asleep.

"Aunt Bessie called me," Jane told her, sensing a faint reproach. "I tried as soon as I could get away from her. She wanted to try that collar thing on me."

"Oh." The apology was accepted. But Beatrice still refused to talk. Jane went over to Emily's bed and put her arm around the little girl.

"Mad at me, Emily?"

"No."

"You are, though. I couldn't help it, honey."

"It was all right," Emily said. "I didn't care."

"All bright and shiny," Charles said sleepily. "Like a Christmas tree."

Beatrice whirled on him. "Shut up!" she cried. "Shut up, Charles! Shut up, shut up, *shut up!*"

Aunt Bessie put her head into the room.

"What's the matter, children?" she asked.

"Nothing, Auntie," Beatrice said. "We were just playing."

Fed, temporarily satiated, it lay torpid in its curious nest. The house was silent, the occupants asleep. Even the Wrong Uncle slept, for Ruggedo was a good mimic.

The Wrong Uncle was not a phantasm, not a mere projection of Ruggedo. As an ameoba extends a pseudo-pod toward food, so Ruggedo had extended and created the Wrong Uncle. But there the parallel stopped. For the Wrong Uncle was not an elastic extension that could be withdrawn at will. Rather, he—it—was a permanent limb, as a man's arm is. From the brain through the neural system the message goes, and the arm stretches out, the fingers constrict—and there is food in the hand's grip.

But Ruggedo's extension was less limited. It was not permanently bound by rigid natural laws of matter. An arm may be painted black. And the Wrong Uncle looked and acted human, except to clear immature eyes.

There were rules to be followed, even by Ruggedo. The natural laws of a world could bind it, to a certain extent. There were cycles. The life-span of a mother-caterpillar is run by cycles, and before it can spin its cocoon and metamorphize, it must eat—eat—eat. Not until the time of change has come can it evade its current incarnation. Nor could Ruggedo change, now, until the end of its cycle had come. Then there would be another metamorphosis, as there had already, in the unthinkable eternity of its past, been a million curious mutations.

But, at present, it was bound by the rules of its current cycle. The extension could not be withdrawn. And the Wrong Uncle was a part of it, and it was a part of the Wrong Uncle.

The Scoodler's body and the Scoodler's head.

Through the dark house beat the unceasing, drowsy waves of satiety— slowly, imperceptibly quickening toward that nervous pulse of avidity that always came after the processes of ingestion and digestion had been completed.

Aunt Bessie rolled over and began to snore. In another room, the Wrong Uncle, without waking, turned on his back and also snored.

The talent of protective mimicry was well developed....

It was afternoon again, though by only half an hour, and the pulse in the house had changed subtly in tempo and mood.

"If we're going up to Santa Barbara," Grandmother Keaton had said, "I'm going to take the children down to the dentist today. Their teeth want cleaning, and it's hard enough to get an appointment with Dr. Hover for one youngster, not to mention four. Jane, your mother wrote me you'd been to the dentist a month ago, so you needn't go."

After that the trouble hung unspoken over the children. But no one mentioned it. Only, as Grandmother Keaton herded the kids out on the porch, Beatrice waited till last. Jane was in the doorway, watching. Beatrice reached behind her without looking, fumbled, found Jane's hand, and squeezed it hard. That was all.

But the responsibility had been passed on. No words had been needed. Beatrice had said plainly that it was Jane's job now. It was her responsibility.

She dared not delay too long. She was too vividly aware of the rising tide of depression affecting the adults. Ruggedo was getting hungry again.

She watched her cousins till they vanished beneath the pepper trees, and the distant rumble of the trolley put a period to any hope of their return. After that, Jane walked to the butcher shop and bought two pounds of meat. She drank a soda. Then she came back to the house.

She felt the pulse beating out faster.

She got a tin pan from the kitchen and put the meat on it, and slipped up to the bathroom. It was hard to reach the attic with her burden and without help, but she did it. In the warm stillness beneath the roof she stood waiting, half-hoping to hear Aunt Bessie call again and relieve her of this duty. But no voice came.

The simple mechanics of what she had to do were sufficiently prosaic to keep fear at a little distance. Besides, she was scarcely nine. And it was not dark in the attic.

She walked along the rafter, balancing, till she came to the plank bridge. She felt its resilient vibration underfoot.

> *"One, two, buckle my shoe,*
> *Three, four, knock at the door,*
> *Five, six, pick up sticks,*
> *Seven, eight—"*

She missed the way twice. The third time she succeeded. The mind had to be at just the right pitch of abstraction.... She crossed the bridge, and turned, and—

It was dim, almost dark, in this place. It smelled cold and hollow, of the underground. Without surprise she knew she was deep down, perhaps beneath the house, perhaps very far away from it. That was as acceptable to her as the rest of the strangeness. She felt no surprise.

Curiously, she seemed to know the way. She was going into a tiny enclosure, and yet at the same time she wandered for a while through low-roofed, hollow spaces, endless, very dim, smelling of cold and moisture. An unpleasant place to the mind, and a dangerous place as well to wander through with one's little pan of meat.

It found the meat acceptable.

Looking back later, Jane had no recollection whatever of *it*. She did not know how she had proffered the food, or how it had been received, or where in that place of paradoxical space and smallness *it* lay dreaming of other worlds and eras.

She only knew that the darkness spun around her again, winking with little lights, as it devoured its food. Memories swirled from its mind to hers as if the two minds were of one fabric. She saw more clearly this time. She saw a great winged thing caged in a glittering pen, and she remembered as Ruggedo remembered, and leaped with Ruggedo's leap, feeling the wings buffet about her and feeling her rending hunger rip into the body, and tasting avidly the hot, sweet, salty fluid bubbling out.

It was a mixed memory. Blending with it, other victims shifted beneath Ruggedo's grip, the feathery pinions becoming the beat of great clawed arms and the writhe of reptilian litheness. All his victims became one in memory as he ate.

One flash of another memory opened briefly toward the last. Jane was aware of a great swaying garden of flowers larger than herself, and of cowled figures moving silently among them, and of a victim with showering pale hair lying helpless upon the lip of one gigantic flower, held down with chains like shining blossoms. And it seemed to Jane that she herself went cowled among those silent figures, and that he—it—Ruggedo—in another guise walked beside her toward the sacrifice.

It was the first human sacrifice he had recalled. Jane would have liked to know more about that. She had no moral scruples, of course. Food was food. But the memory flickered smoothly into another picture and she never saw the end. She did not really need to see it. There was only one end to all these memories. Perhaps it was as well for her that Ruggedo did not dwell overlong on that particular moment of all his bloody meals.

> *"Seventeen, eighteen,*
> *Maids in waiting,*
> *Nineteen, twenty—"*

She tilted precariously back across the rafters, holding her empty pan. The attic smelled dusty. It helped to take away the reek of remembered crimson from her mind. . . .

When the children came back, Beatrice said simply, "Did you?" and Jane nodded. The taboo still held. They would not discuss the matter more fully except in case of real need. And the drowsy, torpid beat in the house, the psychic emptiness of the Wrong Uncle, showed plainly that the danger had been averted again—for a time. . . .

"Read me about Mowgli, Granny," Bobby said. Grandmother Keaton settled down, wiped and adjusted her spectacles, and took up Kipling. Presently the other children were drawn into the charmed circle. Grandmother spoke of Shere Khan's downfall—of the cattle driven into the deep gulch to draw the tiger—and of the earth-shaking stampede that smashed the killer into bloody pulp.

"Well," Grandmother Keaton said, closing the book, "that's the end of Shere Khan. He'd dead now."

"No he isn't," Bobby roused and said sleepily.

"Of course he is. Good and dead. The cattle killed him."

"Only at the end, Granny. If you start reading at the beginning again, Shere Khan's right there."

Bobby, of course, was too young to have any conception of death. You were killed sometimes in games of cowboys-and-Indians, an ending neither regrettable nor fatal. Death is an absolute term that needs personal experience to be made understandable.

Uncle Lew smoked his pipe and wrinkled the brown skin around his eyes at Uncle Bert, who bit his lips and hesitated a long time between moves. But Uncle Lew won the chess game anyway. Uncle James winked at Aunt Gertrude and said he thought he'd take a walk, would she like to come along? She would.

After their departure, Aunt Bessie looked up, sniffed.

"You just take a whiff of their breaths when they come back, Ma," she said. "Why do you stand for it?"

But Grandmother Keaton chuckled and stroked Bobby's hair. He had fallen asleep on her lap, his hands curled into small fists, his cheeks faintly flushed.

Uncle Simon's gaunt figure stood by the window.

He watched through the curtains, and said nothing at all.

"Early to bed," Aunt Bessie said. "If we're going to Santa Barbara in the morning. Children!"

And that was that.

By morning Bobby was running a temperature, and Grandmother Keaton refused to risk his life in Santa Barbara. This made Bobby very sullen, but solved the problem the children had been wondering about for many hours. Also, a telephone call from Jane's father said that he was arriving that day to pick up his daughter, and she had a little brother now. Jane, who had no illusions about the stork, was relieved, and hoped her mother wouldn't be sick any more now

A conclave was held in Bobby's bedroom before breakfast.

"You know what to do, Bobby," Beatrice said. "Promise you'll do it?"

"Promise. Uh-huh."

"You can do it today, Janie, before your father comes. And you'd better get a lot of meat and leave it for Bobby."

"I can't buy any meat without money," Bobby said. Somewhat reluctantly Beatrice counted out what was left of Jane's small hoard, and handed it over. Bobby stuffed the change under his pillow and pulled at the red flannel wound around his neck.

"It scratches," he said. "I'm not sick, anyway."

"It was those green pears you ate yesterday," Emily said very meanly. "You thought nobody saw you, didn't you?"

Charles came in; he had been downstairs. He was breathless.

"Hey, know what happened?" he said. "*He* hurt his foot. Now he can't go to Santa Barbara. I bet he did it on purpose."

"Gosh," Jane said. "How?"

"He said he twisted it on the stairs. But I bet it's a lie. He just doesn't want to go."

"Maybe he *can't* go—that far," Beatrice said, with a sudden flash of intuition, and they spoke no more of the subject. But Beatrice, Emily and Charles were all relieved that the Wrong Uncle was not to go to Santa Barbara with them, after all.

It took two taxis to carry the travelers and their luggage. Grandmother Keaton, the Wrong Uncle, and Jane stood on the front porch and waved. The automobiles clattered off, and Jane promptly got some money from Bobby and went to the butcher store, returning heavy-laden.

The Wrong Uncle, leaning on a cane, hobbled into the sun-parlor and lay down. Grandmother Keaton made a repulsive but healthful drink for Bobby, and Jane decided not to do what she had to do until afternoon. Bobby read *The Jungle Book*, stumbling over the hard words, and, for the while, the truce held.

Jane was not to forget that day quickly. The smells were sharply distinct; the odor of baking bread from the kitchen, the sticky-sweet flower scents from outside, the slightly dusty, rich-brown aroma exhaled by the sun-warmed rugs and furniture. Grandmother Keaton went up to her bedroom to cold-cream her hands and face, and Jane lounged on the threshold, watching.

It was a charming room, in its comfortable, unimaginative way. The curtains were so stiffly starched that they billowed out in crisp whiteness, and the bureau was cluttered with fascinating objects—a pincushion shaped like a doll, a tiny red china shoe, with tinier gray china mice on it, a cameo brooch bearing a portrait of Grandmother Keaton as a girl.

And slowly, insistently, the pulse increased, felt even here, in this bedroom, where Jane felt it was a rather impossible intrusion.

Directly after lunch the bell rang, and it was Jane's father, come to take her back to San Francisco. He was in a hurry to catch the train, and there was time only for a hurried conversation before the two were whisked off in the waiting taxi. But Jane had found time to run upstairs and say goodbye to Bobby—and tell him where the meat was hidden.

"All right, Janie," Bobby said. "Goodbye."

She knew she should not have left the job to Bobby. A nagging sense of responsibility haunted her all the way to the railroad station. She was only vaguely aware of adult voices saying the train would be very late, and of her father suggesting that the circus was in town. . . .

It was a good circus. She almost forgot Bobby and the crisis that would be mounting so dangerously unless he met it as he had promised. Early evening was blue as they moved with the crowd out of the tent. And then through a rift Jane saw a small, familiar figure, and the bottom dropped out of her stomach. She *knew*.

Mr. Larkin saw Bobby in almost the same instant. He called sharply, and a moment later the two children were looking at one another, Bobby's plump face sullen.

"Does your grandmother know you're here, Bobby?" Mr. Larkin said.

"Well, I guess not," Bobby said.

"You ought to be paddled, young man. Come along, both of you. I'll have to phone her right away. She'll be worried to death."

In the drugstore, while he telephoned, Jane looked at her cousin. She was suffering the first pangs of maturity's burden, the knowledge of responsibility misused.

"Bobby," she said. "Did you?"

"You leave me alone," Bobby said with a scowl. There was silence.

Mr. Larkin came back. "Nobody answered. I've called a taxi. There'll be just time to get Bobby back before our train leaves."

In the taxi also there was mostly silence. As for what might be happening at the house, Jane did not think of that at all. The mind has its own automatic protections. And in any case, it was too late now....

When the taxi drew up the house was blazing with orange squares of windows in the dusk. There were men on the porch, and light glinted on a police officer's shield.

"You kids wait here," Mr. Larkin said uneasily. "Don't get out of the car."

The taxi driver shrugged and pulled out a folded newspaper as Mr. Larkin hurried toward the porch. In the back seat Jane spoke to Bobby, her voice very soft.

"You didn't," she whispered. It was not even an accusation.

"I don't care," Bobby whispered back. "I was tired of that game. I wanted to play something else." He giggled. "I won, anyhow," he declared.

"How? What happened?"

"The police came, like I knew they would. *He* never thought of that. So I won."

"But how?"

"Well, it was sort of like *The Jungle Book*. Shooting tigers, remember? They tied a kid to a stake and, when the tiger comes—bang! Only the kids were all gone to Santa Barbara, and you'd gone too. So I used Granny. I didn't think she'd mind. She plays games with us a lot. And anyhow, she was the only one left."

"But Bobby, a kid doesn't mean a kid like us. It means a baby goat. And anyhow—"

"Oh!" Bobby whispered. "Oh—well, anyhow, I thought Granny would be all right. She's too fat to run fast." He grinned scornfully. *"He's* dumb," he said. "He should have know the hunters always come when you tie a kid out for the tiger. He doesn't know anything. When I told him I'd locked Granny in her room and nobody else was around, I thought he might guess." Bobby looked crafty. "I was smart. I told him through the window. I thought he might think about me being a kid. But he didn't. He went right upstairs—fast. He even forgot to limp. I guess he was pretty hungry by then." Bobby glanced toward the swarming porch. "Prob'ly the police have got him now," he added carelessly. "It was easy as pie. I won."

Jane's mind had not followed these fancies.

"Is she dead?" she asked, very softly.

Bobby looked at her. The word had a different meaning for him. It had *no* meaning, beyond a phase in a game. And, to his knowledge, the tiger had never harmed the tethered kid.

Mr. Larkin was coming back to the taxi now, walking very slowly and not very straight.

Jane could not see his face. . . .

It was hushed up, of course, as much as possible. The children, who knew so much more than those who were shielding them, were futilely protected from the knowledge of what had happened. As futilely as they, in their turn, had tried to protect their elders. Except for the two oldest girls, they didn't particularly care. The game was over. Granny had had to go away on a long, long journey, and she would never be back.

They understood what *that* meant well enough.

The Wrong Uncle, on the other hand, had had to go away too, they were told, to a big hospital where he would be taken care of all his life.

This puzzled them all a little, for it fell somewhat outside the limits of their experience. Death they understood very imperfectly, but this other thing was completely mystifying. They didn't greatly care, once their interest faded, though Bobby for some time listened to readings of *The Jungle Book* with unusual attention, wondering if this time they would take the tiger away instead of killing him on the spot. They never did, of course. Evidently in real life tigers were different. . . .

For a long time afterward, in nightmares, Jane's perverse imagination dwelt upon and relived the things she would not let it remember when she was awake. She would see Granny's bedroom as she had seen it last, the starched curtains billowing, the sunshine, the red china shoe, the doll-pincushion. Granny, rubbing cold-cream into her wrinkled hands and looking up more and more nervously from time to time as the long, avid waves of hunger pulsed through the house from the thing in its dreadful hollow place down below.

It must have been very hungry. The Wrong Uncle, pretending to a wrenched ankle downstairs, must have shifted and turned upon the couch, that hollow man, empty and blind of everything but the need for sustenance, the one red food he could not live without. The empty automaton in the sunporch and the ravenous being in its warp below pulsing with one hunger, ravening for one food....

It had been very wise of Bobby to speak through the window when he delivered his baited message.

Upstairs in the locked room, Granny must have discovered presently that she could not get out. Her fat, mottled fingers, slippery from cold-creaming, must have tugged vainly at the knob.

Jane dreamed of the sound of those footsteps many times. The tread she had never heard was louder and more real to her than any which had ever sounded in her ears. She knew very surely how they must have come bounding up the stairs, thump, thump, thump, two steps at a time, so that Granny would look up in alarm, knowing it could not be the Uncle with his wrenched ankle. She would have jumped up then, her heart knocking, thinking wildly of burglars.

It can't have lasted long. The steps would have taken scarcely the length of a heart-beat to come down the hall. And by now the house would be shaking and pulsing with one triumphant roar of hunger almost appeased. The thumping steps would beat in rhythm to it, the long quick strides coming with dreadful purposefulness down the hall. And then the key clicking in the lock. And then—

Usually then Jane awoke....

A little boy isn't responsible. Jane told herself that many times, then and later. She didn't see Bobby again very often, and when she did he had forgotten a great deal; new experiences had crowded out the old. He got a puppy for Christmas, and he started to school. When he heard that the Wrong Uncle had died in the asylum he had had to think hard to remember who they meant, for to the younger children the Wrong Uncle had never been a member of the family, only a part in a game they had played and won.

Gradually the nameless distress which had once pervaded the household faded and ceased. It was strongest, most desperate, in the days just after Granny's death, but everyone attributed that to shock. When it died away they were sure.

By sheer accident Bobby's cold, limited logic had been correct. Ruggedo would not have been playing fair if he had brought still another Wrong Uncle into the game, and Bobby had trusted him to observe the rules. He did observe them, for they were a law he could not break.

Ruggedo and the Wrong Uncle were parts of a whole, indissolubly bound into their cycle. Not until the cycle had been successfully completed could the Wrong Uncle extension be retracted or the cord broken. So, in the end, Ruggedo was helpless.

In the asylum, the Wrong Uncle slowly starved. He would not touch what they offered. He knew what he wanted, but they would not give him that. The head and the body died together, and the house that had been Grandmother Keaton's was peaceful once more.

If Bobby ever remembered, no one knew it. He had acted with perfect logic, limited only by his experience. If you do something sufficiently bad, the policeman will come and get you. And he was tired of the game. Only his competitive instinct kept him from simply quitting it and playing something else.

As it was, he wanted to win—and he had won.

No adult would have done what Bobby did—but a child is of a different species. By adult standards, a child is not wholly sane. Because of the way his mind worked, then—because of what he did, and what he wanted—

Call him demon.

Daemon

C. L. Moore

Padre, the words come slowly. It is a long time now since I have spoken in the Portuguese tongue. For more than a year, my companions here were those who do not speak with the tongues of men. And you must remember, *padre,* that in Rio, where I was born, I was named Luiz *o Bobo,* which is to say, Luiz the Simple. There was something wrong with my head, so that my hands were always clumsy and my feet stumbled over each other. I could not remember very much. But I could see things. Yes, *padre,* I could see things such as other men do not know.

I can see things now. Do you know who stands beside you, *padre,* listening while I talk? Never mind that. I am Luiz *o Bobo* still, though here on this island there were great powers of healing, and I can remember now the things that happened to me years ago. More easily than I remember what happened last week or the week before that. The year has been like a single day, for time on this island is not like time outside. When a man lives with *them,* there is no time.

The *ninfas,* I mean. And the others. . . .

I am not lying. Why should I? I am going to die, quite soon now. You were right to tell me that, *padre*. But I knew. I knew already. Your crucifix is very pretty, *padre*. I like the way it shines in the sun. But that is not for me. You see, I have always known the things that walk beside men—other men. Not me. Perhaps they are souls, and I have no soul, being simple. Or perhaps they are daemons such as only clever men have. Or perhaps they are both these things. I do not know. But I know that I am dying. After the *ninfas* go away, I would not care to live.

Since you ask how I came to this place, I will tell you if the time remains to me. You will not believe. This is the one place on earth, I think, where they lingered still—those things you do not believe.

But before I speak of them, I must go back to an earlier day, when I was young beside the blue bay of Rio, under Sugar Loaf. I remember the docks of Rio, and the children who mocked me. I was big and strong, but I was *o Bobo* with a mind that knew no yesterday or tomorrow.

Minha avó, my grandmother, was kind to me. She was from Ceará, where the yearly droughts kill hope, and she was half blind, with pain in her back always. She worked so that we could eat, and she did not scold me too much. I know that she was good. It was something I could see; I have always had that power.

One morning my grandmother did not waken. She was cold when I touched her hand. That did not frighten me for the—good thing—about her lingered for a while. I closed her eyes and kissed her, and then I went away. I was hungry, and because I was *o Bobo,* I thought that someone might give me food, out of kindness....

In the end, I foraged from the rubbish-heaps.

I did not starve. But I was lost and alone. Have you ever felt that, *padre?* It is like a bitter wind from the mountains and no sheepskin cloak can shut it out. One night I wandered into a sailors' saloon, and I remember that there were many dark shapes with eyes that shone, hovering beside the men who drank there. The men had red, windburned faces and tarry hands. They made me drink *'guardiente* until the room whirled around and went dark.

I woke in a dirty bunk. I heard planks groaning and the floor rocked under me.

Yes, *padre,* I had been shanghaied. I stumbled on deck, half blind in the dazzling sunlight, and there I found a man who had a strange and shining daemon. He was the captain of the ship, though I did not know it then. I scarcely saw the man at all. I was looking at the daemon.

Now, most men have shapes that walk behind them, *padre*. Perhaps you know that, too. Some of them are dark, like the shapes I saw in the saloon. Some of them are bright, like that which followed my grandmother. Some of them are colored, pale colors like ashes or rainbows. But this man had a scarlet daemon. And it was a scarlet beside which blood itself is ashen. The color blinded me. And yet it drew me, too. I could not take my eyes away, nor could I look at it long without pain. I never saw a color more beautiful, nor more frightening. It made my heart shrink within me, and quiver like a dog that fears the whip. If I have a soul, perhaps it was my soul that quivered. And I feared the beauty of the color as much as I feared the terror it awoke in me. It is not good to see beauty in that which is evil.

Other men upon the deck had daemons too. Dark shapes and pale shapes that followed them like their shadows. But I saw all the daemons waver away from the red, beautiful thing that hung above the captain of the ship.

The other daemons watched out of burning eyes. The red daemon had no eyes. Its beautiful, blind face was turned always toward the captain, as if it saw only through his vision. I could see the lines of its closed lids. And my terror of its beauty, and my terror of its evil, were nothing to my terror of the moment when the red daemon might lift those lids and look out upon the world.

The captain's name was Jonah Stryker. He was a cruel man, dangerous to be near. The men hated him. They were at his mercy while we were at sea, and the captain was at the mercy of his daemon. That was why I could not hate him as the others did. Perhaps it was pity I felt for Jonah Stryker. And you, who know men better than I, will understand that the pity I had for him made the captain hate me more bitterly than even his crew hated him.

When I came on deck that first morning, because I was blinded by the sun and by the redness of the scarlet daemon, and because I was ignorant and bewildered, I broke a shipboard rule. What it was, I do not know. There were so many, and I never could remember very clearly in those days. Perhaps I walked between him and the wind. Would that be wrong on a clipper ship, *padre?* I never understood.

The captain shouted at me, in the Yankee tongue, evil words whose meaning I did not know, but the daemon glowed redder when he spoke them. And he struck me with his fist, so that I fell. There was a look of secret bliss on the blind crimson face hovering above his, because of the anger that rose in him. I thought that through the captain's eyes the closed eyes of the daemon were watching me.

I wept. In that moment, for the first time, I knew how truly alone a man like me must be. For I had no daemon. It was not the simple loneliness for my grandmother or for human companionship that brought the tears to my eyes. That I could endure. But I saw the look of joy upon the blind daemon-face because of the captain's evil, and I remembered the look of joy that a bright shape sometimes wears who follows a good man. And I knew that no deed of mine would ever bring joy or sorrow to that which moves behind a man with a soul.

I lay upon the bright, hot deck and wept, not because of the blow, but because I knew suddenly, for the first time, that I was alone. No daemon for good or evil would ever follow me. Perhaps because I have no soul. *That* loneliness, father, is something not even you could understand.

The captain seized my arm and pulled me roughly to my feet. I did not understand, then, the words he spoke in his Yankee tongue, though later I picked up enough of that speech to know what men were saying around me. You may think it strange that *o Bobo* could learn a foreign tongue. It was easy for me. Easier, perhaps, than for a wiser man. Much I read upon the faces of their daemons, and there were many words whose real sounds I did not know, but whose meaning I found in the hum of thoughts about a man's head.

The captain shouted for a man named Barton, and the first mate hurried up, looking frightened. The captain pushed me back against the rail so that I staggered, seeing him and the deck and the watching daemons through the rainbows that tears cast before one's eyes.

There was loud talk, and many gestures toward me and the other two men who had been shanghaied from the port of Rio. The first mate tapped his head when he pointed to me, and the captain cursed again in the tongue of the foreigners, so that his daemon smiled very sweetly at his shoulder.

I think that was the first time I let the captain see pity on my face when I looked at him.

That was the one thing he could not bear. He snatched a belaying pin from the rail and struck me in the face with it, so that I felt the teeth break in my mouth. The blood I spat upon the deck was a beautiful color, but it looked paler than water beside the color of the captain's daemon. I remember all the daemons but the red one leaned a little forward when they saw blood running, snuffing up the smell and the brightness of it like incense. The red one did not even turn his blind face.

The captain struck me again because I had soiled his deck. My first task aboard the *Dancing Martha* was to scrub up my own blood from the planking.

Afterward they dragged me to the galley and threw me into the narrow alley at the cook's feet. I burned my hands on the stove. The captain laughed to see me jump back from it. It is a terrible thing that, though I heard his laughter many times a day, I never heard mirth in it. But there was mirth on his daemon's face.

Pain was with me for many days thereafter, because of the beating and the burns, but I was glad in a way. Pain kept my mind from the loneliness I had just discovered in myself. Those were bad days, *padre*. The worst days of my life. Afterward, when I was no longer lonely, I looked back upon them as a soul in paradise might look back on purgatory.

No, I am still alone. Nothing follows me as things follow other men. But here on the island and I found the *ninfas,* and I was content.

I found them because of the Shaughnessy. I can understand him today in a way I could not do just then. He was a wise man and I am *o Bobo,* but I think I know some of his thoughts now, because today I, too, know I am going to die.

The Shaughnessy lived many days with death. I do not know how long. It was weeks and months in coming to him, though it lived in his lungs and his heart as a child lives within its mother, biding its time to be born. The Shaughnessy was a passenger. He had much money, so that he could do what he willed with his last days of living. Also he came of a great family in a foreign land called Ireland. The captain hated him for many reasons. He scorned him because of his weakness, and he feared him because he was ill. Perhaps he envied him too, because his people had once been kings and because the Shaughnessy was not afraid to die. The captain, I know, feared death. He feared it most terribly. He was right to fear it. He could not know that a daemon rode upon his shoulder, smiling its sweet, secret smile, but some instinct must have warned him that it was there, biding its time like the death in the Shaughnessy's lungs.

I saw the captain die. I know he was right to fear the hour of his daemon....

Those were bad days on the ship. They were worse because of the great beauty all around us. I had never been at sea before, and the motion of the ship was a wonder to me, the clouds of straining sail above us and the sea all about, streaked with the colors of the currents and dazzling where the sun-track lay. White gulls followed us with their yellow feet tucked up as they soared over the deck, and porpoises followed too, playing in great arcs about the ship and dripping diamonds in the sun.

I worked hard, for no more wages than freedom from blows when I did well, and the scraps that were left from the table after the cook had eaten his fill. The cook was not a bad man like the captain, but he was not a good man, either. He did not care. His daemon was smoky, asleep, indifferent to the cook and the world.

It was the Shaughnessy who made my life worth the trouble of living. If it had not been for him, I might have surrendered life and gone into the breathing sea some night when no one was looking. It would not have been a sin for me, as it would be for a man with a soul.

But because of the Shaughnessy I did not. He had a strange sort of daemon himself, mother-of-pearl in the light, with gleams of darker colors when the shadows of night came on. He may have been a bad man in his day. I do not know. The presence of death in him opened his eyes, perhaps. I know only that to me he was very kind. His daemon grew brighter as the man himself grew weak with the oncoming of death.

He told me many tales. I have never seen the foreign country of Ireland, but I walked there often in my dreams because of the tales he told. The foreign isles called Greece grew clear to me too, because the Shaughnessy had dwelt there and loved them.

And he told me of things which he said were not really true, but I thought he said that with only half his mind, because I saw them so clearly while he talked. Great Odysseus was a man of flesh and blood to me, with a shining daemon on his shoulder, and the voyage that took so many enchanted years was a voyage I almost remembered, as if I myself had toiled among the crew.

He told me of burning Sappho, and I knew why the poet used that word for her, and I think the Shaughnessy knew too, though we did not speak of it. I knew how dazzling the thing must have been that followed her through the white streets of Lesbos and leaned upon her shoulder while she sang.

He told me of the nereids and the oceanids, and once I think I saw, far away in the sun-track that blinded my eyes, a mighty head rise dripping from the water, and heard the music of a wreathed horn as Triton called to his fish-tailed girls.

The *Dancing Martha* stopped at Jamaica for a cargo of sugar and rum. Then we struck out across the blue water toward a country called England. But our luck was bad. Nothing was right about the ship on that voyage. Our water-casks had not been cleaned as they should be, and the drinking water became foul. A man can pick the maggots out of his salt pork if he must, but bad water is a thing he cannot mend.

So the captain ordered our course changed for a little island he knew in these waters. It was too tiny to be inhabited, a rock rising out of the great blue deeps with a fresh spring bubbling high up in a cup of the forested crags.

I saw it rising in the dawn like a green cloud on the horizon. Then it was a jewel of green as we drew nearer, floating on the blue water. And my heart was a bubble in my chest, shining with rainbow colors, lighter than the air around me. Part of my mind thought that the island was an isle in Rio Bay, and somehow I felt that I had come home again and would find my grandmother waiting on the shore. I forgot so much in those days. I forgot that she was dead. I thought we would circle the island and come in across the dancing Bay to the foot of the Rua d'Oporto, with the lovely city rising on its hills above the water.

I felt so sure of all this that I ran to tell the Shaughnessy of my delight in homecoming. And because I was hurrying, and blind to all on deck with the vision of Rio in my eyes, I blundered into the captain himself. He staggered and caught my arm to save his footing, and we were so close together that for a moment the crimson daemon swayed above my own head, its eyeless face turned down to mine.

I looked up at that beautiful, smiling face, so near that I could touch it and yet, I knew, farther away than the farthest star. I looked at it and screamed in terror. I had never been so near a daemon before, and I could feel its breath on my face, sweet-smelling, burning my skin with its scorching cold.

The captain was white with his anger and his—his envy? Perhaps it was envy he felt even of me, *o Bobo,* for a man with a daemon like that one hanging on his shoulder may well envy the man without a soul. He hated me bitterly, because he knew I pitied him, and to receive the pity of *o Bobo* must be a very humbling thing. Also he knew that I could not look at him for more than a moment or two, because of the blinding color of his daemon. I think he did not know why I blinked and looked away, shuddering inside, whenever he crossed my path. But he knew it was not the angry fear which other men felt for him which made me avert my eyes. I think he sensed that because he was damned I could not gaze upon him long, and that too made him hate and fear and envy the lowliest man in his crew.

All the color went out of his face as he looked at me, and the daemon above him flushed a deeper and lovelier scarlet, and the captain reached for a belaying pin with a hand that trembled. That which looked out of his eyes was not a man at all, but a daemon, and a daemon that quivered with joy as I was quivering with terror.

I heard the bone crack when the club came down upon my skull. I saw lightning dazzle across my eyes and my head was filled with brightness. I remember almost nothing more of that bad time. A little night closed around me and I saw through it only when the lightning of the captain's blows illumined the dark. I heard his daemon laughing.

When the day came back to me, I was lying on the deck with the Shaughnessy kneeling beside me bathing my face with something that stung. His daemon watched me over his shoulder, bright mother-of-pearl colors, its face compassionate. I did not look at it. The loneliness in me was sharper than the pain of my body, because no daemon of my own hung shining over my hurts, and no daemon ever would.

The Shaughnessy spoke in the soft, hushing Portuguese of Lisboa, that always sounded so strange to me.

"Lie still, Luiz," he was saying. "Don't cry. I'll see that he never touches you again."

I did not know until then that I was weeping. It was not for pain. It was for the look on his daemon's face, and for loneliness.

The Shaughnessy said, "When he comes back from the island, I'll have it out with him." He said more than that, but I was not listening. I was struggling with a thought, and thoughts came hard through the sleepiness that always clouded my brain.

The Shaughnessy meant kindly, but I knew the captain was master upon the ship. And it still seemed to me that we were anchored in the Bay of Rio and my grandmother awaited me on the shore.

I sat up. Beyond the rail the high green island was bright, sunshine winking from the water all around it, and from the leaves that clothed its slopes. I knew what I was going to do.

When the Shaughnessy went away for more water, I got to my feet. There was much pain in my head, and all my body ached from the captain's blows, and the deck was reeling underfoot with a motion the waves could not give it. When I got to the rail, I fell across it before I could jump, and slid into the sea very quietly.

I remember only flashes after that. Salt water burning me, and great waves lifting and falling all around me, and the breath hot in my lungs when the water did not burn even hotter there. Then there was sand under my knees, and I crawled up a little beach and I think I fell asleep in the shelter of a clump of palms.

Then I dreamed that it was dark, with stars hanging overhead almost near enough to touch, and so bright they burned my eyes. I dreamed I heard men calling me through the trees, and I did not answer. I dreamed I heard voices quarreling, the captain's voice loud and angry, the Shaughnessy's tight and thin. I dreamed of oarlocks creaking and water splashing from dipping blades, and the sound of it receding into the warmth and darkness.

I put up a hand to touch a star cluster that hung above my head, and the cluster was bright and tingling to feel. Then I saw that it was the Shaughnessy's face.

I said, "Oh, *s'nhor,*" in a whisper, because I remembered that the captain had spoken from very close by.

The Shaughnessy smiled at me in the starlight. "Don't whisper, Luiz. We're alone now."

I was happy on the island. The Shaughnessy was kind to me, and the days were long and bright, and the island itself was friendly. One knows that of a place. And I thought, in those days, that I would never see the captain again or his beautiful scarlet daemon smiling its blind, secret smile above his shoulder. He had left us to die upon the island, and one of us did die.

The Shaughnessy said that another man might have perished of the blows the captain gave me. But I think because my brain is such a simple thing it mended easily, and perhaps the blow that made my skull crack let in a little more of wit than I had owned before. Or perhaps happiness did it, plenty of food to eat, and the Shaughnessy's tales of the things that—that you do not believe, *meu padre.*

The Shaughnessy grew weak as I grew strong. He lay all day in the shade of a broad tree by the shore, and as his strength failed him, his daemon grew brighter and more remote, as if it were already halfway through the veil of another world.

When I was well again, the Shaughnessy showed me how to build a thatched lean-to that would withstand the rain.

"There may be hurricanes, Luiz," he said to me. "This *barraca* will be blown down. Will you remember how to build another?"

"Sim," I said. "I shall remember. You will show me."

"No, Luiz. I shall not be here. You must remember."

He told me many things, over and over again, very patiently. How to find the shellfish on the rocks when the tide was out, how to trap fish in the stream, which fruit I might eat and what I must never touch. It was not easy for me. When I tried to remember too much it made my head hurt.

I explored the island, coming back to tell him all I had found. At first I was sure that when I had crossed the high hills and stood upon their peaks I would see the beautiful slopes of Rio shining across the water. My heart sank when I stood for the first time upon the heights and saw only more ocean, empty, heaving between me and the horizon.

But I soon forgot again, and Rio and the past faded from my mind. I found the pool cupped high in a hollow of the crags, where clear sweet water bubbled up in the shadow of the trees and the streamlet dropped away in a series of pools and falls toward the levels far below. I found groves of pale trees with leaves like streaming hair, rustling with the noise of the waterfall. I found no people here, and yet I felt always that there were watchers among the leaves, and it seemed to me that laughter sounded sometimes behind me, smothered when I turned my head.

When I told the Shaughnessy this he smiled at me.

"I've told you too many tales," he said. "But if anyone could see them, I think it would be you, Luiz."

"Sim, s'nhor," I said. Tell me again of the forest-women. Could they be here, do you think, *s'nhor?"*

He let sand trickle through his fingers, watching it as if the fall of sand had some meaning to his mind that I could not fathom.

"Ah, well," he said, "they might be. They like the olive groves of Greece best, and the tall trees on Olympus. But every mountain has its oread. Here,

too, perhaps. The Little People left Ireland years ago and for all I know the
oreads have fled from civilization too, and found such places as this to put
them in mind of home. . . .

"There was one who turned into a fountain once, long ago. I saw that
fountain in Greece. I drank from it. There must have been a sort of magic
in the waters, for I always went back to Greece after that. I'd leave, but I
couldn't stay away long." He smiled at me. "Maybe now, because I can't go
back again, the oreads have come to me here."

I looked hard at him to see if he meant what he said, but he shook his
head and smiled again. "I think they haven't come for me. Maybe for you,
Luiz. Belief is what they want. If you believe, perhaps you'll really see
them. I'd be the last man to deny a thing like that. You'll need something
like them to keep you company, my friend—afterward." And he trickled
sand through his fingers again, watching it fall with a look upon his face I
did not understand.

The night came swiftly on that island. It was a lovely place. The
Shaughnessy said islands have a magic all their own, for they are the place
where earth and ocean meet. We used to lie on the shore watching the fire
that burned upon the edges of the waves lap up the beach and breathe
away again, and the Shaughnessy told me many tales. His voice was
growing weaker, and he did not trouble so much any more to test my
memory for the lessons he had taught. But he spoke of ancient magic, and
more and more in these last days, his mind turned back to the wonders of
the country called Ireland.

He told me of the little green people with their lanterns low down
among the ferns. He told me of the *unicórnio,* swift as the swiftest bird, a
magical stag with one horn upon its forehead as long as the shaft of a spear
and as sharp as whatever is sharpest. And he told me of Pan, goat-footed,
moving through the woodland with laughter running before him and panic
behind, the same panic terror which my language and the Shaughnessy's
get from his name. *Pânico,* we Brazilians call it.

One evening he called to me and held up a wooden cross. "Luiz, look at
this," he said. I saw that upon the arms of the cross he had made deep
carvings with his knife. "This is my name," he told me. "If anyone ever
comes here asking for me, you must show them this cross."

I looked at it closely. I knew what he meant about the name—it is that
sort of enchantment in which markings can speak with a voice too tiny for
the ears to hear. I am *o Bobo* and I never learned to read, so that I do not
understand how this may be done.

"Some day," the Shaughnessy went on, "I think someone will come. My
people at home may not be satisfied with whatever story Captain Stryker
invents for them. Or a drunken sailor may talk. If they do find this island,

Luiz, I want this cross above my grave to tell them who I was. And for another reason," he said thoughtfully. "For another reason too. But that need not worry you, *meu amigo.*"

He told me where to dig the bed for him. He did not tell me to put in the leaves and the flowers. I thought of that myself, three days later, when the time came....

Because he had wished it, I put him in the earth. I did not like doing it. But in a way I feared not to carry out his commands, for the daemon of the Shaughnessy still hovered above him, very bright, very bright—so bright I could not look it in the face. I thought there was music coming from it, but I could not be sure.

I put the flowers over him and then the earth. There was more to go back in the grave than I had taken out, so I made a mound above him, as long as the Shaughnessy was long, and I drove in the stake of the wooden cross, above where his head was, as he had told me. Then for a moment I laid my ear to the markings to see if I could hear what they were saying, for it seemed to me that the sound of his name, whispered to me by the marks his hands had made, would lighten my loneliness a little. But I heard nothing.

When I looked up, I saw his daemon glow like the sun at noon, a light so bright I could not bear it upon my eyes. I put my hands before them. When I took them down again, there was no daemon.

You will not believe me when I tell you this, *padre,* but in that moment the—the feel of the island changed. All the leaves, I think, turned the other way on the trees, once, with a rustle like one vast syllable whispered for that time only, and never again.

I think I know what the syllable was. Perhaps I will tell you, later—if you let me.

And the island breathed. It was like a man who has held his breath for a long while, in fear or pain, and let it run out deeply when the fear or the pain departed.

I did not know, then, what it was. But I thought I would go up the steep rocks to the pool, because I wanted a place that would not remind me of the Shaughnessy. So I climbed the crags among the hanging trees. And it seemed to me that I heard laughter when the wind rustled among them. Once I saw what I thought must be a *ninfa,* brown and green in the forest. But she was too shy. I turned my head, and the brown and green stilled into the bark and foliage of the tree.

When I came to the pool, the unicorn was drinking. He was very beautiful, whiter than foam, whiter than a cloud, and his mane lay upon his great shoulders like spray upon the shoulder of a wave. The tip of his long, spiraled horn just touched the water as he drank, so that the ripples ran outward in circles all around it. He tossed his head when he scented me, and I saw the glittering diamonds of the water sparkling from his velvet muzzle. He had eyes as green as a pool with leaves reflecting in it, and a spot of bright gold in the center of each eye.

Very slowly, with the greatest stateliness, he turned from the water and moved away into the forest. I know I heard a singing where he disappeared.

I was still *o Bobo* then. I drank where he had drunk, thinking there was a strange, sweet taste to the water now, and then I went down to the *barraca* on the beach, for I had forgotten already and thought perhaps the Shaughnessy might be there. . . .

Night came, and I slept. Dawn came, and I woke again. I bathed in the ocean. I gathered shellfish and fruit, and drank of the little stream that fell from the mountain pool. And as I leaned to drink, two white dripping arms rose up to clasp my neck, and a mouth as wet and cold as the water pressed mine. It was the kiss of acceptance.

After that the *ninfas* of the island no longer hid their faces from me.

My hair and beard grew long. My garments tore upon the bushes and became the rags you see now. I did not care. It did not matter. It was not my face they saw. They saw my simpleness. And I was one with the *ninfas* and the others.

The oread of the mountain came out to me often, beside the pool where the unicorn came to drink. She was wise and strange, being immortal. The eyes slanted upward in her head, and her hair was a shower of green leaves blowing always backward in a wind that moved about her when no other breezes blew. She used to sit beside the pool in the hot, still afternoons, the unicorn lying beside her and her brown fingers combing out his silver mane. Her wise slanting eyes, the color of shadows in the forest, and his round green eyes the color of the pool, with the flecks of gold in each, used to watch me as we talked.

The oread told me many things. Many things I could never tell you, *padre*. But it was as the Shaughnessy had guessed. Because I believed, they were glad of my presence there. While the Shaughnessy lived, they could not come out into the plane of being, but they watched from the other side. . . . They had been afraid. But they were afraid no longer.

For many years they have been homeless now, blowing about the world in search of some spot of land where no disbelief dwells, and where one other thing has not taken footing. . . . They told me of the isles of Greece, with love and longing upon their tongues, and it seemed to me that I heard the Shaughnessy speak again in their words.

They told me of the One I had not yet seen, or more than glimpsed. That happened when I chanced to pass near the Shaughnessy's grave in the dimness of the evening, and I saw the cross that bore his name had fallen. I took it up and held it to my ear again, hoping the tiny voices of the markings would whisper. But that is a mystery which has never been given me.

I saw the—the One—loitering by that grave. But when I put up the cross, he went away, slowly, sauntering into the dark woods, and a thin piping floated back to me from the spot where he had vanished.

Perhaps the One did not care for my presence there. The others welcomed me. It was not often any more, they said, that men like me were free to move among them. Since the hour of their banishment, they told me, and wept when they spoke of that hour, there had been too few among mankind who really knew them.

I asked about the banishment, and they said that it had happened long ago, very long ago. A great star had stood still in the sky over a stable in a town whose name I do not know. Once I knew it. I do not remember now. It was a town with a beautiful name.

The skies opened and there was singing in the heavens, and after that the gods of Greece had to flee. They have been fleeing ever since.

They were glad I had come to join them. And I was doubly glad. For the first time since my grandmother died, I knew I was not alone. Even the Shaughnessy had not been as close to me as these *ninfas* were. For the Shaughnessy had a daemon. The *ninfas* are immortal, but they have no souls. That, I think, is why they welcomed me so warmly. We without souls are glad of companionship among others of our kind. There is a loneliness among our kind that can only be assuaged by huddling together. The *ninfas* knew it, who must live forever, and I shared it with them, who may die before this night is over.

Well, it was good to live upon the island. The days and months went by beautifully, full of clear colors and the smell of the sea and the stars at night as bright as lanterns just above us. I even grew less *Bobo,* because the *ninfas* spoke wisdom of a kind I never heard among men. They were good months.

And then, one day, Jonah Stryker came back to the island.

You know, *padre,* why he came. The Shaughnessy in his wisdom had guessed that in Ireland men of the Shaughnessy's family might ask questions of Captain Stryker—questions the captain could not answer. But it had not been guessed that the captain might return to the island, swiftly, before the Shaughnessy's people could discover the truth, with the thought in his evil mind of wiping out all traces of the two he had left to die.

I was sitting on the shore that day, listening to the songs of two *ninfas* of the nereid kind as they lay in the edge of the surf, with the waves breaking over them when the water lapped up the slopes of sand. They were swaying their beautiful rainbow-colored fish-bodies as they sang, and I heard the whisper of the surf in their voices, and the long rhythms of the undersea.

But suddenly there came a break in their song, and I saw upon one face before me, and then the other, a look of terror come. The green blood in their veins sank back with fear, and they looked at me, white with pallor and strangely transparent, as if they had halfway ceased to be. With one motion they turned their heads and stared out to sea.

I stared too. I think the first thing I saw was that flash of burning crimson, far out over the waves. And my heart quivered within me like a dog that fears the whip. I knew that beautiful, terrible color too well.

It was only then that I saw the *Dancing Martha,* lying at anchor beyond a ridge of rock. Between the ship and the shore a small boat rocked upon the waves, light flashing from oar-blades as the one man in the boat bent and rose and bent to his work. Above him, hanging like a crimson cloud, the terrible scarlet glowed.

When I looked back, the *ninfas* had vanished. Whether they slid back into the sea, or whether they melted away into nothingness before me I shall never know now. I did not see them again.

I went back a little way into the forest, and watched from among the trees. No dryads spoke to me, but I could hear their quick breathing and the leaves trembled all about me. I could not look at the scarlet daemon coming nearer and nearer over the blue water, but I could not look away long, either. It was so beautiful and so evil.

The captain was alone in the boat. I was not quite so *Bobo* then and I understood why. He beached the boat and climbed up the slope of sand, the daemon swaying behind him like a crimson shadow. I could see its blind eyes and the beautiful, quiet face shut up with bliss because of the thing the captain had come to do. He was carrying in his hand a long shining pistol, and he walked carefully, looking to left and right. His face was anxious, and his mouth had grown more cruel in the months since I saw him last.

I was sorry for him, but I was very frightened, too. I knew he meant to kill whomever he found alive upon the island, so that no tongue could tell the Shaughnessy's people of his wicked deed.

He found my thatched *barraca* at the edge of the shore, and kicked it to pieces with his heavy boots. Then he went on until he saw the long mound above the Shaughnessy's bed, with the cross standing where his head lay. He bent over the cross, and the markings upon it spoke to him as they would never speak to me. I heard nothing, but he heard and knew. He put out his hand and pulled up the cross from the Shaughnessy's grave.

Then he went to the ruins of my *barraca* and to the embers of the fire I kept smouldering there. He broke the cross upon his knee and fed the pieces into the hot coals. The wood was dry. I saw it catch flame and burn. I saw, too, the faint stirring of wind that sprang up with the flames, and I heard the sighing that ran through the trees around me. Now there was nothing here to tell the searchers who might come afterward that the Shaughnessy lay in the island earth. Nothing—except myself.

He saw my footprints around the ruined *barraca*. He stooped to look. When he rose again and peered around the shore and forest, I could see his eyes shine, and it was the daemon who looked out of them, not the man.

Following my tracks, he began to move slowly toward the forest where I was hiding.

Then I was very frightened. I rose and fled through the trees, and I heard the dryads whimpering about me as I ran. They drew back their boughs to let me pass and swept them back after me to bar the way. I ran and ran, upward among the rocks, until I came to the pool of the unicorn, and the oread of the mountain stood there waiting for me, her arm across the unicorn's neck.

There was a rising wind upon the island. The leaves threshed and talked among themselves, and the oread's leafy hair blew backward from her face with its wise slanting eyes. The unicorn's silver mane tossed in that wind and the water ruffled in the pool.

"There is trouble coming, Luiz," the oread told me.

"The daemon. I know." I nodded to her, and then blinked, because it seemed to me that she and the unicorn, like the sea-*ninfas*, were growing so pale I could see the trees behind them through their bodies. But perhaps that was because the scarlet of the daemon had hurt my eyes.

"There is a man with a soul again upon our island," the oread said. "A man who does not believe. Perhaps we will have to go, Luiz."

"The Shaughnessy had a daemon too," I told her. "Yet you were here before his daemon left him to the earth. Why must you go now?"

"His was a good daemon. Even so, we were not fully here while he lived. You must remember, Luiz, that hour I told you of when a star stood above a stable where a child lay, and all our power went from us. Where the souls of men dwell, we cannot stay. This new man has brought a very evil soul with him. It frightens us. Yet since he had burned the cross, perhaps the Master can fight...."

"The Master?" I asked.

"The One we serve. The One you serve, Luiz. The One I think the Shaughnessy served, though he did not know it. The Lord of the opened eyes and the far places. He could not come until the Sign was taken down. Once you had a glimpse of him, when the Sign fell by accident from the grave, but perhaps you have forgotten that."

"I have not forgotten. I am not so *Bobo* now."

She smiled at me, and I could see the tree behind her through the smile. "Then perhaps you can help the Master when the time comes. We cannot help. We are too weak already, because of the presence of the unbeliever, the man with the daemon. See?" She touched my hand, and I felt not the firm, soft brush of fingers but only a coolness like mist blowing across my skin.

"Perhaps the Master can fight him," the oread said, and her voice was very faint, like a voice from far away, though she spoke from so near to me. "I do not know about that. We must go, Luiz. We may not meet again. Good-by, *caro bobo,* while I can still say good-by. . . ." The last of it was faint as the hushing of the leaves, and the oread and the unicorn together looked like smoke blowing from a campfire across the glade.

The knowledge of my loneliness came over me then more painfully than I had felt it since that hour when I first looked upon the captain's daemon and knew at last what my own sorrow was. But I had no time to grieve, for there was a sudden frightened whispering among the leaves behind me, and then the crackle of feet in boots, and then a flicker of terrible crimson among the trees.

I ran. I did not know where I ran. I heard the dryad crying, so it must have been among trees. But at last I came out upon the shore again and I saw the Shaughnessy's long grave without a cross above it. And I stopped short, and a thrill of terror went through me. For there was a Something that crouched upon the grave.

The fear in me then was a new thing. A monstrous, dim fear that moves like a cloud about the Master. I knew he meant me no harm, but the fear was heavy upon me, making my head spin with panic. *Pânico.* . . .

The Master rose upon the grave, and he stamped his goat-hoofed foot twice and set the pipes to his bearded lips. I heard a thin, strange wailing music that made the blood chill inside me. And at the first sound of it there came again what I had heard once before upon the island.

The leaves upon all the trees turned over once, with a great single whispering of one syllable. The syllable was the Master's name. I fled from it in the *pânico* all men have felt who hear that name pronounced. I fled to the edge of the beach, and I could flee no farther. So I crouched behind a hillock of rock on the wet sand, and watched what came after me from the trees.

It was the captain, with his daemon swaying like smoke above his head. He carried the long pistol ready, and his eyes moved from left to right along the beach, seeking like a wild beast for his quarry.

He saw the Master, standing upon the Shaughnessy's grave.

I saw how he stopped, rigid, like a man of stone. The daemon swayed forward above his head, he stopped so suddenly. I saw how he stared. And such was his disbelief, that for an instant I thought even the outlines of the Master grew hazy. There is great power in the men with souls.

I stood up behind my rock. I cried above the noises of the surf, "Master—Great Pan—I believe!"

He heard me. He tossed his horned head and his bulk was solid again. He set the pipes to his lips.

Captain Stryker whirled when he heard me. The long pistol swung up and there was a flash and a roar, and something went by me with a whine of anger. It did not touch me.

Then the music of the pipes began. A terrible music, thin and high, like the ringing in the ears that has no source. It seized the captain as if with thin, strong fingers, making him turn back to the sound. He stood rigid again, staring, straining. The daemon above him turned uneasily from side to side, like a snake swaying.

Then Captain Stryker ran. I saw the sand fly up from under his boots as he fled southward along the shore. His daemon went after him, a red shadow with its eyes still closed, and after them both went Pan, moving delicately on the goathoofs, the pipes to his lips and his horns shining golden in the sun.

And that midday terror I think was greater than any terror that can stalk a man by dark.

I waited beside my rock. The sea was empty behind me except for the *Dancing Martha* waiting the captain's orders at its anchor. But no *ninfas* came in on the foam to keep me company; no heads rose wreathed with seaweed out of the water. The sea was empty and the island was empty too, except for a man and a daemon and the Piper who followed at their heels.

Myself I do not count. I have no soul.

It was nearly dark when they came back along the beach. I think the Piper had hunted them clear around the island, going slowly on his delicate hoofs, never hurrying, never faltering, and that dreadful thin music always in the captain's ears.

I saw the captain's face when he came back in the twilight. It was an old man's face, haggard, white, with deep lines in it and eyes as wild as Pan's. His clothing was torn to ribbons and his hands bled, but he still held the pistol and the red daemon still hung swaying above him.

I think the captain did not know that he had come back to his starting place. By that time, all places must have looked alike to him. He came wavering toward me blindly. I rose up behind my rock.

When he saw me he lifted the pistol again and gasped some Yankee words. He was a strong man, Captain Stryker. With all he had endured in that long chase, he still had the power to remember he must kill me. I did not think he had reloaded the pistol, and I stood up facing him across the sand.

Behind him Pan's pipes shrilled a warning, but the Master did not draw nearer to come between us. The red daemon swayed at the captain's back, and I knew why Pan did not come to my aid. Those who lost their power when the Child was born can never lay hands upon men who possess a soul. Even a soul as evil as the captain's stood like a rock between him and the touch of Pan. Only the pipes could reach a human's ears, but there was that in the sound of the pipes which did all Pan needed to do.

It could not save me. I heard the captain laugh, without breath, a strange, hoarse sound, and I saw the lightning dazzle from the pistol's mouth. The crash it made was like a blow that struck me here, in the chest. I almost fell. That blow was heavy, but I scarcely noticed it then. There was too much to do.

The captain was laughing, and I thought of the Shaughnessy, and I stumbled forward and took the pistol by its hot muzzle with my hand. I am strong. I tore it from the captain's fist and he stood there gaping at me, not believing anything he saw. He breathed in dreadful, deep gasps, and I found I was gasping too, but I did not know why just then.

The captain's eyes met mine, and I think he saw that even now I had no hate for him — only pity. For the man behind the eyes vanished and the crimson daemon of his rage looked out, because I dared to feel sorrow for him. I looked into the eyes that were not his, but the eyes behind the closed lids of the beautiful, blind face above him. It I hated, not him. And it was it I struck. I lifted the pistol and smashed it into the captain's face.

I was not very clear in my head just then. I struck the daemon with my blow, but it was the captain who reeled backward three steps and then fell. I am very strong. One blow was all I needed.

For a moment there was no sound in all the island. Even the waves kept their peace. The captain shuddered and gave one sigh, like that of a man who comes back to living reluctantly. He got his hands beneath him and rose upon them, peering at me through the hair that had fallen across his forehead. He was snarling like an animal.

I do not know what he intended then. I think he would have fought me until one of us was dead. But above him just then I saw the daemon stir. It was the first time I had ever seen it move except in answer to the captain's motion. All his life it had followed him, blind, silent, a shadow that echoed his gait and gestures. Now for the first time it did not obey him.

Now it rose up to a great, shining height above his head, and its color was suddenly very deep, very bright and deep, a blinding thing that hung above him too hot in color to look at. Over the beautiful blind face a look of triumph came. I saw ecstasy dawn over that face in all its glory and its evil.

I knew that this was the hour of the daemon.

Some knowledge deeper than any wisdom warned me to cover my eyes. For I saw its lids flicker, and I knew it would not be good to watch when that terrible gaze looked out at last upon a world it had never seen except through the captain's eyes.

I fell to my knees and covered my face. And the captain, seeing that, must have known at long last what it was I saw behind him. I think now that in the hour of a man's death, he knows. I think in that last moment he knows, and turns, and for the first time and the last, looks his daemon in the face.

I did not see him do it. I did not see anything. But I heard a great, resonant cry, like the mighty music that beats through paradise, a cry full of triumph and thanksgiving, and joy at the end of a long, long, weary road. There was mirth in it, and beauty, and all the evil the mind can compass.

Then fire glowed through my fingers and through my eyelids and into my brain. I could not shut it out. I did not even need to lift my head to see, for that sight would have blazed through my very bones.

I saw the daemon fall upon its master.

The captain sprang to his feet with a howl like a beast's howl, no mind or soul in it. He threw back his head and his arms went up to beat that swooping, beautiful, crimson thing away.

No flesh could oppose it. This was its hour. What sets that hour I do not know, but the daemon knew, and nothing could stop it now.

I saw the flaming thing descend upon the captain like a falling star. Through his defending arms it swept, and through his flesh and his bones and into the hollows where the soul dwells.

He stood for an instant transfixed, motionless, glowing with that bath of crimson light. Then I saw the crimson begin to shine *through* him, so that the shadows of his bones stood out upon the skin. And then fire shot up, wreathing from his eyes and mouth and nostrils. He was a lantern of flesh for that fire of the burning spirit. But he was a lantern that is consumed by the flame it carries. . . .

When the color became too bright for the eyes to bear it, I tried to turn away. I could not. The pain in my chest was too great. I thought of the Shaughnessy in that moment, who knew, too, what pain in the chest was like. I think that was the first moment when it came to me that, like the Shaughnessy, I too was going to die.

Before my eyes, the captain burned in the fire of his daemon, burned and burned, his living eyes looking out at me through the crimson glory, and the laughter of the daemon very sweet above the sound of the whining flame. I could not watch and I could not turn away.

But at last the whine began to die. Then the laughter roared out in one great peal of triumph, and the beautiful crimson color, so dreadfully more crimson than blood, flared in a great burst of light that turned to blackness against my eyeballs.

When I could see again, the captain's body lay flat upon the sand. I know death when I see it. He was not burned at all. He looked as any dead man looks, flat and silent. It was his soul I had watched burning, not his body.

The daemon had gone back again to its own place. I knew that, for I could feel my aloneness on the island.

The Others had gone too. The presence of that fiery daemon was more, in the end, than their power could endure. Perhaps they shun an evil soul more fearfully than a good one, knowing themselves nothing of good and evil, but fearing what they do not understand.

You know, *padre,* what came after. The men from the *Dancing Martha* took their captain away next morning. They were frightened of the island. They looked for that which had killed him, but they did not look far, and I hid in the empty forest until they went away.

I do not remember their going. There was a burning in my chest, and this blood I breathe out ran from time to time, as it does now. I do not like the sight of it. Blood is a beautiful color, but it reminds me of too much that was beautiful also, and much redder. . . .

Then you came, *padre.* I do not know how long thereafter. I know the Shaughnessy's people brought you with their ship, to find him or his grave. You know now. And I am glad you came. It is good to have a man like you beside me at this time. I wish I had a daemon of my own, to grow very bright and vanish when I die, but that is not for *o Bobo* and I am used to that kind of loneliness.

I would not live, you see, now that the *ninfas* are gone. To be with them was good, and we comforted one another in our loneliness but, *padre,* I will tell you this much. It was a chilly comfort we gave each other, at the best. I am a man, though *bobo,* and I know. They are *ninfas,* and will never guess how warm and wonderful it must be to own a soul. I would not tell them if I could. I was sorry for the *ninfas, padre.* They are, you see, immortal.

As for me, I will forget loneliness in a little while. I will forget everything. I would not want to be a *ninfa* and live forever.

There is one behind you, *padre.* It is very bright. It watches me across your shoulder, and its eyes are wise and sad. No, daemon, this is no time for sadness. Be sorry for the *ninfas,* daemon, and for men like him who burned upon this beach. But not for me. I am well content.

I will go now.

The Black Ferris

Ray Bradbury

The carnival had come to town like an October wind, like a dark bat flying over the cold lake, bones rattling in the night, mourning, sighing, whispering up the tents in the dark rain. It stayed on for a month by the gray, restless lake of October, in the black weather and increasing storms and leaden skies.

During the third week, at twilight on a Thursday, the two small boys walked along the lake shore in the cold wind.

"Aw, I don't believe you," said Peter.

"Come on, and I'll show you," said Hank.

They left wads of spit behind them all along the moist brown sand of the crashing shore. They ran to the lonely carnival grounds. It had been raining. The carnival lay by the sounding lake with nobody buying tickets from the flaky black booths, nobody hoping to get the salted hams from the whining roulette wheels, and none of the thin-fat freaks on the big platforms. The midway was silent, all the gray tents hissing on the wind like gigantic prehistoric wings. At eight o'clock perhaps, ghastly lights would flash on, voices would shout, music would go out over the lake. Now there was only a blind hunchback sitting on a black booth, feeling of the cracked china cup from which he was drinking some perfumed brew.

"There," said Hank, pointing.

The black Ferris wheel rose like an immense light-bulbed constellation against the cloudy sky, silent.

"I still don't believe what you said about it," said Peter.

"You wait, I saw it happen. I don't know how, but it did. You know how carnivals are; all funny. Okay; this one's even *funnier*."

Peter let himself be led to the high green hiding place of a tree.

Suddenly, Hank stiffened. "*Hist!* There's Mr. Cooger, the carnival man, now!" Hidden, they watched.

Mr. Cooger, a man of some thirty-five years, dressed in sharp, bright clothes, a lapel carnation, hair greased with oil, drifted under the tree, a brown derby hat on his head. He had arrived in town three weeks before, shaking his brown derby hat at people on the street from inside his shiny red Ford, tooting the horn.

Now Mr. Cooger nodded at the little blind hunchback, spoke a word. The hunchback blindly, fumbling, locked Mr. Cooger into a black seat and sent him whirling up into the ominous twilight sky. Machinery hummed.

"See!" whispered Hank. "The Ferris wheel's going the wrong way. Backwards instead of forwards!"

"So what?" said Peter.

"Watch!"

The black Ferris wheel whirled twenty-five times around. Then the blind hunchback put out his pale hands and halted the machinery. The Ferris wheel stopped, gently swaying, at a certain black seat.

A ten-year-old boy stepped out. He walked off across the whispering carnival ground, in the shadows.

Peter almost fell from his limb. He searched the Ferris wheel with his eyes. "Where's Mr Cooger!"

Hank poked him. "You wouldn't believe! Now *see!*"

"Where's Mr. Cooger at!"

"Come on, quick, run!" Hank dropped and was sprinting before he hit the ground.

Under giant chestnut trees, next to the ravine, the lights were burning in Mrs. Foley's white mansion. Piano music tinkled. Within the warm windows, people moved. Outside, it began to rain, despondently, irrevocably, forever and ever.

"I'm *so* wet," grieved Peter, crouching in the bushes. "Like someone squirted me with a hose. How much longer do we wait?"

"Sh!" said Hank, cloaked in wet mystery.

They had followed the little boy from the Ferris wheel up through town,

down dark streets to Mrs. Foley's ravine house. Now, inside the warm
dining room of the house the strange little boy sat at dinner, forking and
spooning rich lamb chops and mashed potatoes.

"I know his name," whispered Hank, quickly. "My Mom told me about
him the other day. She said, 'Hank, you hear about the li'l orphan boy
moved in Mrs. Foley's? Well, his name is Joseph Pikes and he just came to
Mrs. Foley's one day about two weeks ago and said how he was an orphan
run away and could he have something to eat, and him and Mrs. Foley been
getting on like hot apple pie ever since.' That's what my Mom said,"
finished Hank, peering through the steamy Foley window. Water dripped
from his nose. He held onto Peter who was twitching with cold. "Pete, I
didn't like his looks from the first, I didn't. He looked—mean."

"I'm scared," said Peter, frankly wailing. "I'm cold and hungry and I
don't know what this's all about."

"Gosh, you're dumb!" Hank shook his head, eyes shut in disgust.
"Don't you see, three weeks ago the carnival came. And about the same
time this little ole orphan shows up at Mrs. Foley's. And Mrs. Foley's son
died a long time ago one night one winter, and she's never been the same,
so here's this little ole orphan boy who butters her all around."

"Oh," said Peter, shaking.

"Come on," said Hank. They marched to the front door and banged the
lion knocker.

After awhile the door opened and Mrs. Foley looked out.

"You're all wet, come in," she said. "My land," she herded them into the
hall. "What do you want?" she said, bending over them, a tall lady with
lace on her full bosom and a pale thin face with white hair over it. "You're
Henry Walterson, aren't you?"

Hank nodded, glancing fearfully at the dining room where the strange
little boy looked up from his eating. "Can we see you alone, ma'am?" And
when the old lady looked palely surprised, Hank crept over and shut the
hall door and whispered at her. "We got to warn you about something, it's
about that boy come to live with you, that orphan?"

The hall grew suddenly cold. Mrs. Foley drew herself high and stiff.
"Well?"

"He's from the carnival, and he ain't a boy, he's a man, and he's
planning on living here with you until he finds where your money is and
then run off with it some night, and people will look for him but because
they'll be looking for a little ten-year-old boy they won't recognize him
when he walks by a thirty-five-year man, named Mr. Cooger!" cried Hank.

"What *are* you talking about?" declared Mrs. Foley.

"The carnival and the Ferris wheel and this strange man, Mr. Cooger,
the Ferris wheel going backward and making him younger, I don't know

how, and him coming here as a boy, and you can't trust him, because when he has your money he'll get on the Ferris wheel and it'll go *forward*, and he'll be thirty-five years old again, and the boy'll be gone forever!"

"Good night, Henry Walterson, don't *ever* come back!" shouted Mrs. Foley.

The door slammed. Peter and Hank found themselves in the rain once more. It soaked into and into them, cold and complete.

"Smart guy," snorted Peter. "Now you fixed it. Suppose he heard us, suppose he comes and *kills* us in our beds tonight, to shut us all up for keeps!"

"He wouldn't do that," said Hank.

"Wouldn't he?" Peter seized Hank's arm. "Look."

In the big bay window of the dining room now the mesh curtain pulled aside. Standing there in the pink light, his hand made into a menacing fist, was the little orphan boy. His face was horrible to see, the teeth bared, the eyes hateful, the lips mouthing out terrible words. That was all. The orphan boy was there only a second, then gone. The curtain fell into place. The rain poured down upon the house. Hank and Peter walked slowly home in the storm.

During supper, Father looked at Hank and said, "If you don't catch pneumonia, I'll be surprised. Soaked, you were, by God! What's this about the carnival?"

Hank fussed at his mashed potatoes, occasionally looking at the rattling windows. "You know Mr. Cooger, the carnival man, Dad?"

"The one with the pink carnation in his lapel?" asked Father.

"Yes!" Hank sat up. "You've seen him around?"

"He stays down the street at Mrs. O'Leary's boarding house, got a room in back. Why?"

"Nothing," said Hank, his face glowing.

After supper Hank put through a call to Peter on the phone. At the other end of the line, Peter sounded miserable with coughing.

"Listen, Pete!" said Hank. "I see it all now. When that li'l ole orphan boy, Joseph Pikes, gets Mrs. Foley's money, he's got a good plan."

"What?"

"He'll stick around town as the carnival man, living in a room at Mrs. O'Leary's. That way nobody'll get suspicious of him. Everybody'll be looking for that nasty little boy and he'll be gone. And he'll be walking around, all disguised as the carnival man. That way, nobody'll suspect the carnival at all. It would look funny if the carnival suddenly pulled up stakes."

"Oh," said Peter, sniffling.

"So we got to act fast," said Hank.

"Nobody'll believe us, I tried to tell my folks but they said hogwash!" moaned Peter.

"We got to act tonight, anyway. Because why? Because he's gonna try to kill us! We're the only ones that know and if we tell the police to keep an eye on him, he's the one who stole Mrs. Foley's money in cahoots with the orphan boy, he won't live peaceful. I bet he just tries something tonight. So, I tell you, meet me at Mrs. Foley's in half an hour."

"Aw," said Peter.

"You wanna die?"

"No." Thoughtfully.

"Well, then. Meet me there and I bet we see that orphan boy sneaking out with the money, tonight, and running back down to the carnival grounds with it, when Mrs. Foley's asleep. I'll see you there. So long, Pete!"

"Young man," said Father, standing behind him as he hung up the phone. "You're not going anywhere. You're going straight up to bed. Here." He marched Hank upstairs. "Now hand me out everything you got on." Hank undressed. "There're no other clothes in your room are there?" asked Father.

"No, sir, they're all in the hall closet," said Hank, disconsolately.

"Good," said Dad and shut and locked the door.

Hank stood there, naked. "Holy Cow," he said.

"Go to bed," said Father.

Peter arrived at Mrs. Foley's house at about nine-thirty, sneezing, lost in a vast raincoat and mariner's cap. He stood like a small water hydrant on the street, mourning softly over his fate. The lights in the Foley house were warmly on upstairs. Peter waited for a half an hour, looking at the rain-drenched slick streets of night.

Finally there was a darting paleness, a rustle in wet bushes.

"Hank?" Peter questioned the bushes.

"Yeah." Hank stepped out.

"Gosh," said Peter, staring. "You're—you're *naked!*"

"I ran all the way," said Hank. "Dad wouldn't let me out."

"You'll get pneumonia," said Peter.

The lights in the house went out.

"Duck," cried Hank, bounding behind some bushes. They waited.

"Pete," said Hank. "You're wearing pants, aren't you?"

"Sure," said Pete.

"Well, you're wearing a raincoat, and nobody'll know, so lend me your pants," asked Hank.

A reluctant transaction was made. Hank pulled the pants on.

The rain let up. The clouds began to break apart.

In about ten minutes a small figure emerged from the house, bearing a large paper sack filled with some enormous loot or other.

"There he is," whispered Hank.

"There he goes!" cried Peter.

The orphan boy ran swiftly.

"Get after him!" cried Hank.

They gave chase through the chestnut trees, but the orphan boy was swift, up the hill, through the night streets of town, down past the rail yards, past the factories, to the midway of the deserted carnival. Hank and Peter were poor seconds, Peter weighted as he was with the heavy raincoat, and Hank frozen with cold. The thumping of Hank's bare feet sounded through the town.

"Hurry, Pete! We can't let him get to that Ferris wheel before we do, if he changes back into a man we'll never prove anything!"

"I'm hurrying!" But Pete was left behind as Hank thudded on alone in the clearing weather.

"Yah!" mocked the orphan boy, darting away, no more than a shadow ahead, now. Now vanishing into the carnival yard.

Hank stopped at the edge of the carnival lot. The Ferris wheel was going up and up into the sky, a big nebula of stars caught on the dark earth and turning forward and forward, instead of backward, and there sat Joseph Pikes in a green painted bucket-seat, laughing up and around and down and up and around and down at little old Hank standing there, and the little blind hunchback had his hand on the roaring, oily black machine that made the Ferris wheel go ahead and ahead. The midway was deserted because of the rain. The merry-go-round was still, but its music played and crashed in the open spaces. And Joseph Pikes rode up into the cloudy sky and came down and each time he went around he was a year older, his laughing changed, grew deep, his face changed, the bones of it, the mean eyes of it, the wild hair of it, sitting there in the green bucket-seat whirling, whirling swiftly, laughing into the bleak heavens where now and again a last split of lightning showed itself.

Hank ran forward at the hunchback by the machine. On the way he picked up a tent spike. "Here, now!" yelled the hunchback. The black Ferris wheel whirled around. "You!" stormed the hunchback, fumbling out. Hank hit him in the kneecap and danced away. "Ouch!" screamed the man, falling forward. He tried to reach the machine brake to stop the Ferris wheel. When he put his hand on the brake, Hank ran in and slammed the tent spike against the fingers, mashing them. He hit them twice. The man held his hand in his other hand, howling. He kicked at Hank. Hank grabbed the foot, pulled, the man slipped in the mud and fell. Hank hit him on the head, shouting.

The Ferris wheel went around and around and around.

"Stop, stop the wheel!" cried Joseph Pikes-Mr. Cooger flung up in a stormy cold sky in the bubbled constellation of whirl and rush and wind.

"I can't move," groaned the hunchback. Hank jumped on his chest and they thrashed, biting, kicking.

"Stop, stop the wheel!" cried Mr. Cooger, a man, a different man and voice this time, coming around in panic, going up into the roaring hissing sky of the Ferris wheel. The wind blew through the high dark wheel spokes. "Stop, stop, oh, please stop the wheel!"

Hank leaped up from the sprawled hunchback. He started in on the brake mechanism, hitting it, jamming it, putting chunks of metal in it, tying it with rope, now and again hitting at the crawling weeping dwarf.

"Stop, stop, stop the wheel!" wailed a voice high in the night where the windy moon was coming out of the vaporous white clouds now. "Stop . . ." The voice faded.

Now the carnival was ablaze with sudden light. Men sprang out of tents, came running. Hank felt himself jerked into the air with oaths and beatings rained on him. From a distance there was a sound of Peter's voice and behind Peter, at full tilt, a police officer with pistol drawn.

"Stop, stop the wheel!" In the wind the voice sighed away.

The voice repeated and repeated.

The dark carnival men tried to apply the brake. Nothing happened. The machine hummed and turned the wheel around and around. The mechanism was jammed.

"Stop!" cried the voice one last time.

Silence.

Without a word the Ferris wheel flew in a circle, a high system of electric stars and metal and seats. There was no sound now but the sound of the motor which died and stopped. The Ferris wheel coasted for a minute, all the carnival people looking up at it, the policeman looking up at it, Hank and Peter looking up at it.

The Ferris wheel stopped. A crowd had gathered at the noise. A few fishermen from the wharfhouse, a few switchmen from the rail yards. The Ferris wheel stood whining and stretching in the wind.

"Look," everybody said.

The policeman turned and the carnival people turned and the fishermen turned and they all looked at the occupant in the black-painted seat at the bottom of the ride. The wind touched and moved the black wooden seat in a gentle rocking rhythm, crooning over the occupant in the dim carnival light.

A skeleton sat there, a paper bag of money in its hands, a brown derby hat on its head.

Displaced Person

Eric Frank Russell

He glided out of the gathering dusk and seated himself at the other end of the bench and gazed absently across the lake. The setting sun had dribbled blood in the sky. Mandarin ducks paddled through crimson streaks on the waters. The park held its usual eventide hush; the only sounds were the rustle of leaves and grasses, the murmuring of secluded lovers and the muted tootings of distant cars.

When the bench quivered its announcement of company I had glanced along it half-expecting to find some derelict hoping to cadge the price of a bed. The contrast between the anticipated and the seen was such that I looked again, long, carefully, out of the corners of my eyes so that he wouldn't notice it.

Despite the grey tones of twilight what I saw was a study in black and white. He had thin, sensitive features as white as his gloves and his shirt-front. His shoes and suit were not quite as black as his finely curved eyebrows and well-groomed hair. His eyes were blackest of all: that solid, supernal blackness that can be no deeper or darker. Yet they were alive with an underlying glow.

He had no hat. A slender walking-stick of ebony rested casually against his legs. A black, silk-lined cloak hung from his shoulders. If he had been doing it for the movies he could not have presented a better picture of a distinguished foreigner.

My mind speculated about him in the way minds do when momentarily they have nothing else to occupy them. A European refugee, it decided. Possibly an eminent surgeon or sculptor. Or perhaps a writer or painter, more likely the latter.

I stole another look at him. In the lowering light the pale profile was hawklike. The glow behind the eyes was strengthening with the dark. The cloak lent him a peculiar majesty. The trees were stretching their arms toward him as if to give aid and comfort through the long, long night.

No hint of suffering marked that face. It had nothing in common with the worn, lined features I had seen elsewhere, countenances wearing forever the memories of the manacles, the whip and the horror camp. On the contrary, it held a mixture of boldness and serenity, of confidence in the belief that one day the tide must turn. Impulsively I decided that he was a musician. I could imagine him conducting a tremendous choir of fifty thousand voices.

"I am fond of music," he said in low, rich tones.

His face turned toward me, revealing a pronounced peak in his glossy black hair.

"Really?" The unexpectedness of his remark caught me at a disadvantage. Without knowing it I must have voiced my thoughts aloud. Rather feebly I asked, "Of what kind?"

"This." He used his ebony stick to indicate the world at large. "The sigh of ending day."

"Yes, it is soothing," I agreed.

"It is my time," he said. "The time when the day ends—as all things must end."

"That's true," I said for lack of anything better.

We were silent awhile. Slowly the horizon soaked the blood from the sky. The city put on its lights and a wan moon floated over its towers.

"You're not a native of this place?" I prompted.

"No," resting long, slender hands upon his stick, he gazed meditatively forward. "I have no country. I am a displaced person."

"I'm sorry."

"Thank you," he said.

I couldn't just sit there and leave him to stew in his own juice. The choice was to continue the conversation or depart. There was no need to go. So I continued.

"Care to tell me about it?"

His head came round and he studied me as if only now fully aware of my presence. That weird light in his orbs could almost be felt. He smiled gradually and tolerantly, showing perfect teeth.

"Should I?"

"You don't have to. But sometimes it helps to get things off one's mind."

"I doubt it. Besides, I would be wasting your time."

"Not at all. I'm wasting it anyway."

Smiling again, he used his stick to draw unseeable circles in front of his black shoes.

"In this day and age it is an all too familiar story," he said. "A leader became so blinded by his own glory that he considered himself incapable of making blunders. He rejected all advice and resented all criticism. He developed delusions of grandeur, posed as the final arbiter on everything from birth to death, and thereby brought into being a movement for his overthrow. He created the seeds of his own destruction. It was inevitable in the circumstances."

"And rightly so," I supported. "To hell with dictators!"

The stick slipped from his grasp. He picked it up, juggled it idly, resumed his circle drawing.

"The revolt didn't succeed?" I suggested.

"No." He looked at the circles and struck a line through them. "It proved too early and too weak. It was crushed with the utmost ruthlessness. Then came the purge." His glowing eyes surveyed the sentinel trees. "I created that opposition. I still think it was justified. But I dare not go back. Not yet."

"A fat lot you should care about that. You're in a good country now and you can fit into it comfortably."

"I don't think so. I'm not especially welcome here." His voice was deeper. "Not wanted—anywhere."

"Oh, nonsense!" I retorted. "Everybody is wanted by someone, somewhere. Cheer up. Don't be morbid. After all, it's worth a lot just to be free."

"No man is free until he's beyond his enemy's reach." He glanced at me with an irritating touch of amusement, almost as if he considered that I had yet to learn the facts of life. "When one's foe has gained control of every channel of information and propaganda, when he uses them to present his own case and utterly suppress mine, when he offers calculated lies as truth and damns the truth as a lie, there is little hope for me."

"Well, that's your way of looking at things. I cannot blame you for feeling bitter about bygone experiences. But you've got to forget them. Here, you're living in a different world. We've free speech. A man can say what he likes, write what he likes."

"If only that were true."

"It is true," I asserted, slightly annoyed. "Here you can call the Rajah of Bam an arrogant and overfed parasite if you wish. Nobody can prevent you from doing so, not even the police. We're free, as I've told you."

He stood up, towering amid embracing trees. From my sitting position his height seemed enormous. The moon lit his face in pale ghastliness.

"Your faith is comforting but baseless."

"No!" I denied.

He turned away. His cape swung behind him and billowed in the night breeze until it resembled mighty wings.

"My name," he murmured softly, "is Lucifer."

After that there was only the whisper of the wind.

Our Fair City

Robert A. Heinlein

Pete Perkins turned into the All-Nite Parking Lot and called out, "Hi, Pappy!"

The old parking lot attendant looked up and answered, "Be with you in a moment, Pete." He was tearing a Sunday comic sheet in narrow strips. A little whirlwind waltzed near him, picking up pieces of old newspaper and bits of dirt and flinging them in the faces of passing pedestrians. The old man held out to it a long streamer of the brightly colored funny-paper. "Here, Kitten," he coaxed. "Come, Kitten . . ."

The whirlwind hesitated, then drew itself up until it was quite tall, jumped two parked cars, and landed right near him.

It seemed to sniff at the offering.

"Take it, Kitten," the old man called softly and let the gay streamer slip from his fingers. The whirlwind whipped it up and wound it around its middle. He tore off another and yet another; the whirlwind wound them in a corkscrew through the loose mass of dirty paper and trash that constituted its visible body. Renewed by cold gusts that poured down the canyon of tall buildings, it swirled faster and ever taller, while it lifted the

177

colored paper ribbons in a fantastic upswept hair-do. The old man turned, smiling. "Kitten does like new clothes."

"Take it easy, Pappy, or you'll have me believing in it."

"Eh? You don't have to believe in Kitten—you can *see* her."

"Yeah, sure—but you act as if she—I mean 'it'—could understand what you say."

"You still don't think so?" His voice was gently tolerant.

"Now, Pappy!"

"Hmm. ... Lend me your hat." Pappy reached up and took it. "Here, Kitten," he called. "Come back, Kitten!" The whirlwind was playing around over their heads, several stories high. It dipped down.

"Hey! Where you going with that chapeau?" demanded Perkins.

"Just a moment ... Here, Kitten!" The whirlwind sat down suddenly, spilling its load. The old man handed it the hat. The whirlwind snatched it and started it up a fast, long spiral.

"Hey!" yelped Perkins. "What do you think you're doing? That's not funny—that hat cost me six bucks only three years ago."

"Don't worry," the old man soothed. "Kitten will bring it back."

"She will, huh? More likely she'll dump it in the river."

"Oh, no! Kitten never drops anything she doesn't want to drop. Watch." The old man looked up to where the hat was dancing near the penthouse of the hotel across the street. "Kitten! Oh, Kitten! Bring it back."

The whirlwind hesitated, the hat fell a couple of stories. It swooped, caught it, and juggled it reluctantly. "Bring it *here*, Kitten."

The hat commenced a downward spiral, finishing in a long curving swoop. It hit Perkins full in the face. "She was trying to put it on your head," the attendant explained. "Usually she's more accurate."

"She is, eh?" Perkins picked up his hat and stood looking at the whirlwind, mouth open.

"Convinced?" asked the old man.

" 'Convinced?' Oh, sho' sho.' " He looked back at his hat, then again at the whirlwind. "Pappy, this calls for a drink."

They went inside the lot's little shelter shack; Pappy found glasses; Perkins produced a pint, nearly full, and poured two generous slugs. He tossed his down, poured another, and sat down. "The first was in honor of Kitten," he announced. "This one is to fortify me for the Mayor's banquet."

Pappy cluck-clucked sympathetically. "You have to cover that?"

"Have to write a column about *something*, Pappy. 'Last night Hizzoner the Mayor, surrounded by a glittering galaxy of high-binders, grifters, sycophants, and ballot thieves, was the recipient of a testimonial dinner celebrating ...' Got to write something, Pappy; the cash customers expect it. Why don't I brace up like a man and go on relief?"

"Today's column was good, Pete," the old man comforted him. He picked up a copy of the *Daily Forum*; Perkins took it from him and ran his eye down his own column.

" 'Our Fair City, by Peter Perkins,' " he read, and below that " 'What, No Horsecars? It is the tradition of our civic paradise that what was good enough for the founding fathers is good enough for us. We stumble over the very chuckhole in which great-uncle Tozier broke his leg in '09. It is good to know that the bath water, running out, is not gone forever, but will return through the kitchen faucet, thicker and disguised with chlorine, but the same. (Memo—Hizzoner uses bottled spring water. Must look into this.)

" 'But I must report a dismaying change. Someone has done away with the horsecars!

" 'You may not believe this. Our public conveyances run so seldom and slowly that you may not have noticed it; nevertheless I swear that I saw one wobbling down Grand Avenue with no horses of any sort. It seemed to be propelled by some newfangled electrical device.

" 'Even in the atomic age some changes are too much. I urge all citizens...' " Perkins gave a snort of disgust. "It's tackling a pillbox with a beanshooter, Pappy. This town is corrupt; it'll stay corrupt. Why should I beat out my brains on such piffle? Hand me the bottle."

"Don't be discouraged, Pete. The tyrant fears the laugh more than the assassin's bullet."

"Where'd you pick that up? Okay, so I'm not funny. I've tried laughing them out of office and it hasn't worked. My efforts are as pointless as the activities of your friend the whirling dervish."

The windows rattled under a gusty impact. "Don't talk that way about Kitten," the old man cautioned. "She's sensitive."

"I apologize." He stood up and bowed toward the door. "Kitten, I apologize. Your activities are *more* useful than mine." He turned to his host. "Let's go out and talk to her, Pappy. I'd rather do that than go to the Mayor's banquet, if I had my druthers."

They went outside, Perkins bearing with him the remains of the colored comic sheet. He began tearing off streamers. "Here, Kitty! Here, Kitty! Soup's on!"

The whirlwind bent down and accepted the strips as fast as he tore them. "She's still got the ones you gave her."

"Certainly," agreed Pappy. "Kitten is a pack rat. When she likes something she'll keep it indefinitely."

"Doesn't she ever get tired? There must be some calm days."

"It's never really calm here. It's the arrangement of the buildings and

the way Third Street leads up from the river. But I think she hides her pet
playthings on tops of buildings."

The newspaperman peered into the swirling trash. "I'll bet she's got
newspapers from months back. Say, Pappy, I see a column in this, one about
our trash collection service and how we don't clean our streets. I'll dig up
some papers a couple of years old and claim that they have been blowing
around town since publication."

"Why fake it?" answered Pappy, "Let's see what Kitten has." He
whistled softly. "Come, baby—let Pappy see your playthings." The
whirlwind bulged out; its contents moved less rapidly. The attendant
plucked a piece of old newspaper from it in passing. "Here's one three
months old."

"We'll have to do better than that."

"I'll try again." He reached out and snatched another. "Last June."

"That's better."

A car honked for service and the old man hurried away. When he
returned Perkins was still watching the hovering column. "Any luck?"
asked Pappy.

"She won't let me have them. Snatches them away."

"Naughty Kitten," the old man said. "Pete is a friend of ours. You be
nice to him." The whirlwind fidgeted uncertainly.

"It's all right," said Perkins. "She didn't know. But look, Pappy—see that
piece up there? A front page."

"You want it?"

"Yes. Look closely—the headline reads 'DEWEY' something. You don't
suppose she's been hoarding it since the '44 campaign?"

"Could be. Kitten has been around here as long as I can remember. And
she does hoard things. Wait a second." He called out softly. Shortly the
paper was in his hands. "Now we'll see."

Perkins peered at it. "I'll be a short-term Senator! Can you top that,
Pappy?"

The headline read: "Dewey Captures Manila"; the date was "1898."

Twenty minutes later they were still considering it over the last of
Perkins' bottle. The newspaperman stared at the yellowed, filthy sheet.
"Don't tell me this has been blowing around town for the last half century."

"Why not?"

" 'Why not?' Well, I'll concede that the streets haven't been cleaned in
that time, but this paper wouldn't last. Sun and rain and so forth."

"Kitten is very careful of her toys. She probably put it under cover
during bad weather."

"For the love of Mike, Pappy, you don't really believe... But you do.
Frankly, I don't care where she got it; the official theory is going to be that

this particular piece of paper has been kicking around our dirty streets, unnoticed and uncollected, for the past fifty years. Boy, am I going to have fun!" He rolled the fragment carefully and started to put it in his pocket.

"Say, don't do that!" his host protested.

"Why not? I'm going to take it down and get a pic of it."

"You mustn't! It belongs to Kitten—I just borrowed it."

"Huh? Are you nuts?"

"She'll be upset if she doesn't get it back. Please, Pete—she'll let you look at it any time you want to."

The old man was so earnest that Perkins was stopped. "Suppose we never see it again? My story hangs on it."

"It's no good to *you—she* has to keep it, to make your story stand up. Don't worry—I'll tell her that she mustn't lose it under any circumstances."

"Well—okay." They stepped outside and Pappy talked earnestly to Kitten, then gave her the 1898 fragment. She promptly tucked it into the top of her column. Perkins said good-bye to Pappy, and started to leave the lot. He paused and turned around, looking a little befuddled. "Say, Pappy..."

"Yes, Pete?"

"You don't really think that whirlwind is alive, do you?"

"Why not?"

"Why not? Why not, the man says?"

"Well," said Pappy reasonably, "How do you know *you* are alive?"

"But...Why, because I—well, now, if you put it..." He stopped. "I don't know. You got me, pal."

Pappy smiled. "You see?"

"Uh, I guess so. G'night, Pappy. G'night, Kitten." He tipped his hat to the whirlwind. The column bowed.

The managing editor sent for Perkins. "Look, Pete," he said, chucking a sheaf of gray copy paper at him, "whimsy is all right, but I'd like to see some copy that wasn't dashed off in a gin mill."

Perkins looked over the pages shoved at him. "Our Fair City, by Peter Perkins. Whistle Up The Wind. Walking our streets always is a piquant, even adventurous, experience. We pick our way through the assorted trash, bits of old garbage, cigarette butts, and other less appetizing items that stud our sidewalks while our faces are assaulted by more bouyant souvenirs, the confetti of last Halloween, shreds of dead leaves, and other items too weather-beaten to be identified. However, I had always assumed that a constant turnover in the riches of our streets caused them to renew themselves at least every seven years..." The column then told of the whirlwind that contained the fifty-year-old newspaper and challenged any other city in the country to match it.

" 'Smatter with it?" demanded Perkins.

"Beating the drum about the filth in the streets is fine, Pete, but give it a factual approach."

Perkins leaned over the desk. "Boss, this *is* factual."

"Huh? Don't be silly, Pete."

"Silly, he says. Look ..." Perkins gave him a circumstantial account of Kitten and the 1898 newspaper.

"Pete, you must have been drinking."

"Only Java and tomato juice. Cross my heart and hope to die."

"How about yesterday? I'll bet the whirlwind came right up to the bar with you."

"I was cold, stone ..." Perkins stopped himself and stood on his dignity. "That's my story. Print it, or fire me."

"Don't be like that, Pete. I don't want your job; I just want a column with some meat. Dig up some facts on man-hours and costs for street cleaning, compared with other cities."

"Who'd read that junk? Come down the street with me. I'll *show* you the facts. Wait a moment—I'll pick up a photographer."

A few minutes later Perkins was introducing the managing editor and Clarence V. Weems to Pappy. Clarence unlimbered his camera. "Take a pic of him?"

"Not yet, Clarence. Pappy, can you get Kitten to give us back the museum piece?"

"Why, sure." The old man looked up and whistled. "Oh, Kitten! Come to Pappy." Above their heads a tiny gust took shape, picked up bits of paper and stray leaves, and settled on the lot. Perkins peered into it.

"She hasn't got it," he said in aggrieved tones.

"She'll get it." Pappy stepped forward until the whirlwind enfolded him. They could see his lips move, but the words did not reach them.

"Now?" said Clarence.

"Not yet." The whirlwind bounded up and leapt over an adjoining building. The managing editor opened his mouth, closed it again.

Kitten was soon back. She dropped everything else and had just one piece of paper—*the* paper. "Now!" said Perkins. "Can you get a shot of that paper, Clarence—while it's in the air?"

"Natch," said Clarence, and raised his Speed Graphic. "Back a little, and hold it," he ordered, speaking to the whirlwind.

Kitten hesitated and seemed about to skitter away. "Bring it around slow and easy, Kitten," Pappy supplemented, "and turn it over—no, no! Not that way—the other edge up." The paper flattened out and sailed slowly past them, the headline showing.

"Did you get it?" Perkins demanded.

"Natch," said Clarence. "Is that all?" he asked the editor.

"Natc—I mean, that's all."

"Okay," said Clarence, picked up his case, and left.

The editor sighed. "Gentlemen," he said, "let's have a drink."

Four drinks later Perkins and his boss were still arguing. Pappy had left. "Be reasonable, Boss," Pete was saying, "you can't print an item about a live whirlwind. They'd laugh you out of town."

Managing Editor Gaines straightened himself.

"It's the policy of the *Forum* to print all the news, and print it straight. This is news—we print it." He relaxed. "Hey! Waiter! More of the same—and not so much soda."

"But it's scientifically impossible."

"You saw it, didn't you?"

"Yes, but ..."

Gaines stopped him. "We'll ask the Smithsonian Institution to investigate it."

"They'll laugh at you," Perkins insisted. "Ever hear of mass hypnotism?"

"Huh? No, that's no explanation—Clarence saw it, too."

"What does that prove?"

"Obvious—to be hypnotized you have to have a mind, *Ipso facto.* "

"You mean *Ipse dixit.* "

"Quit hiccuping. Perkins, you shouldn't drink in the daytime. Now start over and say it slowly."

"How do you know Clarence doesn't have a mind?"

"Prove it."

"Well, he's alive—he must have some sort of a mind, then."

"That's just what I was saying. The whirlwind is alive; therefore it has a mind. Perkins, if those longbeards from the Smithsonian are going to persist in their unscientific attitude, I for one will not stand for it. The *Forum* will not stand for it. You will not stand for it."

"Won't I?"

"Not for one minute. I want you to know the *Forum* is behind you, Pete. You go back to the parking lot and get an interview with that whirlwind."

"But I've got one. You wouldn't let me print it."

"Who wouldn't let you print it? I'll fire him! Come on, Pete. We're going to blow this town sky high. Stop the run. Hold the front page. Get busy!" He put on Pete's hat and strode rapidly into the men's room.

Pete settled himself at his desk with a container of coffee, a can of tomato juice, and the Midnight Final (late afternoon) edition. Under a four-column cut of Kitten's toy was his column, boxed and moved to the

front page. Eighteen-point boldface ordered SEE EDITORIAL PAGE
TWELVE. On page twelve another black line enjoined him to SEE OUR
FAIR CITY PAGE ONE. He ignored this and read: MR. MAYOR—
RESIGN!!!!

Pete read it and chuckled. "An ill wind—" "—symbolic of the spiritual
filth lurking in the dark corners of the city hall." "—will grow to cyclonic
proportions and sweep a corrupt and shameless administration from
office." The editorial pointed out that the contract for street cleaning and
trash removal was held by the Mayor's brother-in-law, and then suggested
that the whirlwind could give better service cheaper.

The telephone jingled. He picked it up and said, "Okay—you started it."

"Pete—is that you?" Pappy's voice demanded. "They got me down at
the station house."

"What for?"

"They claim Kitten is a public nuisance."

"I'll be right over." He stopped by the Art Department, snagged
Clarence, and left. Pappy was seated in the station lieutenant's office,
looking stubborn. Perkins shoved his way in. "What's he here for?" he
demanded, jerking a thumb at Pappy.

The lieutenant looked sour. "What are you butting in for, Perkins?
You're not his lawyer."

"Now?" said Clarence.

"Not yet, Clarence. For news, Dumbrosky—I work for a newspaper,
remember? I repeat—what's he in for?"

"Obstructing an officer in the performance of his duty."

"That right, Pappy?"

The old man looked disgusted. "This character—" He indicated one of
the policemen "—comes up to my lot and tries to snatch the Manila-Bay
paper away from Kitten. I tell her to keep it up out of his way. Then he
waves his stick at me and orders me to take it away from her. I tell him what
he can do with his stick." He shrugged. "So here we are."

"I get it," Perkins told him, and turned to Dumbrosky. "You got a call
from the city hall, didn't you? So you sent Dugan down to do the dirty
work. What I don't get is why you sent Dugan. I hear he's so dumb you
don't even let him collect the pay-off on his own beat."

"That's a lie!" put in Dugan. "I do so . . ."

"Shut up, Dugan!" his boss thundered. "Now, see here, Perkins—you
clear out. There ain't no story here."

"No story?" Perkins said softly. "The police force tries to arrest a
whirlwind and you say there's no story?"

"Now?" said Clarence.

"Nobody tried to arrest no whirlwind! Now scram."

"Then how come you're charging Pappy with obstructing an officer?

What was Dugan doing—flying a kite?"

"He's not charged with obstructing an officer."

"He's not, eh? Just what have you booked him for?"

"He's not booked. We're holding him for questioning."

"So? not booked, no warrant, no crime alleged, just pick up a citizen and roust him around, Gestapo style." Perkins turned to Pappy. "You're not under arrest. My advice is to get up and walk out that door."

Pappy started to get up. "Hey!" Lieutenant Dumbrosky bounded out of his chair, grabbed Pappy by the shoulder and pushed him down. "I'm giving the orders around here. You stay . . ."

"Now!" yelled Perkins. Clarence's flashbulb froze them. Then Dumbrosky started up again.

"Who let him in here? Dugan—get that camera."

"Nyannh!" said Clarence and held it away from the cop. They started doing a little Maypole dance, with Clarence as the Maypole.

"Hold it!" yelled Perkins. "Go ahead and grab the camera, Dugan—I'm just aching to write the story. 'Police Lieutenant Destroys Evidence of Police Brutality.' "

"What do you want I should do, Lieutenant?" pleaded Dugan.

Dumbrosky looked disgusted. "Siddown and close your face. Don't use that picture, Perkins—I'm warning you."

"Of what? Going to make me dance with Dugan? Come on, Pappy. Come on, Clarence." They left.

"Our Fair City" read the next day: "City Hall Starts Clean Up. While the city street cleaners were enjoying their usual siesta, Lieutenant Dumbrosky, acting on orders of Hizzoner's office, raided our Third Avenue whirlwind. It went sour, as Patrolman Dugan could not entice the whirlwind into the paddy wagon. Dauntless Dugan was undeterred; he took a citizen standing nearby, one James Metcalfe, parking-lot attendant, into custody as an accomplice of the whirlwind. An accomplice in what, Dugan didn't say—everybody knows that an accomplice is something pretty awful. Lieutenant Dumbrosky questioned the accomplice. See cut. Lieutenant Dumbrosky weighs 215 pounds, without his shoes. The accomplice weighs 119.

"Moral: Don't get underfoot when the police department is playing games with the wind.

"P. S. As we go to press, the whirlwind is still holding the 1898 museum piece. Stop by Third and Main and take a look. Better hurry—Dumbrosky is expected to make an arrest momentarily."

Pete's column continued needling the administration the following day: "Those Missing Files. It is annoying to know that any document needed by the Grand Jury is sure to be mislaid before it can be introduced in evidence. We suggest that Kitten, our Third Avenue Whirlwind, be hired by the city as file clerk extraordinary and entrusted with any item which is likely to be needed later. She could take the special civil exam used to reward the faithful—the one nobody ever flunks.

"Indeed, why limit Kitten to a lowly clerical job? She is persistent—and she hangs on to what she gets. No one will argue that she is less qualified than some city officials we have had.

"Let's run Kitten for Mayor! She's an ideal candidate—she has the common touch, she doesn't mind hurly-burly, she runs around in circles, she knows how to throw dirt, and the opposition can't pin anything on her.

"As to the sort of Mayor she would make, there is an old story—Aesop told it—about King Log and King Stork. We're fed up with King Stork; King Log would be welcome relief.

"Memo to Hizzoner—what *did* become of those Grand Avenue paving bids?

"P. S. Kitten still has the 1898 newspaper on exhibit. Stop by and see it before our police department figures out some way to intimidate a whirlwind."

Pete snagged Clarence and drifted down to the parking lot. The lot was fenced now; a man at a gate handed them two tickets but waved away their money. Inside he found a large circle chained off for Kitten and Pappy inside it. They pushed their way through the crowd to the old man. "Looks like you're coining money, Pappy."

"Should be, but I'm not. They tried to close me up this morning, Pete. Wanted me to pay the $50-a-day circus-and-carnival fee and post a bond besides. So I quit charging for the tickets—but I'm keeping track of them. I'll sue 'em, by gee."

"You won't collect, not in this town. Never mind, we'll make 'em squirm till they let up."

"That's not all. They tried to capture Kitten this morning."

"Huh? Who? How?"

"The cops. They showed up with one of those blower machines used to ventilate manholes, rigged to run backwards and take a suction. The idea was to suck Kitten down into it, or anyhow to grab what she was carrying."

Pete whistled. "You should have called me."

"Wasn't necessary. I warned Kitten and she stashed the Spanish-War paper someplace, then came back. She loved it. She went through that machine about six times, like a merry-go-round. She'd zip through and come out more full of pep than ever. Last time through she took Sergeant Yancel's cap with her and it clogged the machine and ruined his cap. They got disgusted and left."

Peter chortled. "You still should have called me. Clarence should have gotten a picture of that."

"Got it," said Clarence.

"Huh? I didn't know you were here this morning, Clarence."

"You didn't ast me."

Pete looked at him. "Clarence, darling—the idea of a news picture is to print it, not to hide it in the Art Department."

"On your desk," said Clarence.

"Oh. Well, let's move on to a less confusing subject. Pappy, I'd like to put up a big sign here."

"Why not! What do you want to say?"

"Kitten-for-Mayor—Whirlwind Campaign Headquarters. Stick a 24-sheet across the corner of the lot, where they can see it both ways. It fits in with—oh, oh! Company, girls!" He jerked his head toward the entrance.

Sergeant Yancel was back. "All right, all right!" he was saying. "Move on! Clear out of here." He and three cohorts were urging the spectators out of the lot. Pete went to him.

"What goes on, Yancel?"

Yancel looked around. "Oh, it's you, huh? Well, you, too—we got to clear this place out. Emergency."

Pete looked back over his shoulder. "Better get Kitten out of the way, Pappy!" he called out. "*Now*, Clarence."

"Got it," said Clarence.

"Okay," Pete answered. "Now, Yancel, you might tell me what it is we just took a picture of, so we can title it properly."

"Smart guy. You and your stooge had better scram if you don't want your heads blown off. We're setting up a bazooka."

"You're setting up a *what?*" Pete looked toward the squad car, unbelievingly. Sure enough, two of the cops were unloading a bazooka. "Keep shooting, kid," he said to Clarence.

"Natch," said Clarence.

"And quit popping your bubble gum. Now, look, Yancel—I'm just a newsboy. What in the world is the idea?"

"Stick around and find out, wise guy." Yancel turned away. "Okay there! Start doing it—commence firing!"

One of the cops looked up. "At what, Sergeant?"

"I thought you used to be a marine—at the whirlwind, of course."

Pappy leaned over Pete's shoulder. "What are they doing?"

"I'm beginning to get a glimmering. Pappy, keep Kitten out of range—I think they mean to put a rocket shell through her gizzard. It might bust up dynamic stability or something."

"Kitten's safe. I told her to hide. But this is crazy, Pete. They must be absolute, complete and teetotal nuts."

"Any law says a cop has to be sane to be on the force?"

"What whirlwind, Sergeant?" the bazooka man was asking. Yancel started to tell him, forcefully, then deflated when he realized that no whirlwind was available.

"You wait," he told him, and turned to Pappy. "You!" he yelled. "You chased away that whirlwind. Get it back here."

Pete took out his notebook. "This is interesting, Yancel. Is it your professional opinion that a whirlwind can be ordered around like a trained dog? Is that the official position of the police department?"

"I...No comment! You button up, or I'll run you in."

"By all means. But you have that Buck-Rogers cannon pointed so that, after the shell passes through the whirlwind, if any, it should end up just about at the city hall. Is this a plot to assassinate Hizzoner?"

Yancel looked around suddenly, then let his gaze travel an imaginary trajectory.

"Hey, you lugs!" he shouted. "Point that thing the other way. You want to knock off the Mayor?"

"That's better," Pete told the Sergeant. "Now they have it trained on the First National Bank. I can't wait."

Yancel looked over the situation again. "Point it where it won't hurt nobody," he ordered. "Do I have to do all your thinking?"

"But, Sergeant ..."

"Well?"

"You *point* it. We'll fire it."

Pete watched them. "Clarence," he sighed, "you stick around and get a pic of them loading it back into the car. That will be in about five minutes. Pappy and I will be in the Happy Hour Bar-Grill. Get a nice picture, with Yancel's features."

"Natch," said Clarence.

The next installment of "Our Fair City" featured three cuts and was headed "Police Declare War on Whirlwind." Pete took a copy and set out for the parking lot, intending to show it to Pappy.

Pappy wasn't there. Nor was Kitten. He looked around the neighborhood, poking his nose in lunchrooms and bars. No luck.

He headed back toward the *Forum* building, telling himself that Pappy might be shopping, or at a movie. He returned to his desk, made a couple of false starts on a column for the morrow, crumpled them up and went to the Art Department. "Hey! Clarence! Have you been down to the parking lot today?"

"Nah."

"Pappy's missing."

"So what?"

"Well, come along. We got to find him."

"Why?" But he came, lugging his camera.

The lot was still deserted, no Pappy, no Kitten—not even a stray breeze. Pete turned away. "Come on, Clarence—say, what are you shooting now?"

Clarence had his camera turned up toward the sky. "Not shooting," said Clarence. "Light is no good."

"What was it?"

"Whirlwind."

"Huh? Kitten?"

"Maybe."

"Here, Kitten—come Kitten." The whirlwind came back near him, spun faster, and picked up a piece of cardboard it had dropped. It whipped it around, then let him have it in the face.

"That's not funny, Kitten," Pete complained. "Where's Pappy?"

The whirlwind sidled back toward him. He saw it reach again for the cardboard. "No, you don't!" he yelped and reached for it, too.

The whirlwind beat him to it. It carried it up some hundred feet and sailed it back. The card caught him edgewise on the bridge of the nose. "Kitten!" Pete yelled. "Quit the horsing around."

It was a printed notice, about six by eight inches. Evidently it had been tacked up; there were small tears at all four corners. It read: "THE RITZ—CLASSIC" and under that, "Room 2013, Single Occupancy $6.00, Double Occupancy $8.00." There followed a printed list of the house rules.

Pete stared at it and frowned. Suddenly he chucked it back at the whirlwind. Kitten immediately tossed it back in his face.

"Come on, Clarence," he said briskly. "We're going to the Ritz-Classic—room 2013."

"Natch." said Clarence.

The Ritz-Classic was a colossal fleabag, favored by the bookie-and-madame set, three blocks away. Pete avoided the desk by using the basement entrance. The elevator boy looked at Clarence's camera and said, "No, you don't, Doc. No divorce cases in this hotel."

"Relax," Pete told him. "That's not a real camera. We peddle marijuana—that's the hay mow."

"Whyn't you say so? You hadn't ought to carry it in a camera. You make people nervous. What floor?"

"Twenty-one."

The elevator operator took them up nonstop, ignoring other calls. "That'll be two bucks. Special service."

"What do you pay for the concession?" inquired Pete.

"You gotta nerve to beef—with your racket."

They went back down a floor by stair and looked up room 2013. Pete tried the knob cautiously; the door was locked. He knocked on it—no answer. He pressed an ear to it and thought he could hear movement inside. He stepped back, frowning.

Clarence said, "I just remember something," and trotted away. He returned quickly, with a red fire ax. "Now?" he asked Pete.

"A lovely thought, Clarence! Not yet." Pete pounded and yelled, "Pappy! Oh, Pappy!"

A large woman in a pink coolie coat opened the door behind them. "How do you expect a party to sleep?" she demanded.

Pete said, "Quiet, madame! We're on the air." He listened. This time there were sounds of struggling and then, "Pete! Pe——"

"Now!" said Pete. Clarence started swinging.

The lock gave up on the third swing. Pete poured in, with Clarence after him. He collided with someone coming out and sat down abruptly. When he got up he saw Pappy on a bed. The old man was busily trying to get rid of a towel tied around his mouth.

Pete snatched it away. "Get 'em!" yelled Pappy.

"Soon as I get you untied."

"I ain't tied. They took my pants. Boy, I thought you'd never come!"

"Took Kitten a while to make me understand."

"I got 'em," announced Clarence. "Both of 'em."

"Where?" demanded Pete.

"Here," said Clarence proudly, and patted his camera.

Pete restrained his answer and ran to the door. "They went thataway," said the large woman, pointing. He took out, skidded around the corner and saw an elevator door just closing.

Pete stopped, bewildered by the crowd just outside the hotel. He was looking uncertainly around when Pappy grabbed him. "There! That touring car!" The car Pappy pointed out was even then swinging out from the curb just beyond the rank of cabs in front of the hotel; with a deep growl it picked up speed, and headed away. Pete yanked open the door of the nearest cab.

"Follow that car!" he yelled. They all piled in.

"Why?" asked the hackie.

Clarence lifted the fire ax. "Now?" he asked.

The driver ducked. "Forget it," he said. "It was just a yak." He let in his clutch.

The hack driver's skill helped them in the downtown streets, but the driver of the touring car swung right on Third and headed for the river. They streamed across it, fifty yards apart, with traffic snarled behind them, and then were on the no-speed-limit freeway. The cabbie turned his head. "Is the camera truck keeping up?"

"What camera truck?"

"Ain't this a movie?"

"Good grief, no! That car is filled with kidnappers. Faster!"

"A snatch? I don't want no part of it." He braked suddenly.

Pete took the ax and prodded the driver. "You catch 'em!"

The hack speeded up again but the driver protested, "Not in this wreck. They got more power than me."

Pappy grabbed Pete's arm. "There's Kitten!"

"Where? Oh, never mind that now!"

"Slow down!" yelled Pappy. "Kitten, oh, Kitten—over here!"

The whirlwind swooped down and kept pace with them. Pappy called to it. "Here, baby! Go get that car! Up ahead—*get it!*"

Kitten seemed confused, uncertain. Pappy repeated it and she took off—like a whirlwind. She dipped and gathered a load of paper and trash as she flew.

They saw her dip and strike the car ahead, throwing paper in the face of the driver. The car wobbled. She struck again. The car veered, climbed the curb, ricocheted against the crash rail, and fetched up against a lamp post.

Five minutes later Pete, having left Kitten, Clarence, and the fire ax to hold the fort over two hoodlums suffering from abrasion, multiple contusions and shock, was feeding a dime into a pay phone at the nearest filling station. He dialed long distance. "Gimme the F.B.I.'s kidnap number," he demanded. "You know—the Washington, D.C., snatch number."

"My goodness," said the operator, "do you mind if I listen in?"

"Get me that number!"

"Right away!"

Presently a voice answered. "Federal Bureau of Investigation."

"Lemme talk to Hoover! Huh? Okay, okay—I'll talk to you. Listen, this is a snatch case. I've got 'em on ice, for the moment, but unless you get one of your boys from your local office here pronto there won't be any snatch case—not if the city cops get here first. What?" Pete quieted down and explained who he was, where he was, and the more believable aspects of the events that had led up to the present situation. The government man cut in on him as he was urging speed and more speed and more speed and assured him that the local office was already being notified.

Pete got back to the wreck just as Lieutenant Dumbrosky climbed out of a squad car. Pete hurried up. "Don't do it, Dumbrosky," he yelled.

The big cop hesitated. "Don't do what?"

"Don't do anything. The F.B.I. are on their way now—and you're already implicated. Don't make it any worse."

Pete pointed to the two gunsels; Clarence was sitting on one and resting the spike of the ax against the back of the other. "These birds have already sung. This town is about to fall apart. If you hurry, you might be able to get a plane for Mexico."

Dumbrosky looked at him. "Wise guy," he said doubtfully.

"Ask them. They confessed."

One of the hoods raised his head. "We was threatened," he announced. "Take 'em in, lieutenant. They assaulted us."

"Go ahead," Pete said cheerfully. "Take us all in—together. Then you won't be able to lose that pair before the F.B.I. can question them. Maybe you can cop a plea."

"Now?" asked Clarence.

Dumbrosky swung around. "Put that ax down!"

"Do as he says, Clarence. Get your camera ready to get a picture as the G-men arrive."

"You didn't send for no G-men."

"Look behind you!"

A dark blue sedan slid quietly to a stop and four lean, brisk men got out. The first of them said, "Is there someone here named Peter Perkins?"

"Me," said Pete. "Do you mind if I kiss you?"

It was after dark but the parking lot was crowded and noisy. A stand for the new Mayor and distinguished visitors had been erected on one side, opposite it was a bandstand; across the front was a large illuminated sign: "HOME OF KITTEN—HONORARY CITIZEN OF OUR FAIR CITY."

In the fenced-off circle in the middle Kitten herself bounced and spun and swayed and danced. Pete stood on one side of the circle with Pappy opposite him; at four-foot intervals around it children were posted. "All set?" called out Pete.

"All set," answered Pappy. Together, Pete, Pappy and the kids started throwing serpentine into the ring. Kitten swooped, gathered the ribbons up and wrapped them around herself.

"Confetti!" yelled Pete. Each of the kids dumped a sackful toward the whirlwind—little of it reached the ground.

"Balloons!" yelled Pete. "Lights!" Each of the children started blowing up toy balloons; each had a dozen different colors. As fast as they were inflated they fed them to Kitten. Floodlights and searchlights came on; Kitten was transformed into a fountain of boiling, bubbling color, several stories high.

"Now?" said Clarence.

"Now!"

Come and Go Mad

Fredric Brown

He had known it, somehow, when he had awakened that morning. He knew
it more surely now, staring out of the editorial room window into the early
afternoon sunlight slanting down among the buildings to cast a pattern of
light and shadow. He knew that soon, perhaps even today, something
important was going to happen. Whether good or bad he did not know, but
he darkly suspected. And with reason; there are few good things that may
unexpectedly happen to a man, things, that is, of lasting importance.
Disaster can strike from innumerable directions, in amazingly diverse
ways.

A voice said, "Hey, Mr. Vine," and he turned away from the window,
slowly. That in itself was strange for it was not his manner to move slowly;
he was a small, volatile man, almost catlike in the quickness of his
reactions and his movements.

But this time something made him turn slowly from the window, almost
as though he never again expected to see that chiaroscuro of an early
afternoon.

He said, "Hi, Red."

193

The freckled copy boy said, "His Nibs wants to see ya."

"Now?"

"Naw. Atcher convenience. Sometime next week, maybe. If yer busy, give him an apperntment."

He put his fist against Red's chin and shoved, and the copy boy staggered back in assumed distress.

He went over to the water cooler. He pressed his thumb on the button and water gurgled into the paper cup.

Harry Wheeler sauntered over and said, "Hiya, Nappy. What's up? Going on the carpet?"

He said, "Sure, for a raise."

He drank and crumpled the cup, tossing it into the wastebasket. He went over to the door marked Private and went through it.

Walter J. Candler, the managing editor, looked up from the work on his desk and said affably, "Sit down, Vine. Be with you in a moment," and then looked down again.

He slid into the chair opposite Candler, worried a cigarette out of his shirt pocket and lighted it. He studied the back of the sheet of paper of which the managing editor was reading the front. There wasn't anything on the back of it.

The M.E. put the paper down and looked at him. "Vine, I've got a screwy one. You're good on screwy ones."

He grinned slowly at the M.E. He said, "If that's a compliment, thanks."

"It's a compliment, all right. You've done some pretty tough things for us. This one's different. I've never yet asked a reporter to do anything I wouldn't do myself. *I* wouldn't do this, so I'm not asking you to."

The M.E. picked up the paper he'd been reading and then put it down again without even looking at it. "Ever hear of Ellsworth Joyce Randolph?"

"Head of the asylum? Hell yes, I've met him. Casually."

"How'd he impress you?"

He was aware that the managing editor was staring at him intently, that it wasn't too casual a question. He parried. "What do you mean? In what way? You mean is he a good Joe, is he a good politician, has he got a good bedside manner for a psychiatrist, or what?"

"I mean, how sane do you think he is?"

He looked at Candler and Candler wasn't kidding. Candler was strictly deadpan.

He began to laugh, and then he stopped laughing. He leaned forward across Candler's desk. "Ellsworth Joyce Randolph," he said. "You're talking about Ellsworth Joyce Randolph?"

Candler nodded. "Dr. Randolph was in here this morning. He told a rather strange story. He didn't want me to print it. He did want me to check on it, to send our best man to check on it. He said if we found it was true we could print it in hundred and twenty line type in red ink." Candler grinned wryly. "We could, at that."

He stumped out his cigarette and studied Candler's face. "But the story itself is so screwy you're not sure whether Dr. Randolph himself might be insane?"

"Exactly."

"And what's tough about the assignment?"

"The doc says a reporter could get the story only from the inside."

"You mean, go in as a guard or something?"

Candler said, "As something."

"Oh."

He got up out of the chair and walked over to the window, stood with his back to the managing editor, looking out. The sun had moved hardly at all. Yet the shadow pattern in the streets looked different, obscurely different. The shadow pattern inside him was different, too. This, he knew, was what had been going to happen. He turned around. He said, "No. Hell no."

Candler shrugged imperceptibly. "Don't blame you. I haven't even asked you to. I wouldn't do it myself."

He asked, "What does Ellsworth Joyce Randolph think is going on inside his nut-house? It must be something pretty screwy if it made you wonder whether Randolph himself is sane."

"I can't tell you that, Vine. Promised him I wouldn't, whether or not you took the assignment."

"You mean—even if I took the job I still wouldn't know what I was looking for?"

"That's right. You'd be prejudiced. You wouldn't be objective. You'd be looking for something, and you might think you found it whether it was there or not. Or you might be so prejudiced against finding it that you'd refuse to recognize it if it bit you in the leg."

He strode from the window over to the desk and banged his fist down on it.

He said, "Goddamn it, Candler, why *me?* You know what happened to me three years ago."

"Sure. Amnesia."

"Sure, amnesia. Just like that. But I haven't kept it any secret that I never got *over* that amnesia. I'm thirty years old—or am I? My memory goes back three years. Do you know what it feels like to have a blank wall in your memory only three years back?

"Oh, sure, I know what's on the other side of that wall. I know because everybody tells me. I know I started here as a copy boy ten years ago. I know where I was born and when and I know my parents are both dead. I know what they look like—because I've seen their pictures. I know I didn't have a wife and kids, because everybody who knew me told me I didn't. Get that part—everybody who knew me, not everybody I knew. I didn't know anybody.

"Sure, I've done all right since then. After I got out of the hospital—and I don't even remember the accident that put me there—I did all right back here because I still knew how to write news stories, even though I had to learn everybody's name all over again. I wasn't any worse off than a new reporter starting cold on a paper in a strange city. And everybody was as helpful as hell."

Candler raised a placating hand to stem the tide. He said, "Okay, Nappy. You said no, and that's enough. I don't see what all that's got to do with this story, but all you had to do was say no. So forget about it."

The tenseness hadn't gone out of him. He said, "You don't see what *that's* got to do with the story? You ask—or, all right, you don't ask, you suggest—that I get myself certified as a madman, go into an asylum as a patient. When—how much confidence could anyone have in his own mind when he can't remember going to school, can't remember the first time he met any of the people he works with every day, can't remember starting on the job he works at, can't remember—anything back of three years before?"

Abruptly he struck the desk again with his fist, and then looked foolish about it. He said, "I'm sorry. I didn't mean to get wound up about it like that."

Candler said, "Sit down."

"The answer's still no."

"Sit down, anyway."

He sat down and fumbled a cigarette out of his pocket, got it lighted.

Candler said, "I didn't even mean to mention it, but I've got to now. Now that you talked that way. I didn't know you felt like that about your amnesia. I thought that was water under the bridge.

"Listen, when Dr. Randolph asked me what reporter we had that could best cover it, I told him about you. What your background was. He remembered meeting you, too, incidentally. But he hadn't known you had amnesia."

"Is that why you suggested me?"

"Skip that till I make my point. He said that while you were there, he'd be glad to try one of the newer, milder forms of shock treatment on you, and that it might restore your lost memories. He said it would be worth trying."

"He didn't say it would work."

"He said it might; that it wouldn't do any harm."

He stubbed out the cigarette from which he'd taken only three drags. He glared at Candler. He didn't have to say what was in his mind; the managing editor could read it.

Candler said, "Calm down, boy. Remember I didn't bring it up until you yourself started in on how much that memory-wall bothered you. I wasn't saving it for ammunition. I mentioned it only out of fairness to you, after the way you talked."

"Fairness!"

Candler shrugged. "You said no. I accepted it. Then you started raving at me and put me in a spot where I had to mention something I'd hardly thought of at the time. Forget it. How's that graft story coming? Any new leads?"

"You going to put someone else on the asylum story?"

"No. You're the logical one for it."

"What *is* the story? It must be pretty woolly if it makes you wonder if Dr. Randolph is sane. Does he think his patients ought to trade places with his doctors, or what?"

He laughed. "Sure, you can't tell me. That's really beautiful double bait. Curiosity—and hope of knocking down that wall. So what's the rest of it? If I say yes instead of no, how long will I be there, under what circumstances? What chance have I got of getting out again? How do I get in?"

Candler said slowly, "Vine, I'm not sure any more I want you to try it. Let's skip the whole thing."

"Let's not. Not until you answer my questions, anyway."

"All right. You'd go in anonymously, so there wouldn't be any stigma attached if the story wouldn't work out. If it does, you can tell the whole truth—including Dr. Randolph's collusion in getting you in and out again. The cat will be out of the bag, then.

"You might get what you want in a few days—and you wouldn't stay on it more than a couple of weeks in any case."

"How many at the asylum would know who I was and what I was there for, besides Randolph?"

"No one." Candler leaned forward and held up four fingers of his left hand. "Four people would have to be in on it. You." He pointed to one finger. "Me." A second. "Dr. Randolph." The third finger. "And one other reporter from here."

"Not that I'd object, but why the other reporter?"

"Intermediary. In two ways. First, he'll go with you to some psychiatrist; Randolph will recommend one you can fool comparatively easily. He'll be your brother and request that you be examined and certified. You convince the psychiatrist you're nuts and he'll certify you. Of course it takes two doctors to put you away, but Randolph will be the second. Your alleged brother will want Randolph for the second one."

"All this under an assumed name?"

"If you prefer. Of course there's no real reason why it should be."

"That's the way I feel about it. Keep it out of the papers, of course. Tell everybody around here—except my—hey, in that case we couldn't make up a brother. But Charlie Doerr, in Circulation, is my first cousin and my nearest living relative. He'd do, wouldn't he?"

"Sure. And he'd have to be intermediary the rest of the way, then. Visit you at the asylum and bring back anything you have to send back."

"And if, in a couple of weeks, I've found nothing, you'll spring me?"

Candler nodded. "I'll pass the word to Randolph; he'll interview you and pronounce you cured, and you're out. You come back here, and you've been on vacation. That's all."

"What kind of insanity should I pretend to have?"

He thought Candler squirmed a little in his chair. Candler said, "Well—wouldn't this Nappy business be a natural? I mean, paranoia is a form of insanity which Dr. Randolph told me, hasn't any physical symptoms. It's just a delusion supported by a systematic framework of rationalization. A paranoiac can be sane in every way except one."

He watched Candler and there was a faint twisted grin on his lips. "You mean I should think I'm Napoleon?"

Candler gestured slightly. "Choose your own delusion. But—isn't that one a natural? I mean, the boys around the office always kidding you and calling you Nappy. And—" He finished weakly, "—and everything."

And then Candler looked at him squarely. "Want to do it?"

He stood up. "I think so. I'll let you know for sure tomorrow morning after I've slept on it, but unofficially—yes. Is that good enough?"

Candler nodded.

He said, "I'm taking the rest of the afternoon off; I'm going to the library to read up on paranoia. Haven't anything else to do anyway. And I'll talk to Charlie Doerr this evening. Okay?"

"Fine. Thanks."

He grinned at Candler. He leaned across the desk. He said, "I'll let you in on a little secret, now that things have gone this far. Don't tell anyone. I *am* Napoleon!"

It was a good exit line, so he went out.

II

He got his hat and coat and went outside, out of the air-conditioning and into the hot sunlight. Out of the quiet madhouse of a newspaper office after deadline, into the quieter madhouse of the streets on a sultry July afternoon.

He tilted his panama back on his head and ran his handkerchief across his forehead. Where was he going? Not to the library to bone up on paranoia; that had been a gag to get off for the rest of the afternoon. He'd read everything the library had on paranoia—and on allied subjects—over two years ago. He was an expert on it. He could fool any psychiatrist in the country into thinking that he was sane—or that he wasn't.

He walked north to the park and sat down on one of the benches in the shade. He put his hat on the bench beside him and mopped his forehead again.

He stared out at the grass, bright green in the sunlight, at the pigeons with their silly head-bobbing method of walking, at a red squirrel that came down one side of a tree, looked about him and scurried up the other side of the same tree.

And he thought back to the wall of amnesia of three years ago.

The wall that hadn't been a wall at all. The phrase intrigued him: a wall at all. Pigeons on the grass, alas. A wall at all.

It wasn't a wall at all; it was a shift, an abrupt change. A line had been drawn between two lives. Twenty-seven years of a life before the accident. Three years of a life since the accident.

They were not the same life.

But no one knew. Until this afternoon he had never even hinted the truth—if it *was* the truth—to anyone. He'd used it as an exit line in leaving Candler's office, knowing Candler would take it as a gag. Even so, one had to be careful; use a gag-line like that often, and people begin to wonder.

The fact that his extensive injuries from that accident had included a broken jaw was probably responsible for the fact that today he was free and not in an insane asylum. That broken jaw—it had been in a cast when he'd returned to consciousness forty-eight hours after his car had run head-on into a truck ten miles out of town—had prevented him from talking for three weeks.

And by the end of three weeks, despite the pain and the confusion that had filled him, he'd had a chance to think things over. He'd invented the wall. The amnesia, the convenient amnesia that was so much more believable than the truth as he knew it.

But *was* the truth as he knew it?

That was the haunting ghost that had ridden him for three years now, since the very hour when he had awakened to whiteness in a white room and a stranger, strangely dressed, had been sitting beside a bed the like of which had been in no field hospital he'd ever heard of or seen. A bed with an overhead framework. And when he looked from the stranger's face down at his own body, he saw that one of his legs and both of his arms were in casts and that the cast of the leg stuck upward at an angle, a rope running over a pulley holding it so.

He'd tried to open his mouth to ask where he was, what had happened to him, and that was when he discovered the cast on his jaw.

He'd stared at the stranger, hoping the latter would have sense enough to volunteer the information and the stranger had grinned at him and said, "Hi, George. Back with us, huh? You'll be all right."

And there was something strange about the language—until he placed what it was. English. Was he in the hands of the English? And it was a language, too, which he knew little of, yet he understood the stranger perfectly. And why did the stranger call him George?

Maybe some of the doubt, some of the fierce bewilderment, showed in his eyes, for the stranger leaned closer to the bed. He said, "Maybe you're still confused, George. You were in a pretty bad smash-up. You ran that coupe of yours head-on into a gravel truck. That was two days ago, and you're just coming out of it for the first time. You're all right, but you'll be in the hospital for a while, till all the bones you busted knit. Nothing seriously wrong with you."

And then waves of pain had come and swept away the confusion, and he had closed his eyes.

Another voice in the room said, "We're going to give you a hypo, Mr. Vine," but he hadn't dared open his eyes again. It was easier to fight the pain without seeing.

There had been the prick of a needle in his upper arm. And pretty soon there'd been nothingness.

When he came back again—twelve hours later, he learned afterwards— it had been to the same white room, the same strange bed, but this time there was a woman in the room, a woman in a strange white costume standing at the foot of the bed studying a paper that was fastened to a piece of board.

She smiled at him when she saw that his eyes were open. She said, "Good morning, Mr. Vine. Hope you're feeling better. I'll tell Dr. Holt you're back with us."

She went away and came back with a man who was also strangely dressed, in roughly the same fashion as had been the stranger who had called him George.

The doctor looked at him and chuckled. "Got a patient, for once, who can't talk back to me. Or even write notes." Then his face sobered. "Are you in pain, though? Blink once if you're not, twice if you are."

The pain wasn't really very bad this time, and he blinked once. The doctor nodded with satisfaction. "That cousin of yours," he said, "has kept calling up. He'll be glad to know you're going to be back in shape to—well, to listen if not to talk. Guess it won't hurt you to see him a while this evening."

The nurse rearranged his bedclothing and then, mercifully, both she and the doctor had gone, leaving him alone to straighten out his chaotic thoughts.

Straighten them out? That had been three years ago, and he hadn't been able to straighten them out yet:

The startling fact that they'd spoken English and that he'd understood that barbaric tongue perfectly, despite his slight previous knowledge of it. How could an accident have made him suddenly fluent in a language he'd known but slightly?

The startling fact that they'd called him by a different name. "George" had been the name used by the man who'd been beside his bed last night. "Mr. Vine," the nurse had called him. George Vine, an English name, surely.

But there was one thing a thousand times more startling than either of those: It was what last night's stranger (Could he be the "cousin" of whom the doctor had spoken?) had told him about the accident. "You ran that coupe of yours head-on into a gravel truck."

The amazing thing, the contradictory thing, was that he *knew* what a *coupe* was and what a *truck* was. Not that he had any recollection of having driven either, of the accident itself, or of anything beyond that moment when he'd been sitting in the tent after Lodi—but—but how could a picture of a coupe, something driven by a gasoline engine arise to his mind when such a concept had never been *in* his mind before.

There was that mad mingling of two worlds—the one sharp and clear and definite. The world he'd lived his twenty-seven years of life in, the world into which he'd been born twenty-seven years ago, on August 15th, 1769, in Corsica. The world in which he'd gone to sleep—it seemed like last night—in his tent at Lodi, as General of the Army in Italy, after his first important victory in the field.

And then there was this disturbing world into which he had been awakened, this white world in which people spoke an English—now that he thought of it—which was different from the English he had heard spoken at Brienne, in Valence, at Toulon, and yet which he understood perfectly, which he knew instinctively that he could speak if his jaw were not in a cast. This world in which people called him George Vine, and in which, strangest of all, people used words that he did not know, could not conceivably know, and yet which brought pictures to his mind.

Coupe, truck. They were both forms of—the word came to his mind unbidden—automobiles. He concentrated on what an automobile was and how it worked, and the information was there. The cylinder block, the pistons driven by explosions of gasoline vapor, ignited by a spark of electricity from a generator—

Electricity. He opened his eyes and looked upward at the shaded light in the ceiling, and he knew, somehow, that it was an *electric* light, and in a general way he knew what electricity was.

The Italian Galvani—yes, he'd read of some experiments of Galvani, but they hadn't encompassed anything practical such as a light like that. And staring at the shaded light, he visualized behind it water power running dynamos, miles of wire, motors running generators. He caught his breath at the concept that came to him out of his own mind, or part of his own mind.

The faint, fumbling experiments of Galvani with their weak currents and kicking frogs' legs had scarcely foreshadowed the unmysterious mystery of that light up in the ceiling; and that was the strangest thing yet; part of his mind found it mysterious and another part took it for granted and understood in a general sort of way how it all worked.

Let's see, he thought, the electric light was invented by Thomas Alva Edison somewhere around—Ridiculous; he'd been going to say around 1900, and it was now only 1796!

And then the really horrible thing came to him and he tried—painfully, in vain—to sit up in bed. It *had* been 1900, his memory told him, and Edison had died in 1931—and a man named Napoleon Bonaparte had died a hundred and ten years before that, in 1821.

He'd nearly gone insane then.

And, sane or insane, only the fact that he could not speak had kept him out of a madhouse; it gave him time to think things out, time to realize that his only chance lay in pretending amnesia, in pretending that he remembered nothing of life prior to the accident. They don't put you in a madhouse for amnesia. They tell you who you are, let you go back to what they tell you your former life was. They let you pick up the threads and weave them, while you try to remember.

Three years ago he'd done that. Now, tomorrow, he was going to a psychiatrist and say that he was—Napoleon!

III

The slant of the sun was greater. Overhead a big bird of a plane droned by and he looked up at it and began laughing, quietly to himself—not the laughter of madness. True laughter because it sprang from the conception of Napoleon Bonaparte riding in a plane like that and from the overwhelming incongruity of that idea.

It came to him then that he'd never ridden in a plane that he remembered. Maybe George Vine had; at some time in the twenty-seven years of life George Vine had spent, he must have. But did that mean that *he* had ridden in one? That was a question that was part of the big question.

He got up and started to walk again. It was almost five o'clock; pretty soon Charlie Doerr would be leaving the paper and going home for dinner. Maybe he'd better phone Charlie and be sure he'd be home this evening.

He headed for the nearest bar and phoned; he got Charlie just in time. He said, "This is George. Going to be home this evening?"

"Sure, George. I was going to a poker game, but I called it off when I learned you'd be around."

"When you learned— Oh, Candler talked to you?"

"Yeah. Say, I didn't know you'd phone me or I'd have called Marge, but how about coming out for dinner? It'll be all right with her, I'll call her now if you can."

He said, "Thanks, no, Charlie. Got a dinner date. And say, about that card game; you can go. I can get there about seven and we won't have to talk all evening; an hour'll be enough. You wouldn't be leaving before eight anyway."

Charlie said, "Don't worry about it; I don't much want to go anyway, and you haven't been out for a while. So I'll see you at seven, then."

From the phone booth, he walked over to the bar and ordered a beer. He wondered why he'd turned down the invitation to dinner; probably because, subconsciously, he wanted another couple of hours by himself before he talked to anyone, even Charlie and Marge.

He sipped his beer slowly, because he wanted to make it last; he had to stay sober tonight, plenty sober. There was still time to change his mind; he'd left himself a loophole, however small. He could still go to Candler in the morning and say he'd decided not to do it.

Over the rim of his glass he stared at himself in the back-bar mirror. Small, sandy-haired, with freckles on his nose, stocky. The small and stocky part fitted all right; but the rest of it! Not the remotest resemblance.

He drank another beer slowly, and that made it half past five.

He wandered out again and walked, this time toward town. He walked past the *Blade* and looked up to the third floor and at the window he'd been looking out of when Candler had sent for him. He wondered if he'd ever sit by that window again and look out across a sunlit afternoon.

Maybe. Maybe not.

He thought about Clare. Did he want to see her tonight?

Well, no, to be honest about it, he didn't. But if he disappeared for two weeks or so without having even said good-bye to her, then he'd have to write her off his books.

He'd better.

He stopped in at a drugstore and called her home. He said, "This is George, Clare. Listen, I'm being sent out of town tomorrow on an assignment; don't know how long I'll be gone. One of those things that might be a few days or a few weeks. But could I see you late this evening, to say so long?"

"Why sure, George. What time?"

"It might be after nine, but not much after. That be okay? I'm seeing Charlie first, on business; may not be able to get away before nine."

"Of course, George. Any time."

He stopped in at a hamburger stand, although he wasn't hungry, and managed to eat a sandwich and a piece of pie. That made it a quarter after six and, if he walked, he'd get to Charlie's at just about the right time. So he walked.

Charlie met him at the door. With fingers on his lips, he jerked his head backward toward the kitchen where Marge was wiping dishes. He whispered, "I didn't tell Marge, George. It'd worry her."

He wanted to ask Charlie why it would, or should, worry Marge, but he didn't. Maybe he was a little afraid of the answer. It would have to mean that Marge was worrying about him already, and that was a bad sign. He thought he'd been carrying everything off pretty well for three years now.

Anyway, he couldn't ask because Charlie was leading him into the living room and the kitchen was within easy earshot, and Charlie was saying, "Glad you decided you'd like a game of chess, George. Marge is going out tonight; movie she wants to see down at the neighborhood show. I was going to that card game out of self-defense, but I didn't want to."

He got the chessboard and men out of the closet and started to set up a game on the coffee table.

Marge came in with a tray bearing tall cold glasses of beer and put it down beside the chessboard. She said, "Hi, George. Hear you're going away a couple of weeks."

He nodded. "But I don't know where. Candler—the managing editor— asked me if I'd be free for an out of town assignment and I said sure, and he said he'd tell me about it tomorrow."

Charlie was holding out clenched hands, a pawn in each, and he touched Charlie's left hand and got white. He moved pawn to king's fourth and, when Charlie did the same, advanced his queen's pawn.

Marge was fussing with her hat in front of the mirror. She said, "If you're not here when I get back, George, so long and good luck."

He said, "Thanks, Marge. 'Bye."

He made a few more moves before Marge came over, ready to go, kissed Charlie good-bye, and then kissed him lightly on the forehead. She said, "Take care of yourself, George."

For a moment his eyes met her pale blue ones and he thought, she *is* worrying about me. It scared him a little.

After the door had closed behind her, he said, "Let's not finish the game, Charlie. Let's get to the brass tacks, because I've got to see Clare about nine. Dunno how long I'll be gone, so I can't very well not say good-bye to her."

Charlie looked up at him. "You and Clare serious, George?"

"I don't know."

Charlie picked up his beer and took a sip. Suddenly his voice was brisk and businesslike. He said, "All right, let's sit on the brass tacks. We've got an appointment for eleven o'clock tomorrow morning with a guy named Irving, Dr. W. E. Irving, in the Appleton Block. He's a psychiatrist; Dr. Randolph recommended him.

"I called him up this afternoon after Candler talked to me; Candler had already phoned Randolph. I gave my right name. My story was this: I've got a cousin who's been acting queer lately and whom I wanted him to talk to. I didn't give the cousin's name. I didn't tell him in what way you'd been acting queer; I ducked the question and said I'd rather have him judge for himself without prejudice. I said I'd talked you into talking to a psychiatrist and that the only one I knew of was Randolph; that I'd called Randolph, who said he didn't do much private practice and recommended Irving. I told him I was your nearest living relative.

"That leaves the way open to Randolph for the second name on the certificate. If you can talk Irving into thinking you're really insane and he wants to sign you up, I can insist on having Randolph, whom I wanted in the first place. And this time, of course, Randolph will agree."

"You didn't say a thing about what kind of insanity you suspected me of having?"

Charlie shook his head. He said, "So, anyway, neither of us goes to work at the *Blade* tomorrow. I'll leave home the usual time so Marge won't know anything, but I'll meet you downtown—say, in the lobby of the Christina—at a quarter of eleven. And if you can convince Irving that you're commitable—if that's the word—we'll get Randolph right away and get the whole thing settled tomorrow."

"And if I change my mind?"

"Then I'll call the appointment off. That's all. Look, isn't that all there is to talk over? Let's play this game of chess out; it's only twenty after seven."

He shook his head. "I'd rather talk, Charlie. One thing you forgot to cover, anyway. After tomorrow. How often you coming to see me to pick up bulletins for Candler?"

"Oh, sure, I forgot that. As often as visiting hours will permit—three times a week. Monday, Wednesday, Friday afternoons. Tomorrow's Friday, so if you get in, the first time I'll be able to see you is Monday."

"Okay. Say, Charlie, did Candler even hint to you at what the story is that I'm supposed to get in there?"

Charlie Doerr shook his head slowly. "Not a word. What is it? Or is it too secret for you to talk about?"

He stared at Charlie, wondering. And suddenly he felt that he couldn't tell the truth; that he didn't know either. It would make him look so silly. It hadn't sounded so foolish when Candler had given the reason—a reason, anyway—for not telling him, but it would sound foolish now.

He said, "If he didn't tell you, I guess I'd better not either, Charlie." And since that didn't sound too convincing, he added, "I promised Candler I wouldn't."

Both glasses of beer were empty by then, and Charlie took them into the kitchen for refilling.

He followed Charlie, somehow preferring the informality of the kitchen. He sat a-straddle of a kitchen chair, leaning his elbows on the back of it, and Charlie leaned against the refrigerator.

Charlie said, "Prosit!" and they drank, and then Charlie asked, "Have you got your story ready for Doc Irving?"

He nodded. "Did Candler tell you what I'm to tell him?"

"You mean, that you're Napoleon?" Charlie chuckled.

Did that chuckle ring true? He looked at Charlie, and he knew that what he was thinking was completely incredible. Charlie was square and honest as they came. Charlie and Marge were his best friends; they'd been his best friends for three years that he knew of. Longer than that, a hell of a lot longer, according to Charlie. But beyond those three years—that was something else again.

He cleared his throat because the words were going to stick a little. But he had to ask, he had to be sure. "Charlie, I'm going to ask you a hell of a question. Is this business on the up and up?"

"Huh?"

"It's a hell of a thing to ask. But—look, you and Candler don't think I'm crazy, do you? You didn't work this out between you to get me put away— or anyway examined—painlessly, without my knowing it was happening, till too late, did you?"

Charlie was staring at him. He said, "Jeez, George, you don't think I'd do a thing like that, do you?"

"No, I don't. But—you could think it was for my own good, and you might on that basis. Look, Charlie, if it *is* that, if you *think* that, let me point out that this isn't fair. I'm going up against a psychiatrist tomorrow to lie to him, to try to convince him that I have delusions. Not to be honest with him. And that would be unfair as hell, to me. You see that, don't you, Charlie?"

Charlie's face got a little white. He said slowly, "Before God, George, it's nothing like that. All I know about this is what Candler and you have told me."

"You think I'm sane, fully sane?"

Charlie licked his lips. He said, "You want it straight?"

"Yes."

"I never doubted it, until this moment. Unless—well, amnesia is a form of mental aberration, I suppose, and you've never got over that, but that isn't what you mean, is it?"

"No."

"Then, until right now—George, that sounds like a persecution complex, if you really meant what you asked me. A conspiracy to get you to— Surely you can see how ridiculous it is. What possible reason would either Candler or I have to get you to lie yourself into being committed?"

He said, "I'm sorry, Charlie. It was just a screwy momentary notion. No, I don't think that, of course." He glanced at his wristwatch. "Let's finish that chess game, huh?"

"Fine. Wait till I give us a refill to take along."

He played carelessly and managed to lose within fifteen minutes. He turned down Charlie's offer of a chance for revenge and leaned back in his chair.

He said, "Charlie, ever hear of chessmen coming in red and black?"

"N-no. Either black and white, or red and white, any I've ever seen. Why?"

"Well—" He grinned. "I suppose I oughtn't to tell you this after just making you wonder whether I'm really sane after all, but I've been having recurrent dreams recently. No crazier than ordinary dreams except that I've been dreaming the same things over and over. One of them is something about a game between the red and the black; I don't even know whether it's chess. You know how it is when you dream; things seem to make sense whether they do or not. In the dream I don't wonder whether the red-and-black business is chess or not; I know, I guess, or seem to know. But the knowledge doesn't carry over. You know what I mean?"

"Sure. Go on."

"Well, Charlie, I've been wondering if it just might have something to do with the other side of that wall of amnesia I've never been able to cross. This is the first time in my—well, not in my life, maybe, but in the three years I remember of it, that I've had recurrent dreams. I wonder if—if memory may not be trying to get through.

"Did I ever have a set of red and black chessmen, for instance? Or, in any school I went to, did they have intramural basketball or baseball between red teams and black teams, or—or anything like that?"

Charlie thought for a long moment before he shook his head. "No, he said, "nothing like that. Of course there's red and black in roulette—*rouge et noir*. And it's the two colors in a deck of playing cards."

"No, I'm pretty sure it doesn't tie in with cards or roulette. It's not—not like that. It's a game *between* the red and the black. They're the players, somehow. Think hard, Charlie; not about where you might have run into that idea, but where *I* might have."

He watched Charlie struggle and after a while he said, "Okay, don't sprain your brain, Charlie. Try this one. *The brightly shining.*"

"The brightly shining what?"

"Just that phrase, *the brightly shining*. Does it mean anything to you, at all?"

"No."

"Okay," he said. "Forget it."

IV

He was early and he walked past Clare's house, as far as the corner and stood under the big elm there, smoking the rest of his cigarette, thinking bleakly.

There wasn't anything to think about, really; all he had to do was say good-bye to her. Two easy syllables. And stall off her questions as to where he was going, exactly how long he'd be gone. Be quiet and casual and unemotional about it, just as though they didn't mean anything in particular to each other.

It *had* to be that way. He'd known Clare Wilson a year and a half now, and he'd kept her dangling that long; it wasn't fair. This had to be the end, for her sake. He had about as much business asking a woman to marry him as—as a madman who thinks he's Napoleon!

He dropped his cigarette and ground it viciously into the walk with his heel, then went back to the house, up on the porch, and rang the bell.

Clare herself came to the door. The light from the hallway behind her made her hair a circlet of spun gold around her shadowed face.

He wanted to take her into his arms so badly that he clenched his fists with the effort it took to keep his arms down.

Stupidly, he said, "Hi, Clare. How's everything?"

"I don't know, George. How *is* everything? Aren't you coming in?"

She'd stepped back from the doorway to let him past and the light was on her face now, sweetly grave. She knew something was up, he thought; her expression and the tone of her voice gave that away.

He didn't want to go in. He said, "It's such a beautiful night, Clare. Let's take a stroll."

"All right, George." She came out onto the porch. "It is a fine night, such beautiful stars." She turned and looked at him. "Is one of them yours?"

He started a little. Then he stepped forward and took her elbow, guiding her down the porch steps. He said lightly, "All of them are mine. Want to buy any?"

"You wouldn't *give* me one? Just a teeny little dwarf star, maybe? Even one that I'd have to use a telescope to see?"

They were out on the sidewalk then, out of hearing of the house, and abruptly her voice changed, the playful note dropped from it, and she asked another question, "What's wrong, George?"

He opened his mouth to say nothing was wrong, and then closed it again. There wasn't any lie that he could tell her, and he couldn't tell her the truth, either. Her asking of that question, in that way, should have made things easier; it made them more difficult.

She asked another, "You mean to say good-bye for—for good, don't you, George?"

He said, "Yes," and his mouth was very dry. He didn't know whether it came out as an articulate monosyllable or not, and he wetted his lips and tried again. He said, "Yes, I'm afraid so, Clare."

"Why?"

He couldn't make himself turn to look at her, he stared blindly ahead. He said, "I—I can't tell you, Clare. But it's the only thing I can do. It's best for both of us."

"Tell me one thing, George. Are you really going away? Or was that just—an excuse?"

"It's true. I'm going away; I don't know for how long. But don't ask me where, please. I can't tell you that."

"Maybe I can tell you, George. Do you mind if I do?"

He minded all right; he minded terribly. But how could he say so? He didn't say anything, because he couldn't say yes, either.

They were beside the park now, the little neighborhood park that was only a block square and didn't offer much in the way of privacy, but which did have benches. And he steered her—or she steered him; he didn't know which—into the park and they sat down on a bench. There were other people in the park, but not too near. Still he hadn't answered her question.

She sat very close to him on the bench. She said, "You've been worried about your mind, haven't you, George?"

"Well—yes, in a way, yes, I have."

"And your going away has something to do with that, hasn't it? You're going somewhere for observation or treatment, or both?"

"Something like that. It's not as simple as that, Clare, and I—I just can't tell you about it."

She put her hand on his hand, lying on his knee. She said, "I knew it was something like that, George. And I don't ask you to tell me anything about it.

"Just—just don't say what you meant to say. Say so long instead of good-bye. Don't even write me, if you don't want to. But don't be noble and call everything off here and now, for my sake. At least wait until you've been wherever you're going. Will you?"

He gulped. She made it sound so simple when actually it was so complicated. Miserably he said, "All right, Clare. If you want it that way."

Abruptly she stood up. "Let's get back, George."

He stood beside her. "But it's early."

"I know, but sometimes— Well, there's a psychological moment to end a date, George. I know that sounds silly, but after what we've said, wouldn't it be—uh—anticlimactic—to—"

He laughed a little. He said, "I see what you mean."

They walked back to her home in silence. He didn't know whether it was happy or unhappy silence; he was too mixed up for that.

On the shadowed porch, in front of the door, she turned and faced him. "George," she said. Silence.

"Oh, damn you, George; quit being so *noble* or whatever you're being. Unless, of course, you *don't* love me. Unless this is just an elaborate form of—of runaround you're giving me. Is it?"

There were only two things he could do. One was run like hell. The other was what he did. He put his arms around her and kissed her. Hungrily.

When that was over, and it wasn't over too quickly, he was breathing a little hard and not thinking too clearly, for he was saying what he hadn't meant to say at all, "I love you, Clare. I love you; I love you so."

And she said, "I love you, too, dear. You'll come back to me, won't you?" And he said, "Yes, *Yes.*"

It was four miles or so from her home to his rooming house, but he walked, and the walk seemed to take only seconds.

He sat at the window of his room, with the light out, thinking, but the thoughts went in the same old circles they'd gone in for three years.

No new factor had been added except that now he was going to stick his neck out, way out, miles out. Maybe, just maybe, this thing was going to be settled one way or the other.

Out there, out his window, the stars were bright diamonds in the sky. Was one of them his star of destiny? If so, he was going to follow it, follow it even into the madhouse if it led there. Inside him was a deeply rooted conviction that this wasn't accident, that it wasn't coincidence that had led to his being asked to tell the truth under guise of falsehood.

His star of destiny.

Brightly shining? No, the phrase from his dreams did not refer to that; it was not an adjective phrase, but a noun. *The brightly shining.* What was *the brightly shining?*

And the red and the black? He'd thought of everything Charlie had suggested, and other things, too. Checkers, for instance. But it was not that.

The red and the black.

Well, whatever the answer was, he was running full-speed toward it now, not away from it.

After a while he went to bed, but it was a long time before he went to sleep.

V

Charlie Doerr came out of the inner office marked Private and put his hand out. He said, "Good luck, George. The doc's ready to talk to you now."

He shook Charlie's hand and said, "You might as well run along. I'll see you Monday, first visiting day."

"I'll wait here," Charlie said. "I took the day off work anyway, remember? Besides, maybe you won't have to go."

He dropped Charlie's hand, and stared into Charlie's face. He said slowly, "What do you mean, Charlie—maybe I won't have to go."

"Why—" Charlie looked puzzled. "Why, maybe he'll tell you you're all right, or just suggest regular visits to see him until you're straightened out, or—" Charlie finished weakly, "—or something."

Unbelievingly, he stared at Charlie. He wanted to ask, am I crazy or are you, but that sounded crazy under the circumstances. But he had to be sure, sure that Charlie just hadn't let something slip from his mind; maybe he'd fallen into the role he was supposed to be playing when he talked to the doctor just now. He asked, "Charlie, don't you remember that—" And even the rest of that question seemed insane for him to be asking, with Charlie staring blankly at him. The answer was in Charlie's face; it didn't have to be brought to Charlie's lips.

Charlie said again, "I'll wait, of course. Good luck, George."

He looked into Charlie's eyes and nodded, then turned and went through the door marked Private. He closed it behind him, meanwhile studying the man who had been sitting behind the desk and who had risen as he entered. A big man, broad shouldered, iron gray hair.

"Dr. Irving?"

"Yes, Mr. Vine. Will you be seated, please?"

He slid into the comfortable, padded armchair across the desk from the doctor.

"Mr. Vine," said the doctor, "a first interview of this sort is always a bit difficult. For the patient, I mean. Until you know me better, it will be difficult for you to overcome a certain reticence in discussing yourself. Would you prefer to talk, to tell me things your own way, or would you rather I asked questions?"

He thought that over. He'd had a story ready, but those few words with Charlie in the waiting room had changed everything.

He said, "Perhaps you'd better ask questions."

"Very well." There was a pencil in Dr. Irving's hand and paper on the desk before him. "Where and when were you born?"

He took a deep breath. "To the best of my knowledge, in Corsica on August 15th, 1769. I don't actually remember being born, of course. I do remember things from my boyhood on Corsica, though. We stayed there until I was ten, and after that I was sent to school at Brienne."

Instead of writing, the doctor was tapping the paper lightly with the tip of his pencil. He asked, "What month and year is this?"

"August, 1769. Yes, I know that should make me a hundred and seventy-some years old. You want to know how I account for that. I don't. Nor do I account for the fact that Napoleon Bonaparte died in 1821."

He leaned back in the chair and crossed his arms, staring up at the ceiling. "I don't attempt to account for the paradoxes or the discrepancies. I recognize them as such. But according to my own memory, and aside from logic pro or con, I was Napoleon for twenty-seven years. I won't recount what happened during that time; it's all down in the history books.

"But in 1796, after the battle of Lodi, while I was in charge of the armies in Italy, I went to sleep. As far as I knew, just as anyone goes to sleep anywhere, any time. But I woke up—with no sense whatever of duration by the way—in a hospital in town here, and I was informed that my name was George Vine, that the year was 1944, and that I was twenty-seven years old.

"The twenty-seven years old part checked, and that was all. Absolutely all. I have no recollections of any parts of George Vine's life, prior to his—my—waking up in the hospital after the accident. I know quite a bit about his early life now, but only because I've been told.

"I know when and where he was born, where he went to school, and when he started work at the *Blade*. I know when he enlisted in the army and when he was discharged—late in 1943—because he developed a trick knee after a leg injury. Not in combat, incidentally, and there wasn't any 'psycho-neurotic' on my—his—discharge."

The doctor quit doodling with the pencil. He asked, "You've felt this way for three years—and kept it a secret?"

"Yes. I had time to think things over after the accident, and yes, I decided then to accept what they told me about my identity. They'd have locked me up, of course. Incidentally, I've *tried* to figure out an answer. I've studied Dunne's theory of time—even Charles Fort!" He grinned suddenly. "Ever read about Casper Hauser?"

Dr. Irving nodded.

"Maybe he was playing smart the way I did. And I wonder how many other amnesiacs pretended they didn't know what happened prior to a certain date—rather than admit they had memories at obvious variance with the facts."

Dr. Irving said slowly, "Your cousin informs me that you were a bit—ah—'hepped' was his word—on the subject of Napoleon before your accident. How do you account for that?"

"I've told you I don't account for any of it. But I can verify the fact, aside from what Charlie Doerr says about it. Apparently I—the George Vine I, if I was ever George Vine—was quite interested in Napoleon, had read about him, made a hero of him, and had talked about him quite a bit. Enough so that the fellows he worked with at the *Blade* had nicknamed him 'Nappy.' "

"I notice you distinguish between yourself and George Vine. Are you or are you not he?"

"I have been for three years. Before that—I have no recollection of being George Vine. I don't think I was. I think—as nearly as I think anything—that *I,* three years ago, woke up in George Vine's body."

"Having done what for a hundred and seventy-some years?"

"I haven't the faintest idea. Incidentally, I don't doubt that this *is* George Vine's body, and with it I inherited his knowledge—except his personal memories. For example, I knew how to handle his job at the newspaper, although I didn't remember any of the people I worked with there. I have his knowledge of English, for instance, and his ability to write. I knew how to operate a typewriter. My handwriting is the same as his."

"If you think that you are not Vine, how do you account for that?"

He leaned forward. "I think part of me *is* George Vine, and part of me isn't. I think some transference has happened which is outside the run of ordinary human experience. That doesn't necessarily mean that it's supernatural—nor that I'm insane. *Does it?"*

Dr. Irving didn't answer. Instead, he asked, "You kept this secret for three years, for understandable reasons. Now, presumably for other reasons, you decide to tell. What are the other reasons? What has happened to change your attitude?"

It was the question that had been bothering him.

He said slowly, "Because I don't believe in coincidence. Because something in the situation itself has changed. Because I'm willing to risk imprisonment as a paranoiac to find out the truth."

"What in the situation has changed?"

"Yesterday it was suggested—by my employer—that I feign insanity for a practical reason. And the very kind of insanity which I have, if any. Surely, I will admit the possibility that I'm insane. But I can only operate on the theory that I'm not. You know that you're Dr. Willard E. Irving; you can only operate on that theory—but how do you *know* you are? Maybe you're insane, but you can only act as though you're not."

"You think your employer is part of a plot—ah—against you? You think there is a conspiracy to get you into a sanitarium?"

"I don't know. Here's what has happened to me since yesterday noon." He took a deep breath. Then he plunged. He told Dr. Irving the whole story of his interview with Candler, what Candler had said about Dr. Randolph, about his talk with Charlie Doerr last night and about Charlie's bewildering about-face in the waiting room.

When he was through he said, "That's all." He looked at Dr. Irving's expressionless face with more curiosity than concern, trying to read it. He added, quite casually, "You don't believe me, of course. You think I'm insane."

He met Irving's eyes squarely. He said, "You have no choice—unless you would choose to believe I'm telling you an elaborate set of lies to convince you I'm insane. I mean, as a scientist and as a psychiatrist, you cannot even admit the possibility that the things I believe—*know*— are objectively true. Am I not right?"

"I fear that you are. So?"

"So go ahead and sign your commitment. I'm going to follow this thing through. Even to the detail of having Dr. Ellsworth Joyce Randolph sign the second one."

"You make no objection?"

"Would it do any good if I did?"

"On one point, yes, Mr. Vine. If a patient has a prejudice against—or a delusion concerning—one psychiatrist, it is best not to have him under that particular psychiatrist's care. If you think Dr. Randolph is concerned in a plot against you, I would suggest that another one be named."

He said softly, "Even if I choose Randolph?"

Dr. Irving waved a deprecating hand, "Of course, if both you and Mr. Doerr prefer—"

"We prefer."

The iron gray head nodded gravely. "Of course you understand one thing; if Dr. Randolph and I decide you should go to the sanitarium, it will not be for custodial care. It will be for your recovery through treatment."

He nodded.

Dr. Irving stood. "You'll pardon me a moment? I'll phone Dr. Randolph."

He watched Dr. Irving go through a door to an inner room. He thought; there's a phone on his desk right there; but he doesn't want me to overhear the conversation.

He sat there very quietly until Irving came back and said, "Dr. Randolph is free. And I phoned for a cab to take us there. You'll pardon me again? I'd like to speak to your cousin, Mr. Doerr."

He sat there and didn't watch the doctor leave in the opposite direction for the waiting room. He could have gone to the door and tried to catch words in the low-voiced conversation, but he didn't. He just sat there until he heard the waiting room door open behind him and Charlie's voice said, "Come on, George. The cab will be waiting downstairs by now."

They went down in the elevator and the cab was there. Dr. Irving gave the address.

In the cab, about half way there, he said, "It's a beautiful day," and Charlie cleared his throat and said, "Yeah, it is." The rest of the way he didn't try it again and nobody said anything.

VI

He wore gray trousers and a gray shirt, open at the collar and with no necktie that he might decide to hang himself with. No belt, either, for the same reason, although the trousers buttoned so snugly around the waist that there was no danger of them falling off. Just as there was no danger of his falling out any of the windows; they were barred.

He was not in a cell, however; it was a large ward on the third floor. There were seven other men in the ward. His eyes ran over them. Two were playing checkers, sitting on the floor with a board on the floor between them. One sat in a chair, staring fixedly at nothing; two leaned against the bars of one of the open windows, looking out and talking casually and sanely. One read a magazine. One sat in a corner, playing smooth arpeggios on a piano that wasn't there at all.

He stood leaning against the wall, watching the other seven. He'd been here two hours now; it seemed like two years.

The interview with Dr. Ellsworth Joyce Randolph had gone smoothly; it had been practically a duplicate of his interview with Irving. And quite obviously, Dr. Randolph had never heard of him before.

He'd expected that, of course.

He felt very calm, now. For a while, he'd decided, he wasn't going to think, wasn't going to worry, wasn't even going to feel.

He strolled over and stood watching the checker game.

It was a sane checker game; the rules were being followed.

One of the men looked up and asked, "What's your name?" It was a perfectly sane question; the only thing wrong with it was that the same man had asked the same question four times now within the two hours he'd been here.

He said, "George Vine."

"Mine's Bassington, Ray Bassington. Call me Ray. Are you insane?"

"No."

"Some of us are and some of us aren't. He is." He looked at the man who was playing the imaginary piano. "Do you play checkers?"

"Not very well."

"Good. We eat pretty soon now. Anything you want to know, just ask me."

"How do you get out of here? Wait, I don't mean that for a gag, or anything. Seriously, what's the procedure?"

"You go in front of the board once a month. They ask you questions and decide if you go or stay. Sometimes they stick needles in you. What you down for?"

"Down for? What do you mean?"

"Feeble-minded, manic-depressive, dementia praecox, involutional melancholia—"

"Oh. Paranoia, I guess."

"That's bad. Then they stick needles in you."

A bell rang somewhere.

"That's dinner," said the other checker player. "Ever try to commit suicide? Or kill anyone?"

"No."

"They'll let you eat at an A table then, with knife and fork."

The door of the ward was being opened. It opened outward and a guard stood outside and said, "All right." They filed out, all except the man who was sitting in the chair staring into space.

"How about him?" he asked Ray Bassington.

"He'll miss a meal tonight. Manic-depressive, just going into the depressive stage. They let you miss one meal; if you're not able to go to the next they take you and feed you. You a manic-depressive?"

"No."

"You're lucky. It's hell when you're on the down-swing. Here, through this door."

It was a big room. Tables and benches were crowded with men in gray shirts and gray trousers, like his. A guard grabbed his arm as he went through the doorway and said, "There. That seat."

It was right beside the door. There was a tin plate, messy with food, and a spoon beside it. He asked, "Don't I get a knife and fork? I was told—"

The guard gave him a shove toward the seat. "Observation period, seven days. Nobody gets silverware till their observation period's over. Siddown."

He sat down. No one at his table had silverware. All the others were eating, several of them noisily and messily. He kept his eyes on his own plate, unappetizing as that was. He toyed with his spoon and managed to eat a few pieces of potato out of the stew and one or two of the chunks of meat that were mostly lean.

The coffee was in a tin cup and he wondered why until he realized how breakable an ordinary cup would be and how lethal could be one of the heavy mugs cheap restaurants use.

The coffee was weak and cool; he couldn't drink it.

He sat back and closed his eyes. When he opened them again there was an empty plate and an empty cup in front of him and the man at his left was eating very rapidly. It was the man who'd been playing the non-existent piano.

He thought, if I'm here long enough, I'll get hungry enough to eat that stuff. He didn't like the thought of being there that long.

After a while a bell rang and they got up, one table at a time on signals he didn't catch, and filed out. His group had come in last; it went out first.

Ray Bassington was behind him on the stairs. He said, "You'll get used to it. What'd you say your name is?"

What'd you say your name is?"

"George Vine."

Bassington laughed. The door shut on them and a key turned.

He saw it was dark outside. He went over to one of the windows and stared out through the bars. There was a single bright star that showed just above the top of the elm tree in the yard. *His* star? Well, he'd followed it here. A cloud drifted across it.

Someone was standing beside him. He turned his head and saw it was the man who'd been playing piano. He had a dark, foreign-looking face with intense black eyes; just then he was smiling, as though at a secret joke.

"You're new here, aren't you? Or just get put in this ward, which?"

"New. George Vine's the name."

"Baroni. Musician. Used to be, anyway. Now—let it go. Anything you want to know about the place?"

"Sure. How to get out of it."

Baroni laughed, without particular amusement but not bitterly either. "First, convince them you're all right again. Mind telling what's wrong with you—or don't you want to talk about it? Some of us mind, others don't."

He looked at Baroni, wondering which way he felt. Finally he said, "I guess I don't mind. I—think I'm Napoleon."

"Are you?"

"Am I what?"

"*Are* you Napoleon? If you aren't, that's one thing. Then maybe you'll get out of here in six months or so. If you really *are*—that's bad. You'll probably die here."

"Why? I mean, if I *am,* then I'm sane and—"

"Not the point. Point's whether they think you're sane or not. Way they figure, if you think you're Napoleon you're not sane. Q. E. D. You stay here."

"Even if I tell them I'm convinced I'm George Vine?"

"They've worked with paranoia before. And that's what they've got you down for, count on it. And any time a paranoiac gets tired of a place, he'll try to lie his way out of it. They weren't born yesterday. They know that."

"In general, yes, but how—"

A sudden cold chill went down his spine. He didn't have to finish the question. *They stick needles in you—* It hadn't meant anything when Ray Bassington had said it.

The dark man nodded. "Truth serum," he said. "When a paranoiac reaches the stage where he's cured *if* he's telling the truth, they make sure he's telling it before they let him go."

He thought what a beautiful trap it had been that he'd walked into. He'd probably die here, now.

He leaned his head against the cool iron bars and closed his eyes. He heard footsteps walking away from him and knew he was alone.

He opened his eyes and looked out into blackness; now the clouds had drifted across the moon, too.

Clare, he thought; *Clare.*

A trap.

But—if there was a trap, there must be a trapper.

He was sane or he was insane. If he was sane, he'd walked into a trap, and *if there was a trap, there must be a trapper,* or trappers.

If he was insane—

God, let it be that he *was* insane. That way everything made such sweetly simple sense, and someday he might be out of here, he might go back to working for the *Blade,* possibly even with a memory of all the years he'd worked there. Or that George Vine had worked there.

That was the catch. *He* wasn't George Vine.

And there was another catch. He *wasn't* insane.

The cool iron of the bars against his forehead.

After a while he heard the door open and looked around. Two guards had come in. A wild hope, reasonless, surged up inside him. It didn't last.

"Bedtime, you guys," said one of the guards. He looked at the manic-depressive sitting motionless on the chair and said, "Nuts. Hey, Bassington, help me get this guy in."

The other guard, a heavy-set man with hair close-cropped like a wrestler's, came over to the window.

"You. You're the new one in here. Vine, ain't it?"

He nodded.

"Want trouble, or going to be good?" Fingers of the guard's right hand clenched, the fist went back.

"Don't want trouble. Got enough."

The guard relaxed a little. "Okay, stick to that and you'll get along. Vacant bunk's in there." He pointed. "One on the right. Make it up yourself in the morning. Stay in the bunk and mind your own business. If there's any noise or trouble here in the ward, we come in and take care of it. Our own way. You wouldn't like it."

He didn't trust himself to speak, so he just nodded. He turned and went through the door of the cubicle to which the guard had pointed. There were two bunks in there; the manic-depressive who'd been on the chair was lying flat on his back on the other, staring blindly up at the ceiling through wide-open eyes. They'd pulled his shoes off, leaving him otherwise dressed.

He turned to his own bunk, knowing there was nothing on earth he could do for the other man, no way he could reach him through the impenetrable shell of blank misery which is the manic-depressive's intermittent companion.

He turned down a gray sheet-blanket on his own bunk and found under it another gray sheet-blanket atop a hard but smooth pad. He slipped off his shirt and trousers and hung them on a hook on the wall at the foot of his bed. He looked around for a switch to turn off the light overhead and couldn't find one. But, even as he looked, the light went out.

A single light still burned somewhere in the ward room outside, and by it he could see to take his shoes and socks off and get into the bunk.

He lay very quiet for a while, hearing only two sounds, both faint and seeming far away. Somewhere in another cubicle off the ward someone was singing quietly to himself, a wordless monody; somewhere else someone else was sobbing. In his own cubicle, he couldn't hear even the sound of breathing from his roommate.

Then there was a shuffle of bare feet and someone in the open doorway said, "George Vine."

He said, "Yes?"

"Shhhh, not so loud. This is Bassington. Want to tell you about that guard; I should have warned you before. Don't ever tangle with him."

"I didn't."

"I heard; you were smart. He'll slug you to pieces if you give him half a chance. He's a sadist. A lot of guards are; that's why they're bughousers; that's what they call themselves, bughousers. If they get fired one place for being too brutal they get on at another one. He'll be in again in the morning; I thought I'd warn you."

The shadow in the doorway was gone.

He lay there in the dimness, the almost-darkness, feeling rather than thinking. Wondering. Did mad people ever know that they were mad? Could they tell? Was every one of them sure, as he was sure—?

That quiet, still thing lying in the bunk near his, inarticulately suffering, withdrawn from human reach into a profound misery beyond the understanding of the sane—

"Napoleon Bonaparte!"

A clear voice, but had it been within his mind, or from without? He sat up on the bunk. His eyes pierced the dimness, could discern no form, no shadow, in the doorway.

He said, "Yes?"

VII

Only then, sitting up on the bunk and having answered "Yes," did he realize the name by which the voice had called him.

"Get up. Dress."

He swung his legs out over the edge of the bunk, stood up. He reached for his shirt and was slipping his arms into it before he stopped and asked, "Why?"

"To learn the truth."

"Who are you?" he asked.

"Do not speak aloud. I can hear you. I am within you and without. I have no name."

"Then *what* are you?" He said it aloud, without thinking.

"An instrument of The Brightly Shining."

He dropped the trousers he'd been holding. He sat down carefully on the edge of the bunk, leaned over and groped around for them.

His mind groped, too. Groped for he knew not what. Finally he found a question—*the* question. He didn't ask it aloud this time; he thought it, concentrated on it as he straightened out his trousers and thrust his legs in them.

"Am I mad?"

The answer —*No*— came clear and sharp as a spoken word, but had it been spoken? Or was it a sound that was only in his mind?

He found his shoes and pulled them on his feet. As he fumbled the laces into some sort of knots, he thought, "Who—what—is The Brightly Shining?"

"The Brightly Shining is *that which is Earth.* It is the intelligence of our planet. It is one of three intelligences in the solar system, one of many in the universe. Earth is one; it is called The Brightly Shining."

"I do not understand," he thought.

"You will. Are you ready?"

He finished the second knot. He stood up. The voice said, "Come. Walk silently."

It was as though he was being led through the almost darkness, although he felt no physical touch upon him; he saw no physical presence beside him. But he walked confidently, although quietly on tiptoe, knowing he would not walk into anything nor stumble. Through the big room that was the ward, and then his outstretched hand touched the knob of a door.

He turned it gently and the door opened inward. Light blinded him. The voice said, "Wait," and he stood immobile. He could hear sound—the rustle of paper, the turn of a page—outside the door, in the lighted corridor.

Then from across the hall came the sound of a shrill scream. A chair scraped and feet hit the floor of the corridor, walking away toward the sound of the scream. A door opened and closed.

The voice said, "Come," and he pulled the door open the rest of the way and went outside, past the desk and the empty chair that had been just outside the door of the ward.

Another door, another corridor. The voice said, "Wait," the voice said, "Come"; this time a guard slept. He tiptoed past. Down steps.

He thought the question, "Where am I going?"

"Mad," said the voice.

"But you said I wasn't—" He'd spoken aloud and the sound startled him almost more than had the answer to his last question. And in the silence that followed the words he'd spoken there came—from the bottom of the stairs and around the corner—the sound of a buzzing switchboard, and someone said, "Yes? ... Okay, Doctor, I'll be right up." Footsteps and the closing of an elevator door.

He went down the remaining stairs and around the corner and he was in the front main hall. There was an empty desk with a switchboard beside it. He walked past it and to the front door. It was bolted and he threw the heavy bolt.

He went outside, into the night.

He walked quietly across cement, across gravel; then his shoes were on grass and he didn't have to tiptoe any more. It was as dark now as the inside of an elephant; he felt the presence of trees nearby and leaves brushed his face occasionally, but he walked rapidly, confidently, and his hand went forward just in time to touch a brick wall.

He reached up and he could touch the top of it; he pulled himself up and over it. There was broken glass on the flat top of the wall; he cut his clothes and his flesh badly, but he felt no pain, only the wetness of blood and the stickiness of blood.

He walked along a lighted road, he walked along dark and empty streets, he walked down a darker alley. He opened the back gate of a yard and walked to the back door of a house. He opened the door and went in. There was a lighted room at the front of the house; he could see the rectangle of light at the end of a corridor. He went along the corridor and into the lighted room.

Someone who had been seated at a desk stood up. Someone, a man, whose face he knew but whom he could not —

"Yes," said the man, smiling, "you know me, but you do not know me. Your mind is under partial control and your ability to recognize me is blocked out. Other than that and your analgesia — you are covered with blood from the glass on the wall, but you don't feel any pain — your mind is normal and you are sane."

"What's it all about?" he asked. "Why was I brought here?"

"Because you are sane. I'm sorry about that, because you can't be. It is not so much that you retained memory of your previous life, after you'd been moved. That happens. It is that you somehow know something of what you shouldn't — something of The Brightly Shining, and of the Game between the red and the black. For that reason —"

"For that reason, what?" he asked.

The man he knew and did not know smiled gently. "For that reason you must know the rest, so that you will know nothing at all. For everything will add to nothing. The truth will drive you mad."

"That I do not believe."

"Of course you don't. If the truth were conceivable to you, it would not drive you mad. But you cannot remotely conceive the truth."

A powerful anger surged up within him. He stared at the familiar face that he knew and did not know, and he stared down at himself; at the torn and bloody gray uniform, at his torn and bloody hands. The hands hooked like claws with the desire to kill—someone, the someone, whoever it was, who stood before him.

He asked, "What are you?"

"I am an instrument of The Brightly Shining."

"The same which led me here, or another?"

"One is all, all is one. Within the whole and its parts, there is no difference. One instrument is another and the red is the black and the black is the white and there is no difference. The Brightly Shining is the soul of the Earth. I use *soul* as the nearest word in your vocabulary."

Hatred was almost a bright light. It was almost something that he could lean into, lean his weight against.

He asked, "What is The Brightly Shining?" He made the words a curse in his mouth.

"Knowing will make you mad. You want to know?"

"Yes." He made a curse out of that simple, sibilant syllable.

The lights were dimming. Or was it his eyes? The room was becoming dimmer, and at the same time receding. It was becoming a tiny cube of dim light, seen from afar and outside, from somewhere in the distant dark, ever receding, turning into a pin-point of light, and within that point of light ever the hated Thing, the man—or was it a man?—standing beside the desk.

Into darkness, into space, up and apart from the earth—a dim sphere in the night, a receding sphere outlined against the spangled blackness of eternal space, occulting the stars, a disk of black.

It stopped receding, and time stopped. It was as though the clock of the universe stood still. Beside him, out of the void, spoke the voice of the instrument of The Brightly Shining.

"Behold," it said. "The Being of Earth."

He beheld. Not as though an outward change was occurring, but an inward one, as though his senses were being changed to enable him to perceive something hitherto unseeable.

The ball that was Earth began to glow. Brightly to shine.

"You see the intelligence that rules Earth," said the voice. "The sum of the black and the white and the red, that are one, divided only as the lobes of a brain are divided, the trinity that is one."

The glowing ball and the stars behind it faded, and the darkness became deeper darkness and then there was dim light, growing brighter, and he was back in the room with the man standing at the desk.

"You saw," said the man whom he hated. "But you do not understand. You ask, *what* have you seen, *what* is The Brightly Shining? It is a group intelligence, the true intelligence of Earth, one intelligence among three in the Solar system, one among many in the universe.

"What, then, is man? Men are pawns, in games of—to you—unbelievable complexity, between the red and the black, the white and the black, for amusement. Played by one part of an organism against another part, to while away an instant of eternity. There are vaster games, played between galaxies. Not with man.

"Man is a parasite peculiar to Earth, which tolerates his presence for a little while. He exits nowhere else in the cosmos, and he does not exist here for long. A little while, a few chessboard wars, which he thinks he fights himself— You begin to understand."

The man at the desk smiled.

"You want to know of yourself. Nothing is less important. A move was made, before Lodi. The opportunity was there for a move of the red; a stronger, more ruthless personality was needed; it was a turning point in history—which means in the game. Do you understand now? A pinch hitter was put in to become Napoleon."

He managed two words. "And then?"

"The Brightly Shining does not kill. You had to be put somewhere, some time. Long later a man named George Vine was killed in an accident; his body was still usable. George Vine had not been insane, but he had had a Napoleonic complex. The transference was amusing."

"No doubt." Again it was impossible to reach the man at the desk. The hatred itself was a wall between them. "Then George Vine is dead?"

"Yes. And you, because you knew a little too much, must go mad so that you will know nothing. Knowing the truth will drive you mad."

"No!"

The instrument only smiled.

VIII

The room, the cube of light, dimmed; it seemed to tilt. Still standing, he was going over backward, his position becoming horizontal instead of vertical.

His weight was on his back and under him was the soft-hard smoothness of his bunk, the roughness of a gray sheet-blanket. And he could move; he sat up.

Had he been dreaming? Had he really been outside the asylum? He held up his hands, touched one to the other, and they were wet with something sticky. So was the front of his shirt and the thighs and knees of his trousers.

And his shoes were on.

The blood was there from climbing the wall. And now the analgesia was leaving, and pain was beginning to come into his hands, his chest, his stomach and his legs. Sharp biting pain.

He said aloud, *"I am not mad. I am not mad."* Was he screaming it?

A voice said, "No. Not yet." Was it the voice that had been here in the room before? Or was it the voice of the man who had stood in the lighted room? Or had both been the same voice?

It said, "Ask, 'What is man?' "

Mechanically, he asked it.

"Man is a blind alley in evolution, who came too late to compete, who has always been controlled and played with by The Brightly Shining, which was old and wise before man walked erect.

"Man is a parasite upon a planet populated before he came, populated by a Being that is one and many, a billion cells but a single mind, a single intelligence, a single will—as is true of every other populated planet in the universe.

"Man is a joke, a clown, a parasite. He is nothing; he will be less."

"Come and go mad."

He was getting out of bed again; he was walking. Through the doorway of the cubicle, along the ward. To the door that led to the corridor; a thin crack of light showed under it. But this time his hand did not reach out for the knob. Instead he stood there facing the door, and it began to glow; slowly it became light and visible.

As though from somewhere an invisible spotlight played upon it, the door became a visible rectangle in the surrounding blackness; as brightly visible as the crack under it.

The voice said, "You see before you a cell of your ruler, a cell unintelligent in itself, yet a tiny part of a unit which is intelligent, one of a trillion units which make up *the* intelligence which rules the earth—and you. And which earth-wide intelligence is one of a million intelligences which rule the universe."

"The *door?* I don't—"

The voice spoke no more; it had withdrawn, but somehow inside his mind was the echo of silent laughter.

He leaned closer and saw what he was meant to see. An ant was crawling up the door.

His eyes followed it, and numbing horror crawled apace, up his spine. A hundred things that had been told and shown him suddenly fitted into a pattern, a pattern of sheer horror. The black, the white, the red; the black ants, the white ants, the red ants; the players with men, separate lobes of a single group brain, the intelligence that was one. Man an accident, a parasite, a pawn; a million planets in the universe inhabited each by an insect race that was a single intelligence for the planet—and all the intelligences together were the single cosmic intelligence that was—*God!*

The one-syllable word wouldn't come.

He went mad, instead.

He beat upon the now-dark door with his bloody hands, with his knees, his face, with himself, although already he had forgotten why, had forgotten what he wanted to crush.

He was raving mad—dementia praecox, not paranoia—when they released his body by putting it into a straitjacket, released it from frenzy to quietude.

He was quietly mad—paranoia, not dementia praecox—when they released him as sane eleven months later.

Paranoia, you see, is a peculiar affliction; it has no physical symptoms, it is merely the presence of a fixed delusion. A series of metrazol shocks had cleared up the dementia praecox and left only the fixed delusion that he was George Vine, a reporter.

The asylum authorities thought he was, too, so the delusion was not recognized as such and they released him and gave him a certificate to prove he was sane.

He married Clare; he still works at the *Blade*—for a man named Candler. He still plays chess with his cousin, Charlie Doerr. He still sees—for periodic checkups—both Dr. Irving and Dr. Randolph.

Which of them smiles inwardly? What good would it do you to know?

It doesn't matter. Don't you understand? Nothing matters!

There Shall Be No Darkness

James Blish

It was about 10:00 P.M. when Paul Foote decided that there was a monster at Newcliffe's houseparty.

Foote was tight at the time—tighter than he liked to be ever. He sprawled in a too-easy chair in the front room on the end of his spine, his arms resting on the high arms of the chair. A half-empty glass depended laxly from his right hand. A darker spot on one gray trouser-leg showed where some of the drink had gone. Through half-shut eyes he watched Jarmoskowski at the piano.

The pianist was playing, finally, the Scriabin sonata for which the rest of the gathering had been waiting but for Foote, who was a painter with a tin ear, it wasn't music at all. It was a cantrap, whose implications were secret and horrible.

The room was stuffy and was only half as large as it had been during the afternoon and Foote was afraid that he was the only living man in it except for Jan Jarmoskowski. The rest were wax figures, pretending to be humans in an aesthetic trance.

Of Jarmoskowski's vitality there could be no question. He was not handsome but there was in him a pure brute force that had its own beauty—that and the beauty of precision with which the force was

227

controlled. When his big hairy hands came down it seemed that the piano should fall into flinders. But the impact of fingers on keys was calculated to the single dyne.

It was odd to see such delicacy behind such a face. Jarmoskowski's hair grew too low on his rounded head despite the fact that he had avoided carefully any suggestion of Musician's Haircut. His brows were straight, rectangular, so shaggy that they seemed to meet.

From where Foote sat he noticed for the first time the odd way the Pole's ears were placed—tilted forward as if in animal attention, so that the vestigial "point" really was in the uppermost position.

They were cocked directly toward the keyboard, reminding Foote irresistibly of the dog on the His Master's Voice trade-mark.

Where had he seen that head before? In Matthias Grünewald, perhaps—in that panel on the Isenheim Altar that showed the Temptation of St. Anthony. Or was it one of the illustrations in the *Red Grimoire,* those odd old woodcuts that Chris Lundgren called "Rorschach tests of the mediaeval mind"?

Jarmoskowski finished the Scriabin, paused, touched his hands together reflectively, began a work of his own, the *Galliard Fantasque.*

The wax figures did not stir, but a soft eerie sigh of recognition came from their frozen lips. There was another person in the room but Foote could not tell who it was. When he turned his unfocused eyes to count, his mind went back on him and he never managed to reach a total. But somehow there was the impression of another presence that had not been of the party before.

Jarmoskowski was not the presence. He had been there before. But he had something to do with it. There was an eighth presence now and it had something to do with Jarmoskowski.

What was it?

For it was there—there was no doubt about that. The energy which the rest of Foote's senses ordinarily would have consumed was flowing into his instincts now because his senses were numbed. Acutely, poignantly, his instincts told him of the Monster. It hovered around the piano, sat next to Jarmoskowski as he caressed the musical beast's teeth, blended with the long body and the serpentine fingers.

Foote had never had the horrors from drinking before and he knew he did not have them now. A part of his mind which was not drunk had recognized real horror somewhere in this room. And the whole of his mind, its skeptical barriers down, believed and trembled within itself.

The batlike circling of the frantic notes was stilled abruptly. Foote blinked, startled. "Already?" he said stupidly.

"Already?" Jarmoskowski echoed. "But that's a long piece, Paul. Your fascination speaks well for my writing."

His eyes flashed redly as he looked directly at the painter. Foote tried frantically to remember whether or not his eyes had been red during the afternoon. Or whether it was possible for any man's eyes to be as red at any time as this man's were now.

"The writing?" he said, condensing the far-flung diffusion of his brain. Newcliffe's highballs were damn strong. "Hardly the writing, Jan. Such fingers as those could put fascination into *Three Blind Mice.*"

He laughed inside at the parade of emotions which marched across Jarmoskowski's face. Startlement at a compliment from Foote—for there had been an inexplicable antagonism between the two since the pianist had first arrived—then puzzled reflection—then finally veiled anger as the hidden slur bared its fangs in his mind. Nevertheless the man could laugh at it.

"They are long, aren't they?" he said to the rest of the group, unrolling them like the party noisemakers which turn from snail to snake when blown through. "But it's a mistake to suppose that they assist my playing, I assure you. Mostly they stumble over each other. Especially over this one."

He held up his hands for inspection. Suddenly Foote was trembling. On both hands, the index fingers and the middle fingers were exactly the same length.

"I suppose Lundgren would call me a mutation. It's a nuisance at the piano."

Doris Gilmore, once a student of Jarmoskowski in Prague, and still obviously, painfully, in love with him, shook coppery hair back from her shoulders and held up her own hands.

"My fingers are so stubby," she said ruefully. "Hardly pianist's hands at all."

"The hands of a master pianist," Jarmoskowski said. He smiled, scratching his palms abstractedly, and Foote found himself in a universe of brilliant perfectly-even teeth. No, not perfectly even. The polished rows were bounded almost mathematically by slightly longer cuspids. They reminded him of that idiotic Poe story—was it *Berenice*? Obviously Jarmoskowski would not die a natural death. He would be killed by a dentist for possession of those teeth.

"Three fourths of the greatest pianists I know have hands like truck drivers," Jarmoskowski was saying. "Surgeons too, as Lundgren will tell you. Long fingers tend to be clumsy."

"You seem to manage to make tremendous music, all the same," Newcliffe said, getting up.

"Thank you, Tom." Jarmoskowski seemed to take his host's rising as a signal that he was not going to be required to play any more. He lifted his feet from the pedals and swung them around to the end of the bench. Several of the others rose also. Foote struggled up to numb feet from the infernal depths of the armchair. He set his glass cautiously on the side-table and picked his way over to Christian Lundgren.

"I read your paper, the one you read to the Stockholm Congress," he said, controlling his tongue with difficulty. "Jarmoskowski's hands are—"

"Yes," the psychiatrist said, looking at Foote with sharp, troubled eyes. Suddenly Foote was aware of Lundgren's chain of thought. The gray, chubby little man was assessing his drunkenness, and wondering whether or not Foote would have forgotten the whole business in the morning.

Lundgren made a gesture of dismissal. "I saw them," he said, his tone flat. "A mutation probably, as he himself suggests. This is the twentieth century. I'm going to bed and forget it. Which you may take for advice as well as information."

He stalked out of the room, leaving Foote standing alone, wondering whether to be reassured or more alarmed than before. Lundgren should know. Still, if Jarmoskowski was what he seemed—

The party appeared to be surviving quite nicely without Foote. Conversations were starting up about the big room. Jarmoskowski and Doris shared the piano bench and were talking in low tones, punctuated now and then by brilliant arpeggios as the Pole showed her easier ways of handling the work she had played before dinner.

James and Bennington, the American critic, were dissecting James' most recent novel for a fascinated Newcliffe. Blandly innocent Caroline Newcliffe was talking to the air about nothing at all. Nobody missed Lundgren and it seemed unlikely that Foote would be missed.

He walked with wobbly nonchalance into the dining room, where the butler was still clearing the table.

" 'Scuse me," he said. "Little experiment. Return in the morning." He snatched a knife from the table, looked for the door which led from the dining room into the foyer, propelled himself through it. The hallway was dim but intelligible.

As he closed the door to his room he paused for a moment to listen to Jarmoskowski's technical exhibition on the keys. It might be that at midnight Jarmoskowski would give another sort of exhibition. If he did Foote would be glad to have the knife. He shrugged uneasily, closed the door all the way and walked over to his bedroom window.

At 11:30, Jarmoskowski stood alone on the terrace of Newcliffe's country house. Although there was no wind the night was frozen with a piercing cold—but he did not seem to notice it. He stood motionless, like a black statue, with only the long streamers of his breathing, like twin jets of steam from the nostrils of a dragon, to show that he was alive.

Through the haze of lace that curtained Foote's window Jarmoskowski was an heroic pillar of black stone—but a pillar above a fumarole.

The front of the house was entirely dark and the moonlight gleamed dully on the snow. In the dim light the heavy tower which was the central structure was like some ancient donjon-keep. Thin slits of embrasures watched the landscape with a dark vacuity and each of the crowning merlons wore a helmet of snow.

The house huddled against the malice of the white night. A sense of age invested it. The curtains smelt of dust and antiquity. It seemed impossible that anyone but Foote and Jarmoskowski could be alive in it. After a long moment Foote moved the curtain very slightly and drew it back.

His face was drenched in moonlight and he drew back into the dark again, leaving the curtains parted.

If Jarmoskowski saw the furtive motion he gave no sign. He remained engrossed in the acerb beauty of the night. Almost the whole of Newcliffe's estate was visible from where he stood. Even the black border of the forest, beyond the golf course to the right, could be seen through the dry frigid air. A few isolated trees stood nearer the house, casting grotesque shadows on the snow, shadows that flowed and changed shape with infinite slowness as the moon moved.

Jarmoskowski sighed and scratched his left palm. His lips moved soundlessly.

A wandering cloud floated idly toward the moon, its shadow preceding it, gliding in a rush of darkness toward the house. The gentle ripples of the snowbanks contorted in the vast umbra, assumed demon shapes, twisted bodies half-rising from the earth, sinking back, rising again, whirling closer. A damp frigid wind rose briefly, whipping crystalline showers of snow from the terrace flagstones.

The wind died as the shadow engulfed the house. For a long instant the darkness and silence persisted. Then, from somewhere among the stables behind the house, a dog raised his voice in a faint sustained throbbing howl. Others joined him.

Jarmoskowski's teeth gleamed dimly in the occluded moonlight. He stood a moment longer—then his head turned with startling quickness and his eyes flashed a feral scarlet at the dark window where Foote hovered. Foote released the curtains hastily. Even through them he could see the pianist's grim phosphorescent smile. Jarmoskowski went back into the house.

There was a single small light burning in the corridor. Jarmoskowski's room was at the end of the hall next to Foote's. As he walked reflectively toward it the door of the room across from Foote's swung open and Doris Gilmore came out, clad in a housecoat, a towel over her arm and a toothbrush in her hand.

"Oh!" she said. Jarmoskowski turned toward her. Foote slipped behind his back and into Jarmoskowski's room. He did not propose to have Doris a witness to the thing he expected from Jarmoskowski.

In a quieter voice Doris said, "Oh, it's you, Jan. You startled me."

"So I see," Jarmoskowski's voice said. Foote canted one eye around the edge of the door. "It appears that we are the night-owls of the party."

"The rest are tight. Especially that horrible painter. I've been reading the magazines Tom left by my bed and I finally decided to go to sleep too. What have you been doing?"

"Oh, I was just out on the terrace, getting a breath of air. I like the winter night—it bites."

"The dogs are restless, too," she said. "Did you hear them?"

"Yes," Jarmoskowski said and smiled. "Why does a full moon make a dog feel so sorry for himself?"

"Maybe there's a banshee about."

"I doubt it," Jarmoskowski said. "This house isn't old enough to have any family psychopomps. As far as I know none of Tom's or Caroline's relatives have had the privilege of dying in it."

"You talk as if you almost believed it." There was a shiver in her voice. She wrapped the housecoat more tightly about her slim waist.

"I come from a country where belief in such things is common. In Poland most of the skeptics are imported."

"I wish you'd pretend to be an exception," she said. "You give me the creeps."

He nodded seriously. They looked at each other. Then he stepped forward and took her hands in his.

Foote felt a belated flicker of embarrassment. If he were wrong he'd speedily find himself in a position for which no apology would be possible.

The girl was looking up at Jarmoskowski, smiling uncertainly. "Jan," she said.

"No," Jarmoskowski said. "Wait. It has been a long time since Prague."

"I see," she said. She tried to release her hands.

Jarmoskowski said sharply, "You don't see. I was eighteen then. You were—what was it?—eleven, I think. In those days I was proud of your schoolgirl crush but of course infinitely too old for you; I am not so old any more and you are so lovely—no, no, hear me out, please! Doris, I love you now, as I can see you love me, but—"

In the brief pause Foote could hear the sharp indrawn breaths that Doris

Gilmore was trying to control. He writhed with shame for himself. He had no business being—

"But we must wait, Doris—until I warn you of something neither of us could have dreamed in the old days."

"Warn me?"

"Yes," Jarmoskowski paused again. Then he said, "You will find it hard to believe. But if you do we may yet be happy. Doris, I cannot be a skeptic. I am—"

He stopped. He had looked down abstractedly at her hands as if searching for precisely the right words. Then, slowly, he turned her hands over until they rested palms up upon his. An expression of inexpressible shock crossed his face and Foote saw his grip tighten spasmodically.

In that silent moment, Foote knew that he had been right about Jarmoskowski and despite his pleasure he was frightened.

For an instant Jarmoskowski shut his eyes. The muscles along his jaw stood out with the violence with which he was clenching his teeth. Then, deliberately, he folded Doris' hands together and his curious fingers made a fist about them. When his eyes opened again they were red as flame in the weak light.

Doris jerked her hands free and crossed them over her breasts. "Jan— what is it? What's the matter?"

His face, that should have been flying into flinders under the force of the thing behind it, came under control muscle by muscle.

"Nothing," he said. "There's really no point in what I was going to say. Nice to have seen you again, Doris. Good night."

He brushed past her, walked the rest of the way down the corridor, wrenched back the doorknob of his own room. Foote barely managed to get out of his way.

Behind the house a dog howled and was silent again.

II

In Jarmoskowski's room the moonlight played in through the open window upon a carefully turned-down bed and the cold air had penetrated every cranny. He shut the door and went directly across the room to the table beside his bed. As he crossed the path of silvery light his shadow was oddly foreshortened, so that it looked as if it were walking on all fours. There was a lamp on the side table and he reached for it.

Then he stopped dead still, his hand halfway to the switch. He seemed to be listening. Finally, he turned and looked back across the room, directly at the spot behind the door where Foote was standing.

It was the blackest spot of all, for it had its back to the moon. But Jarmoskowski said immediately, "Hello, Paul. Aren't you up rather late?"

Foote did not reply for a while. His senses were still a little alcohol-numbed and he was overwhelmed by the thing he knew to be. He stood silently in the darkness, watching the Pole's barely visible figure beside the fresh bed, and the sound of his own breathing was loud in his ears. The broad flat streamer of moonlight lay between them like a metallic river.

"I'm going to bed shortly," he said at last. His voice sounded flat and dead and faraway, as if belonging to someone else entirely. "I just came to issue a little warning."

"Well, well," said Jarmoskowski pleasantly. "Warnings seem to be all the vogue this evening. Do you customarily pay your social calls with a knife in your hand?"

"That's the warning, Jarmoskowski. The knife is a—*silver* knife."

"You must be drunker than ever," said the pianist. "Why don't you just go to bed? We can talk about it in the morning."

"Don't give me that," Foote snapped savagely. "You can't fool me. I know you for what you are."

"All right. I'll bite, as Bennington would say."

"Yes, you'd bite," Foote said and his voice shook a little despite himself. "Shall I give it a name, Jarmoskowski? In Poland they called you *Vrolok*, didn't they? And in France it was *loup-garou*. In the Carpathians it was *stregoica* or *strega* or *Vlkoslak*."

"Your command of languages is greater than your common sense. But you interest me strangely. Isn't it a little out of season for such things? The aconites do not bloom in the dead of winter. And perhaps the thing you call so many fluent names is also out of the season in nineteen sixty-two."

"The dogs hate you," Foote said softly. "That was a fine display Brucey put on when Tom brought him in from his run and he found you here. Walked sidewise through the room, growling, watching you with every step until Tom dragged him out. He's howling now. And that shock you got from the table silver at dinner—I heard your excuse about rubber-soled shoes.

"I looked under the table, if you recall, and your shoes turned out to be leather-soled. But was a pretty feeble excuse anyhow, for anybody knows that you can't get an electric shock from an ungrounded piece of tableware, no matter how long you've been scuffing rubber. It was the silver that hurt you the first time you touched it. Silver's deadly, isn't it?

"And those fingers—the index fingers as long as the middle ones—you *were* clever about those. You were careful to call everybody's attention to them. It's supposed to be the obvious that everybody misses. But Jarmoskowski, that 'Purloined Letter' gag has been worked too often in detective stories. It didn't fool Lundgren and it didn't fool me."

"Ah," Jarmoskowski said. "Quite a catalogue."

"There's more. How does it happen that your eyes were gray all afternoon and turned red as soon as the moon rose? And the palms of your hands—there was some hair growing there, but you shaved it off, didn't you, Jarmoskowski? I've been watching you scratch them. Everything about you, the way you look, the way you act—everything you say screams your nature in a dozen languages to anyone who knows the signs."

After a long silence Jarmoskowski said, "I see. You've been most attentive, Paul—I see you are what people call the suspicious drunk. But I appreciate your warning, Paul. Let us suppose that what you say of me is true. Have you thought that, knowing that you know, I would have no choice any more? That the first word you said to me about it all might brand *your* palm with the pentagram?"

Foote had not thought about it. He had spent too much time trying to convince himself that it was all a pipe dream. A shock of blinding terror convulsed him. The silver knife clattered to the floor. He snatched up his hands and stared frantically at them, straining his eyes through the blackness. The full horror implicit in Jarmoskowski's suggestion struck him all at once with paralyzing force.

From the other side of his moonlit room, Jarmoskowski's voice came mockingly. "So—you hadn't thought. *Better never* than late, Paul!"

The dim figure of Jarmoskowski began to writhe and ripple in the reflected moonlight. It foreshortened, twisting obscenely, sinking toward the floor, flesh and clothing alike *changing* into something not yet describable.

A cry ripped from Foote's throat and he willed his legs to move with frantic, nightmarish urgency. His clutching hand grasped the doorknob. Tearing his eyes from the hypnotic fascination of the thing that was going on across from him he leaped from his corner and out into the corridor.

A bare second after he had slammed the door, something struck it a frightful blow from the inside. The paneling split. He held it shut with all the strength in his body.

A dim white shape drifted down upon him through the dark corridor and a fresh spasm of fear sent rivers of sweat down on his back, his sides, into his eyes. But it was only the girl.

"Paul! What on earth! What's the *matter!*"

"Quick!" he choked out. "Get something silver—something heavy made out of silver—quick, *quick!*"

Despite her astonishment the frantic urgency in his voice was enough. She darted back into her room.

To Foote it seemed eternity before she returned—an eternity while he listened with abnormally sensitized ears for a sound inside the room. Once he thought he heard a low growl but he was not sure. The sealike hissing and sighing of his blood, rushing through the channels of the inner ear, seemed very loud to him. He couldn't imagine why it was not arousing the whole countryside. He clung to the doorknob and panted.

Then the girl was back, bearing a silver candlestick nearly three feet in length—a weapon that was almost too good, for his fright-weakened muscles had some difficulty in lifting it. He shifted his grip on the knob to his left hand, hefted the candlestick awkwardly.

"All right," he said, in what he hoped was a grim voice. "Now let him come."

"What in heaven's name is this all about?" Doris said. "You're waking everybody in the house with this racket. Look—even one of the dogs is in to see—"

"The dog!"

He swung around, releasing the doorknob. Not ten paces from them, an enormous coal-black animal, nearly five feet in length, grinned at them with polished fangs. As soon as it saw Foote move it snarled. Its eyes gleamed red in the single bulb.

It sprang.

Foote lifted the candlestick high and brought it down—but the animal was not there. Somehow the leap was never completed. There was a brief flash of movement at the open end of the corridor, then darkness and silence.

"He saw the candlestick," Foote panted. "Must have jumped out the window and come around through the front door. Saw the silver and beat it."

"Paul!" Doris cried. "What—how did you know that thing would jump? It was so big! Silver—"

He chuckled, surprising even himself. He had a mental picture of what the truth would sound like to Doris. "That," he said, "was a wolf and a whopping one. Even the usual kind of wolf isn't very friendly and—"

Footsteps sounded on the floor above and the voice of Newcliffe, grumbling loudly, came down the stairs. Newcliffe liked his evenings noisy and his nights quiet. The whole house seemed to have heard the commotion, for in a moment a number of half-clad figures were elbowing out into the corridor, wanting to know what was up.

Abruptly the lights went on, revealing blinking faces and pajama-clad forms struggling into robes. Newcliffe came down the stairs. Caroline was with him, impeccable even in disarray, her face openly and honestly ignorant and unashamedly beautiful. She made an excellent foil for Tom. She was no lion-hunter but she loved parties. Evidently she was pleased that the party was starting again.

"What's all this?" Newcliffe demanded in a gravelly voice. "Foote, are you the center of this whirlpool? Why all the noise?"

"Werewolf," said Foote, suddenly very conscious of how meaningless the word would be here. "We've got a werewolf here. And somebody's marked out for him."

How else could you put it? Let it stand.

There was a chorus of "What's" as the group jostled about him. "Eh? What was that? ... Werewolf, I thought he said ... What's this all about? ... Somebody's been a wolf ... Is that new? What an uproar!"

"Paul," Lundgren's voice cut through. "Details, please."

"Jarmoskowski's a werewolf," Foote said grimly,. making his tone as emotionless and factual as he could. "I suspected it earlier tonight and went into his room and accused him of it. He changed shape, right on the spot while I was watching."

The sweat started out afresh at the recollection of that horrible, half-seen mutation. "He came around into the hall and went for us and I scared him off with a silver candlestick for a club." He realized suddenly that he still held the candlestick, brandished it as proof. "Doris saw the wolf— she'll vouch for that."

"I saw a big doglike thing, all right," Doris admitted. "And it did jump at us. It was black and had huge teeth. But—Paul, was that supposed to be Jan? Why, that's ridiculous!"

"It certainly is," Newcliffe said feelingly. "Getting us all up for a practical joke. Probably one of the dogs is loose."

"Do you have any coal-black dogs five feet long?" Foote demanded desperately. "And where's Jarmoskowski now. Why isn't he here? Answer me that!"

Bennington gave a skeptical grunt from the background and opened Jarmoskowski's door. The party tried to jam itself into the room. Foote forced his way through the jam.

"See? He isn't here, either. And the bed's not been slept in. Doris, you saw him go in there. Did you see him come out?"

The girl looked startled. "No, but I was in my room—"

"All right. Here. Look at this." Foote led the way over to the window and pointed. "See? The prints on the snow?"

One by one the others leaned out. There was no arguing it. A set of animal prints, like large dogtracks, led away from a spot just beneath Jarmoskowski's window—a spot where the disturbed snow indicated the landing of some heavy body.

"Follow them around," Foote said. "They lead around to the front door, and in."

"Have you traced them?" James asked.

"I don't have to. I saw the thing, James."

"Maybe he just went for a walk," Caroline suggested.

"Barefoot? There are his shoes."

Bennington vaulted over the windowsill with an agility astonishing for so round a man and plowed away with slippered feet along the line of tracks. A little while later he entered the room behind their backs.

"Paul's right," he said, above the hub-bub of excited conversation. "The tracks go around to the front door, then come out again and go away around the side of the house toward the golf course." He rolled up his wet pajama-cuffs awkwardly.

"This is crazy," Newcliffe declared angrily. "This is the twentieth century. We're like a lot of little children, panicked by darkness. There's no such thing as a werewolf!"

"I wouldn't place any wagers on that," James said. "Millions of people have thought so for hundreds of years. That's a lot of people."

Newcliffe turned sharply to Lundgren. "Chris, I can depend upon you at least to have your wits about you."

The psychiatrist smiled wanly. "You didn't read my Stockholm paper, did you, Tom? I mean my paper on mental diseases. Most of it dealt with lycanthropy—werewolfism."

"You mean—you believe this idiot story?"

"I spotted Jarmoskowski early in the evening," Lundgren said. "He must have shaved the hair on his palms but he has all the other signs—eyes bloodshot with moonrise, first and second fingers of equal length, pointed ears, domed prefrontal bones, elongated upper cuspids or fangs—in short, the typical hyperpineal type—a lycanthrope."

"Why didn't you say something?"

"I have a natural horror of being laughed at," Lundgren said drily.

"And *I didn't want to draw Jarmoskowski's attention to me.* These endocrine-imbalance cases have a way of making enemies very easily."

Foote grinned ruefully. If he had thought of that part of it before accusing Jarmoskowski he would have kept his big mouth shut.

"Lycanthropy is quite common," Lundgren droned, "but seldom mentioned. It is the little-known aberration of a little-known ductless gland. It appears to enable the victim to control his body."

"I'm still leery of this whole business," Bennington growled, from somewhere deep in his pigeon's chest. "I've known Jan for years. Nice fella—did a lot for me once. And I think there's enough discord in this house so that I won't add to it much if I say I wouldn't trust Paul Foote as far as I could throw him. By heaven, Paul, if this does turn out to be some practical joke of yours—"

"Ask Lundgren," Foote said.

There was dead silence, broken only by heavy breathing. Lundgren was known to every one of them as the world's ultimate authority on hormone-created insanity. Nobody seemed to want to ask him.

"Paul's right," Lundgren said at last. "Take it or leave it. Jarmoskowski is a lycanthrope. A hyperpineal. No other gland could affect the blood-vessels of the eyes like that or make such a reorganization of the cells possible. Jarmoskowski is inarguably a werewolf."

Bennington sagged, the light of righteous incredulity dying from his eyes. "I'll be damned!" he muttered.

"We've got to get him tonight," Foote said. "He's seen the pentagram on somebody's palm—somebody in the party."

"What's that?" asked James.

"Common illusion of lycanthropic seizures," Lundgren said. "Hallucination, I should say. A five-pointed star inscribed in a circle—you find it in all the old mystical books, right back to the so-called fourth and fifth Books of Moses. The werewolf sees it on the palm of his next victim."

There was a gasping little scream from Doris. "So that's it!" she cried. "Dear God, I'm the one! He saw something on my hand tonight while we were talking in the hall. He was awfully startled and went away without another word. He said he was going to warn me about something and then he—"

"Steady," Bennington said in a soft voice that had all the penetrating power of a thunderclap. "There's safety in numbers. We're all here." Nevertheless, he could not keep himself from glancing surreptitiously over his shoulder.

"Well, that settles it," James said in earnest squeaky tones. "We've got to trail the—the beast and kill him. It should be easy to follow his trail in the snow. We must kill him before he kills Doris or somebody else. Even if he misses us it would be just as bad to have him roaming the countryside."

"What are you going to kill him with?" asked Lundgren matter-of-factly.

"Eh?"

"I said, what are you going to kill him with? With that pineal hormone in his blood he can laugh at any ordinary bullet. And since there are no chapels dedicated to St. Hubert around here you can't scare him to death with a church-blessed bullet."

"Silver will do," Foote said.

"Yes, silver will do. It poisons the pinearin-catalysis. But are you going out to hunt a full-grown wolf, a giant wolf, armed with table silver and candlesticks? Or is somebody here metallurgist enough to cast a decent silver bullet?"

Foote sighed. With the burden of proof lifted from him, completely sobered up by shock, he felt a little more like his old self, despite the pall of horror which hung over them.

"Like I always tell my friends," he said, "there's never a dull moment at a Newcliffe houseparty."

III

The clock struck one-thirty. Foote picked up one of Newcliffe's rifles and hefted it. It felt—useless. He said, "How are you coming?"

The group by the kitchen stove shook their heads in comical unison. One of the gas burners had been jury-rigged as a giant Bunsen burner and they were trying to melt down some soft unalloyed silver articles, mostly of Mexican manufacture.

They were using a small earthenware bowl, also Mexican, for a crucible. It was lidded with the bottom of a flower pot, the hole in which had been plugged with a mixture of garden clay and rock wool yanked forcibly out of the insulation in the attic. The awkward flame leapt uncertainly and sent fantastic shadows flickering over their intent faces.

"We've got it melted, all right," Bennington said, lifting the lid cautiously with a pair of kitchen tongs and peering in. "But what do we do now? Drop it from the top of the tower?"

"You can't kill a wolf with buckshot," Newcliffe pointed out. Now that the problem had been reduced temporarily from a hypernatural one to ordinary hunting he was in his element. "And I haven't got a decent shotgun here anyhow. But we ought to be able to whack together a mold. The bullet should be soft enough so that it won't ruin the rifling of my guns."

He opened the door to the cellar stairs and disappeared, carrying several ordinary cartridges in one hand. Faintly the dogs renewed their howling and Doris began to tremble. Foote put his arm around her.

"It's all right," he said. "We'll get him. You're safe enough."

She swallowed. "I know," she agreed in a small voice. "But every time I think of the way he looked at my hands and how red his eyes were— You don't suppose he's prowling around the house? That that's what the dogs are howling about?"

"I don't know," Foote said carefully. "But dogs are funny that way. They can sense things at great distances. I suppose a man with pinearin in his blood would have a strong odor to them. But he probably knows that we're after his scalp, so he won't be hanging around if he's smart."

She managed a tremulous smile. "All right," she said. "I'll try not to be frightened." He gave her an awkward reassuring pat, feeling a little absurd.

"Do you suppose we can use the dogs?" James wanted to know.

"Certainly," said Lundgren. "Dogs have always been our greatest allies against the abnormal. You saw what a rage Jarmoskowski's very presence put Brucey in this afternoon. He must have smelled the incipient seizure. Ah, Tom—what did you manage?"

Newcliffe set a wooden box on the table. "I pried the slug out of one shell for each gun," he said, "and made impressions in clay. The cold has made the stuff pretty hard, so it's a passable mold. Bring the silver over here."

Bennington lifted his improvised crucible from the burner, which immediately shot up a tall blue flame. James carefully turned it off.

"All right, pour," Newcliffe said. "Lundgren, you don't suppose it might help to chant a blessing or something?"

"Not unless Jarmoskowski overheard it—probably not even then since we haven't a priest among us."

"Okay. Pour, Bennington, before the goo hardens."

Bennington decanted sluggishly molten silver into each depression in the clay and Newcliffe cleaned away the oozy residue from the casts before it had time to thicken. At any other time the whole scene would have been funny—now it was grimly grotesque. Newcliffe picked up the box and carried it back down to the cellar, where the emasculated cartridges awaited their new slugs.

"Who's going to carry these things, now?" Foote asked. "There are five rifles. James, how about you?"

"I couldn't hit an elephant's rump at three paces. Tom's an expert shot. So is Bennington here, with a shotgun anyhow."

"I can use a rifle," Bennington said diffidently.

"I've done some shooting," Foote said. "During the Battle of the Bulge I even hit something."

"I," Lundgren said, "am an honorary member of the Swiss Militia."

Nobody laughed. Most of them were aware that Lundgren in his own obscure way was bragging, that he had something to brag about. Newcliffe appeared abruptly from the cellar.

"I pried 'em loose, cooled 'em with snow and rolled 'em out with a file. They're probably badly crystallized but we needn't let that worry us."

He put one cartridge in the chamber of each rifle and shot the bolts home. "There's no sense in loading these any more thoroughly—ordinary bullets are no good anyhow, Chris says. Just make your first shots count. Who's elected?"

Foote, Lundgren and Bennington each took a rifle. Newcliffe took the fourth and handed the last one to his wife.

"I say, wait a minute," James objected. "Do you think that's wise, Tom?

I mean, taking Caroline along?"

"Why certainly," Newcliffe said, looking surprised. "She shoots like a fiend—she's snatched prizes away from me a couple of times. I thought *everybody* was going along."

"That isn't right," Foote said. "Especially not Doris, since the wolf—that is, I don't think she ought to go."

"Are you going to leave her here by herself?"

"Oh no!" Doris cried. "Not here! I've got to go! I don't want to wait all alone in this house. He might come back, and there'd be nobody here. I couldn't stand it!"

"We're *all* going," Newcliffe concluded. "We can't leave Doris here unprotected and we need Caroline's marksmanship. Let's get going. It's two now."

He put on his heavy coat and with the heavy-eyed butler, went out to get the dogs. The rest of the company got out their own heavy clothes. Doris and Caroline climbed into ski-suits. They assembled one by one in the living room. Lundgren's eyes swung on a vase of irislike flowers.

"Hello, what's this?" he said.

"Monkshood," Caroline informed him. "We grow it in the greenhouse. It's pretty, isn't it? Though the gardener says it's poisonous."

"Chris," Foote said. "That isn't wolfsbane, is it?"

The psychiatrist shook his head. "I'm no botanist. I can't tell one aconite from the other. But it hardly matters. Hyperpineals are allergic to the whole group. The pollen, you see. As in hay fever your hyperpineal breathes the pollen, anaphylaxis sets in and—"

"The last twist of the knife," James murmured.

A clamoring of dogs outside announced that Newcliffe was ready. With somber faces the party filed out through the front door. For some reason all of them avoided stepping on the wolf's prints in the snow. Their mien was that of condemned prisoners on the way to the tumbrels. Lundgren took one of the sprigs of flowers from the vase.

The moon had passed its zenith and was almost half-way down the sky, projecting the Bastille-like shadow of the house before it. But there was still plenty of light and the house itself was glowing from basement to tower room. Lundgren located Brucey in the milling yapping pack and abruptly thrust the sprig of flowers under his muzzle. The animal sniffed once, then crouched back and snarled softly.

"Wolfsbane," Lundgren said. "Dogs don't react to the other aconites—basis of the legend, no doubt. Better fire your gardener, Caroline. In the end he's to blame for all this in the dead of winter. Lycanthropy normally is an autumn affliction."

James said,

"Even a man who says his prayers
Before he sleeps each night
May turn to wolf when the wolfsbane blooms
And the moon is high and bright."

"Stop it, you give me the horrors," Foote snapped angrily.

"Well, the dog knows now," said Newcliffe. "Good. It would have been hard for them to pick up the spoor from cold snow but Brucey can lead them. Let's go."

The tracks of the wolf were clear and sharp in the snow. It had formed a hard crust from which fine, powdery showers of tiny ice-crystals were shipped by a fitful wind. The tracks led around the side of the house and out across the golf course. The little group plodded grimly along beside them. The spoor was cold for the dogs but every so often they would pick up a faint trace and go bounding ahead, yanking their master after them. For the most part however the party had to depend upon its eyes.

A heavy mass of clouds had gathered in the west. The moon dipped lower. Foote's shadow, grotesquely lengthened, marched on before him and the crusted snow crunched and crackled beneath his feet. There was a watchful unnaturally still atmosphere to the night and they all moved in tense silence except for a few subdued growls and barks from the dogs.

Once the marks of the werewolf doubled back a short distance, then doubled again as if the monster had turned for a moment to look back at the house before continuing his prowling. For the most part however the trail led directly toward the dark boundary of the woods.

As the brush began to rise about them they stopped by mutual consent and peered warily ahead, rifles held ready for instant action. Far out across the countryside behind them, the great cloud-shadow once more began its sailing. The brilliantly lit house stood out fantastically in the gloom.

"Should have turned those out," Newcliffe muttered, looking back. "Outlines us."

The dogs strained at their leashes. In the black west was an inaudible muttering as of winter thunder. Brucey pointed a quivering nose at the woods and growled.

"He's in there, all right."

"We'd better step on it," Bennington said, whispering. "Going to be plenty dark in about five minutes. Storm."

Still they hesitated, regarding the menacing darkness of the forest. Then Newcliffe waved his gun hand in the conventional deploy-as-skirmishers signal and plowed forward. The rest spread out in a loosely spaced line and followed and Foote's finger trembled over his trigger.

The forest in the shrouded darkness was a place of clutching brittle claws, contorted bodies, and the briefly glimpsed demon-faces of ambushed horrors. It was Dante's jungle, the woods of Purgatory, where each tree was a body frozen in agony and branches were gnarled arms and fingers which groaned in the wind or gave sharp tiny tinkling screams as they were broken off.

The underbrush grasped at Foote's legs. His feet broke jarringly through the crust of snow or were supported by it when he least expected support. His shoulders struck unseen tree-trunks. Imagined things sniffed frightfully at his heels or slunk about him just beyond his range of vision. The touch of a hand was enough to make him jump and smother an involuntary outcry. The dogs strained and panted, weaving, no longer snarling, silent with a vicious intentness.

"They've picked up something, all right," Bennington whispered. "Turn 'em loose, Tom?"

Newcliffe bent and snapped the leashes free. Without a sound the animals shot ahead and disappeared.

Over the forest the oncoming storm-clouds crawled across the moon. Total blackness engulfed them. The beam of a powerful flashlight lanced from Newcliffe's free hand, picking out a path of tracks on the brush-littered snow. The rest of the night drew in closer about the blue-white ray.

"Hate to do this," Newcliffe said. "It gives us away. But he knows we're— Hello, it's snowing."

"Let's go then," Foote said. "The tracks will be blotted out shortly."

A terrible clamorous baying rolled suddenly through the woods. "That's it!" Newcliffe shouted. "Listen to them! Go get him, Brucey!"

They crashed ahead. Foote's heart was beating wildly, his nerves at an impossible pitch. The bellowing cry of the dogs echoed all around him, filling the universe with noise.

"They must have sighted him," he panted. "What a racket! They'll raise the whole countryside."

They plowed blindly through the snow-filled woods. Then, without any interval, they stumbled into a small clearing. Snowflakes flocculated the air. Something dashed between Foote's legs, snapping savagely, and he tripped and fell into a drift.

A voice shouted something indistinguishable. Foote's mouth was full of snow. He jerked his head up—and looked straight into the red rage-glowing eyes of the wolf.

It was standing on the other side of the clearing, facing him, the dogs leaping about it, snapping furiously at its legs. It made no sound at all but crouched tiger-fashion, its lips drawn back in a grinning travesty of Jarmoskowski's smile. It lashed at the dogs as they came closer. One of the dogs already lay writhing on the ground, a dark pool spreading from it, staining the snow.

"Shoot, for heaven's sake!" somebody screamed.

Newcliffe clapped his rifle to his shoulder, then lowered it indecisively. "I can't," he said. "The dogs are in the way."

"The heck with the dogs!" James shouted. "This is no fox-hunt! Shoot, Tom, you're the only one of us that's clear."

It was Foote who fired first. The rifle's flat crack echoed through the woods and snow pulled up in a little explosion by the wolf's left hind pad. A concerted groan arose from the party and Newcliffe's voice thundered above it, ordering his dogs back. Bennington aimed with inexorable care.

The werewolf did not wait. With a screaming snarl he burst through the ring of dogs and charged.

Foote jumped in front of Doris, throwing one arm across his throat. The world dissolved into rolling, twisting pandemonium, filled with screaming and shouting and the frantic hatred of dogs. The snow flew thick. Newcliffe's flashlight rolled away and lay on the snow, regarding the tree-tops with an idiot stare.

Then there was the sound of a heavy body moving swiftly away. The shouting died gradually.

"Anybody hurt?" James' voice asked. There was a general chorus of no's. Newcliffe retrieved his flashlight and played it about but the snowfall had reached blizzard proportions and the light showed nothing but shadows and cold confetti.

"He got away," Bennington said. "And the snow will cover his tracks. Better call your dogs back, Tom."

"They're back," Newcliffe said. "When I call them off they come off."

He bent over the body of the injured animal, which was still twitching feebly. "So—so," he said softly. "So—Brucey. Easy—easy. So, Brucey—so."

Still murmuring, he brought his rifle into position with one arm. The dog's tail beat feebly against the snow.

"So, Brucey."

The rifle crashed.

Newcliffe arose, and looked away. "It looks as if we lose round one," he said tonelessly.

IV

It seemed to become daylight very quickly. The butler went phlegmatically around the house, snapping off the lights. If he knew what was going on he gave no sign of it.

"Cappy?" Newcliffe said into the phone. "Listen and get this straight— it's important. Send a cable to Consolidated Warfare Service—no, no, not the Zurich office, they've offices in London—and place an order for a case of .44 calibre rifle cartridges.

"Listen to me, dammit, I'm not through yet—with *silver slugs*. Yes, that's right—silver—and it had better be the pure stuff, too. No, not sterling, that's too hard. Tell them I want them flown over, and that they've got to arrive here tomorrow. Yes, I know it's impossible but if you offer them enough—yes, of course I'll cover it. Got that?"

"Garlic," Lundgren said to Caroline. She wrote it dutifully on her marketing list. "How many windows does this place have? All right, make it one clove for each and get half a dozen boxes of rosemary, too."

He turned to Foote. "We must cover every angle," he said somberly. "As soon as Tom gets off the phone I'll try to raise the local priest and get him out here with a truckload of silver crucifixes. Understand, Paul, there is a strong physiological basis behind all the mediaeval mumbo-jumbo.

"The herbs are anti-spasmodics—they act rather as ephedrine does in hay fever to reduce the violence of the seizure. It's possible that Jan may not be able to maintain the wolf shape if he gets a good enough sniff. As for the religious trappings, that's all psychological.

"If Jan happens to be a skeptic in such matters they won't bother him but I suspect he's—" Lundgren's English abruptly gave out. The word he wanted obviously was not in his vocabulary. "*Aberglaeubig*," he said. "*Criandre*."

"Superstitious?" Foote suggested, smiling grimly.

"Yes. Yes, certainly. Who has better reason, may I ask?"

"But how does he maintain the wolf shape at all?"

"Oh, that's the easiest part. You know how water takes the shape of a vessel it sits in? Well, protoplasm is a liquid. This pineal hormone lowers the surface tension of the cells and at the same time short-circuits the sympathetic nervous system directly to the cerebral cortex.

"Result, a plastic, malleable body within limits. A wolf is easiest because the skeletons are similar—not much pinearin can do with bone, you see. An ape would be easier, but apes don't eat people."

"And vampires? Are they just advanced cases of the same thing?"

"Vampires," said Lundgren pontifically, "are people we put in padded cells. It's impossible to change the bony structure *that* much. They just think they're bats. But yes, it's advanced hyperpinealism. In the last stages it is quite something to see.

"The surface tension is lowered so much that the cells begin to boil away. Pretty soon there is just a mess. The process is arrested when the vascular system can no longer circulate the hormone but of course the victim is dead long before that."

"No cure?"

"None yet. Someday perhaps, but until then— We will be doing Jan a favor."

"Also," Newcliffe was saying, "drive over and pick me up six Browning automatic rifles. Never mind the bipods, just the rifles themselves. What? Well, you might call it a siege. All right, Cappy. No, I won't be in today. Pay everybody off and send them home until further notice."

"It's a good thing," Foote said, "that Newcliffe has money."

"It's a good thing," said Lundgren, "that he has me—and you. We'll see how twentieth century methods can cope with this Dark-Age disease."

Newcliffe hung up and Lundgren took possession of the phone. "As soon as my man gets back from the village I'm going to set out traps. He may be able to detect hidden metal. I've known dogs that could do it by smell in wet weather but it's worth a try."

"What's to prevent his just going away?" Doris asked. Somehow the shadows of exhaustion and fear around her eyes made her lovelier than ever.

"As I understand it he thinks he's bound by the pentagram," Foote said. At the telephone, where Lundgren evidently was listening to a different conversation with each ear, there was an energetic nod.

"In the old books, the figure is supposed to be a sure trap for demons and such if you can lure them into it. And the werewolf feels compelled to go only for the person whom he thinks is marked with it."

Lundgren said, "Excuse me," and put his hand over the mouth-piece. "Only lasts seven days," he said.

"The compulsion? Then we'll have to get him before then."

"Well, maybe we'll sleep tonight anyhow," Doris said dubiously.

Lundgren hung up and rejoined them. "I didn't have much difficulty selling the good Father the idea," he said. "But he only has crucifixes enough for our groundfloor windows. By the way, he wants a picture of Jan in case he should turn up in the village."

"There are no existing photographs of Jarmoskowski," Newcliffe said positively. "He never allowed any to be taken. It was a headache to his concert manager."

"That's understandable," Lundgren said. "With his cell radiogens under constant stimulation any picture of him would turn out over-exposed anyhow—probably a total blank. And that in turn would expose Jan."

"Well, that's too bad but it's not irreparable," Foote said. He was glad to be of some use again. He opened Newcliffe's desk and took out a sheet of stationery and a pencil. In ten minutes he had produced a head of Jarmoskowski in three-quarter profile as he had seen him at the piano that last night so many centuries ago. Lundgren studied it.

"To the life," he said. "I'll send this over by messenger. You draw well, Paul."

Bennington laughed. "You're not telling him anything he doesn't know," he said. Nevertheless, Foote thought, there was considerably less animosity in the critic's manner.

"What now?" James asked.

"We wait," Newcliffe said. "Bennington's gun was ruined by that one handmade slug. We can't afford to have our weapons taken out of action. If I know Consolidated they'll have the machine-made jobs here tomorrow. Then we'll have some hope of getting him. Right now he's shown us he's more than a match for us in open country."

The group looked at each other. Some little understanding of what it would mean to wait through nervous days and fear-stalked nights, helpless and inactive, already showed on their faces. But there were necessities before which the demands of merely human feelings were forced to yield.

The conference broke up in silence.

For Foote, as for the rest, that night was instilled with dread, pregnant every instant with terror of the outcry that the next moment might bring. The waning moon, greenish and sickly, reeled over the house through a sky troubled with fulgurous clouds. An insistent wind made distant wolf-howls, shook from the trees soft sounds like the padding of stealthy paws, rattled windows with the scrape of claws trying for a hold.

The atmosphere of the house, hot and stuffy because of the closed windows and reeking of garlic, was stretched to an impossible tautness with waiting. In the empty room next to Foote there was the imagined coming and going of thin ghosts and the crouched expectancy of a turned-down bed—awaiting an occupant who might depress the sheets in a shocking pattern, perhaps regardless of the tiny pitiful glint of the crucifix upon the pillow. Above him, other sleepers turned restlessly, or groaned and started up from chilling nightmares.

The boundary between the real and the unreal had been let down in his mind and in the flickering shadows of the moon and the dark errands of the ghosts there was no way of making any selection. He had entered the cobwebby blackness of the borderland between the human and the demon, where nothing is ever more than half true—or half untruth.

After a while, on the threshold of this darkness, the blasphemous voices of the hidden evil things beyond it began to seep through. The wind, abandoning the trees and gables, whispered and echoed the voices, counting the victims slowly as death stalked through the house.

One.

Two.

Three—closer now!

Four—the fourth sleeper struggled a little. Foote could hear a muffled creak of springs over his head.

Five.

Six—who was Six? Who is next? When?

Seven—Oh Lord, I'm next . . . I'm next . . . I'm next.

He curled into a ball, trembling. The wind died away and there was silence, tremendous silence. After a long while he uncurled, swearing at himself but not aloud—because he was afraid to hear his own voice. Cut that out, now. Foote, you bloody fool. You're like a kid hiding from the goblins. You're perfectly safe. Lundgren says so.

Mamma says so.

How the heck does Lundgren know?

He's an expert. He wrote a paper. Go ahead, be a kid. Remember your childhood faith in the printed word? All right then. Go to sleep, will you?

There goes that damned counting again.

But after a while his worn-down nerves would be denied no longer. He slept a little but fitfully, falling in his dreams through such deep pits of evil that he awoke fighting the covers and gasping for the vitiated garlic-heavy air. There was a fetid foulness in his mouth and his heart pounded. He threw off the covers and sat up, lighting a cigarette with trembling hands and trying not to see the shadows the flame threw.

He was no longer waiting for the night to end. He had forgotten that there ever was such a thing as daylight, was waiting only for the inevitable growl that would herald the last horror. Thus it was a shock almost beyond bearing to look out the window and see the brightening of dawn over the forest.

After staring incredulously at it for a moment he snubbed out his cigarette in the candlestick—which he had been carrying around the house as if it had grown to him—and collapsed. With a sigh he was instantly in deep and dreamless sleep.

When he finally came to consciousness he was being shaken and Bennington's voice was in his ear. "Get up, man," the critic was saying. "No, you needn't reach for the candlestick—everything's okay thus far."

Foote grinned. "It's a pleasure to see a friendly expression on your face, Bennington," he said with a faint glow of general relief.

Bennington looked a little abashed. "I misjudged you," he admitted. "I guess it takes a crisis to bring out what's really in a man so that blunt brains like mine can see it. You don't mind if I continue to dislike your latest abstractions, I trust?"

"That's your function," Foote said cheerfully. "To be a gadfly. Now what's happened?"

"Newcliffe got up early and made the rounds of the traps. We got a good-sized rabbit out of one of them and made a stew—very good—you'll see. The other one was empty but there was blood on it and on the snow. Lundgren isn't up yet but we've saved scrapings for him."

James poked his head around the door jamb, then came in. "Hope it cripples him," he said, dextrously snaffling a cigarette from Foote's shirt pocket. "Pardon me. All the servants have deserted us but the butler, and nobody will bring cigarettes up from the village."

"My, my," said Foote. "Everyone feels so chipper. Boy, I never thought I'd be as glad to see any sunrise as I was today's."

"If you—"

There was a sound outside. It sounded like the world's biggest tea-kettle. Something flitted through the sky, wheeled and came back.

"Cripes," Foote said, shading his eyes. "A big jet job. What's he doing here?"

The plane circled silently, jets cut. It lost flying speed and glided in over the golf course, struck and rolled at breakneck speed straight for the forest. At the last minute the pilot spun to a stop expertly.

"By heaven, I'll bet that's Newcliffe's bullets!"

They pounded downstairs. By the time they reached the front room the pilot was coming in with Newcliffe. A heavy case was slung between them.

Newcliffe pried the case open. Then he sighed. "Look at 'em," he said. "Nice, shiny brass cartridges, and dull-silver heads machined for perfect accuracy—yum, yum. I could just stand here and pet them. Where are you from?"

"Croydon," said the pilot. "If you don't mind, Mr. Newcliffe, the company said I was to collect from you. That's a hundred pounds for the cartridges and five hundred for me."

"Cheap enough. Hold on. I'll write you a check."

Foote whistled. He didn't know whether to be more awed by the trans-Atlantic express service or the vast sum it had cost.

The pilot took the check and shortly thereafter the tea-kettle began to whistle again. From another huge wooden crate Newcliffe was handing out brand-new Brownings.

"Now let him come," he said grimly. "Don't worry about wasting shots—there's a full case of clips. As soon as you see him, blaze away like mad. Use it like a hose if you have to."

"Somebody go wake Chris," Bennington said. "He should have lessons too. Doris, go knock on his door like a good girl."

Doris nodded and went upstairs. "Now this stud here," Newcliffe said, "is the fire-control button. You put it in this position and the gun will fire one shot and reload. Put it here and you have to reload it yourself like any rifle. Put it here and it goes into automatic operation, firing every shell in the clip, one after the other."

"Thunder!" James said admiringly. "We could stand off an army."

"Wait a minute—there seem to be two missing."

"Those are all you unpacked," Bennington said.

"Yes but there were two older models of my own. I never used 'em because it didn't seem right to hunt with such a cannon. But I got 'em out last night on account of this trouble."

"Oh," Bennington said with an air of sudden enlightenment. "I thought that thing I had looked odd. I slept with one last night. I think Lundgren has another."

"Where is Lundgren? Doris should have had him up by now. Go see, Bennington, and get that gun."

"Isn't there a lot of recoil?" Foote asked.

"Sure. These are really meant to operate from bipods. Hold the gun at your hip, not your shoulder—what's *that?*"

"Bennington's voice," Foote said, suddenly tense. "Something must be wrong with Doris." The four of them clattered for the stairs.

They found Doris at Bennington's feet in front of Lundgren's open door. Evidently she had fainted without a sound. The critic was in the process of being very sick. On Lundgren's bed lay a crimson horror.

The throat was ripped out and the face and all the soft parts of the body had been eaten away. The right leg had been gnawed in one place all the way to the bone, which gleamed white and polished in the reassuring sunlight.

V

Foote stood in the living room by the piano in the full glare of all the electric lights. He hefted the B. A. R. and surveyed the remainder of his companions, who were standing in a puzzled group before him.

"No," he said, "I don't like that. I don't want you all bunched together. String out in a line, in front of me, so I can see everybody."

He grinned briefly. "Got the drop on you, didn't I? Not a rifle in sight. Of course, there's the big candlestick behind you, Newcliffe, but I can shoot quicker than you can club me." His voice grew ugly. *"And I will,* if you make it necessary. So I would advise everybody—including the women—not to make any sudden moves."

"What is this all about, Paul?" Bennington demanded angrily. "As if things aren't bad enough!"

"You'll see directly. Now line up the way I told you. *Quick!*" He moved the gun suggestively. "And remember what I said about sudden moves. It may be dark outside but I didn't turn on all the lights for nothing."

Quietly the line formed and the eyes that looked at Foote were narrowed with suspicion of madness—or worse.

"Good. Now we can talk comfortably. You see, after what happened to Chris I'm not taking any chances. That was partly his fault and partly mine. But the gods allow no one to err twice in matters like this. He paid a ghastly price for his second error—a price I don't intend to pay or to see anyone else here pay."

"Would you honor us with an explanation of this error?" Newcliffe said icily.

"Yes. I don't blame you for being angry, Tom, since I'm your guest. But you see I'm forced to treat you all alike for the moment. I was fond of Lundgren."

There was silence for a moment, then a thin indrawing of breath from Bennington. "You were fond—my Lord!" he whispered raggedly. "What do you mean?"

"I mean that Lundgren was not killed by Jarmoskowski," Foote said coldly and deliberately. "He was killed by someone else. Another werewolf. *One who is standing before me at this moment.*"

A concerted gasp went up.

"Surprised? But it's true. The error for which Chris paid so dearly, which I made too, was this—we forgot to examine everybody for injuries after the encounter with Jan. We forgot one of the cardinal laws of lycanthropy.

"A man who survives being bitten by a werewolf himself becomes a werewolf. That's how the disease is passed on. The pinearin in the saliva gets in the bloodstream, stimulates the victim's own pineal gland and—"

"But nobody was bitten, Paul," Doris said in a reasonable voice.

"Somebody was, lightly. None of you but Chris and myself could know about the bite-infection. Evidently somebody got a few small scratches, didn't think them worth mentioning, put iodine on them and forgot them—until it was too late."

There were slow movements in the line—heads turning surreptitiously, eyes glancing nervously at persons to left and right.

"Once the attack occurred," Foote said relentlessly, "Chris was the logical first victim. The expert, hence the most dangerous enemy. I wish I had thought of this before lunch. I might have seen which one of you was uninterested in his lunch. In any event Chris' safeguards against letting Jarmoskowski in also keep you from getting out. You won't leave this room ever again."

He gritted his teeth and brought himself back into control. "All right," he said. "This is the showdown. Everybody hold up both hands in plain view."

Almost instantly there was a ravening wolf in the room.

Only Foote, who could see at a glance the order of the people in the line, knew who it was. The frightful tragedy of it struck him such a blow that the gun dropped nervelessly from his hands. He wept convulsively. The monster lunged for his throat like a reddish projectile.

Newcliffe's hand darted back, grasped the candlestick. He leapt forward in a swift, catlike motion and brought it down across the werewolf's side. Ribs burst with a horrible splintering sound. The beast spun, snarling with agony. Newcliffe hit it again across the backbone. It fell, screaming, fangs slashing the air.

Three times, with concentrated viciousness, Newcliffe struck at its head. Then it cried out once in an almost familiar voice—and died.

Slowly the cells of its body groped back toward their natural positions. The awful crawling metamorphosis was never completed. But the hairy-haunched thing with the crushed skull which sprawled at Newcliffe's feet was recognizable.

It had been Caroline Newcliffe.

There was a frozen tableau of wax figures in the yellow lamplight. Tears coursed along Foote's palms, dropped from under them, fell silently to the carpet. After a while he dropped his hands. Bennington's face was gray with illness but rigidly expressionless like a granite statue. James' back was against the wall. He watched the anomalous corpse as if waiting for some new movement.

As for Newcliffe he had no expression at all. He merely stood where he was, the bloody candlestick held loosely in a limp hand.

His eyes were quite empty.

After a moment Doris walked over to Newcliffe and touched his shoulder compassionately. The contact seemed to let something out of him. He shrank visibly into himself, shoulders slumping, his whole body withering visibly into a dry husk.

The candlestick thumped against the floor, rocked wildly on its base, toppled across the body. As it struck, Foote's cigarette butt, which had somehow remained in it all day, tumbled out and rolled crazily along the carpet.

"Tom," Doris said softly. "Come away now. There's nothing you can do."

"Blood," he said emptily. "She had a cut. On her hand. Handled the scrapings from the trap—my trap. I did it. Just a breadknife cut from making canapes. I did it."

"No you didn't, Tom. Let's get some rest." She took his hand. He followed her obediently, stumbling a little as his blood-spattered shoes scuffed over the thick rug, his breath expelling from his lungs with a soft whisper. The two disappeared up the stairs.

Bennington bolted for the kitchen sink.

Foote sat down on the piano bench, his worn face taut with dried tears, and picked at the dusty keys. The lightly struck notes aroused James. He crossed the room and looked down at Foote.

"You did well," the novelist said shakily. "Don't condemn yourself, Paul."

Foote nodded. He felt—nothing. Nothing at all.

"The body?"

"Yes. I suppose so." He got up from the bench. Together they carried the tragic corpse out through the house to the greenhouse.

"We should leave her here," Foote said with a faint return of his old irony. "Here's where the wolfsbane bloomed and started the whole business."

"Poetic justice, I suppose," James said. "But I don't think it's wise. Tom has a toolshed at the other end that isn't steam heated. It should be cold enough."

Gently they placed the body on the cement floor, laying some gunny-sacks under it. "In the morning," Foote said, "we can have someone come for her."

"How about legal trouble?" James said frowning. "Here's a woman whose skull has been crushed with a blunt instrument—"

"I think I can get Lundgren's priest to help us there," Foote said somberly. "They have some authority to make death certificates in this state. Besides, James—is that a woman? Inarguably it isn't Caroline."

James looked sidewise at the hairy, contorted haunches. "Yes. It's— legally it's nothing. I see your point."

Together they went back into the house. "Jarmoskowski?" James said.

"Not tonight. We're all too tired and sick. And we do seem to be safe enough in here. Chris saw to that."

Whatever James had to say in reply was lost in the roar of an automatic rifle somewhere over their heads, exhausting its shots in a quick stream. After a moment there was another burst of ten. Footsteps echoed. Then Bennington came bouncing down the stairs.

"Watch out tonight," he panted. "He's around. I saw him come out of the woods in wolf form. I emptied the clip but missed and he went back again. I sprayed another ten rounds around where I saw him go in but I don't think I hit him."

"Where were you shooting from?"

"The top of the tower." His face was very grim. "Went up for a last look around and there he was. I hope he comes tonight, I want to be the one who kills him."

"How is Tom?"

"Bad. Doesn't seem to know where he is or what he's doing. Well, good night. Keep your eyes peeled."

James nodded and followed him upstairs. Foote remained in the empty room a few minutes longer, looking thoughtfully at the splotch of blood on the priceless Persian carpet. Then he felt of his face and throat, looked at his hands, arms and legs, inside his shirt. Not so much as a scratch—Tom had seen to that.

So hard not to hate these afflicted people, so impossible to remember that lycanthropy was a disease like any other! Caroline, like the man in *The Red Laugh*, had been noble-hearted and gentle and had wished no one evil. Yet—

Maybe God is on the side of the werewolves.

The blasphemy of an exhausted mind. Yet he could not put it from him. Suppose Jarmoskowski should conquer his compulsion and lie out of sight until the seven days were over. Then he could disappear. It was a big country. It would not be necessary for him to kill all his victims—just those he actually needed for food. But he could nip a good many. Every other one, say.

And from wherever he lived the circle of lycanthropy would grow and widen and engulf—

Maybe God had decided that proper humans had made a mess of running the world, had decided to give the *nosferatu*, the undead, a chance at it. Perhaps the human race was on the threshold of that darkness into which he had looked throughout last night.

He ground his teeth and made an exasperated noise. Shock and exhaustion would drive him as crazy as Newcliffe if he kept this up.

He went around the room, making sure that all the windows were tightly closed and the crucifixes in place, turning out the lights as he went. The garlic was getting rancid—it smelled like mercaptan—but he was too tired to replace it. He clicked out the last light, picked up the candlestick and went out into the hall.

As he passed Doris' room, he noticed that the door was ajar. Inside, two voices murmured. Remembering what he had heard before he stopped to eavesdrop.

It was years later that Foote found out exactly what had happened at the very beginning. Doris, physically exhausted by the hideous events of the day, emotionally drained by tending the childlike Newcliffe, feeding him from a spoon and seeing him into bed, had fallen asleep almost immediately.

It was a sleep dreamless except for a vague, dull undercurrent of despair.
When the light tapping against the window-panes finally reached her
consciousness she had no idea how long she had slumbered.

She struggled to a sitting position and forced her eyelids up. Across the
room the moonlight, gleaming in patches against the rotting snow outside,
glared through the window. Silhouetted against it was a tall human figure.
She could not see its face but there was no mistaking the red glint of the
eyes. She clutched for the rifle and brought it awkwardly into position.

Jarmoskowski did not dodge. He moved his arms out a little way away
from his body, palms forward in a gesture that looked almost supplicating,
and waited. Indecisively she lowered the gun again. Was he inviting death?

As she lowered the weapon she saw that the stud was in the continuous-
fire position and carefully she shifted it to *repeat*. She was afraid of the
recoil Newcliffe had mentioned, felt surer of her target if she could throw
one shot at a time at it.

Jarmoskowski tapped again and motioned with his finger. Reasoning
that he would come in if he were able, she took time out to get into her
housecoat. Then, holding her finger against the trigger, she went to the
window. It was closed tightly and a crucifix, suspended from a silk thread,
hung exactly in the center of it. She checked it, and then opened one of the
small panes directly above Jarmoskowski's head.

"Hello, Doris," he said softly.

"Hello." She was more uncertain than afraid. Was this actually
happening or just the recurrent nightmare? "What do you want? I should
shoot you. Can you tell me why I shouldn't?"

"Yes I can. Otherwise I wouldn't have risked exposing myself. That's a
nasty-looking weapon."

"There are ten silver bullets in it."

"I know it. I've seen Brownings before. I would be a good target for you
too, so I have no hope of escape—my nostrils are full of rosemary." He
smiled ruefully. "And Lundgren and Caroline are dead and I am
responsible. I deserve to die. That is why I am here."

"You'll get your wish, Jan," she said. "You have some other reason, I
know. I will back my wits against yours. I want to ask you questions."

"Ask."

"You have your evening clothes on. Paul said they changed with you.
How is that possible?"

"But a wolf has clothes," Jarmoskowski said. "He is not naked like a
man. And surely Chris must have spoken of the effect of the pineal upon
the cell radiogens. These little bodies act upon any organic matter,
including wool or cotton. When I change my clothes change with me. I can
hardly say how, for it is in the blood, like musicianship. Either you can or

you can't. But they change."

His voice took on a darkly somber tone. "Lundgren was right throughout. This werewolfery is now nothing but a disease. It is not pro-survival. Long ago there must have been a number of mutations which brought the pineal gland into use.

"None of them survived but the werewolves and these are dying. Someday the pineal will come into better use and all men will be able to modify their forms without this terrible madness as a penalty. For us, the lycanthropes, the failures, nothing is left.

"It is not good for a man to wander from country to country, knowing that he is a monster to his fellow-men and cursed eternally by his God—if he can claim a God. I went through Europe, playing the piano and giving pleasure, meeting people, making friends—and always, sooner or later, there were whisperings, and strange looks and dawning horror.

"And whether I was hunted down for the beast I was or whether there was merely a vague gradually growing revulsion, they drove me out. Hatred, silver bullets, crucifixes—they are all the same in the end.

"Sometimes, I could spend several months without incident in some one place and my life would take on a veneer of normality. I could attend to my music and have people about me that I liked and be—human. Then the wolfsbane bloomed and the pollen freighted the air and when the moon shone down on that flower my blood surged with the thing I have within me.

"And then I made apologies to my friends and went north to Sweden, where Lundgren was and where spring was much later. I loved him and I think he missed the truth about me until night before last. I was careful.

"Once or twice I did *not* go North and then the people who had been my friends would be hammering silver behind my back and waiting for me in dark corners. After years of this few places in Europe would have me. With my reputation as a musician spread darker rumors.

"Towns I had never visited closed their gates to me without a word. Concert halls were booked up too many months in advance for me to use them, inns and hotels were filled indefinitely, people were too busy to talk to me, to listen to my playing, to write me any letters.

"I have been in love. That—I cannot describe.

"And then I came to this country. Here no one believes in the werewolf. I sought scientific help—not from Lundgren, because I was afraid I should do him some harm. But here I thought someone would know enough to deal with what I had become.

"It was not so. The primitive hatred of my kind lies at the heart of the human as it lies at the heart of the dog. There was no help for me.

"I am here to ask for an end to it."

Slow tears rolled over Doris' cheeks. The voice faded away indefinitely. It did not seem to end at all but rather to retreat into some limbo where men could not hear it. Jarmoskowski stood silently in the moonlight, his eyes burning bloodily, a somber sullen scarlet.

Doris said, "Jan—Jan, I am sorry, I am so sorry. What can I do?"

"Shoot."

"I—can't!"

"Please, Doris."

The girl was crying uncontrollably. "Jan, don't. I can't. You know I can't. Go away, *please* go away."

Jarmoskowski said, "Then come with me, Doris. Open the window and come with me."

"Where?"

"Does it matter? You have denied me the death I ask. Would you deny me this last desperate love, would you deny your own love, your own last and deepest desire? It is too late now, too late for you to pretend revulsion. Come with me."

He held out his hands.

"Say goodbye," he said. "Goodbye to these self-righteous humans. I will give you of my blood and we will range the world, wild and uncontrollable, the last of our race. They will remember us, I promise you."

"Jan—"

"I am here. Come now."

Like a somnambulist she swung the panes out. Jarmoskowski did not move but looked first at her, then at the crucifix. She lifted one end of the thread and let the little thing tinkle to the floor.

"After us there shall be no darkness comparable to our darkness," Jarmoskowski said. "Let them rest—let the world rest."

He sprang into the room with so sudden, so feral a motion that he seemed hardly to have moved at all. From the doorway the automatic rifle yammered with demoniac ferocity. The impact of the slugs hurled Jarmoskowski back against the wall. Foote lowered the smoking muzzle and took one step into the room.

"Too late, Jan," he said stonily.

Doris wailed like a little girl awakened from a dream. Jarmoskowski's lips moved but there was not enough left of his lungs. The effort to speak brought a bloody froth to his mouth. He stood for an instant, stretched out a hand toward the girl. Then the fingers clenched convulsively and the long body folded.

He smiled, put aside that last of all his purposes and died.

The Loom of Darkness

Jack Vance

Through the dim forest came Liane the Wayfarer, passing along the shadowed glades with a prancing light-footed gait. He whistled, he caroled, he was plainly in high spirits. Around his finger he twirled a bit of wrought bronze—a circlet graved with angular crabbed characters, now stained black.

By excellent chance he had found it, banded around the root of an ancient yew. Hacking it free, he had seen the characters on the inner surface—rude forceful symbols, doubtless the cast of a powerful antique rune.... Best take it to a magician and have it tested for sorcery.

Liane made a wry mouth. There were objections to the course. Sometimes it seemed as if all living creatures conspired to exasperate him. Only this morning, the spice merchant—what a tumult he had made dying! How carelessly he had spewed blood on Liane's cockscomb sandals! Still, thought Liane, every unpleasantness carried with it compensation. While digging the grave he had found the bronze ring.

And Liane's spirits soared; he laughed in pure joy. He bounded, he leapt. His green cape flapped behind him, the red feather in his cap winked and blinked.... But still—Liane slowed his step—he was no whit closer to the mystery of the magic, if magic the ring possessed.

Experiment, that was the word!

He stopped where the ruby sunlight slanted down without hindrance from the high foliage, examined the ring, traced the glyphs with his fingernail. He peered through. A faint film, a flicker? He held it at arm's length. It was clearly a coronet. He whipped off his cap, set the band on his brow, rolled his great golden eyes, preened himself. . . . Odd. It slipped down on his ears. It tipped across his eyes. Darkness. Frantically Liane clawed it off. . . . A bronze ring, a hand's-breadth in diameter. Queer.

He tried again. It slipped down over his head, his shoulders. His head was in the darkness of a strange separate space. Looking down, he saw the level of the outside light dropping as he dropped the ring.

Slowly down. . . . Now it was around his ankles—and in sudden panic, Liane snatched the ring up over his body, emerged blinking into the maroon light of the forest.

He saw a blue-white, green-white flicker against the foliage. It was a Twk-man, mounted on a dragon-fly, and light glinted from the dragon-fly's wings.

Liane called sharply, "Here, sir! Here, sir!"

The Twk-man perched his mount on a twig. "Well, Liane, what do you wish?"

"Watch now, and remember what you see." Liane pulled the ring over his head, dropped it to his feet, lifted it back. He looked up to the Twk-man, who was chewing a leaf. "And what did you see?"

"I saw Liane vanish from mortal sight—except for the red curled toes of his sandals. All else was as air."

"Ha!" cried Liane. "Think of it! Have you ever seen the like?"

The Twk-man asked carelessly, "Do you have salt? I would have salt."

Liane cut his exultations short, eyed the Twk-man closely.

"What news do you bring me?"

"Three erbs killed Florejin the Dream-builder, and burst all his bubbles. The air above the manse was colored for many minutes with the flitting fragments."

"A gram."

"Lord Kandive the Golden has built a barge of carven mo-wood ten lengths high, and it floats on the River Scaum for the Regatta, full of treasure."

"Two grams."

"A golden witch named Lith has come to live on Thamber Meadow. She is quiet and very beautiful."

"Three grams."

"Enough," said the Twk-man, and leaned forward to watch while Liane weighed out the salt in a tiny balance. He packed it in small panniers hanging on each side of the ribbed thorax, then twitched the insect into the air and flicked off through the forest vaults.

Once more Liane tried his bronze ring, and this time brought it entirely past his feet, stepped out of it and brought the ring up into the darkness beside him. What a wonderful sanctuary! A hole whose opening could be hidden inside the hole itself! Down with the ring to his feet, step through, bring it up his slender frame and over his shoulders, out into the forest with a small bronze ring in his hand.

Ho! and off to Thamber Meadow to see the beautiful golden witch.

Her hut was a simple affair of woven reeds—a low dome with two round windows and a low door. He saw Lith at the pond bare-legged among the water shoots, catching frogs for her supper. A white kirtle was gathered up tight around her thighs; stock-still she stood and the dark water rippled rings away from her slender knees.

She was more beautiful than Liane could have imagined, as if one of Florejin's wasted bubbles had burst here on the water. Her skin was pale creamed stirred gold, her hair a denser, wetter gold. Her eyes were like Liane's own, great golden orbs, and hers were wide apart, tilted slightly.

Liane strode forward and planted himself on the bank.

She looked up startled, her ripe mouth half-open.

"Behold, golden witch, here is Liane. He has come to welcome you to Thamber; and he offers you his friendship, his love . . ."

Lith bent, scooped a handful of slime from the bank and flung it into his face.

Shouting the most violent curses, Liane wiped his eyes free, but the door to the hut had slammed shut.

Liane strode to the door and pounded it with his fist.

"Open and show your witch's face, or I burn the hut!"

The door opened, and the girl looked forth, smiling. "What now?"

Liane entered the hut and lunged for the girl, but twenty thin shafts darted out, twenty points pricking his chest. He halted, eyebrows raised, mouth twitching.

"Down, steel," said Lith. The blades snapped from view. "So easily could I seek your vitality," said Lith, "had I willed."

Liane frowned and rubbed his chin as if pondering. "You understand," he said earnestly, "what a witless thing you do. Liane is feared by those who fear fear, loved by those who love love. And you—" his eyes swam the golden glory of her body—"you are ripe as a sweet fruit, you are eager, you glisten and tremble with love. You please Liane, and he will spend much warmness on you."

"No, no," said Lith, with a slow smile. "You are too hasty."

Liane looked at her in surprise. "Indeed?"

"I am Lith," said she. "I am what you say I am. I ferment, I burn, I seethe. Yet I may have no lover but him who has served me. He must be brave, swift, cunning."

"I am he," said Liane. He chewed at his lip. "It is not usually thus. I detest this indecision." He took a step forward. "Come, let us—"

She backed away. "No, no. You forget. How have you served me, how have you gained the right to my love?"

"Absurdity!" stormed Liane. "Look at me! Note my perfect grace, the beauty of my form and feature, my great eyes, as golden as your own, my manifest will and power. . . . It is you who should serve me. That is how I will have it." He sank upon a low divan. "Woman, give me wine."

She shook her head. "In my small domed hut I cannot be forced. Perhaps outside on Thamber Meadow—but in here, among my blue and red tassels, with twenty blades of steel at my call, you must obey me. . . . So choose. Either arise and go, never to return, or else agree to serve me on one small mission, and then have me and all my ardor."

Liane sat straight and stiff. An odd creature, the golden witch. But, indeed, she was worth some exertion, and he would make her pay for her impudence.

"Very well, then," he said blandly. "I will serve you. What do you wish? Jewels? I can suffocate you in pearls, blind you with diamonds. I have two emeralds the size of your fist, and they are green oceans, where the gaze is trapped and wanders forever among vertical green prisms . . ."

"No, no jewels—"

"An enemy, perhaps. Ah, so simple. Liane will kill you ten men. Two steps forward, thrust—*thus!*" He lunged. "And souls go thrilling up like bubbles in a beaker of mead."

"No. I want no killing."

He sat back, frowning. "What, then?"

She stepped to the back of the room and pulled at a drape. It swung aside, displaying a golden tapestry. The scene was a valley bounded by two steep mountains, a broad valley where a placid river ran, past a quiet village and so into a grove of trees. Golden was the river, golden the mountains, golden the trees—golds so various, so rich, so subtle that the effect was like a many-colored landscape. But the tapestry had been rudely hacked in half.

Liane was entranced. "Exquisite, exquisite . . ."

Lith said, "It is the Magic Valley of Ariventa so depicted. The other half has been stolen from me, and its recovery is the service I wish of you."

"Where is the other half?" demanded Liane. "Who is the dastard?"

Now she watched him closely. "Have you ever heard of Chun? Chun the Unavoidable?"

Liane considered. "No."

"He stole the half to my tapestry, and hung it in a marble hall, and this hall is in the ruins to the north of Kaiin."

"Ha!" muttered Liane.

"The hall is by the Place of Whispers, and is marked by a leaning column with a black medallion of a phoenix and a two-headed lizard."

"I go," said Liane. He rose. "One day to Kaiin, one day to steal, one day to return. Three days."

Lith followed him to the door. "Beware of Chun the Unavoidable," she whispered.

And Liane strode away whistling, the red feather bobbing in his green cap. Lith watched him, then turned and slowly approached the golden tapestry. "Golden Ariventa," she whispered, "my heart cries and hurts with longing for you . . ."

The Derna is a swifter, thinner river than the Scaum, its bosomy sister to the south. And where the Scaum wallows through a broad dale, purple with horse-blossom, pocked white and gray with crumbling castles, the Derna has sheered a steep canyon, overhung by forested bluffs.

An ancient flint road long ago followed the course of the Derna, but now the exaggeration of the meandering has cut into the pavement, so that Liane, treading the road to Kaiin, was occasionally forced to leave the road and make a detour through banks of thorn and the tube-grass which whistled in the breeze.

The red sun, drifting across the universe like an old man creeping to his death-bed, hung low to the horizon when Liane breasted Porphiron Scar, looked across white-walled Kaiin and the blue bay of Sanreale beyond.

Directly below was the market-place, a medley of stalls selling fruits, slabs of pale meat, molluscs from the slime banks, dull flagons of wine. And the quiet people of Kaiin moved among the stalls, buying their sustenance, carrying it loosely to their stone chambers.

Beyond the market-place rose a bank of ruined columns, like broken teeth—legs to the arena built two hundred feet from the ground by Mad King Shin; beyond, in a grove of bay trees, the glassy dome of the palace was visible, where Kandive the Golden ruled Kaiin and as much of Ascolais as one could see from a vantage on Porphiron Scar.

The Derna, no longer a flow of clear water, poured through a network of dank canals and subterranean tubes, and finally seeped past rotting wharves into the Bay of Sanreale.

A bed for the night, thought Liane; then to his business in the morning.

He leapt down the zig-zag steps—back, forth, back, forth—and came out into the market-place. And now he put on a grave demeanor. Liane the

Wayfarer was not unknown in Kaiin, and many were ill-minded enough to work him harm.

He moved sedately in the shade of the Pannone Wall, turned through a narrow cobbled street, bordered by old wooden houses glowing the rich brown of old stump-water in the rays of the setting sun, and so came to a small square and the high stone face of the Magician's Inn.

The host, a small fat man, sad of eye, with a small fat nose the identical shape of his body, was scraping ashes from the hearth. He straightened his back and hurried behind the counter of his little alcove.

Liane said, "A chamber, well-aired, and a supper of mushrooms, wine and oysters."

The innkeeper bowed humbly.

"Indeed, sir—and how will you pay?"

Liane flung down a leather sack, taken this very morning. The innkeeper raised his eyebrows in pleasure at the fragrance.

"The ground buds of the spase-bush, brought from a far land," said Liane.

"Excellent, excellent.... Your chamber, sir, and your supper at once."

As Liane ate, several other guests of the house appeared and sat before the fire with wine, and the talk grew large, and dwelt on wizards of the past and the great days of magic.

"Great Phandaal knew a lore now forgot," said one old man with hair dyed orange. "He tied white and black strings to the legs of sparrows and sent them veering to his direction. And where they wove their magic woof, great trees appeared, laden with flowers, fruits, nuts, or bulbs of rare liqueurs. It is said that thus he wove Great Da Forest on the shores of Sanra Water."

"Ha," said a dour man in a garment of dark blue, brown and black, "this I can do." He brought forth a bit of string, flicked it, whirled it, spoke a quiet word, and the vitality of the pattern fused the string into a tongue of red and yellow fire, which danced, curled, darted back and forth along the table till the dour man killed it with a gesture.

"And this I can do," said a hooded figure in a black cape sprinkled with silver circles. He brought forth a small tray, laid it on the table and sprinkled therein a pinch of ashes from the hearth. He brought forth a whistle and blew a clear tone, and up from the tray came glittering motes, flashing the prismatic colors red, blue, green, yellow. They floated up a foot and burst in coruscations of brilliant colors, each a beautiful star-shaped pattern, and each burst sounded a tiny repetition of the original tone—the clearest, purest sound in the world. The motes became fewer, the magician blew a different tone, and again the motes floated up to burst in glorious ornamental spangles. Another time—another swarm of motes. At last the magician replaced his whistle, wiped off the tray, tucked it inside his cloak and lapsed back to silence.

Now the other wizards surged forward, and soon the air above the table swarmed with visions, quivered with spells. One showed the group nine new colors of ineffable charm and radiance; another caused a mouth to form on the landlord's forehead and revile the crowd, much to the landlord's discomfiture, since it was his own voice. Another displayed a green glass bottle from which the face of a demon peered and grimaced; another a ball of pure crystal which rolled back and forward to the command of the sorcerer who owned it, and who claimed it to be an earring of the fabled master Sankaferrin.

Liane had attentively watched all, crowing in delight at the bottled imp, and trying to cozen the obedient crystal from its owner, without success.

And Liane became pettish, complaining that the world was full of rock-hearted men, but the sorcerer with the crystal earring remained indifferent, and even when Liane spread out twelve packets of rare spice he refused to part with his toy.

Liane pleaded, "I wish only to please the witch Lith."

"Please her with the spice, then."

Liane said ingenuously, "Indeed, she has but one wish, a bit of tapestry which I must steal from Chun the Unavoidable."

And he looked from face to suddenly silent face.

"What causes such immediate sobriety? Ho, Landlord, more wine!"

The sorcerer with the earring said, "If the floor swam ankle-deep with wine—the rich red wine of Tanvilkat—the leaden print of that name would still ride the air."

"Ha," laughed Liane, "let only a taste of that wine pass your lips, and the fumes would erase all memory."

"See his eyes," came a whisper. "Great and golden."

"And quick to see," spoke Liane. "And these legs—quick to run, fleet as starlight on the waves. And this arm—quick to stab with steel. And my magic—which will set me to a refuge that is out of all cognizance." He gulped wine from a beaker. "Now behold. This is magic from antique days." He set the bronze band over his head, stepped through, brought it up inside the darkness. When he deemed that sufficient time had elapsed, he stepped through once more.

The fire glowed, the landlord stood in his alcove, Liane's wine was at hand. But of the assembled magicians, there was no trace.

Liane looked about in puzzlement. "And where are my wizardly friends?"

The landlord turned his head: "They took to their chambers; the name you spoke weighed on their souls."

And Liane drank his wine in frowning silence.

Next morning he left the inn and picked a roundabout way to the Old Town—a gray wilderness of tumbled pillars, weathered blocks of sandstone, slumped pediments with crumbled inscriptions, flagged terraces overgrown with rusty moss. Lizards, snakes, insects crawled the ruins; no other life did he see.

Threading a way through the rubble, he almost stumbled on a corpse— the body of a youth, one who stared at the sky with empty eye-sockets.

Liane felt a presence. He leapt back, rapier half-bared. A stooped old man stood watching him. He spoke in a feeble, quavering voice: "And what will you have in the Old Town?"

Liane replaced his rapier. "I seek the Place of Whispers. Perhaps you will direct me."

The old man made a croaking sound at the back of his throat. "Another? Another? When will it cease?..." He motioned to the corpse. "This one came yesterday seeking the Place of Whispers. He would steal from Chun the Unavoidable. See him now." He turned away. "Come with me." He disappeared over a tumble of rock.

Liane followed. The old man stood by another corpse with eye-sockets bereft and bloody. "This one came four days ago, and he met Chun the Unavoidable.... And over there behind the arch is still another, a great warrior in cloison armor. And there—and there—" he pointed, pointed. "And there—and there—like crushed flies."

He turned his watery blue gaze back to Liane. "Return, young man, return—lest your body lie here in its green cloak to rot on the flagstones."

Liane drew his rapier and flourished it. "I am Liane the Wayfarer; let them who offend me have fear. And where is the Place of Whispers?"

"If you must know," said the old man, "it is beyond that broken obelisk. But you go to your peril."

"I am Liane the Wayfarer. Peril goes with me."

The old man stood like a piece of weathered statuary as Liane strode off.

And Liane asked himself, suppose this old man were an agent of Chun, and at this minute were on his way to warn him?... Best to take all precautions. He leapt up on a high entablature and ran crouching back to where he had left the ancient.

Here he came, muttering to himself, leaning on his staff. Liane dropped a block of granite as large as his head. A thud, a croak, a gasp—and Liane went his way.

He strode past the broken obelisk, into a wide court—the Place of Whispers. Directly opposite was a long wide hall, marked by a leaning column with a big black medallion, the sign of a phoenix and a two-headed lizard.

Liane merged himself with the shadow of a wall, and stood watching like a wolf, alert for any flicker of motion.

All was quiet. The sunlight invested the ruins with dreary splendor. To all sides, as far as the eye could reach, was broken stone, a wasteland leached by a thousand rains, until now the sense of man had departed and the stone was one with the natural earth.

The sun moved across the dark-blue sky. Liane presently stole from his vantage-point and circled the hall. No sight nor sign did he see.

He approached the building from the rear and pressed his ear to the stone. It was dead, without vibration. Around the side—watching up, down, to all sides; a breach in the wall. Liane peered inside. At the back hung half a golden tapestry. Otherwise the hall was empty.

Liane looked up, down, this side, that. There was nothing in sight. He continued around the hall.

He came to another broken place. He looked within. To the rear hung the golden tapestry. Nothing else, to right or left, no sight or sound.

Liane continued to the front of the hall and sought into the eaves; dead as dust.

He had a clear view of the room. Bare, barren, except for the bit of golden tapestry.

Liane entered, striding with long soft steps. He halted in the middle of the floor. Light came to him from all sides except the rear wall. There were a dozen openings from which to flee and no sound except the dull thudding of his heart.

He took two steps forward. The tapestry was almost at his fingertips.

He stepped forward and swiftly jerked the tapestry down from the wall.

And behind was Chun the Unavoidable.

Liane screamed. He turned on paralyzed legs and they were leaden, like legs in a dream which refused to run.

Chun dropped out of the wall and advanced. Over his shiny black back he wore a robe of eyeballs threaded on silk.

Liane was running, fleetly now. He sprang, he soared. The tips of his toes scarcely touched the ground. Out the hall, across the square, into the wilderness of broken statues and fallen columns. And behind came Chun, running like a dog.

Liane sped along the crest of a wall and sprang a great gap to a shattered fountain. Behind came Chun.

Liane darted up a narrow alley, climbed over a pile of refuse, over a roof, down into a court. Behind came Chun.

Liane sped down a wide avenue lined with a few stunted old cypress trees, and he heard Chun close at his heels. He turned into an archway, pulled his bronze ring over his head, down to his feet. He stepped through, brought the ring up inside the darkness. Sanctuary. He was alone in a dark magic space, vanished from earthly gaze and knowledge. Brooding silence, dead space ...

He felt a stir behind him, a breath of air. At his elbow a voice said, "I am Chun the Unavoidable."

Lith sat on her couch near the candles, weaving a cap from frogskins. The door to her hut was barred, the windows shuttered. Outside, Thamber Meadow dwelled in darkness.

A scrape at her door, a creak as the lock was tested. Lith became rigid and stared at the door.

A voice said, "Tonight, O Lith, tonight it is two long bright threads for you. Two because the eyes were so great, so large, so golden ..."

Lith sat quiet. She waited an hour; then, creeping to the door, she listened. The sense of presence was absent. A frog croaked nearby.

She eased the door ajar, found the threads and closed the door. She ran to her golden tapestry and fitted the threads into the ravelled warp.

And she stared at the golden valley, sick with longing for Ariventa, and tears blurred out the peaceful river, the quiet golden forest. "The cloth slowly grows wider ... One day it will be done, and I will come home...."

The Rag Thing

Donald A. Wollheim

It would have been all right if spring had never come. During the winter nothing had happened and nothing was likely to happen as long as the weather remained cold and Mrs. Larch kept the radiators going. In a way, though, it is quite possible to hold Mrs. Larch to blame for everything that happened. Not that she had what people would call malicious intentions, but just that she was two things practically every boarding-house landlady is—thrifty and not too clean.

She shouldn't have been in such a hurry to turn the heat off so early in March. March is a tricky month and she should have known that the first warm day is usually an isolated phenomenon. But then you could always claim that she shouldn't have been so sloppy in her cleaning last November. She shouldn't have dropped that rag behind the radiator in the third-floor front room.

As a matter of fact, one could well wonder what she was doing using such a rag anyway. Polishing furniture doesn't require a clean rag to start with, certainly not the rag you stick into the furniture polish, that's going to be greasy anyway—but she didn't have to use that particular rag. The one that had so much dried blood on it from the meat that had been lying on it in the kitchen.

On top of that, it is probable that she had spit into the filthy thing, too. Mrs. Larch was no prize package. Gross, dull, unkempt, widowed, and careless, she fitted into the house—one of innumerable other brownstone fronts in the lower sixties of New York. Houses that in former days, fifty or sixty years ago, were considered the height of fashion and the residences of the well-to-do, now reduced to dingy rooming places for all manner of itinerants, lonely people with no hope in life other than dreary jobs, or an occasional young and confused person from the hinterland seeking fame and fortune in a city that rarely grants it.

So it was not particularly odd that when she accidentally dropped the filthy old rag behind the radiator in the room on the third-floor front late in November, she had simply left it there and forgotten to pick it up.

It gathered dust all winter, unnoticed. Skelty, who had the room, might have cleaned it out himself save that he was always too tired for that. He worked at some indefinite factory all day and when he came home he was always too tired to do much more than read the sports and comics pages of the newspapers and then maybe stare at the streaky brown walls a bit before dragging himself into bed to sleep the dreamless sleep of the weary.

The radiator, a steam one oddly enough (for most of these houses used the older hot-air circulation), was in none too good condition. Installed many, many years ago by the house's last Victorian owner, it was given to knocks, leaks, and cantankerous action. Along in December it developed a slow drip, and drops of hot water would fall to seep slowly into the floor and leave the rag lying on a moist hot surface. Steam was constantly escaping from a bad valve that Mrs. Larch would have repaired if it had blown off completely but, because the radiator always managed to be hot, never did.

Because Mrs. Larch feared drafts, the windows were rarely open in the winter, and the room would become oppressively hot at times when Skelty was away.

It is hard to say what is the cause of chemical reactions. Some hold that all things are mechanical in nature, others that life has a psychic side which cannot be duplicated in laboratories. The problem is one for metaphysicians; everyone knows that some chemicals are attracted to heat, others to light, and they may not necessarily be alive at all. Tropism is the scientific term used, and if you want to believe that living matter is stuff with a great number of tropisms and dead matter is stuff with little or no tropisms, that's one way of looking at it. Heat and moisture and greasy chemical compounds were the sole ingredients of the birth of life in some ancient unremembered swamp.

Which is why it probably would have been all right if spring had never come. Because Mrs. Larch turned the radiators off one day early in March. The warm hours were but few. It grew cold with the darkness and by night it was back in the chill of February again. But Mrs. Larch had turned the heat off and, being lazy, decided not to turn it on again till the next morning, provided of course that it stayed cold the next day (which it did).

Anyway Skelty was found dead in bed the next morning. Mrs. Larch knocked on his door when he failed to come down to breakfast and when he hadn't answered, she turned the knob and went in. He was lying in bed, blue and cold, and he had been smothered in his sleep.

There was quite a to-do about the whole business but nothing came of it. A few stupid detectives blundered around the room, asked silly questions, made a few notes, and then left the matter to the coroner and the morgue. Skelty was a nobody, no one cared whether he lived or died, he had no enemies and no friends, there were no suspicious visitors, and he had probably smothered accidentally in the blankets. Of course the body was unusually cold when Mrs. Larch found it, as if the heat had been sucked out of him, but who notices a thing like that? They also discounted the grease smudge on the top sheet, the grease stains on the floor, and the slime on his face. Probably some grease he might have been using for some imagined skin trouble, though Mrs. Larch had not heard of his doing so. In any case, no one really cared.

Mrs. Larch wore black for a day and then advertised in the papers. She made a perfunctory job of cleaning the room. Skelty's possessions were taken away by a drab sister-in-law from Brooklyn who didn't seem to care much either, and Mrs. Larch was all ready to rent the room to someone else.

The weather remained cold for the next ten days and the heat was kept up in the pipes.

The new occupant of the room was a nervous young man from upstate who was trying to get a job in New York. He was a high-strung young man who entertained any number of illusions about life and society. He thought that people did things for the love of it and he wanted to find a job where he could work for that motivation rather than the sort of things he might have done back home. He thought New York was different, which was a mistake.

He smoked like fury which was something Mrs. Larch did not like because it meant ashes on the floor and burned spots on her furniture (not that there weren't plenty already), but there was nothing Mrs. Larch would do about it because it would have meant exertion.

After four days in New York, this young man, Gorman by name, was more nervous than ever. He would lie in bed nights smoking cigarette after cigarette thinking and thinking and getting nowhere. Over and over he was facing the problem of resigning himself to a life of gray drab. It was a thought he had tried not to face and now that it was thrusting itself upon him, it was becoming intolerable.

The next time a warm day came, Mrs. Larch left the radiators on because she was not going to be fooled twice. As a result, when the weather stayed warm, the rooms became insufferably hot because she was still keeping the windows down. So that when she turned the heat off finally, the afternoon of the second day, it was pretty tropical in the rooms.

When the March weather turned about suddenly again and became chilly about nine at night, Mrs. Larch was going to bed and figured that no one would complain and that it would be warm again the next day. Which may or may not be true, it does not matter.

Gorman got home about ten, opened the window, got undressed, moved a pack of cigarettes and an ashtray next to his bed on the floor, got into bed, turned out the light and started to smoke.

He stared at the ceiling, blowing smoke upwards into the darkened room trying to see its outlines in the dim light coming in from the street. When he finished one cigarette, he let his hand dangle out the side of the bed and picked up another cigarette from the pack on the floor, lit it from the butt in his mouth, and dropped the butt into the ashtray on the floor.

The rag under the radiator was getting cold, the room was getting cold, there was one source of heat radiation in the room. That was the man in the bed. Skelty had proven a source of heat supply once. Heat attraction was chemical force that could not be denied. Strange forces began to accumulate in the long-transformed fibers of the rag.

Gorman thought he heard something flap in the room but he paid it no attention. Things were always creaking in the house. Gorman heard a swishing noise and ascribed it to the mice.

Gorman reached down for a cigarette, fumbled for it, found the pack, deftly extracted a smoke in the one-handed manner chain smokers become accustomed to, lifted it to his mouth, lit it from the burning butt in his mouth, and reached down with the butt to crush it out against the tray.

He pressed the butt into something wet like a used handkerchief, there was a sudden hiss, something coiled and whipped about his wrist; Gorman gasped and drew his hand back fast. A flaming horror, twisting and writhing, was curled around it. Before Gorman could shriek, it had whipped itself from his hand and fastened over his face, over the warm, heat-radiating skin and the glowing flame of the cigarette.

Mrs. Larch was awakened by the clang of fire engines. When the fire was put out, most of the third floor had been gutted. Gorman was an unrecognizable charred mass.

The fire department put the blaze down to Gorman's habit of smoking in bed. Mrs. Larch collected on the fire insurance and bought a new house, selling the old one to a widow who wanted to start a boarding-house.

Sail On! Sail On!

Philip José Farmer

Friar Sparks sat wedged between the wall and the realizer. He was motionless except for his forefinger and his eyes. From time to time his finger tapped rapidly on the key upon the desk, and now and then his irises, gray-blue as his native Irish sky, swiveled to look through the open door of the *toldilla* in which he crouched, the little shanty on the poop deck. Visibility was low.

Outside was dusk and a lantern by the railing. Two sailors leaned on it. Beyond them bobbed the bright lights and dark shapes of the *Niña* and the *Pinta*. And beyond them was the smooth horizon-brow of the Atlantic, edged in black and blood by the red dome of the rising moon.

The single carbon filament bulb above the monk's tonsure showed a face lost in fat—and in concentration.

The luminiferous ether crackled and hissed tonight, but the phones clamped over his ears carried, along with them, the steady dots and dashes sent by the operator at the Las Palmas station on the Grand Canary.

"Zzisss! So you are out of sherry already.... *Pop!* ... Too bad.... *Crackle* ... you hardened old winebutt.... *Zzz* ... May God have mercy on your sins....

"Lots of gossip, news, et cetera.... *Hisses!* ... Bend your ear instead of your neck, impious one.... The Turks are said to be gathering ... *crackle* ... an army to march on Austria. It is rumored that the flying sausages, said by so many to have been seen over the capitals of the Christian world, are of Turkish origin. The rumor goes they have been invented by a renegade Rogerian who was converted to the Muslim religion.... I say ... *zziss* ... to that. No one of us would do that. It is a falsity spread by our enemies in the Church to discredit us. But many people believe that....

"How close does the Admiral calculate he is to Cipangu now?"

"Flash! Savonarola today denounced the Pope, the wealthy of Florence, Greek art and literature, and the experiments of the disciples of Saint Roger Bacon.... *Zzz!* ... The man is sincere but misguided and dangerous.... I predict he'll end up on the stake he's always prescribing for us....

"Pop. ... This will kill you.... Two Irish mercenaries by the name of Pat and Mike were walking down the street of Granada when a beautiful Saracen lady leaned out of a balcony and emptied a pot of ... *hiss!* ... and Pat looked up and ... *Crackle.* ... Good, hah? Brother Juan told that last night....

"PV ... PV ... Are you coming in? ... PV ... PV ... Yes, I know it's dangerous to bandy such jests about, but nobody is monitoring us tonight.... *Zzz.* ... I think they're not, anyway...."

And so the ether bent and warped with their messages. And presently Friar Sparks tapped out the PV that ended their talk—the *"Pax vobiscum."* Then he pulled the plug out that connected his earphones to the set and, lifting them from his ears, clamped them down forward over his temples in the regulation manner.

After sidling bent-kneed from the *toldilla,* punishing his belly against the desk's hard edge as he did so, he walked over to the railing. De Salcedo and de Torres were leaning there and talking in low tones. The big bulb above gleamed on the page's red-gold hair and on the interpreter's full black beard. It also bounced pinkishly off the priest's smooth-shaven jowls and the light scarlet robe of the Rogerian order. His cowl, thrown back, served as a bag for scratch paper, pens, an ink bottle, tiny wrenches and screwdrivers, a book on cryptography, a slide rule, and a manual of angelic principles.

"Well, old rind," said young de Salcedo familiarly, "what do you hear from Las Palmas?"

"Nothing now. Too much interference from that." He pointed to the moon riding the horizon ahead of them. "What an orb!" bellowed the priest. "It's as big and red as my revered nose!"

The two sailors laughed, and de Salcedo said, "But it will get smaller and paler as the night grows, Father. And your proboscis will, on the contrary, become larger and more sparkling in inverse proportion according to the square of the ascent—"

He stopped and grinned, for the monk had suddenly dipped his nose, like a porpoise diving into the sea, raised it again, like the same animal jumping from a wave, and then once more plunged it into the heavy currents of their breath. Nose to nose, he faced them, his twinkling little eyes seeming to emit sparks like the realizer in his *toldilla.*

Again, porpoiselike, he sniffed and snuffed several times, quite loudly. Then, satisfied with what he had gleaned from their breaths, he winked at them. He did not, however, mention his findings at once, preferring to sidle toward the subject.

He said, "This Father Sparks on the Grand Canary is so entertaining. He stimulates me with all sorts of philosophical notions, both valid and fantastic. For instance, tonight, just before we were cut off by that"—he gestured at the huge bloodshot eye in the sky—"he was discussing what he called worlds of parallel time tracks, an idea originated by Dysphagius of Gotham. It's his idea there may be other worlds in coincident but not contacting universes, that God, being infinite and of unlimited creative talent and ability, the Master Alchemist, in other words, has possibly— perhaps necessarily—created a plurality of continua in which every probable event has happened."

"Huh?" grunted de Salcedo.

"Exactly. Thus, Columbus was turned down by Queen Isabella, so this attempt to reach the Indies across the Atlantic was never made. So we would not now be standing here plunging ever deeper into Oceanus in our three cockleshells, there would be no booster buoys strung out between us and the Canaries, and Father Sparks at Las Palmas and I on the *Santa Maria* would not be carrying on our fascinating conversations across the ether.

"Or, say, Roger Bacon was persecuted by the Church, instead of being encouraged and giving rise to the order whose inventions have done so much to insure the monopoly of the Church on alchemy and its divinely inspired guidance of that formerly pagan and hellish practice."

De Torres opened his mouth, but the priest silenced him with a magnificent and imperious gesture and continued.

"Or, even more ridiculous, but thought-provoking, he speculated just this evening on universes with different physical laws. One, in particular, I thought very droll. As you probably don't know, Angelo Angelei has proved, by dropping objects from the Leaning Tower of Pisa, that different weights fall at different speeds. My delightful colleague on the Grand Canary is writing a satire which takes place in a universe where Aristotle is made out to be a liar, where all things drop with equal velocities, no matter what their size. Silly stuff, but it helps to pass the time. We keep the ether busy with our little angels."

De Salcedo said, "Uh, I don't want to seem too curious about the secrets of your holy and cryptic order, Friar Sparks. But these little angels your machine realizes intrigue me. Is it a sin to presume to ask about them?"

The monk's bull roar slid to a dove cooing. "Whether it's a sin or not depends. Let me illustrate, young fellows. If you were concealing a bottle of, say, very scarce sherry on you, and you did not offer to share it with a very thirsty old gentleman, that would be a sin. A sin of omission. But if you were to give that desert-dry, that pilgrim-weary, that devout, humble, and decrepit old soul a long, soothing, refreshing, and stimulating draught of lifegiving fluid, daughter of the vine, I would find it in my heart to pray for you for that deed of loving-kindness, of encompassing charity. And it would please me so much I might tell you a little of our realizer. Not enough to hurt you, just enough so you might gain more respect for the intelligence and glory of my order."

De Salcedo grinned conspiratorially and passed the monk the bottle he'd hidden under his jacket. As the friar tilted it, and the chug-chug-chug of vanishing sherry became louder, the two sailors glanced meaningfully at each other. No wonder the priest, reputed to be so brilliant in his branch of the alchemical mysteries, had yet been sent off on this half-baked voyage to devil-knew-where. The Church had calculated that if he survived, well and good. If he didn't, then he would sin no more.

The monk wiped his lips on his sleeve, belched loudly as a horse, and said, *"Gracias,* boys. From my heart, so deeply buried in this fat, I thank you. An old Irishman, dry as a camel's hoof, choking to death with the dust of abstinence, thanks you. You have saved my life."

"Thank rather that magic nose of yours," replied de Salcedo. "Now, old rind, now that you're well greased again, would you mind explaining as much as you are allowed about that machine of yours?"

Friar Sparks took fifteen minutes. At the end of that time, his listeners asked a few permitted questions.

"...and you say you broadcast on a frequency of eighteen hundred k.c.?" the page asked. "What does 'k.c.' mean?"

"K stands for the French *kilo,* from a Greek word meaning thousand. And *c* stands for the Hebrew *cherubim,* the 'little angels.' Angel comes from the Greek *angelos,* meaning messenger. It is our concept that the ether is crammed with these cherubim, these little messengers. Thus, when we Friar Sparkses depress the key of our machine, we are able to realize some

of the infinity of 'messengers' waiting for just such a demand for service.

"So, eighteen hundred k.c. means that in a given unit of time one million, eight hundred thousand cherubim line up and hurl themselves across the ether, the nose of one being brushed by the feathertips of the cherub's wings ahead. The height of the wing crests of each little creature is even, so that if you were to draw an outline of the whole train, there would be nothing to distinguish one cherub from the next, the whole column forming that grade of little angels known as C.W."

"C.W.?"

"Continuous wingheight. My machine is a C.W. realizer."

Young de Salcedo said, "My mind reels. Such a concept! Such a revelation! It almost passes comprehension. Imagine, the aerial of your realizer is cut just so long, so that the evil cherubim surging back and forth on it demand a predetermined and equal number of good angels to combat them. And this seduction coil on the realizer crowds 'bad' angels into the left-hand, the sinister, side. And when the bad little cherubim are crowded so closely and numerously that they can't bear each other's evil company, they jump the spark gap and speed around the wire to the 'good' plate. And in this racing back and forth they call themselves to the attention of the 'little messengers,' the yea-saying cherubim. And you, Friar Sparks, by manipulating your machine thus and so, and by lifting and lowering your key, you bring these invisible and friendly lines of carriers, your etheric and winged postmen, into reality. And you are able, thus, to communicate at great distances with your brothers of the order."

"Great God!" said de Torres.

It was not a vain oath but a pious exclamation of wonder. His eyes bulged; it was evident that he suddenly saw that man was not alone, that on every side, piled on top of each other, flanked on every angle, stood a host. Black and white, they presented a solid chessboard of the seemingly empty cosmos, black for the nay-sayers, white for the yea-sayers, maintained by a Hand in delicate balance and subject as the fowls of the air and the fish of the sea to exploitation by man.

Yet de Torres, having seen such a vision as has made a saint of many a man, could only ask, "Perhaps you could tell me how many angels may stand on the point of a pin?"

Obviously, de Torres would never wear a halo. He was destined, if he lived, to cover his bony head with the mortarboard of a university teacher.

De Salcedo snorted. "I'll tell you. Philosophically speaking, you may put as many angels on a pinhead as you want to. Actually speaking, you may put only as many as there is room for. Enough of that. I'm interested in facts, not fancies. Tell me, how could the moon's rising interrupt your reception of the cherubim sent by the Sparks at Las Palmas?"

"Great Caesar, how would I know? Am I a repository of universal knowledge? No, not I! A humble and ignorant friar, I! All I can tell you is that last night it rose like a bloody tumor on the horizon, and that when it was up I had to quit marshaling my little messengers in their short and long columns. The Canary station was quite overpowered, so that both of us gave up. And the same thing happened tonight."

"The moon sends messages?" asked de Torres.

"Not in a code I can decipher. But it sends, yes."

"Santa Maria!"

"Perhaps," suggested de Salcedo, "there are people on that moon, and they are sending."

Friar Sparks blew derision through his nose. Enormous as were his nostrils, his derision was not small-bore. Artillery of contempt laid down a barrage that would have silenced any but the strongest of souls.

"Maybe—" de Torres spoke in a low tone—"maybe, if the stars are windows in heaven, as I've heard said, the angels of the higher hierarchy, the big ones, are realizing—uh—the smaller? And they only do it when the moon is up so we may know it is a celestial phenomenon?"

He crossed himself and looked around the vessel.

"You need not fear," said the monk gently. "There is no Inquisitor leaning over your shoulder. Remember, I am the only priest on this expedition. Moreover, your conjecture has nothing to do with dogma. However, that's unimportant. Here's what I don't understand: How can a heavenly body broadcast? Why does it have the same frequency as the one I'm restricted to? Why—"

"I could explain," interrupted de Salcedo with all the brashness and impatience of youth. "I could say that the Admiral and the Rogerians are wrong about the earth's shape. I could say the earth is not round but is flat. I could say the horizon exists, not because we live upon a globe, but because the earth is curved only a little ways, like a greatly flattened-out hemisphere. I could also say that the cherubim are coming, not from Luna, but from a ship such as ours, a vessel which is hanging in the void off the edge of the earth."

"What?" gasped the other two.

"Haven't you heard," said de Salcedo, "that the King of Portugal secretly sent out a ship after he turned down Columbus' proposal? How do we know he did not, that the messages are from our predecessor, that he sailed off the world's rim and is now suspended in the air and becomes exposed at night because it follows the moon around Terra—is, in fact, a much smaller and unseen satellite?"

The monk's laughter woke many men on the ship. "I'll have to tell the Las Palmas operator your tale. He can put it in that novel of his. Next you'll be telling me those messages are from one of those fire-shooting sausages so many credulous laymen have been seeing flying around. No, my dear de Salcedo, let's not be ridiculous. Even the ancient Greeks knew the earth was round. Every university in Europe teaches that. And we Rogerians have measured the circumference. We know for sure that the Indies lie just across the Atlantic. Just as we know for sure, through mathematics, that heavier-than-air machines are impossible. Our Friar Ripskulls, our mind doctors, have assured us these flying creations are mass hallucinations or else the tricks of heretics or Turks who want to panic the populace.

"That moon radio is no delusion, I'll grant you. What it is, I don't know. But it's not a Spanish or Portuguese ship. What about its different code? Even if it came from Lisbon, that ship would still have a Rogerian operator. And he would, according to our policy, be of a different nationality from the crew so he might the easier stay out of political embroilments. He wouldn't break our laws by using a different code in order to communicate with Lisbon. We disciples of Saint Roger do not stoop to petty boundary intrigues. Moreover, that realizer would not be powerful enough to reach Europe, and must, therefore, be directed at us."

"How can you be sure?" said de Salcedo. "Distressing though the thought may be to you, a priest could be subverted. Or a layman could learn your secrets and invent a code. I think that a Portuguese ship is sending to another, a ship perhaps not too distant from us."

De Torres shivered and crossed himself again. "Perhaps the angels are warning us of approaching death? Perhaps?"

"Perhaps? Then why don't they use our code? Angels would know it as well as I. No, there is no perhaps. The order does not permit perhaps. It experiments and finds out; nor does it pass judgment until it knows."

"I doubt we'll ever know," said de Salcedo gloomily. "Columbus has promised the crew that if we come across no sign of land by evening tomorrow, we shall turn back. Otherwise—" he drew a finger across his throat— "*kkk!* Another day, and we'll be pointed east and getting away from that evil and bloody-looking moon and its incomprehensible messages."

"It would be a great loss to the order and to the Church," sighed the friar. "But I leave such things in the hands of God and inspect only what He hands me to look at."

With which pious statement Friar Sparks lifted the bottle to ascertain the liquid level. Having determined in a scientific manner its existence, he next measured its quantity and tested its quality by putting all of it in that best of all chemistry tubes, his enormous belly.

Afterward, smacking his lips and ignoring the pained and disappointed looks on the faces of the sailors, he went on to speak enthusiastically of the water screw and the engine which turned it, both of which had been built recently at the St. Jonas College at Genoa. If Isabella's three ships had been equipped with those, he declared, they would not have to depend upon the wind. However, so far, the fathers had forbidden its extended use because it was feared the engine's fumes might poison the air and the terrible speeds it made possible might be fatal to the human body. After which he plunged into a tedious description of the life of his patron saint, the inventor of the first cherubim realizer and receiver, Jonas of Carcassonne, who had been martyred when he grabbed a wire he thought was insulated.

The two sailors found excuses to walk off. The monk was a good fellow, but hagiography bored them. Besides, they wanted to talk of women....

If Columbus had not succeeded in persuading his crews to sail one more day, events would have been different.

At dawn the sailors were very much cheered by the sight of several large birds circling their ships. Land could not be far off; perhaps these winged creatures came from the coast of fabled Cipangu itself, the country whose houses were roofed with gold.

The birds swooped down. Closer, they were enormous and very strange. Their bodies were flattish and almost saucer-shaped and small in proportion to the wings, which had a spread of at least thirty feet. Nor did they have legs. Only a few sailors saw the significance of that fact. These birds dwelt in the air and never rested upon land or sea.

While they were meditating upon that, they heard a slight sound as of a man clearing his throat. So gentle and far off was the noise that nobody paid any attention to it, for each thought his neighbor had made it.

A few minutes later, the sound had become louder and deeper, like a lute string being twanged.

Everybody looked up. Heads were turned west.

Even yet they did not understand that the noise like a finger plucking a wire came from the line that held the earth together, and that the line was stretched to its utmost, and that the violent finger of the sea was what had plucked the line.

It was some time before they understood. They had run out of horizon.

When they saw that, they were too late.

The dawn had not only come up *like* thunder, it *was* thunder. And though the three ships heeled over at once and tried to sail close-hauled on the port tack, the suddenly speeded-up and relentless current made beating hopeless.

Then it was the Rogerian wished for the Genoese screw and the wood-burning engine that would have made them able to resist the terrible muscles of the charging and bull like sea. Then it was that some men prayed, some raved, some tried to attack the Admiral, some jumped overboard, and some sank into a stupor.

Only the fearless Columbus and the courageous Friar Sparks stuck to their duties. All that day the fat monk crouched wedged in his little shanty, dot-dashing to his fellow on the Grand Canary. He ceased only when the moon rose like a huge red bubble from the throat of a dying giant. Then he listened intently all night and worked desperately, scribbling and swearing impiously and checking cipher books.

When the dawn came up again in a roar and a rush, he ran from the *toldilla,* a piece of paper clutched in his hand. His eyes were wild, and his lips were moving fast, but nobody could understand that he had cracked the code. They could not hear him shouting, "It is the Portuguese! It is the Portuguese!"

Their ears were too overwhelmed to hear a mere human voice. The throat clearing and the twanging of the string had been the noises preliminary to the concert itself. Now came the mighty overture; as compelling as the blast of Gabriel's horn was the topple of Oceanus into space.

One Ordinary Day, with Peanuts

Shirley Jackson

Mr. John Philip Johnson shut his front door behind him and came down his front steps into the bright morning with a feeling that all was well with the world on this best of all days, and wasn't the sun warm and good, and didn't his shoes feel comfortable after the resoling, and he knew that he had undoubtedly chosen the precise very tie which belonged with the day and the sun and his comfortable feet, and, after all, wasn't the world just a wonderful place? In spite of the fact that he was a small man, and the tie was perhaps a shade vivid, Mr. Johnson irradiated this feeling of well-being as he came down the steps and onto the dirty sidewalk, and he smiled at people who passed him, and some of them even smiled back. He stopped at the newsstand on the corner and bought his paper, saying *"Good* morning" with real conviction to the man who sold him the paper and the two or three other people who were lucky enough to be buying papers when Mr. Johnson skipped up. He remembered to fill his pockets with candy and peanuts, and then he set out to get himself uptown. He stopped in a flower shop and bought a carnation for his buttonhole, and stopped almost immediately afterward to give the carnation to a small child in a carriage, who looked at him dumbly, and then smiled, and Mr. Johnson smiled, and the child's mother looked at Mr. Johnson for a minute and then smiled too.

When he had gone several blocks uptown, Mr. Johnson cut across the avenue and went along a side street, chosen at random; he did not follow the same route every morning, but preferred to pursue his eventful way in wide detours, more like a puppy than a man intent upon business. It happened this morning that halfway down the block a moving van was parked, and the furniture from an upstairs apartment stood half on the sidewalk, half on the steps, while an amused group of people loitered, examining the scratches on the tables and the worn spots on the chairs, and a harassed woman, trying to watch a young child and the movers and the furniture all at the same time, gave the clear impression of endeavoring to shelter her private life from the people staring at her belongings. Mr. Johnson stopped, and for a moment joined the crowd, and then he came forward and, touching his hat civilly, said, "Perhaps I can keep an eye on your little boy for you?"

The woman turned and glared at him distrustfully, and Mr. Johnson added hastily, "We'll sit right here on the steps." He beckoned to the little boy, who hesitated and then responded agreeably to Mr. Johnson's genial smile. Mr. Johnson brought out a handful of peanuts from his pocket and sat on the steps with the boy, who at first refused the peanuts on the grounds that his mother did not allow him to accept food from strangers; Mr. Johnson said that probably his mother had not intended peanuts to be included, since elephants at the circus ate them, and the boy considered, and then agreed solemnly. They sat on the steps cracking peanuts in a comradely fashion, and Mr. Johnson said, "So you're moving?"

"Yep," said the boy.

"Where you going?"

"Vermont."

"Nice place. Plenty of snow there. Maple sugar, too; you like maple sugar?"

"Sure."

"Plenty of maple sugar in Vermont. You going to live on a farm?"

"Going to live with Grandpa."

"Grandpa like peanuts?"

"Sure."

"Ought to take him some," said Mr. Johnson, reaching into his pocket. "Just you and Mommy going?"

"Yep."

"Tell you what," Mr. Johnson said. "You take some peanuts to eat on the train."

The boy's mother, after glancing at them frequently, had seemingly decided that Mr. Johnson was trustworthy, because she had devoted herself wholeheartedly to seeing that the movers did not — what movers rarely do, but every housewife believes they will — crack a leg from her good table, or set a kitchen chair down on a lamp. Most of the furniture was loaded by now, and she was deep in that nervous stage when she knew there was something she had forgotten to pack — hidden away in the back of a closet somewhere, or left at a neighbor's and forgotten, or on the clothesline — and was trying to remember under stress what it was.

"This all, lady?" the chief mover said, completing her dismay.

Uncertainly, she nodded.

"Want to go on the truck with the furniture, sonny?" the mover asked the boy, and laughed. The boy laughed too and said to Mr. Johnson, "I guess I'll have a good time at Vermont."

"Fine time," said Mr. Johnson, and stood up. "Have one more peanut before you go," he said to the boy.

The boy's mother said to Mr. Johnson, "Thank you so much; it was a great help to me."

"Nothing at all," said Mr. Johnson gallantly. "Where in Vermont are you going?"

The mother looked at the little boy accusingly, as though he had given away a secret of some importance, and said unwillingly, "Greenwich."

"Lovely town," said Mr. Johnson. He took out a card, and wrote a name on the back. "Very good friend of mine lives in Greenwich," he said. "Call on him for anything you need. His wife makes the best doughnuts in town," he added soberly to the little boy.

"Swell," said the little boy.

"Goodbye," said Mr. Johnson.

He went on, stepping happily with his new-shod feet, feeling the warm sun on his back and on the top of his head. Halfway down the block he met a stray dog and fed him a peanut.

At the corner, where another wide avenue faced him, Mr. Johnson decided to go on uptown again. Moving with comparative laziness, he was passed on either side by people hurrying and frowning, and people brushed past him going the other way, clattering along to get somewhere quickly. Mr. Johnson stopped on every corner and waited patiently for the light to change, and he stepped out of the way of anyone who seemed to be in any particular hurry, but one young lady came too fast for him, and crashed wildly into him when he stooped to pat a kitten which had run out onto the sidewalk from an apartment house and was now unable to get back through the rushing feet.

"Excuse me," said the young lady, trying frantically to pick up Mr.

Johnson and hurry on at the same time, "terribly sorry."

The kitten, regardless now of danger, raced back to its home. "Perfectly all right," said Mr. Johnson, adjusting himself carefully. "You seem to be in a hurry."

"Of course I'm in a hurry," said the young lady. "I'm late."

She was extremely cross and the frown between her eyes seemed well on its way to becoming permanent. She had obviously awakened late, because she had not spent any extra time in making herself look pretty, and her dress was plain and unadorned with collar or brooch, and her lipstick was noticeably crooked. She tried to brush past Mr. Johnson, but, risking her suspicious displeasure, he took her arm and said, "Please wait."

"Look," she said ominously, "I ran into you and your lawyer can see my lawyer and I will gladly pay all damages and all inconveniences suffered therefrom but please this minute let me go because *I am late.*"

"Late for what?" said Mr. Johnson; he tried his winning smile on her but it did no more than keep her, he suspected, from knocking him down again.

"Late for work," she said between her teeth. "Late for my employment. I have a job and if I am late I lose exactly so much an hour and I cannot really afford what your pleasant conversation is costing me, be it *ever* so pleasant."

"I'll pay for it," said Mr. Johnson. Now these were magic words, not necessarily because they were true, or because she seriously expected Mr. Johnson to pay for anything, but because Mr. Johnson's flat statement, obviously innocent of irony, could not be, coming from Mr. Johnson, anything but the statement of a responsible and truthful and respectable man.

"What *do* you mean?" she asked.

"I said that since I am obviously responsible for your being late I shall certainly pay for it."

"Don't be silly," she said, and for the first time the frown disappeared. *"I* wouldn't expect you to pay for anything—a few minutes ago I was offering to pay *you.* Anyway," she added, almost smiling, "it *was* my fault."

"What happens if you don't go to work?"

She stared. "I don't get paid."

"Precisely," said Mr. Johnson.

"What do you mean, precisely? If I don't show up at the office exactly twenty minutes ago I lose a dollar and twenty cents an hour, or two cents a minute on...." She thought. "...Almost a dime for the time I've spent talking to you."

Mr. Johnson laughed, and finally she laughed, too. "You're late already," he pointed out. "Will you give me another four cents worth?"

"I don't understand why."

"You'll see," Mr. Johnson promised. He led her over to the side of the walk, next to the buildings, and said, "Stand here," and went out into the rush of people going both ways. Selecting and considering, as one who must make a choice involving perhaps whole years of lives, he estimated the people going by. Once he almost moved, and then at the last minute thought better of it and drew back. Finally, from half a block away, he saw what he wanted, and moved out into the center of the traffic to intercept a young man, who was hurrying, and dressed as though he had awakened late, and frowning.

"Oof," said the young man, because Mr. Johnson had thought of no better way to intercept anyone than the one the young woman had unwittingly used upon him. "Where do you think you're going?" the young man demanded from the sidewalk.

"I want to speak to you," said Mr. Johnson ominously.

The young man got up nervously, dusting himself and eyeing Mr. Johnson. "What for?" he said. "What'd *I* do?"

"That's what bothers me most about people nowadays," Mr. Johnson complained broadly to the people passing. "No matter whether they've done anything or not, they always figure someone's after them. About what you're going to do," he told the young man.

"Listen," said the young man, trying to brush past him, "I'm late, and I don't have any time to listen. Here's a dime, now get going."

"Thank you," said Mr. Johnson, pocketing the dime. "Look," he said, "what happens if you stop running?"

"I'm late," said the young man, still trying to get past Mr. Johnson, who was unexpectedly clinging.

"How much you make an hour?" Mr. Johnson demanded.

"A communist, are you?" said the young man. "Now will you please let me—"

"No," said Mr. Johnson insistently, "*how* much?"

"Dollar fifty," said the young man. "And *now* will you—"

"You like adventure?"

The young man stared, and, staring, found himself caught and held by Mr. Johnson's genial smile; he almost smiled back and then repressed it and made an effort to tear away. "I got to *hurry*," he said.

"Mystery? Like surprises? Unusual and exciting events?"

"You selling something?"

"Sure," said Mr. Johnson. "You want to take a chance?"

The young man hesitated, looked longingly up the avenue toward what might have been his destination and then, when Mr. Johnson said, "I'll pay for it," with his own peculiar convincing emphasis, turned and said, "Well, okay. But I got to *see* it first, what I'm buying."

Mr. Johnson, breathing hard, led the young man over to the side where the girl was standing; she had been watching with interest Mr. Johnson's capture of the young man and now, smiling timidly, she looked at Mr. Johnson as though prepared to be surprised at nothing.

Mr. Johnson reached into his pocket and took out his wallet. "Here," he said, and handed a bill to the girl. "This about equals your day's pay."

"But no," she said, surprised in spite of herself. "I mean, I *couldn't*."

"Please do not interrupt," Mr. Johnson told her. "And *here*," he said to the young man, "this will take care of *you*." The young man accepted the bill dazedly, but said, "Probably counterfeit," to the young woman out of the side of his mouth. "Now," Mr. Johnson went on, disregarding the young man, "what is your name, miss?"

"Kent," she said helplessly. "Mildred Kent."

"Fine," said Mr. Johnson. "And you, sir?"

"Arthur Adams," said the young man stiffly.

"Splendid," said Mr. Johnson. "Now, Miss Kent, I would like you to meet Mr. Adams. Mr. Adams, Miss Kent."

Miss Kent stared, wet her lips nervously, made a gesture as though she might run, and said, "How do you do?"

Mr. Adams straightened his shoulders, scowled at Mr. Johnson, made a gesture as though he might run, and said, "How do you do?"

"Now *this*," said Mr. Johnson, taking several bills from his wallet, "should be enough for the day for both of you. I would suggest, perhaps, Coney Island—although I personally am not fond of the place—or perhaps a nice lunch somewhere, and dancing, or a matinee, or even a movie, although take care to choose a really *good* one; there are *so* many bad movies these days. You might," he said, struck with an inspiration, "visit the Bronx Zoo, or the Planetarium. Anywhere, as a matter of fact," he concluded, "that you would like to go. Have a nice time."

As he started to move away Arthur Adams, breaking from his dumfounded stare, said, "But see here, mister, you *can't* do this. Why—how do you know—I mean, *we* don't even know—I mean, how do you know we won't just take the money and not do what you said?"

"You've taken the money," Mr. Johnson said. "You don't have to follow any of my suggestions. You may know something you prefer to do—perhaps a museum, or something."

"But suppose I just run away with it and leave her here?"

"I know you won't," said Mr. Johnson gently, "because you remembered to ask *me* that. Goodbye," he added, and went on.

As he stepped up the street, conscious of the sun on his head and his good shoes, he heard from somewhere behind him the young man saying,

"Look, you know you don't *have* to if you don't want to," and the girl saying, "But unless *you* don't want to...." Mr. Johnson smiled to himself and then thought that he had better hurry along; when he wanted to he could move very quickly, and before the young woman had gotten around to saying, "Well, *I* will if *you* will," Mr. Johnson was several blocks away and had already stopped twice, once to help a lady lift several large packages into a taxi and once to hand a peanut to a seagull. By this time he was in an area of large stores and many more people and he was buffeted constantly from either side by people hurrying and cross and late and sullen. Once he offered a peanut to a man who asked him for a dime, and once he offered a peanut to a bus driver who had stopped his bus at an intersection and had opened the window next to his seat and put out his head as though longing for fresh air and the comparative quiet of the traffic. The man wanting a dime took the peanut because Mr. Johnson had wrapped a dollar bill around it, but the bus driver took the peanut and asked ironically, "You want a transfer, Jack?"

On a busy corner Mr. Johnson encountered two young people—for one minute he thought they might be Mildred Kent and Arthur Adams—who were eagerly scanning a newspaper, their backs pressed against a storefront to avoid the people passing, their heads bent together. Mr. Johnson, whose curiosity was insatiable, leaned onto the storefront next to them and peeked over the man's shoulder; they were scanning the "Apartments Vacant" columns.

Mr. Johnson remembered the street where the woman and her little boy were going to Vermont and he tapped the man on the shoulder and said amiably, "Try down on West Seventeen. About the middle of the block, people moved out this morning."

"Say, what do you—" said the man, and then, seeing Mr. Johnson clearly, "Well, thanks. Where did you say?"

"West Seventeen," said Mr. Johnson. "About the middle of the block." He smiled again and said, "Good luck."

"Thanks," said the man.

"Thanks," said the girl, as they moved off.

"Goodbye," said Mr. Johnson.

He lunched alone in a pleasant restaurant, where the food was rich, and only Mr. Johnson's excellent digestion could encompass two of their whipped-cream-and-chocolate-and-rum-cake pastries for dessert. He had three cups of coffee, tipped the waiter largely, and went out into the street again into the wonderful sunlight, his shoes still comfortable and fresh on his feet. Outside he found a beggar staring into the windows of the restaurant he had left and, carefully looking through the money in his pocket, Mr. Johnson approached the beggar and pressed some coins and a couple of bills into his hand. "It's the price of the veal cutlet lunch plus tip," said Mr. Johnson. "Goodbye."

After his lunch he rested; he walked into the nearest park and fed peanuts to the pigeons. It was late afternoon by the time he was ready to start back downtown, and he had refereed two checker games and watched a small boy and girl whose mother had fallen asleep and awakened with surprise and fear which turned to amusement when she saw Mr. Johnson. He had given away almost all of his candy, and had fed all the rest of his peanuts to the pigeons, and it was time to go home. Although the late afternoon sun was pleasant, and his shoes were still entirely comfortable, he decided to take a taxi downtown.

He had a difficult time catching a taxi, because he gave up the first three or four empty ones to people who seemed to need them more; finally, however, he stood alone on the corner and—almost like netting a frisky fish—he hailed desperately until he succeeded in catching a cab which had been proceeding with haste uptown and seemed to draw in towards Mr. Johnson against its own will.

"Mister," the cab driver said as Mr. Johnson climbed in, "I figured you was an omen, like. I wasn't going to pick you up at all."

"Kind of you," said Mr. Johnson ambiguously.

"If I'd of let you go it would of cost me ten bucks," said the driver.

"Really?" said Mr. Johnson.

"Yeah," said the driver. "Guy just got out of the cab, he turned around and give me ten bucks, said take this and bet it in a hurry on a horse named Vulcan, right away."

"Vulcan?" said Mr. Johnson, horrified. "A fire sign on a Wednesday?"

"What?" said the driver. "Anyway, I said to myself if I got no fare between here and there I'd bet the ten, but if anyone looked like they needed the cab I'd take it as an omen and I'd take the ten home to the wife."

"You were very right," said Mr. Johnson heartily. "This is Wednesday, you would have lost your money. Monday, yes, or even Saturday. But never never never a fire sign on a Wednesday. Sunday would have been good, now."

"Vulcan don't run on Sunday," said the driver.

"You wait till another day," said Mr. Johnson. "Down this street, please, driver. I'll get off on the next corner."

"He *told* me Vulcan, though," said the driver.

"I'll tell you," said Mr. Johnson, hesitating with the door of the cab half open. "You take that ten dollars and I'll give you another ten dollars to go with it, and you go right ahead and bet that money on any Thursday on any horse that has a name indicating . . . let me see, Thursday . . . well, grain. Or any growing food."

"Grain?" said the driver. "You mean a horse named, like, Wheat or something?"

"Certainly," said Mr. Johnson. "Or, as a matter of fact, to make it even easier, any horse whose name includes the letters, C, R, L. Perfectly simple."

"Tall Corn?" said the driver, a light in his eye. "You mean a horse named, like, Tall Corn?"

"Absolutely," said Mr. Johnson. "Here's your money."

"Tall Corn," said the driver. "Thank *you*, mister."

"Goodbye," said Mr. Johnson.

He was on his own corner and went straight up to his apartment. He let himself in and called "Hello?" and Mrs. Johnson answered from the kitchen, "Hello, dear, aren't you early?"

"Took a taxi home," Mr. Johnson said. "I remembered the cheesecake, too. What's for dinner?"

Mrs. Johnson came out of the kitchen and kissed him; she was a comfortable woman, and smiling as Mr. Johnson smiled. "Hard day?" she asked.

"Not very," said Mr. Johnson, hanging his coat in the closet. "How about you?"

"So-so," she said. She stood in the kitchen doorway while he settled into his easy chair and took off his good shoes and took out the paper he had bought that morning. "Here and there," she said.

"I didn't do so badly," Mr. Johnson said. "Couple young people."

"Fine," she said. "I had a little nap this afternoon, took it easy most of the day. Went into a department store this morning and accused the woman next to me of shoplifting, and had the store detective pick her up. Sent three dogs to the pound—*you* know, the usual thing. Oh, and listen," she added, remembering.

"What?" asked Mr. Johnson.

"Well," she said, "I got onto a bus and asked the driver for a transfer, and when he helped someone else first I said that he was impertinent, and quarreled with him. And then I said why wasn't he in the army, and I said it loud enough for everyone to hear, and I took his number and I turned in a complaint. Probably got him fired."

"Fine," said Mr. Johnson. "But you do look tired. Want to change over tomorrow?"

"I *would* like to," she said. "I could do with a change."

"Right," said Mr. Johnson. "What's for dinner?"

"Veal cutlet."

"Had it for lunch," said Mr. Johnson.

That Hell-Bound Train

Robert Bloch

When Martin was a little boy, his Daddy was a Railroad Man. Daddy never rode the high iron, but he walked the tracks for the *CB&Q,* and he was proud of his job. And every night when he got drunk, he sang this old song about *That Hell-Bound Train.*

Martin didn't quite remember any of the words, but he couldn't forget the way his Daddy sang them out. And when Daddy made the mistake of getting drunk in the afternoon and got squeezed between a Pennsy tank-car and an *AT&SF* gondola, Martin sort of wondered why the Brotherhood didn't sing the song at his funeral.

After that, things didn't go so good for Martin, but somehow he always recalled Daddy's song. When Mom up and ran off with a traveling salesman from Keokuk (Daddy must have turned over in his grave, knowing she'd done such a thing, and with a *passenger,* too!) Martin hummed the tune to himself every night in the Orphan Home. And after Martin himself ran away, he used to whistle the song softly at night in the jungles, after the other bindlestiffs were asleep.

Martin was on the road for four-five years before he realized he wasn't getting anyplace. Of course he'd tried his hand at a lot of things—picking fruit in Oregon, washing dishes in a Montana hash-house, stealing hub-caps in Denver and tires in Oklahoma City—but by the time he'd put in six months on the chain-gang down in Alabama he knew he had no future drifting around this way on his own.

So he tried to get on the railroad like his Daddy had and they told him that times were bad.

But Martin couldn't keep away from the railroads. Wherever he traveled, he rode the rods; he'd rather hop a freight heading north in sub-zero weather than lift his thumb to hitch a ride with a Cadillac headed for Florida. Whenever he managed to get hold of a can of Sterno, he'd sit there under a nice warm culvert, think about the old days, and often as not he'd hum the song about *That Hell-Bound Train*. That was the train the drunks and the sinners rode—the gambling men and the grifters, the big-time spenders, the skirt-chasers, and all the jolly crew. It would be really fine to take a trip in such good company, but Martin didn't like to think of what happened when that train finally pulled into the Depot Way Down Yonder. He didn't figure on spending eternity stoking boilers in Hell, without even a Company Union to protect him. Still, it would be a lovely ride. If there was *such* a thing as a Hell-Bound Train. Which, of course, there wasn't.

At least Martin didn't *think* there was, until that evening when he found himself walking the tracks heading south, just outside of Appleton Junction. The night was cold and dark, the way November nights are in the Fox River Valley, and he knew he'd have to work his way down to New Orleans for the winter, or maybe even Texas. Somehow he didn't much feel like going, even though he'd heard tell that a lot of those Texas automobiles had solid gold hub-caps.

No sir, he just wasn't cut out for petty larceny. It was worse than a sin—it was unprofitable, too. Bad enough to do the Devil's work, but then to get such miserable pay on top of it! Maybe he'd better let the Salvation Army convert him.

Martin trudged along humming Daddy's song, waiting for a rattler to pull out of the Junction behind him. He'd have to catch it—there was nothing else for him to do.

But the first train to come along came from the other direction, roaring towards him along the track from the south.

Martin peered ahead, but his eyes couldn't match his ears, and so far all he could recognize was the sound. It *was* a train, though; he felt the steel shudder and sing beneath his feet.

And yet, how could it be? The next station was Neenah-Menasha, and there was nothing due out of there for hours.

The clouds were thick overhead, and the field-mists rolled like a cold fog in a November midnight. Even so, Martin should have been able to see the headlight as the train rushed on. But there was only the whistle, screaming out of the black throat of the night. Martin could recognize the equipment of just about any locomotive ever built, but he'd never heard a whistle that sounded like this one. It wasn't signalling; it was screaming like a lost soul.

He stepped to one side, for the train was almost on top of him now. And suddenly there it was, looming along the tracks and grinding to a stop in less time than he'd believed possible. The wheels hadn't been oiled, because they screamed too, screamed like the damned. But the train slid to a halt and the screams died away into a series of low, groaning sounds, and Martin looked up and saw that this was a passenger train. It was big and black, without a single light shining in the engine cab or any of the long string of cars; Martin couldn't read any lettering on the sides, but he was pretty sure this train didn't belong on the Northwestern Road.

He was even more sure when he saw the man clamber down out of the forward car. There was something wrong about the way he walked, as though one of his feet dragged, and about the lantern he carried. The lantern was dark, and the man held it up to his mouth and blew, and instantly it glowed redly. You don't have to be a member of the Railway Brotherhood to know that this is a mighty peculiar way of lighting a lantern.

As the figure approached, Martin recognized the conductor's cap perched on his head, and this made him feel a little better for a moment—until he noticed that it was worn a bit too high, as though there might be something sticking up on the forehead underneath it.

Still, Martin knew his manners, and when the man smiled at him, he said, "Good evening, Mr. Conductor."

"Good evening, Martin."

"How did you know my name?"

The man shrugged. "How did you know I was the Conductor?"

"You *are,* aren't you?"

"To you, yes. Although other people, in other walks of life, may recognize me in different roles. For instance, you ought to see what I look like to the folks out in Hollywood." The man grinned. "I travel a great deal," he explained.

"What brings you here?" Martin asked.

"Why, you ought to know the answer to that, Martin. I came because you needed me. Tonight, I suddenly realized you were backsliding. Thinking of joining the Salvation Army, weren't you?"

"Well—" Martin hesitated.

"Don't be ashamed. To err is human, as somebody-or-other once said.

Reader's Digest, wasn't it? Never mind. The point is, I felt you needed me. So I switched over and came your way."

"What for?"

"Why, to offer you a ride, of course. Isn't it better to travel comfortably by train than to march along the cold streets behind a Salvation Army band? Hard on the feet, they tell me, and even harder on the eardrums."

"I'm not sure I'd care to ride your train, sir," Martin said. "Considering where I'm likely to end up."

"Ah, yes. The old argument." The Conductor sighed. "I suppose you'd prefer some sort of bargain, is that it?"

"Exactly," Martin answered.

"Well, I'm afraid I'm all through with that sort of thing. There's no shortage of prospective passengers any more. Why should I offer you any special inducements?"

"You must want me, or else you wouldn't have bothered to go out of your way to find me."

The Conductor sighed again. "There you have a point. Pride was always my besetting weakness, I admit. And somehow I'd hate to lose you to the competition, after thinking of you as my own all these years." He hesitated. "Yes, I'm prepared to deal with you on your own terms, if you insist."

"The terms?" Martin asked.

"Standard proposition. Anything you want."

"Ah," said Martin.

"But I warn you in advance, there'll be no tricks. I'll grant you any wish you can name—but in return, you must promise to ride the train when the time comes."

"Suppose it never comes?"

"It will."

"Suppose I've got the kind of a wish that will keep me off forever?"

"There is no such wish."

"Don't be too sure."

"Let me worry about that," the Conductor told him. "No matter what you have in mind, I warn you that I'll collect in the end. And there'll be none of this last-minute hocus-pocus, either. No last-hour repentances, no blonde *fräuleins* or fancy lawyers showing up to get you off. I offer a clean deal. That is to say, you'll get what you want, and I'll get what I want."

"I've heard you trick people. They say you're worse than a used-car salesman."

"Now, wait a minute—"

"I apologize," Martin said, hastily. "But it *is* supposed to be a fact that you can't be trusted."

"I admit it. On the other hand, you seem to think you have found a way out."

"A sure-fire proposition."

"Sure-fire? Very funny!" The man began to chuckle, then halted. "But we waste valuable time, Martin. Let's get down to cases. What do you want from me?"

Martin took a deep breath. "I want to be able to stop Time."

"Right now?"

"No. Not yet. And not for everybody. I realize that would be impossible, of course. But I want to be able to stop Time for myself. Just once, in the future. Whenever I get to a point where I know I'm happy and contented, that's where I'd like to stop. So I can just keep on being happy forever."

"That's quite a proposition," the Conductor mused. "I've got to admit I've never heard anything just like it before—and believe me, I've listened to some lulus in my day." He grinned at Martin. "You've really been thinking about this, haven't you?"

"For years," Martin admitted. Then he coughed. "Well, what do you say?"

"It's not impossible, in terms of your own *subjective* time-sense," the Conductor murmured. "Yes, I think it could be arranged."

"But I mean *really* to stop. Nor for me just to *imagine* it."

"I understand. And it can be done."

"Then you'll agree?"

"Why not? I promised you, didn't I? Give me your hand."

Martin hesitated. "Will it hurt very much? I mean, I don't like the sight of blood, and—"

"Nonsense! You've been listening to a lot of poppycock. We already have made our bargain, my boy. I merely intend to put something into your hand. The ways and means of fulfilling your wish. After all, there's no telling at just what moment you may decide to exercise the agreement, and I can't drop everything and come running. So it's better if you can regulate matters for yourself."

"You're going to give me a Time-stopper?"

"That's the general idea. As soon as I can decide what would be practical." The Conductor hesitated. "Ah, the very thing! Here, take my watch."

He pulled it out of his vest-pocket; a railroad watch in a silver case. He opened the back and made a delicate adjustment; Martin tried to see just exactly what he was doing, but the fingers moved in a blinding blur.

"There we are," the Conductor smiled. "It's all set, now. When you finally decide where you'd like to call a halt, merely turn the stem in reverse and unwind the watch until it stops. When it stops, Time stops, for you. Simple enough?" And the Conductor dropped the watch into Martin's hand.

The young man closed his fingers tightly around the case. "That's all there is to it, eh?"

"Absolutely. But remember—you can stop the watch only once. So you'd better make sure that you're satisfied with the moment you choose to prolong. I caution you in all fairness; make very certain of your choice."

"I will." Martin grinned. "And since you've been so fair about it, I'll be fair, too. There's one thing you seem to have forgotten. It doesn't really matter *what* moment I choose. Because once I stop Time for myself, that means I stay where I am forever. I'll never have to get any older. And if I don't get any older, I'll never die. And if I never die, then I'll never have to take a ride on your train."

The Conductor turned away. His shoulders shook convulsively, and he may have been crying. "And you said *I* was worse than a used-car salesman," he gasped, in a strangled voice.

Then he wandered off into the fog, and the train-whistle gave an impatient shriek, and all at once it was moving swiftly down the track, rumbling out of sight in the darkness.

Martin stood there, blinking down at the silver watch in his hand. If it wasn't that he could actually see it and feel it there, and if he couldn't smell that peculiar odor, he might have thought he'd imagined the whole thing from start to finish—train, Conductor, bargain, and all.

But he had the watch, and he could recognize the scent left by the train as it departed, even though there aren't many locomotives around that use sulphur and brimstone as fuel.

And he had no doubts about his bargain. That's what came of thinking things through to a logical conclusion. Some fools would have settled for wealth, or power, or Kim Novak. Daddy might have sold out for a fifth of whiskey.

Martin knew that he'd made a better deal. Better? It was foolproof. All he needed to do now was choose his moment.

He put the watch in his pocket and started back down the railroad track. He hadn't really had a destination in mind before, but he did now. He was going to find a moment of happiness. . . .

Now young Martin wasn't altogether a ninny. He realized perfectly well that happiness is a relative thing; there are conditions and degrees of contentment, and they vary with one's lot in life. As a hobo, he was often satisfied with a warm handout, a double-length bench in the park, or a can of Sterno made in 1957 (a vintage year). Many a time he had reached a state of momentary bliss through such simple agencies, but he was aware that there were better things. Martin determined to seek them out.

Within two days he was in the great city of Chicago. Quite naturally, he drifted over to West Madison Street, and there he took steps to elevate his role in life. He became a city bum, a panhandler, a moocher. Within a week he had risen to the point where happiness was a meal in a regular one-arm luncheon joint, a two-bit flop on a real army cot in a real flophouse, and a full fifth of muscatel.

There was a night, after enjoying all three of these luxuries to the full, when Martin thought of unwinding his watch at the pinnacle of intoxication. But he also thought of the faces of the honest johns he'd braced for a handout today. Sure, they were squares, but they were prosperous. They wore good clothes, held good jobs, drove nice cars. And for them, happiness was even more ecstatic—they ate dinner in fine hotels, they slept on innerspring mattresses, they drank blended whiskey.

Squares or no, they had something there. Martin fingered his watch, put aside the temptation to hock it for another bottle of muscatel, and went to sleep determined to get himself a job and improve his happiness-quotient.

When he awoke he had a hangover, but the determination was still with him. Before the month was out Martin was working for a general contractor over on the South Side, at one of the big rehabilitation projects. He hated the grind, but the pay was good, and pretty soon he got himself a one-room apartment out on Blue Island Avenue. He was accustomed to eating in decent restaurants now, and he bought himself a comfortable bed, and every Saturday night he went down to the corner tavern. It was all very pleasant, but—

The foreman liked his work and promised him a raise in a month. If he waited around, the raise would mean that he could afford a secondhand car. With a car, he could even start picking up a girl for a date now and then. Other fellows on the job did, and they seemed pretty happy.

So Martin kept on working, and the raise came through and the car came through and pretty soon a couple of girls came through.

The first time it happened, he wanted to unwind his watch immediately. Until he got to thinking about what some of the older men always said. There was a guy named Charlie, for example, who worked alongside him on the hoist. "When you're young and don't know the score, maybe you get a kick out of running around with those pigs. But after a while, you want something better. A nice girl of your own. That's the ticket."

Martin felt he owed it to himself to find out. If he didn't like it better, he could always go back to what he had.

Almost six months went by before Martin met Lillian Gillis. By that time he'd had another promotion and was working inside, in the office. They made him go to night school to learn how to do simple bookkeeping, but it meant another fifteen bucks extra a week, and it was nicer working indoors.

And Lillian *was* a lot of fun. When she told him she'd marry him, Martin was almost sure that the time was now. Except that she was sort of—well, she was a *nice* girl, and she said they'd have to wait until they were married. Of course, Martin couldn't expect to marry her until he had a little more money saved up, and another raise would help, too.

That took a year. Martin was patient, because he knew it was going to be worth it. Every time he had any doubts, he took out his watch and looked at it. But he never showed it to Lillian, or anybody else. Most of the other men wore expensive wristwatches and the old silver railroad watch looked just a little cheap.

Martin smiled as he gazed at the stem. Just a few twists and he'd have something none of these other poor working slobs would ever have. Permanent satisfaction, with his blushing bride—

Only getting married turned out to be just the beginning. Sure, it was wonderful, but Lillian told him how much better things would be if they could move into a new place and fix it up. Martin wanted decent furniture, a TV set, a nice car.

So he started taking night courses and got a promotion to the front office. With the baby coming, he wanted to stick around and see his son arrive. And when it came, he realized he'd have to wait until it got a little older, started to walk and talk and develop a personality of its own.

About this time the company sent him out on the road as a troubleshooter on some of those other jobs, and now he *was* eating at those good hotels, living high on the hog and the expense-account. More than once he was tempted to unwind his watch. This was the good life. . . . Of course, it would be even better if he just didn't have to *work*. Sooner or later, if he could cut in on one of the company deals, he could make a pile and retire. Then everything would be ideal.

It happened, but it took time. Martin's son was going to high school before he really got up there into the chips. Martin got a strong hunch that it was now or never, because he wasn't exactly a kid any more.

But right about then he met Sherry Westcott, and she didn't seem to think he was middle-aged at all, in spite of the way he was losing hair and adding stomach. She taught him that a *toupee* would cover the bald spot and a cummerbund could cover the potgut. In fact, she taught him quite a lot and he so enjoyed learning that he actually took out his watch and prepared to unwind it.

Unfortunately, he chose the very moment that the private detectives broke down the door of the hotel room, and then there was a long stretch of time when Martin was so busy fighting the divorce action that he couldn't honestly say he was enjoying any given moment.

When he made the final settlement with Lil he was broke again, and

Sherry didn't seem to think he was so young, after all. So he squared his shoulders and went back to work.

He made his pile, eventually, but it took longer this time, and there wasn't much chance to have fun along the way. The fancy dames in the fancy cocktail lounges didn't seem to interest him any more, and neither did the liquor. Besides, the Doc had warned him off that.

But there were other pleasures for a rich man to investigate. Travel, for instance—and not riding the rods from one hick burg to another, either. Martin went around the world by plane and luxury liner. For a while it seemed as though he would find his moment after all, visiting the Taj Mahal by moonlight. Martin pulled out the battered old watchcase, and got ready to unwind it. Nobody else was there to watch him—

And that's why he hesitated. Sure, this was an enjoyable moment, but he was alone. Lil and the kid were gone, Sherry was gone, and somehow he'd never had time to make any friends. Maybe if he found new congenial people, he'd have the ultimate happiness. That must be the answer—it wasn't just money or power or sex or seeing beautiful things. The real satisfaction lay in friendship.

So on the boat trip home, Martin tried to strike up a few acquaintances at the ship's bar. But all these people were much younger, and Martin had nothing in common with them. Also they wanted to dance and drink, and Martin wasn't in condition to appreciate such pastimes. Nevertheless, he tried.

Perhaps that's why he had the little accident the day before they docked in San Francisco. "Little accident" was the ship's doctor's way of describing it, but Martin noticed he looked very grave when he told him to stay in bed, and he'd called an ambulance to meet the liner at the dock and take the patient right to the hospital.

At the hospital, all the expensive treatment and the expensive smiles and the expensive words didn't fool Martin any. He was an old man with a bad heart, and they thought he was going to die.

But he could fool them. He still had the watch. He found it in his coat when he put on his clothes and sneaked out of the hospital.

He didn't have to die. He could cheat death with a single gesture—and he intended to do it as a free man, out there under a free sky.

That was the real secret of happiness. He understood it now. Not even friendship meant as much as freedom. This was the best thing of all—to be free of friends or family or the furies of the flesh.

Martin walked slowly beside the embankment under the night sky. Come to think of it, he was just about back where he'd started, so many years ago. But the moment was good, good enough to prolong forever. Once a bum, always a bum.

He smiled as he thought about it, and then the smile twisted sharply and suddenly, like the pain twisting sharply and suddenly in his chest. The world began to spin and he fell down on the side of the embankment.

He couldn't see very well, but he was still conscious, and he knew what had happened. Another stroke, and a bad one. Maybe this was it. Except that he wouldn't be a fool any longer. He wouldn't wait to see what was around the corner.

Right now was his chance to use his power and save his life. And he was going to do it. He could still move, nothing could stop him.

He groped in his pocket and pulled out the old silver watch, fumbling with the stem. A few twists and he'd cheat death, he'd never have to ride that Hell-Bound Train. He could go on forever.

Forever.

Martin had never really considered the word before. To go on forever — but *how?* Did he *want* to go on forever, like this; a sick old man, lying helplessly here in the grass?

No. He couldn't do it. He wouldn't do it. And suddenly he wanted very much to cry, because he knew that somewhere along the line he'd outsmarted himself. And now it was too late. His eyes dimmed, there was a roaring in his ears. . . .

He recognized the roaring, of course, and he wasn't at all surprised to see the train come rushing out of the fog up there on the embankment. He wasn't surprised when it stopped, either, or when the Conductor climbed off and walked slowly towards him.

The Conductor hadn't changed a bit. Even his grin was still the same.

"Hello, Martin," he said. "All aboard."

"I know," Martin whispered. "But you'll have to carry me. I can't walk. I'm not even really talking any more, am I?"

"Yes you are," the Conductor said. "I can hear you fine. And you can walk, too." He leaned down and placed his hand on Martin's chest. There was a moment of icy numbness, and then, sure enough, Martin could walk after all.

He got up and followed the Conductor along the slope, moving to the side of the train.

"In here?" he asked.

"No, the next car," the Conductor murmured. "I guess you're entitled to ride Pullman. After all, you're quite a successful man. You've tasted the joys of wealth and position and prestige. You've known the pleasures of marriage and fatherhood. You've sampled the delights of dining and drinking and debauchery, too, and you traveled high, wide and handsome. So let's not have any last-minute recriminations."

"All right," Martin sighed. "I can't blame you for my mistakes. On the other hand, you can't take credit for what happened, either. I worked for everything I got. I did it all on my own. I didn't even need your watch."

"So you didn't," the Conductor said, smiling. "But would you mind giving it back to me now?"

"Need it for the next sucker, eh?" Martin muttered.

"Perhaps."

Something about the way he said it made Martin look up. He tried to see the Conductor's eyes, but the brim of his cap cast a shadow. So Martin looked down at the watch instead.

"Tell me something," he said, softly. "If I give you the watch, what will you do with it?"

"Why, throw it into the ditch," the Conductor told him. "That's all I'll do with it." And he held out his hand.

"What if somebody comes along and finds it? And twists the stem backwards, and stops Time?"

"Nobody would do that," the Conductor murmured. "Even if they knew."

"You mean, it was all a trick? This is only an ordinary, cheap watch?"

"I didn't say that," whispered the Conductor. "I only said that no one has ever twisted the stem backwards. They've all been like you, Martin—looking ahead to find that perfect happiness. Waiting for the moment that never comes."

The Conductor held out his hand again.

Martin sighed and shook his head. "You cheated me after all."

"You cheated yourself, Martin. And now you're going to ride that Hell-Bound Train."

He pushed Martin up the steps and into the car ahead. As he entered, the train began to move and the whistle screamed. And Martin stood there in the swaying Pullman, gazing down the aisle at the other passengers. He could see them sitting there, and somehow it didn't seem strange at all.

Here they were; the drunks and the sinners, the gambling men and the grifters, the big-time spenders, the skirt-chasers, and all the jolly crew. They knew where they were going, of course, but they didn't seem to give a damn. The blinds were drawn on the windows, yet it was light inside, and they were all living it up—singing and passing the bottle and roaring with laughter, throwing the dice and telling their jokes and bragging their big brags, just the way Daddy used to sing about them in the old song.

"Mighty nice traveling companions," Martin said. "Why, I've never seen such a pleasant bunch of people. I mean, they seem to be really enjoying themselves!"

The Conductor shrugged. "I'm afraid things won't be quite so jazzy when we pull into that Depot Way Down Yonder."

For the third time, he held out his hand. "Now, before you sit down, if you'll just give me that watch. A bargain's a bargain—"

Martin smiled. "A bargain's a bargain," he echoed. "I agreed to ride your train if I could stop Time when I found the right moment of happiness. And I think I'm about as happy right here as I've ever been."

Very slowly, Martin took hold of the silver watch-stem.

"No!" gasped the Conductor. "No!"

But the watch-stem turned.

"Do you realize what you've done?" the Conductor yelled. "Now we'll never reach the Depot! We'll just go on riding, all of us—forever!"

Martin grinned. "I know," he said. "But the fun is in the trip, not the destination. You taught me that. And I'm looking forward to a wonderful trip. Look, maybe I can even help. If you were to find me another one of those caps, now, and let me keep this watch—"

And that's the way it finally worked out. Wearing his cap and carrying his battered old silver watch, there's no happier person in or out of this world—now and forever—than Martin. Martin, the new Brakeman on That Hell-Bound Train.

Nine Yards of Other Cloth

Manly Wade Wellman

High up that almighty steep rocky slope with the sun just sunk, I turned as I knelt by my little campfire. Looking down slope and down to where the river crawled like a snake in the valley bottom, I saw her little black figure splash across the shallow place I'd found an hour back. At noontime I'd looked from the mountain yonder across the valley and I'd seen her then, too, on another height I'd left behind. And I'd thought of a song with my name in it:

> *On yonder hill there stands a creature,*
> *Who she is I do not know . . .*
> *Oh no, John, no, John, no! . . .*

But I knew she was Evadare. I'd fled from before her pretty face as never I'd fled from any living thing, not from evil spell-throwers nor murder-doers, nor either from my country's enemies when I'd soldiered in foreign parts and seen battle as the Bible prophet-book tells it, confused noises and garments rolled in blood. Since dawn I'd run from Evadare like a rabbit from a fox, and still she followed, climbing now along the trail I'd tried not to leave, toward the smoke of the fire I'd built before I knew she was still coming.

No getaway from her now, for night dropped on the world, and to climb higher would be to fall from some steep hidden place. I could wait where I was or I could head down and face her. Wondering which to do, I recollected how first we'd come on each other in Hosea's Hollow.

I'd not rightly known how I'd wandered there—Hosea's Hollow. I hadn't meant to, that was certain sure. No good-sensed man or woman would mean to. Folks wished Hosea's Hollow was a lost hollow, tried to stay out of it and not think about it.

Not even the old Indians relished to go there. When the white folks ran the Indians off, the Indians grinned over their shoulders as they went, calling out how Kalu would give white men the same hard times he'd given Indians.

Kalu. The Indian word means a bone. Why Kalu was named that nobody could rightly say, for nobody who saw him lived to tell what he looked to be. He came from his place when he was mad or just hungry. Who he met he snatched away, to eat or worse than eat. The folks who'd stolen the Indians' country near about loaded their wagons to go the way they'd come. Then—and this was before the time of the oldest man I'd heard tell of it—young Hosea Palmer said he'd take Kalu's curse away.

Folks hadn't wanted Hosea to try such. Hosea's father was a preacher— he begged him. So did Hosea's mother and so did a girl who'd dreamed to marry Hosea. They said if Hosea went where Kalu denned, he'd not come back, but Hosea allowed Kalu was the downright evil and couldn't prevail against a pure heart. He went in the hollow, and true he didn't come out, but no more did Kalu, from that day on. Both vanished from folks' sight and knowledge, and folks named the place Hosea's Hollow, and nary path led there.

How I myself had come to the hollow, the first soul in long years as I reckoned, it wondered me. What outside had been the broad open light of the day was cloudy gray light here among funny-growing trees. Somewhere I heard an owl hoot, not waiting for night. Likewise I half-heard music, and it came to me that was why I'd walked there without meaning to.

Later, while I watched Evadare climb up trail to me, I recollected how, in Hosea's Hollow, I'd recollected hearing the sure enough music, two days before and forty-fifty miles off.

At Haynie's Fork, hunters had shot a hog that belonged to nobody, and butched it up while the lady-folks baked pones of corn bread and sliced up coleslaw, and from here and yonder came folks carrying jugs of beady white liquor and music instruments. I was there, too, I enjoy to aid at such doings. We ate and drank and had dancing, and the most skilled men gave us music. Obray Ramsey picked his banjo and sang *O where is pretty Polly, O yonder she stands, with rings on the fingers of her lily-white hands*, on to the last line that's near about the frighteningest last line ary song had. Then they devilled me to play my silver-strung guitar and give them *Vandy, Vandy* and *The Little Black Train*. That led to tale-tellings, and one tale was of Hosea's Hollow and fifty different notions of what might could have gone with Hosea and whatever bore the name of Kalu. Then more music, with Byard Ray fiddling his possible best, the way we never thought to hear better.

But a tall thin stranger was there, with a chin like a skinny fist and sooty-colored hair. When Byard Ray had done, the stranger took from a bag a shiny black fiddle. I offered to pick guitar to harmony with him, but he said sharp, "No, I thank you." Alone he fiddled, and, gentlemen, he purely fiddled better than Byard Ray. When he'd done, I inquired him his name.

"Shull Cobart," he replied me. "You're John, is that right? We'll meet again, it's possible, John."

His smile was no way likeable as he walked off, while folks swore no living soul could fiddle Byard Ray down without some special fiddle-secret. That had been two days before, and here I was in Hosea's Hollow, seeming to hear music that was some way like the music of Shull Cobart's black fiddle.

The gray air shimmered, but not the least hot or bright, there where owls hooted by day. I looked at a funny-growing tree, and such flowers as it had I'd not seen before. Might be they grew from the tree, might be from a vine scrabbled up. They were cup-shape, shiny black like new shoes—or like Shull Cobart's shiny-black fiddle, and I felt I could hear him still play, could see him still grin.

Was that why I half-heard the ghost of his music, why I'd come to these black-flowered trees in the shimmery gray air? Anyway, there was a trail, showing that something moved in Hosea's Hollow, between the trees so close-grown on each side you wondered could you put a knife blade among them. I headed along the trail, and the gray dancing shimmer seemed to slow me as I walked.

That tune in my head; I swung my guitar around from where it hung with my soogin sack and blanket roll, and tweaked the music from the silver strings. The shimmer dulled off, or at least I moved faster, picking up my feet to my own playing, around a curve bunched with more black flowers. And there, under the trees to one side, was a grave.

Years old it had to be, for vines and scrub grew on it. A wooden cross showed it was sure enough a grave. The straight stick was as tall as my chin and as big around as my both hands could grab, and the crosspiece wasn't nailed or tied on, it grew on. I stopped.

You've seen branches grown to each other like that. Two sorts of wood, the straight-up piece darker than the crosspiece. But both pieces looked alive, though the ends had been cut or broken so long back the raw was gone and the splinters rubbed off. Little-bitty twigs sprouted, with broad light-green leaves on the crosspiece and narrow dark laurel-looking ones on the straight pole. Roots reached into the grave, to sprout the cross. And letters were carved on, shaky and deep-dug and different sizes:

PRay
foR
HosEA PALMeR

So here was where Hosea Palmer had lain down the last time, and some friend had buried him with the word to pray for him. Standing alone in the unchanciness, I did what the cross bade. In my heart I prayed, *Let the good man rest as he's earned the right and when it's my time, O Lord, let me rest as I've earned the right; and bless the kind soul who made and marked a long home for Hosea Palmer, amen.*

While always my hands moved to pick that inner-heard tune, slow and quiet like a hymn. Still picking, I strolled around another curve, and there before me was a cabin.

I reckoned one main room with clay chinking, with a split-plank door on leather hinges and a window curtained inside with tanned hide. A shed-roofed leanto was tacked to the left, and it and the main cabin had shake shingles pegged on.

The door opened, and I popped behind a tree as a girl came out.

Small-made; yet you saw she was grown and you saw she was proud, though the color was faded from her cotton dress till it was gray as a dove. Her bright, sun-colored hair was tied behind her neck with a blue ribbon. She brought a rusty old axe with her, walking proud toward a skimpy woodpile, and on her feet were flat, homemade shoes with the hair still on the cowhide. The axe was wobble-handled, but there was strength in her little round arms. She made the axe chew the wood into pieces enough for an armful, carried the wood back into the cabin, and came out again with an old hoe on her shoulder.

From the dug well she drew the bucket—it was old, too, with a couple of silver trickles leaking from it. She dipped a drink with a gourd dipper and lowered the bucket again. Then she went to the clear patch past the cabin, and leaned on the hoe to look at the plants growing.

There was shin-high corn, and what looked like cabbages. She studied them, and her face was lovely. I saw that she yearned for her little crop to grow into food for her. She began to chop the ground up along a row, and I slid off down trail again, past the grave to where I heard water talking to itself.

I found a way through the trees to the waterside. Lay flat and took a big drink, and washed my face and hands. I dropped my gear on a flat rock, then unlaced my shoes and let the water wash my feet. Finally I cut a pole, tied on a string and hook and baited it with a scrap of smoke meat.

Fishing was good. Gentlemen, fresh fish are pretty things, they show you the reason for the names they've earned—shiner, sunfish, rainbow trout. Not that I caught any such, but what I caught was all right. When I had six I opened my knife to clean them, and built a fire and propped a stone beside it to fry meat on and then a couple of fish for supper. They ate good, just as the sun went down across the funny trees, and I wondered about the bright-haired girl, if she had a plenty to eat.

Finally, in the last dim light, I took my handaxe and chopped as much dry wood as I could tote. I wrapped the four other fish in leaves. I slung on my guitar, for I never walk off from that. Back I went along the trail to the cabin. Firelight danced in the window as I sneaked through the dooryard, and bent to stack the wood by the threshold log and lay the fish on it.

"What are you doing?"

She'd ripped the door open, and she had the axe in her hand. I took a long jump away before she could swing that rusty blade.

She stood with feet apart and elbows square, to fill the door as much as her small self could. Her hair was down around her shoulders, and shone like gold fire in the light from inside.

"Oh," she said, and let the axe sink. "You're not—"

"Whom am I not?" I inquired her, trying hard to sound laughy.

She leaned tired on the axe. "Not Shull Cobart," she said.

"No, ma'am," I said. "You can say for me that I'm not Shull Cobart, nor I wouldn't be. I saw him once, and I'm honest to tell you he doesn't suit me." I pointed at what I'd brought. "I'm camped by the branch yonder. Had more fish and wood than I needed, and figured you might like them." I bowed to her. "Good night."

"Wait." There was a plea in that, and I waited. "What brought you here, Mr.—"

"I'm named John. And I just roamed in here, without thought of why."

"I'm wondered, Mr.—"

"John," I named myself again.

"I'm wondered if you're the man I've heard tell of, named John, with a silver-strung guitar."

"Why," I said, "I'd not be amazed if I had the only silver-strung guitar there is. Nobody these days strings with silver but me."

"Then I've heard you called a good man." She looked down at the wood and the fish. "You've had your supper?" she asked, soft.

"Yes, ma'am, I've had my supper."

She picked up a fish. "I've not eaten. If you—maybe you'd like some coffee—"

"Coffee," I repeated her. "I'd mightily relish a cup."

She picked up the rest of the fish. "Come in, John," she bade me, and I gathered the wood in my arms and walked in after her.

"My name's Evadare," she told me.

The inside of the cabin was what I might expect from the outside. Chinked walls, a stone fireplace with wood burning in it, a table home-pegged together, two stools made of split chunks with tough branches for legs. In a corner was a pallet bed, made up on the floor with two old patch quilts. A mirror was stuck to the wall-chinking—a woman purely has to have a mirror. Evadare took a fire-splinter from the hearth and lighted a candle stuck on the table in its own tallow. I saw by the glow how pinky-soft her skin was, how young and pretty; and bigger, bluer eyes than Evadare's you couldn't call for. At last she smiled, just a little hopeful smile.

I laid more wood to the fire, found a skillet and a chunk of fat meat. I rolled two fish in cornmeal and commenced frying them. She poured coffee from a tin pot into two tin cups. Watching, I had it in mind that the bottom of the pot was as sooty black as Shull Cobart's hair.

Finally I forked the fish on to an old cracked white plate for her. She ate, and I saw she was hungry. Again she smiled that little small smile, and filled my cup again.

"I'd not expected ary soul to come into Hosea's Hollow," she finally said.

"You expected Shull Cobart," I told her to recollect. "You said so."

"He'd come if anybody would, John."

"He didn't," I said. "And I did. Do you care to talk about it?"

She acted glad to talk about it, once she started.

She'd worked at weaving for Shull Cobart, with maybe nine-ten others, in a little town off in the hills. He took the cloth to places like Asheville and sold at a high mark to the touristers that came there. Once or twice he made to court Evadare, but she paid him no mind. But one day he went on a trip, and came again with the black fiddle.

"And he was different," she said. "He'd been scared and polite to folks before that. But the fiddle made him somebody else. He played at dances and folks danced their highest and fastest, but they were scared by his music, even when they flocked to it. He won prizes at fiddle-playing. He'd stand by the shop door and play to us girls, and the cloth we wove was more cloth and better cloth — but it was strange. Funny feel and funny look to it."

"Did the touristers still buy it?" I inquired her.

"Yes, and payed more for it, but they seemed scared while they were buying it. So I've heard tell from folks who saw."

"And Shull Cobart made you run off."

"It was when he said he wanted me to light his darkness."

I saw what those words meant. An evil man speaking them to a good girl, because his evil was hungry for good. "What did you reply him?"

"I said I wanted to be quiet and good, he wanted to be showy and scary. And he said that was just his reason, he wanted me for my goodness to his scariness." She shivered, the way folks shiver when ice falls outside the window. "I swore to go where he'd not follow. Then he played his fiddle, it somehow made to bind me hand and foot. I felt he'd tole me off with him then and there, but I pretended—"

She looked sad and ashamed of pretending, even in peril.

"I said I'd go with him next day. He was ready to wait. That night I ran off."

"And you came to Hosea's Hollow," I said. "How did you make yourself able?"

"I feared Kalu another sight less than I fear Shull Cobart," Evadare replied me. "And I've not seen Kalu—I've seen nothing. I heard a couple of things, though. Once something knocked at the door at night."

"What was it knocked, Evadare?"

"I wasn't so foolish for the lack of sense that I went to see." She shivered again, from her little toes up to her bright hair. "I dragged up the quilt and spoke the strongest prayer I remember, the old-timey one about God gives His angels charge over us by day and by night." Her blue eyes fluttered, remembering. "Whatever knocked gave one knock more and never again, that night or ary night since."

I was purely ready to talk of something else. "Who made this cabin for you?" I asked, looking around.

"It was here when I came — empty. But I knew good folks had made it, by the cross."

I saw where her eyes went, to the inside of the half-shut door. A cross was cut there, putting me in mind of the grave by the trail.

"It must have been Hosea Palmer's cabin. He's dead and buried now. Who buried him?"

She shook her head. "That wonders me, too. All I know is, a good friend did it years ago. Sometimes, when I reckon maybe it's a Sunday, I say a prayer by the grave and sing a hymn. It seems brighter when I sing, looking up to the sky."

"Maybe I can guess the song you sing, Evadare." And I touched the guitar again, and both of us sang it:

> *Lights in the valley outshine the sun—*
> *Look away beyond the blue!*

As we sang I kept thinking in my heart—how pretty her voice, and how sweet the words in Evadare's mouth.

She went on to tell me how she hoped to live. She'd fetched in meal and salt and not much else, and she'd stretched it by picking wild greens, and there were some nuts here and there around the old cabin, poked away in little handfuls like the work of squirrels; though neither of us had seen a squirrel in Hosea's Hollow. She had planted cabbages and seed corn, and reckoned these would be worth eating by deep summer. She was made up in her mind to stay in Hosea's Hollow till she had some notion that Shull Cobart didn't lie in wait for her coming back.

"He's waiting," she felt sure. "He laughed when I spoke of running off. Said he'd know all I meant to do, all he needed was to wonder a thing while he played his fiddle and the answer was in his mind." Her pink tongue wet her lips. "He had a song he played, said it had power—"

"Was it maybe this one?" I asked, trying to jolly her, and again I touched the strings. I sang old words to the music I heard inside:

> *My pretty little pink, I once did think*
> *That you and I would marry,*
> *But now I've lost all hope of you,*
> *And I've no time to tarry.*
>
> *I'll take my sack upon my back,*
> *My rifle on my shoulder,*
> *And I'll be off to the Western States*
> *To view the country over . . .*

"That's the tune," she said, "but not the words." Again she shivered. "They were like something in a dream, while he played and sang along, and I felt I was trapped and tangled and webbed."

"Like something in a dream," I repeated her, and made up words like another thing I'd heard once, to fit the same music:

> *I dreamed last night of my true love,*
> *All in my arms I had her,*
> *And her locks of hair, all long and fair,*
> *Hung round me like a shadow . . .*

"That's not his song, either," said Evadare.

"No, it isn't," a voice I'd heard before came to agree her.

In through the half-open door stepped Shull Cobart, with his sooty hair and his grin, and his shiny black fiddle in his hand.

"Why don't you say me a welcome?" he asked Evadare, and cut his eyes across at me. "John, I counted on you being here, too."

Quick I leaned my guitar to the wall and got up. "Then you counted on trouble with me," I said. "Lay aside that fiddle so I won't break it when I break you."

But it was to his chin, and the bow across. "Hark before we fight," he said, and gentlemen, hush! how Shull Cobart could play.

It was the same tune, fiddled beyond my tongue's power to tell how wild and lovely. And the cabin that had had red-gold light from the fire and soft-gold light from Evadare's hair, it looked that quick to glow silver-pale, in jumping, throbbing sweeps as he played. Once, a cold clear dry winter night, I saw in the sky the Northern Lights; and the air in that cabin beat and throbbed and quivered the same way, but pale silver, I say, not warm red. And it came to my mind, harking helpless, that the air turned colder all at once than that winter night when I'd watched the Northern Lights in the sky.

I couldn't come at Shull Cobart. Somehow, to move at him was like moving neck-deep against a flooding river. I couldn't wear my way a foot closer. I sat on the stool again, and he stripped his teeth at me, grinning like a dog above a trapped rabbit.

"I wish the best for you, John," he said through the music. "Look how I make you welcome and at rest here."

I knew what way he wanted me to rest, the same way Hosea Palmer rested out yonder. I knew it wouldn't help to get up again, so I took back my guitar and sat quiet. I looked him up and down. He wore a suit of dark cloth with a red stripe, a suit that looked worth money, and his shoes were as shiny as his fiddle, ready to make manners before rich city folks. His mean dark eyes, close together above that singing, spell-casting fiddle, read my thoughts inside me.

"Yes, John, it's good cloth," he said. "My own weaving."

"I know how it was woven," Evadare barely whispered, the first words she'd spoken since Shull came in.

She'd moved halfway into a corner. Scared white—but she was a prettier thing than I'd ever seen in my life.

"Like me to weave for you?" he inquired me, mocking; and then he sang a trifly few words to his tune:

I wove this suit and I cut this suit,
And I put this suit right on,
And I'll weave nine yards of other cloth
To make a suit for John . . .

"Nine yards," I repeated after him.

"Would that be enough fine cloth for your suit?" he grinned across the droning fiddle strings. "You're long and tall, a right much of a man, but—"

"Nobody needs nine yards but for one kind of suit," I kept on figuring. "And that's no suit at all."

"A shroud," said Evadare, barely making herself heard, and how Shull Cobart laughed at her wide eyes and the fright in her voice!

"You reckon there'll be a grave for him here in Kalu's own place, Evadare?" he gobbled at her. "Would Kalu leave enough of John to be worth burying? I know about old Barebones Kalu."

"He's not hereabouts," Evadare half-begged to be believed. "Never once he bothered me."

"Maybe he's just spared you, hoping for something better," said Shull. "But he won't be of a mind to spare all of us that came here making a fuss in his home place. That's why I toled John here."

"You toled me?" I asked, and again he nodded.

"I played a little tune so you'd come alone, John. I reckoned Kalu would relish finding you here. Being he's the sort he is, and I'm the sort I am, it's you he'd make way with instead of me. That lets me free to take Evadare away."

"I'll not go with you," Evadare said, sharper and louder than I thought possible for her.

"Won't you, though?" Shull laughed.

His fiddle-music came up, and Evadare drew herself tight and strong, as if she leaned back against ropes on her. The music took on wild-sounding notes to fit into itself. Evadare's hands made fists, her teeth bit together, her eyes shut tight. She took a step, or maybe she was dragged. Another step she took, another, toward Shull.

I tried to get up, too, but I couldn't move as she was moving. I had to sit and watch, and I had the thought of that saying about how a snake draws a bird to his coil. I'd never believed such a thing till I saw Evadare move, step by step she didn't want to take, toward Shull Cobart.

Suddenly he stopped playing, and breathed hard, like a man who's been working in the fields. Evadare stood still and rocked on her feet. I took up my muscles to make a jump, but Shull pointed his fiddle-bow at me, like a gun.

"Have sense!" he slung out. "You've both learned I can make you go or stay, whichever I want, when I fiddle as I know how. Sit down, Evadare, and I'll silence my playing for the time. But make a foolish move, John, and I might play a note that would have the bones out of your body without ary bit of help from Kalu."

Bad man as he was, he told the truth, and both of us knew it. Evadare sat on the other stool, and I put my guitar across my knees. Shull Cobart leaned against the door jamb, his fiddle low against his chest, and looked sure of himself. At that instant I was dead sure I'd never seen a wickeder face, not among all the wicked faces of the wide world.

"Know where I got this fiddle, you two?" he asked.

"I can guess," I said, "and it spoils my notion of how good a trader a certain old somebody is. He didn't make much of a swap, that fiddle for your soul; for the soul was lost before you bargained."

"It wasn't a trade, John." He plucked a fiddle-string with his thumbnail. "Just a sort of little present between friends."

"I've heard the fiddle called the devil's instrument," said Evadare, back to her soft whisper; and once again Shull Cobart laughed at her, and then at me.

"Folks have got a sight to learn about fiddles. This fiddle will make you and me rich, Evadare. We'll go to the land's great cities, and I'll play the dollars out of folks' pockets and the hearts out of folks' bodies. They'll honor me, and they'll bow their faces in the dirt before your feet."

"I'll not go with you," she told him again.

"No? Want me to play you right into my arms this minute? The only reason I don't, Evadare—and my arms want you, and that's a fact—I'd have to put down my fiddle to hold you right."

"And I'd be on you and twist your neck around like the stem on a watch," I added onto that. "You know I can do it, and so do I. Any moment it's liable to happen."

As he'd picked his fiddle-string, I touched a silver string of my guitar, and it sang like a honeybee.

"Don't do that any more, John," he snapped. "Your guitar and my fiddle don't tune together. I'm a lone player."

To his chin went that shiny black thing, and the music he made lay heavy on me. He sang:

> *I'll weave nine yards of other cloth*
> *For John to have and keep,*
> *He'll need it where he's going to lie,*
> *To warm him in his sleep. . . .*

"What are we waiting for?" I broke in. "You might kill me somehow with your fiddling, but you won't scare me."

"Kalu will do the scaring," he said as he stopped again. "Scare you purely to death. We're just a-waiting for him to come."

"How will we know—" began Evadare.

"We'll know," said Shull, the way he'd promise a baby child something. "We'll hear him. Then I'll play John out of here to stand face to face with Kalu, if it's really a face Kalu has."

I laughed myself, and heaven pardon me the lie I put into my laugh, trying to sound as if naught pestered me. Shull frowned; he didn't like how my laugh hit his ear.

"Just for argument's sake," I said to him, "how do you explain what you say your music can do?"

"I don't do any explaining. I just do the playing."

"I've heard tell how a fiddler can be skilled to where he plays a note and breaks a glass window," I recollected. "I've heard tell that he might possibly even make a house fall down."

"Dogs howl when fiddles play," said Evadare. "From pain it makes."

Shull nodded at us both. "You folks are right. There's been power-music long before this. Ever hear of a man named Orpheus?"

"He was an old-timey Greek," I said.

"He played his harp, and trees danced for him. He played his way down to the floor of hell, and back out again. Maybe I've got some of that power. A fiddle can sing extra sharp or extra sweet, and its sound's solid—like a knife or club or rope, if you can work it."

I remembered in my mind that sound goes in waves like light, and can be measured; and a wave is power, whether of sound or light. Waves can wash, like the waves of the sea that strike down tall walls and strong men. Too bad, I decided, that educated folks couldn't use that black fiddle, to make its power good and useful. In devil-taught hands, it was the devil's instrument. Not like my silver-strung guitar, the way harps, certain harps in a certain high place, are said to be strung with gold....

Shull listened. You could almost see his ears stick up, like the ears of an animal. "Something's out there," he said.

I heard it, too. Not a step or a scramble, but a movement.

"Kalu," said Evadare, her eyes the widest yet in the firelight.

"Yes, it's Kalu," said Shull. "John, wouldn't it be kindlier to the lady if you met him outside?"

"Much kindlier," I agreed him, and got up.

"You know this isn't personal, John," Shull said, fiddle at his chin. "But Kalu's bound to have somebody. It won't be Evadare, because some way he's let her be. And it won't be me, with you here. You've got a reputation, John, for doing things against what Kalu stands to represent. I figure he wants something good, because he's got plenty of the strong evil."

"The way you think you've got to have Evadare," I said.

"That's it. You're in the line of what he wants to devour." He began to play again. "Come on, John."

I was coming. I'd made up my mind. The weight of the music was on me, but not quite as deadening and binding as before. Shull Cobart walked out, fiddling. I just winked at Evadare, as if I figured it would be all right. Then I walked out, too.

The light was greeny-pale, though I saw no moon. Maybe the trees hid it, or the haze in the sky.

"Where will you face him?" asked Shull, almost polite above his soft playing.

"There's a grave down yonder—" I began to say.

"Yes, just the place. Come on."

I followed after him on the trail. My left hand chorded my guitar at the neck, my right-hand fingers found the strings. What was it Evadare had told me? . . . *I say a prayer by the grave and sing a hymn. It seems brighter when I sing.* . . .

Then there could be two kinds of power-music.

I began to pick the tune along with Shull, softer even than Evadare's whisper. He didn't hear; and, because I followed him like a calf to the slaughter-pen, he didn't guess.

Around the bend was the grave, the green light paler around it. Shull stopped. All of a quick, I knew Kalu was in the trees over us. Somewhere up there, he made a heaviness in the branches.

"Stand where you want to, John. I vow, you've played the man so far."

I moved past him, close to the cross, though there wasn't light enough to see the name or the prayer.

"Drop that guitar!" Shull howled at me.

For I began to play loud, and I sang to his tune, changing the rhythm for my own quick-made-up words:

> *I came to where the pilgrim lay,*
> *Though he was dead and gone,*
> *And I could hear his comrade say,*
> *He rests in peace alone—*

"Hush up with that!"

Shull Cobart stopped playing and ran at me. I ducked away and around the cross, and quick I sang the second verse:

Winds may come and thunders roll
And stormy tempests rise,
But here he sleeps with a restful soul
And the tears wiped from his eyes—

"Come for him, Kalu!" Shull screamed.

Kalu drop-leaped out of the branches between us.

Gentlemen, don't ask me to say too much what Kalu was. Bones, yes—
something like man-bones, but bigger and thicker, also something like
bear-bones, or big ape-bones from a foreign land. And a rotten light to
them, so I saw for a moment that the bones weren't empty. Inside the ribs
were caged puffy things, like guts and lungs and maybe a heart that
skipped and wiggled. The skull had a snout like I can't say what, and in its
eye-holes burned blue-green fire. Out came the arm-bones, and the finger-
bones were on Shull Cobart.

I heard Shull Cobart scream one more time, and then Kalu had him, like
a bullfrog with a minnow. And Kalu was back up in the branches. Standing
by the grave, still tweaking my strings, I heard the branches rustle, and no
more sounds after that from Shull Cobart.

After while, I walked to where the black fiddle lay. I stomped with my
foot, heard it smash, and kicked the pieces away.

Walking back to the cabin seemed to take an hour. I stopped at the door.

"No!" moaned Evadare, and then she just looked at me. "John—but—"

"That's twice you thought I was Shull Cobart," I said.

"Kalu—"

"Kalu took *him,* not me."

"But—" She stopped again.

"I figured the truth about Kalu and Hosea Palmer, walking out with
Shull," I began to explain. "All at once I knew why Kalu never pestered
you. You'll wonder why you didn't know it, too."

"But—" she tried once more.

"Think," I bade her. "Who buried Hosea Palmer, with a cross and a
prayer? What dear friend could he have, when he came in here alone?
Who was left alive here when it was Hosea Palmer's time to die?"

She just shook her head from side to side.

"It was Kalu," I said. "Remember the story, all of it. Hosea Palmer said
he knew how to stop Kalu's wickedness. Folks think Hosea destroyed Kalu
some way. But what he did was teach him the good part of things. They
weren't enemies. They were friends."

"Oh," she said. "Then—"

"Kalu buried Hosea Palmer," I finished for her, "and cut his name and
the prayer. Hosea must have taught him his letters. But how could Shull

Cobart understand that? It wasn't for us to know, even, till the last minute. And Kalu took the evil man, to punish him."

I sat on the door-log, my arms around my guitar.

"You can go home now, Evadare," I said. "Shull Cobart won't vex you again, by word of mouth or by sight of his face."

She'd been sitting all drawn up, as small as she could make herself. Now she managed to stand.

"Where will you go, John?"

"There's all the world for me to go through. I'll view the country over. Think me a kind thought once in a while when we're parted."

"Parted?" she said after me, and took a step, but not as if a web of music dragged her. "John. Let me come with you."

I jumped up. "With me? You don't want to go with me, Evadare."

"Let me come." Her hand touched my arm, trembling like a bird.

"How could I do that, take you with me? I live hard."

"I've not lived soft, John." But she said it soft and lovely, and it made my heart ache with what I hadn't had time before to feel for her.

"I don't have a home," I said.

"Folks make you welcome everywhere. You're happy. You have enough of what you need. There's music wherever you go. John, I want to hear the music and help the song."

I wanted to try to laugh that thought away, but I couldn't laugh. "You don't know what you say. Listen, I'll go now. Back to my camp, and I'll be out of here before sunup. Evadare, God bless you wherever you go."

"Don't you want me to go with you, John?"

I couldn't dare reply her the truth of that. Make her a wanderer of the earth, like me? I ran off. She called my name once, but I didn't stop. At my camp again, I sat by my died-out fire, wondering, then wishing, then driving the wish from me.

In the black hour before dawn, I got my stuff together and started out of Hosea's Hollow. I came clear of it as the light rose, and mounted up a trail to a ridge above. Something made me look back.

Far down the trail I'd come, I saw her. She leaned on a stick, and she carried some kind of bundle—maybe her quilts, and what little food she had. She was following.

"That fool-headed girl," I said, all alone to myself, and I up and ran down the far side. It was hours until I crossed the bottom below and mounted another ridge beyond. On the ridge I'd left behind I saw Evadare still moving after me, her little shape barely bigger than a fly. Then I thought of that song I've told you before:

> *On yonder hill there stands a creature,*
> *Who she is I do not know,*
> *I will ask her if she'll marry . . .*
> *Oh, no, John, no, John, no!*

But she didn't stand, she came on. And I knew who she was. And if I asked her to marry she wouldn't answer no.

The rest of that day I fled from her, not stopping to eat, only to grab mouthfuls of water from streams. And in the dusky last end of the day I sat quiet and watched her still coming, leaning on her stick for weariness, and knew I must go down trail to meet her.

She was at the moment when she'd drop. She'd lost her ribbon, and the locks of her hair fell round her like a shadow. Her dress was torn, her face was white-tired, and the rocks had cut her shoes to pieces and the blood seeped out of her torn feet.

She couldn't even speak. She just sagged into my arms when I held them out to her.

I carried her to my camp. The spring trickled enough so I could wash her poor cut feet. I put down her quilt and my blanket for her to sit on, with her back to a big rock. I mixed a pone of cornmeal to bake on a flat stone, and strung a few pieces of meat on a green twig. I brought her water in my cupped hand.

"John," she managed at last to speak my name.

"Evadare," I said, and we both smiled at each other, and I sat down beside her.

"I'll cease from wandering," I vowed to her. "I'll get a piece of land and put up a cabin. I'll plant and hoe a crop for us—"

"No such thing, John! I'm tired now—so tired—but I'll get over that. Let's just—view the country over."

I pulled my guitar to me, and remembered another verse to the old song that fitted Shull Cobart's tune:

> *And don't you think she's a pretty little pink,*
> *And don't you think she's clever,*
> *And don't you think that she and I*
> *Could make a match forever?*

The Montavarde Camera

Avram Davidson

Mr. Azel's shop was set in between a glazier's establishment and a woolen draper's; three short steps led down to it. The shopfront was narrow; a stranger hurrying by would not even notice it, for the grimy brick walling of the glazier's was part of a separate building, and extended farther out.

Three short steps down, and there was a little areaway before the door, and it was always clean, somehow. The slattern wind blew bits of straw and paper scraps in circles up and down the street, leaving its discarded playthings scattered all about, but not in the areaway in front of the shop door. Just above the height of a man's eye there was a rod fastened to the inside of the door, and from it descended, in neat folds, a red velveteen curtain. The shop's window, to the door's left, was veiled in the same way. In old-fashioned lettering the gold-leaf figures of the street number stood alone on the glass pane.

There was no slot for letters, no name or sign, nothing displayed on door or window. The shop was a blank, it made no impression on the eye, conveyed no message to brain. If a few of the many people scurrying by noticed it at all, it was only to assume it was empty.

No cats took advantage of this quiet backwater to doze in the sun, although at least two of them always reclined under the projecting window of the draper. On this particular day the pair were jolted out of their calm by the running feet of Mr. Lucius Collins, who was chasing his hat. It was a high-crowned bowler, a neat and altogether proper hat, and as he chased it indignantly Mr. Collins puffed and breathed through his mouth—a small, full, red-lipped mouth, grazed on either side by a pair of well-trimmed, sandy, mutton chop whiskers.

Outrageous! Mr. Collins thought, his stout little legs pumping furiously. *Humiliating!* And no one to be blamed for it, either, not even the Government, or the Boers, or Mrs. Collins, she of the sniffles and rabbity face. *Shameful!* The gold seals on his watchchain jingled and clashed together and beat against the stomach it confined, and the wind carried the hat at a rapid clip along the street.

Just as the wind had passed the draper's, it abruptly abandoned the object of its game, and the forsaken bowler fell with a thud in front of the next shop. It rolled down the first, the second, and the third step, and leaned wearily against the door.

Mr. Collins trotted awkwardly down the steps and knelt down to seize the hat. His head remained where it was, as did his hands and knees. About a foot of uncurtained glass extended from the lower border of the red velveteen to the wooden doorframe, and through this Mr. Lucius Collins looked. It almost seemed that he gaped.

Inside the shop, looking down at Mr. Collins' round and red face, was a small, slender gentleman, who leaned against a showcase as if he were (the thought flitted through Mr. Collins' mind) posing for his photograph. The mild amusement evident on his thin features brought to Mr. Collins anew the realization that his position was, at best, undignified. He took up his hat, arose, brushed the errant bowler with his sleeve, dusted his knees, and entered the shop. Somewhere in the back a bell tinkled as he did so.

A red rug covered the floor and muffled his footsteps. The place was small, but well furnished, in the solid style more fashionable in past days. Nothing was shabby or worn, yet nothing was new. A gas jet with mantle projected from a paneled wall whose dark wood had the gleam of much polishing, but the burner was not lit, although the shop was rather dark. Several chairs upholstered in leather were set at intervals around the shop. There was no counter, and no shelves, and only the one showcase. *It* was empty, and only a well-brushed Ascot top hat rested on it.

Mr. Collins did not wish the slender little gentleman to receive the impression that he, Lucius, made a practice of squatting down and peering beneath curtained shop windows.

"Are you the proprietor?" he asked. The gentleman, still smiling, said that he was. It was a dry smile, and its owner was a dry-looking person. His was a long nose set in a long face. His chin was cleft.

The gentleman's slender legs were clad in rather baggy trousers, but it was obvious that they were the aftermath of the period when baggy trousers were the fashion, and were not the result of any carelessness in attire. The cloth was of a design halfway between plaid and checkered, and a pair of sharply pointed and very glossy shoes were on his small feet. A gray waistcoat, crossed by a light gold watchchain, a rather short frock coat, and a wing collar with a black cravat completed his dress. No particular period was stamped on his clothes, but one felt that in his prime— whenever that had been—this slender little gentleman had been a dandy, in a dry, smiling sort of way.

From his nose to his chin two deep lines were etched, and there were laughter wrinkles about the corners of his eyes. His hair was brown and rather sparse, cut in the conventional fashion. Its only unusual feature was that the little gentleman had on his forehead, after the manner of the late Lord Beaconsfield, a ringlet of the type commonly known as a "spit curl." And his nicely appointed little shop contained, as far as Mr. Collins could see, absolutely no merchandise at all.

"The wind, you know, it—ah, blew my hat off and carried it away. Dropped it at your door, so to speak."

Mr. Collins spoke awkwardly, aware that the man seemed still to be somewhat amused, and believed that this was due to his own precipitate entry. In order to cover his embarrassment and justify his continued presence inside, he asked in a rush, "What is it exactly that you sell here?" and waved his arm at the unstocked room.

"What is it you wish to buy?" the man asked.

Mr. Collins flushed again, and gaped again, and fumbled about for an answer.

"Why what I meant was: in what line *are* you? You have nothing displayed whatsoever, you know. Not a thing. How is one to know what sort of stock you have, if you don't put it about where it can be seen?" As he spoke, Mr. Collins felt his self-possession returning, and went on with increased confidence to say: "Now, just for example, my own particular avocation is photography. But if you have nothing displayed to show you sell anything in that line, I daresay I would pass by here every day and never think to stop in."

The proprietor's smile increased slightly, and his eyebrows arched up to his curl.

"But it so happens that I, too, am interested in photography, and although I have no display or sign to beguile you, in you came. I do not care for advertising. It is, I think, vulgar. My equipment is not for your tuppenytintype customer, nor will I pander to his tastes."

"Your equipment?" Mr. Collins again surveyed the place. "Where is it?" A most unusual studio—if studio it was—or shop, he thought; but he was impressed by what he considered a commendable attitude on the part of the slender gentleman—a standard so elevated that he refused to lower it by the most universally accepted customs of commerce.

The proprietor pointed to the most shadowy corner of the shop. There, in the semidarkness between the showcase and the wall, a large camera of archaic design stood upon a tripod. Mr. Collins approached it with interest, and began to examine it in the failing light.

Made out of some unfamiliar type of hardwood, with its lens piece gleaming a richer gold than ordinary brass, the old camera was in every respect a museum piece; yet, despite its age, it seemed to be in good working order. Mr. Collins ran his hand over the smooth surface; as he did so, he felt a rough spot on the back. It was evidently someone's name, he discovered, burned or carved into the wood, but now impossible to read in the thickening dusk. He turned to the proprietor.

"It is rather dark back here."

"Of course. I beg your pardon; I was forgetting. It is something remarkable, isn't it? There is no such workmanship nowadays. Years of effort that took, you know." As he spoke, he lit the jet and turned up the gas. The soft, yellow light of the flame filled the shop, hissing quietly to itself. More and more shops now had electric lights; this one, certainly, never would.

Mr. Collins reverently bowed his head and peered at the writing. In a flourishing old-fashioned script, someone long ago had engraved the name of *Gaston Montavarde*. Mr. Collins looked up in amazement.

"Montavarde's camera? Here?"

"Here, before you. Montavarde worked five years on his experimental models before he made the one you see now. At that time he was still—so the books tell you—the pupil of Daguerre. But to those who knew him, the pupil far excelled the master; just as Daguerre himself far excelled Niepce. If Montavarde had not died just as he was nearing mastery of the technique he sought, his work would be world famous. As it is, appreciation of Montavarde's style and importance is largely confined to the few—of whom I count myself one. You, sir, I am pleased to note, are one of the others. One of the few others." Here the slender gentleman gave a slight bow. Mr. Collins was extremely flattered, not so much by the bow—all shopkeepers bowed—but by the implied compliment to his knowledge.

In point of fact, he knew very little of Montavarde, his life, or his work. Who does? He was familiar, as are all students of photography, with Montavarde's study of a street scene in Paris during the 1848 Revolution.

Barricades in the Morning, which shows a ruined embattlement and the still bodies of its defenders, is perhaps the first war photograph ever taken; it is usually, and wrongly, called a Daguerrotype. Perhaps not more than six or eight, altogether, of Montavarde's pictures are known to the general public, and all are famous for that peculiar luminous quality that seems to come from some unknown source within the scene. Collins was also aware that several more Montavardes in the possession of collectors of the esoteric and erotic could not be published or displayed. One of the most famous of these is the so-called *La Messe Noire.*

The renegade priest of Lyons, Du Val, who was in the habit of conducting the Black Mass of the Demonolaters, used for some years as his "altar" the naked body of the famous courtesan, La Manchette. It was this scene that Montavarde was reputed to have photographed. Like many popular women of her type, La Manchette might have eventually retired to grow roses and live to a great age, had she not been murdered by one of her numerous lovers. Montavarde's photographs of the guillotine (*The Widow*) before and after the execution, had been banned by the French censor under Louis Napoleon as a matter of public policy.

All this is a digression, of course. These asides are mentioned because they were known to Mr. Lucius Collins, and largely explained his awe and reverence on seeing the—presumably—same camera which had photographed these scenes.

"How did you get this?" he asked, not troubling to suppress or conceal his eagerness.

"For more than thirty years," explained the proprietor, "it was the property of a North American. He came to London, met with financial reverses and pawned his equipment. He did not know, one assumes, that it was *the* Montavarde camera. Nor did he redeem. I had little or no competition at the auction. Later I heard he had gone back to America, or done away with himself, some said; but no matter: the camera was a *bon marché.* I never expected to see it again. I sold it soon after, but the payments were not kept up, and so here it is."

On hearing that the camera could be purchased, Mr. Collins began to treat for its sale (though he knew he could really not afford to buy) and would not take no for an answer. In short, an agreement was drawn up, whereby he was to pay a certain sum down, and something each month for eight months.

"Shall I make out the check in pounds or in guineas?" he asked.

"Guineas, of course. I do not consider myself a tradesman." The slender gentleman smiled and fingered his watchchain as Mr. Collins drew out his checkbook.

"What name am I to write, sir? I do not—"

"My name, sir, is Azel. The initials, A. A. Ah, just so. Can you manage the camera by yourself? Then I bid you a good evening, Mr. Collins. You have made a rare acquisition, indeed. Allow me to open the door."

Mr. Collins brought his purchase home in a four-wheeler, and spent the rest of the evening dusting and polishing. Mrs. Collins, a wispy, weedy little figure, who wore her hair in what she imagined was the manner of the Princess of Wales—Mrs. Collins had a cold, as usual. She agreed that the camera *was* in excellent condition, but, with a snuffle, she pointed out that he had spent far too much money on it. In her younger days, as one of the Misses Wilkins, she had done quite a good bit of amateur photography herself, but she had given it up because it cost far too much money.

She repeated her remarks some evenings later when her brother, the Reverend Wycliffe Wilkins, made his weekly call.

"Mind you," said Mr. Collins to his brother-in-law, "I don't know just what process the inventor used in developing his plates, but I did the best I could, and I don't think it's half bad. See here. This is the only thing I've done so far. One of those old Tudor houses in Great Cumberland Street. They say it was one of the old plague houses. Pity it's got to be torn down to make way for that new road. I thought I'd beat the wreckers to it."

"Very neatly done, I'm sure," said his brother-in-law. "I don't know much about photography myself. But evidently you haven't heard about this particular house. No? Happened yesterday. My cook was out marketing, and just as she came up to the corner, the house collapsed in a pile of dust. Shoddy worksmanship somewhere; I mean, the house couldn't have been more than three hundred years old. Of course, there was no one in it, but still, it gave the cook quite a turn. I suppose there's no harm in your having this camera, but, as for me, considering its associations, I wouldn't have it in the house. Naked women, indeed!— saving your presence, Mary."

"Oh, come now," said Mr. Collins. "Montavarde was an artist."

"Many artists have been pious, decent people, Lucius. There can be no compromise between good and evil." Mrs. Collins snuffled her agreement. Mr. Collins pursed his little mouth and said no more until his good humor was restored by the maid's coming in with the tea tray.

"I suppose, then, Wycliffe, you wouldn't think of letting me take your picture."

"Well, I don't know why ever not," Mrs. Collins protested. "After the amount of money Lucius spent on the camera, we ought to make *some* use out of it, I think. Lucius will take your likeness whenever it's convenient. He has a great deal of free time. Raspberry jam or gooseberry, Wycliffe?"

Mr. Collins photographed his brother-in-law in the vicarage garden— alone, and then with his curate, the Reverend Osias Gomm. Both clerical gentlemen were very active in the temperance movement, and this added a note of irony to the tragic events of the following day. It was the carriage of Stout, the brewer; there was no doubt about that. The horses had shied at a scrap of paper. The witnesses (six of them) had described seeing the two clergymen start across the street, deep in conversation. They described how the carriage came flying around the corner.

"They never knew wot 'it 'em," the witnesses agreed. Mrs. Collins said that was the only thing that comforted her. She said nothing, of course, about the estate (three thousand pounds in six percent bonds), but she did mention the picture.

"How bright it is, Lucius," she said. "Almost shining."

After the funeral she felt free to talk about the financial affairs of her late brother, and until the estate was close to being settled, Mr. Collins had no time for photography. He did keep up the monthly payments on the camera, however, although he found them rather a drain. After all, it had not been *his* income which had just been increased 180 pounds per annum.

It was almost November before Mrs. Collins would consent to have a fire laid. The inheritance of her brother's share of their patrimony had not changed her habits for what her husband, if no one else, would have considered the better. Although he still transferred the same amount each quarter from his personal account to the household funds, there was less and less to show for it each week. Meat appeared on the table less often, and it was much more likely to be a piece of the neck than a cut off the joint. The tea grew dustier and the pieces of butter shrank in size, and more than once Mr. Collins had asked for another bit of cake at tea and been told (truthfully, as he learned by prowling around the kitchen late at night) that there wasn't another bit of cake in the house. (Perhaps it was his going to sleep on an empty—and hence, nervous, stomach—that caused the odd dreams which began about this time: confused scenes he could never remember, come daylight, and a voice—flat, resonant—repeating over and over, *"The life is in the light . . . the life is in the light."*)

He had, of course, protested, and it had, of course, done him no good at all. Mrs. Collins, with a snuffle, spoke of increased prices, the unsteady condition of World Affairs, and the necessity of Setting Something Aside For the Future, because, she said, who knows?

So, at any rate, here it was November, and a nice sea-coal fire in the grate, with Mr. Collins sitting by it in his favorite chair, reading the newspaper (there had formerly been two, but Mrs. Collins had stopped one of them in the interests of domestic economy). There were a number of interesting bits in the paper that evening, and occasionally Mr. Collins would read one of them aloud. Mrs. Collins was unraveling some wool with an eye toward reknitting it.

"Dear me!" said Mr. Collins.

"What is that, Lucius?"

" 'Unusual Pronouncement By the Bishop of Lyons.' " He looked over at his wife. "Shall I read it to you?"

"Do."

His Grace the Bishop of Lyons had found it necessary to warn all the faithful against a most horrible series of crimes that had recently been perpetrated in the City and See of Lyons. It was a sign of the infamy and decadence of the age that not once but six times in the course of the past year, consecrated wafers had been stolen from churches and rectories in the City and See of Lyons. The purpose of these thefts could only indicate one thing, and it behooved all of the faithful, and so forth. There was little doubt (wrote the Paris correspondent of Mr. Collins' newspaper) that the bishop referred to the curious ceremony generally called the Black Mass, which, it would appear, was still being performed in parts of France; and not merely, as might be assumed, among the more uneducated elements of the population.

"Dear me!" said Mr. Collins.

"Ah, those French!" said Mrs. Collins. "Wasn't it Lyons—wasn't that the place that this unpleasant person came from? The camera man?"

"Montavarde?" Mr. Collins looked up in surprise. "Perhaps. I don't know. What makes you think so?"

"Didn't poor Wycliffe say so on that last night he was here?"

"Did he? I don't remember."

"He must have. Else how could I know?"

This was a question which required no answer, but it aroused other questions in Mr. Collins' mind. That night he had the dream again, and he recalled it very clearly on awakening. There was a woman, a foreign woman ... though how he knew she was foreign, he could not say. It was not her voice, for she never spoke, only gestured: horrid, wanton gestures, too! Nor was it in her clothes, for she wore none. And she had something in her hand, about the size of a florin, curiously marked, and she offered it to him. When he went to take it, she snatched it back, laughing, and thrust it into her red, red mouth. And all the while the voice—inflectionless, echoing—repeated over and again, *"The light is in the life ... the light is in the life."* It seemed, somehow, a familiar voice.

The next day found him at his bookdealer's, the establishment of little Mr. Pettigew, the well-known antiquary, known among younger and envious members of the trade as "the well-known antiquity." There, under pretense of browsing, Mr. Collins read as much as he could on demonolatry in general, and the Black Mass in particular. It was most interesting, but, as the books all dated from the previous century, there was no mention of either Duval or Montavarde. Mr. Collins tipped his hat to the bookdealer (it was the same bowler) and left the shop.

He bought an *Illustrated London News* at a tobacconist's, got a seat on top of the omnibus, and prepared to enjoy the ride home. It was a bright day despite the time of year, one of the brightest Guy Fawkes' Days that Mr. Collins could remember.

The *Illustrated,* he noted, was showing more and more photographs as time went on, and fewer drawings. Progress, progress, thought Mr. Collins, looking with approval and affection at a picture of the Duke of York and his sons, the little princes, all in Highland costume. Then he turned the page, and saw something which almost caused him to drop the paper. It was a picture of a dreadnought, but it was the style and not the subject that fixed his attention to the page.

"The above photograph," read the caption, "of the ill-fated American battleship, the *U.S.S. Maine,* was taken shortly before it left on its last voyage for Havana. Those familiar with photography will be at once attracted by the peculiar luminosity of the photograph, which is reminiscent of the work of the Frenchman, Montavarde. The *Maine* was built at—" Mr. Collins read no further. He began to think, began to follow a train of thought alien to his mind. Shying away from any wild and outrageous fantasies, Mr. Collins began to enumerate as best he could all the photographs known to him to have been taken by the Montavarde camera.

Barricades in the Morning proved nothing, and neither did *The Widow;* no living person appeared in either. On the other hand, consider the matter of La Manchette, the subject of Montavarde's picture *La Messe Noire;* consider the old house in Great Cumberland Street, and the Reverends Wilkins and Gomm. Consider also the battleship *Maine.*

After considering all this, Mr. Collins found himself at his stop. He went directly home, took the camera in his arms, and descended with it to the basement.

Was there some quality in the camera which absorbed the life of its subjects? Some means whereby that life was transmuted into light, a light impressed upon the photograph, leaving the subjects to die?

Mr. Collins took an ax and began to destroy the camera. The wood was intensely hard, and he removed his coat before falling to work again. Try as he might, Mr. Collins could not dent the camera, box, brass or lens. He stopped at last, sweat pouring down his face, and heard his wife's voice calling to him. What*ever* was he doing?

"I'm breaking up a box for kindling wood," he shouted back. And then, even as she warned him not to use too much wood, that the wood had to last them another fortnight, that wood had gone up—even as she chattered away, Mr. Collins had another idea. He carried the camera up to the fire and thrust it in. He heaped on the coals, he threw in kerosene at the cost of his eyebrows, and he plied the bellows.

Half an hour's effort saw the camera not only unconsumed, but unscorched. He finally removed it from the fire in despair, and stood there, hot and disheveled, not knowing what to do. All doubts that he had felt earlier were now removed. Previously he had been uncertain as to the significance of Montavarde's presence with his dreadful camera at the Rites of Lucifer, at the foul ritual conducted by the renegade priest Duval. It was *not* merely as a spectator that the cameraman had attended these blasphemous parodies. The spitting on the crucifix, the receiving of the witch mar, the signing of the compact with his own blood, the ceremonial stabbing of the stolen Host while awaiting the awful moment when the priest or priestess of the unholy sect declared manifest in his or her own body the presence of the Evil One—surely Montavarde had *done* all these things, and not just seen them.

Mr. Collins felt that he needed some air. He put on his hat and coat and went down to the street. The breeze cooled his hot face and calmed his thoughts. Several children came down the street toward him, lighting firecrackers and tossing them into the air.

> *"Remember, remember, the 5th of November*
> *Was gunpowder, treason, and plot"*

the children began to chant as they came up to him. They were wheeling a tatterdemalion old bath chair, and in it was a scarecrow of a Guy Fawkes, clad in old clothes; just as Mr. Collins had done as a boy.

> *"I see no reason why gunpowder treason*
> *Should ever be forgot"*

ended the traditional phrases, and then the outstretched, expectant grimy paws, and a general cry of "Remember the Guy, sir! Remember the Guy!" Mr. Collins distributed some money to the eager group, even though he could see that his wife, who had come down and was now looking out of the first floor window, was shaking her head at him and pursing her lips, pantomiming that he wasn't to give them a farthing. He looked away and glanced at the Guy.

Its torn trousers were of a plaid design, its scuffed shoes were sharply pointed. A greasy gray waistcoat, a ragged sort of frock coat, a drooping and dirty wing collar, and a battered Ascot top hat completed its dress. The costume seemed unpleasantly familiar to Mr. Collins, but he could not quite place it. Just then a gust of wind blew off the old topper and revealed the Guy's head. It was made of one of those carven coconuts that visitors from southern countries sometimes bring back, and its carven features were a horrible parody of the face of the slender gentleman who had sold the camera.

The children went on their way while Mr. Collins remained standing, his mind a maze of strange thoughts, and Mrs. Collins frowned down at him from the window. She seemed to be busy with something; her hands moved. It seemed to him that an age passed as he stood there, hand in pocket, thinking of the long-dead Montavarde. (How did he die? "Untimely" was the word invariably used) who had purchased, at a price unknown and scarcely to be guessed at, unsurpassable skill in building and using his camera. What should one do? One might place the camera in a large sack, or encase it in concrete, and throw it in the Thames.

Or one might keep it hidden in a safe place that one knew of.

He turned to his house and looked up at Mrs. Collins, there at the window. (What *had* she been busied with?) It seemed to him that she had never looked so much like a rabbit before, and it also occurred to him how much he disliked rabbits and always had, since he was a boy. That, after all, was not so very long ago. He was still a comparatively young man. Many attractive women might still find him attractive too.

Should he submit, like some vegetable, while his wife nibbled, nibbled away at him forever? No. The way had been shown him; he had fought, but that sort of victory was plainly not to be his. So be it; he would follow the way which had been open to him since the moment he took the camera. And he would use it again, this time with full knowledge.

He started up the steps, and had just reached the top one when a searing pain stabbed him in the chest, and the sun went out. His hat fell off as he dropped. It rolled down the first, the second, and the third step. Mrs. Collins began to scream. It occurred to him, even in that moment of dark agony, how singularly unconvincing those screams sounded.

For some reason the end did not come at once.

"I'm not completely satisfied with that likeness I took of you just before you were stricken," Mrs. Collins said. "Of course, it *was* the first time I had used a camera since we were married. And the picture, even while you look at it, seems to be growing brighter."

Logically, Mr. Collins thought; for at the same time he was growing weaker. Well, it did not matter.

"Your affairs *are* in order, aren't they, Lucius?" Her eyes, as she gazed at him, were bright, birdlike. A bird, of course, is not human. He made no reply. "Yes, to be sure they are. I made certain. Except for this unpleasant Mr. Azel asking me for money he claims is still owing on the camera. Well,

I shan't pay it. I have all I can do to keep myself. But I mean to show him. He can have his old camera back, and much good may it do him. I took my mother's ring and I scratched the nasty lens up completely with the diamond."

Her voice was growing weaker now. "It's a tradition in our family, you know. It's an old diamond, an heirloom; it has been in our family ever so long, and they say that it was once set in a jeweled monstrance that stood upon the high altar at Canterbury before the days of good King Harry.

"*That* will teach that Mr. A. A. Azel a good lesson."

Man Overboard

John Collier

Glenway Morgan Abbott had the sort of face that is associated with New England by those who like New England. It was so bony, so toothly even, so modest, so extremely serious, and so nearly flinchingly unflinching, that one hardly noticed that he was actually a very good-looking man.

He also had the yacht *Zenobia,* which was handsome enough to take one's breath away at the very first glance; it showed its seriousness only on a closer inspection. Once in a very great while, I used to go on a long cruise with Glenway. I was his best, and his only intimate, friend.

Those who have seen the *Zenobia,* or seen even its picture in books on sailing, may be impolite enough to wonder how I came to be so specially friendly with the owner of a three-masted schooner which is certainly among the dozen, perhaps among the half-dozen, most famous of the great yachts of the world.

Such people should realize that, though I may lack wealth and grace and charm, I do so in a special and superior way. Moreover, in spite of the glorious *Zenobia* and the impressive association of his name, Glenway's way of life was far from being sophisticated or luxurious. His income, though still very large, was only large enough to pay for her enormous upkeep and her numerous crew. When he wanted to get a piece of research done, he had to dip into his capital.

The fact is, Glenway had at one time been married, and to a film star, and in highly romantic circumstances. As if this wasn't enough, he had at once got divorced. The star in question was Thora Vyborg, whose beauty and personality are among the legends, or the myths, of our time. All this happened before I met him, but I had gathered, though not from Glenway, that the divorce had been distinguished by a settlement such as can only result from the cruelest heartbreak, the bitterest injury; and the most efficient lawyers on the one side, and honest eyes and rather prominent front teeth on the other.

Therefore if the word yacht suggests music, ladies, awnings, white-jacketed stewards, caviar, and champagne, the suggestion is altogether misleading. The only music was the wind in the rigging; there were no ladies; the solitary steward wore no jacket, and the crew wore no shirts either. They were all natives of different parts of the Pacific with different complexions and different tongues. The language used on board was sort of sub-basic English, adequate for work, expressive in song, but not very suitable for conversation. Glenway might have had an American or a British captain or mate; however, he did not.

Anyway, every man on board knew his job. It was a pity that the cook's job was all too often only the opening of cans of frankfurters or baked beans. This was not so much due to New English frugality as to that gastronomical absent-mindedness which is so often found linked with honesty, teeth, and devotion to a cause.

Glenway was devoted to a cause, and so was the *Zenobia*. All these great yachts are, of course, capable of ocean cruising; this one was used for it, and for nothing else at all. She was used and hard-used, and, though as clean as a pin, she was by no means as shiny. On the horizon, she looked like a cloud; at her mooring like a swan to the poetically minded, or to the materialistic, like a floating palace. But as soon as you stepped aboard she had more the appearance of something sent out by an oceanographical institute. All manner of oddly shaped nets and trawls and scoops were hung, or spread, or stowed around her deck. On either side of the foremast there were two objects on pedestals, shoulder-high, and made of that ugly, gray, rust-resisting alloy which was used everywhere on this boat in place of brass or chromium. These objects were not ventilators. They had rotating tops; these tops were hooded or cowled, or whatever you'd call it, and closely shuttered against the salty spray. If you turned one of the tops toward you, and slid open the shutter, and looked inside, you would find yourself being looked back at, quietly, by the darkly gleaming eye of a movie camera.

Up in the bow there was a bulky object lashed down under quickly removable canvas. This was a searchlight. Long chests, seated high, almost as high as the low gunwale into which they were built, contained rockets and flares. Glenway was hoping to photograph something which he believed might be nocturnal in its habits. He thought that otherwise, being a very large, noticeable creature, and being a reptile, and breathing air, it would have been seen more often by daylight.

Glenway, in a word, was looking for the sea serpent. As he detested the sensational newspaper stories and the tiresome jokes associated with the term, he preferred to think of it as a *large marine saurian*. For short, we called it, not inaptly, *it*.

People all over the Pacific knew of Glenway's quest. They were, though tactful about it, rather too obviously so. Something about Glenway caused them to refrain from guffaws; but they put on leaky masks of politeness over their grins, or, if they took the matter seriously, they seriously sought to reclaim him from his folly. Either way, they made it all too clear that they thought him a crank and perhaps a zany because he believed in such a creature. For this reason he avoided ports as far as possible, and when taking in supplies or docked for overhaul he avoided the society of his kind. Now it so happens that, though I am of skeptical nature in most matters, I am strongly inclined to suspend disbelief when it comes to a large marine saurian. Without at least the possibility of such a creature, it seems to me that the world would be a poor and a narrow place. Glenway perceived this at our very first meeting, and it was the reason for at least the beginning of our friendship. I was forced to tell him I thought the chances were a million to one against him ever seeing his quarry, and I thought he was crazy to waste his time and his lovely money on hunting for it. This didn't worry him in the least.

"I shall find it sooner or later," said he, when first we debated the question, "because I know where to look."

His theory was a simple one, and made sense up to a point. If you know how an animal is constructed you can deduce a great deal as to how it lives, and especially as to what it lives on. When you know what it eats, and where that particular food abounds, you have already a very good clue as to where to look for it.

Glenway had taken all the best authenticated reports, and he had an outline drawn up from each of them. Almost all these reports, from whatever corner of the world they may come, describe more or less the same sort of creature, so he had no trouble in getting a composite picture made by an expert hand. This, of course, showed a reptile of the plesiosaur type, but very much larger than any of the fossil plesiosaurs, being only a few inches under eighty feet in length. But here there was a snag.

Glenway had every reason to know what each extra foot on the length of a yacht adds to its maintenance bills, and he knew that an eighty-foot plesiosaur is not a practicable proposition. It was not hard to calculate what its weight would be, or the size of its bite, or how large a fish could pass down its narrow gullet. "It would spend more energy just picking up fish of that size one by one," said Glenway, "than it would gain by eating them. Also, schools of herrings, mackerel, haddock, and so forth are mostly found in coastal waters, and fishermen have been after them by day and by night ever since fishermen existed. An air-breathing creature has to show itself on the suface fairly often; if it followed fish of that sort it would be as familiar to us as the barking shark. And finally, it would be extinct, because with those jaws it couldn't defend itself against killer whales, or threshers, and certainly not against the big sharks of the late Pleistocene."

"Glenway, if all this is correct, you've slain your own goddamn Jabberwock."

"I was afraid I had," said he. "It depressed the hell out of me. But one day it struck me that people who see something very surprising, in bad visibility and so forth, will naturally tend to exaggerate the most surprising aspect of whatever it is they see. Thus an astonishingly long, snaky neck will look longer and snakier than it actually is, a small head smaller, and so forth. So I had a couple of young chaps from Uncle Fred's Institute of Industrial Psychology do a series of tests. They found a deviation running up to about twenty-five percent. Then I told them what I wanted it for, and asked them to modify this outline accordingly. We got this." He handed me a second sheet. "We can take it this is what was actually seen."

"Why, this damned thing's only sixty feet long!" said I rather discontentedly. "It seems to me you're correcting eye-witness reports on pure speculation."

"No, I'm not," said he. "I double-checked it. I hired a reptile man and an ichthyologist, and I asked them to work out what the nearest thing to a sixty-foot plesiosaur would be like if it were to be a practical proposition in terms of food, energy, defense, and all that. They came up with two or three alternatives; the one that interested me was this." He pulled out a third outline. "If you put this on top of the psychologists' version," said he, "you'll see they correspond in everything essential."

"All the same, if I'm going to believe in a large marine saurian, I'd rather have an eighty-footer."

"This one weighs more than an eighty-footer," said Glenway, "and he's probably ten times as powerful. Those jaws have a bite of over three feet. This fellow could swallow a barracuda at a gulp. He might have to make two snaps at a porpoise. He'll follow schools of tuna, albacore, any sort of fish ranging from fifty to a hundred and fifty pounds. Not cod, of course."

"And why not cod?"

"Fishermen. He'd have been seen."

"Oh!"

"So evidently he doesn't follow cod."

"And evidently you can sweat a positive out of a couple of demolished negatives. Even so, it may make some sort of sense."

Glenway accepted this, which at least was better than he got from other people. He eagerly showed me innumerable charts he had drawn up, and had amended by his own observation. These showed the seasonal movements of deep-sea fish in the east Pacific, and where these movements weren't known he had what data there was on the smaller fish that the larger ones preyed on. He went on down through the food chains, and down to plankton drifts and current temperatures and so forth, and with all these, modified by all sorts of other factors, he had marked out a great oval, with dates put in here and there, which tilted through those immense solitudes of ocean which stretch from the coast of Chile up to the Aleutians.

This was his beat, and two or three times I sailed it with him. There were almost no islands, almost no shipping lanes. I used to take a regular spell in the crow's nest; two hours in the morning and two more in the late afternoon. You can't sit day after day looking for something without an admission, deep in your mind, of the possibility of seeing it. Anyway, I was extremely fond of Glenway, and it would have given me great pleasure to have been the one who sighted this saurian for him somewhere far out on the flat green or the rolling blue. The very wish lent a sinewy twist to every waterlogged palm trunk that drifted across our bows, and every distant dolphin leap offered the arc of a black, wet, and leathery neck.

At the first sight of such things, my hand, more wishful even than my thoughts, would move towards the red button on the rail of the crow's nest. This, like another in the bow, and a third by the wheel, was connected with a loud buzzer in Glenway's cabin. However, the buzzer remained silent; the immense horizon, day after day, was empty.

Glenway was an excellent navigator. One morning when I was aloft he called up to ask if I could see anything ahead. I told him there was nothing, but I had no sooner raised my glasses again than I discerned a thickening, a long hump gathering itself in the infinitely faint pencil line that marked the juncture of sky and sea. "There's something. It's land! Land ahead!"

"That's Paumoy."

He had not bothered to mention that he was going to touch at Paumoy, the main island of an isolated group northeast of the Marquesas. I had heard of the place; there were eight or ten Americans there, and someone had said that since the war they almost never got their mail. Glenway's boat took him within fifty miles of the island, and he now told me he had agreed to touch there as he passed. Sensitive as he was to crude jokes about the sea serpent, he was still a New Englander, and he felt that people should have their mail.

The island, as we drew nearer, revealed itself as several miles of whaleback, covered with that hot froth of green which suggests coconut palms and boredom. I put down the light binoculars I was using and took up the telescope, which had a much greater range. I could see the harbor, the white bungalows spaced out around it, and I could even see the people quite clearly. Before long I saw a man catch sight of the yacht. He stared under his hand, and waved and pointed; another man came out of a bungalow with a pair of glasses. I saw the two of them go off at a run to where a jeep was standing. The jeep crawled off round the harbor, stopped at another bungalow; someone got out, someone got in. The jeep moved off again, disappeared into a grove, came out on the other side, and went toiling up a little threadlike track until it went out of sight over the ridge.

By this time other people on the shore level had turned out to look at us. They had plenty of time to do so, for the breeze fell off almost to nothing as we stood in towards the island. It was already late afternoon when the *Zenobia,* with every sail set, floated as softly as an enormous thistledown to her anchorage in the harbor of Paumoy.

"What a dreary-looking dump!" I said. "What do they do here? Copra?"

"That, and shell. One fellow dries a sort of sea-slug and sells it to Chinese dealers all over the world. There was a Gauguin from San Francisco, but he didn't stay very long."

"You'd think they'd cut each other's throats out of sheer boredom."

"Well, they play poker every night of their lives, and I guess they've developed a technique of not getting on each other's nerves."

"They must need it." There seemed to be nothing on the island but coconut palms, which I don't like, and the blistering bungalows, all of which might have been prefabricated by the same mail order house. What I had taken from a greater distance to be banks of vari-colored flowers beside the bungalows, were now recognizable as heaps of tin cans, some rusty, some with their labels still on.

But I had no more time to look about me; we were on the quay, and being greeted by men in shorts and old-fashioned sun helmets, and the greeting was hearty.

"Now listen to me," said Victor Brewer, "we've got two new guys here who've been in Java. We've had them working like dogs ever since we sighted you, fixing a *rikstafel.* So you've got to stay to dinner. Or those guys are going to be hurt. Hell, you're not going to insult a couple of fellows who are slaving over a hot stove, fixing you a dinner."

Glenway wanted nothing but to pick up the outgoing mail bag and be gone. On the other hand he hated the idea of hurting anyone. He looked at me as if in the faint hope that I might step in and do it for him. It was at such moments, very rare with Glenway, that I felt Fitzgerald was right about the rich being different, or half-right, or a quarter right, and the thought of this, and the thought of the *rikstafel,* prevented me from obliging him. Instead, I pointed out there'd probably be no wind till nightfall, so we'd be losing hardly any time. Glenway at once surrendered, and we settled down to drinks and chat.

Listening to the chat, I remembered Glenway's remark about the technique of not getting on each other's nerves. It seemed to me that this technique was being exercised, and especially for Glenway's benefit. At the end of almost every remark our hosts made I felt myself dropping in the air pocket of a pulled punch; I experienced that disconcerting absence of impact which is the concomitant of velvet paws. It was clear they knew what Glenway was after, and they even referred to it, but with such collective tact that if one of them seemed likely to dwell on it for more than a few seconds he would be steam-rollered out of the conversation, generally by Mr. Brewer. It was he who asked, very casually, when we had been sitting some time at dinner, if Glenway was sailing the same course as usual; if he was going to pass, give or take a hundred miles, the northern extremity of Japan.

Glenway having replied that he always followed the same course: "You know," said Vic Brewer, letting the words fall as casually as one lets fall the poker chips when the hands are high and the stakes are higher. "You know, you could do the hell of a good turn to a guy. If you felt like it, that is."

"What sort of a turn?" asked Glenway. "And which guy?"

"You don't know him," said the man on Brewer's left. "He's a fellow called Geisecker. He's Charlie's brother-in-law's brother-in-law, if you can work that one out."

"He dropped in here to say hello," said the next man. "He came on the copra boat and he didn't know the mailboat doesn't call any more. So he's stuck."

"The point is, this poor guy is going to be in big trouble if he doesn't get to Tokyo in the next few weeks."

"When you get up in those latitudes you're certain to sight some boat or other bound for Japan."

"Any little tramp; a crab fisher or anything. He'll be tickled to death."

They spoke one after another all the way round the table, and, remembering that Glenway had said they played poker every night of their lives, I was irresistibly reminded of the process of doubling up.

"We hate to see him go," said Brewer, collecting the whole matter into his hands with the genial authority of the dealer. "He's wonderful company, Bob Geisecker. But it's almost life or death for him, poor fellow! Look, he'll pay for his passage—anything you like—if *that's* the obstacle."

"It isn't that," said Glenway. "But I haven't seen him yet."

"He's over on the other side of the island," said Brewer. "He went off with Johnny Ray in the jeep less than half an hour before we sighted you."

"That's funny," said I, thinking of what I'd seen through the telescope.

"Damned funny," said Brewer, "if going off to give Johnny a hand makes him miss his chance of passage." And turning to Glenway, he added, "If you'd only seen old Bob I know you'd have been glad to help him."

"I'll take him," said Glenway, "if he's back in time. But the wind's been failing us, and we're behind schedule, and ..."

"Fair enough," said Brewer. "If he's back in time you'll take him. If he isn't, that's his hard luck. More rice? More chicken? More shrimp? Boy, fill up that glass for Mr. Abbott."

The dinner went on and on, and not another word was said about Mr. Geisecker. At last the heavy frondage above the table drew a deep breath and began to live and move. The wind was up, and Glenway said we could wait no longer. We all walked together down to the quay. Glenway and I were just stepping into the dinghy when someone pointed, and looking back, as people were rightly warned not to do in the old stories, we saw, like a moonrise, the glow of headlights in the sky. The jeep was coming up on the far side of the ridge. "That's Bob," said Brewer. "But don't wait. We'll get him packed up in no time, and bring him out in the launch before you can up anchor."

Sure enough, just as we were ready to move out, the launch came alongside with Mr. Bob Geisecker and his bags. The latter had pieces of pajamas hanging out at their sides like the tongues of panting dogs Geisecker himself seemed a little breathless. His face, as he came up the steps into the light hanging above, had something strange about it. At first I thought it was just the flustered and confused expression of a man who had to pack and get off in such a hurry; then I thought it was the fact that, after weeks and months under an equatorial sun, this considerable face still peeled and glowed as if fresh from a weekend at Atlantic City. Finally, still unsatisfied, I thought of that massive, opulently curved, wide-mouthed instrument which is included in every brass band, and which, when it is not playing at full blast, looks as if it ought to be, or at least is about to be. Mr. Geisecker greatly resembled this instrument, but he was very silent, and it was this that was strange.

There was a quick introduction, a brief welcome from Glenway, who was busy, an uncertain mumble of thanks from our guest, and a very hasty farewell from Brewer. Glenway had to give all his attention to taking the yacht out, and Geisecker stood neglected on deck, staring after the launch, his mouth open, looking something worse than lost. I took him down to his cabin, told him we breakfasted at seven, and asked him if there was anything he wanted before turning in. He seemed only vaguely aware that I was talking to him.

"Those guys," said he, speaking like a man in a state of shock, "I kept them in stitches. In stitches—all the time!"

"Good night," I said. "I'll see you in the morning."

Next morning Geisecker joined us at breakfast. He acknowledged our greeting soberly, sat down, and looked at his plate. Glenway apologized for having been so much occupied overnight and began to discuss where and when we might hope to encounter a boat headed for Tokyo or Yokohama. Geisecker lifted a face on which dawning enlightenment made me think of the rapid change from the blue-gray hush of the tropic night to the full glare and blare of tropic day; light, warmth, life, and laughter all came flooding in faster than one would think believable or even desirable.

"I knew it all the time!" said he exultantly. "Only I just didn't happen to think of it. I knew it was a gag. When those guys hustled me aboard this lugger I got the idea they were—you know—giving me the brush-off. They just about had me fooled. Now I get it. Anything for a laugh! They swore to me last night you were heading for Lima, Peru."

"They told me very definitely," said Glenway, staring, "that it was of the greatest importance that you should get to Tokyo."

Geisecker slapped his plump and crimson thigh with startling effect. "Those guys," said he, "they'd ship a fellow to the moon on one of these goddamn spaceships if they could get a laugh out of it. And that's what they've done to me! Tokyo's where I came from. Lima, Peru is where I was going to move on to. *That's* why they kept me all day over on the other side of the island. So I shouldn't hear which way you were going."

"We're short of time," said Glenway, "but I'll put about and take you back to Paumoy if you want me to."

"Not on your life," said Geisecker. "It's a good gag and I'll be goddamned if I spoil it. All I'm doing is just going around the world saying hello to people, and to tell you the truth there's a little kimono lady back in Tokyo I shan't mind saying hello to once again." With that he obliged us with a few bars from *Madame Butterfly*.

"Glenway," said I, "it's just on eight. I think I'll be getting up aloft."

"Aloft?" cried Geisecker. "That sounds like the real salt water stuff. I've never been on one of these windjammers before. You've got to give me the dope on marlinspikes, splicing the main brace and all the rest of the nonsense. I tell you, boys, I'm going to learn to be a sailor. Now what's all this about going up aloft?"

"I'm just going to the crow's nest for a couple of hours."

"What for? Looking for something?" Even as he asked the question he turned, first on me and then on Glenway, a face which now resembled a thespian as well as a porcine ham, it so overacted the simple feat of putting two and two together. Fixing his eyes on Glenway, he slowly raised and extended an index finger of great substance. The lower joint of this finger was adorned with curving hairs, very strong and serviceable and of a ruddy gold which glinted in the morning sun. The finger stopped about a foot short of Glenway's ribs, but its quality was so potent that it seemed to make itself felt here. In fact, I even felt it in my own.

"Abbott!" cried Geisecker triumphantly. "Now that shows you how miffed I was last night when I thought those guys had given me the brush—it didn't ring any sort of a bell. Glenway Morgan Abbott! Christ, I've heard about you, pal. Those birds told me all sorts of yarns. *You're* the guy who goes around looking for the sea serpent!"

At this point he became aware of Glenway's regard, which was, for one naked moment at least, quite deadly. Geisecker drew back a little. "But maybe," said he, "maybe they were pulling my leg. I ought to have seen it right away. A fellow with your education wouldn't fall for that cheesy old bit of hokum."

By this time Glenway had recovered himself, which is to say that he was once more subject to his customary inhibitions and compulsions. These forbade him to be discourteous to a guest; and forced him to bear witness like a zealot in favor of his large marine saurian. "Perhaps," said he, after a painful swallow or two, "you haven't considered the evidence."

He went on to summarize the affidavits of numbers of worthy citizens, all describing what was obviously the same sort of creature, seen at widely dispersed times and places. He stressed especially the sworn evidence of naval officers and sea captains, and crowned the list with a reference to the reptile clearly seen by the bearded and impeccable gentlemen in charge of Queen Victoria's own yacht, the *Osborne*.

Geisecker, who had been listening with a widening smile, here heartily slapped Glenway on the back. "You know what it is *they* saw, brother? They saw the old girl herself, flopped overboard for a dip. What do you say, boys?" said he, addressing the question to me and to the man who was clearing the table. "That's about the size of it, believe you me! *Splash me, Albert!*"

He accompanied this last sentence with a flapping mimicry of regal and natatory gambols, which, considering he was neither on a throne nor in the water, seemed to me to show talent. Glenway, like the august personage represented, was not amused. There was such a contest between displeasure and hospitality visible on his face that it looked for a moment like a wrestling match seen on television, only, of course, the pain was genuine.

This, and the thought that I had rather let him down over the dinner on Paumoy, moved me to an unwonted self-sacrifice. "Glenway," said I, "you take my spell in the crow's nest, and I'll take the wheel this morning."

Glenway, being one of nature's martyrs, refused this handsome offer, and elected to stay down in the arena. As I went aloft I realized how those patricians must have felt, who, though inclined to early Christian sympathies, were nevertheless pressured into taking a box in the Colosseum on a gala night in Nero's Rome.

Every now and then I heard a roar below me, and it was not merely that of a lion; it was that of Geisecker's laughter. Before long I saw Glenway come forward, and pretend to busy himself with the little nets that were used for taking up plankton and algae. In a very few minutes Geisecker came after him, smiling, and spoke with jovial camaraderie to the two sailors who were spreading the nets. These men looked uneasily at Glenway before they laughed; it was sufficiently obvious that the jests were concerned with the sea serpent. Glenway then dropped his work and went aft, and below. Geisecker went bellowing along the deck and, getting no response, he went down after Glenway. There was a period of calm; deceptive calm, which is calmer than the other sort. Then Glenway burst up out of the forward hatch and looked around him as if for refuge. But there is no refuge on a yacht, not even on a yacht like the *Zenobia*. I realized that he must have slipped through the pantry, into the galley, and thence into the men's quarters, leaving Geisecker ditched in the saloon. Geisecker was, of all men, the least likely to remain ditched more than three minutes. At the expiration of that time I leaned far out and looked back, and saw his mighty, sweating torso emerge from the companionway.

There are certain big fat men who, when they joke with you, seem almost to enfold you in a physical embrace. This caused me to wish we were farther from the equator, but it did not prevent me going down to try to run a little interference for Glenway.

I soon found that it was next door to impossible to draw Geisecker away from Glenway. There are certain people who, if they become dimly aware they are offensive to another, will fasten on that unfortunate with all the persistence of a cat which seeks out the one cat-hater in a crowded room. They can't believe it; they think you really love them; they are tickled and fascinated and awesomely thrilled by the fantastic improbability of your dislike. They'll pluck at your attention and finger your very flesh for the unbelievable spectacle of your recoil, and they'll press yet closer for the marvel of your shudder, for all the world as if recoil and shudder were rapturous spasms induced by some novel form of lovemaking, to be evoked in wonder and in triumph again and again and again.

"Good old Glen!" said Geisecker, one afternoon when Glenway had

jumped up with what I can call a muttered exclamation, and sought refuge
in his cabin. "I love that guy. I love the way he takes a bit of ribbing. You
know—straight, deadpan, and yet you can tell that underneath he just loves
it."

"Not on that subject," I said. "He detests it. And so do I. It's making him
miserable. It's driving him just about crazy."

"Ah, don't give me that baloney!" said he with a goodhumored flap of
his hand. Geisecker was not in the least interested in what I said about my
own reaction. Sensitive to nothing else on earth, he had, unconsciously of
course, better than a dog's nose for the exact nature of the feeling he
inspired. This keen sense told thim that I am of a type not offended by his
sort of humor, and that my mounting anger was entirely on behalf of
Glenway. To him, therefore, it was vicarious, secondhand, and as flavorless
as a duenna's kiss. It gave him no sort of thrill, and he had no itch to
increase it. I felt quite rejected.

I went down to see if I could be more effective with Glenway. I said, "If
you had the least sense of humor, you'd enjoy this monster. After all, he's
the sort of thing you're looking for. He belongs to a species thought to be
extinct."

"I wish to God he was," said Glenway.

"He may not come from the Pleistocene, but he's at least a survival
from the Joke Book Age. He's a human coelacanth. He's a specimen of
Comic Picture Postcard Man. He's a living Babbitt. You ought to turn your
cameras on him. People'll think you're making it all up."

It was like trying to skip and run over soft sand. Each new sentence got
off to a worse start and sank deeper into Glenway's depression. At last I
was altogether bogged down, and we sat there just looking at each other.
Then, like the last trump, there arose an urgent, heart-stopping stridulation
in the buzzer box on the wall over the bed. Glenway was out of his
depression, out of his chair, into the doorway, and up the companion so
quickly that one felt certain intervening movements must have been left
out. I followed as fast as I could; after all, it was either the sea serpent or
Geisecker, and in either case I thought I'd better be there.

It was Geisecker. He was standing by the wheel, hooting with laughter,
pointing out over the ocean, shouting. "Thar she blows! Flukes on the
starboard bow!"

Then the laughter doubled him up completely. I noticed that it can be
true about people getting purple in the face. I noticed also that, even
doubled up, Geisecker seemed bigger; there seemed to be more of him,
than at any other times.

Sadder still, there seemed to be less of Glenway. He seemed to be
shrunken and concentrated into a narrower and grayer column of tissue

than was natural. I had time to think, "He'll be driven completely out of his mind if this continues," and then he turned and went down the companion out of sight.

I went over to Geisecker, wondering on the way what sort of words could possibly pierce his thick hide. "Jesus Christ!" said he. "I knew it was true. When those boys on Paumoy told me, I knew it was true, but I just felt I had to check up on it."

"What the hell are you talking about?" I asked.

"About old Glen and Thora Vyborg," replied Geisecker, still gasping with mirth. "Don't you know about Glen and Thora Vyborg?"

I knew they had been married. I vaguely remembered something about a dramatic love-at-first-sight encounter in Honolulu. I had some sort of a picture in my mind of the more-than-famous film star; of her unfathomable personality, her unknowable beauty, and the fact that she talked to no one and traveled with no one and dined with no one except her Svengali, her current director, and her publicity man. I had a fairly clear idea of what these types were like, and I could imagine that Glenway, younger then, tall, angular, already dedicated, with the ocean behind him, winged with sail and haloed with sun and money, must have seemed to offer her a part in a rather better production.

I remembered, too, that the marriage had been extremely short-lived. Someone had said something about them sailing away with the sunset and returning with the dawn. No statement had been made by either party. There had been rumors, as there always are, but these were weak, uncertain; they had been drowned in a flood of better-authenticated adulteries long before I ever knew Glenway. Now it seemed that some of them had been washed ashore, horribly disfigured, swollen and salty, on the ultimate beaches of Paumoy.

"You know what the boys there told me?" said Geisecker, watching me closely. "Seems they got married in no time flat and started out on this very same boat, on a big, frontpage honeymoon. Believe it or not, the very first night out—round about eleven o'clock, if you get what I mean, pal—some fellow on deck sees something or other, maybe porpoises or kelp or any damn thing you like, and he gets the idea it's the old brontosaurus in person. So he presses the buzzer, and Glen comes rushing up on deck in ten seconds flat. Don't ask me any questions, pal; all I know is that first thing next morning the lugger was turned right around, and it's full steam ahead back to Honolulu, and Reno, and points in opposite directions."

I realized at once that this was true, and had a certain beauty. However, that was for my private contemplation and had nothing to do with Geisecker. He was regarding me with a sort of arrested gloat, his eyes triumphant and his nose tilted up ready to join in the expected peal of laughter. "Geisecker," I said, and for the first time I heard, and he heard, a note of direct and personal hatred in my voice, "Geisecker, I'm not going to discuss the whys and wherefores, but from now on you're going to stay right away from Glenway. You can come on deck; you can have a chair on the port side there, between the masts. But if you step one inch ..."

"Hold it!" said Geisecker. "Who's talking? The owner? Skipper? First mate? Or what the hell else do you think you are? I'd like to hear what old Glen's got to say."

I am no good at all at a row. When my first damp squib of wrath has exploded I am always overwhelmed by an immense weariness and blankness. At that moment I had neither the will nor the power to go on. But Geisecker obligingly came to my assistance. I could never decide whether he was a sadist, avid for the discomfort of his victim, or a masochist, indecently eager for the wound of being disliked. Whichever it was, he watched me with his little eyes, and he actually passed his tongue over his lips. "Anyway," said he, "I'm going down to ask him if there's any truth in that yarn."

The lip-licking was so crude and so banal that it transposed everything into a different key. There was a sailor of great good nature and phenomenal size, a man called Wiggam, a native of Hawaii, who was mending a net a little way along the deck. I called him and told him, in phrases which normally appear only in balloons in comic strips, to take his net and work on it outside Abbott's door, and, in the event of Geisecker approaching that door, to cut his belly open.

I gave the deplorable instructions in a rather cold, staccato tone, assumed in order to overcome a tendency to squeakiness, and I was reminded, even as I heard myself speak, of a small boy's imitation of a tommy gun. Had Geisecker laughed, or had the sailor looked surprised or reluctant, I should have been in a very ludicrous situation. However, it seems that sailors are simple folk; this one showed alacrity, his teeth, and a spring knife that seemed all the more purposeful for being of very moderate dimensions. He glanced at Geisecker, or rather at the belly in question, as if making certain precise and workmanlike calculations, and then he went and gathered up the long net and carried it below. Geisecker watched all this with growing seriousness.

"Look," said he, "maybe I got things wrong somehow, but ..."

"Listen, Fatso," said I, "if you get anything else wrong you're going to be put on a little Jap crab-fisher boat, see? And the name of that boat's going to be screwed up when we write it down in the log. 'Cause it'll be a Japanese name that means *the boat that never returned*. Or never existed. Work that one out next time you feel like kidding."

I went down and found Glenway lying on his bed, not reading. I said,

"I've fixed him. I can't believe it, but I have."

"How?" said Glenway.

When I had told him, he said, "He won't stay fixed, not by that sort of thing."

I said, "You think so because I've related it with a twinkle. When I spoke to Geisecker my voice was cold and dead, like steel, and I let my eyelids droop a little. Like this."

"He certainly won't stay fixed," said Glenway.

"In that case his belly will be cut open," said I. "Because to Hill Wiggam, who is sitting right out there in the passage, this is his moment of fulfillment. Or it will be if Geisecker tries to get past him. It's a case of a man suddenly finding his vocation."

"I don't want Wiggam getting into trouble," said Glenway.

"Nor," said I, "does Geisecker." With that I went up and did my afternoon spell in the crow's nest, and later I had a drink with Geisecker, to whom I said as little as possible, not knowing what to say nor how to say it. I then dined with Glenway, in his cabin, and then had a smoke with Geisecker on the port deck, and at about ten o'clock, I went to spend the last hour of the evening with Glenway, who was still extremely tense.

"What's the night like?" he asked.

I said, "It's the most wonderful night of the whole cruise. The moon's just on full, and someone's let it down on an invisible wire, and you can see the curve of the stars going up behind it. The wind's light, but there's a hell of a big swell rolling in from somewhere. She's still got everything on but her balloon jib, and she's riding it like a steeplechaser. Why don't you go up and take the wheel for a bit?"

"Where's Geisecker?" asked Glenway.

"Amidships, on the port side, fenced in invisibly by threats," I said with some pride.

"I'll stay down here," said Glenway.

"Glenway," said I, "you're making altogether too much of this. The fact is, you've led a sheltered life; people like Geisecker have always treated you with far too much respect. It sets you apart, and I find it rather offensive. Remember what Fitzgerald said about the rich. He said you are different. Think of that! It's almost worse than being the same."

"You forget what Hemingway said," replied Glenway, who perhaps found little attraction in either alternative.

"The Hemingway rebuttal," said I, "proves only what it was intended to prove. That is, that Hemingway is a fine, upstanding, independent citizen, and probably with a magnificent growth of hair on his chest. All the same, Fitzgerald had a point. Just because your iniquitous old grandfather happened to build a few railways—"

"First of all," interrupted Glenway, "it was not my grandfather but my great grandfather. What's more—"

And at that moment, just as I was exulting in having induced him to unclench his hands, and look out of his eyes, and stick his neck out, the buzzer sounded again. I had forgotten to have it disconnected.

What was quite pathetic was that Glenway couldn't control an instinctive movement towards leaping off the bed. He arched up like a tetanus victim, and then collapsed as flat as an empty sack. The buzzer went on. I had a panicky feeling that he might arch up again at any moment. I lost my head and picked up a stool that stood in front of the dressing table and pounded that rattlesnake box into silence.

The silence, once achieved, seemed deep and complete. This was an illusion; we soon noticed that there were all sorts of noises here and there in the large emptiness left by the death of the outrageous buzzer. We could hear the patter of running feet on deck, and voices, and especially Geisecker's voice, spouting large jets of urgent sound.

I opened the door and the words came rushing in. "Glen! Glen! Come up, for God's sake! Can't you hear me? Come quick!"

"My God!" I said. "Maybe they *are* cutting his belly open."

With that, I ran up. Geisecker was at the head of the companionway. He turned his head briefly to send another shout down the stairs; then he turned it back again to stare out over the sea. I barged into him. He blindly clutched at my arm and dragged me to the side of the boat, and pointed.

I saw something already disappearing into the great smooth side of one of the enormous waves. It was black, wet, shining, and very large. These words can be applied to a whale or a whale-shark, and maybe to two or three other things. I can summon up with absolute precision the way Geisecker's face was turning as I came up the companionway; I can remember exactly how his shout went on a little after he had turned his head back to look over the sea again. But I haven't the same perfect mental photograph of what I saw disappearing into the wave. To the very best of my recollection I saw the hinder half of an enormous back and, following on a curve, already half lost in the black and moon-glitter, a monstrous tail.

The men who had run up were standing three or four paces away. I looked at them, and they nodded. As they did so I heard Glenway's voice speaking to the men. "You saw it?" He had come up after all, and had seen my look and their response as he came toward us. One of them said, "Yes, but he shout," pointing to Geisecker. "He shout, shout, shout, and it go under."

Glenway stepped towards Geisecker, thus turning his back on the men. They couldn't see his face, but I could see it, and so could Geisecker. I don't think Glenway even raised his hand. Geisecker stepped backwards, which brought him, at what I would have thought a very slight and harmless angle, against the low gunwale. His big, fat heavy torso went on and over; his feet went up, and he was gone. He was overboard.

I don't remember putting my hand on the life belt, but I can remember flinging it, skimming it almost parallel with the side of the boat, and feeling sure it hit the water within a very few feet of Geisecker. Then the boat, whose six knots or so had been like nothing at all a moment earlier, seemed to be racing ahead faster than any boat had ever gone before.

Glenway shouted; the helmsman put the helm over and spilled the wind out of her sails. There was always a boat ready to be lowered at record speed. Two men were at the oars, Glenway took the tiller, and I stood in the bows looking out for Geisecker, who could be no more than two or three hundred yards away.

The night was clear beyond all description. The enormous, smooth swells gleamed and flashed under the moon. The yacht, when we had drawn away from it, stood up like a snowy alp on the water, and when, at the top of each swell, the men lifted their oars for a moment, it was a moment of unbelievable silence, as if some tremendous creature was holding its breath.

Then I saw Geisecker. We were lifted high on one of the great glassy hills of sea, and he was beginning to slide down the slope of another. He had the life belt. I couldn't see his real features at that distance, but the white moonlight gave him such great hollow black eyes, and made such a crater of his open mouth, that I got the picture of a clown in comic distress. Then he went down, and we went down, and two or three ridges twenty feet high humped themselves between us.

I said, "He's ahead of us; a couple of hundred feet. You'll see him from the top of the next one."

But we didn't. I began to wonder if a man and a life belt rise and fall faster or slower on a rolling sea than does a fourteen-foot boat. Before I could work out an answer we had gone up and down again and had arrived at a spot which was extremely close to where I had seen him.

"You misjudged the distance," said Glenway after perhaps half a puzzled minute.

"I must have. Anyway, he's got the lifebuoy. He'll be all right. Let's row around in a circle."

One of the men put out a bailing can as a marker. The giant swells were so smooth that, ballasted with a couple of inches of water, the can floated up and down without shipping another drop. We went round it on a hundred-foot radius and then at a hundred and fifty feet. Geisecker was not to be seen. And we could see, at one time or another, every square foot of water where he could possibly be.

"He's sunk!" said Glenway. "A cramp . . . a shark . . ."

"No shark would have taken the life belt down. It'd be floating right here. We'd see it."

The words were scarcely out of my mouth when we saw it. It breached up, right out of the water—it must have come up from God knows how many fathoms—and it fell back with a splash just a boat's length ahead of us. Next moment it was beside our bow and I reached out and lifted it aboard. I turned, holding it in my hands, and showed it to Glenway. It was easier than speaking, and not so silly. We both knew perfectly well that no known creature, except possibly a sperm whale, could have taken Geisecker and the life belt down to that sort of depth. And we knew that what I had seen, and what the men had seen, was not a sperm whale.

We rowed around in circles for a little longer, and then we pulled back to the yacht. When we were aboard again, I said to Glenway, "You didn't as much as touch him. You didn't even mean to touch him. You didn't even raise your hand."

"And some of the men were watching," said Glenway with the utmost calm. "They can testify to that."

If not the railway tycoon, his great grandfather, it might certainly have been his grandfather, the banker, speaking. He saw my surprise, and smiled. "From the most scrupulous legal point of view," he said, "it was a pure accident. And we'll make a report accordingly. Of course, I killed the man."

"Now wait a minute," said I.

"Excuse me," said he. We were near the wheel. He took it from the man who was steering, and said something to him, and the man ran forward calling to the rest of the crew who were still on deck. Next minute the helm went up, the booms swung over, the sails bellied out on the other side, and the great boat was jibbed and sweeping round on to a new course.

"Where are we heading now?" said I to Glenway.

"Due east," said he. "To San Francisco."

"To make the report? Can't you . . . ?"

"To put the boat up for sale."

I said, "Glenway, you're upset. You've got to see this business in proportion."

He said, "He was alive and enjoying himself, and now he's dead. I didn't like him; I detested him, but that's got nothing to do with it."

I said, "Don't be completely psychological illiterate. It's got every-thing in the world to do with it. You hated his guts, a little too intensely, perhaps, but very understandably. You wished he was dead. In fact, you more or less said so. Now you've got guilt feelings; you're going to take the blame for it. Glenway, you're an obsessive type; you're a Puritan, a New

Englander, any early Christian. Be reasonable. Be moderate."

"Suppose you were driving a car," said Glenway, "and you knocked a man down and killed him?"

"I'd be very sorry, but I think I'd go on driving."

"If you were a speed demon, and it was because of that? Or a drunk? Or if you were mentally unfit to handle a car?"

"Well..." I said.

But Glenway wasn't listening. He beckoned the man who had been steering, and turned the wheel over to him. He gave him the course and told him who was to relieve him in each watch. Then he turned away and walked forward. He walked like a passenger. He walked like a man walking on a street. He was walking away from his mania, and in the very hour of its justification.

I followed him, eager to bring him back to himself, but he walked away from me too.

I said to him considerably later, "I've found out something very interesting, talking to the men. Shall I tell you?"

"Please do," said he.

I said, "I thought they rather liked Geisecker because he made them laugh. But they didn't. Not a bit. Are you listening?"

"Of course," said he as politely as a banker who has already decided not to make a loan.

I said, "They hated him almost as much as you did, and for the same reason, for making fun of it. They believed in it, all the time. They've all got different names for it, according to where they come from. Almost every man's got an uncle who's seen it, or a wife's grandfather, or someone. And it's quite clear it's the same sort of beast."

Glenway said, "I've decided I'm going to buy a farm or a ranch as far from the ocean as I can get. I'll breed cattle or hybridize corn or something."

I said, "You've been over seven years on this boat with these men, or most of them. Did you know they believed in it?"

"No," he said. "Or I might go in for soil biology. There's still a tremendous amount to be discovered in that field."

This made me feel very sick. I felt Glenway was indeed different; different from me, different from himself. The beautiful *Zenobia* had to be sold, the crew disbanded and the large marine saurian left to dwindle into a figure on an old map, distant and disregarded in its watery solitude. As for myself, all my friendship with Glenway had been aboard the boat; I was part of it; I was one of these things. I had been nothing but the accomplice of his obsession, and now he was, in a way I didn't like, cured. I felt that I too was up for sale, and we talked amiably and politely and quite meaninglessly all the way back to San Francisco, and there we said good-by to each other and promised to write.

We didn't write in over three years. One can't write to the ghost of a banker, nor expect a letter from one. But this summer, when I was in New York, I got home one night and found a letter awaiting me. The postmark was Gregory, South Dakota, which is about as far from either ocean as you can get.

He was there; he wondered if I knew those parts; he wondered if I was likely to be free; there were some interesting things to talk about. The lines were extremely few but there was all the more space to read between them. I took up the telephone.

It was nearly midnight, but of course it was two hours earlier in South Dakota. All the same Glenway was a very long time coming to the phone. "I hope I didn't get you out of bed," I told him.

"Heavens no!" said he. "I was on the roof. We get wonderful nights here; as clear as Arizona."

I remembered that clear night in the Pacific, and the flash and glitter of the enormous glassy waves, and the silence, and the boat rising and falling so high and so low, and the yacht like a hill of snow in the distance, and the little bailing can visible at over a hundred feet. I said, "I'd like to come out right away."

"I rather hoped you would," said Glenway, and began to tell me about planes and trains.

I asked him if there was anything he wanted from New York.

"There most certainly is," said he. "There's a man called Emil Schroeder; you'll find his address in the book; he's out in Brooklyn; he's the best lens grinder that ever got out of Germany, and he's got a package for me that I don't want sent through the mail because it's fragile."

"What is it?" I asked. "A microscope? Did you go in for soil biology after all?"

"Well, I did for a time," said Glenway. "But this is something different. It's lenses for a binocular telescope a fellow's designed for me. You see, a single eyepiece is no good for following anything that moves at all fast. But this binocular thing will be perfect. I can use it on the roof, or I can set it in a mounting I've had built into the plane."

"Glenway, do you mind telling me what the hell you're talking about?"

"Haven't you read the government report on unidentified flying objects? ... Hello! Are you there?"

"Yes, I'm here, Glenway. And you're there. You're there, sure enough!"

"Listen, if you haven't read that report, do please get hold of it first thing tomorrow, and read it on the way out here. I don't want to hear you talking like that unfortunate Geisecker. Will you read it?"

"All right, Glenway, I will. I most certainly will."

My Dear Emily

Joanna Russ

San Francisco, 188—

I am so looking forward to seeing my dear Emily at last, now she is grown, a woman, although I'm sure I will hardly recognize her. She must not be proud (as if she could be!) but will remember her friends, I know, and have patience with her dear Will who cannot help but remember the girl she was, and the sweet influence she had in her old home. I talked to your father about you every day, dear, and he longs to see you as I do. Think! a learned lady in our circle! But I know you have not changed...

Emily came home from school in April with her bosom friend Charlotte. They had loved each other in school, but they didn't speak much on the train. While Emily read Mr. Emerson's poems, Charlotte examined the scenery through opera-glasses. She expressed her wish to see "savages."

"That's foolish," says Emily promptly.

"If we were carried off," says Charlotte, "I don't think you would notice it in time to disapprove."

"That's very foolish," says Emily, touching her round lace collar with

355

one hand. She looks up from Mr. Emerson to stare Charlotte out of countenance, properly, morally, and matter-of-course young lady. It has always been her style.

"The New England look," Charlotte snaps resentfully. She makes her opera-glasses slap shut.

"I should like to be carried off," she proposes; "but then I don't have an engagement to look forward to. A delicate affair."

"You mustn't make fun," says Emily. Mr. Emerson drops into her lap. She stares unseeing at Charlotte's opera-glasses.

"Why do they close?" she asks helplessly.

"I beg your pardon?" blankly, from Charlotte.

"Nothing. You're much nicer than I am," says Emily.

"Look," urges Charlotte kindly, pressing the toy into her friend's hand.

"For savages?"

Charlotte nods, Emily pushes the spring that will open the little machine, and a moment later drops them into her lap where they fall on Mr. Emerson. There is a cut across one of her fingers and a blue pinch darkening the other.

"They hurt me," she says without expression, and as Charlotte takes the glasses up quickly, Emily looks with curious sad passivity at the blood from her little wound, which has bled an incongruous passionate drop on Mr. Emerson's clothbound poems. To her friend's surprise (and her own, too) she begins to cry, heavily, silently, and totally without reason.

He wakes up slowly, mistily, dizzily, with a vague memory of having fallen asleep on plush. He is intensely miserable, bound down to his bed with hoops of steel, and the memory adds nausea to his misery, solidifying ticklishly around his bare hands and the back of his neck as he drifts towards wakefulness. His stomach turns over with the dry brushy filthiness of it. With the caution of the chronically ill, he opens his eyelids, careful not to move, careful even to keep from focusing his gaze until—he thinks to himself—his bed stops holding him with the force of Hell and this intense miserable sickness goes down, settles.... Darkness. No breath. A glimmer of light, a stone wall. He thinks: *I'm dead and buried, dead and buried, dead and*— With infinite care he attempts to breathe, sure that this time it will be easy; he'll be patient, discreet, sensible, he won't do it all at once—

He gags. Spasmodically, he gulps, cries out, and gags again, springing convulsively to his knees and throwing himself over the low wall by his bed, laboring as if he were breathing sand. He starts to sweat. His heartbeat comes back, then pulse, then seeing, hearing, swallowing.... High in the wall a window glimmers, a star is out, the sky is pale evening blue.

Trembling with nausea, he rises to his feet, sways a little in the gloom, then puts out one arm and steadies himself against the stone wall. He sees the window, sees the door ahead of him. In his tearing eyes the star suddenly blazes and lengthens like a knife; his head is whirling, his heart painful as a man's; he throws his hands over his face, longing for life and strength to come back, the overwhelming flow of force that will crest at sunrise, leaving him raging at the world and ready to kill anyone, utterly proud and contemptuous, driven to sleep as the last resort of a balked assassin. But it's difficult to stand, difficult to breathe: *I wish I were dead and buried, dead and buried, dead and buried— But there!* he whispers to himself like a charm, *There, it's going, it's going away.* He smiles slyly round at his companionable, merciful stone walls. With an involuntarily silent, gliding gait he moves towards the door, opens the iron gate, and goes outside. Life is coming back. The trees are black against the sky, which yet holds some light; far away in the West lie the radiant memories of a vanished sun. An always vanished sun.

"Alive!" he cries, in triumph. It is—as usual—his first word of the day.

Dear Emily, sweet Emily, met Martin Guevara three days after she arrived home. She had been shown the plants in the garden and the houseplants in stands and had praised them; she had been shown the sunpictures and praised *them;* she had fingered antimacassars, promised to knit, exclaimed at gaslights, and passed two evenings at home, doing nothing. Then in the hall that led to the pantry Sweet Will had taken her hand and she had dropped her eyes because you were supposed to and that was her style. Charlotte (who slept in the same room as her friend) embraced her at bedtime, wept over the handtaking, and then Emily said to her dear, dear friend (without thinking):

"Sweet William."

Charlotte laughed.

"It's not a joke!"

"It's so funny."

"I love Will dearly." She wondered if God would strike her dead for a hypocrite. Charlotte was looking at her oddly, and smiling.

"You mustn't be full of levity," said Emily, peeved. It was then that Sweet William came in and told them of tomorrow's garden-party, which was to be composed of her father's congregation. They were lucky, he said, to have acquaintances of such position and character. Charlotte slipped out on purpose, and Will, seeing they were alone, atempted to take Emily's hand again.

"Leave me alone!" Emily said angrily. He stared.

"I said leave me alone!"

And she gave him such a look of angry pride that, in fact, he did.

Emily sees Guevara across the parlor by the abominable cherry-red sofa, talking animatedly and carelessly. In repose he is slight, undistinguished, and plain, but no one will ever see him in repose; Emily realizes this. His strategy is never to rest, to bewilder, he would (she thinks) slap you if only to confuse you, and when he can't he's always out of the way and attacking, making one look ridiculous. She knows nobody and is bored; she starts for the door to the garden.

At the door his hand closes over her wrist; he has somehow gotten there ahead of her.

"The lady of the house," he says.

"I'm back from school."

"And you've learned—?"

"Let me go, please."

"Never." He drops her hand and stands in the doorway. She says:

"I want to go outside."

"Never."

"I'll call my father."

"Do." She tries and can't talk; I wouldn't *bother,* she thinks to herself, loftily. She goes out into the garden with him. Under the trees his plainness vanishes like smoke.

"You want lemonade," he says.

"I'm not going to talk to you," she responds. "I'll talk to Will. Yes! I'll make him—"

"In trouble," says Mr. Guevara, returning silently with lemonade in a glass cup.

"No thank you."

"She wants to get away," says Martin Guevara. "I know."

"If I had your trick of walking like a cat," she says, "I could get out of anything."

"I *can* get out of anything," says the gentleman, handing Emily her punch, "out of an engagement, a difficulty. I can even get *you* out of anything."

"I loathe you," whispers Emily suddenly. "You walk like a cat. You're ugly."

"Not out here," he remarks.

"Who has to be afraid of lights?" cries Emily energetically. He stands away from the paper lanterns strung between the trees, handsome, comfortable and collected, watching Emily's cut-glass cup shake in her hand.

"I can't move," she says miserably.

"Try." She takes a step towards him. "See; you can."

"But I wanted to go *away!*" With sudden hysteria she flings the lemonade (cup and all) into his face, but he is no longer there.

"What are you doing at a church supper, you hypocrite!" she shouts tearfully at the vacancy.

Sweet William has to lead her in to bed.

"You thought better of it," remarks Martin, head framed in an evening window, sounds of footsteps outside, ladies' heels clicking in the streets.

"I don't know you," she says miserably, "I just don't." He takes her light shawl, a pattern in India cashmere.

"That will come," he says, smiling. He sits again, takes her hand, and squeezes the skin on the wrist.

"Let me go, please?" she says like a child.

"I don't know."

"You talk like the smart young gentlemen at Andover; they were all fools."

"Perhaps you overawed them." He leans forward and puts his hand around the back of her neck for a moment. "Come on, dear."

"What are you talking about!" Emily cries.

"San Francisco is a lovely city. I had ancestors here three hundred years ago."

"Don't think that because I came here—"

"She doesn't," he whispers, grasping her shoulder, "she doesn't know a thing."

"Goddamn you!"

He blinks and sits back. Emily is weeping. The confusion of the room—an over-stuffed, over-draped hotel room—has gotten on her nerves. She snatches for her shawl, which is still in his grasp, but he holds it out of her reach, darting his handsome, unnaturally young face from side to side as she tries to reach round him. She falls across his lap and lies there, breathless with terror.

"You're cold," she whispers, horrified, "you're cold as a corpse." The shawl descends lightly over her head and shoulders. His frozen hands help her to her feet. He is delighted; he bares his teeth in a smile.

"I think," he says, tasting it, "that I'm going to visit your family."

"But you don't—" she stumbles—"you don't want to ... sleep with me. I know it."

"I can be a suitor like anyone else," he says.

That night Emily tells it all to Charlotte, who, afraid of the roué, stays up and reads a French novel as the light drains from the windows and the true black dark takes its place. It is almost dawn and Charlotte has been dozing, when Emily shakes her friend awake, kneeling by the bed with innocent blue eyes reflecting the dying night.

"I had a terrible dream," she complains.

"Hmmmm?"

"I dreamed," says Emily tiredly. "I had a nightmare. I dreamed I was walking by the beach and I decided to go swimming and then a . . . a thing, I don't know . . . it took me by the neck."

"Is that all?" says Charlotte peevishly.

"I'm sick," says Emily with childish satisfaction. She pushes Charlotte over in the bed and climbs in with her. "I won't have to see that man again if I'm sick."

"Pooh, why not?" mumbles Charlotte.

"Because I'll have to stay home."

"He'll visit you."

"William won't let him."

"Sick?" says Charlotte then, suddenly waking up. She moves away from her friend, for she has read more bad fiction than Emily and less moral poetry.

"Yes, I feel awful," says Emily simply, resting her head on her knees. She pulls away in tired irritation when her friend reaches for the collar of her nightdress. Charlotte looks and jumps out of bed.

"Oh," says Charlotte. "Oh—goodness—oh—" holding out her hands.

"What on earth's the matter with you?"

"He's—" whispers Charlotte in horror, "he's—"

In the dim light her hands are black with blood.

"You've come," he says. He is lying on his hotel sofa, reading a newspaper, his feet over one arm and a hand trailing on the rug.

"Yes," she answers, trembling with resolution.

"I never thought this place would have such a good use. But I never know when I'll manage to pick up money—"

With a blow of her hand, she makes a fountain of the newspaper; he lies on the sofa, mildly amused.

"Nobody knows I came," she says rapidly. "But I'm going to finish you off. I know how." She hunts feverishly in her bag.

"I wouldn't," he remarks quietly.

"Ah!" Hauling out her baby cross (silver), she confronts him with it like Joan of Arc. He is still amused, still mildly surprised.

"In your hands?" he says delicately. Her fingers are loosening, her face pitiful.

"My dear, the significance is in the feeling, the faith, not the symbol. You use that the way you would use a hypodermic needle. Now in your father's hands—"

"I dropped it," she says in a little voice. He picks it up and hands it to her.

"You can touch—" she says, her face screwing up for tears.

"I can."

"Oh my God!" she cries in despair.

"My dear." He puts one arm around her, holding her against him, a very strong man for she pushes frantically to free herself. "How many times have *I* said that! But you'll learn. Do I sound like the silly boys at Andover?" Emily's eyes are fixed and her throat contracts; he forces her head between her knees. "The way you go on, you'd think I was bad luck."

"I—I—"

"And you without the plentiful lack of brains that characterizes your friend. She'll be somebody's short work and I think I know whose."

Emily turns white again.

"I'll send her around to you afterwards. Good God! What do you think will happen to her?"

"She'll die," says Emily clearly. He grasps her by the shoulders.

"Ah!" he says with immense satisfaction. "And after that? Who lives forever after that? Did you know that?"

"Yes, people like you don't die," whispers Emily. "But you're not people—"

"No," he says intently, "no. We're not." He stands Emily on her feet. "We're a passion!" Smiling triumphantly, he puts his hands on each side of her head, flattening the pretty curls, digging his fingers into the hair, in a grip Emily can no more break than she could break a vise.

"We're passion," he whispers, amused. "Life is passion. Desire makes life."

"Ah, let me go," says Emily.

He smiles ecstatically at the sick girl.

"Desire," he says dreamily, "lives; *that* lives when nothing else does, and we're desire made purely, desire walking the Earth. Can a dead man walk? Ah! If you want, want, want ..."

He throws his arms around her, pressing her head to his chest and nearly suffocating her, ruining her elaborate coiffure and crushing her lace at her throat. Emily breathes in the deadness about him, the queer absence of odor, or heat, or presence; her mouth is pressed against the cloth of his fashionable suit, expensive stuff, a good dollar a yard, gotten by—what? But his hands are strong enough to get anything.

"You see," he says gently, "I enjoy someone with intelligence, even with morals; it adds a certain— And besides—" here he releases her and holds her face up to his— "we like souls that come to us; these visits to the bedrooms of unconscious citizens are rather like frequenting a public brothel."

"I abhor you," manages Emily. He laughs. He's delighted.

"Yes, yes, dear," he says, "but don't imagine we're callous parasites. Followers of the Marquis de Sade, perhaps—you see Frisco has evening hours for its bookstores!—but sensitive souls, really, and apt to long for a little conscious partnership." Emily shuts her eyes. "I said," he goes on, with a touch of hardness, "that I am a genuine seducer. I flatter myself that I'm not an animal."

"You're a monster," says Emily, with utter conviction. Keeping one hand on her shoulder, he steps back a pace.

"Go." She stands, unable to believe her luck, then makes what seems to her a rush for the door; it carries her into his arms.

"You see?" He's pleased; he's proved a point.

"I can't," she says, with wide eyes and wrinkled forehead . . .

"You will." He reaches for her and she faints.

Down in the dark where love and some other things make their hidingplace, Emily drifts aimlessly, quite alone, quite cold, like a dead woman without a passion in her soul to make her come back to life.

She opens her eyes and finds herself looking at his face in the dark, as if the man carried his own light with him.

"I'll die," she says softly.

"Not for a while," he drawls, sleek and content.

"You've killed me."

"I've loved."

"Love!"

"Say 'taken' then, if you insist."

"I do! I do!" she cried bitterly.

"You decided to faint."

"Oh the hell with you!" she shouts.

"Good girl!" And as she collapses, weeping hysterically, "Now, now, come here, dear . . ." nuzzling her abused little neck. He kisses it in the tenderest fashion with an exaggerated, mocking sigh; she twists away, but is pulled closer and as his lips open over the teeth of inhuman, dead desire, his victim finds—to her surprise—that there is no pain. She braces herself and then, unexpectedly, shivers from head to foot.

"Stop it!" she whispers, horrified. "Stop it! Stop it!"

But a vampire who has found a soul-mate (even a temporary one) will be immoderate. There's no stopping them.

Charlotte's books have not prepared her for *this*.

"You're to stay in the house, my dear, because you're ill."

"I'm not," Emily says, pulling the sheet up to her chin.

"Of course you are." The Reverend beams at her, under the portrait of

Emily's dead mother which hangs in Emily's bedroom. "You've had a severe chill."

"But I have to get out!" says Emily, sitting up. "Because I have an appointment, you see."

"Not now," says the Reverend.

"But I *can't* have a severe chill in the *summer!*"

"You look so like your mother," says the Reverend, musing. After he has gone away, Charlotte comes in.

"I have to stay in the damned bed," says Emily forcefully, wiggling her toes under the sheet. Charlotte, who has been carrying a tray with tea and a posy on it, drops it on the washstand.

"Why, Emily!"

"I have to stay in the damned bed the whole damned day," Emily adds.

"Dear, why do you use those words?"

"Because the whole world's damned!"

After the duties of his employment were completed at six o'clock on a Wednesday, William came to the house with a doctor and introduced him to the Reverend and Emily's bosom friend. The street lamps would not be lit for an hour but the sun was just down and the little party congregated in the garden under remains of Japanese paper lanterns. No one ever worried that these might set themselves on fire. Lucy brought tea—they were one of the few civilized circles in Frisco—and over the tea, in the darkening garden, to the accompaniment of sugar-tongs and plopping cream (very musical) they talked.

"Do you think," says the Reverend, very worried, "that it might be consumption?"

"Perhaps the lungs are affected," says the doctor.

"She's always been such a robust girl." This is William, putting down the teapot which has a knitted tube about the handle, for insulation. Charlotte is stirring her tea with a spoon.

"It's very strange," says the doctor serenely, and he repeats "it's very strange" as shadows advance in the garden. "But young ladies, you know— especially at twenty—young ladies often take strange ideas into their heads; they do, they often do; they droop; they worry." His eyes are mild, his back sags, he hears the pleasant gurgle of more tea. A quiet consultation, good people, good solid people, a little illness, nothing serious—

"No," says Charlotte. Nobody hears her.

"I knew a young lady once—" ventures the doctor mildly.

"No," says Charlotte, more loudly. Everyone turns to her, and Lucy, taking the opportunity, insinuates a plate of small-sized muffins in front of Charlotte.

"I can tell you all about it," mutters Charlotte, glancing up from under her eyebrows. "But you'll *laugh.*"

"Now, dear—" says the Reverend.

"Now, miss—" says the doctor.

"As a friend—" says William.

Charlotte begins to sob.

"Oh," she says, "I'll—I'll tell you about it."

Emily meets Mr. Guevara at the Mansion House at seven, having recovered an appearance of health (through self-denial) and a good solid record of spending the evenings at home (through self-control). She stands at the hotel's wrought-iron gateway, her back rigid as a stick, drawing on white gloves. Martin materializes out of the blue evening shadows and takes her arm.

"I shall like living forever," says Emily, thoughtfully.

"God deliver me from Puritans," says Mr. Guevara.

"What?"

"You're a lady. You'll swallow me up."

"I'll do anything I please," remarks Emily severely, with a glint of teeth. "Ah."

"I will." They walk through the gateway. "You don't care two pins for me."

"Unfortunately," says he, bowing.

"It's not unfortunate as long as *I* care for me," says Emily, smiling with great energy. "Damn them all."

"You proper girls would overturn the world." Along they walk in the evening, in quiet, respectable rustle of clothes. Halfway to the restaurant she stops and says breathlessly:

"Let's go—somewhere else!"

"My dear, you'll ruin your health!"

"You know better. Three weeks ago I was sick as a dog and much you cared; I haven't slept for days and I'm fine."

"You look fine."

"Ah! You mean I'm beginning to look dead, like you." She tightens her hold on his arm, to bring him closer.

"Dead?" says he, slipping his arm around her.

"Fixed. Bright-eyed. Always at the same heat and not a moment's rest."

"It agrees with you."

"I adore you," she says.

When Emily gets home, there's a reckoning. The Reverend stands in the doorway and sad William, too, but not Charlotte, for she is on the parlor sofa, having had hysterics.

"Dear Emily," says the Reverend. "We don't know how to tell you this—"

"Why, Daddy, *what?*" exclaims Emily, making wide-eyes at him.

"Your little friend told us—"

"Has something happened to Charlotte?" cries Emily. "Oh tell me, tell me, what happened to Charlotte?" And before they can stop her she has flown into the parlor and is kneeling beside her friend, wondering if she dares pinch her under cover of her shawl. William, quick as a flash, kneels on one side of her and Daddy on the other.

"Dear Emily!" cries William with fervor.

"Oh sweetheart!" says Charlotte, reaching down and putting her arms around her friend.

"You're well!" shouts Emily, sobbing over Charlotte's hand and thinking perhaps to bite her. But the Reverend's arms lift her up.

"My dear," says he, "you came home unaccompanied. You were not at the Society."

"But," says Emily, smiling dazzlingly, "two of the girls took all my hospital sewing to their house because we must finish it right away and I have not—"

"You have been lying to us," the Reverend says. *Now,* thinks Emily, *Sweet William will cover his face.* Charlotte sobs.

"She can't help it," says Charlotte brokenly. "It's the spell."

"Why, I think everyone's gone out of their minds," says Emily, frowning. Sweet William takes her from Daddy, leading her away from Charlotte.

"Weren't you with a gentleman tonight?" says Sweet Will firmly. Emily backs away.

"For shame!"

"She doesn't remember it," explains Charlotte; "it's part of his spell."

"I think you ought to get a doctor for *her,*" observes Emily.

"You were with a gentleman named Guevara," says Will, showing less tenderness than Emily expects. "Weren't you? Well—weren't you?"

"Bad cess to you if I was!" snaps Emily, surprised at herself. The other three gasp. "I won't be questioned," she goes on, "and I won't be spied upon. And I think you'd better take some of Charlotte's books away from her; she's getting downright silly."

"You have too much color," says Will, catching her hands. "You're ill but you don't sleep. You stay awake all night. You don't eat. But look at you!"

"I don't understand you. Do you want me to be ugly?" says Emily, trying to be pitiful. Will softens; she sees him do it.

"My dear Emily," he says. "My dear girl—we're afraid for you."

"Me?" says Emily, enjoying herself.

"We'd better put you to bed," says the Reverend kindly.

"You're so kind," whispers Emily, blinking as if she held back tears.

"That's a good girl," says Will, approving. "We know you don't understand. But we'll take care of you, Em."

"*Will* you?"

"Yes, dear. You've been near very grave danger, but luckily we found out in time, and we found out what to do; we'll make you well, we'll keep you safe, we'll—"

"Not with *that* you won't," says Emily suddenly, rooting herself to the spot, for what William takes out of his vest pocket (where he usually keeps his watch) is a broad-leaved, prickle-faced dock called wolfsbane; it must distress any vampire of sense to be so enslaved to pure superstition. But enslaved they are, nonetheless.

"Oh, no!" says Emily swiftly. "That's silly, perfectly silly!"

"Common sense must give way in such a crisis," remarks the Reverend gravely.

"You bastard!" shouts Emily, turning red, attempting to tear the charm out of her fiancé's hand and jump up and down on it. But the Reverend holds one arm and Charlotte the other and between them they pry her fingers apart and William puts his property gently in his vest pocket again.

"She's far gone," says the Reverend fearfully, at his angry daughter. Emily is scowling, Charlotte stroking her hair.

"Ssssh" says Will with great seriousness. "We must get her to bed," and between them they half-carry Emily up the stairs and put her, dressed as she is, in the big double bed with the plush headboard that she has shared so far with Charlotte. Daddy and fiancé confer in the room across the long, low rambling hall, and Charlotte sits by her rebellious friend's bed and attempts to hold her hand.

"I won't permit it; you're a damned fool!" says Emily.

"Oh, Emmy!"

"Bosh."

"It's true!"

"Is it?" With extraordinary swiftness, Emily turns round in the bed and rises to her knees. "Do you know anything about it?"

"I know it's horrid, I—"

"Silly!" Playfully Emily puts her hands on Charlotte's shoulders. Her eyes are narrowed, her nostrils widened to breathe; she parts her lips a little and looks archly at her friend. "You don't know anything about it," she says insinuatingly.

"I'll call your father," says Charlotte quickly.

Emily throws an arm around her friend's neck.

"Not yet! Dear Charlotte!"

"We'll save you," says Charlotte doubtfully.

"Sweet Charrie; you're my friend, aren't you?"

Charlotte begins to sob again.

"Give me those awful things, those leaves."

"Why, Emily, I *couldn't!*"

"But he'll come for me and I have to protect myself, don't I?"

"I'll call your father," says Charlotte firmly.

"No, I'm *afraid.*" Emily wrinkles her forehead sadly.

"Well—"

"Sometimes I—I—" falters Emily. "I can't move or run away and everything looks so—so strange and *horrible—*"

"Oh, here!" Covering her face with one hand, Charlotte holds out her precious dock leaves in the other.

"Dear, dear! Oh, sweet! Oh thank you! Don't be afraid. He isn't after you."

"I hope not," says the bosom friend.

"Oh no, he told me. It's me he's after."

"How awful," says Charlotte, sincerely.

"Yes," says Emily. "Look." And she pulls down the collar of her dress to show the ugly marks, white dots unnaturally healed up, like the pockmarks of a drug addict.

"Don't!" chokes Charlotte.

Emily smiles mournfully. "We really ought to put the lights out," she says.

"Out!"

"Yes, you can see him better that way. If the lights are on, he could sneak in without being seen; he doesn't mind lights, you know."

"I don't know, dear—"

"I do." (Emily is dropping the dock leaves into the washstand, under cover of her skirt.) "I'm afraid. Please."

"Well—"

"Oh, you must!" And leaping to her feet, she turns down the gas to a dim glow; Charlotte's face fades into the obscurity of the deepening shadows.

"So. The lights are out," says Emily quietly.

"I'll ask Will—" Charlotte begins . . .

"No, dear."

"But, Emily—"

"He's coming, dear."

"You mean Will is coming."

"No, not Will."

"Emily, you're a—"

"I'm a sneak," says Emily, chuckling. "Sssssh!" And, while her friend sits paralyzed, one of the windows swings open in the night breeze, a lead-paned window that opens on a hinge, for the Reverend is fond of culture and old architecture. Charlotte lets out a little noise in her throat; and then—with the smash of a pistol shot—the gaslight shatters and the flame goes out. Gas hisses into the air, quietly, insinuatingly, as if explaining the same thing over and over. Charlotte screams with her whole heart. In the dark a hand clamps like a vise on Emily's wrist. A moment passes.

"Charlotte?" she whispers.

"Dead," says Guevara.

Emily has spent most of the day asleep in the rubble, with his coat rolled under her head where he threw it the moment before sunrise, the moment before he staggered to his place and plunged into sleep. She has watched the dawn come up behind the rusty barred gate, and then drifted into sleep herself with his face before her closed eyes—his face burning with a rigid, constricted, unwasting vitality. Now she wakes aching and bruised, with the sun of late afternoon in her face. Sitting against the stone wall, she sneezes twice and tries, ineffectually, to shake the dust from her silk skirt.

Oh, how—she thinks vaguely—*how messy.* She gets to her feet. *There's something I have to do.* The iron gate swings open at a touch. *Trees and gravestones tilted every which way. What did he say? Nothing would disturb it but a Historical Society.*

Having tidied herself as best she can, with his coat over her arm and the address of his tailor in her pocket, she trudges among the erupted stones, which tilt crazily to all sides as if in an earthquake. Blood (Charlotte's, whom she does not think about) has spread thinly on to her hair and the hem of her dress, but her hair is done up with fine feeling, despite the absence of a mirror, and her dress is dark gray; the spot looks like a spot of dust. She folds the coat into a neat package and uses it to wipe the dust off her shoes, then lightens her step past the cemetery entrance, trying to look healthy and respectable. She aches all over from sleeping on the ground.

Once in town and having ascertained from a shop window that she will pass muster in a crowd, Emily trudges up hills and down hills to the tailor, the evidence over her arm. She stops at other windows, to look or to admire herself; thinks smugly of her improved coloring; shifts the parcel on her arm to show off her waist. In one window there is a display of religious objects—beads and crosses, books with fringed gilt bookmarks, a colored chromo of Madonna and Child. In this window Emily admires herself.

"It's Emily, dear!"

A Mrs. L—— appears in the window beside her, with Constantia, Mrs. L——'s twelve-year-old offspring.

"Why, dear, whatever happened to you?" says Mrs. L——, noticing no hat, no gloves, and no veil.

"Nothing; whatever happened to you?" says Emily cockily. Constantia's eyes grow wide with astonishment at the fine, free audacity of it.

"Why, you look as if you'd been—"

"Picnicking," says Emily, promptly. "One of the gentlemen spilled beer on his coat." And she's in the shop now and hanging over the counter, flushed, counting the coral and amber beads strung around a crucifix.

Mrs. L—— knocks doubtfully on the window-glass.

Emily waves and smiles.

Your father—form Mrs. L——'s lips in the glass.

Emily nods and waves cheerfully.

They do go away, finally.

"A fine gentleman," says the tailor earnestly, "a very fine man." He lisps a little.

"Oh very fine," agrees Emily, sitting on a stool and kicking the rungs with her feet. "Monstrous fine."

"But very careless," says the tailor fretfully, pulling Martin's coat nearer the window so he can see it, for the shop is a hole-in-the-wall and dark. "He shouldn't send a lady to this part of the town."

"I was a lady once," says Emily.

"Mmmmm."

"It's fruit stains—something awful, don't you think?"

"I cannot have this ready by tonight," looking up.

"Well, you must, that's all," says Emily calmly. "You always have and he has a lot of confidence in you, you know. He'd be awfully angry if he found out."

"Found out?" sharply.

"That you can't have it ready by tonight."

The tailor ponders.

"I'll positively stay in the shop while you work," says Emily flatteringly.

"Why, Reverend, I saw her on King Street as dirty as a gypsy, with her hair loose and the wildest eyes and I *tried* to talk to her, but she dashed into a shop—"

The sun goes down in a broad belt of gold, goes down over the ocean, over the hills and the beaches, makes shadows lengthen in the street near the quays where a lisping tailor smooths and alters, working against the sun (and very uncomfortable he is, too), watched by a pair of unwinking eyes that glitter a little in the dusk inside the stuffy shop. (*I think I've changed, meditates Emily.*)

He finishes, finally, with relief, and sits with an *ouf!* handing her the coat, the new and beautiful coat that will be worn as soon as the eccentric gentleman comes out to take the evening air. The eccentric gentleman, says Emily incautiously, will do so in an hour by the Mansion House when the last traces of light have faded from the sky.

"Then, my dear Miss," says the tailor unctuously, "I think a little matter of pay—"

"You don't think," says Emily softly, "or you wouldn't have gotten yourself into such a mess as to be this eccentric gentleman's tailor." And out she goes.

Now nobody can see the stains on Emily's skirt or in her hair; street lamps are being lit, there are no more carriages, and the number of people in the streets grows—San Francisco making the most of the short summer nights. It is perhaps fifteen minutes back to the fashionable part of the town where Emily's hatless, shawlless state will be looked on with disdain; here nobody notices. Emily dawdles through the streets, fingering her throat, yawning, looking at the sky, thinking: *I love, I love, I love—*

She has fasted for the day but she feels fine; she feels busy, busy inside as if the life inside her is flowering and bestirring itself, populated as the streets. She remembers—

I love you. I hate you. You enchantment, you degrading necessity, you foul and filthy life, you promise of endless love and endless time . . .

What words to say with Charlotte sleeping in the same room, no, the same bed, with her hands folded under her face! Innocent sweetheart, whose state must now be rather different.

Up the hills she goes, where the view becomes wider and wider, and the lights spread out like sparkles on a cake, out of the section which is too dangerous, too low, and too furtive to bother with a lady (or is it something in her eyes?), into the broader bystreets where shore-leave sailors try to make her acquaintance by falling into step and seizing her elbow; she snakes away with unbounded strength, darts into shadows, laughs in their faces: "I've got what I want!"

"Not like me!"

"Better!"

This is the Barbary Coast, only beginning to become a tourist attraction; there are barkers outside the restaurants advertising pretty waiter girls, dance halls, spangled posters twice the height of a man, crowds upon crowds of people, one or two guides with tickets in their hats, and Emily— who keeps to the shadows. She nearly chokes with laughter: *What a field of ripe wheat!* One of the barkers hoists her by the waist onto his platform.

"Do you see this little lady? Do you see this—"

"Let me go, Goddamn you!" she cries indignantly.

"This angry little lady—" pushing her chin with one sun-burned hand to make her face the crowd. "This—" But here Emily hurts him, slashing his palm with her teeth, quite pleased with herself, but surprised, too, for the man was holding his hand cupped and the whole thing seemed to happen of itself. She escapes instantly into the crowd and continues up through the Coast, through the old Tenderloin, drunk with self-confidence, slipping like a shadow through the now genteel streets and arriving at the Mansion House gate having seen no family spies and convinced that none has seen her.

But nobody is there.

Ten by the clock, and no one is there, either; eleven by the clock and still no one. *Why didn't I leave this life when I had the chance!* Only one thing consoles Emily, that by some alchemy or nearness to the state she longs for, no one bothers or questions her and even the policemen pass her by as if in her little corner of the gate there is nothing but a shadow. Midnight and no one, half-past and she dozes; perhaps three hours later, perhaps four, she is startled awake by the sound of footsteps. She wakes: nothing. She sleeps again and in her dream hears them for the second time, then she wakes to find herself looking into the face of a lady who wears a veil.

"What!" Emily's startled whisper.

The lady gestures vaguely, as if trying to speak.

"What is it?"

"Don't—" and the lady speaks with feeling but, it seems, with difficulty also—"don't go home."

"Home?" echoes Emily, stupefied, and the stranger nods, saying:

"In danger."

"Who?" Emily is horrified.

"He's in danger." Behind her veil her face seems almost to emit a faint light of its own.

"You're one of them," says Emily. "Aren't you?" and when the woman nods, adds desperately, "Then you must save him!"

The lady smiles pitifully; that much of her face can be seen as the light breeze plays with her net veil.

"But you must!" exclaims Emily. "You know how; I don't; you've got to!"

"I don't dare," very softly. Then the veiled woman turns to go, but Emily—quite hysterical now—seizes her hand, saying:

"Who are you? Who are you?"

The lady gestures vaguely and shakes her head.

"Who are you!" repeats Emily with more energy. "You tell me, do you hear?"

Sombrely the lady raises her veil and stares at her friend with a tragic, dignified, pitiful gaze. In the darkness her face burns with unnatural and beautiful color.

It is Charlotte.

Dawn comes with a pellucid quickening, glassy and ghostly. Slowly, shapes emerge from darkness and the blue pours back into the world—twilight turned backwards and the natural order reversed. Destruction, which is simple, logical, and easy, finds a kind of mocking parody in the morning's creation. Light has no business coming back, but light does.

Emily reaches the cemetery just as the caldron in the east overflows, just as the birds (*idiots!* she thinks) begin a tentative cheeping and chirping. She sits at the gate for a minute to regain her strength, for the night's walking and worry have tried her severely. In front of her the stones lie on graves, almost completely hard and real, waiting for the rising of the sun to finish them off and make complete masterpieces of them. Emily rises and trudges up the hill, slower and slower as the ground rises to its topmost swell, where three hundred years of peaceful Guevaras fertilize the grass and do their best to discredit the one wild shoot that lives on, the only disrespectful member of the family. Weeping a little to herself, Emily lags up the hill, raising her skirts to keep them off the weeds, and murderously hating in her heart the increasing light and the happier celebrating of the birds. She rounds the last hillock of ground and raises her eyes to the Guevaras' eternal mansion, expecting to see nobody again. There is the corner of the building, the low iron gate—

In front of it stands Martin Guevara between her father and Sweet Sweet Will, captived by both arms, his face pale and beautiful between two gold crosses that are just beginning to sparkle in the light of day.

"We are caught," says Guevara, seeing her, directing at her his fixed, white smile.

"You let him go," says Emily—very reasonably.

"You're safe, my Emily!" cries Sweet Will.

"Let him go!" She runs to them, stops, looks at them, perplexed to the bottom of her soul.

"Let him go," she says. "Let him go, let him go!"

Between the two bits of jewelry, Emily's life and hope and only pleasure smiles painfully at her, the color drained out of his face, desperate eyes fixed on the east.

"You don't understand," says Emily, inventing. "He isn't dangerous now. If you let him go, he'll run inside and then you can come back any time during the day and finish him off. I'm sick. You—"

The words die in her throat. All around them, from every tree and hedge, from boughs that have sheltered the graveyard for a hundred years, the birds begin their morning noise. A great hallelujah rises; after all, the birds have nothing to worry about. Numb, with legs like sticks, Emily sees sunlight touch the top of the stone mausoleum, sunlight slide down its face, sunlight reach the level of a standing man—

"I adore you," says Martin to her. With the slow bending over of a drowning man, he doubles up, like a man stuck with a knife in a dream; he doubles up, falls—

And Emily screams; what a scream! as if her soul were being haled out through her throat; and she is running down the other side of the little hill to regions as yet untouched by the sun, crying inwardly: I need help! help! help!— She knows where she can get it. Three hundred feet down the hill in a valley, a wooded protected valley sunk below the touch of the rising sun, there she runs through the trees, past the fence that separates the old graveyard from the new, expensive, polished granite—Charlotte is her friend, she loves her: Charlotte in her new home will make room for her.

Descending

Thomas M. Disch

Catsup, mustard, pickle relish, mayonnaise, two kinds of salad dressing, bacon grease, and a lemon. Oh yes, two trays of ice cubes. In the cupboard it wasn't much better: jars and boxes of spice, flour, sugar, salt—and a box of raisins!

An empty box of raisins.

Not even any coffee. Not even tea, which he hated. Nothing in the mailbox but a bill from Underwood's: *Unless we receive the arrears on your account...*

$4.75 in change jingled in his coat pocket—the plunder of the Chianti bottle he had promised himself never to break open. He was spared the unpleasantness of having to sell his books. They had all been sold. The letter to Graham had gone out a week ago. If his brother intended to send something this time, it would have come by now.

—I should be desperate, he thought—Perhaps I am.

He might have looked in the *Times*. But, no, that was too depressing—applying for jobs at $50 a week and being turned down. Not that he blamed them; he wouldn't have hired himself himself. He had been a grasshopper for years. The ants were on to his tricks.

Thomas M. Disch

He shaved without soap and brushed his shoes to a high polish. He whitened the sepulchre of his unwashed torso with a fresh, starched shirt and chose his somberest tie from the rack. He began to feel excited and expressed it, characteristically, by appearing statuesquely, icily calm.

Descending the stairway to the first floor, he encountered Mrs. Beale, who was pretending to sweep the well-swept floor of the entrance.

"Good afternoon—or I s'pose it's good morning for you, eh?"

"Good afternoon, Mrs. Beale."

"Your letter come?"

"Not yet."

"The first of the month isn't far off."

"Yes indeed, Mrs. Beale."

At the subway station he considered a moment before answering the attendant: One token or two? Two, he decided. After all, he had no choice, but to return to his apartment. The first of the month was still a long way off.

—If Jean Valjean had had a charge account, he would have never gone to prison.

Having thus cheered himself, he settled down to enjoy the ads in the subway car. *Smoke. Try. Eat. Live. See. Drink. Use. Buy.* He thought of Alice with her mushrooms: Eat me.

At 34th Street he got off and entered Underwood's Department Store directly from the train platform. On the main floor he stopped at the cigar stand and bought a carton of cigarettes.

"Cash or charge?"

"Charge." He handed the clerk the laminated plastic card. The charge was rung up.

Fancy groceries was on 5. He made his selection judiciously. A jar of instant and a 2-pound can of drip-ground coffee, a large tin of corned beef, packaged soups and boxes of pancake mix and condensed milk. Jam, peanut butter, and honey. Six cans of tuna fish. Then, he indulged himself in perishables: English cookies, and Edam cheese, a small frozen pheasant—even fruitcake. He never ate so well as when he was broke. He couldn't afford to.

"$14.87."

This time after ringing up his charge, the clerk checked the number on his card against her list of closed or doubtful accounts. She smiled apologetically and handed the card back.

"Sorry, but we have to check."

"I understand."

The bag of groceries weighed a good twenty pounds. Carrying it with the exquisite casualness of a burglar passing before a policeman with his loot, he took the escalator to the bookshop on 8. His choice of books was determined by the same principle as his choice of groceries. First, the staples: two Victorian novels he had never read, *Vanity Fair* and *Middlemarch;* the Sayers' translation of Dante, and a two-volume anthology of German plays none of which he had read and few he had even heard of. Then the perishables: a sensational novel that had reached the best seller list via the Supreme Court, and two mysteries.

He had begun to feel giddy with self-indulgence. He reached into his jacket pocket for a coin.

—Heads a new suit; tails the Sky Room.

Tails.

The Sky Room on 15 was empty of all but a few women chatting over coffee and cakes. He was able to get a seat by a window. He ordered from the à la Carte side of the menu and finished his meal with Espresso and baklava. He handed the waitress his credit card and tipped her fifty cents.

Dawdling over his second cup of coffee, he began *Vanity Fair.* Rather to his surprise, he found himself enjoying it. The waitress returned with his card and a receipt for the meal.

Since the Sky Room was on the top floor of Underwood's there was only one escalator to take now—Descending. Riding down, he continued to read *Vanity Fair.* He could read anywhere—in restaurants, on subways, even walking down the street. At each landing he made his way from the foot of one escalator to the head of the next without lifting his eyes from the book. When he came to the Bargain Basement, he would be only a few steps from the subway turnstile.

He was halfway through Chapter VI (on page 55, to be exact) when he began to feel something amiss.

—How long does this damn thing take to reach the basement?

He stopped at the next landing, but there was no sign to indicate on what floor he was nor any door by which he might re-enter the store. Deducing from this that he was between floors, he took the escalator down one more flight only to find the same perplexing absence of landmarks.

There was, however, a water fountain, and he stopped to take a drink.

—I must have gone to a sub-basement. But this was not too likely after all. Escalators were seldom provided for janitors and stockboys.

He waited on the landing watching the steps of the escalators slowly descend toward him and, at the end of their journey, telescope in upon themselves and disappear. He waited a long while, and no one else came down the moving steps.

—Perhaps the store has closed. Having no wristwatch and having rather lost track of the time, he had no way of knowing. At last, he reasoned that he had become so engrossed in the Thackeray novel that he had simply stopped on one of the upper landings—say, on 8—to finish a chapter and had read on to page 55 without realizing that he was making no progress on the escalators.

When he read, he could forget everything else.

He must, therefore, still be somewhere above the main floor. The absence of exits, though disconcerting, could be explained by some quirk of the floor plan. The absence of signs was merely a carelessness on the part of the management.

He tucked *Vanity Fair* into his shopping bag and stepped onto the grilled lip of the down-going escalator—not, it must be admitted, without a certain degree of reluctance. At each landing, he marked his progress by a number spoken aloud. By *eight* he was uneasy; by *fifteen* he was desperate.

It was, of course, possible that he had to descend two flights of stairs for every floor of the department store. With this possibility in mind, he counted off fifteen more landings.

—No.

Dazedly and as though to deny the reality of this seemingly interminable stairwell, he continued his descent. When he stopped again at the forty-fifth landing, he was trembling. He was afraid.

He rested the shopping bag on the bare concrete floor of the landing, realizing that his arm had gone quite sore from supporting the twenty pounds and more of groceries and books. He discounted the enticing possibility that "it was all a dream," for the dream-world is the reality of the dreamer, to which he could not weakly surrender, no more than one could surrender to the realities of life. Besides, he was not dreaming; of that he was quite sure.

He checked his pulse. It was fast—say, eighty a minute. He rode down two more flights, counting his pulse. Eighty almost exactly. Two flights took only one minute.

He could read approximately one page a minute, a little less on an escalator. Suppose he had spent one hour on the escalators while he had read: sixty minutes—one hundred and twenty floors. Plus forty-seven that he had counted. One hundred sixty-seven. The Sky Room was on 15.

$167 - 15 = 152$.

He was in the one-hundred-fifty-second sub-basement. That was impossible.

The appropriate response to an impossible situation was to deal with it as though it were commonplace—like Alice in Wonderland. Ergo, he would return to Underwood's the same way he had (apparently) left it. He would walk up one hundred fifty-two flights of down-going escalators.

Taking the steps three at a time and running, it was almost like going up a regular staircase. But after ascending the second escalator in this manner, he found himself already out of breath.

There was no hurry. He would not allow himself to be overtaken by panic.

No.

He picked up the bag of groceries and books he had left on that landing, waiting for his breath to return, and darted up a third and fourth flight. While he rested on the landing, he tried to count the steps between floors, but this count differed depending on whether he counted with the current or against it, down or up. The average was roughly eighteen steps, and the steps appeared to be eight or nine inches deep. Each flight was, therefore, about twelve feet.

It was one-third of a mile, as the plumb drops, to Underwood's main floor.

Dashing up the ninth escalator, the bag of groceries broke open at the bottom, where the thawing pheasant had dampened the paper. Groceries and books tumbled onto the steps, some rolling of their own accord to the landing below, others being transported there by the moving stairs and forming a neat little pile. Only the jam jar had been broken.

He stacked the groceries in the corner of the landing, except for the half-thawed pheasant, which he stuffed into his coat pocket, anticipating that his ascent would take him well past his dinner hour.

Physical exertion had dulled his finer feelings—to be precise, his capacity for fear. Like a cross-country runner in his last laps, he thought single-mindedly of the task at hand and made no effort to understand what he had in any case already decided was not to be understood. He mounted one flight, rested, mounted and rested again. Each mount was wearier; each rest longer. He stopped counting the landings after the twenty-eighth, and some time after that—how long he had no idea—his legs gave out and he collapsed to the concrete floor of the landing. His calves were hard aching knots of muscle; his thighs quivered erratically. He tried to do knee-bends and fell backward.

Despite his recent dinner (assuming that it had been recent), he was hungry and he devoured the entire pheasant, completely thawed now, without being able to tell if it were raw or had been pre-cooked.

—This is what it's like to be a cannibal, he thought as he fell asleep.

Sleeping, he dreamed he was falling down a bottomless pit. Waking, he discovered nothing had changed, except the dull ache in his legs, which had become a sharp pain.

Overhead, a single strip of fluorescent lighting snaked down the stairwell. The mechanical purr of the escalators seemed to have heightened to the roar of a Niagara, and their rate of descent seemed to have increased proportionately.

Fever, he decided. He stood up stiffly and flexed some of the soreness from his muscles.

Halfway up the third escalator, his legs gave way under him. He attempted the climb again and succeeded. He collapsed again on the next flight. Lying on the landing where the escalator had deposited him, he realized that his hunger had returned. He also needed to have water—and to let it.

The latter necessity he could easily—and without false modesty—satisfy. Also he remembered the water fountain he had drunk from yesterday and he found another three floors below.

—It's so much easier going down.

His groceries were down there. To go after them now, he would erase whatever progress he had made in his ascent. Perhaps Underwood's main floor was only a few more flights up. Or a hundred. There was no way to know.

Because he was hungry and because he was tired and because the futility of mounting endless flights of descending escalators was, as he now considered it, a labor of Sisyphus, he returned, descended, gave in.

At first, he allowed the escalator to take him along at its own mild pace, but he soon grew impatient of this. He found that the exercise of running down the steps three at a time was not so exhausting as running *up*. It was refreshing, almost. And, by swimming with the current instead of against it, his progress, if such it can be called, was appreciable. In only minutes he was back at his cache of groceries.

After eating half the fruitcake and a little cheese, he fashioned his coat into a sort of a sling for the groceries, knotting the sleeves together and buttoning it closed. With one hand at the collar and the other about the hem, he could carry all his food with him.

He looked up the descending staircase with a scornful smile, for he had decided with the wisdom of failure to abandon *that* venture. If the stairs wished to take him down, then down, giddily, he would go.

Then, down he did go, down dizzily, down, down and always, it seemed, faster, spinning about lightly on his heels at each landing so that there was hardly any break in the wild speed of his descent. He whooped and halooed and laughed to hear his whoopings echo in the narrow, low-vaulted corridors, following him as though they could not keep up his pace.

Down, ever deeper down.

Twice he slipped at the landings and once he missed his footing in mid-leap on the escalator, hurtled forward, letting go of the sling of groceries and falling, hands stretched out to cushion him, onto the steps, which, imperturbably, continued their descent.

He must have been unconscious then, for he woke up in a pile of groceries with a split cheek and a splitting headache. The telescoping steps of the escalator gently grazed his heels.

He knew then his first moment of terror—a premonition that there was no *end* to his descent, but this feeling gave way quickly to a laughing fit.

"I'm going to hell!" he shouted, though he could not drown with his voice the steady purr of the escalators. "This is the way to hell. Abandon hope all ye who enter here."

—If only I were, he reflected— If that were the case, it would make sense. Not quite orthodox sense, but some sense, a little.

Sanity, however, was so integral to his character that neither hysteria nor horror could long have their way with him. He gathered up his groceries again, relieved to find that only the jar of instant coffee had been broken this time. After reflection he also discarded the can of drip-ground coffee, for which he could conceive no use—under the present circumstances. And he would allow himself, for the sake of sanity, to conceive of no other circumstances than those.

He began a more deliberate descent. He returned to *Vanity Fair,* reading it as he paced down the down-going steps. He did not let himself consider the extent of the abyss into which he was plunging, and the vicarious excitement of the novel helped him keep his thoughts from his own situation. At page 235, he lunched (that is, he took his second meal of the day) on the remainder of the cheese and fruitcake; at 523 he rested and dined on the English cookies dipped in peanut butter.

—Perhaps I had better ration my food.

If he could regard this absurd dilemma merely as a struggle for survival, another chapter in his own Robinson Crusoe story, he might get to the bottom of this mechanized vortex alive and sane. He thought proudly that many people in his position could not have adjusted, would have gone mad.

Of course, he *was* descending . . .

But he was still sane. He had chosen his course and now he was following it.

There was no night in the stairwell, and scarcely any shadows. He slept when his legs could no longer bear his weight and his eyes were tearful from reading. Sleeping, he dreamed that he was continuing his descent on the escalators. Waking, his hand resting on the rubber railing that moved along at the same rate as the steps, he discovered this to be the case.

Somnambulistically, he had ridden the escalators further down into this mild, interminable hell, leaving behind his bundle of food and even the still-unfinished Thackeray novel.

Stumbling up the escalators, he began, for the first time, to cry. Without the novel, there was nothing to *think* of but this, this ...

—How far? How long did I sleep?

His legs, which had only been slightly wearied by his descent, gave out twenty flights up. His spirit gave out soon after. Again he turned around, allowed himself to be swept up by current—or, more exactly, swept down.

The escalator seemed to be traveling more rapidly, the pitch of the steps to be more pronounced. But he no longer trusted the evidence of his senses.

—I am, perhaps, insane—or sick from hunger. Yet, I would have run out of food eventually. This will bring the crisis to a head. Optimism, that's the spirit!

Continuing his descent, he occupied himself with a closer analysis of his environment, not undertaken with any hope of bettering his condition but only for lack of other diversions. The walls and ceilings were hard, smooth, and off-white. The escalator steps were a dull nickel color, the treads being somewhat shinier, the crevices darker. Did that mean that the treads were polished from use? Or were they designed in that fashion? The treads were half an inch wide and spaced apart from each other by the same width. They projected slightly over the edge of each step, resembling somewhat the head of a barber's shears. Whenever he stopped at a landing, his attention would become fixed on the illusory "disappearance" of the steps, as they sank flush to the floor and slid, tread in groove, into the grilled baseplate.

Less and less would he run, or even walk, down the stairs, content merely to ride his chosen step from top to bottom of each flight and, at the landing, step (left foot, right, and left again) onto the escalator that would transport him to the floor below. The stairwell now had tunneled, by his calculations, miles beneath the department store—so many miles that he began to congratulate himself upon his unsought adventure, wondering if he had established some sort of record. Just so, a criminal will stand in awe of his own baseness and be most proud of his vilest crime, which he believes unparalleled.

In the days that followed, when his only nourishment was the water from the fountains provided at every tenth landing, he thought frequently of food, preparing imaginary meals from the store of groceries he had left behind, savoring the ideal sweetness of the honey, the richness of the soup which he would prepare by soaking the powder in the emptied cookie tin, licking the film of gelatin lining the opened can of corned beef. When he thought of the six cans of tuna fish, his anxiety became intolerable, for he had (would have had) no way to open them. Merely to stamp on them would not be enough. What, then? He turned the question over and over in his head, like a squirrel spinning the wheel in its cage, to no avail.

Then a curious thing happened. He quickened again the speed of his descent, faster now than when first he had done this, eagerly, headlong, absolutely heedless. The several landings seemed to flash by like a montage of Flight, each scarcely perceived before the next was before him. A demonic, pointless race—and why? He was running, so he thought, toward his store of groceries, either believing that they had been left *below* or thinking that he was running *up*. Clearly, he was delirious.

It did not last. His weakened body could not maintain the frantic pace, and he awoke from his delirium confused and utterly spent. Now began another, more rational delirium, a madness fired by logic. Lying on the landing, rubbing a torn muscle in his ankle, he speculated on the nature, origin and purpose of the escalators. Reasoned thought was of no more use to him, however, than unreasoning action. Ingenuity was helpless to solve a riddle that had no answer, which was its own reason, self-contained and whole. He—not the escalators—needed an answer.

Perhaps his most interesting theory was the notion that these escalators were a kind of exercise wheel, like those found in a squirrel cage, from which, because it was a closed system, there could be no escape. This theory required some minor alterations in his conception of the physical universe, which had always appeared highly Euclidean to him before, a universe in which his descent seemingly along a plumb-line was, in fact, describing a loop. This theory cheered him, for he might hope, coming full circle, to return to his store of groceries again, if not to Underwood's. Perhaps in his abstracted state he had passed one or the other already several times without observing.

There was another, and related, theory concerning the measures taken by Underwood's Credit Department against delinquent accounts. This was mere paranoia.

—Theories! I don't need theories. I must get on with it.

So, favoring his good leg, he continued his descent, although his speculations did not immediately cease. They became, if anything, more metaphysical. They became vague. Eventually, he could regard the escalators as being entirely matter-of-fact, requiring no more explanation than, by their sheer existence, they offered him.

He discovered that he was losing weight. Being so long without food (by the evidence of his beard, he estimated that more than a week had gone by), this was only to be expected. Yet, there was another possibility that he could not exclude: that he was approaching the center of the earth where, as he understood, all things were weightless.

—Now *that*, he thought, is something worth striving for.

He had discovered a goal. On the other hand, he was dying, a process he did not give all the attention it deserved. Unwilling to admit this eventuality and yet not so foolish as to admit any other, he side-stepped the issue by pretending to hope.

—Maybe someone will rescue me, he hoped.

But his hope was as mechanical as the escalators he rode—and tended, in much the same way, to sink.

Waking and sleeping were no longer distinct states of which he could say: "Now I am sleeping," or "Now I am awake." Sometimes he would discover himself descending and be unable to tell whether he had been waked from sleep or roused from inattention.

He hallucinated.

A woman, loaded with packages from Underwood's and wearing a trim, pillbox-style hat, came down the escalator toward him, turned around on the landing, high heels clicking smartly, and rode away without even nodding to him.

More and more, when he awoke or was roused from his stupor, he found himself, instead of hurrying to his goal, lying on a landing, weak, dazed, and beyond hunger. Then he would crawl to the down-going escalator and pull himself onto one of the steps, which he would ride to the bottom, sprawled head foremost, hands and shoulders braced against the treads to keep from skittering bumpily down.

—At the bottom, he thought—at the bottom ... I will ... when I get there ...

From the bottom, which he conceived of as the center of the earth, there would be literally nowhere to go but up. Probably another chain of escalators, ascending escalators, but preferably by an elevator. It was important to believe in a bottom.

Thought was becoming as difficult, as demanding and painful, as once his struggle to ascend had been. His perceptions were fuzzy. He did not know what was real and what imaginary. He thought he was eating and discovered he was gnawing at his hands.

He thought he had come to the bottom. It was a large high-ceilinged room. Signs pointed to another escalator: *Ascending*. But there was a chain across it and a small typed announcement.

"Out of order. Please bear with us while the escalators are being repaired. Thank you. The Management."

He laughed weakly.

He devised a way to open the tuna fish cans. He would slip the can sideways beneath the projecting treads of the escalator, just at the point where the steps were sinking flush to the floor. Either the escalator would split the can open or the can would jam the escalator. Perhaps if one escalator were jammed the whole chain of them would stop. He should have thought of that before, but he was, nevertheless, quite pleased to have thought of it at all.

—I might have escaped.

His body seemed to weigh so little now. He must have come hundreds of miles. Thousands.

Again, he descended.

Then, he was lying at the foot of the escalator. His head rested on the cold metal of the baseplate and he was looking at his hand, the fingers of which were pressed into the creviced grille. One after another, in perfect order, the steps of the escalator slipped into these crevices, tread in groove, rasping at his fingertips, occasionally tearing away a sliver of his flesh.

That was the last thing he remembered.

Four Ghosts in Hamlet

Fritz Leiber

Actors are a superstitious lot, probably because chance plays a big part in
the success of a production of a company or merely an actor—and because
we're still a little closer than other people to the gypsies in the way we live
and think. For instance, it's bad luck to have peacock feathers on stage or
say the last line of a play at rehearsals or whistle in the dressing room (the
one nearest the door gets fired) or sing God Save the Sovereign on a railway
train. (A Canadian company got wrecked that way.)

Shakespearean actors are no exceptions. They simply travel a few extra
superstitions, such as the one which forbids reciting the lines of the Three
Witches, or anything from *Macbeth*, for that matter, except at performances, rehearsals, and on other legitimate occasions. This might be a
good rule for outsiders too—then there wouldn't be the endless flood of
books with titles taken from the text of *Macbeth*—you know, *Brief Candle*,
Tomorrow and Tomorrow, *The Sound and the Fury*, *A Poor Player*, *All Our
Yesterdays*, and those are all just from one brief soliloquy.

And our company, the Governor's company, has a rule against the Ghost
in *Hamlet* dropping his greenish cheesecloth veil over his helmet-framed

face until the very moment he makes each of his entrances. Hamlet's dead
father mustn't stand veiled in the darkness of the wings.

This last superstition commemorates something which happened not
too long ago, an actual ghost story. Sometimes I think it's the greatest ghost
story in the world—though certainly not from my way of telling it, which is
gossipy and poor, but from the wonder blazing at its core.

It's not only a true tale of the supernatural, but also very much a story
about people, for after all—and before everything else—ghosts are people.

The ghostly part of the story first showed itself in the tritest way
imaginable: three of our actresses (meaning practically all the ladies in a
Shakespearean company) took to having sessions with a Ouija board in the
hour before curtain time and sometimes even during a performance when
they had long offstage waits, and they became so wrapped up in it and
conceited about it and they squeaked so excitedly at the revelations which
the planchette spelled out—and three or four times almost missed
entrances because of it—that if the Governor weren't such a tolerant
commander-in-chief, he would have forbidden them to bring the board to
the theater. I'm sure he was tempted to and might have, except that Props
pointed out to him that our three ladies probably wouldn't enjoy Ouija
sessions one bit in the privacy of a hotel room, that much of the fun in
operating a Ouija board is in having a half-exasperated, half-intrigued
floating audience, and that when all's done the basic business of all ladies is
glamour, whether of personal charm or of actual witchcraft, since the word
means both.

Props—that is, our property man, Billy Simpson—was fascinated by
their obsession, as he is by any new thing that comes along, and might very
well have broken our Shakespearean taboo by quoting the Three Witches
about them, except that Props has no flair for Shakespearean speech at all,
no dramatic ability whatsoever, in fact he's the one person in our company
who never acts even a bit part or carries a mute spear on stage, though he
has other talents which make up for this deficiency—he can throw
together a papier-mâché bust of Pompey in two hours, or turn out a
wooden prop dagger all silvery-bladed and hilt-gilded, or fix a zipper, and
that's not all.

As for myself, I was very irked at the ridiculous alphabet board, since it
seemed to occupy most of Monica Singleton's spare time and satisfy all her
hunger for thrills. I'd been trying to promote a romance with her—a long
touring season becomes deadly and cold without some sort of heart-
tickle—and for a while I'd made progress. But after Ouija came along, I
became a ridiculous Guildenstern mooning after an unattainable unseeing
Ophelia—which were the parts I and she actually played in *Hamlet*.

I cursed the idiot board with its childish corner-pictures of grinning suns

and smirking moons and windblown spirits, and I further alienated Monica
by asking her why wasn't it called a Nenein or No-No board (Ninny
board!) instead of a Yes-Yes board? Was that, I inquired, because all
spiritualists are forever accentuating the positive and behaving like a pack
of fawning yes-men? —yes, we're here; yes, we're your uncle Harry; yes,
we're happy on this plane; yes, we have a doctor among us who'll diagnose
that pain in your chest; and so on.

Monica wouldn't speak to me for a week after that.

I would have been even more depressed except that Props pointed out
to me that no flesh-and-blood man can compete with ghosts in a girl's
affections, since ghosts being imaginary have all the charms and
perfections a girl can dream of, but that all girls eventually tire of ghosts, or
if their minds don't, their bodies do. This eventually did happen, thank
goodness, in the case of myself and Monica, though not until we'd had a
grisly, mind-wrenching experience—a night of terrors before the nights of
love.

So Ouija flourished and the Governor and the rest of us put up with it
one way or another, until there came that three-night-stand in Wolverton,
when its dismal uncanny old theater tempted our three Ouija-women to
ask the board who was the ghost haunting the spooky place and the
swooping planchette spelled out the name S-H-A-K-E-S-P-E-A-R-E ....

But I am getting ahead of my story. I haven't introduced our company
except for Monica, Props, and the Governor—and I haven't identified the
last of those three.

We call Gilbert Usher the Governor out of sheer respect and affection.
He's about the last of the old actor-managers. He hasn't the name of
Gielgud or Olivier or Evans or Richardson, but he's spent most of a
lifetime keeping Shakespeare alive, spreading that magical a-religious
gospel in the more remote counties and the Dominions and the United
States, like Benson once did. Our other actors aren't names at all—I refuse
to tell you mine!—but with the exception of myself they're good troupers,
or if they don't become that the first season, they drop out. Gruelingly long
seasons, much uncomfortable traveling, and small profits are our destiny.

This particular season had got to that familiar point where the plays are
playing smoothly and everyone's a bit tireder than he realizes and the
restlessness sets in. Robert Dennis, our juvenile, was writing a novel of
theatrical life (he said) mornings at the hotel—up at seven to slave at it,
our Robert claimed. Poor old Guthrie Boyd had started to drink again, and
drink quite too much, after an abstemious two months which had
astonished everyone.

Francis Farley Scott, our leading man, had started to drop hints that he
was going to organize a Shakespearean repertory company of his own next

year and he began to have conspiratorial conversations with Gertrude Grainger, our leading lady, and to draw us furtively aside one by one to make us hypothetical offers, no exact salary named. F. F. is as old as the Governor—who is our star, of course—and he has no talents at all except for self-infatuation and a somewhat grandiose yet impressive fashion of acting. He's portly like an opera tenor and quite bald and he travels with an assortment of thirty toupees, ranging from red to black shot with silver, which he alternates with shameless abandon—they're for wear offstage, not on. It doesn't matter to him that the company knows all about his multi-colored artificial toppings, for we're part of his world of illusion, and he's firmly convinced that the stage-struck local ladies he squires about never notice, or at any rate mind the deception. He once gave me a lecture on the subtleties of suiting the color of your hair to the lady you're trying to fascinate—her own age, hair color, and so on.

Every year F. F. plots to start a company of his own—it's a regular midseason routine with him—and every year it comes to nothing, for he's as lazy and impractical as he is vain. Yet F. F. believes he could play any part in Shakespeare or all of them at once in a pinch; perhaps the only F. F. Scott Company which would really satisfy him would be one in which he would be the only actor—a Shakespearean monologue; in fact, the one respect in which F. F. is not lazy is in his eagerness to double as many parts as possible in any single play.

F. F.'s yearly plots never bother the Governor a bit—he keeps waiting wistfully for F. F. to fix him with an hypnotic eye and in a hoarse whisper ask *him* to join the Scott company.

And I of course was hoping that now at last Monica Singleton would stop trying to be the most exquisite ingenue that ever came tripping Shakespeare's way (rehearsing her parts even in her sleep, I guessed, though I was miles from being in a position to know that for certain) and begin to take note and not just advantage of my devoted attentions.

But then old Sybil Jameson bought the Ouija board and Gertrude Grainger dragooned an unwilling Monica into placing her fingertips on the planchette along with theirs "just for a lark." Next day Gertrude announced to several of us in a hushed voice that Monica had the most amazing undeveloped mediumistic talent she'd ever encountered, and from then on the girl was a Ouija-addict. Poor tight-drawn Monica, I suppose she had to explode out of her self-imposed Shakespearean discipline somehow, and it was just too bad it had to be the board instead of me. Though come to think of it, I shouldn't have felt quite so resentful of the board, for she might have exploded with Robert Dennis, which would have been infinitely worse, though we were never quite sure of Robert's sex. For that matter I wasn't sure of Gertrude's and suffered agonies of uncertain jealousy when she captured my beloved. I was obsessed with the vision of Gertrude's bold knees pressing Monica's under the Ouija board, though with Sybil's bony ones for chaperones, fortunately.

Francis Farley Scott, who was jealous too because this new toy had taken Gertrude's mind off their annual plottings, said rather spitefully that Monica must be one of those grabby girls who have to take command of whatever they get their fingers on, whether it's a man or a planchette, but Props told me he'd bet anything that Gertrude and Sybil had "followed" Monica's first random finger movements like the skillfulest dancers guiding a partner while seeming to yield, in order to coax her into the business and make sure of their third.

Sometimes I thought that F. F. was right and sometimes Props and sometimes I thought that Monica had a genuine supernatural talent, though I don't ordinarily believe in such things, and that last really frightened me, for such a person might give up live men for ghosts forever. She was such a sensitive, subtle, wraith-cheeked girl and she could get so keyed up and when she touched the planchette her eyes got such an empty look, as if her mind had traveled down into her fingertips or out to the ends of time and space. And once the three of them gave me a character reading from the board which embarrassed me with its accuracy. The same thing happened to several other people in the company. Of course, as Props pointed out, actors can be pretty good character analysts whenever they stop being egomaniacs.

After reading characters and foretelling the future for several weeks, our Three Weird Sisters got interested in reincarnation and began asking the board and then telling us what famous or infamous people we'd been in past lives. Gertrude Grainger had been Queen Boadicea, I wasn't surprised to hear. Sybil Jameson had been Cassandra. While Monica was once mad Queen Joanna of Castile and more recently a prize hysterical patient of Janet at the Salpetriere—touches which irritated and frightened me more than they should have. Billy Simpson—Props—had been an Egyptian silversmith under Queen Hatshepsut and later a servant of Samuel Pepys; he heard this with a delighted chuckle. Guthrie Boyd had been the Emperor Claudius and Robert Dennis had been Caligula. For some reason I had been both John Wilkes Booth and Lambert Simnel, which irritated me considerably, for I saw no romance but only neurosis in assassinating an American president and dying in a buring barn, or impersonating the Earl of Warwick, pretending unsuccessfully to the British throne, being pardoned for it—of all things!—and spending the rest of my life as a scullion in the kitchen of Henry VII and his son. The fact that both Booth and Simnel had been actors of a sort—a poor sort— naturally irritated me the more. Only much later did Monica confess to me that the board had probably made those decisions because I had had such a "tragic, dangerous, defeated look"—a revelation which surprised and flattered me.

Francis Farley Scott was flattered too, to hear he'd once been Henry VIII—he fancied all those wives and he wore his golden blond toupee after the show that night—until Gertrude and Sybil and Monica announced that the Governor was a reincarnation of no less than William Shakespeare himself. That made F. F. so jealous that he instantly sat down at the prop table, grabbed up a quill pen, and did an impromptu rendering of Shakespeare composing Hamlet's "To be or not to be" soliloquy. It was an effective performance, though with considerably more frowning and eye-rolling and trying of lines for sound that I imagine Willy S. himself used originally, and when F. F. finished, even the Governor, who'd been standing unobserved in the shadows beside Props, applauded with the latter.

Governor kidded the pants off the idea of himself as Shakespeare. He said that if Willy S. were ever reincarnated it ought to be as a world-famous dramatist who was secretly in his spare time the world's greatest scientist and philosopher and left clues to his identity in his mathematical equations—that way he'd get his own back at Bacon, rather the Baconians.

Yet I suppose if you had to pick someone for a reincarnation of Shakespeare, Gilbert Usher wouldn't be a bad choice. Insofar as a star and director ever can be, the Governor is gentle and self-effacing—as Shakespeare himself must have been, or else there would never have arisen that ridiculous Bacon-Oxford-Marlowe-Elizabeth-take-your-pick-who-wrote-Shakespeare controversy. And the Governor has a sweet melancholy about him, though he's handsomer and despite his years more athletic than one imagines Shakespeare being. And he's generous to a fault, especially where old actors who've done brave fine things in the past are concerned.

This season his mistake in that last direction had been in hiring Guthrie Boyd to play some of the more difficult older leading roles, including a couple F. F. usually handles: Brutus, Othello, and besides those Duncan in *Macbeth,* Kent in *King Lear*, and the Ghost in *Hamlet*.

Guthrie was a bellowing hard-drinking bear of an actor, who'd been a Shakespearean star in Australia and successfully smuggled some of his reputation west—he learned to moderate his bellowing, while his emotions were always simple and sincere, though explosive—and finally even spent some years in Hollywood. But there his drinking caught up with him, probably because of the stupid film parts he got, and he failed six times over. His wife divorced him. His children cut themselves off. He married a starlet and she divorced him. He dropped out of sight.

Then after several years the Governor ran into him. He'd been rusticating in Canada with a stubborn teetotal admirer. He was only a shadow of his former self, but there was some substance to the shadow —and he wasn't drinking. The Governor decided to take a chance on him— although the company manager Harry Grossman was dead set against it —and during rehearsals and the first month or so of performances it was wonderful to see how old Guthrie Boyd came back, exactly as if Shakespeare were a restorative medicine.

It may be stuffy or sentimental of me to say so, but you know, I think Shakespeare's good for people. I don't know of an actor, except myself, whose character hasn't been strengthened and his vision widened and charity quickened by working in the plays. I've heard that before Gilbert Usher became a Shakespearean, he was a more ruthlessly ambitious and critical man, not without malice, but the plays mellowed him, as they've mellowed Props's philosophy and given him a zest for life.

Because of his contact with Shakespeare, Robert Dennis is a less strident and pettish swish (if he is one), Gertrude Grainger's outbursts of cold rage have an undercurrent of queenly make-believe, and even Francis Farley Scott's grubby little seductions are probably kinder and less insultingly illusionary.

In fact I sometimes think that what civilized serenity the British people possess, and small but real ability to smile at themselves, is chiefly due to their good luck in having had William Shakespeare born one of their company.

But I was telling how Guthrie Boyd performed very capably those first weeks, against the expectations of most of us, so that we almost quit holding our breaths—or sniffing at his. His Brutus was workmanlike, his Kent quite fine—that bluff rough honest part suited him well—and he regularly got admiring notices for his Ghost in *Hamlet.* I think his years of living death as a drinking alcoholic had given him an understanding of loneliness and frozen abilities and despair that he put to good use— probably unconsciously—in interpreting that small role.

He was really a most impressive figure in the part, even just visually. The Ghost's basic costume is simple enough—a big all-enveloping cloak that brushes the groundcloth, a big dull helmet with the tiniest battery light inside its peak to throw a faint green glow on the Ghost's features, and over the helmet a veil of greenish cheesecloth that registers as mist to the audience. He wears a suit of stage armor under the cloak, but that's not important and at a pinch he can do without it, for his cloak can cover his entire body.

The Ghost doesn't switch on his helmet-light until he makes his entrance, for fear of it being glimpsed by an edge of the audience, and nowadays because of that superstition or rule I told you about, he doesn't drop the cheesecloth veil until the last second either, but when Guthrie Boyd was playing the part that rule didn't exist and I have a vivid recollection of him standing in the wings, waiting to go on, a big bearish inscrutable figure about as solid and un-supernatural as a bushy seven-foot evergreen covered by a gray tarpaulin. But then when Guthrie would switch on the tiny light and stride smoothly and silently on stage and his hollow distant tormented voice boom out, there'd be a terrific shivery thrill, even for us backstage, as if we were listening to words that really had traveled across black windy infinite gulfs from the Afterworld or the Other Side.

At any rate Guthrie was a great Ghost, and adequate or a bit better than that in most of his other parts— for those first nondrinking weeks. He seemed very cheerful on the whole, modestly buoyed up by his comeback, though sometimes something empty and dead would stare for a moment out of his eyes—the old drinking alcoholic wondering what all this fatiguing sober nonsense was about. He was especially looking forward to our three-night-stand at Wolverton, although that was still two months in the future then. The reason was that both his children—married and with families now, of course—lived and worked at Wolverton and I'm sure he set great store on proving to them in person his rehabilitation, figuring it would lead to a reconciliation and so on.

But then came his first performance as Othello. (The Governor, although the star, always played Iago—an equal role, though not the title one.) Guthrie was almost too old for Othello, of course, and besides that, his health wasn't good—the drinking years had taken their toll of his stamina and the work of rehearsals and of first nights in eight different plays after years away from the theater had exhausted him. But somehow the old volcano inside him got seething again and he gave a magnificent performance. Next morning the papers raved about him and one review rated him even better than the Governor.

That did it, unfortunately. The glory of his triumph was too much for him. The next night—*Othello* again—he was drunk as a skunk. He remembered most of his lines—though the Governor had to throw him about every sixth one out of the side of his mouth—but he weaved and wobbled, he planked a big hand on the shoulder of every other character he addressed to keep from falling over, and he even forgot to put in his false teeth the first two acts, so that his voice was mushy. To cap that, he started really to strangle Gertrude Grainger in the last scene, until that rather brawny Desdemona, unseen by the audience, gave him a knee in the gut; then, after stabbing himself, he flung the prop dagger high in the flies so that it came down with two lazy twists and piercing the groundcloth buried its blunt point deep in the soft wood of the stage floor not three feet from

Monica, who plays Iago's wife Emilia and so was lying dead on the stage at that point in the drama, murdered by her villainous husband—and might have been dead for real if the dagger had followed a slightly different trajectory.

Since a third performance of *Othello* was billed for the following night, the Governor had no choice but to replace Guthrie with Francis Farley Scott, who did a good job (for him) of covering up his satisfaction at getting his old role back. F.F., always a plushy and lascivious-eyed Moor, also did a good job with the part, coming in that way without even a brush-up rehearsal, so that one critic, catching the first and third shows, marveled how we could change big roles at will, thinking we'd done it solely to demonstrate our virtuosity.

Of course the Governor read the riot act to Guthrie and carried him off to a doctor, who without being prompted threw a big scare into him about his drinking and his heart, so that he just might have recovered from his lapse, except that two nights later we did *Julius Caesar* and Guthrie, instead of being satisfied with being workmanlike, decided to recoup himself with a really rousing performance. So he bellowed and groaned and bugged his eyes as I suppose he had done in his palmiest Australian days. His optimistic self-satisfaction between scenes was frightening to behold. Not too terrible a performance, truly, but the critics all panned him and one of them said, "Guthrie Boyd played Brutus—a bunch of vocal cords wrapped up in a toga."

That tied up the package and knotted it tight. Thereafter Guthrie was medium pie-eyed from morning to night—and often more than medium. The Governor had to yank him out of Brutus too (F. F. again replacing), but being the Governor he didn't sack him. He put him into a couple of bit parts—Montano and the Soothsayer—in *Othello* and *Caesar* and let him keep on at the others and he gave me and Joe Rubens and sometimes Props the job of keeping an eye on the poor old sot and making sure he got to the theater by the half hour and if possible not too plastered. Often he played the Ghost or the Doge of Venice in his street clothes under cloak or scarlet robe, but he played them. And many were the nights Joe and I made the rounds of half the local bars before we corraled him. The Governor sometimes refers to Joe Rubens and me in mild derision as "the American element" in his company, but just the same he depends on us quite a bit; and I certainly don't mind being one of his trouble-shooters—it's a joy to serve him.

All this may seem to contradict my statement about our getting to the point, about this time, where the plays were playing smoothly and the monotony setting in. But it doesn't really. There's always something going wrong in a theatrical company—anything else would be abnormal; just as the Samoans say no party is a success until somebody's dropped a plate or spilled a drink or tickled the wrong woman.

Besides, once Guthrie had got Othello and Brutus off his neck, he didn't do too badly. The little parts and even Kent he could play passably whether drunk or sober. King Duncan, for instance, and the Doge in *The Merchant* are easy to play drunk because the actor always has a couple of attendants to either side of him, who can guide his steps if he weaves and even hold him up if necessary—which can turn out to be an effective dramatic touch, registering as the infirmity of extreme age.

And somehow Guthrie continued to give that same masterful performance as the Ghost and get occasional notices for it. In fact Sybil Jameson insisted he was a shade better in the Ghost now that he was invariably drunk; which could have been true. And he still talked about the three-night-stand coming up in Wolverton, though now as often with gloomy apprehension as with proud fatherly anticipation.

Well, the three-night-stand eventually came. We arrived at Wolverton on a non-playing evening. To the surprise of most of us, but especially Guthrie, his son and daughter were there at the station to welcome him with their respective spouses and all their kids and numerous in-laws and a great gaggle of friends. Their cries of greeting when they spotted him were almost an organized cheer and I looked around for a brass band to strike up.

I found out later that Sybil Jameson, who knew them, had been sending them all his favorable notices, so that they were eager as weasels to be reconciled with him and show him off as blatantly as possible.

When he saw his childrens' and grandchildrens' faces and realized the cries were for him, old Guthrie got red in the face and beamed like the sun, and they closed in around him and carried him off in triumph for an evening of celebrations.

Next day I heard from Sybil, whom they'd carried off with him, that everything had gone beautifully. He'd drunk like a fish, but kept marvellous control, so that no one but she noticed, and the warmth of the reconciliation of Guthrie to everyone, complete strangers included, had been wonderful to behold. Guthrie's son-in-law, a pugnacious chap, had got angry when he'd heard Guthrie wasn't to play Brutus the third night, and he declared that Gilbert Usher must be jealous of his magnificent father-in-law. Everything was forgiven twenty times over. They'd even tried to put old Sybil to bed with Guthrie, figuring romantically, as people will about actors, that she must be his mistress. All this was very fine, and of course wonderful for Guthrie, and for Sybil too in a fashion, yet I suppose the unconstrained nightlong bash, after two months of uninterrupted semi-controlled drunkenness, was just about the worst thing anybody could have done to the old boy's sodden body and laboring heart.

Meanwhile on that first evening I accompanied Joe Rubens and Props to the theater we were playing at Wolverton to make sure the scenery got stacked right and the costume trunks were all safely arrived and stowed. Joe is our stage manager besides doing rough or Hebraic parts like Caliban and Tubal—he was a professional boxer in his youth and got his nose smashed crooked. Once I started to take boxing lessons from him, figuring an actor should know everything, but during the third lesson I walked into a gentle right cross and although it didn't exactly stun me there were bells ringing faintly in my head for six hours afterwards and I lived in a world of faery and that was the end of my fistic career. Joe is actually a most versatile actor—for instance, he understudies the Governor in Macbeth, Lear, Iago, and of course Shylock—though his brutal moon-face is against him, especially when his make-up doesn't include a beard. But he dotes on being genial and in the States he often gets a job by day playing Santa Claus in big department stores during the month before Christmas.

The Monarch was a cavernous old place, very grimy backstage, but with a great warren of dirty little dressing rooms and even a property room shaped like an L stage left. Its empty shelves were thick with dust.

There hadn't been a show in the Monarch for over a year, I saw from the yellowing sheets thumbtacked to the callboard as I tore them off and replaced them with a simple black-crayoned HAMLET: TONIGHT AT 8:30.

Then I noticed, by the cold inadequate working lights, a couple of tiny dark shapes dropping down from the flies and gliding around in wide swift circles—out into the house too, since the curtain was up. Bats, I realized with a little start—the Monarch was really halfway through the lich gate. The bats would fit very nicely with *Macbeth,* I told myself, but not so well with *The Merchant of Venice,* while with *Hamlet* they should neither help nor hinder, provided they didn't descend in nightfighter squadrons; it would be nice if they stuck to the Ghost scenes.

I'm sure the Governor had decided we'd open at Wolverton with *Hamlet* so that Guthrie would have the best chance of being a hit in his children's home city.

Billy Simpson, shoving his properties table into place just in front of the dismal L of the prop room, observed cheerfully, "It's a proper haunted house. The girls'll find some rare ghosts here, I'll wager, if they work their board."

Which turned out to be far truer than he realized at the time—I think.

"Bruce!" Joe Rubens called to me. "We better buy a couple of rat traps and set them out. There's something scuttling back of the drops."

But when I entered the Monarch next night, well before the hour, by the creaky thick metal stage door, the place had been swept and tidied a bit. With the groundcloth down and the *Hamlet* set up, it didn't look too terrible, even though the curtain was still unlowered, dimly showing the house and its curves of empty seats and the two faint green exit lights with no one but myself to look at them.

There was a little pool of light around the callboard stage right, and another glow the other side of the stage beyond the wings, and lines of light showing around the edges of the door of the second dressing room, next to the star's.

I started across the dark stage, sliding my shoes softly so as not to trip over a cable or stage-screw and brace, and right away I got the magic electric feeling I often do in an empty theater the night of a show. Only this time there was something additional, something that started a shiver crawling down my neck. It wasn't, I think, the thought of the bats which might now be swooping around me unseen, skirling their inaudibly shrill trumpet calls, or even of the rats which *might* be watching sequin-eyed from behind trunks and flats, although not an hour ago Joe had told me that the traps he'd actually procured and set last night had been empty today.

No, it was more as if all of Shakespeare's characters were invisibly there around me—all the infinite possibilities of the theater. I imagined Rosalind and Falstaff and Prospero standing arm-in-arm watching me with different smiles. And Caliban grinning down from where he silently swung in the flies. And side by side, but unsmiling and not arm-in-arm: Macbeth and Iago and Dick the Three Eyes—Richard III. And all the rest of Shakespeare's myriad-minded good-evil crew.

I passed through the wings opposite and there in the second pool of light Billy Simpson sat behind his table with the properties for *Hamlet* set out on it: the skulls, the foils, the lantern, the purses, the parchmenty letters, Ophelia's flowers, and all the rest. It was odd Props having everything ready quite so early and a bit odd too that he should be alone, for Props has the un-actorish habit of making friends with all sorts of locals, such as policemen and porters and flower women and newsboys and shopkeepers and tramps who claim they're indigent actors, and even inviting them backstage with him—a fracture of rules which the Governor allows since Props is such a sensible chap. He has a great liking for people, especially low people, Props has, and for all the humble details of life. He'd make a good writer, I'd think, except for his utter lack of dramatic flair and story-skill—a sort of prosiness that goes with his profession.

And now he was sitting at his table, his stooped shoulders almost inside the doorless entry to the empty-shelfed prop room—no point in using it for a three-night-stand—and he was gazing at me quizzically. He has a big forehead—the light was on that—and a tapering chin—that was in shadow—and rather large eyes, which were betwixt the light and the dark.

Sitting there like that, he seemed to me for a moment (mostly because of the outspread props, I guess) like the midnight Master of the Show in *The Rubaiyat* round whom all the rest of us move like shadow shapes.

Usually he has a quick greeting for anyone, but tonight he was silent, and that added to the illusion.

"Props," I said, "this theater's got a supernatural smell."

His expression didn't change at that, but he solemnly sniffed the air in several little whiffles adding up to one big inhalation, and as he did so he threw his head back, bringing his weakish chin into the light and shattering the illusion.

"Dust," he said after a moment. "Dust and old plush and scenery waterpaint and sweat and drains and gelatin and greasepaint and powder and a breath of whisky. But the supernatural ... no, I can't smell that. Unless ..." And he sniffed again, but shook his head.

I chuckled at his materialism—although that touch about whisky did seem fanciful, since I hadn't been drinking and Props never does and Guthrie Boyd was nowhere in evidence. Props has a mind like a notebook for sensory details—and for the minutiae of human habits too. It was Props, for instance, who told me about the actual notebook in which John McCarthy (who would be playing Fortinbras and the Player King in a couple of hours) jots down the exact number of hours he sleeps each night and keeps totting them up, so he knows when he'll have to start sleeping extra hours to average the full nine he thinks he must get each night to keep from dying.

It was also Props who pointed out to me that F. F. is much more careless gumming his offstage toupees to his head than his theater wigs—a studied carelessness, like that in tying a bowtie, he assured me; it indicated, he said, a touch of contempt for the whole offstage world.

Props isn't *only* a detail-worm, but it's perhaps because he is one that he has sympathy for all human hopes and frailties, even the most trivial, like my selfish infatuation with Monica.

Now I said to him, "I didn't mean an actual smell, Billy. But back there just now I got the feeling anything might happen tonight."

He nodded slowly and solemnly. With anyone but Props I'd have wondered if he weren't a little drunk. Then he said, "You were on a stage. You know, the science-fiction writers are missing a bet there. We've got time machines right now. Theaters. Theaters are time machines and spaceships too. They take people on trips through the future and the past and the elsewhere and the might-have-been—yes, and if it's done well enough, give them glimpses of Heaven and Hell."

I nodded back at him. Such grotesque fancies are the closest Props ever comes to escaping from prosiness.

I said, "Well, let's hope Guthrie gets aboard the spaceship before the curtain up-jets. Tonight we're depending on his children having the sense to deliver him here intact. Which from what Sybil says about them is not to be taken for granted."

Props stared at me owlishly and slowly shook his head. "Guthrie got here about ten minutes ago," he said, "and looking no drunker than usual."

"That's a relief," I told him, meaning it.

"The girls are having a Ouija session," he went on, as if he were determined to account for all of us from moment to moment. "They smelt the supernatural here, just as you did, and they're asking the board to name the culprit." Then he stooped so that he looked almost hunchbacked and he felt for something under the table.

I nodded. I'd guessed the Ouija part from the lines of light showing around the door of Gertrude Grainger's dressing room.

Props straightened up and he had a pint bottle of whisky in his hand. I don't think a loaded revolver would have dumbfounded me as much. He unscrewed the top.

"There's the Governor coming in," he said tranquilly, hearing the stage door creak and evidently some footsteps my own ears missed. "That's seven of us in the theater before the hour."

He took a big slow swallow of whisky and recapped the bottle, as naturally as if it were a nightly action. I goggled at him without comment. What he was doing was simply unheard of—for Billy Simpson.

At that moment there was a sharp scream and a clatter of thin wood and something twangy and metallic falling and a scurry of footsteps. Our previous words must have cocked a trigger in me, for I was at Gertrude Grainger's dressing-room door as fast as I could sprint—no worry this time about tripping over cables or braces in the dark.

I yanked the door open and there by the bright light of the bulbs framing the mirror were Gertrude and Sybil sitting close together with the Ouija board face down on the floor in front of them along with a flimsy wire-backed chair, overturned. While pressing back into Gertrude's costumes hanging on the rack across the little room, almost as if she wanted to hide behind them like bedclothes, was Monica, pale and staring-eyed. She didn't seem to recognize me. The dark-green heavily brocaded costume Gertrude wears as the Queen in *Hamlet*, into which Monica was chiefly pressing herself, accentuated her pallor. All three of them were in their streetclothes.

I went to Monica and put an arm around her and gripped her hand. It was cold as ice. She was standing rigidly.

While I was doing that Gertrude stood up and explained in rather haughty tones what I told you earlier: about them asking the board who the

ghost was haunting the Monarch tonight and the planchette spelling out
S-H-A-K-E-S-P-E-A-R-E ..:

"I don't know why it startled you so, dear," she ended crossly, speaking
to Monica. "It's very natural his spirit should attend performances of his
plays."

I felt the slim body I clasped relax a little. That relieved me. I was
selfishly pleased at having got an arm around it, even under such public
and unamorous circumstances, while at the same time my silly mind was
thinking that if Props had been lying to me about Guthrie Boyd having
come in no more drunken than usual (this new Props who drank straight
whisky in the theater could lie too, I supposed) why then we could
certainly use William Shakespeare tonight, since the Ghost in *Hamlet* is the
one part in all his plays Shakespeare himself is supposed to have acted on
the stage.

"I don't know why myself now," Monica suddenly answered from
beside me, shaking her head as if to clear it. She became aware of me at last,
started to pull away, then let my arm stay around her.

The next voice that spoke was the Governor's. He was standing in the
doorway, smiling faintly, with Props peering around his shoulder. Props
would be as tall as the Governor if he ever straightened up, but his stoop
takes almost a foot off his height.

The Governor said softly, a comic light in his eyes, "I think we should be
content to bring Shakespeare's plays to life, without trying for their author.
It's hard enough on the nerves just to *act* Shakespeare."

He stepped forward with one of his swift, naturally graceful movements
and kneeling on one knee he picked up the fallen board and planchette.
"At all events I'll take these in charge for tonight. Feeling better now, Miss
Singleton?" he asked as he straightened and stepped back.

"Yes, quite all right," she answered flusteredly, disengaging my arm and
pulling away from me rather too quickly.

He nodded. Gertrude Grainger was staring at him coldly, as if about to
say something scathing, but she didn't. Sybil Jameson was looking at the
floor. She seemed embarrassed, yet puzzled too.

I followed the Governor out of the dressing room and told him, in case
Props hadn't, about Guthrie Boyd coming to the theater early. My
momentary doubt of Props's honesty seemed plain silly to me now,
although his taking that drink remained an astonishing riddle.

Props confirmed me about Guthrie coming in, though his manner was a
touch abstracted.

The Governor nodded his thanks for the news, then twitched a nostril
and frowned. I was sure he'd caught a whiff of alcohol and didn't know to
which of us two to attribute it—or perhaps even to one of the ladies, or to

an earlier passage of Guthrie this way.

He said to me, "Would you come into my dressing room for a bit, Bruce?"

I followed him, thinking he'd picked me for the drinker and wondering how to answer—best perhaps simply silently accept the fatherly lecture—but when he'd turned on the lights and I'd shut the door, his first question was, "You're attracted to Miss Singleton, aren't you, Bruce?"

When I nodded abruptly, swallowing my morsel of surprise, he went on softly but emphatically, "Then why don't you quit hovering and playing Galahad and really go after her? Ordinarily I must appear to frown on affairs in the company, but in this case it would be the best way I know of to break up those Ouija sessions, which are obviously harming the girl."

I managed to grin and tell him I'd be happy to obey his instructions—and do it entirely on my own initiative too.

He grinned back and started to toss the Ouija board on his couch, but instead put it and the planchette carefully down on the end of his long dressing table and put a second question to me.

"What do you think of some of this stuff they're getting over the board, Bruce?"

I said, "Well, that last one gave me a shiver, all right—I suppose because ..." and I told him about sensing the presence of Shakespeare's characters in the dark. I finished, "But of course the whole idea is nonsense," and I grinned.

He didn't grin back.

I continued impulsively, "There was one idea they had a few weeks back that impressed me, though it didn't seem to impress you. I hope you won't think I'm trying to butter you up, Mr. Usher. I mean the idea of you being a reincarnation of William Shakespeare."

He laughed delightedly and said, "Clearly you don't yet know the difference between a player and a playwright, Bruce. Shakespeare striding about romantically with head thrown back?—and twirling a sword and shaping his body and voice to every feeling handed him? Oh no! I'll grant he might have played the Ghost—it's a part within the scope of an average writer's talents, requiring nothing more than that he stand still and sound off sepulchrally."

He paused and smiled and went on. "No, there's only one person in this company who might be Shakespeare come again, and that's Billy Simpson. Yes, I mean Props. He's a great listener and he knows how to put himself in touch with everyone and then he's got that rat-trap mind for every hue and scent and sound of life, inside or out the mind. And he's very analytic. Oh, I know he's got no poetic talent, but surely Shakespeare wouldn't have that in *every* reincarnation. I'd think he'd need about a dozen lives in which to gather material for every one in which he gave it dramatic form. Don't you find something very poignant in the idea of a mute inglorious Shakespeare spending whole humble lifetimes collecting the necessary stuff for one great dramatic burst? Think about it some day."

I was doing that already and finding it a fascinating fantasy. It crystalized so perfectly the feeling I'd got seeing Billy Simpson behind his property table. And then Props did have a high-foreheaded poet-schoolmaster's face like that given Shakespeare in the posthumous engravings and woodcuts and portraits. Why, even their initials were the same. It made me feel strange.

Then the Governor put his third question to me.

"He's drinking tonight, isn't he? I mean Props, not Guthrie."

I didn't say anything, but my face must have answered for me—at least to such a student of expressions as the Governor—for he smiled and said, "You needn't worry. I wouldn't be angry with him. In fact, the only other time I know of that Props drank spirits by himself in the theater, I had a great deal to thank him for." His lean face grew thoughtful. "It was long before your time, in fact it was the first season I took out a company of my own. I had barely enough money to pay the printer for the three-sheets and get the first-night curtain up. After that it was touch and go for months. Then in mid-season we had a run of bad luck—a two-night heavy fog in one city, an influenza scare in another, Harvey Wilkins' Shakespearean troupe two weeks ahead of us in a third. And when in the next town we played it turned out the advance sale was very light—because my name was unknown there and the theater was an unpopular one—I realized I'd have to pay off the company while there was still money enough to get them home, if not the scenery.

"That night I caught Props swigging, but I hadn't the heart to chide him for it—in fact I don't think I'd have blamed anyone, except perhaps myself, for getting drunk that night. But then during the performance the actors and even the union stagehands we travel with began coming to my dressing room by ones and twos and telling me they'd be happy to work without salary for another three weeks, if I thought that might give us a chance of recouping. Well, of course I grabbed at their offers and we got a spell of brisk pleasant weather and we hit a couple of places starved for Shakespeare, and things worked out, even to paying all the back salary owed before the season was ended.

"Later on I discovered it was Props who had put them all up to doing it."

Gilbert Usher looked up at me and one of his eyes was wet and his lips were working just a little. "I couldn't have done it myself," he said, "for I wasn't a popular man with my company that first season—I'd been riding everyone much too hard and with nasty sarcasms—and I hadn't yet learned how to ask anyone for help when I really needed it. But Billy Simpson did what I couldn't, though he had to nerve himself for it with spirits. He's quick enough with his tongue in ordinary circumstances, as you know, particularly when he's being the friendly listener, but apparently when something very special is required of him, he must drink himself to the proper pitch. I'm wondering . . ."

His voice trailed off and then he straightened up before his mirror and started to unknot his tie and he said to me briskly, "Better get dressed now, Bruce. And then look in on Guthrie, will you?"

My mind was churning some rather strange thoughts as I hurried up the iron stairs to the dressing room I shared with Robert Dennis. I got on my Guildenstern make-up and costume, finishing just as Robert arrived; as Laertes, Robert makes a late entrance and so needn't hurry to the theater on *Hamlet* nights. Also, although we don't make a point of it, he and I spend as little time together in the dressing room as we can.

Before going down I looked into Guthrie Boyd's. He wasn't there, but the lights were on and the essentials of the Ghost's costume weren't in sight—impossible to miss that big helmet!—so I assumed he'd gone down ahead of me.

It was almost the half hour. The house lights were on, the curtain down, more stage lights on too, and quite a few of us about. I noticed that Props was back in the chair behind his table and not looking particularly different from any other night—perhaps the drink had been a once-only aberration and not some symptom of a crisis in the company.

I didn't make a point of hunting for Guthrie. When he gets costumed early he generally stands back in a dark corner somewhere, wanting to be alone—perchance to sip, aye, there's the rub!—or visits with Sybil in her dressing room.

I spotted Monica sitting on a trunk by the switchboard, where backstage was brightest lit at the moment. She looked ethereal yet springlike in her blonde Ophelia wig and first costume, a pale green one. Recalling my happy promise to the Governor, I bounced up beside her and asked her straight out about the Ouija business, pleased to have something to the point besides the plays to talk with her about—and really not worrying as much about her nerves as I suppose I should have.

She was in a very odd mood, both agitated and abstracted, her gaze going back and forth between distant and near and very distant. My questions didn't disturb her at all, in fact I got the feeling she welcomed them, yet she genuinely didn't seem able to tell me much about why she'd been so frightened at the last name the board had spelled. She told me that she actually did get into a sort of dream state when she worked the board and that she'd screamed before she'd quite comprehended what had shocked her so; then her mind had blacked out for a few seconds, she thought.

"One thing though, Bruce," she said. "I'm not going to work the board any more, at least when the three of us are alone like that."

"That sounds like a wise idea," I agreed, trying not to let the extreme heartiness of my agreement show through.

She stopped peering around as if for some figure to appear that wasn't in the play and didn't belong backstage, and she laid her hand on mine and said, "Thanks for coming so quickly when I went idiot and screamed."

I was about to improve this opportunity by telling her that the reason I'd come so quickly was that she was so much in my mind, but just then Joe Rubens came hurrying up with the Governor behind him in his Hamlet black to tell me that neither Guthrie Boyd nor his Ghost costume was to be found anywhere in the theater.

What's more, Joe had got the phone numbers of Guthrie's son and daughter from Sybil and rung them up. The one phone hadn't answered, while on the other a female voice—presumably a maid's—had informed him that everyone had gone to see Guthrie Boyd in *Hamlet*.

Joe was already wearing his cumbrous chain-mail armor for Marcellus—woven cord silvered—so I knew I was elected. I ran upstairs and in the space of time it took Robert Dennis to guess my mission and advise me to try the dingiest bars first and have a drink or two myself in them, I'd put on my hat, overcoat, and wristwatch and left him.

So garbed and as usual nervous about people looking at my ankles, I sallied forth to comb the nearby bars of Wolverton. I consoled myself with the thought that if I found Hamlet's father's ghost drinking his way through them, no one would ever spare a glance for my own costume.

Almost on the stroke of curtain I returned, no longer giving a damn what anyone thought about my ankles. I hadn't found Guthrie or spoken to a soul who'd seen a large male imbiber—most likely of Irish whisky—in great-cloak and antique armor, with perhaps some ghostly green light cascading down his face.

Beyond the curtain the overture was fading to its sinister close and the backstage lights were all down, but there was an angry hushed-voice dispute going on stage left, where the Ghost makes all his entrances and exits. Skipping across the dim stage in front of the blue-lit battlements of Elsinore—I still in my hat and overcoat—I found the Governor and Joe Rubens and with them John McCarthy all ready to go on as the Ghost in his Fortinbras armor with a dark cloak and some green gauze over it.

But alongside them was Francis Farley Scott in a very similar get-up—no armor, but a big enough cloak to hide his King costume and a rather more impressive helmet than John's.

They were all very dim in the midnight glow leaking back from the dimmed-down blue floods. The five of us were the only people I could see on this side of the stage.

F. F. was arguing vehemently that he must be allowed to double the Ghost with King Claudius because he knew the part better than John and because—this was the important thing—he could imitate Guthrie's voice perfectly enough to deceive his children and perhaps save their illusions about him. Sybil had looked through the curtain hole and seen them and all of their yesterday crowd, with new recruits besides, occupying all of the second, third, and fourth rows center, chattering with excitement and beaming with anticipation. Harry Grossman had confirmed this from the front of the house.

I could tell that the Governor was vastly irked at F. F. and at the same time touched by the last part of his argument. It was exactly the sort of sentimental heroic rationalization with which F. F. cloaked his insatiable yearnings for personal glory. Very likely he believed it himself.

John McCarthy was simply ready to do what the Governor asked him. He's an actor untroubled by inward urgencies—except things like keeping a record of the hours he sleeps and each penny he spends—though with a natural facility for portraying on stage emotions which he doesn't feel one iota.

The Governor shut up F. F. with a gesture and got ready to make his decision, but just then I saw that there was a sixth person on this side of the stage.

Standing in the second wings beyond our group was a dark figure like a tarpaulined Christmas tree topped by a big helmet of unmistakable general shape despite its veiling. I grabbed the Governor's arm and pointed at it silently. He smothered a large curse and strode up to it and rasped, "Guthrie, you old Son of a B! Can you go on?" The figure gave an affirmative grunt.

Joe Rubens grimaced at me as if to say "Show business!" and grabbed a spear from the prop table and hurried back across the stage for his entrance as Marcellus just before the curtain lifted and the first nervous, superbly atmospheric lines of the play rang out, loud at first, but then going low with unspoken apprehension.

"Who's there?"

"Nay, answer me; stand, and unfold yourself."

"Long live the king!"

"Bernardo?"

"He."

"You come most carefully upon your hour."

"'Tis now struck twelve; get thee to bed, Francisco."

"For this relief much thanks; 'tis bitter cold and I am sick at heart."

"Have you had quiet guard?"

"Not a mouse stirring."

With a resigned shrug, John McCarthy simply sat down. F. F. did the same, though *his* gesture was clench-fisted and exasperated. For a moment it seemed to me very comic that two Ghosts in *Hamlet* should be sitting in the wings, watching a third perform. I unbuttoned my overcoat and slung it over my left arm.

The Ghost's first two appearances are entirely silent ones. He merely goes on stage, shows himself to the soldiers, and comes off again. Nevertheless there was a determined little ripple of handclapping from the audience—the second, third, and fourth rows center greeting their patriarchal hero, it seemed likely. Guthrie didn't fall down at any rate and he walked reasonably straight—an achievement perhaps rating applause, if anyone out there knew the degree of intoxication Guthrie was probably burdened with at this moment—a cask-bellied Old Man of the Sea on his back.

The only thing out of normal was that he had forgot to turn on the little green light in the peak of his helmet—an omission which hardly mattered, certainly not on his first appearance. I hurried up to him when he came off and told him about it in a whisper as he moved off toward a dark backstage corner. I got in reply, through the inscrutable green veil, an exhalation of whisky and three affirmative grunts: one, that he knew it; two, that the light was working; three, that he'd remember to turn it on next time.

Then the scene had ended and I darted across the stage as they changed to the room-of-state set. I wanted to get rid of my overcoat. Joe Rubens grabbed me and told me about Guthrie's green light not being on and I told him that was all taken care of.

"Where the hell was he all the time we were hunting for him?" Joe asked me.

"I don't know," I answered.

By that time the second scene was playing, with F. F., his Ghost-coverings shed, playing the King as well as he always does (it's about his best part) and Gertrude Grainger looking very regal beside him as the Queen, her namesake, while there was another flurry of applause, more scattered this time, for the Governor in his black doublet and tights beginning about his seven hundredth performance of Shakespeare's longest and meatiest role.

Monica was still sitting on the trunk by the switchboard, looking paler than ever under her make-up, it seemed to me, and I folded my overcoat and silently persuaded her to use it as a cushion. I sat beside her and she took my hand and we watched the play from the wings.

After a while I whispered to her, giving her hand a little squeeze, "Feeling better now?"

She shook her head. Then leaning toward me, her mouth close to my ear, she whispered rapidly and unevenly, as if she just had to tell someone, "Bruce, I'm frightened. There's something in the theater. I don't think that was Guthrie playing the Ghost."

I whispered back, "Sure it was. I talked with him."

"Did you see his face?" she asked.

"No, but I smelled his breath," I told her and explained to her about him forgetting to turn on the green light. I continued, "Francis and John were both ready to go on as the Ghost, though, until Guthrie turned up. Maybe you glimpsed one of them before the play started and that gave you the idea that it was Guthrie."

Sybil Jameson in her Player costume looked around at me warningly. I was letting my whispering get too loud.

Monica put her mouth so close that her lips for an instant brushed my ear and she mouse-whispered, "I don't mean another *person* playing the Ghost—not that exactly. Bruce, there's *something* in the theater."

"You've got to forget that Ouija nonsense," I told her sharply. "And buck up now," I added, for the curtain had just gone down on Scene Two and it was time for her to get on stage for her scene with Laertes and Polonius.

I waited until she was launched into it, speaking her lines brightly enough, and then I carefully crossed the stage behind the backdrop. I was sure there was no more than nerves and imagination to her notions, though they'd raised shivers on me, but just the same I wanted to speak to Guthrie again and see his face.

When I'd completed my slow trip (you have to move rather slowly, so the drop won't ripple or bulge), I was dumbfounded to find myself witnessing the identical backstage scene that had been going on when I'd got back from my tour of the bars. Only now there was a lot more light because the scene being played on stage was a bright one. And Props was there behind his table, watching everything like the spectator he basically is. But beyond him were Francis Farley Scott and John McCarthy in their improvised Ghost costumes again, and the Governor and Joe with them, and all of them carrying on that furious lip-reader's argument, now doubly hushed.

I didn't have to wait to get close to them to know that Guthrie must have disappeared again. As I made my way toward them, watching their silent antics, my silly mind became almost hysterical with the thought that Guthrie had at last discovered that invisible hole every genuine alcoholic wishes he had, into which he could decorously disappear and drink during the times between his absolute necessary appearances in the real world.

As I neared them, Donald Fryer (our Horatio) came from behind me, having made the trip behind the backdrop faster than I had, to tell the

Governor in hushed gasps that Guthrie wasn't in any of the dressing rooms or anywhere else stage right.

Just at that moment the bright scene ended, the curtain came down, the drapes before which Ophelia and the others had been playing swung back to reveal again the battlements of Elsinore, and the lighting shifted back to the midnight blue of the first scene, so that for the moment it was hard to see at all. I heard the Governor say decisively, "*You* play the Ghost," his voice receding as he and Joe and Don hurried across the stage to be in place for their proper entrance. Seconds later there came the dull soft hiss of the main curtain opening and I heard the Governor's taut resonant voice saying, "The air bites shrewdly; it is very cold," and Don responding as Horatio with, "It is a nipping and an eager air."

By that time I could see again well enough—see Francis Farley Scott and John McCarthy moving side by side toward the back wing through which the Ghost enters. They were still arguing in whispers. The explanation was clear enough: each thought the Governor had pointed at him in the sudden darkness—or possibly in F. F.'s case was pretending he so thought. For a moment the comic side of my mind, grown a bit hysterical by now, almost collapsed me with the thought of twin Ghosts entering the stage side by side. Then once again, history still repeating itself, I saw beyond them that other bulkier figure with the unmistakable shrouded helmet. They must have seen it too for they stopped dead just before my hands touched a shoulder of each of them. I circled quickly past them and reached out my hands to put them lightly on the third figure's shoulders, intending to whisper, "Guthrie, are you okay?" It was a very stupid thing for one actor to do to another—startling him just before his entrance—but I was made thoughtless by the memory of Monica's fears and by the rather frantic riddle of where Guthrie could possibly have been hiding.

But just then Horatio gasped, "Look, my lord, it comes," and Guthrie moved out of my light grasp onto the stage without so much as turning his head—and leaving me shaking because where I'd touched the rough buckram-braced fabric of the Ghost's cloak I'd felt only a kind of insubstantiality beneath instead of Guthrie's broad shoulders.

I quickly told myself that was because Guthrie's cloak had stood out from his shoulders and his back as he had moved. I had to tell myself something like that. I turned around. John McCarthy and F. F. were standing in front of the dark prop table and by now my nerves were in such a state that their paired forms gave me another start. But I tiptoed after them into the downstage wings and watched the scene from there.

The Governor was still on his knees with his sword held hilt up like a cross doing the long speech that begins, "Angels and ministers of grace defend us!" And of course the Ghost had his cloak drawn around him so you couldn't see what was under it—and the little green light still wasn't lit in his helmet. Tonight the absence of that theatric touch made him a more frightening figure—certainly to me, who wanted so much to see Guthrie's ravaged old face and be reassured by it. Though there was still enough comedy left in the ragged edges of my thoughts that I could imagine Guthrie's pugnacious son-in-law whispering angrily to those around him that Gilbert Usher was so jealous of his great father-in-law that he wouldn't let him show his face on the stage.

Then came the transition to the following scene where the Ghost has led Hamlet off alone with him—just a five-second complete darkening of the stage while a scrim is dropped—and at last the Ghost spoke those first lines of "Mark me" and "My hour is almost come, When I to sulphurous and tormenting flames Must render up myself."

If any of us had any worries about the Ghost blowing up on his lines or slurring them drunkenly, they were taken care of now. Those lines were delivered with the greatest authority and effect. And I was almost certain that it was Guthrie's rightful voice—at least I was at first—but doing an even better job than the good one he had always done of getting the effect of distance and otherworldliness and hopeless alienation from all life on Earth. The theater became as silent as death, yet at the same time I could imagine the soft pounding of a thousand hearts, thousands of shivers crawling—and I *knew* that Francis Farley Scott, whose shoulder was pressed against mine, was trembling.

Each word the Ghost spoke was like a ghost itself, mounting the air and hanging poised for an impossible extra instant before it faded towards eternity.

Those great lines came: "I am thy father's spirit; Doomed for a certain term to walk the night..." and just at that moment the idea came to me that Guthrie Boyd might be dead, that he might have died and be lying unnoticed somewhere between his children's home and the theater—no matter what Props had said or the rest of us had seen—and that his ghost might have come to give a last performance. And on the heels of that shivery impossibility came the thought that similar and perhaps even eerier ideas must be frightening Monica. I knew I had to go to her.

So while the Ghost's words swooped and soared in the dark— marvellous black-plumed birds—I again made that nervous cross behind the backdrop.

Everyone stage right was standing as frozen and absorbed—motionless loomings—as I'd left John and F. F. I spotted Monica at once. She'd moved forward from the switchboard and was standing, crouched a little, by the big floodlight that throws some dimmed blue on the backdrop and across the back of the stage. I went to her just as the Ghost was beginning his exit stage left, moving backward along the edge of the light from the flood, but not quite in it, and reciting more lonelily and eerily than I'd ever heard them before those memorable last lines:

> *"Fare thee well at once!*
> *"The glow-worm shows the matin to be near,*
> *"And 'gins to pale his uneffectual fire;*
> *"Adieu, adieu! Hamlet, remember me."*

One second passed, then another, and then there came two unexpected bursts of sound at the same identical instant: Monica screamed and a thunderous applause started out front, touched off by Guthrie's people, of course, but this time swiftly spreading to all the rest of the audience.

I imagine it was the biggest hand the Ghost ever got in the history of the theater. In fact, I never heard of him getting a hand before. It certainly was a most inappropriate place to clap, however much the performance deserved it. It broke the atmosphere and the thread of the scene.

Also, it drowned out Monica's scream, so that only I and a few of those behind me heard it.

At first I thought I'd made her scream, by touching her as I had Guthrie, suddenly, like an idiot, from behind. But instead of dodging away she turned and clung to me, and kept clinging too even after I'd drawn her back and Gertrude Grainger and Sybil Jameson had closed in to comfort her and hush her gasping sobs and try to draw her away from me.

By this time the applause was through and Governor and Don and Joe were taking up the broken scene and knitting together its finish as best they could, while the floods came up little by little, changing to rosy, to indicate dawn breaking over Elsinore.

Then Monica mastered herself and told us in quick whispers what had made her scream. The Ghost, she said, had moved for a moment into the edge of the blue floodlight, and she had seen for a moment through his veil, and what she had seen had been a face like Shakespeare's. Just that and no more. Except that at the moment when she told us—later she became less certain—she was sure it was Shakespeare himself and no one else.

I discovered that when you hear something like that you don't exclaim or get outwardly excited. Or even inwardly, exactly. It rather shuts you up. I know I felt at the same time extreme awe and a renewed irritation at the Ouija board. I was deeply moved, yet at the same time pettishly irked, as if some vast adult creature had disordered the toy world of my universe.

It seemed to hit Sybil and even Gertrude the same way. For the moment we were shy about the whole thing, and so, in her way, was Monica, and so were the few others who had overheard in part or all what Monica had said.

I knew we were going to cross the stage in a few more seconds when the curtain came down on that scene, ending the first act, and stagelights came up. At least I knew that I was going across. Yet I wasn't looking forward to it.

When the curtain did come down—with another round of applause from out front—and we started across, Monica beside me with my arm still tight around her, there came a choked-off male cry of horror from ahead to shock and hurry us. I think about a dozen of us got stage left about the same time, including of course the Governor and the others who had been on stage.

F. F. and Props were standing inside the doorway to the empty prop room and looking down into the hidden part of the L. Even from the side, they both looked pretty sick. Then F. F. knelt down and almost went out of view, while Props hunched over him with his natural stoop.

As we craned around Props for a look—myself among the first, just beside the Governor, we saw something that told us right away that this Ghost wasn't ever going to be able to answer that curtain call they were still fitfully clapping for out front, although the house lights must be up by now for the first intermission.

Guthrie Boyd was lying on his back in this street clothes. His face looked gray, the eyes staring straight up. While swirled beside him lay the Ghost's cloak and veil and the helmet and an empty fifth of whisky.

Between the two conflicting shocks of Monica's revelation and the body in the prop room, my mind was in a useless state. And from her helpless incredulous expression I knew Monica felt the same. I tried to put things together and they wouldn't fit anywhere.

F. F. looked up at us over his shoulder. "He's not breathing," he said. "I think he's gone." Just the same he started loosing Boyd's tie and shirt and pillowing his head on the cloak. He handed the whisky bottle back to us through several hands and Joe Rubens got rid of it.

The Governor sent out front for a doctor and within two minutes Harry Grossman was bringing us one from the audience who'd left his seat number and bag at the box office. He was a small man—Guthrie would have made two of him—and a bit awestruck, I could see, though holding himself with greater professional dignity because of that, as we made way for him and then crowded in behind.

He confirmed F. F.'s diagnosis by standing up quickly after kneeling only for a few seconds where F. F. had. Then he said hurriedly to the Governor, as if the words were being surprised out of him against his professional caution, "Mr. Usher, if I hadn't heard this man giving that great performance just now, I'd think he'd been dead for an hour or more."

He spoke low and not all of us heard him, but I did and so did Monica, and there was Shock Three to go along with the other two, raising in my mind for an instant the grisly pricture of Guthrie Boyd's spirit, or some other entity, willing his dead body to go through with the last performance. Once again I unsuccessfully tried to fumble together the parts of this night's mystery.

The little doctor looked around at us slowly and puzzledly. He said, "I take it he just wore the cloak over his street clothes?" He paused. Then, "He *did* play the Ghost?" he asked us.

The Governor and several others nodded, but some of us didn't at once and I think F. F. gave him a rather peculiar look, for the doctor cleared his throat and said, "I'll have to examine this man as quickly as possible in a better place and light. Is there—?" The Governor suggested the couch in his dressing room and the doctor designated Joe Rubens and John McCarthy and Francis Farley Scott to carry the body. He passed over the Governor, perhaps out of awe, but Hamlet helped just the same, his black garb most fitting.

It was odd the doctor picked the older men—I think he did it for dignity. And it was odder still that he should have picked two ghosts to help carry a third, though he couldn't have known that.

As the designated ones moved forward, the doctor said, "Please stand back, the rest of you."

It was then that the very little thing happened which made all the pieces of this night's mystery fall into place—for me, that is, and for Monica too, judging from the way her hand trembled in and then tightened around mine. We'd been given the key to what had happened. I won't tell you what it was until I've knit together the ends of this story.

The second act was delayed perhaps a minute, but after that we kept to schedule, giving a better performance than usual—I never knew the Graveyard Scene to carry so much feeling or the bit with Yorick's skull to be so poignant.

Just before I made my own first entrance, Joe Rubens snatched off my street hat—I'd had it on all this while—and I played all of Guildenstern wearing a wristwatch, though I don't imagine anyone noticed.

F. F. played the Ghost as an off-stage voice when he makes his final brief appearance in the Closet Scene. He used Guthrie's voice to do it, imitating him very well. It struck me afterwards as ghoulish—but right.

Well before the play ended, the doctor had decided he could say that Guthrie had died of a heart seizure, not mentioning the alcoholism. The minute the curtain came down on the last act, Harry Grossman informed Guthrie's son and daughter and brought them backstage. They were much moved, though hardly deeply smitten, seeing they'd been out of touch with the old boy for a decade. However, they quickly saw it was a Grand and Solemn Occasion and behaved accordingly, especially Guthrie's pugnacious son-in-law.

Next morning the two Wolverton papers had headlines about it and Guthrie got his biggest notices ever in the Ghost. The strangeness of the event carried the item around the world—a six-line filler, capturing the mind for a second or two, about how a once-famous actor had died immediately after giving a performance as the Ghost in *Hamlet*, though in some versions, of course, it became Hamlet's Ghost.

The funeral came on the afternoon of the third day, just before our last performance in Wolverton, and the whole company attended along with Guthrie's children's crowd and many other Wolvertonians. Old Sybil broke down and sobbed.

Yet to be a bit callous, it was a neat thing that Guthrie died where he did, for it saved us the trouble of having to send for relatives and probably take care of the funeral ourselves. And it did give old Guthrie a grand finish, with everyone outside the company thinking him a hero-martyr to the motto The Show Must Go On. And of course we knew too that in a deeper sense he'd really been that.

We shifted around in our parts and doubled some to fill the little gaps Guthrie had left in the plays, so that the Governor didn't have to hire another actor at once. For me, and I think for Monica, the rest of the season was very sweet. Gertrude and Sybil carried on with the Ouija sessions alone.

And now I must tell you about the very little thing which gave myself and Monica a satisfying solution to the mystery of what had happened that night.

You'll have realized that it involved Props. Afterwards I asked him straight out about it and he shyly told me that he really couldn't help me there. He'd had this unaccountable devilish compulsion to get drunk and his mind had blanked out entirely from well before the performance until he found himself standing with F. F. over Guthrie's body at the end of the first act. He didn't remember the Ouija-scare or a word of what he'd said to me about theaters and time machines—or so he always insisted.

F. F. told us that after the Ghost's last exit he'd seen him—very vaguely in the dimness—lurch across backstage into the empty prop room and that he and Props had found Guthrie lying there at the end of the scene. I think the queer look F. F.—the old reality-fuddling rogue!—gave the doctor was to hint to him that *he* had played the Ghost, though that wasn't something I could ask him about.

But the very little thing— When they were picking up Guthrie's body and the doctor told the rest of us to stand back, Props turned as he obeyed and straightened his shoulders and looked directly at Monica and myself, or rather a little over our heads. He appeared compassionate yet smilingly serene as always and for a moment transfigured, as if he were the eternal observer of the stage of life and this little tragedy were only part of an infinitely vaster, endlessly interesting pattern.

I realized at that instant that Props could have done it, that he'd very effectively guarded the doorway to the empty prop room during our searches, that the Ghost's costume could be put on or off in seconds (though Prop's shoulders wouldn't fill the cloak like Guthrie's), and that I'd never once before or during the play seen him and the Ghost at the same time. Yes, Guthrie had arrived a few minutes before me ... and died ... and Props, nerved to it by drink, had covered for him.

While Monica, as she told me later, knew at once that here was the great-browed face she'd glimpsed for a moment through the greenish gauze.

Clearly there had been four ghosts in *Hamlet* that night—John McCarthy, Francis Farley Scott, Guthrie Boyd, and the fourth who had really played the role. Mentally blacked out or not, knowing the lines from the many times he'd listened to *Hamlet* performed in this life, or from buried memories of times he'd taken the role in the days of Queen Elizabeth the First, Billy (or Willy) Simpson, or simply Willy S., had played the Ghost, a good trouper responding automatically to an emergency.

Divine Madness

Roger Zelazny

"...I is this *?hearers wounded-wonder like stand them makes and stars wandering the conjures sorrow of phrase Whose ...*"

He blew smoke through the cigarette and it grew longer.

He glanced at the clock and realized that its hands were moving backwards.

The clock told him that it was 10:33, going on 10:32 in the P.M.

Then came the thing like despair, for he knew there was not a thing he could do about it. He was trapped, moving in reverse through the sequence of actions past. Somehow, he had missed the warning.

Usually, there was a prism-effect, a flash of pink static, a drowsiness, then a moment of heightened perception ...

He turned the pages, from left to right, his eyes retracing their path back along the lines.

"*?emphasis an such bears grief whose he is What*"

Helpless, there behind his eyes, he watched his body perform.

The cigarette had reached its full length. He clicked on the lighter, which sucked away its glowing point, and then he shook the cigarette back into the pack.

He yawned in reverse: first an exhalation, then an inhalation.

It wasn't real—the doctor had told him. It was grief and epilepsy, meeting to form an unusual syndrome.

He'd already had the seizure. The Dilantin wasn't helping. This was a post-traumatic locomotor hallucination, elicited by anxiety, precipitated by the attack.

But he did not believe it, could not believe it—not after twenty minutes had gone by, in the other direction—not after he had placed the book upon the reading stand, stood, walked backward across the room to his closet, hung up his robe, redressed himself in the same shirt and slacks he had worn all day, backed over to the bar and regurgitated a Martini, sip by cooling sip, until the glass was filled to the brim and not a drop spilled.

There was an impending taste of olive, and then everything was changed again.

The second-hand was sweeping around his wristwatch in the proper direction.

The time was 10:07.

He felt free to move as he wished.

He redrank his Martini.

Now, if he would be true to the pattern, he would change into his robe and try to read. Instead, he mixed another drink.

Now the sequence would not occur.

Now the things would not happen as he thought they had happened, and un-happened.

Now everything was different.

All of which went to prove it had been an hallucination.

Even the notion that it had taken twenty-six minutes each way was an attempted rationalization.

Nothing had happened.

...Shouldn't be drinking, he decided. It might bring on a seizure.

He laughed.

Crazy, though, the whole thing...

Remembering, he drank.

In the morning he skipped breakfast, as usual, noted that it would soon stop being morning, took two aspirins, a lukewarm shower, a cup of coffee, and a walk.

The park, the fountain, the children with their boats, the grass, the pond, he hated them; and the morning, and the sunlight, and the blue moats around the towering clouds.

Hating, he sat there. And remembering.

If he was on the verge of a crackup, he decided, then the thing he wanted most was to plunge ahead into it, not to totter halfway out, halfway in.

He remembered why.

But it was clear, so clear, the morning, and everything crisp and distinct and burning with the green fires of spring, there in the sign of the Ram, April.

He watched the winds pile up the remains of winter against the far gray fence, and he saw them push the boats across the pond, to come to rest in shallow mud the children tracked.

The fountain jetted its cold umbrella above the green-tinged copper dolphins. The sun ignited it whenever he moved his head. The wind rumpled it.

Clustered on the concrete, birds pecked at part of a candy bar stuck to a red wrapper.

Kites swayed on their tails, nosed downward, rose again, as youngsters tugged at invisible strings. Telephone lines were tangled with wooden frames and torn paper, like broken G clefs and smeared glissandos.

He hated the telephone lines, the kites, the children, the birds.

Most of all, though, he hated himself.

How does a man undo that which has been done? He doesn't. There is no way under the sun. He may suffer, remember, repent, curse, or forget. Nothing else. The past, in this sense, is inevitable.

A woman walked past. He did not look up in time to see her face, but the dusky blonde fall of her hair to her collar and the swell of her sure, sheer-netted legs below the black hem of her coat and above the matching click of her heels heigh-ho, stopped his breath behind his stomach and snared his eyes in the wizard-weft of her walking and her posture and some more, like a rhyme to the last of his thoughts.

He half-rose from the bench when the pink static struck his eyeballs, and the fountain became a volcano spouting rainbows.

The world was frozen and served up to him under glass.

... The woman passed back before him and he looked down too soon to see her face.

The hell was beginning once more, he realized, as the backward-flying birds passed before.

He gave himself to it. Let it keep him until he broke, until he was all used up and there was nothing left.

He waited, there on the bench, watching the slithey toves be brillig, as the fountain sucked its waters back within itself, drawing them up in a great arc above the unmoving dolphins, and the boats raced backward across the pond, and the fence divested itself of stray scraps of paper, as the birds replaced the candy bar within the red wrapper, bit by crunchy bit.

His thoughts only were inviolate, his body belonged to the retreating tide.

Eventually, he rose and strolled backwards out of the park.

On the street a boy backed past him, unwhistling snatches of a popular song.

He backed up the stairs to his apartment, his hangover growing worse again, undrank his coffee, unshowered, unswallowed his aspirins, and got into bed, feeling awful.

Let this be it, he decided.

A faintly remembered nightmare ran in reverse through his mind, giving it an undeserved happy ending.

It was dark when he awakened.

He was very drunk.

He backed over to the bar and began spitting out his drinks, one by one into the same glass he had used the night before, and pouring them from the glass back into the bottles again. Separating the gin and vermouth was no trick at all. The proper liquids leapt into the air as he held the uncorked bottles above the bar.

And he grew less and less drunk as this went on.

Then he stood before an early Martini and it was 10:07 in thé P.M. There, within the hallucination, he wondered about another hallucination. Would time loop-the-loop, forward and then backward again, through his previous seizure?

No.

It was as though it had not happened, had never been.

He continued on back through the evening, undoing things.

He raised the telephone, said "good-bye," untold Murray that he would not be coming to work again tomorrow, listened a moment, recradled the phone and looked at it as it rang.

The sun came up in the west and people were backing their cars to work.

He read the weather report and the headlines, folded the evening paper and placed it out in the hall.

It was the longest seizure he had ever had, but he did not really care. He settled himself down within it and watched as the day unwound itself back to morning.

His hangover returned as the day grew smaller, and it was terrible when he got into bed again.

When he awakened the previous evening the drunkenness was high upon him. Two of the bottles he refilled, recorked, resealed. He knew he would take them to the liquor store soon and get his money back.

As he sat there that day, his mouth uncursing and undrinking and his eyes unreading, he knew that new cars were being shipped back to Detroit and disassembled, that corpses were awakening into their death-throes, and that priests the world over were saying black mass, unknowing.

He wanted to chuckle but he could not tell his mouth to do it.

He unsmoked two and a half packs of cigarettes.

Then came another hangover and he went to bed. Later, the sun set in the east.

Time's winged chariot fled before him as he opened the door and said "good-bye" to his comforters and they came in and sat down and told him not to grieve overmuch.

And he wept without tears as he realized what was to come.

Despite his madness, he hurt.

... Hurt, as the days rolled backward.

... Backward, inexorably.

... Inexorably, until he knew the time was near at hand.

He gnashed the teeth of his mind.

Great was his grief and his hate and his love.

He was wearing his black suit and undrinking drink after drink, while somewhere the men were scraping the clay back onto the shovels which would be used to undig the grave.

He backed his car to the funeral parlor, parked it, and climbed into the limousine.

They backed all the way to the graveyard.

He stood among his friends and listened to the preacher.

"dust to dust; ashes to Ashes," the man said, which is pretty much the same whichever way you say it.

The casket was taken back to the hearse and returned to the funeral parlor.

He sat through the service and went home and unshaved and unbrushed his teeth and went to bed.

He awakened and dressed again in black and returned to the parlor.

The flowers were all back in place.

Solemn-faced friends unsigned the Sympathy Book and unshook his hand. Then they went inside to sit awhile and stare at the closed casket. Then they left, until he was alone with the funeral director.

Then he was alone with himself.

The tears ran up his cheeks.

His suit and shirt were crisp and unwrinkled again.

He backed home, undressed, uncombed his hair. The day collapsed around him into morning, and he returned to bed to unsleep another night.

The previous evening, when he awakened, he realized where he was headed.

Twice, he exerted all of his will power in an attempt to interrupt the sequence of events. He failed.

He wanted to die. If he had killed himself that day, he would not be headed back toward it now.

There were tears within his mind as he realized the past which lay less than twenty-four hours before him.

The past stalked him that day as he unnegotiated the purchase of the casket, the vault, the accessories.

Then he headed home into the biggest hangover of all and slept until he was awakened to undrink drink after drink and then return to the morgue and come back in time to hang up the telephone on that call, that call which had come to break . . .

. . . The silence of his anger with its ringing.

She was dead.

She was lying somewhere in the fragments of her car on Interstate 90 now.

As he paced, unsmoking, he knew she was lying there bleeding.

. . . Then dying, after that crash at 80 miles an hour.

. . . Then alive?

Then re-formed, along with the car, and alive again, arisen? Even now backing home at a terrible speed, to re-slam the door on their final argument? To unscream at him and to be unscreamed at?

He cried out within his mind. He wrung the hands of his spirit.

It couldn't stop at this point. No. Not now.

All his grief and his love and his self-hate had brought him back this far, this near to the moment . . .

It *couldn't* end now.

After a time, he moved to the living room, his legs pacing, his lips cursing, himself waiting.

The door slammed open.

She stared in at him, her mascara smeared, tears upon her cheeks.

"!hell to go Then," he said.

"!going I'm," she said.

She stepped back inside, closed the door.

She hung her coat hurriedly in the hall closet.

".it about feel you way the that's If," he said, shrugging.

"!yourself but anybody about care don't You," she said.

"!child a like behaving You're," he said.

"!sorry you're say least at could You"

Her eyes flashed like emeralds through the pink static, and she was lovely and alive again. In his mind he was dancing.

The change came.

"You could at least say you're sorry!"

"I am," he said, taking her hand in a grip that she could not break. "How much, you'll never know."

"Come here," and she did.

Narrow Valley

R. A. Lafferty

In the year 1893, land allotments in severalty were made to the remaining eight hundred and twenty-one Pawnee Indians. Each would receive one hundred and sixty acres of land and no more, and thereafter the Pawnees would be expected to pay taxes on their land, the same as the White-Eyes did.

"Kitkehahke!" Clarence Big-Saddle cussed. "You can't kick a dog around proper on a hundred and sixty acres. And I sure am not hear before about this pay taxes on land."

Clarence Big-Saddle selected a nice green vally for his allotment. It was one of the half dozen plots he had always regarded as his own. He sodded around the summer lodge that he had there and made it an all-season home. But he sure didn't intend to pay taxes on it.

So he burned leaves and bark and made a speech:

"That my valley be always wide and flourish and green and such stuff as that!" he orated in Pawnee chant style. "But that it be narrow if an intruder come."

425

He didn't have any balsam bark to burn. He threw on a little cedar bark instead. He didn't have any elder leaves. He used a handful of jack-oak leaves. And he forgot the word. How you going to work it if you forget the word?

"Petahauerat!" he howled out with the confidence he hoped would fool the fates.

"That's the same long of a word," he said in a low aside to himself. But he was doubtful. "What am I, a White Man, a burr-tailed jack, a new kind of nut to think it will work?" he asked. "I have to laugh at me. Oh well, we see."

He threw the rest of the bark and the leaves on the fire, and he hollered the wrong word out again.

And he was answered by a dazzling sheet of summer lightning.

"Skidi!" Clarence Big-Saddle swore. "It worked. I didn't think it would."

Clarence Big-Saddle lived on his land for many years, and he paid no taxes. Intruders were unable to come down to his place. The land was sold for taxes three times, but nobody ever came down to claim it. Finally, it was carried as open land on the books. Homesteaders filed on it several times, but none of them fulfilled the qualification of living on the land.

Half a century went by. Clarence Big-Saddle called his son.

"I've had it, boy," he said. "I think I'll just go in the house and die."

"Okay, Dad," the son Clarence Little-Saddle said. "I'm going in to town to shoot a few games of pool with the boys. I'll bury you when I get back this evening."

So the son Clarence Little-Saddle inherited. He also lived on the land for many years without paying taxes.

There was a disturbance in the courthouse one day. The place seemed to be invaded in force, but actually there were but one man, one woman, and five children. "I'm Robert Rampart," said the man, "and we want the Land Office."

"I'm Robert Rampart Junior," said a nine-year-old gangler, "and we want it pretty blamed quick."

"I don't think we have anything like that," the girl at the desk said. "Isn't that something they had a long time ago?"

"Ignorance is no excuse for inefficiency, my dear," said Mary Mabel Rampart, an eight-year-old who could easily pass for eight and a half. "After I make my report, I wonder who will be sitting at your desk tomorrow."

"You people are either in the wrong state or the wrong century," the girl said.

"The Homestead Act still obtains," Robert Rampart insisted. "There is one tract of land carried as open in this county. I want to file on it."

Cecilia Rampart answered the knowing wink of a beefy man at the distant desk. "Hi," she breathed as she slinked over. "I'm Cecilia Rampart, but my stage name is Cecilia San Juan. Do you think that seven is too young to play ingenue roles?"

"Not for you," the man said. "Tell your folks to come over here."

"Do you know where the Land Office is?" Cecilia asked.

"Sure. It's the fourth left-hand drawer of my desk. The smallest office we got in the whole courthouse. We don't use it much any more."

The Ramparts gathered around. The beefy man started to make out the papers.

"This is the land description," Robert Rampart began. "Why, you've got it down already. How did you know?"

"I've been around here a long time," the man answered.

They did the paper work, and Robert Rampart filed on the land.

"You won't be able to come onto the land itself, though," the man said.

"Why won't I?" Rampart demanded. "Isn't the land description accurate?"

"Oh, I suppose so. But nobody's ever been able to get to the land. It's become a sort of joke."

"Well, I intend to get to the bottom of that joke," Rampart insisted. "I will occupy the land, or I will find out why not."

"I'm not sure about that," the beefy man said. "The last man to file on the land, about a dozen years ago, wasn't able to occupy the land. And he wasn't able to say why he couldn't. It's kind of interesting, the look on their faces after they try it for a day or two, and then give it up."

The Ramparts left the courthouse, loaded into their camper, and drove out to find their land. They stopped at the house of a cattle and wheat farmer named Charley Dublin. Dublin met them with a grin which indicated he'd been tipped off.

"Come along if you want to, folks," Dublin said. "The easiest way is on foot across my short pasture here. Your land's directly west of mine."

They walked the short distance to the border.

"My name is Tom Rampart, Mr. Dublin." Six-year-old Tom made conversation as they walked. "But my name is really Ramires, and not Tom. I am the issue of an indiscretion of my mother in Mexico several years ago."

"The boy is a kidder, Mr. Dublin," said the mother, Nina Rampart, defending herself. "I have never been in Mexico, but sometimes I have the urge to disappear there forever."

"Ay yes, Mrs. Rampart. And what is the name of the youngest boy here?" Charley Dublin asked.

"Fatty," said Fatty Rampart.

"But surely that is not your given name?"

"Audifax," said five-year-old Fatty.

"Ah well, Audifax, Fatty, are you a kidder too?"

"He's getting better at it, Mr. Dublin," Mary Mabel said. "He was a twin till last week. His twin was named Skinny. Mama left Skinny unguarded while she was out tippling, and there were wild dogs in the neighborhood. When Mama got back, do you know what was left of Skinny? Two neck bones and an ankle bone. That was all."

"Poor Skinny," Dublin said. "Well, Rampart, this is the fence and the end of my land. Yours is just beyond."

"Is that ditch on my land?" Rampart asked.

"That ditch *is* your land."

"I'll have it filled in. It's a dangerous deep cut even if it is narrow. And the other fence looks like a good one, and I sure have a pretty plot of land beyond it."

"No, Rampart, the land beyond the second fence belongs to Holister Hyde," Charley Dublin said. "That second fence is the *end* of your land."

"Now, just wait a minute, Dublin! There's something wrong here. My land is one hundred and sixty acres, which would be a half mile on a side. Where's my half-mile width?"

"Between the two fences."

"That's not eight feet."

"Doesn't look like it, does it, Rampart? Tell you what—there's plenty of throwing-sized rocks around. Try to throw one across it."

"I'm not interested in any such boys' games," Rampart exploded. "I want my land."

But the Rampart children *were* interested in such games. They got with it with those throwing rocks. They winged them out over the little gully. The stones acted funny. They hung in the air, as it were, and diminished in size. And they were small as pebbles when they dropped down, down into the gully. None of them could throw a stone across that ditch, and they were throwing kids.

"You and your neighbor have conspired to fence open land for your own use," Rampart charged.

"No such thing, Rampart," Dublin said cheerfully. "My land checks perfectly. So does Hyde's. So does yours, if we knew how to check it. It's like one of those trick topological drawings. It really is half a mile from here to there, but the eye gets lost somewhere. It's your land. Crawl through the fence and figure it out."

Rampart crawled through the fence, and drew himself up to jump the gully. Then he hesitated. He got a glimpse of just how deep that gully was. Still, it wasn't five feet across.

There was a heavy fence post on the ground, designed for use as a corner post. Rampart up-ended it with some effort. Then he shoved it to fall and bridge the gully. But it fell short, and it shouldn't have. An eight-foot post should bridge a five-foot gully.

The post fell into the gully, and rolled and rolled and rolled. It spun as though it were rolling outward, but it made no progress except vertically. The post came to rest on a ledge of the gully, so close that Rampart could almost reach out and touch it, but it now appeared no bigger than a match stick.

"There is something wrong with that fence post, or with the world, or with my eyes," Robert Rampart said. "I wish I felt dizzy so I could blame it on that."

"There's a little game that I sometimes play with my neighbor Hyde when we're both out," Dublin said. "I've a heavy rifle and I train it on the middle of his forehead as he stands on the other side of the ditch apparently eight feet away. I fire it off then (I'm a good shot), and I hear it whine across. It'd kill him dead if things were as they seem. But Hyde's in no danger. The shot always bangs into that little scuff of rocks and boulders about thirty feet below him. I can see it kick up the rock dust there, and the sound of it rattling into those little boulders comes back to me in about two and a half seconds."

A bull-bat (poor people call it the night-hawk) raveled around in the air and zoomed out over the narrow ditch, but it did not reach the other side. The bird dropped below ground level and could be seen against the background of the other side of the ditch. It grew smaller and hazier as though at a distance of three or four hundred yards. The white bars on its wings could no longer be discerned; then the bird itself could hardly be discerned; but it was far short of the other side of the five-foot ditch.

A man identified by Charley Dublin as the neighbor Hollister Hyde had appeared on the other side of the little ditch. Hyde grinned and waved. He shouted something, but could not be heard.

"Hyde and I both read mouths," Dublin said, "so we can talk across the ditch easy enough. Which kid wants to play chicken? Hyde will barrel a good-sized rock right at your head, and if you duck or flinch you're chicken."

"Me! Me!" Audifax Rampart challenged. And Hyde, a big man with big hands, did barrel a fearsome jagged rock right at the head of the boy. It would have killed him if things had been as they appeared. But the rock diminished to nothing and disappeared into the ditch. Here was a phenomenon: things seemed real-sized on either side of the ditch, but they diminished coming out over the ditch either way.

"Everybody game for it?" Robert Rampart Junior asked.

"We won't get down there by standing here," Mary Mabel said.

"Nothing wenchered, nothing gained," said Cecilia. "I got that from an ad for a sex comedy."

Then the five Rampart kids ran down into the gully. Ran *down* is right. It was almost as if they ran down the vertical face of a cliff. They couldn't do that. The gully was no wider than the stride of the biggest kids. But the gully diminished those children, it ate them alive. They were doll-sized. They were acorn-sized. They were running for minute after minute across a ditch that was only five feet across. They were going, deeper in it, and getting smaller. Robert Rampart was roaring his alarm, and his wife Nina was screaming. Then she stopped. "What am I carrying on so loud about?" she asked herself. "It looks like fun. I'll do it too."

She plunged into the gully, diminished in size as the children had done, and ran at a pace to carry her a hundred yards away across a gully only five feet wide.

That Robert Rampart stirred things up for a while then. He got the sheriff there, and the highway patrolmen. A ditch had stolen his wife and five children, he said, and maybe killed them. And if anybody laughs, there may be another killing. He got the colonel of the State National Guard there, and a command post set up. He got a couple of airplane pilots. Robert Rampart had one quality: when he hollered, people came.

He got the newsmen out from T-Town, and the eminent scientists, Dr. Velikof Vonk, Arpad Arkabaranan, and Willy McGilly. That bunch turns up every time you get on a good one. They just happen to be in that part of the country where something interesting is going on.

They attacked the thing from all four sides and the top, and by inner and outer theory. If a thing measures half a mile on each side, and the sides are straight, there just has to be something in the middle of it. They took pictures from the air, and they turned out perfect. They proved that Robert Rampart had the prettiest hundred and sixty acres in the country, the larger part of it being a lush green valley, and all of it being half a mile on a side, and situated just where it should be. They took ground-level photos then, and it showed a beautiful half-mile stretch of land between the boundaries of Charley Dublin and Hollister Hyde. But a man isn't a camera. None of them could see that beautiful spread with the eyes in their heads. Where was it?

Down in the valley itself everything was normal. It really was half a mile wide and no more than eighty feet deep with a very gentle slope. It was warm and sweet, and beautiful with grass and grain.

Nina and the kids loved it, and they rushed to see what squatter had built that little house on their land. A house, or a shack. It had never known paint, but paint would have spoiled it. It was built of split timbers dressed near smooth with ax and draw knife, chinked with white clay, and sodded up to about half its height. And there was an interloper standing by the little lodge.

"Here, here what are you doing on our land?" Robert Rampart Junior demanded of the man. "Now you just shamble off again wherever you came from. I'll bet you're a thief too, and those cattle are stolen."

"Only the black-and-white calf," Clarence Little-Saddle said. "I couldn't resist him, but the rest are mine. I guess I'll just stay around and see that you folks get settled all right."

"Is there any wild Indians around here?" Fatty Rampart asked.

"No, not really. I go on a bender about every three months and get a little bit wild, and there's a couple Osage boys from Gray Horse that get noisy sometimes, but that's about all," Clarence Little-Saddle said.

"You certainly don't intend to palm yourself off on us as an Indian," Mary Mabel challenged. "You'll find us a little too knowledgeable for that."

"Little girl, you might as well tell this cow there's no room for her to be a cow since you're so knowledgeable. She thinks she's a short-horn cow named Sweet Virginia. I think I'm a Pawnee Indian named Clarence. Break it to us real gentle if we're not."

"If you're an Indian where's your war bonnet? There's not a feather on you anywhere."

"How you be sure? There's a story that we got feathers instead of hair on— Aw, I can't tell a joke like that to a little girl! How come you're not wearing the Iron Crown of Lombardy if you're a white girl? How you expect me to believe you're a little white girl and your folks came from Europe a couple hundred years ago if you don't wear it? There are six hundred tribes, and only one of them, the Oglala Sioux, had the war bonnet, and only the big leaders, never more than two or three alive at one time, wore it."

"Your analogy is a little strained," Mary Mabel said. "Those Indians we saw in Florida and the ones at Atlantic City had war bonnets, and they couldn't very well have been the kind of Sioux you said. And just last night on the TV in the motel, those Massachusetts Indians put a war bonnet on the President and called him the Great White Father. You mean to tell me that they were all phonies? Hey, who's laughing at who here?"

"If you're an Indian where's your bow and arrow?" Tom Rampart interrupted. "I bet you can't even shoot one."

"You're sure right there," Clarence admitted. "I never shot one of those things but once in my life. They used to have an archery range in Boulder Park over in T-Town, and you could rent the things and shoot at targets tied to hay bales. Hey, I barked my whole forearm and nearly broke my thumb when the bow-string thwacked home. I couldn't shoot that thing at all. I don't see how anybody ever could shoot one of them."

"Okay, kids," Nina Rampart called to her brood. "Let's start pitching this junk out of the shack so we can move in. Is there any way we can drive our camper down here, Clarence?"

"Sure, there's a pretty good dirt road, and it's a lot wider than it looks from the top. I got a bunch of green bills in an old night charley in the shack. Let me get them, and I'll clear out for a while. The shack hasn't been cleaned out for seven years, since the last time this happened. I'll show you the road to the top, and you can bring your car down it."

"Hey, you old Indian, you lied!" Cecilia Rampart shrilled from the doorway of the shack. "You *do* have a war bonnet. Can I have it?"

"I didn't mean to lie, I forgot about that thing," Clarence Little-Saddle said. "My son Clarence Bareback sent that to me from Japan for a joke a long time ago. Sure, you can have it."

All the children were assigned tasks carrying the junk out of the shack and setting fire to it. Nina Rampart and Clarence Little-Saddle ambled up to the rim of the valley by the vehicle road that was wider than it looked from the top.

"Nina, you're back! I thought you were gone forever," Robert Rampart jittered at seeing her again. "What—where are the children?"

"Why, I left them down in the valley, Robert. That is, ah, down in that little ditch right there. Now you've got me worried again. I'm going to drive the camper down there and unload it. You'd better go on down and lend a hand too, Robert, and quit talking to all these funny-looking men here."

And Nina went back to Dublin's place for the camper.

"It would be easier for a camel to go through the eye of a needle than for that intrepid woman to drive a car down into that narrow ditch," the eminent scientist Dr. Velikof Vonk said.

"You know how that camel does it?" Clarence Little-Saddle offered, appearing all of a sudden from nowhere. "He just closes one of his own eyes and flops back his ears and plunges right through. A camel is mighty narrow when he closes one eye and flops back his ears. Besides, they use a big-eyed needle in the act."

"Where'd this crazy man come from?" Robert Rampart demanded, jumping three feet in the air. "Things are coming out of the ground now. I want my land! I want my children! I want my wife! Whoops, here she comes driving it. Nina, you can't drive a loaded camper into a ditch like that! You'll be killed or collapsed!"

Nina Rampart drove the loaded camper into the little ditch at a pretty good rate of speed. The best of belief is that she just closed one eye and plunged right through. The car diminished and dropped, and it was smaller than a toy car. But it raised a pretty good cloud of dust as it bumped for several hundred yards across a ditch that was only five feet wide.

"Rampart, it's akin to the phenomenon known as looming, only in reverse," the eminent scientist Arpad Arkabaranan explained as he attempted to throw a rock across the narrow ditch. The rock rose very high in the air, seemed to hang at its apex while it diminished to the size of a grain of sand, and then fell into the ditch not six inches of the way across. There isn't anybody going to throw across a half-mile valley even if it looks five feet. "Look at a rising moon sometimes, Rampart. It appears very large, as though covering a great sector of the horizon, but it only covers one-half of a degree. It is hard to believe that you could set seven hundred and twenty of such large moons side by side around the horizon, or that it would take one hundred and eighty of the big things to reach from the horizon to a point overhead. It is also hard to believe that your valley is five hundred times as wide as it appears, but it has been surveyed, and it is."

"I want my land. I want my children. I want my wife," Robert chanted dully. "Damn, I let her get away again."

"I'll tell you, Rampy," Clarence Little-Saddle squared on him, "a man that lets his wife get away twice doesn't deserve to keep her. I give you till nightfall; then you forfeit. I've taken a liking to the brood. One of us is going to be down there tonight."

After a while a bunch of them were off in that little tavern on the road between Cleveland and Osage. It was only a half a mile away. If the valley had run in the other direction, it would have been only six feet away.

"It is a psychic nexus in the form of an elongated dome," said the eminent scientist Velikof Vonk. "It is maintained subconsciously by the concatenation of at least two minds, the stronger of them belonging to a man dead for many years. It has apparently existed for a little less than a hundred years, and in another hundred years it will be considerably weakened. We know from our checking out folk tales of Europe as well as Cambodia that these ensorceled areas seldom survive for more than two hundred and fifty years. The person who first set such a thing in being will usually lose interest in it, and in all worldly things, within a hundred years of his own death. This is a simple thanato-psychic limitation. As a short-term device, the thing has been used several times as a military tactic.

"This psychic nexus, as long as it maintains itself, causes group illusion, but it is really a simple thing. It doesn't fool birds or rabbits or cattle or cameras, only humans. There is nothing meteorological about it. It is strictly psychological. I'm glad I was able to give a scientific explanation to it or it would have worried me."

"It is continental fault coinciding with a noospheric fault," said the eminent scientist Arpad Arkabaranan. "The valley really is half a mile wide, and at the same time it really is only five feet wide. If we measured correctly, we would get these dual measurements. Of course it is meteorological! Everything including dreams is meteorological. It is the animals and cameras which are fooled, as lacking a true dimension; it is only humans who see the true duality. The phenomenon should be common along the whole continental fault where the earth gains or loses half a mile that has to go somewhere. Likely it extends through the whole sweep of the Cross Timbers. Many of those trees appear twice, and many do not appear at all. A man in the proper state of mind could farm that land or raise cattle on it, but it doesn't really exist. There is a clear parallel in the Luftspiegelungthal sector in the Black Forest of Germany which exists, or does not exist, according to the circumstances and to the attitude of the beholder. Then we have the case of Mad Mountain in Morgan County, Tennessee, which isn't there all the time, and also the Little Lobo Mirage south of Presidio, Texas, from which twenty thousand barrels of water were pumped in one two-and-a-half-year period before the mirage reverted to a mirage status. I'm glad I was able to give a scientific explanation to this or it would have worried me."

"I just don't understand how he worked it," said the eminent scientist Willy McGilly. "Cedar bark, jack-oak leaves, and the word 'Petahauerat.' The thing's impossible! When I was a boy and we wanted to make a hideout, we used bark from the skunk-spruce tree, the leaves of a box-elder, and the word was 'Boadicea.' All three elements are wrong here. I cannot find a scientific explanation for it, and it does worry me."

They went back to Narrow Valley. Robert Rampart was still chanting dully: "I want my land. I want my children. I want my wife."

Nina Rampart came chugging up out of the narrow ditch in the camper and emerged through that little gate a few yards down the fence row.

"Supper's ready and we're tired of waiting for you, Robert," she said. "A fine homesteader you are! Afraid to come onto your own land! Come along now; I'm tired of waiting for you."

"I want my land! I want my children! I want my wife!" Robert Rampart still chanted. "Oh, there you are, Nina. You stay here this time. I want my land! I want my children! I want an answer to this terrible thing!"

"It is time we decided who wears the pants in this family," Nina said stoutly. She picked up her husband, slung him over her shoulder, carried him to the camper and dumped him in, slammed (as it seemed) a dozen doors at once, and drove furiously into the Narrow Valley, which already seemed wider.

Why, the place was getting normaler and normaler by the minute! Pretty soon it looked almost as wide as it was supposed to be. The psychic nexus in the form of an elongated dome had collapsed. The continental fault that coincided with the noospheric fault had faced facts and decided to conform. The Ramparts were in effective possession of their homestead, and Narrow Valley was as normal as any place anywhere.

"I have lost my land," Clarence Little-Saddle moaned. "It was the land of my father Clarence Big-Saddle, and I meant it to be the land of my son Clarence Bareback. It looked so narrow that people did not notice how wide it was, and people did not try to enter it. Now I have lost it."

Clarence Little-Saddle and the eminent scientist Willy McGilly were standing on the edge of Narrow Valley, which now appeared its true half-mile extent. The moon was just rising, so big that it filled a third of the sky. Who would have imagined that it would take a hundred and eight of such monstrous things to reach from the horizon to a point overhead, and yet you could sight it with sighters and figure it so.

"I had a little bear-cat by the tail and I let go," Clarence groaned. "I had a fine valley for free, and I have lost it. I am like that hard-luck guy in the funny-paper or Job in the Bible. Destitution is my lot."

Willy McGilly looked around furtively. They were alone on the edge of the half-mile-wide valley.

"Let's give it a booster shot," Willy McGilly said.

Hey, those two got with it! They started a snapping fire and began to throw the stuff onto it. Bark from the dog-elm tree—how do you know it won't work?

It *was* working! Already the other side of the valley seemed a hundred yards closer, and there were alarmed noises coming up from the people in the valley.

Leaves from a black locust tree—and the valley narrowed still more! There was, moreover, terrified screaming of both children and big people from the depths of Narrow Valley, and the happy voice of Mary Mabel Rampart chanting "Earthquake! Earthquake!"

"That my valley be always wide and flourish and such stuff, and green with money and grass!" Clarence Little-Saddle orated in Pawnee chant style, "but that it be narrow if intruders come, smash them like bugs!"

People, that valley wasn't over a hundred feet wide, now, and the screaming of the people in the bottom of the valley had been joined by the hysterical coughing of the camper car starting up.

Willy and Clarence threw everything that was left on the fire. But the word? The word? Who remembers the word?

"Corsicanatexas!" Clarence Little-Saddle howled out with confidence he hoped would fool the fates.

He was answered not only by a dazzling sheet of summer lightning, but also by thunder and raindrops.

"Chahiksi!" Clarence Little-Saddle swore. "It worked. I didn't think it would. It will be all right now. I can use the rain."

The valley was again a ditch only five feet wide.

The camper car struggled out of Narrow Valley through the little gate. It was smashed flat as a sheet of paper, and the screaming kids and people in it had only one dimension.

"It's closing in! It's closing in!" Robert Rampart roared, and he was no thicker than if he had been made out of cardboard.

"We're smashed like bugs," the Rampart boys intoned. "We're thin like paper."

"Mort, ruine, ecrasement!" spoke-acted Cecilia Rampart like the great tragedienne she was.

"Help! Help!" Nina Rampart croaked, but she winked at Willy and Clarence as they rolled by. "This homesteading jag always did leave me a little flat."

"Don't throw those paper dolls away. They might be the Ramparts," Mary Mabel called.

The camper car coughed again and bumped along on level ground. This couldn't last forever. The car was widening out as it bumped along.

"Did we overdo it, Clarence?" Willy McGilly asked. "What did one flat-lander say to the other?"

"Dimension of us never got around," Clarence said. "No, I don't think we overdid it, Willy. That car must be eighteen inches wide already, and they all ought to be normal by the time they reach the main road. The next time I do it, I think I'll throw wood-grain plastic on the fire to see who's kidding who."

Timothy

Keith Roberts

Anita was bored; and when she was bored odd things were liable to happen. Granny Thompson, who studied her granddaughter far more closely than she would have cared to admit, had been noticing a brooding look in her eyes for some days. She cast about for chores that would keep her mind off more exotic mischief for a time. "There's the 'en run" intoned the old lady. "That wants a good gooin'-uvver fer a start. 'Arf the posts orl of a tip, 'oles everywheer.... An' the path up ter the you-know-wot. Nearly *went* on that yisdey. Place gooin' orl of 'eap, an' yer sits there *moanin'....*"

Anita sneered. "Chicken runs. Paths up to you-know-whats. I want to do something *interesting,* Gran. Like working a brand-new spell. Can't we—"

"No we *kent!*" snapped the old lady irritably. "Spells, spells, kent think o' nothink but *spells.* You wants ter look a bit lively, my gel. Goo on out an' earn yer kep, sit there chopsin'.... Goo on, git summat *done.* Git some o' that fat orf yer...."

Anita hissed furiously. She was very proud of her figure.

"Mackle up that there chair-back in the wosh'ouse," snarled Granny, warming to her theme. "Tek the truck down to ole Goody's place an' git them line props wot's bin cut an' waitin' arf a month. Git rid of orl that muck an' jollop yer chucked down by the copper 'ole a week larst *Toosdey.* Git the three o'clock inter Ket'rin', save my legs fere a change. 'Ole 'eap o' stuff we're run out on...."

"Oh *please* Gran, not today...."

Granny Thompson softened a little. She didn't like going to Kettering either. "Well goo on uvver to Aggie Everett's then an' git a couple of 'andfuls o' flour ... an' watch she dunt put no chiblins o' nuthink in *with* it. Aggie's sense o' wot's funny ent the same as anybody normal.... An' when yer gits back yer kin goo up an' git orl that birdsnest muck out o' the *thack.* I ent avin' that game agin, wadn't the same fer a month larst time I went up that there ladder...."

Anita fled, partly to escape her Granny's inventiveness, partly because there was some truth in the crack about her weight. In the winter she seemed to store fat like a dormouse, there was no answer to it; she'd tried a summer dress on only a day before and there had been too much Anita nearly everywhere. She decided to make a start on the chicken run. Levitation and spellraising were all very well in their way but there was something peculiarly satisfying once in a while in taking ordinary wood and nails and a perfectly normal hammer and lashing about as vigorously as possible. She rapidly tired of the job though. The rolls of wire netting were recalcitrant, possessed of a seemingly infinite number of hooks and snags that all but defied unravelment; once undone, they buried themselves gleefully in her palms. And the ground was soaked and nasty so that worms spurted out whenever she tried to drive a post. Anita leaned on the somewhat disheveled end frame of the run and yawned. She probed the mind of the nearest of its occupants and got back the usual moronic burbling about the next feeding-time. Hens are easily the most boring of companions.

Anita snorted, pushed back her hair, wiped her hot face and decided to go to Aggie's for the flour. She knew her Granny still had a good stock of practically everything in the larder and that the errand was only an excuse to get her out from underfoot for a while, but that didn't matter. She could take the long path round the far side of Foxhanger; perhaps the wood creatures were waking up by now.

She walked between the trees, well muffled in jeans, boots and donkey jacket. As she moved she scuffed irritably at twigs and leaves. She hated this time of the year with a peculiar loathing. February is a pointless sort of month: neither hot nor cold, neither winter nor spring. No animals, no birds, the sky a dull, uniform gray.... Anita hung her head and frowned. If only things would get a move on.... There were creatures in old tree stumps and deep in the ground but the few she was able to contact were dozy and grumpy and made it quite clear they wanted to be left alone for another six weeks, longer if possible. Anita decided she would like to hibernate, curled paws over nose in some brown crackling lair of leaves. Another year she really must try it; at least she might wake up feeling like doing something.

If she had expected any comfort from Aggie Everett she was disappointed. The old lady was morose; she had recently developed a head cold, and treated herself with a variety of ancient remedies and felt as she put it "wuss in consiquence." She was wearing a muffler knotted several times round her thin neck; her face was pale and even more scrinched-looking than usual while her nose, always a delicate member, glowed like a stoplight. She confided to Anita that things "orl wanted a good shove, like"; her nephews would be coming down for the spring equinox and there were great plans for festivities but until then the Witches' Calendar was empty. The boys were away making cardboard boxes in far-off Northamptom and there was nothing to do, nothing to do at all. . . .

On the way back Anita took a shortcut across part of the Johnsons' land and saw Timothy on the horizon. Lacking anything better to do, she detoured so as to pass close by where he stood. She couldn't help noticing that Timothy looked as depressed as she felt. He had been made the previous spring to keep the birds off the new crops, so he was nearly a year old; and for nine months now he had had nothing to do but stand and be rained on and blown about by the wind and stars at the crown of Foxhanger wood away across the fields. Anita nodded mechanically as she trudged past. "Afternoon, Timothy. . . ." But it seemed he was too tired even to flap a ragged sleeve at her. She walked on.

Twenty yards away she stopped, struck by a thought. She stood still for a moment, weighing possibilities and feeling excited for the first time in weeks. Then she went back, stepping awkwardly on the chunky soil. She set the flour down, put her hands on her hips and looked at Timothy with her head on one side and her eyes narrowed appraisingly.

His face was badly weathered, of course, but that was unimportant; if anything, it tended to give him character. She walked up to him, brushed the laps of his coat and tilted his old floppy hat to a more rakish angle. She made motions as if parting his wild straw hair. Timothy watched her enigmatically from his almond-shaped slits of eyes. He was a very well built scarecrow; the Johnson boys had put him together one weekend when they were home from College and Anita, who loved dolls and effigies, had watched the process with delight. She prodded and patted him, making sure his baling-wire tendons had not rotted from exposure. Timothy was still in good order; and although he was actually held up by a thick stake driven into the ground he had legs of his own, which was a great advantage. Anita walked round him, examining him with the air of a connoisseur. There were great possibilities in Timothy.

She moved back a few paces. Her boredom was forgotten now; she saw the chance of a brand new and very interesting spell. She squatted on her heels, folded her arms and rocked slightly to aid concentration. Around her, winter-brown fields and empty sky waited silently; there was no breath of wind. Anita opened her eyes, and ran through the incantation quickly to make sure she had it firmly set in her mind. Then she waved a hand and began to mutter rapidly.

A strange thing happened. Although the day remained still, something like a breeze moved across the ground to Timothy. Had there been grass it might have waved; but there was no grass, and the soil twinkled and shifted and was still again. The wind touched the scarecrow and it seemed his shoulders stiffened, his head came up a trifle. One of his outstretched arms waved; a wisp of straw dropped from his cuff and floated to the ground. The stake creaked faintly to itself.

Anita was vastly pleased. She stood and did a little jig; then she looked around carefully. For a moment she was tempted to finish the job on the spot and activate Timothy; but the Johnson farmhouse was in sight and scarecrows that talk and walk and sing maybe and dance, are best not seen by ordinary folk. Anita scurried off with her head full of plans. Twenty yards away she remembered the flour and went back for it. Timothy stirred impatiently on his post and a wind that was not a wind riffled the ragged tails of his coat. "Sorry," called Anita. "I'll come back tonight; we can talk then. Besides, I'd better look up the rest of the trick, just to be sure." She skipped away, not turning back again, and Timothy might or might not have waved. . . .

The sky was deep gray when she returned, and the swell of land on which the scarecrow stood looked dark and rough as a dog's back. Timothy was silhouetted against the last of the light, a black drunken shape looking bigger than he really was. Anita breathed words over him, made passes; then she undid the wire and cord that held him to his stake and Timothy slid down and stood a little uncertainly on his curious feet. Anita held his arm in case he tumbled and broke himself apart. "How do you feel?" she asked.

"Stiff," said Timothy. His voice had a musty, earthy sort of quality and when he opened his mouth there was an old smell of dry soil and libraries. Anita walked slowly with him across the furrows; for a time he tottered and reeled like an old man or a sick one, then he began to get more assurance and strode out rapidly. At first his noseless round face looked odd in the twilight but Anita soon got used to it. After all, Timothy was a personality, and personalities do not need to be conventionally handsome. She crossed the field with the scarecrow jolting beside her, headed for the cover of the nearest trees.

She found Timothy's mind was as empty as a thing could be; but that was part of his charm, because Anita could stock it with whatever she wanted him to know. At first the learning process was difficult because one question had a knack of leading to a dozen others and often the simplest things are hardest to explain. Thus:

"What's night?"

"Night is now. When it's dark."

"What's dark?"

"When there isn't any light."

"What's light?"

"Er.... Light is when you can see Foxhanger across the fields. Dark is when you can't."

"What's 'see'.... ?"

Anita was on firmer ground when it came to the question of scarecrows.

"What's a scarecrow?"

"A thing they put in a field when there are crops. The birds don't come because they think it's a man."

"I was in a field. Am I a scarecrow?"

"No, you're not. Well, maybe once on a time, but not any more, I changed you."

"Am I a man?"

"You will be...." And Anita leaned on the arm of the giant and felt the firmness of his wooden bones, and was very proud.

Timothy was back in his place by first light and Anita spent some time scuffing out tracks. When the scarecrow walked he had a way of plonking his feet down very hard so they sank deeply into the ground. If old Johnson saw the marks he might take it into his head to wait up and see what queer animal was on the prowl, and Anita hated the thought of Timothy being parted by a charge from a twelve bore. She was only just beginning to find out how interesting he could be.

During the following weeks Granny Thompson had little cause for complaint. She rarely saw her granddaughter; in the daytime Anita was usually mugging up fresh spellwork, or trying with the aid of a hugely battered Britannica to solve some of the more brilliant of Timothy's probings; and at night she was invariably and mysteriously absent. Her granny finally raised the question of these absences.

"Gallivantin'!" snorted the elder Thompson. "Yore got summat *on,* I knows that. The question iss *wot?"*

"But Gran, I don't know what you mean...."

"Kep me up 'arf the night larst night," pronounced Granny. "I could 'ear yer, gooin' on. Chelp chelp chelp, ev'ry night alike, but I kent 'ear nothing *answer....*" And then with a suddenly gimlet-like expression, "Yore got a *bloke* agin my gel, that's wot...."

"Really, Gran," said Anita primly. "The very *idea*. . . ."

"Anita, what's a witch?"

"I've told you a dozen times, Timothy. A witch is somebody like me or Gran, or Aggie Everett I suppose. We can . . . talk to all sorts of people. Like yourself. Normal folk can't."

"Why can't other people talk to me?"

"Well, the . . . it's hard to explain. It doesn't matter anyway; you've got me. I talk to you. I made you."

"Yes, Anita. . . ."

"I've got a new dress," said Anita, pirouetting. Timothy stood stiffly by the gate and watched her. "An' new shoes . . . but I'm not wearing them tonight because I don't want the damp to spoil them. I've got all new things because it's spring." She held her hand out to Timothy and felt the brittle strength in him as he helped her over the gate. He had a sort of clumsy courtesy that was all his own.

"Anita, what's spring?"

Anita was exasperated. "It's when . . . ah, the birds come back from Africa, don't ask me where's Africa because I shan't tell you . . . and there's nice scents in the air at night and the leaves come on the trees and you get new clothes and you can go out and everything feels different. I like spring."

"What's 'like'?"

Anita stopped, puzzled. "Well, it's . . . I don't know. It's a feeling you have about people. I like you, for instance. Because you're gentle and you think about the things I think about." Overhead a bat circled and dipped and the evening light showed redly through his wings and for a moment he almost spoke to Anita; then he saw the gauntness walking with her along the path and spun back up into the sky. "I shall have to teach you about liking," said Anita. "There's still so many things you don't know." She pelted ultrasonics after the noctule but if he was still in range he didn't answer. "Come on, Timothy," she said. "I think we'll go to Deadman's Copse and see if the badgers are out yet."

"Spells," said Anita. "Marjoram and wormsblood and quicksilver and cinnabar. Mandrakes and tar and honey. Divination by sieve and shears. Can you remember all that?"

"Yes, Anita."

"You've got a very good brain, Timothy; you remember practically everything now. You've got most of the standard manual word for word, and I only read it through to you once. You really could be very useful. . . I think you're developing what they call a Balanced Personality. Though there's so much to put in, I still keep remembering bits I haven't done.... Would you like to learn poetry?"

"What's poetry?"

Anita fumed momentarily, then started to laugh. "I'm tired of defining things; it gets harder all the time. We shall just have to do some, that's all; I'll bring a book tomorrow." And the day after she brought the book; it was one of her treasures, heavy and old and bound with leather. She opened Timothy's mind till he could read Shakespeare better than a man, then they went to Drawback Hill to get a dramatic setting and Anita found Timothy's withered lips were just right for the ringing utterances of the old mad Lear. Next night they did a piece of *Tempest,* choosing for it the ghostly locale of Deadman's Copse. Anita read Ariel, although as she pointed out she was a little too well-developed for the part. Timothy made a fine Prospero; the cursing boomed out in great style although the bit about pegging people in oaks was if anything rather too realistic. When Timothy spoke the words Anita could see quite clearly how bad it would be to get mixed up with the knotty entrails of a tree as big as that.

The next day it rained, making the ground soggy and heavy. Mud covered Anita's ankles before she was halfway across the field. Timothy looked a little sullen and there was a pungent, rotting smell about his clothing that she found alarming. "It's no good," she said, "we shall just have to get you under cover. I hate the idea of you standing out all the time; I don't expect you mind, though."

"Anita, what's 'mind'?"

By mid-April Anita would normally have been busying herself about a hundred and one things connected with the field creatures and their affairs, but she was still mainly preoccupied with Timothy. Somehow she had stopped thinking of him as a scarecrow; the thing she had woken up was beginning to work by itself now and often when she came to release him he would bubble with notions of his own that had come to him in the gray time before the sun drained away his power. He asked her how she knew the bats called each other and why she was always sure when the weasel was too close for comfort; so she gave him a sixth sense, and portions of the seventh, eighth and ninth for good measure. Then she could leave him standing on watch in his field and scurry off on her own business and Timothy would tattle and wheeze out the night's news when next he saw her. He found out where the fieldmice were building, and how the hedgepigs were faring on their rounds; then one of the hares under Drawback was taken by a lurcher and Timothy heard the scream and told Anita stiffly, making the death seem like a lab report; and Anita angrily gave him emotions and after that the tears would squeeze from somewhere and roll down his football face whenever he thought about killing.

A week later Anita came home with the dawn to find her Granny waiting for her. "This," said the old lady without preamble, " 'as gotta *stop*."

Anita flung herself down in one of the big armchairs and yawned. "Wha', Gran...."

"Gallivantin' " said Granny Thompson sternly. "Muckin' about wi' that gret thing uvver at the Johnsonses. *Ugghhh*.... Giz me the creeps it does straight.... Gret mucky thing orl straw an' stuff, sets yer teeth on edge ter *think* on it...." She crossed to one of the little windows and opened it. A breeze moved cold and sweet, ruffling Anita's hair. The room was shadowy, but the sky outside was bright; somewhere a bird started to sing, all on his own. *"Gallivantin'!"* said Granny again, as if to clinch matters.

Anita was nearly asleep; she'd used a lot of power that night and she was very tired. She said dreamily, "He's not a thing, Gran. He's Timothy. He's very sweet. I invented him, he knows about everything...." Then a little more sharply, *"Gran!* How did you know—"

Granny Thompson sniffed. "I knows wot I *knows*.... There's ways an' means, my gel.... Some as even you dunt know, artful though yer might be...."

Anita had a vision of something skulking in hedgerows, pouring itself across open ground like spilled jam. A very particular vision this, it lashed its tail and spat. She said reproachfully "You didn't play fair. You used a Familiar...."

Granny looked virtuous. "I ent sayin' I *did,* an' there agin I ent sayin' I *didn't*...."

"It was Vortigern," said Anita, pouting. "It must have been. None of the others would peach on me. But *him*...."

"Never mind 'ow I *knows*," said Granny Thompson sternly. "Or 'oo tole me. The thing is, yore gone fur *enough*. Any more an' I wunt be responsible, straight I wunt...."

"But Gran, he's nice, And...well, I'm sorry for him. I don't like to think of him being left on his own now. It would be...well, like somebody dying almost. He's too clever now, can't just...*eeeooohhh*...jus' leave him like that...."

"Clever," muttered Granny, looking at the wall and not seeing it. "That ent no call for pity.... You save yer pity fer the next world me gel, there ent no place fer it 'ere.... Brains, pah. Straw an' dirt an' muck orf the fields, that's brains. Same with 'im, same with 'em orl. You'll learn...."

But the homily was lost on Anita; she had incontinently fallen asleep.

She dreamed of Timothy that morning, woke and slept again to see if he would come back. He did; he was standing far away in his field and waving his arms to her and calling but his voice was so thick and distant she couldn't hear the words. But he wanted something, that was plain; and

Anita woke and blinked, thought she knew what it was, and forgot again. She rubbed her eyes, saw the sunlight, felt the warmth of the air. It was lunchtime, and the day was as hot as June.

The fields were dark and rough and a full moon was rising. Anita crossed the open ground behind Foxhanger. A hunting bird called, close and low; she stopped and saw distant woods humped on their hills, looking like palls of smoke in the moonhaze. Timothy was waiting for her, a tiny speck a long way off in the night. When she reached him he looked gaunter than ever; his fingers stuck out in bundles from his sleeve, and his hat was askew. The night wind stirred his coat, moonlight oozed through the tatters and rags. Anita felt a queer stirring inside her; but she released him as usual and Timothy wriggled from the stake and dropped awkwardly to the ground. He said, "It's a lovely night, Anita." He took an experimental step or two. "After you'd gone this morning my leg broke; but I mended it with wire and it's all right again now." Anita nodded, her mind on other things. "Good," she said. "Good, Timothy, that's fine...."

In February the ground had been bare and red-brown; now the harshness was lost under a new green hair. That was the corn Timothy had been made to protect. She took his arm. "Timothy," she said. "Let's walk. I'm afraid I've got an awful lot to say."

They paced the field, on the path that was beaten hard where the tractor came each day; and Anita told Timothy about the world. Everything she knew, about people dying, and living, and hoping; and how all things, even good things, get old and dirty and worn-out, and the winds blow through them, and the rain washes them away. As it has always been, as it will be forever until the sun is cold. "Timothy," she said gently, "one day ... even my great Prince will be dust. It will be as though He had never been. He, and all the people of His house. Nobody knows why; nobody ever will. It's just the way things are."

Timothy jolted gravely alongside; Anita held his thin arm and although he had no real face she could tell by his expression that he understood what she was saying. "Timothy," she said. "I've got to go away...."

"Yes, Anita...."

She swallowed. "It's right what Gran says. You're old now and nearly finished and there are so many things to do. I haven't been fair, Timothy. You've just been a ... well, a sort of toy. You know ... I wasn't ever really interested in you. You were just something I made when I was bored. You sort of grew on me."

"Yes, Anita...."

They turned at the farthest end of their walk. The air was wine-warm on her face and arms and Timothy smelled faintly of old brass spoons and what he was thinking about it was impossible to say. "It's spring now," said Anita. "It's the time you put on a new dress and do your hair and find someone nice you can drive with or talk with or just walk along with and watch the night coming and the owls and the stars. They're the things that have to be done because they start right deep down inside you, in the blood. It's the same with animals nearly, they wake up and everything's fresh and green, and it's as if winter was the night and summer is one great long day...."

They had reached Timothy's stake. In the west the sky was still turquoise; an owl dropped down against the light like a black flake of something burned. Anita propped Timothy against his post. He seemed stiffer already and more lifeless somehow. She put his hat right; it was always flopping down. As she reached up she saw something shine silver on his wizened-turnip face. She was startled, until she remembered she had given him feelings. Timothy was crying.

She hugged him then, not knowing what to do. She felt the hardness of him and the crackling dryness, the knobs and angles of his bits-and-pieces body. "Oh, Timothy," she said. "Timothy I'm sorry, but I just can't go with you any more. There won't be any spells for you after this, I've taken the power off...." She stepped back, not looking at him. "I'll go now," she said. "This way's best, honestly. I won't tie you back onto your stick or anything, you can just stand here awhile and watch the bats and the owl. And in the morning you'll just sort of fade away; it won't hurt or anything...." She started to walk off down the slope, feeling the blades of new corn touch her calves. "Goodbye, Timothy," she called.

Something iron-hard snagged at her. She fell, rolled over horrified and tried to get up. Her ankles were caught; she wriggled and the night vanished, shut away by rough cloth that smelled of earth. "Love," croaked Timothy. "Please, Anita, love...." And she felt his twiggy fingers move up and close over her breasts.

She looped like a caterpillar caught by the tail and her fists hit Timothy squarely, bang-bang. Dust flew, and the seeds of grass; then Anita was up and running down the hill, stumbling over the rough ground, and Timothy was close behind her, a flapping patch of darkness with his musty old head bobbing and his arms reaching out. His voice floated to her through the night. "Anita ... *love*...."

She reached the bottom of the field tousled and too shocked to defend herself at all, cut across the Johnsons' stackyard with Timothy still hard on her heels. A dog volleyed barks, subsided whimpering as he caught the strange scent on the air. Back up the hill, a doubling across Home Paddock; a horse bolted in terror as old cloth flapped at his eyes. Near the hedge Timothy gained once more, but he lost time climbing the gate. Anita spun round fifty yards away. "Timothy, *go back! Timothy, no!*"

He came on again; she took three deep breaths, lifted her arm and flung something at him that crackled and fizzed and knocked a great lump of wadding from his shoulder. One arm flopped down uselessly but the rest of him still thumped towards her. Anita was angry now; her face was white in moonlight and there was a little burning spot on each cheek and her mouth was compressed till her lips were hardly visible at all. "Scarecrow!" she shouted. "Old dirty thing made of straw! *Spiders' home!*" She'd had time to aim; her next shot took Timothy full in the chest and bowled him backwards. He got up and came on again although he was much slower.

Anita waited for him on the little bridge over the Fynebrook. She stood panting and pushing the hair out of her eyes with each hand in turn and the rage was white-hot now and choking her. Around her, brightnesses fizzed and sparkled; as Timothy came within range she hit him again and again, arms and legs and head. Pieces flew from him and bounced across the grass. He reached the bridge but he was only a matchstick man now, his thin limbs glinting under tatters of cloth. Anita took a breath and held it, shut her eyes then opened them very wide, made a circle with her hands, thrust fire at Timothy. His wooden spine broke with a great sound; what was left of him folded in the middle, tumbled against the handrail of the bridge. He fell feet over head into the stream. The current seized him, whirling him off; he fetched up twenty yards away and lay quiet, humped in a reedbed like a heap of broken umbrellas.

Anita moved forward one foot at a time, ready to bolt again or throw more magic; but there was no need. Timothy was finished; he stayed still, the water rippling through his clothes. A little bright beetle shot from somewhere into his coatsleeve, came out at the elbow and sculled away down the stream. Timothy's face was pressed into mud so he could see nothing, but his voice still whispered in Anita's mind. *"Please ... please...."*

She ran again, faster than ever. Along beside the brook, across the meadow, through Foxhanger, up the garden path. She burst into the kitchen of the cottage, spinning Granny Thompson completely round. Took the stairs three at a time and banged her bedroom door shut behind her. She flung herself on the bed and sobbed and wrapped blankets around her ears; but all night long, until the last of the power ran down, she could hear Timothy thinking old moldy thoughts about rooks and winds, and worms in the thick red ground.

Through a Glass—Darkly

Zenna Henderson

I finally got so frightened that I decided to go to Dr. Barstow and have my eyes checked.

Dr. Barstow has been my eye doctor for years—all the way from when a monkey bit and broke one lens of my first glasses, up to the current encouraging me through getting used to bifocals. Although I still take them off to thread a needle and put them back on to see across the room, I take his word for it that someday I'll hardly notice the vast no-vision slash across the middle of everywhere I look.

But it wasn't the bifocals that took me to Dr. Barstow. And he knew it. He didn't know that the real reason I went to him was the cactus I saw in my front room. And I could have adjusted to a cactus—even in the front room, but not to the roadrunner darting from my fireplace to my hall door and disappearing with the last, limp two inches of a swallowed snake flapping from his smirking beak.

So Dr. Barstow finished his most thorough investigation of my eyes. Then he sat straddling his little stool and looked at me mildly. "It takes time," he said, "to make the adjustment. Some people take longer—"

"It's not that, Doctor," I said miserably, "even though I could smash the

things happily some times. No, it's—it's—" Well, there was no helping it.
I'd come purposely to tell him. "It's what I see. It's that cactus in my front
room." His eyes flicked up quickly to mine. "And right now I'm seeing a
prickly pear cactus with fruit on it where your desk is." I swallowed
rackingly and he looked at his desk.

For a moment he twiddled with whatever ophthalmologists twiddle
with and then he said, "Have you had a physical check-up recently?" His
eyes were a little amused.

"Yes," I replied. "For exactly this reason. And I truly don't think I'm
going mad." I paused and mentally rapped a few spots that might have gone
soft, but they rang reassuringly sound. "Unless I'm just starting and this is
one of the symptoms."

"So it's all visual," he said, briskly.

"So far," I said, feeling a flood of relief that he was listening without
laughter. It had been frightening, being alone. How can you tell your
husband casually that he is relaxing into a cholla cactus with his
newspaper? Even a husband like Peter. "All visual except sometimes I
think I hear the wind through the cactus."

Dr. Barstow blinked. "You say there's a cactus where my desk is?"

I checked. "Yes, a prickly pear. But your desk is there, too. It's—it's—"

"Superimposed?" he suggested.

"Yes," I said, checking again. "And if you sat down there, it'd be your
desk, but—but there's the cactus—" I spread my hands helplessly, "With a
blue tarantula hawk flying around over it."

"Tarantula hawk?" he asked.

"Yes, you know, those waspy looking things. Some are bright blue and
some are orangy—"

"Then you see movement, too," he said.

"Oh yes," I smiled feebly. Now that I was discussing it, it wasn't even
remotely a funny story any more. I hadn't realized how frightened I had
been. To go blind! Or mad! "That's one reason I asked for an emergency
appointment. Things began to move. Saturday it was a horny toad on the
mantel, which is a ledge along a sand wash. But yesterday it was a
roadrunner with a snake in his beak, coming out of the fireplace. The
hearth is a clump of chaparral."

"Where is the wasp now?" asked Dr. Barstow.

I checked briefly. "It's gone." And I sat and looked at him forlornly.

He twiddled some more and seemed to be reading his diploma on the
wall behind me. I noticed the thin line across his glasses that signaled
bifocals and I wondered absently how long it had taken him to get used to
them.

"Did you know that every time you look at your—um—cactus, you look away from where you say it is?" he finally asked.

"Away from it!" I exclaimed. "But—"

"How many fruits on the prickly pear?" he asked.

I checked. "Four green ones and a withered—"

"Don't turn your head," he said. "Now what do you see in front of you?"

My eyes swam through a change of focus. "You, holding up three fingers," I said.

"And yet the cactus is where my desk is and I'm almost at right angles to it." He put down his three fingers. "Every time you've checked the cactus, you've looked at me, and that's completely away from where you say."

"But what—" I felt tears starting and I turned away, ashamed.

"Now turn your head and look directly at my desk," he said. "Do you see the cactus now?"

"No," my voice jerked forlornly. "Just the desk."

"Keep your eyes on the desk," he said. "Don't move your head. Now check my position."

I did—and then I did cry—big sniffy tears. "You're sitting on a rock under a mesquite tree!" I choked, pulling my glasses off blindly.

He handed me a tissue. And another when that became sodden. And a third to wipe those blasted bifocals.

"Does having the glasses off make a difference in what you see?" he asked.

"No," I sniffed. "Only I can see better with them." And I laughed shakily, remembering the old joke about spots-before-the-eyes.

"Well, Mrs. Jessymin," he said. "There's nothing in the condition of your eyes to account for what you're seeing. And this—um—visual manifestation is apparently not in your direct vision, but in your peripheral vision."

"You mean my around-the-edges sight?" I asked.

"Yes," he said. "Incidentally you have excellent peripheral vision. Much better than most people—"

"Of my advanced age!" I finished, mock bitterly. "These dern bifocals!"

"But bifocals aren't necessarily a sign of age—"

"I know, I know," I said, "Only of getting old."

We had automatically dropped into our usual bifocal speech pattern while our minds busied themselves elsewhere.

"Does this thing bother you when you drive?" he asked.

I was startled. What if they took my license! "No," I hastened. "Most of the time I don't even notice it. Then sometimes I catch a glimpse of something interesting and then's when I focus in on it. But it's all voluntary—so far. Paying attention to it, I mean."

"And you focus in as long as you look away from it." Dr. Barstow smiled. "As a matter of fact, some things can be seen more sharply in peripheral vision than by looking directly at them. But I'm at a loss to explain your cactus. That sounds like hallucination—"

"Well," I twisted the tissue in my fingers. "I have a sort of idea. I mean—where our house is—it's in a new housing development—it was all desert not too long ago. I've—well—I've wondered if maybe I was seeing the same place, only before. I mean, when it was still desert." I tried a smile, but Dr. Barstow didn't notice.

"Hmmm," he said, looking absently again at his diploma. "That would certainly put cactus almost anywhere you looked, in Tucson," he said. "But how long ago are you seeing? This office building is fifteen years old."

"I—I don't know," I faltered. "I haven't thought it out that far."

Dr. Barstow looked at me and smiled his infrequent, wide smile. "Well, there doesn't seem to be anything wrong with you," he said. "If I were having an experience as interesting as the one you're having, I'd just enjoy it. I'd start a little research into it. Or at least start compiling a few statistics. How long ago *are* you seeing? Is it the same time period every time? What else can you see? People? Big animals? Enjoy it while you can. It arrived out of nowhere, and it might go back to the same place." He stood up.

So did I. "Then I don't have to worry—"

"Not about your eyes, anyway," he assured me. "Keep me posted if anything new develops." I turned to the door. His voice paused me there. "By the way, if Tucson were wiped out, eventually the cactus would come back. Are you seeing *ago* or *to come?*"

We looked at each other levelly a moment, then we both smiled and I left.

Of course I told Peter, passing on the latest greetings from our old friend. And Peter, after a few sharp, anxious questions to be sure that I wasn't concealing from him some Monstrous Doom, accepted my odd affliction with his usual slight grin and glint of interest. He has long since realized that I don't see quite eye-to-eye with the usual maturing-into-bifocals groups.

Since I didn't have to worry about it anymore, I mostly ignored my side vision. However, there were a few more 'sharpenings' in the days that followed.

Once in a Bayless supermarket on double stamp day, I caused a two-aisle jam of shopping carts because I became so engrossed in one of my peripheral pictures. There I stood at a strategic junction, staring fixedly at a stack of tuna cans while the rising murmur of voices and the muted *clish-clish* of colliding carts faded away.

There were people this time, two women and an assortment of small nearly naked children whose runnings and playings took them in and out of my range of vision like circling, romping puppies. It was a group of Indians. The women were intent on their work. They had a very long slender sahuaro rib and were busy harvesting the fruit from the top of an enormously tall sahuaro cactus, right in the middle of canned tomatoes. One woman was dislodging the reddish egg-shaped fruit from the top of the cactus with the stick, and the other was gathering it up from the ground into a basket, using a tong like arrangement of sticks to avoid the thorns that cover the fruit.

I was watching, fascinated, when suddenly I *heard!* There was a soft, singing voice in my mind, and my mind knew it was the woman who knelt in the sandy dust and lifted the thorny fruit.

> *"Good, good, good! softly she sang.*
> *"Food for now. Food for later.*
> *Sing good, sing good,*
> *Sing praise, sing praise!"*

"Lady, are you all right?" An anxious hand on my elbow brought me back to Bayless and the traffic jam. I blinked and drew a deep breath.

The manager repeated, "Are you all right?" He had efficiently rerouted the various carts and they were moving away from me now, with eyes looking back, curious, avid, or concerned.

"Oh, I'm so sorry," I said, clutching the handle of my shopping cart. "I— I suddenly remembered something and forgot where I was." I smiled into the manager's anxious face. "I'm all right, thank you. I'm sorry I caused trouble."

"No trouble," he answered my smile a little tentatively. "You're sure—"

"Oh, certainly," I hastened. "Thank you for your kindness." And I moved away briskly to look for the pizza mix that was on sale.

Up and down the aisles through the towering forest of food I hurried, echoing in my mind, as I contrasted the little lifting sticks and my chrome-bright cart—

> *Good, good*
> *Food for now,*
> *Food for later.*
> *Sing praise! Sing praise!*

Several days later I stood in one of those goldfish-bowl telephone booths on a service station corner and listened to the purr as Dr. Barstow's office phone rang. Finally his secretary, Miss Kieth, answered briskly, and he eventually came on the line, probably between eyelashes.

"I'm downtown," I said hastily after identifying myself. "I know you're busy, but—but—how long have your people been in Tucson?"

There was a slight digestive pause and then he said slowly, "My folks came out here before the turn of the century."

"What—what did they do? I mean, to earn a living? What I mean is, I'm seeing again, right now. There's a big sign over a store, JAS. R. BARSTOW AND SONS GENERAL MERCHANDISE. And if *Jas.* means James, well, that's you—" I wiped a tissue across my oozing forehead and grimaced at the grime. Dr. Barstow broke the breathing silence.

"That was my great grandfather. At least he's the one long enough ago with the right name. Can you still see the place?" His voice quickened.

"Yes," I said, concentrating on the telephone mouthpiece. "I'm dying to go in it and see all that General Merchandise. But I don't think I can go in—not yet. What I wanted to know is, *when* is the store?"

After a minute he asked, "Does it have a porch over the sidewalk?"

I stared studiously at the dial of the phone. "Yes," I said, "with peeled pine porch posts"—I dabbled my lips—"holding up the roof."

"Then it's after 1897," he said. "That was one of our favorite 'olden days' stories—the one about the store burning down. And the magnificent one that arose from the ashes. It boasted a porch."

"Then that's when I'm seeing!" I cried. "Around the turn of the century!"

"If," came his voice cautiously, "if all your seeing is in the same period of time."

"Someday," I said determinedly after a slight pause, "someday I'm going to get a flat 'yes' or 'no' from you about something!"

"And won't that be dull?" I heard him chuckle as he hung up.

I walked over to the store on the next scramble WALK signal at the corner. The concrete clicked under my hurried feet, but, when I stepped up to the far sidewalk, my feet rang hollowly on a wooden porch floor. Hastily, lest a change should come, I hurried across uneven planks to the door. I grabbed the handle. Then I paused, taking a deep breath of a general-store smell that was instantly recognizable—I could smell now!

"Oh!" I thought, the pit of my stomach cold with excitement. "To see all the things we keep in museums and collections now! Just walk in and—"

Then I heard Peter, vigorously and decisively, *"Don't you dare take one step into this—!"*

Caught in midstep, I turned my full gaze on the handle I held. Jarringly, I thumped down several inches to the sidewalk. I removed my hand from where it was pressed against a dusty, empty store window. Automatically I read the sign propped against the stained sagging back of the display window— *You'll wonder where the yellow went—*

The week following came an odd sort of day. It had rained in the night—torrents of rain that made every upside-down drainage street in Tucson run curb to curb. The thirsty earth drank and drank and couldn't keep up with the heavy fall, so now the runoff was making Rillito Creek roar softly to itself as it became again, briefly, a running stream. The dust had been beautifully settled. An autumn-like sky cover of heavy gray clouds hid the sun.

Peter and I decided this was the time for us to relearn the art of bicycling and to do something about my black belt that never lied when it pinched me the news that I was increasing around the middle. It was also time for Peter to stop being critical of the Laundromat for shrinking his pants. So, on this cool, moist morning we resurrected the bikes from the accumulation in the garage. We stacked them awkwardly in the car trunk and drove across the Rillito, stopping briefly at the bridge to join others who stood around enjoying the unusual sight of Water-in-a-River! Then we went on up through the mushrooming foothills land developments, until we finally arrived at a narrow, two-rutted, sandy road that looped out of sight around the low hills and abrupt arroyos. We parked the car and got the bikes out.

It was a wonderful day, fragrant with wet greasewood-after-a-rain. The breeze was blowing, cool enough for sleeves to feel good. It was a dustless, delightful breeze.

"I love days like this," I said, as I wobbled away from the car on my bike. I made ten feet before I fell. "I get so lonesome for rain."

Peter patiently untangled me from the bike, flexed my arms to see if they were broken, flexed my neck to kiss the end of my nose, then tried to steady my bike with both hands and, at the same time, help me get back on. "I get so tired of sun, sun, sun—"

"You talk like a native," said Peter, making nice straight tracks in the damp sand of the road.

"So I am," I said, my tracks scalloping back and forth across his as I tried to follow him. "It's only you fotched-on-furriners that find perpetual sun so delightful."

I fell again, this time contriving to have the bike fall one way and me the other with the pedals and my feet twined together.

Peter was extricating me, muttering something about a donkey being better for me since it's braced at all four corners, when I saw it—on the next loop of the road where it topped the rise above us.

"Peter," I said softly, staring at him, "I can see a horse pulling a buggy on the road over there. There's another and another and a hay wagon-looking vehicle. Peter, it's a procession of some sort."

Peter straightened my legs and sat down on the ground near me. "Go on," he said, taking my hands.

"There's something on the hay wagon," I said. "It looks—it's a coffin, Peter!" The back of my neck chilled.

"A coffin?" Peter was startled, too.

"They're going down the other side of the hill now. There are three buggies and the wagon. They're gone—"

"Come on," said Peter, getting up and lifting the bikes, "let's follow them."

"Follow them?" I grabbed my bike and tried to remember which side to mount from—or does that only matter for horses? "Did you see them, too?"

"No," he said, flinging himself up onto the bike seat. "But you did. Let's see if you *can* follow them."

And behold! I could ride my bike! All sorts of muscular memories awoke and I forgot the problems of aiming and balancing, and I whizzed—slowly—through the sand at the bottom of a rise, as I followed Peter.

"I don't see them!" I called to Peter's bobbing back. "I guess they're gone."

"Are you looking over there?" he called back.

"Of course I am!" I cried. "Oh!" I murmured. "Oh, of course." And I looked out over the valley. I noticed one slender column of smoke rising from Davis-Monthan Air Base before my peripheral vision took over.

"Peter," I said, "it is a coffin. I'm right by the wagon. Don't go so fast. You're leaving us behind."

Peter dropped back to ride beside me. "Go on," he said. "What kind of buggies are they?"

I stared out over the valley again, and my bike backed up over a granite knob in the sand and I fell. Peter swung back toward me as I scrambled to my feet. "Leave the bikes," I said. "Let's walk. They're going slow enough—"

A fine rain had begun. With it came the soft sense of stillness I love so about the rain. Beside me, within my vision, moved the last buggy of the procession, also through a fine rain that was not even heavy enough to make a sound on its faded black top, but its color began to darken and to shine.

There were two people in the buggy, one man driving the single horse, the other man, thin, wrinkled, smelling of musty old age and camphor, huddled in his heavy overcoat, under a laprobe. A fine tremor stirred his knotted hands and his toothless mouth grinned a little to show the pink smoothness of his lower gums.

I lengthened my stride to keep up with the slow moving procession, hearing the gritty grind of the metal tires through the sand. I put out my hand to rest it on the side of the buggy, but drew it back again, afraid I might feel Something. Then I sensed the insistent seep of a voice, soundless, inside my mind.

Seventeen trips to the cemetery—and back again! That's more than anyone else around here can say. I'll see them all underground yet! There—and back! I go there and come back. They all stay!

The rain was heavier. I could feel its gnatlike insistence against my face. The road was swinging around the base of a long, low hill now.

So this is what she came to. Another thought began. *She was a pretty little thing. Thought sure some young feller around here would have spoke for her. They say she was bad. Shipped her back from the city to bury her. Women sure had a fit about burying her with their honored dead. Honored dead! Honored because they* are *dead. Every evil in the book safely underground here in the graveyard. Hope Papa's having a good time. Sure likes funerals.*

I reeled away from the buggy. I had walked full tilt into a fence post. Peter grabbed me before I fell.

"Well?" he asked, pushing a limp wet strand of my hair off my forehead.

"I'm okay," I said. "Peter, is there a cemetery around here anywhere? You've hunted these foothills often enough to know."

"A cemetery?" Peter's eyes narrowed. "Well, there are a few graves in a fence corner around here some place. Come on!"

We abandoned the road and started across country. As we trudged up one hill and scurried down another, treading our way through cactus and mesquite, I told Peter what I'd seen and heard.

"There!" Peter gestured to the left and we plunged down into a sand wash that walked firmly because the night rain had packed the sand and up the other steep side and topped out onto a small flat. Half a dozen forlorn sunken mounds lay in the corner of two barbed-wire fences meeting. Gray, wordless slabs of weathered wood splintered at the heads of two of them. Small rocks half outlined another.

I looked up at the towering Santa Catalinas and saw Peter. "Move, Peter," I said. "You're standing on a grave. There are dozens of them."

"Where can I stand?" Peter asked.

"In the fence corner," I said. "There's no fence there—only a big rock. Here they come."

I moved over to where the procession was coming through the barbed-wire fence. I stood there, hearing the waves of voices breaking over me.

The first buggy—

Bad—bad! Rouged, even in her coffin. I should have wiped it off the way I started to. Disgraceful! Why did she have to humiliate me like this by coming back? They've got places in the city for people like her. She was dead to respectability a long time ago. Why did she come back?

The woman pinched her lips together more tightly behind the black veil and thought passionately, *Punish her! Punish her! The wages of sin!*

The next buggy was passing me now. *Poor child—oh, poor child—to come back so unwanted. Please, God, cleanse her of all her sins—*

There were two women and a man in this buggy.

Good rain. Needed it. Oughta be home getting things done, not trailing after a fancy woman. Good rain for this time of year.

The metal tires gritted past me.

They'll be bringing me out here next. I'm dying! I'm dying! I know. I know. Mama died of the same thing. I'm afraid to tell. All they could do would be to tell me I'll be the next one to come out here. I'm afraid! I'm afraid! I'm crying for myself, not her!

A woman alone was driving the next buggy—a smart, shiny vehicle. She was easily controlling the restless horse.

At least she has had someone love her, whether it was good or bad. How many wanted her and had her doesn't matter now. Someone cared about what she did and liked the way she looked. Someone loved her.

By now the men had got out of the buggies—all except the old one—and I heard the grating sound as they dragged the coffin from the hayrack. It thumped to an awkward angle against the mound of desert dirt, rocks, caliche and the thin sandy soil of the hillside. It was seized and lowered quickly and ungently to the bottom of the grave. The men got shovels from their vehicles. They took off their coats, hitched their sleeve garters higher and began to fill in the grave.

"Isn't anyone going to pray?" The shocked cry came from the one woman. "Isn't anyone going to pray?"

There was a short, uneasy pause.

"Preacher's prayed over her already," said one of the men. "For her kind, that's enough."

The woman stumbled to the half-filled grave and fell to her knees. Maybe I was the only one who heard her. *"She loved much—forgive her much."*

Peter and I sat warming our hands by cradling our coffee mugs in them. We were in a little hamburger joint halfway back home. Outside the rain purred down, seething on the blacktop road, thrumming insistently on metal somewhere out back. We sat, each busy with his own thoughts, and watched the rain furrow the sandy shoulder of the road. It *was* an unusual rain for this time of year.

"Well." My voice lifted Peter's eyes from his coffee. He lifted one brow inquiringly. "I have Told All," I went on. "What is your considered opinion?"

"Interesting," he said. "Not everyone's aberrant wife has such interesting aberrations."

"No, I mean," I carefully balanced the tinny spoon on my forefinger, "what—why—"

"Let's not try to explain anything," said Peter. "In the first place, I know I can't and I don't think you can either. Let's enjoy, as Dr. Barstow suggested."

"Where do you suppose they shipped Gayla home from?" I asked.

"Gayla?" said Peter. "Where did you get that name? Did someone call her by it?"

I felt goose bumps run down my arms to the elbows. "No," I said, thinking back over the recent events. "No one mentioned any names, but—but her name is—was—is Gayla!"

We eyed one another and I plunged back into words.

"Maybe from Phoenix," I said. "It was rather fleshpotty in the old days."

"Or Tombstone, maybe?" suggested Peter. "It was even more so."

"Did Tombstone have a railway?" I asked, lifting my cup. "I don't remember seeing a depot there even nowadays. I think Benson would be the closest."

"Maybe it wasn't by rail," said Peter. "Maybe freight. You know, those big wagons."

"It was by rail," I said, grimacing at the taste of cold coffee. Peter laughed. "Well," I said, "I don't like cold coffee."

"It wasn't that," said Peter. "You're sure her name is Gayla and that she came home by rail, but you can't remember whether or not Tombstone has a depot and we were through there last week!"

"Peter," I said through the pluming steam of a fresh cup of coffee. "That brings up something interesting. This—this *thing* is progressive. First I only saw still things. Then moving things. Then people. Then I heard thoughts. Today I heard two people talk out loud. And now I know something about them that I didn't see or hear. How far do you suppose—"

Peter grabbed both my hands, sloshing coffee over our tight fingers. "Don't you dare!" he said tensely, "Don't you dare take one step into whatever this is! Look if you want to and listen when you can, but stay out of it!"

My jaw dropped. "Peter!" My breath wasn't working very well. "Peter, that's what you said when I was going to go into that store. Peter, how could I hear then what you didn't say until now? Or are you just saying again what you said then—Peter!"

Peter mopped my hands and his. "You didn't tell me that part about the store." So I did. And it shook him, too. Peter suddenly grinned and said, "Whenever I said it, it's worth repeating. *Stay* out of this!" His grin died and his hands tightened on mine. His eyes were troubled.

"Let's go home," I said, tears suddenly biting the back of my eyes. "I don't call this enjoying."

As we left the cafe, I said, "Peter, do you think that if we went back up there we could pick up the procession again and follow it again—"

"No," he said. "Not unless we could duplicate everything—time, temperature, humidity, mental state—maybe even the color of lipstick you had on once today." He grinned at me. "You look a little bedraggled."

"*Look* bedraggled?" I eased myself into the car. "How do you suppose I feel? And the bicycling hasn't helped matters much, either. I think I sprained something."

Later that week I was trying to find an address in a new subdivision of curved streets, cul-de-sacs too narrow to turn in, and invisible house numbers. Finally I even forgot the name of the stravenue I was looking for. I pulled up to park along a school fence on Fort Lowell Road. I was rummaging in my purse, trying to find the paper I had written the address on, when I stopped in mid-rummage.

From the corner of my eye I could see the school grounds—hard packed adobe around a swing and teeter-totter, and the front door of a tiny, one-roomed schoolhouse. The children were outside for a ghostly recess. I heard no sound. I studiously kept my eyes on the city map spread out on the steering wheel as I counted twelve children, though one hyper-active little boy might have been number one, nine and twelve, he moved so fast.

I was parked next to a three-strand, barbed-wire fence lined by chaparral more than head-high in places. It formed a rough hedge around the school grounds. Right by my car was a break in the brush through which I could see the school. Clouds were stacking above the school in tumbled blue and white. Over the Catalinas a silent lightning flicked and flicked again. With the squeal of the children spattered by a brief gust of raindrops, the audio of the scene began to function.

The clang of a handbell caught all the children in mid-stride and then pulled them, running, toward the schoolhouse. I smiled and went back to comparing the map that stubbornly insisted that the east-west stravenue I sought was a north-south calle, with the address on the paper.

A side movement brought the playground back into my periphery. A solid chunk of a child was trudging across the playground, exasperation implicit in the dangling jerk of her arms as she plodded, her nondescript skirts catching her shins and flapping gracelessly behind her. She was headed straight for me and I wondered ruefully if I was going to get walked through, body, bones, and car. Then the barbed-wire fence and the clumps of brush focused in.

Gayla—I knew her as I would a long-time acquaintance—was crouched under a bush on ground that had been worn floor-hard and smooth by small bodies. She was hidden from the school by the bushes but sat, leaning forearms—careful of the barbs—on the second strand of wire that sagged with repetitions of such scenes. She was looking, dreamy-faced, through me and beyond me.

"Make my own way," she murmured. "Doesn't that sound lovely! A highway. Make my own way along the highway, away, away—"

"Gayla!" The plodding girl had reached the bushes. "The bell rang a long time ago! Miss Pederson's awful mad at you. This is the third time this week she's had to send for you! And it's going to rain—" The girl dropped to all fours and scrambled by one of the well-worn paths into the tiny roomlike enclosure with Gayla. "You better watch out!" She snatched her wadded skirts from under her knees. "Next thing you know she'll be telling your Aunt Faith on you."

"Aunt Faith—" Gayla stirred and straightened. With both hands she put back the dark curling of her front hair. "Know what she said this morning, Vera? This is my last year in school. She said I'm getting old enough to make my own way—" She savored the words.

"Oh, Gayla!" Vera sank back against her heels. "Isn't she going to let you finish with me? Only another year and then we'll be fourteen—"

"No. I've been a burden long enough, she said, taking food out of her own children's mouths. No—" Her eyes dreamed through me again. "I'm going to make my own way. To the City. I'm going to find a job there—"

"The City!" Vera laughed shortly. "Silly! As if your Aunt would let you go! And what kind of job do you think you could find, being so young?"

"Ben Collins is looking for a girl again. I'll bet your Aunt Faith—"

"Ben Collins!" Gayla's startled face swung about to look at Vera. "What's the matter with Ruth?"

"She's going to live with her uncle in Central. She'd rather milk cows and chop cotton than tend that Collins bunch. You think sleeping four to a bed is crowded. At least there's room for two at each end. At Collins' you'll sleep five to a bed—cross-wise."

"Come on, Gayla! Miss Pederson's throwing a fit—"

She began to back out of the playhouse.

"If Aunt Faith tries to make me go there, I'll run away." Gayla was following slowly, the two girls face to face on hands and knees. "And don't you go telling, either, Vera. I'll run away to the City and get rich and when I come back, she'll be sorry she was so mean. But I'll forgive her and give her a magnificent gift and she'll cry and beg my—"

"Your Aunt Faith cry!" Vera snickered. "Not that I believe for one minute that you'll ever run away, but if you do, don't ever come back. You know your Aunt Faith better than that!"

The two girls emerged from the bushes and stood erect. Vera towed the reluctant Gayla toward the schoolhouse. Gayla looked wistfully back over her shoulder at the dusty road leading away from the school. *Make my own way.* I heard the thought trail behind her like a banner. *Seek my fortune, and someone who'll love me. Someone who'll want me.*

Lightning stabbed out of the darkening sky. A sudden swirling wind and an icy spate of stinging raindrops that came with the thunder jolting across the hills, sent the two girls racing for the schoolhouse and—

My windshield was speckling with rain. I blinked down at my street map. There was my stravenue, right under my thumb, neither north-and-south nor east-and-west, but sidling off widdershins across the subdivision. I started my car and looked for a moment at the high cyclone fence that now enclosed the huge sprawl of the modern school. "Her own way! Was it *her* way—"

I suppose I could have started all sorts of scholarly research to find out who Gayla was, but I didn't, mostly because I knew it would be unproductive. Even in my birthtime, a birth registration was not required around here. Neither were death certificates or burial permits. It was not only possible, but very commonplace in those days to be one whose name was "writ in water." And an awful lot of water had been writ in since the turn of the century—if so she lived then. Then, too, I didn't care to make a cold black and white business of this seeing business. I agreed with Dr. Barstow. I preferred to enjoy. I'd rather have Gayla and girl friend swept away from me diagonally across a windy playground under a thunder-heavy sky.

Well, in the days that followed, a cactus wren built a nest roughly where the upper right corner of Peter's easy chair came, and for a while I couldn't help laughing every time I saw her tiny head peering solemnly over Peter's ear as she earnestly sat and sat.

"But no worms," said Peter firmly. "She'd better not dribble worms on me and my chair when her fine-feathered infants arrive."

"I imagine worms would be the least of your worry as far as dribbling goes," I said. "Baby birds are so messy!"

Occasionally I wondered about Gayla, my imagination trying to bridge the gap between *making my own way* and the person over whom no one had cared to pray. Had she become a full-fledged Scarlet Woman with all the sinful luxury associated with the primrose path, or had she slipped once or been betrayed by some Ben Collins? Too often a community will, well, play down the moral question if the sin is large—and profitable—enough, but a small sin is never let to die. Maybe it's because so few of us have the capacity to sin in the grand manner, but we all can sin sordidly. And we can't forgive people for being as weak as we are.

You understand, of course, that any number of ordinary things were happening during this time. These peripheral wanderings were a little like recurring headaches. They claimed my whole attention while they were in progress, but were speedily set aside when they were over.

Well, Fall came and with it, the hunting season. Peter decided to try for his deer in the rapidly diminishing wilds of the foothills of the Catalinas. He went out one Saturday to look the ground over and came back fit to be tied.

"Two new fences!" he roared. "One of them straight across Flecha Cayendo Wash and the other running right along the top of the hills above Fool's Pass! And that's not all. A road! They've 'dozed out a road! You know that little flat where we like to picnic? Well, the road goes right through it!"

"Not where we wait for the lights in town to come on!" I cried.

"And now they'll use those same lights to sell those quarter million dollar houses with huge picture windows that look out over the valley and have good heavy curtains to pull across as soon as the sun goes down—"

So, in the week following, Peter found another way into the Catalinas. It involved a lot of rough mileage and a going-away before a returning-to the area he wanted to hunt. We went out one early morning armed with enthusiasm, thirty-ought-sixes and hunting licenses, but we walked the hills over all day and didn't get a glimpse of a deer, let alone a shot.

We came back that evening, exhausted, to the flat where we had left the car. We had planned, in case of just such luck, to spend the night under the stars and start out again the next day, so we unloaded.

We built our campfire of splintered, warped odds and ends of lumber we salvaged from the remnants of a shack that sagged and melted to ruin in the middle of a little flat. We ate our supper and were relaxing against a sun-warmed boulder in the flicker of a firelight when the first raindrops fell and hissed in the fire.

"Rain?" Peter held out his hand incredulously. The sunset had been almost cloudless.

"Rain," I said resignedly, having been whacked on my dusty bifocals with two big drops.

"I might have known," said Peter morosely. "I suspected all afternoon that your muttering and scrambling was some sort of incantation, but did it have to be a rain dance?"

"It wasn't," I retorted. "It was a hole in my left sock and I have the blister to prove it."

"Well, let's get the tarp out," said Peter. " 's probably just a sprinkle, but we might as well have something overhead."

We busied ourselves arranging our sleeping bags and stretching the tarp over them. I poured what was left of the coffee into the thermos and put the rest of the food back into the chuck box.

But it wasn't a sprinkle. The thrum on the tarp over us got louder and louder. Muffled thunder followed the flash of lightning. Rain was a solid curtain between us and the edge of our flat. I felt a flutter of alarm as the noise increased steadily. And increased again.

"Boy! This is a gulley-washer!" Peter ducked his dripping head back into the shelter after a moment's glance out in the downpour. "The bottom's dropped out of something!"

"I think it's our camp floor," I said. "I just put my hand up to the wrist in running water!"

We scrambled around bundling things back into the car. My uneasiness was increased by the stinging force of the rain on my head and shoulders as we scrambled, and by the wading we had to do to get into the car. I huddled in the front seat, plucking at the tight, wet knot of my soaked scarf as Peter slithered off in the darkness to the edge of the flat and sloshed back a little quicker than he had gone. Rain came into the car with him.

"The run-off's here already," he said. "We're marooned—on a desert island. Listen to the roar!"

Above and underlying the roar of the rain on the car roof, I could hear a deeper tone—a shaking, frightening roar of narrow sand washes trying to channel off a cloudburst.

"Oh, Peter!" My hand shook on his arm. "Are we safe here? Is this high enough?" Rain was something our area prayed for, but often when it came, it did so in such huge punishing amounts in such a short time that it was terrifying. And sometimes the Search And Rescue units retrieved bodies far downstream, not always sure whether they had died of thirst or were drowned.

"I think we're okay," Peter said. "I doubt if the whole flat would cave into the washes, but I think I'd better move the car more nearly into the middle, just in case."

"Don't get too close to that old shack," I warned, peering through a windshield the wipers couldn't clear. "We don't want to pick up a nail."

"The place was mostly 'dobe, anyway," said Peter, easing the car to a stop and setting the hand brake. "This storm'll probably finish melting it down."

We finally managed to make ourselves a little foreshortenedly comfortable in the car for the night. Peter had the back seat and I had the front. I lay warm and dry in my flannel gown—Peter despaired of ever making me a genuine camper, *A nightgown?*—my head propped on the arm rest. Pulling up the blanket, I let the drumming roar of the rain wash me past my prayers in steadily deepening waves into sleep.

The light woke me. Struggling, I freed one elbow from the cocoon of my blanket and lifted myself, gasping a little from a stiff neck. I was lost. I couldn't square the light with any light in our house nor the stiff neck with my down pillow nor the roar around me with any familiar home noise. For a moment I was floating in a directionless, timeless warm bath of Not Being. Then I pulled myself up a little higher and suddenly the car and all the circumstances were back and I blinked sleepily at the light.

The light? I sat up and fumbled for the shoe where I'd left my glasses. What was a light doing on this flat? And so close that it filled the whole of my window? I wiped my glasses on a fold of my gown and put them on. The wide myopic flare of a light concentrated then to a glow, softer, but still close. I rolled the car window down and leaned my arms on the frame.

The room was small. The floor was dirt, beaten hard by use. Rain was roaring on a tin roof and it had come in under the unpainted wooden door, darkening the sill and curling in a faintly silver wetness along one wall. A steady dripping leak from the ceilingless roof had dug a little crater in the floor in one corner and each heavy drop exploded muddily in its center. Steam plumed up from the spout of a granite-ware teakettle on the small cast-iron stove that glowed faintly pink through its small isinglass window on the front. The light was on the table. It was a kerosene lamp, its flame, turned too high, was yellow and jagged, occasionally smoking the side of the glass chimney. It was so close to me that the faint flare of light was enough to make shadowy the room beyond the table.

"It's that peripheral thing again," I thought and looked straight at the lamp. But it didn't fade out! The car did instead! I blinked, astonished. This wasn't peripheral—it was whole sight! I looked down at my folded arms. My sleeves were muddy from a damp adobe window sill.

Movement caught my attention—movement and sound. I focused on the dim interior of the room. There was an iron bedstead in the far corner. And someone was in it—in pain. And someone was by it—in fear and distress.

"It hurts! It hurts!" the jerky whisper was sexless and ageless because of pain. "Where's Jim?"

"I told you. He went to see if he could get help. Maybe Gramma Nearing or even a doctor." The voice was patient. "He can't get back because of the storm. Listen to it?"

We three listened to the roar of the flooded washes, the drum of the rain and, faintly, the plash of the leaking roof.

"I wish he was—" The voice lost its words and became a smothered, exhausted cry of pain.

I closed my eyes—and lost the sound along with the sight. I opened my eyes hastily. The room was still there, but the dampness by the door was a puddle now, swelling slowly in the lamplight. The leak in the corner was a steady trickle that had overrun its crater and become a little dust-covered snake that wandered around, seeking the lowest spot on the floor.

The person on the bed cried out again, and, tangled in the cry, came the unmistakable thin wail of the new-born. A baby! I hitched myself higher on my folded arms. My involuntary blinking as I did so moved time again in the small room. I peered into the pale light.

A woman was busy with the baby on the table. As she worked, she glanced anxiously and frequently over at the bed corner. She had reached for some baby clothes when a sound and movement from the corner snatched her away from the table so hastily that the corner of the blanket around the baby was flipped back, leaving the tiny chest uncovered. The baby's face turned blindly, and its mouth opened in a soundless cry. The soft lamplight ran across its wet, dark hair as the head turned.

"It won't stop!" I don't know whether I caught the panting words or the thought. "I can't stop the blood! Jim! Get here! God help me!"

I tried to see past the flair of light but could only sense movement. If only I could—but what could I do? I snatched my attention back to the baby. Its mouth was opening and closing in little gasping motions. Its little chest was laboring but it wasn't breathing!

"Come back!" I cried—silently?—aloud? "Come back! Quick! The baby's dying!"

The vague figure moving beyond the light paid no attention. I heard her again, desperately, "Vesta! What am I supposed to do? I can't—"

The baby was gasping still, its face shadowing over with a slatey blue. I reached. The table was beyond my finger tips. I pulled myself forward over the sill until the warped board of the wide framing cut across my stomach. My hand hovered over the baby.

Somewhere, far, far behind me, I heard Peter cry out sleepily and felt a handful of my flannel gown gathered up and pulled. But I pulled too, and, surging forward, wide-eyed, afraid to blink and thus change time again, I finally touched the thin little subsiding chest.

My reach was awkward. The fingers of my one hand were reaching beyond their ability, the other was trying to keep me balanced on the window sill as I reached. But I felt the soft, cold skin, the thin hush of the turned back blanket, the fragile baby body under my palm.

I began a sort of one-handed respiration attempt. Two hands would probably have crushed the tiny rib cage. Compress—release—compress—release. I felt sweat break out along my hairline and upper lip. It wasn't working. Peter's tug on me was more insistent. My breath cut off as the collar of my gown was pulled tightly backward.

"Peter!" I choked voicelessly. "Let me go!" I scrambled through the window, fighting every inch of the way against the backward tug, and reached for the child. There was a sudden release that staggered me across the table. Or over the table? My physical orientation was lost.

I bent over the child, tilting its small quiet face up and back. In a split second I reviewed everything I had heard or read about mouth-to-mouth resuscitation and then sent my fervent petitionary prayer into the lungs of the child with the first breath.

I had never tried this before, but I breathed—not too hard! It's a baby— and paused and breathed and paused and breathed, losing myself in the rhythm, losing my sight in a too-close blur, afraid to close my eyes.

Then there was movement! *Breathe.* And a gasp! *Breathe.* And a turning! *Breathe.* And a thin wail that strengthened and lifted and filled the room.

My eyes ached with keeping them wide and I was gasping Blessedly the room swam grayly. I thought, *Peter! Oh, Peter!* And felt a small twitch at the hem of my gown. And felt the flannel tug me back to awareness. There was a movement beyond the lamp.

"My baby." The voice was hardly audible. "Hattie, let me see my baby before I die."

"Vesta!" Hattie's voice was sharp with anxiety. "Don't talk about dying! And I can't leave you now. Not even to—"

"I want to see my baby," the faint voice persisted. "Hattie, please—"

I looked down at the still wailing child, its face, reddening with life, its clenched fists blindly beating the air. Then I was with the baby near the bed. The young face in the shadows below was a vague white blur. The baby fit into the thin curve of the young shoulder.

"I can't see!" The pale suffering face fretted in the shadows of the bed corner. "It's too dark."

Hattie whirled from the empty table, the lamp she had just lifted tilting heavy black smoke against one side of the chimney, slanting heavily in her hands. She righted it, her eyes terrified, and looked quickly back over her shoulder. Her face, steadied by the determined set of her mouth, was white as she brought the lamp to the bed, her free hand curving around the top of the chimney to cut the draft. She held the lamp high above Vesta.

Vesta weakly brought herself up to one elbow above the baby and peered down at the crumpled face and the smudge of dark hair.

"A girl," she smiled softly. "Name her Gayla, Hattie. It's a happy name. Maybe she will be—" Her face whitened and she slid slowly down from her elbow. "Oh, I wish," she whispered. "I wish I could see her grown up!"

The sound of the rain filled the silence that followed, and the tug on my own gown was no longer a tug, it was an insistence, an imperative. My gown was straining back so that I felt as if I were a figurehead on a ship. I moved involuntarily backward.

"Who came?" Vesta's fading voice was drowsy.

"There's nobody here but me." Hattie's voice jerked.

"I thought someone came." Now she was fading and the whole room was stirring like a bowl full of smoke and I was being drawn back through it, hearing Hattie's, "There's nobody here but me—"

The sound of the baby's cry cut through the rain-sound, the swirling smoke and Hattie's voice. I heard Vesta's tender crooning, "There, there, Gayla, there, there."

Then I faded—and could finally close my eyes. I faded into an intolerable stretching from adobe window sill to car window, a stretching from Then to Now, a stretching across impossibility. I felt pulled out so thin and tight that it seemed to me the sudden rush of raindrops thrummed on me as on the tightened strings of some instrument. I think I cried out. Then there was a terrific tug and a feeling of coming unstuck and then I was face down, halfway out of the car window, rain parting my hair with wet insistent hands, hearing Peter's angry, frightened voice, "Not even sense enough to come in out of the rain!"

It took quite a while to convince Peter that I was all there. And quite a time to get my wet hair dried. And to believe that there were no mud stains on the sleeves of my gown. And an even longer, disjointed time to fill Peter in on what had happened.

He didn't have much to say about what happened from his point of view. "Bless the honest flannel!" He muttered as he wrapped me in a scratchy blanket and the warmth of his arms. "I was sure it was going to tear before I could get you back. I held on like grim death with that flannel stretching like a rubber band out the window and into the dark—into nothing! There I was, like hanging onto a kite string! A flannel one! Or a fishing line! A flannel one! Wondering what would happen if I had let go? If I'd had to let go!"

We comforted each other for the unanswerable terror of the question. And I told him all of it again and together we looked once more at the memory of the white, young face floating in the darkness. And the reddening small face, topped by its smudge of black, floating in the yellow flood of lamp light.

Then I started up, crying, "Oh Peter, what did I save her for?"

"Because you couldn't let her die," he said, pulling me back.

"I don't mean why did I save her. I mean for what did I save her? For making her own way? For that's enough for her kind? For what did I save her?" I felt sorrow flood over me.

Peter took my shoulders and shook me. "Now, look here," he said sternly. "What makes you think you had anything to do with whether she lived or died? You may have been an instrument. On the other hand, you may have just wanted so badly to help that you thought you did. Don't go appointing yourself judge and jury over the worth of anyone's life. You only know the little bit that touched you. And for all you know, that little bit is all hallucination."

I caught my breath in a hiccoughy sob and blinked in the dark. "Do you think it's all hallucination?" I asked quietly.

Peter tucked me back into the curve of his shoulder. "I don't know what I think," he said. "I'm just the observer. And most likely that's all you are. Let's wait until morning before we decide.

"Go to sleep. We have hunting to do in the morning, too."

"In all this rain and mud?" I protested.

"Wait till morning," he repeated.

Long after his steady sleeping breath came and went over my head, I lay and listened to the intermittent rain on the roof—and thought.

Finally the tight knot inside me dissolved and I relaxed against Peter.

Now that I had seen Gayla born, I could let her be dead. Or I could keep her forever the dreaming child in the playhouse on the school grounds. Why I had become involved in her life, I didn't need to know any more than I needed to know why I walked through the wrong door one time and met Peter. I tucked my hand against my cheek, then roused a little. Where were my glasses?

I groped on the car floor. My shoe. Yes, the glasses were there, where I always put them when we're camping. I leaned again and slept.

Jeffty Is Five

Harlan Ellison

When I was five years old, there was a little kid I played with: Jeffty. His real name was Jeff Kinzer, and everyone who played with him called him Jeffty. We were five years old together, and we had good times playing together.

When I was five, a Clark Bar was as fat around as the gripping end of a Louisville Slugger, and pretty nearly six inches long, and they used real chocolate to coat it, and it crunched very nicely when you bit into the center, and the paper it came wrapped in smelled fresh and good when you peeled off one end to hold the bar so it wouldn't melt onto your fingers. Today, a Clark Bar is as thin as a credit card, they use something artificial and awful-tasting instead of pure chocolate, the thing is soft and soggy, it costs fifteen or twenty cents instead of a decent, correct nickel, and they wrap it so you think it's the same size it was twenty years ago, only it isn't; it's slim and ugly and nasty tasting and not worth a penny, much less fifteen or twenty cents.

When I was that age, five years old, I was sent away to my Aunt Patricia's home in Buffalo, New York, for two years. My father was going through "bad times" and Aunt Patricia was very beautiful, and had married a stockbroker. They took care of me for two years. When I was seven, I came back home and went to find Jeffty, so we could play together.

I was seven. Jeffty was still five. I didn't notice any difference. I didn't know: I was only seven.

When I was seven years old, I used to lie on my stomach in front of our Atwater-Kent radio and listen to swell stuff. I had tied the ground wire to the radiator, and I would lie there with my coloring books and my Crayolas (when there were only sixteen colors in the big box), and listen to the NBC red network: Jack Benny on the Jell-O Program, Amos 'n' Andy, Edgar Bergen and Charlie McCarthy on the Chase and Sanborn Program, One Man's Family, First Nighter; the NBC blue network: Easy Aces, the Jergens Program with Walter Winchell, Information Please, Death Valley Days; and best of all, the Mutual network with The Green Hornet, The Lone Ranger, The Shadow and Quiet Please. Today, I turn on my car radio and go from one end of the dial to the other and all I get is 100 strings orchestras, banal housewives and insipid truckers discussing their kinky sex lives with arrogant talk show hosts, country and western drivel and rock music so loud it hurts my ears.

When I was ten, my grandfather died of old age and I was "a troublesome kid," and they sent me off to military school, so I could be "taken in hand."

I came back when I was fourteen. Jeffty was still five.

When I was fourteen years old, I used to go to the movies on Saturday afternoons and a matinee was ten cents and they used real butter on the popcorn and I could always be sure of seeing a western like Lash LaRue, or Wild Bill Elliott as Red Ryder with Bobby Blake as Little Beaver, or Roy Rogers, or Johnny Mack Brown; a scary picture like *House of Horrors* with Rondo Hatton as the Strangler, or *The Cat People*, or *The Mummy*, or *I Married a Witch* with Fredric March and Veronica Lake; plus an episode of a great serial like The Shadow with Victor Jory, or Dick Tracy or Flash Gordon; and three cartoons; a James Fitzpatrick Travel-Talk; Movietone News; a singalong and, if I stayed on till evening, Bingo or Keeno; and free dishes. Today, I go to movies and see Clint Eastwood blowing people's heads apart like ripe cantaloupes.

At eighteen, I went to college. Jeffty was still five. I came back during the summers, to work at my Uncle Joe's jewelry store. Jeffty hadn't changed. Now I knew there was something different about him, something wrong, something weird. Jeffty was still five years old, not a day older.

At twenty-two, I came home for keeps. To open a Sony television franchise in town, the first one. I saw Jeffty from time to time. He was five.

Things are better in a lot of ways. People don't die from some of the old diseases any more. Cars go faster and get you there more quickly on better roads. Shirts are softer and silkier. We have paperback books even though they cost as much as a good hardcover used to. When I'm running short in the bank I can live off credit cards till things even out. But I still think we've lost a lot of good stuff. Did you know you can't buy linoleum any more, only vinyl floor covering? There's no such thing as oilcloth any more; you'll never again smell that special, sweet smell from your grandmother's kitchen. Furniture isn't made to last thirty years or longer, because they took a survey and found that young homemakers like to throw their furniture out and bring in all new, color-coded borax every seven years. Records don't feel right; they're not thick and solid like old ones, they're thin and you can bend them . . . that doesn't seem right to me. Restaurants don't serve cream in pitchers any more, just that artificial glop in little plastic tubs, and one is never enough to get coffee the right color. You can make a dent in a car fender with only a sneaker. Everywhere you go, all the towns look the same with Burger Kings and McDonald's and 7-Elevens and Taco Bells and motels and shopping centers. Things may be better, but why do I keep thinking about the past?

What I mean by five years old is not that Jeffty was retarded. I don't think that's what it was. Smart as a whip for five years old; very bright, quick, cute, a funny kid.

But he was three feet tall, small for his age, and perfectly formed: no big head, no strange jaw, none of that. A nice, normal-looking five-year-old kid. Except that he was the same age as I was: twenty-two.

When he spoke it was with the squeaking, soprano voice of a five-year-old; when he walked it was with the little hops and shuffles of a five-year-old; when he talked to you it was about the concerns of a five-year-old . . . comic books, playing soldier, using a clothespin to attach a stiff piece of cardboard to the front fork of his bike so the sound it made when the spokes hit was like a motorboat, asking questions like *why does that thing do that like that,* how high is up, how old is old, why is grass green, what's an elephant look like? At twenty-two, he was five.

Jeffty's parents were a sad pair. Because I was still a friend of Jeffty's, still let him hang around with me, sometimes took him to the county fair or miniature golf or the movies, I wound up spending time with *them.* Not that I much cared for them, because they were so awfully depressing. But then, I suppose one couldn't expect much more from the poor devils. They had an alien thing in their home, a child who had grown no older than five in twenty-two years, who provided the treasure of that special childlike state indefinitely, but who also denied them the joys of watching the child grow into a normal adult.

Five is a wonderful time of life for a little kid ... or it *can* be, if the child is relatively free of the monstrous beastliness other children indulge in. It is a time when the eyes are wide open and the patterns are not yet set; a time when one has not yet been hammered into accepting everything as immutable and hopeless; a time when the hands can not do enough, the mind can not learn enough, the world is infinite and colorful and filled with mysteries. Five is a special time before they take the questing, unquenchable, quixotic soul of the young dreamer and thrust it into dreary schoolroom boxes. A time before they take the trembling hands that want to hold everything, touch everything, figure everything out, and make them lie still on desktops. A time before people begin saying "act your age" and "grow up" or "you're behaving like a baby." It is a time when a child who acts adolescent is still cute and responsive and everyone's pet. A time of delight, of wonder, of innocence.

Jeffty had been stuck in that time, just five, just so.

But for his parents it was an ongoing nightmare from which no one—not social workers, not priests, not child psychologists, not teachers, not friends, not medical wizards, not psychiatrists, no one—could slap or shake them awake. For seventeen years their sorrow had grown through stages of parental dotage to concern, from concern to worry, from worry to fear, from fear to confusion, from confusion to anger, from anger to dislike, from dislike to naked hatred, and finally, from deepest loathing and revulsion to a stolid, depressive acceptance.

John Kinzer was a shift foreman at the Balder Tool & Die plant. He was a thirty-year man. To everyone but the man living it, his was a spectacularly uneventful life. In no way was he remarkable ... save that he had fathered a twenty-two-year-old five-year-old.

John Kinzer was a small man; soft, with no sharp angles; with pale eyes that never seemed to hold mine for longer than a few seconds. He continually shifted in his chair during conversations, and seemed to see things in the upper corners of the room, things no one else could see ... or wanted to see. I suppose the word that best suited him was *haunted*. What his life had become ... well, *haunted* suited him.

Leona Kinzer tried valiantly to compensate. No matter what hour of the day I visited, she always tried to foist food on me. And when Jeffty was in the house she was always at *him* about eating: "Honey, would you like an orange? A nice orange? Or a tangerine? I have tangerines. I could peel a tangerine for you." But there was clearly such fear in her, fear of her own child, that the offers of sustenance always had a faintly ominous tone.

Leona Kinzer had been a tall woman, but the years had bent her. She seemed always to be seeking some area of wallpapered wall or storage niche into which she could fade, adopt some chintz or rose-patterned protective coloration and hide forever in plain sight of the child's big brown eyes, pass her a hundred times a day and never realize she was there, holding her breath, invisible. She always had an apron tied around her waist, and her hands were red from cleaning. As if by maintaining the environment immaculately she could pay off her imagined sin: having given birth to this strange creature.

Neither of them watched television very much. The house was usually dead silent, not even the sibilant whispering of water in the pipes, the creaking of timbers settling, the humming of the refrigerator. Awfully silent, as if time itself had taken a detour around that house.

As for Jeffty, he was inoffensive. He lived in that atmosphere of gentle dread and dulled loathing, and if he understood it, he never remarked in any way. He played, as a child plays, and seemed happy. But he must have sensed, in the way of a five-year-old, just how alien he was in their presence.

Alien. No, that wasn't right. He was *too* human, if anything. But out of phase, out of sync with the world around him, and resonating to a different vibration than his parents, God knows. Nor would other children play with him. As they grew past him, they found him at first childish, then uninteresting, then simply frightening as their perceptions of aging became clear and they could see he was not affected by time as they were. Even the little ones, his own age, who might wander into the neighborhood, quickly came to shy away from him like a dog in the street when a car backfires.

Thus, I remained his only friend. A friend of many years. Five years. Twenty-two years. I liked him; more than I can say. And never knew exactly why. But I did, without reserve.

But because we spent time together, I found I was also—polite society— spending time with John and Leona Kinzer. Dinner, Saturday afternoons sometimes, an hour or so when I'd bring Jeffty back from a movie. They were grateful: slavishly so. It relieved them of the embarrassing chore of going out with him, of having to pretend before the world that they were loving parents with a perfectly normal, happy, attractive child. And their gratitude extended to hosting me. Hideous, every moment of their depression, hideous.

I felt sorry for the poor devils, but I despised them for their inability to love Jeffty, who was eminently lovable.

I never let on, of course, even during the evenings in their company that were awkward beyond belief.

We would sit there in the darkening living room—*always* dark or darkening, as if kept in shadow to hold back what the light might reveal to the world outside through the bright eyes of the house—we would sit and silently stare at one another. They never knew what to say to me.

"So how are things down at the plant?" I'd say to John Kinzer.

He would shrug. Neither conversation nor life suited him with any ease or grace. "Fine, just fine," he would say, finally.

And we would sit in silence again.

"Would you like a nice piece of coffee cake?" Leona would say. "I made it fresh just this morning." Or deep-dish green apple pie. Or milk and tollhouse cookies. Or a brown betty pudding.

"No, no, thank you, Mrs. Kinzer; Jeffty and I grabbed a couple of cheeseburgers on the way home." And again, silence.

Then, when the stillness and the awkwardness became too much even for them (and who knew how long that total silence reigned when they were alone, with that thing they never talked about any more, hanging between them), Leona Kinzer would say, "I think he's asleep."

John Kinzer would say, "I don't hear the radio playing."

Just so, it would go on like that, until I could politely find excuse to bolt away on some flimsy pretext. Yes, that was the way it would go on, every time, just the same . . . except once.

"I don't know what to do any more," Leona said. She began crying. "There's no change, not one day of peace."

Her husband managed to drag himself out of the old easy chair and went to her. He bent and tried to soothe her, but it was clear from the graceless way in which he touched her graying hair that the ability to be compassionate had been stunted in him. "Shhh, Leona, it's all right. Shhh." But she continued crying. Her hands scraped gently at the antimacassars on the arms of the chair.

Then she said, "Sometimes I wish he had been stillborn."

John looked up into the corners of the room. For the nameless shadows that were always watching him? Was it God he was seeking in those spaces? "You don't mean that," he said to her, softly, pathetically, urging her with body tension and trembling in his voice to recant before God took notice of the terrible thought. But she meant it; she meant it very much.

I managed to get away quickly that evening. They didn't want witnesses to their shame. I was glad to go.

And for a week I stayed away. From them, from Jeffty, from their street, even from that end of town.

I had my own life. The store, accounts, suppliers' conferences, poker with friends, pretty women I took to well-lit restaurants, my own parents, putting anti-freeze in the car, complaining to the laundry about too much starch in the collars and cuffs, working out at the gym, taxes, catching Jan or David (whichever one it was) stealing from the cash register. I had my own life.

But not even *that* evening could keep me from Jeffty. He called me at the store and asked me to take him to the rodeo. We chummed it up as best a twenty-two-year-old with other interests *could*...with a five-year-old. I never dwelled on what bound us together; I always thought it was simply the years. That, and affection for a kid who could have been the little brother I never had. (Except I *remembered* when we had played together, when we had both been the same age; I *remembered* that period, and Jeffty was still the same.)

And then, one Saturday afternoon, I came to take him to a double feature, and things I should have noticed so many times before, I first began to notice only that afternoon.

I came walking up to the Kinzer house, expecting Jeffty to be sitting on the front porch steps, or in the porch glider, waiting for me. But he was nowhere in sight.

Going inside, into that darkness and silence, in the midst of May sunshine, was unthinkable. I stood on the front walk for a few moments, then cupped my hands around my mouth and yelled, "Jeffty? Hey, Jeffty, come on out, let's go. We'll be late."

His voice came faintly, as if from under the ground.

"Here I am, Donny."

I could hear him, but I couldn't see him. It was Jeffty, no question about it: as Donald H. Horton, President and Sole Owner of The Horton TV & Sound Center, no one but Jeffty called me Donny. He had never called me anything else.

(Actually, it isn't a lie. I *am,* as far as the public is concerned, Sole Owner of the Center. The partnership with my Aunt Patricia is only to repay the loan she made me, to supplement the money I came into when I was twenty-one, left to me when I was ten by my grandfather. It wasn't a very big loan, only eighteen thousand, but I asked her to be a silent partner, because of when she had taken care of me as a child.)

"Where are you, Jeffty?"

"Under the porch in my secret place."

I walked around the side of the porch, and stooped down and pulled away the wicker grating. Back in there, on the pressed dirt, Jeffty had built himself a secret place. He had comics in orange crates, he had a little table and some pillows, it was lit by big fat candles, and we used to hide there when we were both...five.

"What'cha up to?" I asked, crawling in and pulling the grate closed behind me. It was cool under the porch, and the dirt smelled comfortable, the candles smelled clubby and familiar. Any kid would feel at home in such a secret place: there's never been a kid who didn't spend the happiest, most productive, most deliciously mysterious times of his life in such a secret place.

"Playin'," he said. He was holding something golden and round. It filled the palm of his little hand.

"You forget we were going to the movies?"

"Nope. I was just waitin' for you here."

"Your mom and dad home?"

"Momma."

I understood why he was waiting under the porch. I didn't push it any further. "What've you got there?"

"Captain Midnight Secret Decoder Badge," he said, showing it to me on his flattened palm.

I realized I was looking at it without comprehending what it was for a long time. Then it dawned on me what a miracle Jeffty had in his hand. A miracle that simply could *not* exist.

"Jeffty," I said softly, with wonder in my voice, "where'd you get that?"

"Came in the mail today. I sent away for it."

"It must have cost a lot of money."

"Not so much. Ten cents an' two inner wax seals from two jars of Ovaltine."

"May I see it?" My voice was trembling, and so was the hand I extended. He gave it to me and I held the miracle in the palm of my hand. It was *wonderful* .

You remember. *Captain Midnight* went on the radio nationwide in 1940. It was sponsored by Ovaltine. And every year they issued a Secret Squadron Decoder Badge. And every day at the end of the program, they would give you a clue to the next day's installment in a code that only kids with the official badge could decipher. They stopped making those wonderful Decoder Badges in 1949. I remember the one I had in 1945: it was beautiful. It had a magnifying glass in the center of the code dial. *Captain Midnight* went off the air in 1950, and though I understand it was a short-lived television series in the mid-fifties, and though they issued Decoder Badges in 1955 and 1956, as far as the *real* badges were concerned, they never made one after 1949.

The Captain Midnight Code-O-Graph I held in my hand, the one Jeffty said he had gotten in the mail for ten cents *(ten cents!!!)* and two Ovaltine labels, was brand new, shiny gold metal, not a dent or a spot of rust on it like the old ones you can find at exorbitant prices in collectible shoppes from time to time . . . it was a *new* Decoder. And the date on it was *this* year.

But *Captain Midnight* no longer existed. Nothing like it existed on the radio. I'd listened to the one or two weak imitations of old-time radio the networks were currently airing, and the stories were dull, the sound effects bland, the whole feeling of it wrong, out of date, cornball. Yet I held a *new* Code-O-Graph.

"Jeffty, tell me about this," I said.

"Tell you what, Donny? It's my new Capt'n Midnight Secret Decoder Badge. I use it to figger out what's gonna happen tomorrow."

"Tomorrow how?"

"On the program."

"What program?!"

He stared at me as if I was being purposely stupid. "On Capt'n *Mid*night! Boy!" I was being dumb.

I still couldn't get it straight. It was right there, right out in the open, and I still didn't know what was happening. "You mean one of those records they made of the old-time radio programs? Is that what you mean, Jeffty?"

"What records?" he asked. He didn't know what *I* meant.

We stared at each other, there under the porch. And then I said, very slowly, almost afraid of the answer, "Jeffty, how do you hear *Captain Midnight?"*

"Every day. On the radio. On my radio. Every day at five-thirty."

News. Music, dumb music, and news. That's what was on the radio every day at 5:30. Not *Captain Midnight*. The Secret Squadron hadn't been on the air in twenty years

"Can we hear it tonight?" I asked.

"Boy!" he said. I was being dumb. I knew it from the way he said it; but I didn't know *why.* Then it dawned on me: this was Saturday. *Captain Midnight* was on Monday through Friday. Not on Saturday or Sunday.

"We goin' to the movies?"

He had to repeat himself twice. My mind was somewhere else. Nothing definite. No conclusions. No wild assumptions leapt to. Just off somewhere trying to figure it out, and concluding—as *you* would have concluded, as *any*one would have concluded rather than accepting the truth, the impossible and wonderful truth—just finally concluding there was a simple explanation I didn't yet perceive. Something mundane and dull, like the passage of time that steals all good, old things from us, packratting trinkets and plastic in exchange. And all in the name of Progress.

"We goin' to the movies, Donny?"

"You bet your boots we are, kiddo," I said. And I smiled. And I handed him the Code-O-Graph. And he put it in his side pants pocket. And we crawled out from under the porch. And we went to the movies. And neither of us said anything about *Captain Midnight* all the rest of that day. And there wasn't a ten-minute stretch, all the rest of that day, that I didn't think about it.

It was inventory all that next week. I didn't see Jeffty till late Thursday. I confess I left the store in the hands of Jan and David, told them I had some errands to run, and left early. At 4:00. I got to the Kinzers' right around 4:45. Leona answered the door, looking exhausted and distant. "Is Jeffty around?" She said he was upstairs in his room . . .

. . . listening to the radio.

I climbed the stairs two at a time.

All right, I had finally made that impossible, illogical leap. Had the stretch of belief involved anyone but Jeffty, adult or child, I would have reasoned out more explicable answers. But it *was* Jeffty, clearly another kind of vessel of life, and what he might experience should not be expected to fit into the ordered scheme.

I admit it: I *wanted* to hear what I heard.

Even with the door closed, I recognized the program.

"There he goes, Tennessee! Get him!"

There was the heavy report of a squirrel-rifle shot and the keening whine of the slug ricocheting, and then the same voice yelled triumphantly, *"Got him! D-e-a-a-a-d center!"*

He was listening to the American Broadcasting Company, 790 kilohertz, and he was hearing *Tennessee Jed,* one of my most favorite programs from the forties, a western adventure I had not heard in twenty years, because it had not existed for twenty years.

I sat down on the top step of the stairs, there in the upstairs hall of the Kinzer home, and I listened to the show. It wasn't a rerun of an old program; I knew every one of them by heart, had never missed an episode. Further evidence that this was a new installment: there were occasional references during the integrated commercials to current cultural and technological developments, and phrases that had not existed in common usage in the forties: aerosol spray cans, laserasing of tattoos, Tanzania, the word "uptight."

I couldn't ignore it. Jeffty was listening to a *new* segment of *Tennessee Jed.*

I ran downstairs and out the front door to my car. Leona must have been in the kitchen. I turned the key and punched on the radio and spun the dial to 790 kilohertz. The ABC station. Rock music.

I sat there for a few moments, then ran the dial slowly from one end to the other. Music, news, talk shows. No *Tennessee Jed.* And it was a

Blaupunkt, the best radio I could get. I wasn't missing some perimeter station. It simply was not there!

After a few moments I turned off the radio and the ignition and went back upstairs quietly. I sat down on the top step and listened to the entire program. It was *wonderful*.

Exciting, imaginative, filled with everything I remembered as being most innovative about radio drama. But it was modern. It wasn't an antique, rebroadcast to assuage the need of that dwindling listenership who longed for the old days. It was a new show, with all the old voices, but still young and bright. Even the commercials were for currently available products, but they weren't as loud or as insulting as the screamer ads one heard on radio these days.

And when *Tennessee Jed* went off at 5:00, I heard Jeffty spin the dial on his radio till I heard the familiar voice of the announcer Glenn Riggs proclaim, *"Presenting Hop Harrigan! America's ace of the airwaves!"* There was the sound of an airplane in flight. It was a prop plane, *not* a jet! Not the sound kids today have grown up with, but the sound *I* grew up with, the *real* sound of an airplane, the growling, revving, throaty sound of the kind of airplanes G-8 and His Battle Aces flew, the kind Captain Midnight flew, the kind Hop Harrigan flew. And then I heard Hop say, *"CX-4 calling control tower. CX-4 calling control tower. Standing by!"* A pause, then, *"Okay, this is Hop Harrigan . . . coming in!"*

And Jeffty, who had the same problem all of us kids had had in the forties with programming that pitted equal favorites against one another on different stations, having paid his respects to Hop Harrigan and Tank Tinker, spun the dial and went back to ABC, where I heard the stroke of a gong, the wild cacophony of nonsense Chinese chatter, and the announcer yelled, *"T-e-e-e-rry and the Pirates!"*

I sat there on the top step and listened to Terry and Connie and Flip Corkin and, so help me God, Agnes Moorehead as the Dragon Lady, all of them in a new adventure that took place in a Red China that had not existed in the days of Milton Caniff's 1937 version of the Orient, with river pirates and Chiang Kai-shek and warlords and the naive Imperialism of American gunboat diplomacy.

Sat, and listened to the whole show, and sat even longer to hear *Superman* and part of *Jack Armstrong, the All-American Boy* and part of *Captain Midnight*, and John Kinzer came home and neither he nor Leona came upstairs to find out what had happened to me, or where Jeffty was, and sat longer, and found I had started crying, and could not stop, just sat there with tears running down my face, into the corners of my mouth, sitting and crying until Jeffty heard me and opened his door and saw me and came out and looked at me in childish confusion as I heard the station break for the Mutual Network and they began the theme music of *Tom Mix*, "When It's Round-up Time in Texas and the Bloom Is on the Sage," and Jeffty touched my shoulder and smiled at me, with his mouth and his big brown eyes, and said, "Hi, Donny. Wanna come in an' listen to the radio with me?"

Hume denied the existence of an absolute space, in which each thing has its place; Borges denies the existence of one single time, in which all events are linked.

Jeffty received radio programs from a place that could not, in logic, in the natural scheme of the space-time universe as conceived by Einstein, exist. But that wasn't all he received. He got mail-order premiums that no one was manufacturing. He read comic books that had been defunct for three decades. He saw movies with actors who had been dead for twenty years. He was the receiving terminal for endless joys and pleasures of the past that the world had dropped along the way. On its headlong suicidal flight toward New Tomorrows, the world had razed its treasurehouse of simple happinesses, had poured concrete over its playgrounds, had abandoned its elfin stragglers, and all of it was being impossibly, miraculously shunted back into the present through Jeffty. Revivified, updated, the traditions maintained but contemporaneous. Jeffty was the unbidding Aladdin whose very nature formed the magic lampness of his reality.

And he took me into his world with him.

Because he trusted me.

We had breakfast of Quaker Puffed Wheat Sparkies and warm Ovaltine we drank out of *this* year's Little Orphan Annie Shake-Up Mugs. We went to the movies and while everyone else was seeing a comedy starring Goldie Hawn and Ryan O'Neal, Jeffty and I were enjoying Humphrey Bogart as the professional thief Parker in John Huston's brilliant adaptation of the Donald Westlake novel *Slayground*. The second feature was Spencer Tracy, Carole Lombard and Laird Cregar in the Val Lewton-produced film of *Leinengen Versus the Ants*.

Twice a month we went down to the newsstand and bought the current pulp issues of *The Shadow, Doc Savage* and *Startling Stories*. Jeffty and I sat together and I read to him from the magazines. He particularly liked the new short novel by Henry Kuttner, *The Dreams of Achilles,* and the new Stanley G. Weinbaum series of short stories set in the subatomic particle universe of Redurna. In September we enjoyed the first installment of the new Robert E. Howard Conan novel, ISLE OF THE BLACK ONES, in *Weird Tales;* and in August we were only mildly disappointed by Edgar Rice Burroughs's fourth novella in the Jupiter series featuring John Carter of

Barsoom—"Corsairs of Jupiter." But the editor of *Argosy All-Story Weekly* promised there would be two more stories in the series, and it was such an unexpected revelation for Jeffty and me that it dimmed our disappointment at the lessened quality of the current story.

We read comics together, and Jeffty and I both decided—separately, before we came together to discuss it—that our favorite characters were Doll Man, Airboy and The Heap. We also adored the George Carlson strips in *Jingle Jangle Comics*, particularly the Pie-Face Prince of Old Pretzleburg stories, which we read together and laughed over, even though I had to explain some of the esoteric puns to Jeffty, who was too young to have that kind of subtle wit.

How to explain it? I can't. I had enough physics in college to make some offhand guesses, but I'm more likely wrong than right. The laws of the conservation of energy occasionally break. These are laws that physicists call "weakly violated." Perhaps Jeffty was a catalyst for the weak violation of conservation laws we're only now beginning to realize exist. I tried doing some reading in the area—muon decay of the "forbidden" kind: gamma decay that doesn't include the muon neutrino among its products—but nothing I encountered, not even the latest readings from the Swiss Institute for Nuclear Research near Zurich gave me an insight. I was thrown back on a vague acceptance of the philosophy that the real name for "science" is *magic*.

No explanations, but enormous good times.

The happiest time of my life.

I had the "real" world, the world of my store and my friends and my family, the world of profit&loss, of taxes and evenings with young women who talked about going shopping or the United Nations, of the rising cost of coffee and microwave ovens. And I had Jeffty's world, in which I existed only when I was with him. The things of the past he knew as fresh and new, I could experience only when in his company. And the membrane between the two worlds grew ever thinner, more luminous and transparent. I had the best of both worlds. And knew, somehow, that I could carry nothing from one to the other.

Forgetting for just a moment, betraying Jeffty by forgetting, brought an end to it all.

Enjoying myself so much, I grew careless and failed to consider how fragile the relationship between Jeffty's world and my world really was. There is a reason why the present begrudges the existence of the past. I never really understood. Nowhere in the beast books, where survival is shown in battles between claw and fang, tentacle and poison sac, is there recognition of the ferocity the present always brings to bear on the past. Nowhere is there a detailed statement of how the Present lies in wait for

What-Was, waiting for it to become Now-This-Moment so it can shred it
with its merciless jaws.

Who could know such a thing . . . at any age . . . and certainly not at my
age . . . who could understand such a thing?

I'm trying to exculpate myself. I can't. It was my fault.

It was another Saturday afternoon.

"What's playing today?" I asked him, in the car, on the way downtown.

He looked up at me from the other side of the front seat and smiled one
of his best smiles. "Ken Maynard in *Bullwhip Justice* an' *The Demolished
Man*." He kept smiling, as if he'd really put one over on me. I looked at him
with disbelief.

"You're *kid*ding!" I said, delighted. "Bester's THE DEMOLISHED
MAN?" He nodded his head, delighted at my being delighted. He knew it
was one of my favorite books. "Oh, that's super!"

"Super *duper*," he said.

"Who's in it?"

"Franchot Tone, Evelyn Keyes, Lionel Barrymore and Elisha Cook, Jr."
He was much more knowledgeable about movie actors than I'd ever been.
He could name the character actors in any movie he'd ever seen. Even the
crowd scenes.

"And cartoons?" I asked.

"Three of 'em: a *Little Lulu*, a *Donald Duck* and a *Bugs Bunny*. An' a *Pete
Smith Specialty* an' a Lew Lehr *Monkeys is da C-r-r-r-aziest Peoples*."

"Oh boy!" I said. I was grinning from ear to ear. And then I looked down
and saw the pad of purchase order forms on the seat. I'd forgotten to drop it
off at the store.

"Gotta stop by the Center," I said. "Gotta drop off something. It'll only
take a minute."

"Okay," Jeffty said. "But we won't be late, will we?"

"Not on your tintype, kiddo," I said.

When I pulled into the parking lot behind the Center, he decided to come
in with me and we'd walk over to the theater. It's not a large town. There
are only two movie houses, the Utopia and the Lyric. We were going to the
Utopia and it was only three blocks from the Center.

I walked into the store with the pad of forms, and it was bedlam. David
and Jan were handling two customers each, and there were people standing
around waiting to be helped. Jan turned a look on me and her face was a
horror-mask of pleading. David was running from the stockroom to the
showroom and all he could murmur as he whipped past was "Help!" and
then he was gone.

"Jeffty," I said, crouching down, "listen, give me a few minutes. Jan and David are in trouble with all these people. We won't be late, I promise. Just let me get rid of a couple of these customers." He looked nervous, but nodded okay.

I motioned to a chair and said, "Just sit down for a while and I'll be right with you."

He went to the chair, good as you please, though he knew what was happening, and he sat down.

I started taking care of people who wanted color television sets. This was the first really substantial batch of units we'd gotten in—color television was only now becoming reasonably priced and this was Sony's first promotion—and it was bonanza time for me. I could see paying off the loan and being out in front for the first time with the Center. It was business.

In my world, good business comes first.

Jeffty sat there and stared at the wall. Let me tell you about the wall.

Stanchion and bracket designs had been rigged from the floor to within two feet of the ceiling. Television sets had been stacked artfully on the wall. Thirty-three television sets. All playing at the same time. Black and white, color, little ones, big ones, all going at the same time.

Jeffty sat and watched thirty-three television sets, on a Saturday afternoon. We can pick up a total of thirteen channels including the UHF educational stations. Golf was on one channel; baseball was on a second; celebrity bowling was on a third; the fourth channel was a religious seminar; a teen-age dance show was on the fifth; the sixth was a rerun of a situation comedy; the seventh was a rerun of a police show; eighth was a nature program showing a man flycasting endlessly; ninth was news and conversation; tenth was a stock car race; eleventh was a man doing logarithms on a blackboard; twelfth was a woman in a leotard doing sitting-up exercises; and on the thirteenth channel was a badly animated cartoon show in Spanish. All but six of the shows were repeated on three sets. Jeffty sat and watched that wall of television on a Saturday afternoon while I sold as fast and as hard as I could, to pay back my Aunt Patricia and stay in touch with my world. It was business.

I should have known better. I should have understood about the present and the way it kills the past. But I was selling with both hands. And when I finally glanced over at Jeffty, half an hour later, he looked like another child.

He was sweating. That terrible fever sweat when you have stomach flu. He was pale, as pasty and pale as a worm, and his little hands were gripping the arms of the chair so tightly I could see his knuckles in bold relief. I dashed over to him, excusing myself from the middle-aged couple looking at the new 21" Mediterranean model.

"Jeffty!"

He looked at me, but his eyes didn't track. He was in absolute terror. I pulled him out of the chair and started toward the front door with him, but the customers I'd deserted yelled at me, "Hey!" The middle-aged man said, "You wanna sell me this thing or don't you?"

I looked from him to Jeffty and back again. Jeffty was like a zombie. He had come where I'd pulled him. His legs were rubbery and his feet dragged. The past being eaten by the present, the sound of something in pain.

I clawed some money out of my pants pocket and jammed it into Jeffty's hand. "Kiddo...listen to me...get out of here right now!" He still couldn't focus properly. *"Jeffty,"* I said as tightly as I could, *"listen* to me!" The middle-aged customer and his wife were walking toward us. "Listen, kiddo, get out of here right this minute. Walk over to the Utopia and buy the tickets. I'll be right behind you." The middle-aged man and his wife were almost on us. I shoved Jeffty through the door and watched him stumble away in the wrong direction, then stop as if gathering his wits, turn and go back past the front of the Center and in the direction of the Utopia. "Yes, sir," I said, straightening up and facing them, "yes, ma'am, that is one terrific set with some sen*sa*tional features! If you'll just step back here with me..."

There was a terrible sound of something hurting, but I couldn't tell from which channel, or from which set, it was coming.

Most of it I learned later, from the girl in the ticket booth, and from some people I knew who came to me to tell me what had happened. By the time I got to the Utopia, nearly twenty minutes later, Jeffty was already beaten to a pulp and had been taken to the manager's office.

"Did you see a very little boy, about five years old, with big brown eyes and straight brown hair...he was waiting for me?"

"Oh, I think that's the little boy those kids beat up?"

"What!?! *Where is he?*"

"They took him to the manager's office. No one knew who he was or where to find his parents—"

A young girl wearing an usher's uniform was kneeling down beside the couch, placing a wet paper towel on his face.

I took the towel away from her and ordered her out of the office. She looked insulted and snorted something rude, but she left. I sat on the edge of the couch and tried to swab away the blood from the lacerations without opening the wounds where the blood had caked. Both his eyes were swollen shut. His mouth was ripped badly. His hair was matted with dried blood.

He had been standing in line behind two kids in their teens. They started selling tickets at 12:30 and the show started at 1:00. The doors weren't opened till 12:45. He had been waiting, and the kids in front of him had had a portable radio. They were listening to the ball game. Jeffty had wanted to hear some program, God knows what it might have been, *Grand Central Station, Let's Pretend, The Land of the Lost,* God only knows which one it might have been.

He had asked if he could borrow their radio to hear the program for a minute, and it had been a commercial break or something, and the kids had given him the radio, probably out of some malicious kind of courtesy that would permit them to take offense and rag the little boy. He had changed the station . . . and they'd been unable to get it to go back to the ball game. It was locked into the past, on a station that was broadcasting a program that didn't exist for anyone but Jeffty.

They had beaten him badly . . . as everyone watched.

And then they had run away.

I had left him alone, left him to fight off the present without sufficient weaponry. I had betrayed him for the sale of a 21″ Mediterranean console television, and now his face was pulped meat. He moaned something inaudible and sobbed softly.

"Shhh, it's okay, kiddo, it's Donny. I'm here. I'll get you home, it'll be okay."

I should have taken him straight to the hospital. I don't know why I didn't. I should have. I should have done that.

When I carried him through the door, John and Leona Kinzer just stared at me. They didn't move to take him from my arms. One of his hands was hanging down. He was conscious, but just barely. They stared, there in the semi-darkness of a Saturday afternoon in the present. I looked at them. "A couple of kids beat him up at the theater." I raised him a few inches in my arms and extended him. They stared at me, at both of us, with nothing in their eyes, without movement. "Jesus Christ," I shouted, "he's been beaten! He's your son! Don't you even want to touch him? What the hell kind of people are you?!"

Then Leona moved toward me very slowly. She stood in front of us for a few seconds, and there was a leaden stoicism in her face that was terrible to see. It said, *I have been in this place before, many times, and I cannot bear to be in it again; but I am here now.*

So I gave him to her. God help me, I gave him over to her.

And she took him upstairs to bathe away his blood and his pain.

John Kinzer and I stood in our separate places in the dim living room of their home, and we stared at each other. He had nothing to say to me.

I shoved past him and fell into a chair. I was shaking.

I heard the bath water running upstairs.

After what seemed a very long time Leona came downstairs, wiping her hands on her apron. She sat down on the sofa and after a moment John sat down beside her. I heard the sound of rock music from upstairs.

"Would you like a piece of nice pound cake?" Leona said.

I didn't answer. I was listening to the sound of the music. Rock music. On the radio. There was a table lamp on the end table beside the sofa. It cast a dim and futile light in the shadowed living room. *Rock music from the present, on a radio upstairs?* I started to say something, and then *knew . . .* Oh, God . . . *no!*

I jumped up just as the sound of hideous crackling blotted out the music, and the table lamp dimmed and dimmed and flickered. I screamed something, I don't know what it was, and ran for the stairs.

Jeffty's parents did not move. They sat there with their hands folded, in that place they had been for so many years.

I fell twice rushing up the stairs.

There isn't much on television that can hold my interest. I bought an old cathedral-shaped Philco radio in a second-hand store, and I replaced all the burnt-out parts with the original tubes from old radios I could cannibalize that still worked. I don't use transistors or printed circuits. They wouldn't work. I've sat in front of that set for hours sometimes, running the dial back and forth as slowly as you can imagine, so slowly it doesn't look as if it's moving at all sometimes.

But I can't find *Captain Midnight* or *The Land of the Lost* or *The Shadow* or *Quiet, Please.*

So she did love him, still, a little bit, even after all those years. I can't hate them: they only wanted to live in the present world again. That isn't such a terrible thing.

It's a good world, all things considered. It's much better than it used to be, in a lot of ways. People don't die from the old diseases any more. They die from new ones, but that's Progress, isn't it?

Isn't it?

Tell me.

Somebody please tell me.

Within the Walls of Tyre

Michael Bishop

As she eased her Nova into the lane permitting access to the perimeter highway, Marilyn Odau reflected that the hardest time of year for her was the Christmas season. From late November to well into January her nerves were invariably as taut as harp strings. The traffic on the expressway— lane-jumping vans and pickups, sleek sports cars, tailgating semis, and all the blurred, indistinguishable others—was no help, either. Even though she could see her hands on the wheel, trembling inside beige, leather-tooled gloves, her Nova seemed hardly to be under her control; instead, it was a piece of machinery given all its impetus and direction by an invisible slot in the concrete beneath it. Her illusion of control was exactly that—an illusion.

Looking quickly over her left shoulder, Marilyn Odau had to laugh at herself as she yanked the automobile around a bearded young man on a motorcycle. If your car's in someone else's control, why is it so damn hard to steer?

Nerves; balky Yuletide nerves.

Marilyn Odau was fifty-five; she had lived in this city—*her* city—ever since leaving Greenville during the first days of World War II to begin her

489

own life and to take a job clerking at Satterwhite's. Ten minutes ago, before reaching the perimeter highway, she had passed through the heart of the city and driven beneath the great, gray cracking backside of Satterwhite's (which was now a temporary warehouse for an electronics firm located in a suburban industrial complex). Like the heart of the city itself, Satterwhite's was dead—its great silver escalators, its pneumatic message tubes, its elevator bell tones, and its perfume-scented mezzanines as surely things of the past as ... well, as Tojo, Tarawa Atoll, and a young marine named Jordan Burk. That was why, particularly at this time of year, Marilyn never glanced at the old department store as she drove beneath it on her way to Summerstone.

For the past two years she had been the manager of the Creighton's Corner Boutique at Summerstone Mall, the largest self-contained shopping facility in the five-county metropolitan area. Business had been shifting steadily, for well over a decade, from downtown to suburban and even quasi-rural commercial centers. And when a position had opened up for her at the new tri-level mecca bewilderingly dubbed Summerstone, Marilyn had shifted too, moving from Creighton's original franchise near Capitol Square to a second-level shop in an acre-square monolith sixteen miles to the city's northwest—a building more like a starship hangar than a shopping center.

Soon, she supposed, she ought also to shift residences. There were town houses closer to Summerstone, after all, with names just as ersatz-elegant as that of the Brookmist complex in which she now lived: Chateau Royale, Springhaven, Tivoli, Smoke Glade, Eden Manor, Sussex Wood... *There,* she told herself, glancing sidelong at the Matterhorn Heights complex nestled below the highway to her left, its cheesebox-and-cardboard-shingle chalets distorted by a teepee of glaring window panes on a glass truck cruising abreast of her.

Living at Matterhorn Heights would have put Marilyn fifteen minutes closer to her job, but it would have meant enduring a gaudier lapse of taste than she had opted for at Brookmist. There were degrees of artificiality, she knew, and each person found his own level... Above her, a green and white highway sign indicated the Willowglen and Summerstone exits. Surprised as always by its sudden appearance, she wrestled the Nova into an off-ramp lane and heard behind her the inevitable blaring of horns.

Pack it in, she told the driver on her bumper—an expression she had learned from Jane Sidney, one of her employees at the boutique. Pack it in, laddie.

Intent on the traffic light at the end of the off-ramp, conscious too of the wetness under the arms of her pantsuit jacket, Marilyn managed to giggle at the incongruous *feel* of these words. In her rearview mirror she could see the angry features of a modishly long-haired young man squinting at her over the hood of a Le Mans—and it was impossible to imagine herself confronting him, outside their automobiles, with the imperative, "Pack it in, laddie!" Absolutely impossible. All she could do was giggle at the thought and jab nervously at her clutch and brake pedals. Morning traffic—Christmas traffic—was bearable only if you remembered that impatience was a self-punishing sin.

At 8:50 she reached Summerstone and found a parking place near a battery of army-green trash bins. A security-guard was passing in mall employees through a second-tier entrance near Montgomery-Ward's; and when Marilyn showed him her ID card, he said almost by way of ritual shibboleth, "Have a good day, Miss Odau." Then, with a host of people to whom she never spoke, she was on the enclosed promenade of machined wooden beams and open carpeted shops. As always, the hour could have been high noon or twelve midnight—there was no way to tell. The season was identifiable only because of the winter merchandise on display and the Christmas decorations suspended overhead or twining like tinfoil helixes through the central shaft of the mall. The smells of ammonia, confectionary goods, and perfumes commingled piquantly, even at this early hour, but Marilyn scarcely noticed.

Managing Creighton's Corner had become her life, the enterprise for which she lived; and because Summerstone contained Creighton's Corner, she went into it daily with less philosophical scrutiny than a coal miner gives his mine. Such speculation, Marilyn knew from thirty-five years on her own, was worse than useless—it imprisoned you in doubts and misapprehensions largely of your own devising. She was glad to be but a few short steps from Creighton's, glad to feel her funk disintegrating beneath the prospect of an efficient day at work....

"Good morning, Ms. Odau," Jane Sidney said as she entered Creighton's.

"Good morning. You look nice today."

The girl was wearing a green and gold jersey, a kind of gaucho skirt of imitation leather, and suede boots. Her hair was not much longer than a military cadet's. She always pronounced "Ms." as a muted buzz—either out of feminist conviction or, more likely, her fear that "Miss" would betray her more-than-middle-aged superior as unmarried ... as if that were a shameful thing in one of Marilyn's generation. Only Cissy Campbell of the three girls who worked in the boutique could address her as "Miss Odau" without looking flustered. Or maybe Marilyn imagined this. She didn't try to plumb the personal feelings of her employees, and they in turn didn't try to cast her in the role of a mother confessor. They liked her well enough, though. Everyone got along.

"I'm working for Cissy until three, Ms. Odau. We've traded shifts. Is that all right?" Jane followed her toward her office.

"Of course it is. What about Terri?"

The walls were mercury-colored mirrors; there were mirrors overhead. Racks of swirl-patterned jerseys, erotically tailored jumpsuits, and flamboyant scarves were reiterated around them like the refrain of a toothpaste or cola jingle. Macramé baskets with plastic flowers and exotic bath soaps hung from the ceiling. Black-light and pop-art posters went in and out on the walls, even though they never moved—and looking up at one of them, Marilyn had a vision of Satterwhite's during the austere days of 1942-43, when the war had begun to put money in people's pockets for the first time since the twenties but it was unpatriotic to spend it. She remembered the Office of Price Administration and ration-stamp booklets. Because of leather shortages, you couldn't have more than two pairs of shoes a year....

Jane was looking at her fixedly.

"I'm sorry, Jane. I didn't hear you."

"I said Terri'll be here at twelve, but she wants to work all day tomorrow too, if that's okay. There aren't any Tuesday classes at City College, and she wants to get in as many hours as she can before final exams come up." Terri was still relatively new to the boutique.

"Of course, that's fine. Won't you be here too?"

"Yes, ma'am. In the afternoon."

"Okay, good.... I've got some order forms to look over and a letter or two to write." She excused herself and went behind a tie-dyed curtain into an office as plain and practical as Creighton's decor was peacockish and orgiastic. She sat down to a small metal filing cabinet with an audible moan—a moan at odds with the satisfaction she felt in getting down to work. What was wrong with her? She knew, she knew, dear God wasn't she perfectly aware.... Marilyn pulled her gloves off. As her fingers went to the onion-skin order forms and bills of lading in her files, she was surprised by the deep oxblood color of her nails. Why? She had worn this polish for a week, since well before Thanksgiving....

The answer of course was Maggie Hood. During the war Marilyn and Maggie had roomed together in a clapboard house not far from Satterwhite's, a house with two poplars in the small front yard but not a single blade of grass. Maggie had worked for the telephone company (an irony, since they had no phone in their house), and she always wore oxblood nail polish. Several months before the Axis surrender, Maggie married a 4-F telephone-company official and moved to Mobile. The little house on Greenbriar Street was torn down during the mid-fifties to make way for an office building. Maggie Hood and oxblood nail polish—

Recollections that skirted the heart of the matter, Marilyn knew. She shook them off and got down to business.

Tasteful rock was playing in the boutique, something from Stevie Wonder's *Songs in the Key of Life*—Jane had flipped the music on. Through it, Marilyn could hear the morning herds passing along the concourses and interior bridges of Summerstone. Sometimes it seemed that half the population of the state was out there. Twice the previous Christmas season the structural vibrations had become so worrisome that security-guards were ordered to keep new shoppers out until enough people had left to avert the danger of collapse. That was the rumor, anyway, and Marilyn almost believed it. Summerstone's several owners, on the other hand, claimed that the doors had been locked simply to minimize crowding. But how many times did sane business people turn away customers solely to "minimize crowding"?

Marilyn helped Jane wait on shoppers until noon. Then Terri Bready arrived, and she went back to her office. Instead of eating she checked outstanding accounts and sought to square away records. She kept her mind wholly occupied with the minutiae of running her business for its semi-retired owners, Charlie and Agnes Creighton. It didn't bother her at all that they were ten years younger than she, absentee landlords with a condominium apartment on the Gulf Coast. She did a good job for them, working evenings as well as lunch hours, and the Creightons were smart enough to realize her worth. They trusted her completely and paid her well.

At one o'clock Terri Bready stepped through Marilyn's curtain and made an apologetic noise in her throat.

"Hey, Terri. What is it?"

"There's a salesman out here who'd like to see you." Bending a business card between her thumb and forefinger, the girl gave an odd baritone chuckle. Tawny-haired and lean, she was a freshman drama major who made the most fashionable clothes look like off-the-racks from a Salvation Army outlet. But she was sweet—so sweet that Marilyn had been embarrassed to hear her discussing with Cissy Campbell the boy she was living with.

"Is he someone we regularly buy from, Terri?"

"I don't know. I don't know who we buy from."

"Is that his card?"

"Yeah, it is."

"Why don't you let me see it, then?"

"Oh. Okay. Sorry, Ms. Odau. Here." Trying to hand it over, the girl popped the card out of her fingers; it struck Marilyn's chest and fluttered into her lap. "Sorry again. Sheesh, I really am." Terri chuckled her baritone chuckle and Marilyn, smiling briefly, retrieved the card.

It said: *Nicholas Anson / Products Consultant & Sales Representative / Latter-Day Novelties / Los Angeles, California.* Also on the card were two telephone numbers and a zip code.

Terri Bready wet her lips with her tongue. "He's a hunk, Ms. Odau, I'm not kidding you—he's as pretty as a naked Swede."

"Is that right? How old?"

"Oh, he's too old for me. He's got to be in his thirties at least."

"Decrepit, dear."

"Oh, he's not decrepit, any. But I'm out of the market. You know."

"Off the auction block?"

"Yes, ma'am. Yeah."

"What's he selling? We don't often work through independent dealers—the Creightons don't, that is—and I've never heard of this firm."

"Jane says she thinks he's been hitting the stores up and down the mall for the last couple of days. Don't know what he's pushing. He's got a samples case, though—and really the most incredible kiss-me eyes."

"If he's been here two days, I'm surprised he hasn't already sold those."

"Do you want me to send him back? He's too polite to burst in. He's been calling Jane and me Ms. Sidney and Ms. Bready, like that."

"Don't send him back yet." Marilyn had a premonition, almost a fear. "Let me take a look at him first."

Terri Bready barked a laugh and had to cover her mouth. "Hey, Ms. Odau, I wouldn't talk him up like Robert Redford and then send you a bald frog. I mean, why would I?"

"Go on, Terri. I'll talk to him in a couple of minutes."

"Yeah. Okay." The girl was quickly gone, and at the curtain's edge Marilyn looked out. Jane was waiting on a heavy-set woman in a fire-engine-red pantsuit, and just inside the boutique's open threshold the man named Nicholas Anson was watching the crowds and counter-crowds work through each other like grim armies.

Anson's hair was modishly long, and he reminded Marilyn a bit of the man who had grimaced at her on the off-ramp. Then, however, the sun had been richocheting off windshields, grilles, and hood ornaments, and any real identification of the man in the Le Mans with this composed sales representative was impossible, if not downright pointless. A person in an automobile was not the same person you met on common ground. . . . Now Terri was approaching this Anson fellow, and he was turning toward the girl.

Marilyn Odau felt her fingers tighten on the curtain. Already she had taken in the man's navy-blue leisure jacket and, beneath it, his silky shirt the color and pattern of a cumulus-filled sky. Already she had noted the length and the sun-flecked blondness of his hair, the etched-out quality of his profile.... But when he turned, the only thing apparent to her was Anson's resemblance to a dead marine named Jordan Burk, even though he was older than Jordan had lived to be. Ten or twelve years older, at the very least. Jordan Burk had died at twenty-four taking an amphibious tractor ashore at Betio, a tiny island near Tarawa Atoll in the Gilbert Islands. Nicholas Anson, however, had crow's-feet at the corners of his eyes and glints of silver in his sideburns. These things didn't matter much—the resemblance was still a heart-breaking one, and Marilyn found that she was staring at Anson like a star-struck teenager. She let the curtain fall.

This has happened before, she told herself. In a world of four billion people, over a period of thirty-five years, it isn't surprising that you should encounter two or more young men who look like each other. For God's sake, Odau, don't go to pieces over the sight of still another man who reminds you of Jordan—a stranger from Los Angeles who in just a couple of years is going to be old enough to be the *father* of your forever-twenty-four Jordan darling.

It's the season, Marilyn protested, answering her relentlessly rational self. It's especially cruel that this should happen now.

It happens all the time. You're just more susceptible at this time of year. Odau, you haven't outgrown what amounts to a basically childish syndrome, and it's beginning to look as if you never will.

Old enough in just a couple of years to be Jordan's father? He's old enough right now to be Jordan's and my child. *Our* child.

Marilyn could feel tears welling up from some ancient spring; susceptible, she had an unexpected mental glimpse of the upstairs bedroom in her Brookmist townhouse, the bedroom next to hers, the bedroom she had made a sort of shrine. In its corner, a white wicker bassinet—

That's enough, Odau!

"That's enough!" she said aloud, clenching a fist at her throat.

The curtain drew back, and she was again face to face with Terri Bready. "I'm sorry, Ms. Odau. You talkin' to me?"

"No, Terri. To myself."

"He's a neat fella, really. Says he played drums for a rock band in Haight-Ashbury once upon a time. Says he was one of the original hippies. He's been straight since Nixon resigned, he says—his faith was restored—. Whyn't you talk to him, Ms. Odau? Even if you don't place an order with him, he's an interesting person to talk to. Really. He says he's heard good things about you from the other managers on the mall. He thinks our place is just the sort of place to handle one of his products."

496   Michael Bishop

"I bet he does. You certainly got a lot out of him in the short time he's
been here."

"Yeah. All my doing, too. I thought maybe, being from Los Angeles, he
knew somebody in Hollywood. I sorta told him I was a drama major. You
know... Let me send him back, okay?"

"All right. Send him back."

Marilyn sat down at her desk. Almost immediately Nicholas Anson came
through the curtain with his samples case. They exchanged polite
greetings, and she was struck again by his resemblance to Jordan. Seeing
him at close range didn't dispel the illusion of an older Jordan Burk, but
intensified it. This was the reverse of the way it usually happened, and
when he put his case on her desk, she had to resist a real urge to reach out
and touch his hand.

No wonder Terri had been snowed. Anson's presence was a mature and
amiable one, faintly sexual in its undertones. Haight-Ashbury? No, that
was wrong. Marilyn couldn't imagine this man among Jesus freaks and
flower children, begging small change, the ankles of his grubby blue jeans
frayed above a pair of falling-to-pieces sandals. Altogether wrong. Thank
God, he had found his calling. He seemed born to move gracefully among
boutiques and front-line department stores, making recommendations,
giving of his smile. Was it possible that he had once turned his gaunt young
face upward to the beacon of a strobe and howled his heart out to the
rhythms of his own acid drumming? Probably. A great many things had
changed since the sixties....

"You're quite far afield," Marilyn said, to be saying something. "I've
never heard of Latter-Day-Novelties."

"It's a consortium of independent business people and manufacturers,"
Anson responded. "We're trying to expand our markets, go nation-wide.
I'm not really used to acting as—what does it say on my card?—a sales
representative. My first job—my real love—is being a products consultant.
If your company is a novelties company, it has to have novelties, products
that are new and appealing and unusual. Prior to coming East on this trip,
my principal responsibility was making product suggestions. That seems to
be my forte, and that's what I really like to do."

"Well, I think you'll be an able enough sales representative too."

"Thank you, Miss Odau. Still, I always feel a little hesitation opening
this case and going to bat for what it contains. There's an element of
egotism in going out and pushing your own brain-children on the world."

"There's an element of egotism in almost every human enterprise. I
don't think you need to worry."

"I suppose not."

"Why don't you show me what you have?"

Nicholas Anson undid the catches on his case. "I've only brought you a single product. It was my judgment you wouldn't be interested in celebrity T-shirts, cartoon-character paperweights—products of that nature. Have I judged fairly, Miss Odau?"

"We've sold novelty T-shirts and jerseys, Mr. Anson, but the others sound like gift-shop gimcracks and we don't ordinarily stock that sort of thing. Clothing, cosmetics, toiletries, a few handicraft or decorator items if they correlate well with the Creightons' image of their franchise."

"Okay." Anson removed a glossy cardboard package from his case and handed it across the desk to Marilyn. The kit was blue and white, with two triangular windows in the cardboard. Elegant longhand lettering on the package spelled out the words *Liquid Sheers*. Through one of the triangular windows she could see a bottle of mahogany-colored liquid, a small foil tray, and a short-bristled brush with a grip on its back; through the other window was visible an array of colored pencils.

" 'Liquid Sheers?' "

"Yes, ma'am. The idea struck me only about a month ago, I drew up a marketing prospectus, and the Latter-Day consortium rushed the concept into production so quickly that the product's already selling quite well in a number of West Coast boutiques. Speed is one of the keynotes of our company's early success. By cutting down the elapsed time between concept-visualization and actual manufacture of the product, we've been able to stay ahead of most of our California competitors.... If you like Liquid Sheers, we have the means to keep you in a good supply."

Marilyn was reading the instructions on the kit. Her attention refused to stay fixed on the words and they kept slipping away from her. Anson's matter-of-fact monologue about his company's business practices didn't help her concentration. She gave up and set the package down.

"But what are? These Liquid Sheers?"

"They're a novel substitute—a decorator substitute—for pantyhose or nylons, Miss Odau. A woman mixes a small amount of the Liquid Sheer solution with water and rubs or paints it on her legs. The pencils can be used to draw on seams or color in some of the applicator designs we've included with the kit—butterflies, flowers, that sort of thing. Placement's up to the individual.... We have kits for dark- as well as light-complexioned women, and the application process takes much less time than you might expect. It's fun too, some of our products-testers have told us. Several boutiques have even reported increased sales of shorts, abbreviated skirts, and short culotte outfits once they began stocking Liquid Sheers. This, I ought to add, right here at the beginning of winter."

Anson stopped, his spiel dutifully completed and his smile expectant.

"They're bottled stockings," Marilyn said.

"Yes, ma'am. I suppose you could phrase it that way."

"We sold something very like this at Satterwhite's during the war," Marilyn went on, careful not to look at Anson. "Without the design doodads and the different colored pencils, at any rate. Women painted on their stockings and set the seams with mascara pencils."

Anson laughed. "To tell you the truth, Miss Odau, that's where I got part of my original idea. I rummage old mail-order catalogues and the ads in old magazines. Of course, Liquid Sheers also derive a little from the body-painting fad of the sixties—but in our advertising we plan to lay heavy stress on their affinity to the World War era."

"Why?"

"Nostalgia sells. Girls who don't know World War II from the Peloponnesian War—girls who've worn seamless stockings all their lives, if they've worn stockings at all—are painting on Liquid Sheers and setting grease-pencil seams because they've seen Lauren Bacall and Ann Sheridan in Bogart film revivals and it makes them feel vaguely heroic. It's amazing, Miss Odau. In the last few years we've had sales and entertainment booms featuring nostalgia for the twenties, the thirties, the fifties, and the sixties. The forties—if you except Bogart—have been pretty much bypassed, and Liquid Sheers purposely play to that era while recalling some of the art-deco creations of the Beatles period too."

Marilyn met Anson's gaze and refused to fall back from it. "Maybe the forties have been 'pretty much bypassed' because it's hard to recall World War II with unfettered joy."

"I don't really buy that," Anson replied, earnest and undismayed. "The twenties gave us Harding and Coolidge, the thirties the Great Depression, the fifties the Cold War, and the sixties Vietnam. There's no accounting what people are going to remember with fondness—but I can assure you that Liquid Sheers are doing well in California."

Marilyn pushed her chair back on its coasters and stood up. "I sold bottled stockings, Mr. Anson. I painted them on my legs. You couldn't *pay* me to use a product like that again—even with colored pencils and butterflies thrown in gratis."

Seemingly out of deference to her Anson also stood. "Oh, no, Miss Odau—I wouldn't expect you to. This is a product aimed at adolescent girls and post-adolescent young women. We fully realize it's a fad product. We expect booming sales for a year and then a rapid tapering off. But it won't matter—our overhead on Liquid Sheers is low and when sales have bottomed out we'll drop 'em and move on to something else. You understand the transience of items like this."

"Mr. Anson, do you know why bottled stockings existed at all during the Second World War?"

"Yes, ma'am. There was a nylon shortage."

"The nylon went into the war effort—parachutes, I don't know what else." She shook her head, trying to remember. "All I know is that you didn't see them as often as you'd been used to. They were an important commodity on the domestic black market, just like alcohol and gasoline and shoes."

Anson's smile was sympathetic, but he seemed to know he was defeated. "I guess you're not interested in Liquid Sheers?"

"I don't see how I could have them on my shelves, Mr. Anson."

He reached across her desk, picked up the kit he had given her, and dropped it in his samples case. When he snapped its lid down, the reports of the catches were like distant gunshots. "Maybe you'll let me try you with something else, another time."

"You don't have anything else with you?"

"To tell you the truth, I was so certain you'd like these I didn't bring another product along. I've placed Liquid Sheers with another boutique on the first level, though, and sold a few things to gift and novelty stores. Not a complete loss, this trip." He paused at the curtain. "Nice doing business with you, Miss Odau."

"I'll walk you to the front."

Together they strolled through an aisleway of clothes racks and toiletry shelves over a mulberry carpet. Jane and Terri were busy with customers.... *Why am I being so solicitous?* Marilyn asked herself. Anson didn't look a bit broken by her refusal, and Liquid Sheers were definitely offensive to her—she wanted nothing to do with them. Still, any rejection was an intimation of failure, and Marilyn knew how this young man must feel. It was a shame her visitor would have to plunge himself back into the mall's motivelessly surging bodies on a note, however small, of defeat. He would be lost to her, borne to oblivion on the tide....

"I'm sorry, Jordan," she said. "Please do try us again with something else."

The man beside her flinched and cocked his head. "You called me Jordan, Miss Odau."

Marilyn covered the lower portion of her face with her hand. She spread her fingers and spoke through them. "Forgive me." She dropped her hand. "Actually, I'm surprised it didn't happen before now. You look very much like someone I once knew. The resemblance is uncanny."

"You did say Jordan, didn't you?"

"Yes, I guess I did—that was his name."

"Ah." Anson seemed on the verge of some further comment but all he came out with was, "Goodbye, Miss Odau. Hope you have a good Christmas season," after which he set himself adrift and disappeared in the crowd.

The tinfoil decorations in the mall's central shaft were like columns of a strange scarlet coral, and Marilyn studied them intently until Terri Bready spoke her name and returned her to the present. She didn't leave the boutique until ten that evening.

Tuesday, ten minutes before noon.

He wore the same navy-blue leisure jacket, with an open collar shirt of gentle beige and bold indigo. He carried no samples case, and speaking with Cissy Campbell and then Terri, he seemed from the vantage of Marilyn's office, her curtain partially drawn back, less certain of his ground. Marilyn knew a similar uncertainty—Anson's presence seemed ominous, a challenge. She put a hand to her hair, then rose and went through the shop to meet him.

"You didn't bring me something else to look at, did you?"

"No; no, I didn't." He revealed his empty hands. "I didn't come on business at all...unless..." He let his voice trail away. "You haven't changed your mind about Liquid Sheers, have you?"

This surprised her. Marilyn could hear the stiffness in her voice. "I'm afraid I haven't."

Anson waved a hand. "Please forget that. I shouldn't have brought it up—because I *didn't* come on business." He raised his palm, like a Boy Scout pledging his honor. "I was hoping you'd have lunch with me."

"Why?"

"Because you seem *simpático*—that's the Spanish word for the quality you have. And it would be nice to sit down and talk with someone congenial about something other than Latter-Day Novelties. I've been on the road a week."

Out of the corner of her eye she could see Terri Bready straining to interpret her response to this proposal. Cissy Campbell, Marilyn's black clerk, had stopped racking a new supply of puff-sleeved blouses, and Marilyn had a glimpse of orange eyeliner and iridescent lipstick—the girl's face was that of an alert and self-confident panther.

"I don't usually eat lunch, Mr. Anson."

"Make an exception today. Not a word about business, I promise you."

"Go with him," Terri urged from the cash computer. "Cissy and I can take care of things here, Ms. Odau." Then she chuckled.

"Excellent advice," Anson said. "If I were you, I'd take it."

"Okay," Marilyn agreed. "So long as we don't leave Summerstone and don't stay gone too long. Let me get my bag."

Inevitably, they ended up at the McDonald's downstairs—yellow and orange wall paneling, trash bins covered with wood-grained contact paper, rows of people six and seven deep at the shiny metal counters. Marilyn found a two-person table and eased herself into one of the attached, scoop-shaped plastic chairs. It took Anson almost fifteen minutes to return with two cheeseburgers and a couple of softdrinks, which he nearly spilled squeezing his way out of the crowd to their tiny table.

"Thank God for plastic tops. Is it always like this?"

"Worse at Christmas. Aren't there any McDonalds in Los Angeles?"

"Nothing but. But it's three whole weeks till Christmas. Have these people no piety?"

"None."

"It's the same in Los Angeles."

They ate. While they were eating, Anson asked that she use his first name and she in turn felt obligated to tell him hers. Now they were Marilyn and Nicholas, mother and son on an outing to McDonald's. Except that his attention to her wasn't filial—it was warm and direct, with a wooer's deliberately restrained urgency. His manner reminded her again of Jordan Burk, and at one point she realized that she had heard nothing at all he'd said for the last several minutes. Listen to this man, she cautioned herself. Come back to the here and now. After that, she managed better.

He told her that he'd been born in the East, raised singlehandedly by his mother until her remarriage in the late forties, and, after his new family's removal to Encino, educated entirely on the West Coast. He told her of his abortive career as a rock drummer, his early resistance to the war in Southeast Asia, and his difficulties with the United States military.

"I had no direction at all until my thirty-second birthday, Marilyn. Then I discovered where my talent lay and I haven't looked back since. I tell you, if I had the sixties to do over again—well, I'd gladly do them. I'd finagle myself a place in an Army reserve unit, be a weekend soldier, and get right down to products-consulting on a full-time basis. If I'd done that in '65 I'd probably be retired by now."

"You have plenty of time. You're still young."

"I've just turned thirty-six."

"You look less."

"But not much. Thanks anyway, though—it's nice to hear."

"Did you fight in Vietnam?" Marilyn asked on impulse.

"I *went* there in '68. I don't think you could say I fought. I was one of the oldest enlisted men in my unit, with a history of anti-war activity and draft-card burning. I'm going to tell you something, though—once I got home and turned myself around, I wept when Saigon fell. That's the truth—I wept. Saigon was some city, if you looked at it right."

Mentally counting back, Marilyn realized that Nicholas was the right age to be her and Jordan's child. Exactly. In early December, 1942, she and Jordan had made their last farewells in the little house on Greenbriar

Street.... She attached no shame to this memory, had no regrets about it. The shame had come twenty-six years later—the same year, strangely enough, that Nicholas Anson was reluctantly pulling a tour of duty in Vietnam. The white wicker bassinet in her upstairs shrine was a perpetual reminder of this shame, of her secret monstrousness, and yet she could not dispose of the evidence branding her a freak, if only to herself, for the simple reason that she loved it. She loved it because she had once loved Jordan Burk.... Marilyn put her cheeseburger down. There was no way— no way at all—that she was gong to be able to finish eating.

"Are you all right?"

"I need to get back to the boutique."

"Let me take you out to dinner this evening. You can hardly call this a relaxed and unhurried get-together. I'd like to take you somewhere nice. I'd like to buy you a snifter of brandy and a nice rare cut of prime rib."

"Why?"

"You use that word like a stiletto, Marilyn. Why not?"

"Because I don't go out. My work keeps me busy. And there's a discrepancy in our ages that embarrasses me. I don't know whether your motives are commercial, innocently social, or.... Go ahead, then—laugh." She was wadding up the wrapper from her cheeseburger, squeezing the paper tighter and tighter, and she could tell that her face was crimsoning.

"I'm not laughing," Nicholas said. "I don't either—know what my motives are, I mean. Except that they're not blameworthy or unnatural."

"I'd better go." She eased herself out of the underslung plastic chair and draped her bag over her shoulder.

"When can I see you?" His eyes were full of remonstrance and appeal. "The company wants me here another week or so—problems with a delivery. I don't know anyone in this city. I'm living out of a suitcase. And I've never in my life been married, if that's worrying you."

"Maybe I should worry because you haven't."

Nicholas smiled at her, a self-effacing charmer's smile. "When?"

"Wednesdays and Sundays are the only nights I don't work. And tomorrow's Wednesday."

"What time?"

"I don't know," she said distractedly. "Call me. Or come by the boutique. Or don't. Whatever you want."

She stepped into the aisle beside their table and quickly worked her way through the crowd to the capsule-lift outside McDonald's. Her thoughts were jumbled, and she hoped feebly—willing the hope—that Nicholas Anson would simply disappear from her life.

The next morning, before any customers had been admitted to the mall, Marilyn Odau went down to Summerstone's first level and walked past the boutique whose owner had elected to sell Nicholas' Liquid Sheers. The kits were on display in two colorful pyramids just inside the shop's entrance.

That afternoon a leggy, dark-haired girl came into Creighton's Corner to browse, and when she let her fur-trimmed coat fall open Marilyn saw a small magenta rose above her right knee. The girl's winter tan had been rubbed or brushed on, and there were magenta seams going up the backs of her legs. Marilyn didn't like the effect, but she understood that others might not find it unattractive.

At six o'clock Nicholas Anson showed up in sports clothes and an expensive deerskin coat. Jane Sidney and Cissy Campbell left, and Marilyn had a mall attendant draw the shop's movable grating across its entrance. Despite the early Wednesday closing time, people were still milling about as shopkeepers transacted last-minute business or sought to shoo away their last heel-dragging customers. This was the last Wednesday evening before Christmas that Summerstone would be closed.

Marilyn began walking, and Nicholas fell in beside her like an assigned escort at a military ball. "Did you think I wasn't coming?"

"I didn't know. What now?"

"Dinner."

"I'd like to go home first. To freshen up."

"I'll drive you."

"I have a car."

"Lock it and let it sit. This place is about as well guarded as Fort Knox. I've rented a car from the service at the airport."

Marilyn didn't want to see Nicholas Anson's rental car. "Let *yours* sit. You can drive me home in mine." He started to protest. "It's either that or an early goodbye. I worry about my car."

So he drove her to Brookmist in her '68 Nova. The perimeter highway was yellow-grey under its ghostly lamps and the traffic was bewilderingly swift. Twilight had already edged over into evening—a drear winter evening. The Nova's gears rattled even when Nicholas wasn't touching the stick on the steering column.

"I'm surprised you don't have a newer car. Surely you can afford one."

"I could, I suppose, but I like this one. It's easy on gas, and during the oil embargo I felt quite smart.... What's the matter with it?"

"Nothing. It's just that I'd imagined you in a bigger or a sportier one. I shouldn't have said anything." He banged his temple with the heel of his right hand. "I'm sorry, Marilyn."

"Don't apologize. Jane Sidney asked me the same thing one day. I told her that my parents were dirt-poor during the Depression and that as soon as I was able to sock any money away for them, that's what I did. It's a habit I haven't been able to break—even today, with my family dead and no real financial worries."

They rode in silence beneath the haloed lamps on the overpass and the looming grey shadow of Satterwhite's.

"A girl came into the boutique this afternoon wearing Liquid Sheers," Marilyn said. "It does seem your product's selling."

"Hooo," Nicholas replied, laughing mirthlessly. "Just remember that *I* didn't bring that up, okay?"

They left the expressway and drove down several elm-lined residential streets. The Brookmist complex of townhouses came into the Nova's headlights like a photographic image emerging from a wash of chemicals, everything gauzy and indistinct at first. Marilyn directed Nicholas to the community carport against a brick wall behind one of the rows of houses, and he parked the car. They walked hunch-shouldered in the cold to a tall redwood fence enclosing a concrete patio not much bigger than a phone booth. Marilyn pushed the gate aside, let the latch fall behind them, and put her key into the lock on the kitchen door. Two or three flower pots with drooping, unrecognizable plants in them sat on a peeling windowsill beside the door.

"I suppose you think I could afford a nicer place to live, too."

"No, but you do give yourself a long drive to work."

"This place is paid for, Nicholas. It's mine."

She left him sitting under a table lamp with several old copies of *McCall's* and *Cosmopolitan* in front of him on her stonework coffee table and went upstairs to change clothes. She came back down wearing a long-sleeved black jumpsuit with a peach-colored sweater and a single polished-stone pendant at her throat. The heat had kicked on, and the downstairs was cozily warm.

Nicholas stood up. "You've set things up so that I'm going to have to drive your car and you're going to have to navigate. I hope you'll let me buy the gas."

"Why couldn't I drive and you just sit back and enjoy the ride?" Her voice was tight again, with uneasiness and mild disdain. For a products consultant Nicholas didn't seem quite as imaginative as he ought. Liquid Sheers were a rip-off of an idea born out of necessity during World War II, and the "novelties" he'd mentioned in his spiel on Monday were for the most part variations on the standard fare of gift shops and bookstores. He wasn't even able to envision her doing the driving while he relaxed and played the role of a passenger. And *he* was the one who'd come to maturity during the sixties, that fabled decade of egalitarian upheaval and heightened social awareness. . . .

"The real point, Marilyn, is that I wanted to do something for *you*. But you've taken the evening out of my hands."

All right, she could see that. She relented. "Nicholas, I'm not trying to stage-manage this—this *date,* if that's what it is. I was surprised that you came by the shop. I wasn't ready. And I'm not ready to go out this evening, either—I'm cold and I'm tired. I have a pair of steaks and a bottle of cold duck in the refrigerator, and enough fixings for a salad. Let me make dinner."

"A *pair* of steaks?"

"There's a grocery store off the perimeter highway that stays open night and day. I stopped there last night after work."

"But you didn't think I'd come by today?"

"No. Not really. And despite buying the steaks, I'm not sure I really wanted you to. I know that sounds backwards somehow, but it's the truth."

Nicholas ignored this. "But you'll have to cook. I wanted to spare you that. I wanted to do something *for* you."

"Spare me another trip down the highway in my car and the agony of waiting for service in one of this city's snooty night spots."

He gave in, and she felt kindlier toward him. They ate at the coffee table in the living room, sitting on the floor in their stocking feet and listening to an FM radio station. They talked cursorily about sports and politics and movies, which neither of them was particularly interested in anymore; and then, because they had both staked their lives to it, Marilyn lifted the taboo that Nicholas had promised to observe and they talked business. They didn't talk about Liquid Sheers or profit margins or tax shelters, they talked about the involvement of their feelings with what they were doing and the sense of satisfaction that they derived from their work. That was common ground, and the evening passed—as Jane Sidney might have put it—"like sixty."

They were finishing the bottle of Cold Duck. Nicholas shifted positions, catching his knees with his right arm and rocking back a little.

"Marilyn?"

"Mmm?"

"You would never have let me drive you over here if I hadn't reminded you of this fellow you once knew, would you? This fellow named Jordan? Tell me the truth. No bet-hedging."

Her uneasiness returned. "I don't know."

"Yes, you do. Your answer won't hurt my feelings. I'd like to think that now that you know me a little better my resemblance to this person doesn't matter anymore—that you like me for myself." He waited.

"Okay, then. You're right."

"I'm right," he echoed her dubiously.

"I wouldn't have let you bring me home if you hadn't looked like
Jordan. But now that I know you a little better it doesn't make any
difference."

Not much, Marilyn told herself. At least I've stopped putting you in a
marine uniform and trimming back the hair over your ears.... She felt a
quiet tenderness for both men, the dead Jordan and the boyish Nicholas
Anson who in many ways seemed younger than Jordan ever had.... That's
because Jordan was almost three years older than you, Odau, and Nicholas
is almost twenty years younger. Think a little.

The young man who resembled Jordan Burk drained his glass and
hoisted himself nimbly off the floor.

"I'm staying at the Holiday Inn near the airport," he said. "Let me call a
cab so you won't have to get out again."

"Cabs aren't very good about answering night calls anymore. The
drivers are afraid to come."

"I hate for you to have to drive me, Marilyn." His look was expectant,
and she hated to disappoint him.

"Why don't you just spend the night here?" she said.

They went upstairs together, and she was careful to close the door to the
bedroom containing the wicker bassinet before following him into her
own. They undressed in the greenish light sifting through her curtains
from the arc lamp in the elm trees. Her heart raced. Then his body covered
its beating, and afterwards she lay staring wide-eyed and bemused at her
acoustic ceiling panels as he slept beside her with a hand on her hip. Then
she fell asleep too, and woke when her sleeping mind noted that his hand
was gone, and sat up to discover that Nicholas was no longer there. The
wind in the leafless elms was making a noise like angry surf.

"Nick!" she called.

He didn't answer.

She swung her feet to the carpet, put on her gown, and found him
standing in a pair of plaid boxer shorts beside the wicker bassinet. He had
put on a desk lamp, and its glow made a pool of light that contained and
illuminated everything in that corner of the room. There was no doubt that
he had discovered the proof of her monstrousness there, even if he didn't
know what it meant.

Instead of screaming or flying at him like a drunken doxy, she sank to
the floor in the billow of her dressing gown, shamefully conscious of her
restraint and too well satisfied by Nicholas' snooping to be shocked by it. If
she hadn't wanted this to happen, she would never have let him come. Or
she would have locked the door to her shrine. Or she would have murdered
Nicholas in the numb sleep of his fulfillment. Any number of things. But
this was what she had wanted.

Confession and surcease.

"I was looking for the bathroom," Nicholas said. "I didn't know where the upstairs bathroom was. But when I saw the baby bed ... well, I didn't know why you'd have a baby bed and—" He broke off.

"Don't explain, Nicholas." She gave him an up-from-under look and wondered what her own appearance must suggest. Age, promiscuousness, dissolution? You grew old, that you couldn't stop. But the others ... those were lies. She wanted confession and surcease, that was all, and he was too intent on the bassinet to escape giving them to her, too intent to see how downright *old* she could look at two in the morning. Consumed by years. Consumed by that which life itself is nourished by. Just one of a world of consumer goods.

Nicholas lifted something from the bassinet. He held it in the palm of one hand. "What is this?" he asked. "Marilyn ... ?"

"Lithopedion," she said numbly. "The medical term is lithopedion. And lithopedion is the word I use when I want to put myself at a distance from it. With you here, that's what I think I want to do—put myself at a distance from it. I don't know. Do you understand?"

He stared at her blankly.

"It means stone child, Nicholas. I was delivered of it during the first week of December, 1968. A petrified fetus."

" 'Delivered of it'?"

"That's wrong. I don't know why I said that. It was removed surgically, cut from my abdominal cavity. Lithopedion." Finally she began to cry. "Bring him to me."

The unfamiliar man across from her didn't move. He held the stone child questioningly on his naked palm.

"Damn it, Nicholas, I asked you to bring him to me! He's mine! Bring him here!"

She put a fist to one of her eyes and drew it away to find black makeup on the back of her hand. Anson brought her the lithopedion, and she cradled it against the flimsy bodice of her dressing gown. A male child, calcified, with a tiny hand to the side of its face and its eyes forever shut; a fossil before it had ever really begun to live.

"This is Jordan's son," Marilyn told Anson, who was still standing over her. "Jordan's and mine."

"But how could that be? He died during the Pacific campaign."

Marilyn took no notice of either the disbelief in Anson's voice or his unaccountable knowledge of the circumstances of Jordan's death. "We had a honeymoon in the house on Greenbriar while Maggie was off for Christmas," she said, cradling her son. "Then Jordan had to return to his Division. In late March of '43 I collapsed while I was clerking at

Satterwhite's. I was stricken with terrible cramps and I collapsed. Maggie drove me home to Greenville, and I was treated for intestinal flu. That was the diagnosis of a local doctor. I was in a coma for a while. I had to be forcibly fed. But after a while I got well again, and the manager of the notions department at Satterwhite's let me have my job back. I came back to the city."

"And twenty-five years later you had your baby?"

Even the nastiness that Anson imparted to this question failed to dismay her. "Yes. It was an ectopic pregnancy. The fetus grew not in my womb, you see, but in the right Fallopian tube—where there isn't much room for it to grow. I didn't know, I didn't suspect anything. There were no signs."

"Until you collapsed at Satterwhite's?"

"Dr. Rule says that was the fetus bursting the Fallopian tube and escaping into the abdominal cavity. I didn't know. I was twenty years old. It was diagnosed as flu, and they put me to bed. I had a terrible time. I almost died. Later in the year, just before Thanksgiving, Jordan was killed at Tarawa, and I wished that I had died before him."

"He never lived to see his son," Anson said bitterly.

"No. I was frightened of doctors. I'm still frightened by them. But in 1965 I went to work for the Creightons at Capitol Square, and when I began having severe pains in my side a couple of years later, they *made* me go to Dr. Rule. They told me I'd have to give up my job if I didn't go." Marilyn brought a fold of her nightgown around the calcified infant in her arms. "He discovered what was wrong. He delivered my baby. A lithopedion, he said.... Do you know that there've been only a few hundred of them in all recorded history? That makes me a freak, all my love at the beck and call of a father and son who'll never be able to hear me." Marilyn's shoulders began to heave and her mouth fell slack to let the sounds of her grief work clear. "A freak," she repeated, sobbing.

"No more a freak than that thing's father."

She caught Anson's tone and turned her eyes up to see his face through a blur of tears.

"Its father was Jordan Burk," Anson told her. "My father was Jordan Burk. He even went so far as to *marry* my mother, Miss Odau. But when he discovered she was pregnant, he deserted her to enlist in a Division bound for combat. But he came here first and found another pretty piece to slip it to before he left. You."

"No," Marilyn said, her sobs suddenly stilled.

"Yes. My mother found Burk in this city and asked him to come back to her. He pleaded his overmastering love for another woman and refused. *I* was no enticement at all—I was an argument for remaining with you. Once during her futile visit here Burk took my mother into Satterwhite's by a side-street entrance and pointed you out to her from one of the mezzanines. The 'other woman' was prettier than she was, my mother said. She gave up and returned home. She permitted Burk to divorce her without alimony while he was in the Pacific. Don't ask me why. I don't know. Later my mother married a man named Samuel Anson and we moved with him to California. . . . That thing in your arms, Miss Odau, is my half-brother."

It was impossible to cry now. Marilyn could hear her voice growing shrill and accusative. "That's why you asked me to lunch yesterday, isn't it? And why you asked me to dinner this evening. A chance for revenge. A chance to defile a memory you could have easily left untouched." She slapped Anson across the thigh, harmlessly. "I didn't know anything about your mother or you! I never suspected and I wasn't responsible! I'm not that kind of freak! Why have you set out to destroy both me and one of the few things in my life I've truly been able to cherish? Why do you turn on me with a nasty 'truth' that doesn't have any significance for me and never can? What kind of vindictive jackal are you?"

Anson looked bewildered. He dropped onto his knees in front of her and tried to grip her shoulders. She shook his hands away.

"Marilyn, I'm sorry. I asked you to lunch because you called me Jordan, just like you let me drive you home because I resembled him."

" 'Marilyn?' What happened to 'Miss Odau'?"

"Never mind that." He tried to grip her shoulders again, and she shook him off. "Is my crime greater than yours? If I've spoiled your memory of the man who fathered me, it's because of the bitterness I've carried against him for as long as I can remember. My intention wasn't to hurt you. The 'other woman' that my mother always used to talk about, even after she married Anson, has always been an abstract to me. Revenge wasn't my motive. Curiosity, maybe. But not revenge. Please believe me."

"You have no imagination, Nicholas."

He looked at her searchingly. "What does that mean?"

"It means that if you'd only. . . . Why should I explain this to you? I want you to get dressed and take my car and drive back to your motel. You can drop it off at Summerstone tomorrow when you come to get your rental car. Give the keys to one of the girls, I don't want to see you."

"Out into the cold, huh?"

"Please go, Nicholas. I might resort to screaming if you don't."

He rose, went into the other room, and a few minutes later descended the carpeted stairs without saying a word. Marilyn heard the flaring of her Nova's engine and a faint grinding of gears. After that, she heard nothing but the wind in the skeletal elm trees.

Without rising from the floor in her second upstairs bedroom, she sang a lullaby to the fossil child in her arms. "Dapples and grays," she crooned. "Pintos and bays, / All the pretty little horses...."

It was almost seven o'clock of the following evening before Anson returned her key case to Cissy Campbell at the cash computer up front. Marilyn didn't hear him or see him, and she was happy that she had been in her office when he at last came by. The episode was over. She hoped that she never saw Anson again, even if he was truly Jordan's son—and she believed that Anson understood her wishes.

Four hours later she pulled into the carport at Brookmist and crossed the parking lot to her small patio. The redwood gate was standing open. She pulled it shut behind her and set its latch. Then, inside, she felt briefly on the verge of swooning because there was an odor in the air like that of a man's cologne, a fragrance Anson had worn. For a moment she considered running back onto the patio and shouting for assistance. If Anson was upstairs waiting for her, she'd be a fool to go up there alone. She'd be a fool to go up there at all. Who could read the mind of an enigma like Anson?

He's not up there waiting for you, Marilyn told herself. He's been here and gone.

But why?

Your baby, Marilyn—see to your baby. Who knows what Anson might have done for spite? Who knows what sick destruction he might have—

"Oh, God!" Marilyn cried aloud. She ran up the stairs unmindful of the intensifying smell of cologne and threw the door to her second bedroom open. The wicker bassinet was not in its corner but in the very center of the room. She ran to it and clutched its side, very nearly tipping it over.

Unharmed, her and Jordan's tiny child lay on the satin bolster she had made for him.

Marilyn stood over the baby trying to catch her breath. Then she moved his bed back into the corner where it belonged. Not until the following morning was the smell of that musky cologne dissipated enough for her to forget that Anson—or someone—had been in her house. Because she had no evidence of theft, she rationalized that the odor had drifted into her apartment through the ventilation system from the townhouse next to hers.

The fact that the bassinet had been moved she conveniently put out of her mind.

Two weeks passed. Business at Creighton's Corner Boutique was brisk, and if Marilyn thought of Nicholas Anson at all, it was to console herself with the thought that by now he was back in Los Angeles. A continent away. But on the last weekend before Christmas, Jane Sidney told Marilyn that she thought she had seen Anson going through the center of one of Summerstone's largest department stores carrying his samples case. He looked tan and happy, Jane said.

"Good. But if he shows up here, I'm not in. If I'm waiting on a customer and he comes by, you or Terri will have to take over for me. Do you understand?"

"Yes, ma'am."

But later that afternoon the telephone in her office rang, and when she answered it, the voice coming through the receiver was Anson's.

"Don't hang up, Miss Odau. I knew you wouldn't see me in person, so I've been reduced to telephoning."

"What do you want?"

"Take a walk down the mall toward Davner's. Take a walk down the mall and meet me there."

"Why should I do that? I thought that's why you phoned."

Anson hung up.

You can wait forever, then, she told him. The phone didn't ring again, and she busied herself with the onion-skin order forms and bills of lading. It was hard to pay attention to them, though.

At last she got up and told Jane she was going to stroll down the mall to stretch her legs. The crowd was shoulder to shoulder. She saw old people being pushed along in wheelchairs and, as if they were dogs or monkeys, small children in leather harnesses. There were girls whose legs had been painted with Liquid Sheers, and young men in Russian hats and low-heeled shoes who made no secret of their appreciation of these girls' legs. The benches lining the shaft at the center of the promenade were all occupied, and the people sitting on them looked fatigued and irritable.

A hundred or so yards ahead of her, in front of the jewelry store called Davner's, there was a Santa Claus and a live reindeer.

She kept walking.

An odd display caught Marilyn's eye. She did a double-take and halted amid the traffic surging in both directions around her.

"Hey," a man said. He shoved past.

The shop window to her right was lined with eight or ten chalk-white effigies not much longer than her hand. They were eyeless. A small light played on them like the revolving blue strobe on a police vehicle. A sign in the window said *Stone Children for Christmas, from Latter-Day Novelties.* Marilyn put a hand to her mouth and made a gagging sound that no one else on the mall paid any mind. She spun around. It seemed that Summerstone itself was swaying under her. Across from the gift shop, on one of the display cases of the bookstore located there, were a dozen more of these minute statuettes. Tiny fingers, tiny feet, tiny eyeless faces. She looked down the collapsing mall and saw still another window displaying replicas of her and Jordan's baby. And in the windows that they weren't displayed, they were endlessly reflected.

Tiny fingers, tiny feet, tiny eyeless faces.

"Anson!" Marilyn shouted hoarsely, trying to find something to hang on to. "Anson, God damn you! God *damn* you!" She rushed on the gift-shop window and broke it with her fists. Then, not knowing what else to do, she withdrew her hands—with their worn oxblood nail polish—and held them bleeding above her head. A woman screamed, and the crowd fell back from her aghast.

In front of Davner's, only three or four stores away now, Nicholas Anson was stroking the head of the live reindeer. When he saw Marilyn, he gave her a friendly boyish smile.